A Dictionary of

Accounting

FOURTH EDITION

OXFORD
UNIVERSITY PRESS

OXFORD
UNIVERSITY PRESS

Great Clarendon Street, Oxford OX2 6DP

Oxford University Press is a department of the University of Oxford.
It furthers the University's objective of excellence in research, scholarship,
and education by publishing worldwide in

Oxford New York
Auckland Cape Town Dar es Salaam Hong Kong Karachi
Kuala Lumpur Madrid Melbourne Mexico City Nairobi
New Delhi Shanghai Taipei Toronto

With offices in
Argentina Austria Brazil Chile Czech Republic France Greece
Guatemala Hungary Italy Japan Poland Portugal Singapore
South Korea Switzerland Thailand Turkey Ukraine Vietnam

Oxford is a registered trade mark of Oxford University Press
in the UK and in certain other countries

Published in the United States
by Oxford University Press Inc., New York

British Library Cataloguing in Publication Data
Data available

Library of Congress Cataloging in Publication Data
Data available

Typeset by Market House Books Ltd.
Printed in Great Britain by
Clays Ltd, St Ives plc

ISBN 978-0-19-956305-0

10 9 8 7

A Dictionary of

Accounting

WITHDRAWN

 SEE WEB LINKS

For recommended web links for this title, visit
www.oxfordreference.com/page/acc when you see this sign.

The most authoritative and up-to-date reference books for both students and the general reader.

Accounting
Animal Behaviour
Archaeology
Architecture and Landscape Architecture
Art and Artists
Art Terms
Arthurian Literature and Legend
Astronomy
Battles
Bible
Biology
Biomedicine
British History
British Place-Names
Business and Management
Card Games
Chemical Engineering
Chemistry
Christian Art and Architecture
Christian Church
Classical Literature
Computing
Construction, Surveying, and Civil Engineering
Cosmology
Countries of the World
Critical Theory
Dance
Dentistry
Ecology
Economics
Education
English Etymology
English Grammar
English Idioms
English Literature
English Surnames
Environment and Conservation
Everyday Grammar
Film Studies
Finance and Banking
Foreign Words and Phrases
Forensic Science
Geography
Geology and Earth Sciences
Hinduism
Human Geography
Humorous Quotations

Irish History
Islam
Journalism
Kings and Queens of Britain
Law
Law Enforcement
Linguistics
Literary Terms
London Place-Names
Mathematics
Marketing
Mechanical Engineering
Media and Communication
Medical
Modern Poetry
Modern Slang
Music
Musical Terms
Nursing
Opera Characters
Philosophy
Physics
Plant Sciences
Plays
Pocket Fowler's Modern English Usage
Political Quotations
Politics
Popes
Proverbs
Psychology
Quotations
Quotations by Subject
Reference and Allusion
Rhyming
Rhyming Slang
Saints
Science
Scottish History
Shakespeare
Slang
Social Work and Social Care
Sociology
Statistics
Synonyms and Antonyms
Weather
Weights, Measures, and Units
Word Origins
Zoology

Many of these titles are also available online at www.Oxfordreference.com

Contents

Preface

This dictionary, now in its fourth edition, is a companion volume to *A Dictionary of Business and Management* and *A Dictionary of Finance and Banking*. It is intended for students of accounting and related fields at all levels and for business people and other professionals who require an authoritative and up-to-date guide to the subject.

The dictionary provides extensive coverage of the terms commonly used in financial accounting, management accounting, taxation, treasury management, financial management, and audit. It also includes a selection of terms from the wider fields of commerce, finance, law, computing, and statistics.

Since its first appearance in 1995 the book has been repeatedly revised and updated to keep abreast of the latest developments. In particular, the third edition was greatly expanded to reflect such major changes as the growing importance of international accounting standards, the rise of activity-based costing systems, European Monetary Union, and the ongoing globalization of financial markets. Similarly, this latest edition has been thoroughly revised to reflect the financial crisis of 2008–09 and the new and comprehensive UK Companies Act. International coverage has been broadened and there is an increased emphasis on corporate governance issues.

The book includes worked examples where these seem a particularly useful way of explaining a topic; it also features special pages on a number of broader – chiefly financial and legal – subjects that an accountant may well be required to understand.

J.L., 2009

Note: an asterisk (*) placed before a term in a definition indicates that this term can be found as an entry in the dictionary and that further information may be found there. Synonyms and abbreviations are usually found within brackets immediately following a headword.

Credits

Editor of the fourth edition

Jonathan Law (Market House Books Ltd)

Editors of the earlier editions

Professor Roger Hussey
Gary Owen MSc, FFIS

Contributors

John Smullen BSc, MA, MSc, MBA
Nicholas Hand MSc, BComm
David Collison CTA (Fellow), FCA, TEP

AAA Abbreviation for *American Accounting Association.

AADB Abbreviation for *Accountancy and Actuarial Discipline Board.

A & M trust Abbreviation for accumulation and maintenance trust. *See* DISCRETIONARY TRUST; 18–25 TRUST.

AAPA **1.** Abbreviation for *Association of Authorized Public Accountants. **2.** Abbreviation for Associate of the Association of Authorized Public Accountants.

AAT Abbreviation for *Association of Accounting Technicians.

abacus An ancient device for performing arithmetic calculations by sliding beads along rods or in grooves. Despite the spread of electronic calculators and computers, the abacus is still widely used in the Far East.

ABB Abbreviation for *activity-based budgeting.

abbreviated accounts A shorter form of *annual accounts that may be filed by a company qualifying as a small or medium-sized company under the Companies Act. The use of abbreviated accounts can cut costs and save time. It can also minimize the information made available to others, especially business rivals. *See also* SUMMARY FINANCIAL STATEMENT.

ABC method *See* ACTIVITY-BASED COSTING.

ABCP Abbreviation for asset-backed *commercial paper.

ability-to-pay The principle that taxes should be levied on the basis of the taxpayer's ability to pay. This normally leads to the view that as income or wealth increases, its marginal utility (its value to its owner) decreases, so that higher rates of tax can be levied on the higher slices. A typical *progressive tax of this sort is UK *income tax. *See also* FLAT TAX.

ABMTN Abbreviation for asset-backed *medium-term note.

abnormal loss The loss arising from a manufacturing or chemical process through abnormal waste, shrinkage, seepage, or spoilage in excess of the *normal loss. It may be expressed as a weight or volume or in other units appropriate to the process; it is usually valued on the same basis as the *good output. An **abnormal gain** is an unexpected surplus of output that may occur if the actual loss is less than anticipated.

above par *See* PAR VALUE.

above-the-line Denoting those entries printed above the horizontal line on a company's *profit and loss account that separates the profit (or loss) from the entries showing how the profit is distributed. *Compare* BELOW-THE-LINE.

  Prior to the introduction of *Financial Reporting Standard (FRS) 3, Reporting

Financial Performance, in October 1992, it was understood that any *exceptional items that were within the ordinary activities of the business were shown above the line, while any *extraordinary items that were outside the ordinary activities of the business were shown below it. There was, however, criticism that the definitions of extraordinary and exceptional items could be manipulated to improve the *earnings per share figure. For example, if a building was sold for a large profit it could be interpreted as being exceptional and included in the earnings per share, whereas if it was sold at a loss it could be interpreted as being extraordinary and not included in the earnings per share. With the introduction of FRS 3, virtually all previously extraordinary items have been redefined as exceptional and are therefore shown above the line and included in the earnings per share.

abridged accounts *See* NON-STATUTORY ACCOUNTS.

absorb To assimilate or incorporate amounts in an account or a group of accounts so that they are absorbed and lose their identity. *See* ABSORPTION COSTING.

absorbed overhead (applied overhead; recovered overhead) The amount of the *overhead of an organization charged to, or borne by, the *production of that organization for the accounting period under consideration when the technique of *absorption costing is used. The absorbed overhead is obtained by multiplying the actual production for the period by the *absorption rate.

absorption (cost absorption; overhead absorption) An accounting process used in *absorption costing in which the *overhead of an organization is borne by the production of that organization by the use of *absorption rates.

absorption account An account opened when a system of *double-entry cost accounting is in operation to show the amount of *overhead that has been absorbed by the production.

absorption costing (full absorption costing; total absorption costing) The cost accounting system in which the *overheads of an organization are charged to the production by means of the process of *absorption. Costs are first apportioned to *cost centres, where they are absorbed using *absorption rates. Although this method has the advantage of simplicity, it involves an essentially *arbitrary allocation of costs; for this reason the system of *activity-based costing is now widely preferred. *Compare* MARGINAL COSTING.

absorption rate (overhead absorption rate; recovery rate) The rate or rates calculated in an *absorption costing system in advance of an accounting period for the purpose of charging the *overheads to the *production of that period. Absorption rates are calculated for the accounting period in question using the following formula:

budgeted overhead/budgeted production.

In absorption costing production may be expressed in a number of different ways; the way chosen to express production will determine the absorption rate to be used. The seven major methods of measuring production, together with their associated absorption rate, are given in the table below. The rate is used during the accounting period to obtain the *absorbed overhead by multiplying the actual production achieved by the absorption rate.

Production measure	Absorption rate
units, weight, or volume	rate per unit, weight, or volume
direct labour hours	rate per direct labour hour
machine hours	rate per machine hour
direct labour cost	% on direct labour cost
direct material cost	% on direct material cost
prime cost	% on prime cost
standard hours	rate per standard hour

These rates have been used by accountants for over a century and they are still widely applied. Many, however, would argue that they cannot provide the accurate *cause-and-effect allocations of costs that modern managers require; for this a system of *activity-based costing must be used. *See also* TRADITIONAL COSTING SYSTEM.

abuse of a dominant position Unlawful activities by large businesses, i.e. usually those having a market share of at least 40% in at least one EU state. Examples of such activities, which are contrary to Article 82 of the Treaty of Rome and the UK Competition Act 1998, include refusing to supply an existing customer and engaging in predatory pricing. The European Commission and the *Office of Fair Trading can fine businesses up to 10% of annual worldwide group turnover for breach of Article 82.

abusive tax shelter In the USA, a limited partnership that the *Internal Revenue Service (IRS) considers is claiming illegal tax deductions, often by increasing the value of purchased property as a basis for inflated *depreciation write-offs. In recent years the IRS and the US Department of Justice have taken concerted action against abusive *tax shelters.

ACA Abbreviation for Associate of the *Institute of Chartered Accountants in England and Wales.

ACCA Abbreviation for *Association of Chartered Certified Accountants.

accelerated cost recovery system (ACRS) In the USA, a system of *depreciation designed to encourage capital investment by businesses. It permits a quicker recovery of an asset's cost to provide higher tax benefits in the earlier years of its use. A higher depreciation charge is made to the *profit and loss account in the early years, thus reducing the amount of profit assessable for tax. The **modified accelerated cost recovery system** (**MACRS**) was introduced in 1986.

accelerated depreciation A rate of *depreciation of assets that is faster than the useful-life basis normally used to calculate depreciation. For example, a computer may be expected to have a useful life of four years when it is purchased; however, as a result of new product innovation, it is replaced after two years. If the useful-life basis had been used, the full cost would not have been charged to the accounts until the end of the fourth year; by accelerating the depreciation the full charge would be made earlier, reflecting the short life cycle of high-tech products. In the USA, the accelerated depreciation may be used to gain tax advantages (*see* ACCELERATED COST RECOVERY SYSTEM).

acceleration The action of a lender in demanding early repayment when a borrower defaults.

acceptance commission *See* ACCEPTANCE CREDIT.

acceptance credit A means of financing the sale of goods, particularly in international trade. It involves a commercial bank or merchant bank extending credit to a foreign importer whom it deems creditworthy. An acceptance credit is opened against which the exporter can draw a *bill of exchange. Once accepted by the bank, the bill can be discounted on the *money market or allowed to run to maturity. In return for this service the exporter pays the bank a fee known as the **acceptance commission.**

acceptance supra protest (acceptance for honour) The acceptance or payment of a *bill of exchange, after it has been dishonoured, by a person wishing to save the honour of the drawer or an endorser of the bill.

accommodation bill A *bill of exchange signed by a person (the accom-modation party) who acts as a guarantor. The accommodation party is liable for the bill should the acceptor fail to pay at maturity. Accommodation bills are sometimes known as **windbills** or **windmills**. *See also* KITE.

accommodation party The person who signs an *accommodation bill as drawer, acceptor, or endorser and acts as the guarantor.

accord and satisfaction A device enabling one party to a contract to avoid an obligation that arises under the contract, provided that the other party agrees. The accord is the agreement by which the contractual obligation is discharged and the satisfaction is the *consideration making the agreement legally operative. Such an agreement only discharges the contractual obligation if it is accompanied by consideration. For example, under a contract of sale the seller of goods may discharge the contractual obligation by delivering goods of different quality to that specified in the contract, provided there is agreement with the buyer (the accord) and a reduction in the contract price (the satisfaction) is offered. The seller has therefore 'purchased' release from the obligation. Accord and satisfaction refer to the discharge of an obligation arising under the law of tort.

account **1.** A statement of indebtedness from one person to another. A provider of goods or services may render an account to a client or customer (*see* SALES INVOICE). **2.** A named segment of a *ledger recording transactions relevant to the person or matter named. *See* BOOKS OF ACCOUNT; LEDGER ACCOUNT. **3.** An account maintained by a bank or building society in which a depositor's money is kept. *See* CHEQUE ACCOUNT; CURRENT ACCOUNT; DEPOSIT ACCOUNT; SAVINGS ACCOUNT. **4.** *See* ANNUAL ACCOUNTS.

accountability An obligation to give an account. For limited companies, it is assumed that the directors of the company are accountable to the shareholders and that this responsibility is discharged, in part, by the directors providing an annual report and accounts (*see* ANNUAL ACCOUNTS). In an accountability relationship there will be at least one principal and at least one agent. This forms the basis of an *agency relationship.

accountancy **1.** The profession in which *accountancy bodies regulate the activities of accountants. **2.** The process of *accounting.

Accountancy and Actuarial Discipline Board (AADB) The UK body responsible for investigating those cases of alleged misconduct by members of the accounting and actuarial professions that are held to raise issues of public concern; cases that do not raise such issues are dealt with by the relevant professional body. The AADB superseded the **Accountancy Investigation and Discipline Board (AIDB)**, in 2007, the AIDB having itself replaced the former **Joint Disciplinary Scheme (JDS)** in 2004. The Board is an operating body of the *Financial Reporting Council.

((⊕)) SEE WEB LINKS
• Website of the AADB: includes full text of the Board's disciplinary Scheme and the associated Regulations

accountancy bodies Organizations, established in most countries in the world, to regulate the activities of accountants; their members are normally entitled to use the title *chartered accountant, *chartered certified accountant, or *certified public accountant. Membership is normally controlled by examination and the members are expected to comply with the regulations of their body. In the UK and the USA the accountancy profession is powerful and active. It takes a significant role in the regulation of financial accounting and reporting by issuing *accounting standards. In the UK, the profession is somewhat fragmented due to the number of separate accountancy bodies. Although there have been attempts to integrate these into one body, this has not yet been achieved. The professional bodies in the UK making up the *Consultative Committee of Accountancy Bodies are the *Association of Chartered Certified Accountants, the *Chartered Institute of Management Accountants, the *Chartered Institute of Public Finance and Accountancy, the *Institute of Chartered Accountants in England and Wales, the *Institute of Chartered Accountants in Ireland, and the *Institute of Chartered Accountants of Scotland. *See also* DESIGNATED PROFESSIONAL BODY; RECOGNIZED QUALIFYING BODY; RECOGNIZED SUPERVISORY BODY.

Accountancy Investigation and Discipline Board (AIDB) *See* ACCOUNTANCY AND ACTUARIAL DISCIPLINE BOARD.

accountant A person who has passed the accountancy examinations of one of the recognized *accountancy bodies and completed the required work experience. Each of the bodies varies in the way they train their students and the type of work expected to be undertaken. For example, accountants who are members of the *Chartered Institute of Public Finance and Accountancy generally work in local authorities, the National Health Service, or other similar public bodies, while members of the *Chartered Institute of Management Accountants work in industry and commerce. Wherever accountants work, their responsibilities centre on the collating, recording, and communicating of financial information and the preparation of analyses for decision-making purposes.

Accountant's Index *See* ACCOUNTING AND TAX INDEX.

accountant's lien The right to retain possession of goods or property that belongs to another until that person pays debts due to the possessor of the goods or property.

accountants' report 1. A report prepared by accountants that the London

Stock Exchange requires to be included in the *prospectus of a company. It must include certain financial information for a period of at least three years up to the end of the latest audited financial period. The information must be in a form consistent with that which would be adopted in the company's *annual accounts, unless the Stock Exchange agrees otherwise. The report is intended to assist potential investors in making a decision based on the information in the prospectus. *See* REPORTING ACCOUNTANT. **2.** An *audit exemption report.

account code A number given to an account from a *chart of accounts. Each number in the code will represent some feature; for example, asset type, location, department with responsibility for maintaining it, etc.

accounting The process of identifying, measuring, recording, and communicating economic transactions. Measurement is normally made in monetary terms and the accountant will prepare records in the form of *financial statements, such as a *profit and loss account and *balance sheet. Accounting can be subdivided into *financial accounting, which is mainly concerned with the legal aspects of the subject and reporting to parties external to an organization, and *management accounting, which is mainly concerned with providing information helpful to managers running a business. Accounting includes various activities, such as conducting *audits, *book-keeping, and *taxation.

Accounting and Finance Association of Australia and New Zealand (AFAANZ) A professional association formed in 2002 from the Accounting Association of Australia and New Zealand (AAANZ) and the Australian Association of University Teachers in Accounting (AAUTA). It represents the interests of those involved in finance and accounting education.

Accounting and Tax Index A bibliography of books and articles on accounting and tax subjects published by the *American Institute of Certified Public Accountants. Issued on a quarterly basis, it represents a major reference source for all aspects of accounting. Before 1992 it was known as the **Accountants' Index**.

accounting bases The methods used for applying fundamental *accounting concepts to financial transactions and items when preparing *financial statements. The particular bases adopted by an organization will form its *accounting policies.

accounting code (cost code; expenditure code; income code) In modern accounting systems, a numerical reference given to each account to facilitate the recording of voluminous accounting transactions by computer.

accounting concepts (accounting principles; fundamental accounting concepts) The basic theoretical ideas devised to support the activity of accounting. As accounting developed largely from a practical base, it has been argued that it lacks a theoretical framework. Accountants have therefore tried to develop such a framework; although various concepts have been suggested, few have found universal agreement. However, four are often deemed to be fundamental:

• the *going-concern concept assumes that the business is a going concern until there is evidence to the contrary, so that assets are not stated at their break-up value;

- the *accruals concept involves recording income and expenses as they accrue, as distinct from when they are received or paid;
- the *consistency concept demands that accounts be prepared on a basis that clearly allows comparability from one period to another;
- the *prudence concept calls for accounts to be prepared on a conservative basis, not taking credit for profits or income before they are realized but making provision for losses when they are foreseen.

These four principles were laid down in *Statement of Standard Accounting Practice (SSAP) 2, Disclosure of Accounting Policies; they are also recognized in the EU's *Fourth Company Law Directive and the UK Companies Acts together with a fifth principle, the *accounting entity concept. SSAP 2 has now been superseded by *Financial Reporting Standard (FRS) 18, which was issued in December 2000: this states that the consistency concept and the prudence concept should no longer be regarded as fundamental. FRS 18 also identifies four key objectives of financial information that can be regarded as fundamental principles: *comparability, *relevance, *reliability, and *understandability. These objectives are also explicitly identified in the *Framework for the Preparation and Presentation of Financial Statements, the document that sets out the accounting concepts informing *International Accounting Standards and *International Financial Reporting Standards. *See also* CONCEPTUAL FRAMEWORK.

accounting cushion In the USA, the practice of making larger provisions for expenses in one year, in order to minimize them in future years. Effectively, earnings will be understated in the present year but will be overstated in a subsequent year.

accounting cycle The sequence of steps in accounting for a financial transaction entered into by an organization. First, it is recorded in the *books of account and finally it will be aggregated with other transactions in the *financial statements for a financial period.

accounting entity (entity; business entity; reporting entity) The unit for which accounting records are maintained and for which *financial statements are prepared. The **accounting entity concept** (or **entity concept** or **separate entity concept**) is the principle that financial records are prepared for a distinct unit or entity regarded as separate from the individuals that own it. This will often be an incorporated *company, whose treatment as a separate accounting entity is required by law. For sole traders and partnerships accounts are also prepared to reflect the transactions of the business as an accounting entity, not those of the owner(s) of the business. Changing the boundaries of the accounting entity can have a significant impact on the accounts themselves, as these will reflect the purpose of the accounts and for whom they are prepared.

accounting equation (balance-sheet equation) The formula underlying a *balance sheet; it can be expressed as:

assets = liabilities + capital.

An increase or decrease in the total assets of a concern must be accompanied by an equal increase or decrease in the liabilities and capital in order to ensure that a balance sheet will always balance. This formula expresses an *entity view of the business, whereas the *proprietary view would deduct liabilities from assets to calculate the owners' stake in the business.

accounting event A transaction or change (internal or external) recognized by the accounting recording system. Events are recorded as debit and credit entries. For example, when a sale is made for cash the double entry for the sales transaction would be debit bank, credit sales (*see* DOUBLE-ENTRY BOOK-KEEPING).

accounting exposure *See* TRANSLATION EXPOSURE.

accounting manual A document that gives details of a business's accounting policies and procedures; it often includes a list of account codes or a *chart of accounts. An example of an accounting policy would be the way in which the company treats *depreciation, including the method selected and the *useful economic life used for each asset type. The procedure would explain how to apply the policy; for example, how to work out the depreciation charge for the year, which is then debited to the *profit and loss account and credited to the provision for depreciation. Other procedures relating to depreciation would show how to deal with both the revaluation of assets and the sale of assets.

accounting package *See* BUSINESS SOFTWARE PACKAGE.

accounting period 1. (financial period; period of account) The period for which a business prepares its accounts. Internally, management accounts may be produced monthly or quarterly. Externally, *financial statements are produced for a period of 12 months, although this may vary when a business is set up or ceases or if it changes its accounting year end. *See* ACCOUNTING REFERENCE DATE. **2. (chargeable account period)** A period in respect of which a *corporation tax assessment is raised. It cannot be more than 12 months in length. An accounting period starts when a company begins to trade or immediately after a previous accounting period ends. An accounting period ends at the earliest of:
- 12 months after the start date,
- at the end of the company's period of account,
- the start of a winding-up,
- on ceasing to be UK resident.

accounting plan A detailed accounting guide provided by a number of European countries, such as France and Spain. The guide gives definitions of accounting terms, rules for valuation and measurement, model financial statements, and a *chart of accounts. This legalistic approach to the preparation of *financial statements contrasts with the approach in the UK, where greater emphasis is placed on ensuring that the financial statements present a *true and fair view of the financial status of a particular organization.

accounting policies The specific *accounting bases adopted and consistently followed by an organization in the preparation of its *financial statements. These bases will have been determined by the organization to be the most appropriate for presenting fairly its financial results and operations; they will concentrate on such specific topics as pension schemes, *goodwill, *research and development costs, and *foreign exchange. Under *Financial Reporting Standard 18, companies are required to disclose their accounting

policies in their *annual accounts. This is also required under *International
Accounting Standard 1.

accounting principles See ACCOUNTING CONCEPTS.

Accounting Principles Board (APB) In the USA, the forerunner of the
*Financial Accounting Standards Board. It was established by the *Institute of
Certified Public Accountants in 1959 and issued Opinions until 1973. Several of
the 31 Opinions issued significantly improved the theory and practice of
accounting and still form part of *generally accepted accounting principles
(GAAP).

accounting profit The amount of *profit calculated by using *generally
accepted accounting principles instead of tax rules. At its simplest the profit is
the revenue for an accounting period less the expenses incurred, using the
concept of *accrual accounting. There are a number of theoretical and practical
problems in arriving at the amount, for both revenue and expenses; the result is
that the accounting profit has less precision than many believe. One of the
consequences of this imprecision is that a number of organizations are tempted
to present profits in their best light. *Accounting standards attempt to prevent
any abuses.

accounting rate of return (ARR) An *accounting ratio that expresses the
profit of an organization before interest and taxation, usually for a year, as a
percentage of the capital employed at the end of the period. Variants of the
measure include using profit after interest and taxation, equity capital
employed, and the average of opening and closing capital employed for the
period. Although it can be used to forecast return on an investment project,
*discounted cash flow measures are acknowledged to be superior for this
purpose.

accounting ratio (financial ratio) A ratio calculated from two or more figures
taken from the *financial statements of a company in order to provide an
indication of the financial performance and position of that company. Ratios
may be expressed as a percentage (e.g. *return on capital employed), in days (e.g.
*debtor collection period), or as a multiple (e.g. *inventory turnover). See
COMMON-SIZE FINANCIAL STATEMENTS; FINANCIAL STATEMENT ANALYSIS;
PERFORMANCE MEASUREMENT; RATIO ANALYSIS.

accounting records See PROPER ACCOUNTING RECORDS; STATUTORY BOOKS.

accounting reference date (ARD) The date at the end of an **accounting
reference period**, i.e. the *financial year for a company, as notified to the
*Registrar of Companies. For companies incorporated after 1 April 1990, it is
normally taken as the last day of the month in which the anniversary of
incorporation falls. Companies wishing to change their ARD must notify
Companies House in advance.

Accounting Series Release In the USA, the former name for a *Financial
Reporting Release.

accounting standard A definitive standard for financial accounting and
reporting established in the form of a *Statement of Standard Accounting
Practice (SSAP) issued by the *Accounting Standards Committee or, since 1990, a

*Financial Reporting Standard (FRS) issued by the *Accounting Standards Board in the UK. In the USA the issue of *Statements of Financial Accounting Standards is the responsibility of the *Financial Accounting Standards Board. Standards set out rules and procedures relating to the measurement, valuation, and disclosure of accounting transactions. In recent years there have been attempts in a number of countries to improve accounting standards by developing a *conceptual framework. It can be argued that national accounting standards are becoming steadily less important with the development of *international accounting standards.

Accounting Standards Board (ASB) The recognized body for setting accounting standards in the UK. It was established in 1990 to replace the *Accounting Standards Committee (ASC) following the recommendations contained in the *Dearing Report. Under the Companies Act, companies (except certain *small companies and *medium-sized companies) must state whether their accounts have been prepared in accordance with the relevant *accounting standards and give details and reasons for any material departures from those standards. The ASB issues *Financial Reporting Exposure Drafts (FREDs), Financial Reporting Standards (FRS), and through its offshoot, the *Urgent Issues Task Force, reports known as Abstracts. The ASB is a subsidiary of the *Financial Reporting Council.

(())) SEE WEB LINKS
• Website of the ASB: includes a list of standards in issue with summaries

Accounting Standards Committee (ASC) A joint committee of the *Consultative Committee of Accountancy Bodies set up in 1976 as a successor to the Accounting Standards Steering Committee. Membership of the ASC was part-time and unpaid; because serious doubts concerning its effectiveness were raised, in 1990 it was replaced by the *Accounting Standards Board. In its life the ASC issued 25 *Statements of Standard Accounting Practice (SSAPs), many of which were adopted by the ASB. The ASC was also responsible for issuing *Statements of Recommended Practice (SORPs). Despite its failings, the ASC did much to improve the general level of financial reporting and accounting in the UK.

accounting system The system designed to record the accounting transactions and events of a business and account for them in a way that complies with its policies and procedures. The basic elements of the accounting system are concerned with collecting, recording, evaluating, and reporting transactions and events.

accounting technician Another name for a *book-keeper. *See also* ASSOCIATION OF ACCOUNTING TECHNICIANS; CERTIFIED ACCOUNTING TECHNICIAN.

account payee only Words printed between two vertical lines in the centre of a UK cheque that, in accordance with the Cheque Act 1992, make the cheque non-transferable. This is to avoid cheques being endorsed and paid into an account other than that of the payee, although it should be noted that banks may argue in some circumstances that they acted in good faith and without negligence if an endorsed cheque is honoured by the bank. In spite of this most cheques are now overprinted 'account payee only' or 'A/C payee', and the words 'not negotiable' are sometimes added.

account reconciliation **1.** A procedure for confirming that the *balance in a chequebook matches the corresponding *bank statement. This is normally done by preparing a *bank reconciliation statement. **2.** A procedure for confirming the reliability of a company's accounting records by regularly comparing balances of transactions. An account reconciliation may be prepared on a daily, monthly, or annual basis.

accounts **1.** The *profit and loss account, *balance sheet, and *cash-flow statements of a company. *See* ANNUAL ACCOUNTS; PUBLISHED ACCOUNTS. *See also* FINANCIAL STATEMENTS. **2.** *See* BOOKS OF ACCOUNT.

Accounts Modernization Directive An EU directive (2003) that requires companies to publish information that provides a 'balanced and comprehensive' analysis of their development and performance during the financial year. This should include not only key financial performance indicators but also, where appropriate, non-financial indicators, including information relating to environmental and employee matters. The directive, which is binding on publicly listed companies for financial years beginning on or after 1 January 2005, has necessitated changes to the UK regulations on the *directors' report.

accounts payable (**trade creditors**) The amounts owed by a business to suppliers (e.g. for raw materials). Accounts payable are classed as *current liabilities on the balance sheet but distinguished from *accruals and other non-trade creditors (such as HM Revenue and Customs).

accounts receivable (**trade debtors**) The amounts owing to a business from customers for invoiced amounts. Accounts receivable are classed as *current assets on the balance sheet, but distinguished from prepayments and other non-trade debtors. A *provision for bad debts is often shown against the accounts receivable balance in line with the *prudence concept. This provision is based on the company's past history of bad debts and its current expectations. A general provision is often based on a percentage of the total credit sales, for example 2% of credit sales made during the period.

accounts receivable collection period The time given to customers in which to pay their accounts. It is common to require customers to pay within 30 days, although in practice the collection period is often not respected. As late-paying customers can often cause major cash-flow problems, a chronological analysis of outstanding debtor amounts should be produced monthly to ensure that all outstanding amounts are followed up by reminders.

accretion An increase in the value of an asset as a result of a physical change (e.g. a growing crop), as opposed to an increase in value as a result of a change in its market price.

accrual (**accrued charge; accrued expense; accrued liability**) An estimate in the accounts of a business of a liability that is not supported by an invoice or a request for payment at the time the accounts are prepared. An accrual is a *current liability on the *balance sheet and will be charged under expenses in the *profit and loss account. Expenses are accrued as set out in the *accruals concept outlined in Statement of Standard Accounting Practice 2. An example of an accrual would be telephone expenses, which are billed in arrears. At the end of the accounting period, if no bill has been received, an estimate (based on past bills) would be made and credited to an accruals account; the corresponding debit would be made to the telephone expense account. The telephone expense account is then cleared to the profit and loss account.

accrual accounting A system of accounting in which *revenue is recognized when it is earned and expenses are recognized as they are incurred. The *accruals concept is a basic *accounting concept used in the preparation of the *profit and loss account and *balance sheet of a business. Accrual accounting differs from *cash accounting, which recognizes transactions when cash has been received or paid. In preparing *financial statements for an *accounting period using accrual accounting, there will inevitably be some estimation and uncertainty in respect of transactions. The reader of the financial statements therefore cannot have the same high level of confidence in these statements as in those using cash-flow accounting.

accruals concept (matching concept) One of the four fundamental *accounting concepts laid down in *Statement of Standard Accounting Practice (SSAP) 2, Disclosure of Accounting Policies; it is also recognized in the Companies Act and the EU's *Fourth Company Law Directive. It requires that revenue and costs are recognized as they are earned or incurred, not as money is received or paid. Income and expenses should be matched with one another, as far as their relationship can be established or justifiably assumed, and dealt with in the *profit and loss account of the period to which they relate. *Accruals and *prepayments are examples of the application of the accruals concept in practice. For example, if a rates bill for both a current and future period is paid, that part relating to the future period is carried forward as a current asset (a prepayment) until it can be matched to the future periods.

The importance of the accruals concept was reaffirmed in *Financial Reporting Standard 18, which superseded SSAP 2, and *International Accounting Standard 18.

accrued benefits Benefits due under a *defined-benefit pension scheme in respect of service up to a given time. Accrued benefits may be calculated in relation to current earnings or protected final earnings. *Statement of Standard Accounting Practice 24 and *Financial Reporting Standard 17, Retirement Benefits, contain regulations on accounting for pension costs in financial accounts. From January 2005 listed companies have to comply with *International Accounting Standard 19, Employee Benefits. *See also* POST-RETIREMENT BENEFITS.

accrued benefits method An actuarial method used in accounting for pension costs in which the actuarial value of liabilities relates at a given date to:
- the benefits, including future increases promised by the rules, for current and deferred pensioners and their dependants;
- the benefits that the members assumed to be in service on the given date will receive for service up to that date only.

Allowance may be made for expected increases in earnings after the given date, and for additional pension increases not promised by the rules. The given date may be a current or future date. The further into the future the adopted date lies, the closer the results will be to those obtained by a prospective benefits valuation method.

accrued charge *See* ACCRUAL.

accrued expense *See* ACCRUAL.

accrued income (accrued revenue) Income that has been earned during an accounting period but not received by the end of it. Accrued income is dealt with as set out in the *accruals concept outlined in *Statement of Standard Accounting Practice 2. For example, interest may have been earned but not received; it should be included in the profit figure (subject to the overriding *prudence concept) and classified as a *current asset on the balance sheet.

accrued liability *See* ACCRUAL.

accrued revenue *See* ACCRUED INCOME.

accumulated depreciation (aggregate depreciation) The total amount of the *depreciation written off the cost price or valuation of a *fixed asset since it was brought into the balance sheet of an organization.

accumulated dividend A dividend that has not been paid to a holder of *cumulative preference shares and is carried forward (i.e. accumulated) to the next accounting period. It represents a liability to the company. The Companies Act requires that where any fixed cumulative dividends on a company's shares are in arrears, both the amount of the arrears and the period(s) in arrears must be disclosed for each class of shares.

accumulated earnings *See* ACCUMULATED PROFITS.

accumulated fund (capital fund) A fund held by a non-profit making organization (such as a club or society) to which a surplus of income over expenditure is credited and to which any deficit is debited. The value of the accumulated funds can be calculated at any time by valuing the net assets (i.e. assets less liabilities) of the organization. The accumulated fund is the equivalent of the capital of a profit-making organization.

accumulated profits (accumulated earnings) The amount showing in the *appropriation of profits account that can be carried forward to the next year's accounts, i.e. after paying dividends, taxes, and putting some to reserve.

accumulating shares Additional *ordinary shares issued to holders of ordinary shares in a company, instead of a dividend. Accumulating shares are a way of replacing annual income with capital growth; they avoid income tax but not capital gains tax. Usually tax is deducted by the company from the declared dividend, in the usual way, and the net dividend is then used to buy additional ordinary shares for the shareholder.

accumulation and maintenance trust *See* DISCRETIONARY TRUST; 18–25 TRUST.

acid-test ratio *See* LIQUID RATIO.

ACIS Abbreviation for Associate of the *Institute of Chartered Secretaries and Administrators.

ACMA Abbreviation for Associate of the *Chartered Institute of Management Accountants.

acquisition accounting (purchase accounting) The accounting procedures followed when one company is taken over by another. The *fair value of the purchase consideration should, for the purpose of consolidated financial statements, be allocated between the underlying net tangible and intangible assets, other than *goodwill, on the basis of the fair value to the acquiring company. Any difference between the fair value of the consideration and the aggregate of the fair values of the separable net assets (including identifiable intangibles, such as patents, licences, and trademarks) will represent goodwill. The results of the acquired company should be brought into the *consolidated profit and loss account from the date of acquisition only.

Acquisition accounting is covered by *Financial Reporting Standard 6, Acquisitions and Mergers, and Financial Reporting Standard 7, Fair Values in Acquisition Accounting. However, for UK listed companies these have now been superseded by *International Financial Reporting Standard 3, Business Combinations. *See also* MERGER ACCOUNTING.

acquisition fraud *See* MISSING TRADER INTRA-COMMUNITY FRAUD.

Acrobat (Adobe Acrobat) A software application produced by Adobe Inc., used for producing and viewing electronic documents. The file format, known as **PDF** (portable document format), allows an exact reproduction of printed text, including fonts. It is widely used for Internet publication of official documents (e.g. annual accounts).

ACRS Abbreviation for *accelerated cost recovery system.

ACT **1.** Abbreviation for *Association of Corporate Treasurers. **2.** Abbreviation for *advance corporation tax.

acting in concert The situation in which a number of persons act collectively in the affairs of an undertaking, whether on the basis of a formal agreement or an informal understanding.

active stocks Securities that have been actively traded on a particular stock exchange during a particular period.

activity In *activity-based costing systems, any operation performed within an organization that causes *costs to be incurred. Examples of activities therefore include processing an order, writing a letter, designing a product, and visiting a customer. The number of activities identified as such will vary from organization to organization. Activity-based costing is founded on the recognition that resources generate costs, activities consume resources, and *cost objects (products, services, or customers) consume activities.

For purposes of *cost allocation, activities may be divided into several different categories:
- **batch-level activities**, i.e. those activities that are performed each time a batch of goods is handled or processed. The cost incurred depends on the number of batches run rather than on the number of units in the batch. The cost is not therefore dependent on the volume of units. *See* BATCH COSTING.
- **product-sustaining-level activities**, i.e. activities relating to specific products that must be carried out regardless of how many units are produced and sold.
- **unit-level activities**, i.e. activities that must be performed for each unit of production.

- **customer-level activities**, i.e. activities that are carried out for a customer but are not related to a specific product.
  See also FACILITY-SUSTAINING ACTIVITY.

activity analysis In *activity-based costing, the identification and description of *activities in an organization. Each department will determine the key activities, how many people work on the activities, and what resources are required to perform the activities. Some activities may be performed in a number of different departments. *See* ACTIVITY DICTIONARY.

activity-based budgeting (ABB) Establishing the *activities that incur costs in each function of an organization, defining the relationships between activities, and using the information to decide how much resource should be allowed for each activity in the *budget. ABB also attempts to determine how well a particular section of the budget is being managed and to explain any variances from budgeted expenditure.

activity-based costing (ABC method; activity costing) A system of *cost allocation proposed by Professors Johnson and Kaplan in their book *Relevance Lost: The Rise and Fall of Management Accounting* (1987), in which they questioned accounting techniques based on *absorption costing. Their method recognizes that costs are incurred by each *activity that takes place within an organization and that products (or customers) should bear costs according to the activities they use. *Cost drivers are identified, together with the appropriate *activity cost pools, which are used to charge costs to products. Adherents of activity-based costing maintain that it provides accurate *cause-and-effect allocations of costs that cannot be obtained from *traditional costing systems.

activity-based management The use made by the management of an organization of *activity-based costing. The identification of *activities and *cost drivers encourages the management to review how projected cost levels compare with the activity levels achieved.

activity costing *See* ACTIVITY-BASED COSTING.

activity cost pool (cost pool) In *activity-based costing, a collection of *indirect costs grouped according to the activity involved. To identify the costs of each activity, cost pool managers will have to ask such questions as:
  - What staff are involved with the activity?
  - What machinery, equipment, vehicles, and computers are used by staff?
  - What materials are used for the activity?

Each activity cost pool has one or more relevant *activity measures (or *cost drivers) that are used in allocating costs, for example:

Activity cost pool	Activity measure
Order processing	Number of orders
Product design	Number of product designs
Deliveries	Number of deliveries
Other costs not included	Not applicable

The size of a particular cost pool will vary widely from one organization to another. For example, a cost pool for order processing may include hundreds of staff in a large organization, whereas a smaller organization may not have a separate cost pool for this activity as it involves only one or two staff. Note that some costs may not be included in any activity cost pool, usually because they are too minor or too difficult to allocate in this way.

activity dictionary A complete listing of the *activities included in an organization's *activity-based costing system. The activity dictionary will give a precise definition of each activity. This will help managers to calculate a cost for each activity. *See* ACTIVITY ANALYSIS.

activity measure In *activity-based costing systems, a measure of the volume or rate of *activity in an *activity cost pool used as a basis for allocating costs. Ideally, the activity measure chosen will be such that any rise or fall in the measure correlates closely with a rise or fall in the total cost of the activity. The terms activity measure and *cost driver are therefore often used synonymously (*see also* ALLOCATION BASE). Examples of activity measures include *direct labour hours, *machine hours, number of deliveries, units of output, and number of production run set-ups. In a large international organization there may be thousands of activity measures, whereas a smaller organization may identify only 20–30 such measures. It is important to state that there is no optimal number of activity measures for an organization. Note also that managers often identify more than one activity measure for each activity.

Some activity measures, such as labour hours, are very closely related to the volume of production, whereas others, such as the number of orders, are not.

activity ratio A ratio used in *management accounting consisting of the *production achieved for an accounting period divided by the production level regarded as achievable for that period.

actual cost The actual expenditure incurred in carrying out any of the activities of an organization, especially as compared with the budgeted or *standard cost.

actuals (physicals) 1. Commodities that can be purchased and used, rather than goods traded on a *futures contract. **2.** Expenses or receipts that have actually occurred, as opposed to targets, budgets, or other projections.

actuarial method A method used in *lease accounting to apportion rentals on the basis of compound *interest; it is also used in accounting for pensions to determine the charge to the *profit and loss account.

actuary A professional trained in the application of statistics and probability theory to issues relating to general insurance and *life assurance. Some are employed by insurance companies to calculate probable lengths of life and advise insurers on the amounts that should be put aside to pay claims and the amount of premium to be charged for each type of risk. They advise on the pricing of insurance contracts and also on the administration of pension funds. The work of the actuary is separate from that of the accountant, although there are certain areas in which they are required to collaborate, particularly in accounting for pension costs (now governed by *Financial Reporting Standard 17 and *International Accounting Standard 19).

added-value statement *See* VALUE-ADDED STATEMENT.

additional paid-in capital In the USA, the excess received from stockholders over the *par value of the stock issued.

additional voluntary contribution (AVC) Additional pension-scheme contributions that employees can make, at their discretion, in order to increase the benefits available from their pension fund on retirement. Additional voluntary contributions can be paid into an employers' scheme or to a scheme of the employee's choice (a free-standing AVC). The employee's total pension contributions must not exceed the limit of 15% of current salary. AVCs are restricted to the difference between 15% of salary and the standard pension contributions. AVCs will be used to increase the pension payable and only in exceptional circumstances will they increase the tax-free lump sum payable on retirement.

adjudication 1. The judgment or decision of a court, especially in bankruptcy proceedings. 2. An assessment by the Stamp Office of the amount of *stamp duty due on a document. A document sent for adjudication will either be stamped as having no duty to pay or the taxpayer will be advised how much is due. An appeal may be made to the High Court if the taxpayer disagrees with the adjudication. The adjudication system no longer applies in the case of *stamp duty land tax.

adjusted gross income In the USA, the difference between the gross income of a taxpayer and the adjustments to income.

adjusted present value A calculation of the *all-equity net present value of an investment or project that is then adjusted to allow for any other impacts, for example any tax concessions on financing. *See also* NET PRESENT VALUE; PRESENT VALUE.

adjusted trial balance A *trial balance to which adjustments have been made; for example, there may be *prepayments and *accruals that need to be taken into account. Separate columns are used for these adjustments, one for debits and one for credits. Once the trial balance has been adjusted in this way, it forms the basis for the *profit and loss account and *balance sheet.

adjusting entries Entries made at a *balance-sheet date under an *accrual accounting system to ensure that the income and expenditure of the business concerned are included in the correct period. Examples of adjustments include those made for *depreciation, *prepayments, *accruals, and closing stock (items that will not be sold until future periods).

adjusting events (post-balance-sheet events) Events that occur between a balance-sheet date and the date on which *financial statements are approved, providing additional evidence of conditions existing at the balance-sheet date. For example, a valuation of a property held at the balance-sheet date that provides evidence of a permanent diminution in value would need to be adjusted in the financial statements. Such events include those that, because of statutory or conventional requirements, are reflected in financial statements. The traditional UK practice is set out in *Statement of Standard Accounting Practice 17, Accounting for Post Balance Sheet Events, which requires that such material events should be reflected in the actual account balances in the financial accounts, where they purport to give a *true and fair view. In 2004 SSAP 17 was replaced by *Financial Reporting Standard 21, Events After the Balance Sheet, which includes a stricter definition of adjusting events based on that in *International Accounting Standard 10. *Compare* NON-ADJUSTING EVENTS.

adjusting journal entry (AJE) An entry made in a *journal to record a movement, such as a prepayment at year end, which has to be posted to a *ledger account.

administration cost variance The difference between the *administration overheads budgeted for in an accounting period and those actually incurred.

administration expenses *See* ADMINISTRATION OVERHEAD.

administration order **1.** An order made in a county court for the administration of the estate of a *judgment debtor. The order normally requires the debtor to pay the debts by instalments; so long as this is done, the creditors referred to in the order cannot enforce their individual claims by other methods without the leave of the court. Administration orders are issued when the debtor has multiple debts but it is thought that *bankruptcy can be avoided. **2.** An order of the court under the Insolvency Act 1986 made in relation to a company in financial difficulties with a view to securing its survival as a going concern or, failing that, to achieving a more favourable realization of its assets than would be possible on a *liquidation. While the order is in force, the affairs of the company are managed by an *administrator and the firm is protected from legal action by the creditors to wind up the business. Since 2003 a form of **out-of-court administration** has also been possible. Under this procedure a company, its directors, or the holder of a floating *charge can appoint an administrator with a view to achieving the same purposes as an administrator appointed by a court.

administration overhead (administration expenses) That part of the general *overhead of an organization that is incurred in carrying out its administrative activities. It includes general office salaries, stationery, telephones, etc.

administrative receiver A *receiver appointed by the holder of a floating *charge covering the whole, or substantially all, of a company's assets. The administrative receiver has the power to sell the assets that are secured by the charge or to carry on the company's business. Subject to certain exceptions, an administrative receiver cannot be appointed by the holder of a floating charge created after 15 September 2003; it is now possible, however, for the holder of such a charge to appoint an *administrator without obtaining a court order.

administrator **1.** Any person appointed by the courts, or by private arrangement, to manage the property of another. **2.** Any person appointed by the courts to take charge of the affairs of a deceased person, who died without making a will. This includes collection of assets, payment of debts, and distribution of the surplus to those persons entitled to inherit, according to the laws of intestacy (*see* INTESTATE). The administrator must be in possession of *letters of administration as proof of the authority vested by the courts. **3.** Any person appointed by the courts to implement an *administration order or undertake the duty of an *administrative receiver, or appointed to carry out an out-of-court administration of the affairs of a person or a company. Debt administration is now recognized as an *ancillary credit business.

Adobe Acrobat *See* ACROBAT.

ADR Abbreviation for *American depositary receipt.

ad valorem (Latin: according to value) Denoting a tax, duty, or commission calculated as a percentage of the total invoice value of goods or services. *Value added tax is an *ad valorem* tax.

advance A payment on account or a loan. In a *partnership it refers to any amount paid into the partnership in excess of the agreed capital contributions. Under the Partnership Act 1890 interest is payable on advances, unless the partners agree to the contrary. On dissolution the advance would be repaid after any external creditors were paid but before the distribution of capital to the partners.

advance corporation tax (ACT) Formerly, an advance payment of *corporation tax payable when a company made a *qualifying distribution. ACT was abolished on 6 April 1999, although rules exist to permit the recovery of payments prior to this date. Larger companies must now pay corporation tax in instalments.

advancement Payment by a parent (during his or her lifetime) to a child of an amount that the child would receive as beneficiary, or as heir, on the death of that parent.

advance payment bond A guarantee that any advance payments made by a customer will be reimbursed if the company cannot fulfil its obligations under the relevant contract. Such guarantees are normally given by the company's bankers, who are indemnified by the company.

adverse opinion An opinion expressed in an *auditors' report to the effect that the financial statements do not give a *true and fair view of the organization's activities. This situation usually arises when there is a disagreement between the auditor and the directors, and the auditor considers the effect of the disagreement so material or pervasive that the financial statements are seriously misleading. Audit reports are covered by the *Auditing Practices Board's Statement of Auditing Standards 600, Auditors' Reports on Financial Statements. *See* QUALIFIED AUDIT REPORT.

adverse variance (unfavourable variance) In *standard costing and *budgetary control, the differences between actual and budgeted performance of an organization where the differences create a deduction from the budgeted profit. For example, this may occur if the actual sales revenue is less than that budgeted or the actual costs exceed budgeted costs. *Compare* FAVOURABLE VARIANCE. *See also* ANALYSIS OF VARIANCE; VARIANCE.

advice note A document issued by a supplier of goods advising the customer that the goods have been sent. The advice note is generally received before the goods themselves.

AFAANZ Abbreviation for *Accounting and Finance Association of Australia and New Zealand.

affiliate A company linked in some sense to another company. The concept has no legal status in the UK. *See also* ASSOCIATED UNDERTAKING.

affinity card A *credit card issued to members of a particular group (such as a club, college, etc.) or to supporters of a particular charity; the credit-card company pledges to make a donation to the charity or organization for each card issued and may also donate a small proportion of the money spent by card users. In the UK, affinity cards are sometimes called **charity cards**.

after date The words used in a *bill of exchange to indicate that the period of the bill should commence from the date inserted on the bill, e.g. '… 30 days after date, we promise to pay …'. *Compare* AFTER SIGHT; AT SIGHT.

after sight The words used in a *bill of exchange to indicate that the period of the bill should commence from the date on which the drawee is presented with it for acceptance, i.e. has sight of it. *Compare* AFTER DATE; AT SIGHT.

age allowance The increased *personal allowance available to taxpayers aged 65 and over. The age allowance for taxpayers aged 65–74 is £9490 and for those 75 and over it is £9640 (2010–11). There is an income limit of £22,900 for age allowance. The allowance is reduced at a rate of £1 off the allowance for every £2 by which the income exceeds the income limit, until the basic personal allowance is reached.

age analysis A listing of debtors' accounts (i.e. the amounts owing to a business), usually produced monthly, which analyses the age of the debts by splitting them into such categories as those up to one month old, two months old, and more than two months old. As a basic part of the credit control system, the analysis should be regularly examined so that any appropriate follow-up action may be taken.

agency agreement **1.** An agreement between a customer and a bank allowing the customer to bank cheques at one of its branches even though he or she does not have an account with that bank. It is usually entered into for logistical reasons. A charge is made by the bank for this service. **2.** Any agreement between an agent and a principal. *See* AGENCY RELATIONSHIP.

agency fee (facility fee) An annual fee paid to an agent for the work and responsibility involved in managing a loan after it has been signed.

agency relationship A relationship in which a principal engages an agent to perform some service on his or her behalf; this involves delegating authority by the principal. As it has to be assumed that the agent may not always act in the best interests of the principal, the principal incurs costs in monitoring and controlling the behaviour of the agent. In turn, the agent will incur bonding costs in convincing the principal that his or her interests will not be harmed. Even when carefully monitored, the agent may still take decisions that do not always maximize the welfare of the principal; these decisions can result in what is called a residual loss. The sum of the monitoring and bonding costs together with the residual loss forms the **agency costs**. Even in an unregulated economy managers may choose to provide financial statements, examined by independent auditors, to shareholders and creditors in order to reduce agency costs. By supplying informative financial statements to external parties on the basis of information held by them, managers may avoid costly disputes and more expensive mechanisms for controlling their actions. These aspects of an agency relationship are sometimes referred to as **agency theory**. The so-called **agency problem** that arises when shareholders and managers have different interests and 'asymmetric information' was brought into sharp focus by the collapse of the US companies Enron and WorldCom in 2002. *See also* GOAL CONGRUENCY.

agent A person appointed by another person, known as the *principal, to act on his or her behalf. The directors of a company are agents of the shareholders (the principal). *See* AGENCY RELATIONSHIP.

aggregate depreciation *See* ACCUMULATED DEPRECIATION.

aggregator A firm that collates and presents information about an individual's bank accounts, investments, insurance policies, etc. so that the person concerned can manage all his or her financial affairs via a single website.

AGM Abbreviation for *annual general meeting.

agreed bid A *takeover bid that is supported by a majority of the shareholders of the target company, whereas a **hostile bid** is not welcomed by the majority of the shareholders of the target company.

agricultural property relief An *inheritance tax relief available on the transfer of agricultural property when certain conditions are met. Since March 1992 the relief has been at a rate of 100% or 50%. The 100% rate applies if the transferor has vacant possession of the property or the right to vacant possession within the following 12 months; it may also apply if the property was let after 31 August 1995. Otherwise the 50% rate applies. Houses or cottages on farmland may qualify for the relief if the Revenue is satisfied that they are occupied for the purposes of agriculture.

AIA **1.** Abbreviation for *Association of International Accountants.
2. Abbreviation for *Annual Investment Allowance.

AIAB Abbreviation for Associate of the *International Association of Book-keepers.

AICPA Abbreviation for *American Institute of Certified Public Accountants.

AIDB Abbreviation for Accountancy Investigation and Discipline Board. *See* ACCOUNTANCY AND ACTUARIAL DISCIPLINE BOARD.

AIFA Abbreviation for *Association of Independent Financial Advisers.

AIM Abbreviation for *Alternative Investment Market.

AJE Abbreviation for *adjusting journal entry.

alienation of assets The sale by a borrower of some or all of the assets that form the actual or implied security for a loan. It is therefore common practice to include a clause in the document setting up a loan, which restricts the disposal of the borrower's assets to specific circumstances.

alimony payment In the USA, payments in a divorce settlement. They are treated as deductions from *adjusted gross income by the payer, but the recipient treats them as income for tax purposes.

all-equity net present value A calculation of *net present value made as if the firm, project, or investment were funded entirely by equity. In such cases, the *discount rate is the discount rate for equity. *See also* ADJUSTED PRESENT VALUE; PRESENT VALUE.

all-financial resources concept In the USA, the basis for preparing a *statement of changes in financial position. The statement presents transactions affecting *working capital and transactions not affecting working capital if they are of a material noncurrent nature, such as the acquisition of a fixed asset in exchange for a long-term liability.

Allfinanz *See* BANCASSURANCE.

all-inclusive income concept A concept used in drawing up a *profit and loss account, in which all items of profit and loss are included in the statement to arrive at a figure of *earnings; this is the approach adopted in the UK and the USA. Although it is claimed that this basis gives the fullest picture of the operation of an enterprise, it does lead to a volatility in earnings figures as one-off costs, such as redundancies and sale of assets, will be included. To assist prediction of future profits, users are often more interested in the sustainable profits, which are shown using *reserve accounting, which is the alternative basis for drawing up a profit and loss account.

allocation 1. *See* COST ALLOCATION. 2. The number of shares in a new issue allotted (*see* ALLOTMENT) to an investor or syndicate of investors.

allocation base In *management accounting, the basis that is used to allocate costs to *cost objects. In a *traditional costing system there may be a single allocation base for each cost object, whereas in an *activity-based costing system there may be many such bases. In practice the term allocation base is often used synonymously with *activity measure or *cost driver. *See* COST ALLOCATION.

allotment A method of distributing previously unissued shares in a limited company in exchange for a contribution of capital. An application for such shares will often be made after the issue of a prospectus on the *flotation of a public company or on the privatization of a state-owned industry. The company accepts the application by dispatching a **letter of allotment** to the applicant stating how many shares have been allotted; the applicant then has an unconditional right to be entered in the *register of members in respect of those shares. If the number of shares applied for exceeds the number available (oversubscription), allotment is made by a random draw or by a proportional allocation. Applicants that have been allotted fewer shares than they applied for receive a cheque for the unallotted balance (an application must be accompanied by a cheque for the full value of the shares applied for).

allotted shares Shares distributed by *allotment to new shareholders (allottees). The shares form part of the **allotted share capital**. *See also* ISSUED SHARE CAPITAL.

allowable capital loss *See* CAPITAL LOSS.

allowance 1. An amount deducted from an invoice; for example, to compensate for damaged goods. 2. An amount given to an employee for expenses, such as the cost of travel. 3. A tax allowance. *See* CAPITAL ALLOWANCES; INCOME TAX ALLOWANCES.

allowance for doubtful accounts *See* PROVISION FOR BAD DEBTS.

all-purpose financial statements *See* GENERAL PURPOSE FINANCIAL
STATEMENTS.

alpha coefficient A measure of the expected return on a particular share
compared to the expected return on shares with a similar *beta coefficient. It
identifies the specific risk associated with a share as opposed to the systematic
risk associated with securities of the same class.

alpha risk and beta risk Risks that occur in the sampling procedure
undertaken by an *auditor. An auditor may reject a population that should have
been accepted (alpha risk) or accept it when it should have been rejected (beta
risk). *See* AUDIT RISK; SAMPLE.

alteration of share capital An increase, reduction (*see* REDUCTION OF
CAPITAL), or any other change in the *authorized share capital of a company. If
acting in accordance with the Companies Act, a limited company can increase
its authorized capital as appropriate. It can also rearrange its existing authorized
capital (e.g. by consolidating 100 shares of £1 into 25 shares of £4 or by
subdividing 100 shares of £1 into 200 of 50p) and cancel unissued shares.

alternative accounting rules Alternative rules for valuing certain assets
under the Companies Act. These rules modify the *historical-cost convention.
According to the modified rules *intangible assets may be valued at current cost
(with the exception of *goodwill). Tangible fixed assets may be included at
market value, determined as at their last valuation date, or at current cost. Fixed-
asset investments may be valued at market value, determined as at their last
valuation date, or at a value determined on any basis considered by the directors
to be appropriate to the circumstances. Current-asset investments and stock
may be included at current cost, unless the *net realizable value is lower, in
which case this must be used. Any *permanent diminution in value must be
provided for. Accounts prepared under the alternative accounting rules are
described as being prepared under the *modified historical-cost convention.

alternative budgets Financial or quantitative budgets produced for
consideration by the management of an organization in addition to the budgets
adopted. The alternative budgets are based upon alternative policies, which may
or may not be pursued by the organization at a later date.

alternative costs **1.** The costs that would apply if an alternative set of
assumptions were adopted. **2.** The benefits foregone when a second ranked
alternative is compared to the chosen alternative. *See* OPPORTUNITY COST.

alternative finance arrangements A term applied in the UK Finance Acts
to certain lending arrangements that comply with Islamic law (*see* ISLAMIC
FINANCE). The Finance Act 2005 introduced a tax code under which tax is levied
on the lender and relief is granted to the borrower as if (broadly) a proportion of
each payment were interest.

Alternative Investment Market (AIM) A market of the *London Stock
Exchange that opened in June 1995 to replace the Unlisted Securities Market. It
provides an opportunity for smaller growing companies to raise capital and have
their shares traded in a market, without the expense of a full market listing. Since

its formation nearly 3000 smaller companies have traded their shares on this market and the number of institutions investing in the market is increasing.

((⊕)) SEE WEB LINKS

• Information for companies, traders, and investors from the website of the London Stock Exchange

Altman's Z score *See* Z SCORE. *See also* CORPORATE FAILURE PREDICTION.

amalgamation The combination of two or more companies. The combination may be effected by one company acquiring others, by the merging of two or more companies, or by existing companies being dissolved and a new company formed to take over the combined business. The relevant accounting standards are *Financial Reporting Standard 6, Acquisitions and Mergers, and *International Financial Reporting Standard 3, Business Combinations. *See also* ACQUISITION ACCOUNTING; MERGER ACCOUNTING.

American Accounting Association (AAA) An influential organization with a membership consisting primarily of academic accountants. Originally founded in 1916 as the American Association of University Instructors in Accounting, the Association adopted its present name in 1936. The Association has contributed to the development of accounting theory through the publication of reports, papers, and journals (notably *The Accounting Review*) and gives a number of awards.

((⊕)) SEE WEB LINKS

• Website of the AAA

American depositary receipt (ADR) A receipt issued by a US bank to a member of the US public who has bought shares in a foreign country. The certificates are denominated in US dollars and can be traded as a security in US markets. The advantages of ADRs are the reduction in administration costs and the avoidance of stamp duty on each transaction.

American Institute of Certified Public Accountants (AICPA) The professional organization of practising certified public accountants. The Institute, which was founded in 1887, provides technical advice and guidance to its members and such government bodies as the *Securities and Exchange Commission. It issues many influential publications in the areas of accounting, auditing, and taxation.

((⊕)) SEE WEB LINKS

• Website of the AICPA: includes advice on personal finance as well as a wide range of professional resources

American option An *option that can be exercised on any business day prior to its expiry date. *Compare* EUROPEAN OPTION.

American Society of Women Accountants An organization whose membership consists of practising women accountants; its aim is to promote women's interests in the accounting profession.

amortization 1. The process of treating as an expense the annual amount deemed to waste away from a fixed asset. The concept is particularly applied to leases, which are acquired for a given sum for a specified term at the end of which the lease will have no value. It is customary to divide the cost of the lease by the number of years of its term and treat the result as an annual charge against profit. While this method does not necessarily reflect the value of the lease at any given time, it is an equitable way of allocating the original cost between periods. *Compare* DEPRECIATION.

*Goodwill may also be amortized. *Financial Reporting Standard 10, Goodwill and Intangible Assets, requires the writing-off of goodwill to the *profit and loss account in regular instalments over the period of its economic life. However, non-amortization is an option in exceptional circumstances.

2. The repayment of debt by a borrower in a series of instalments over a period. Each payment includes interest and part repayment of the capital.

3. The spreading of the *front-end fee charged on taking out a loan over the life of a loan for accounting purposes.

4. In the USA, another word for *depreciation.

amortization schedule A schedule that summarizes the dates on which specified amounts must be paid in the repayment of a loan.

amortized cost That part of the value of an asset that has been written off; it represents the *accumulated depreciation to date.

amortizing loan A loan in which the repayment is made in more than one instalment. *Compare* BULLET LOAN.

AMPS Abbreviation for *auction market preferred stock.

analysis of variance **(ANOVA; variance analysis)** In *standard costing and *budgetary control, the analysis of *variances in order to seek their causes. The total *profit variance or *production cost variance is analysed into sub-variances to indicate the major reasons for the difference between budgeted figures and actual figures. The most important sub-variances include:
  *direct labour total cost variance
  *direct labour efficiency variance
  *direct labour rate of pay variance
  *direct materials total cost variance
  *direct materials price variance
  *direct materials usage variance
  *overhead total variance
  *overhead efficiency variance
  *overhead expenditure variance
  *fixed overhead total variance
  *variable overhead total variance
  *sales margin price variance
  *sales margin volume variance.

analytical auditing An analytical approach to an audit that compares figures and other financial and non-financial data, either internally or with external data, to decide whether the picture presented appears to be reasonable. Analytical auditing is used in the initial planning stage of an audit, during the audit, or in its final stages when the tests of details have been completed. *See also* ANALYTICAL REVIEW.

analytical review An audit test designed to provide evidence of the completeness, accuracy, and validity of accounting records and *financial statements. Analytical review is a type of *substantive test that may be used in planning and undertaking an audit. It works by comparing figures and other financial and non-financial data, either internally or with external data, to decide whether they are reasonable. Procedures range from simple comparisons (e.g. comparing current amounts with those of earlier years) to more sophisticated methods using computer *audit software and advanced statistical techniques (e.g. multiple regression analysis).

ancillary credit business A business involved in credit brokerage, debt adjusting, debt counselling, debt collecting, debt administration, or the operation of a credit-reference agency (*see* CREDIT RATING).
• **Credit brokerage** involves the introduction of individuals wishing to obtain credit to persons carrying on a consumer-credit business.
• **Debt adjusting** is the process by which a third party negotiates terms for the discharge of a debt due under consumer-credit agreements or consumer-hire agreements with the creditor or owner on behalf of the debtor or hirer. The latter may also pay a third party to take over an obligation to discharge a debt or to undertake any similar activity concerned with its liquidation.
• **Debt counselling** is the giving of advice (other than by the original creditor and certain others) to debtors or hirers about the liquidation of debts due under consumer-credit agreements or consumer-hire agreements.
• In **debt collecting** someone other than the creditor takes steps to procure the payment of debt owing. A creditor may engage a debt collector for this purpose.
• A **credit-reference agency** collects information concerning the financial standing of individuals and supplies this information to those seeking it.
• **Debt administration**, which was legally recognized as a form of ancillary credit business in 2006, is the process in which an *administrator is appointed to manage the property of a debtor, including his or her salary or wages. The debt administrator may be appointed by court order (*see* ADMINISTRATION ORDER) or by a voluntary decision of the debtor.
The Consumer Credit Act 1974 provides for the licensing of ancillary credit businesses and regulates their activities.

anergy *See* SYNERGY.

Annual Abstract of Statistics An annual publication of the *Office for National Statistics giving UK industrial, vital, legal, and social statistics. It is now available in both online and print versions.

annual accounts (annual report; report and accounts) The *financial statements of an organization, generally published annually. In the UK, incorporated bodies have a legal obligation to publish annual accounts and file them at Companies House. Annual accounts consist of a *profit and loss account, *balance sheet, *cash-flow statement (if required), and *statement of total recognized gains and losses, together with supporting notes and the *directors' report and *auditors' report. Companies falling into the legally defined *small companies and *medium-sized companies categories may file *abbreviated accounts and small companies may also enjoy *audit exemption. Some bodies are regulated by other statutes; for example, many financial institutions and their accounts will have to comply with their own regulations. Non-incorporated bodies, such as partnerships, are not legally obliged to produce accounts but may do so for their own information, for their banks if funding is being sought, and for the HM Revenue for taxation purposes. Under the Companies Act 2006 listed companies are now required to make their accounts available on a website. *See also* ANNUAL RETURN; GENERAL PURPOSE FINANCIAL STATEMENTS; PUBLISHED ACCOUNTS.

annual exemption An *exempt transfer under *inheritance tax legislation allowing £3000 to be given each year as a gift without liability to inheritance tax. This has remained unchanged since 6 April 1981. Spouses or civil partners each have their own exemption. If the exemption is not used or not fully used during a *fiscal year, the amount not used can be carried forward to the next tax year only, to cover gifts made in that following year.

annual general meeting (AGM) A meeting of the members of a *public limited company required to be held each calendar year. Not more than 18 months should elapse between meetings, and 21 days' written notice (specifying the meeting as the annual general meeting) must usually be given. AGMs are principally concerned with the presentation of the accounts and the directors' and auditor's reports, recommendations for the payment of dividends, the election of directors, and the appointment and remuneration of the auditor. Other matters may be treated if notice has been given to shareholders. Under the Companies Act 2006 private companies are no longer required to hold an AGM. *See also* GENERAL MEETING.

Annual Investment Allowance (AIA) A *capital allowance available from April 2008. It enables a business to offset 100% of its capital expenditure in any one year against corporation tax, to a limit of £50,000. The allowance, which is available to businesses of any size or legal form, replaces the various *first-year allowances on specified *plant and machinery previously available to small and medium-sized companies. It cannot be claimed on non-commercial motor vehicles.

annualization In the USA, a procedure specified by the Internal Revenue Code in which taxable income for part of a year is multiplied by 12 and divided by the number of months involved to give a monthly amount.

annual percentage rate (APR) The annual equivalent *rate of return on a loan or investment in which the rate of interest and charges are specified in terms of an annual rate of interest. Most investment institutions are now required by law to specify the APR when the interest intervals are more frequent than annual. Similarly those charge cards that advertise monthly rates of interest (say, 2%) must state the equivalent APR. In this case it would be $[(1.02)^{12} - 1] = 26.8\%$.

annual report *See* ANNUAL ACCOUNTS.

annual return A document that must be filed with the *Registrar of Companies within seven months of the end of the relevant accounting period (ten months for private companies). Information required on the annual return includes the address of the registered office of the company and the names, addresses, nationality, and occupations of its directors and secretary: details of the share capital and shareholders must also be included. The *directors' report must be annexed to the return, as must the *annual accounts (or *abbreviated accounts) and the *auditors' report (unless exempt from statutory audit).

annuitant A person receiving an *annuity.

annuity 1. A contract in which a person pays a premium to an insurance company, usually in one lump sum, and in return receives periodic payments for an agreed period or for the rest of his or her life. An annuity has been described as the opposite of *life assurance as the policyholder pays the lump sum and the insurer makes the regular payments. Annuities form the basis for private pensions in most developed countries. *See also* ANNUITY CERTAIN; DEFERRED ANNUITY. **2.** A payment made on such a contract.

annuity certain An *annuity in which payments continue for a specified period irrespective of the life or death of the person covered. In general, annuities cease on the death of the policyholder unless they are annuities certain.

annuity method A method of calculating the *depreciation on a fixed asset. The objective of the method is to produce an approximately constant annual charge for the total depreciation and cost of capital of an asset. It is calculated in such a way that a low depreciation charge is made in the earlier years when interest costs are high, and a higher charge is made in the later years when interest costs are lower. It is less popular than the *straight-line method or the *diminishing-balance method.

annulment The cancellation by a court of a bankruptcy order, which occurs when it considers that the debtor was wrongly made bankrupt, when all the debts have been paid in full, or when the court approves a *voluntary arrangement. The power of annulment is discretionary. Annulment does not affect the validity of any sale of property or other action that has already taken place as a result of the bankruptcy order. See feature BANKRUPTCY LAW on p. 52.

ANOVA *Acronym for* *analysis of variance.

antedate To date a document before the date on which it is drawn up. This is not necessarily illegal or improper. For instance, an ante-dated cheque is not in law invalid. *Compare* POST-DATE.

anti-avoidance provisions A cluster of statutory provisions designed to stop certain arrangements that would otherwise reduce the taxpayer's tax liability. The main anti-avoidance provisions, as found in the Taxes Act 1988, are:
• a clause dealing with so-called dividend stripping and bond washing;
• a clause concerning manufactured dividends;
• a clause dealing with transactions in securities;
• the so-called 'Beatles clause' designed to counter an arrangement entered into by the group whereby they sold their future income to a company in exchange for a (pre-1965 non-taxable) capital sum received.
See TAX AVOIDANCE.

anti-trust laws Laws passed in the USA, from 1890 onwards, making it illegal to do anything in restraint of trade, set up monopolies, or otherwise interfere with free trade and competition.

APACS Abbreviation for *Association for Payment Clearing Services.

APB 1. Abbreviation for *Accounting Principles Board. **2.** Abbreviation for *Auditing Practices Board.

APC Abbreviation for *Auditing Practices Committee.

application and allotment account A *ledger account used in the process of applications for and *allotment of a company's share capital. When the shares are offered, potential shareholders (applicants) apply to buy them on an *application form with a cheque to cover the cost of the shares. This is known as the **application process**. On receipt of the applicants' money, the company debits the bank account with the cash received and credits an application and allotment account. When the shares are allocated to the applicants they become the **allottees**, i.e. the new shareholders; this is known as the **process of allotment**. The book-keeping entries on allotment involve debiting the application and allotment account and crediting the share capital or share premium, as appropriate. If the applications exceed the number of shares available, each applicant receives a scaled down number of shares and the excess application money is returned. The application and allotment account may also be split into two separate accounts: the application account and the allotment account.

application controls Controls relating to the transactions and *standing data for each computer-based accounting system; they are, therefore, specific to each such application. Application controls, which may be manual or programmed, are designed to ensure the completeness and accuracy of the accounting records and the validity of the entries made. An example of an application control designed to check completeness would be a manual or programmed agreement of control totals, i.e. the total of the source documents and the total of the amounts input would be compared. Other examples of application controls include checks to ensure that the correct *master files are used, that data has been updated, and that output reports are both complete and accurate. *Compare* GENERAL CONTROLS. *See also* COMPUTER-ASSISTED AUDIT TECHNIQUES.

application for listing The process by which a company applies to a stock exchange for its securities to be traded on that exchange. In obtaining the listing a company will be required to abide by the rules of the exchange. The advantage for a company in obtaining a listing is that it will be able to raise funds by issuing shares on the stock exchange and the marketability of the shares it issues will attract investors. *See also* FLOTATION; LISTING REQUIREMENTS.

application form A form, issued by a newly floated company with its *prospectus, on which members of the public apply for shares in the company. *See also* ALLOTMENT.

applications software Computer programs that are designed for a particular purpose or application. Accounts programs are therefore applications software, as is *audit software. *See also* BUSINESS SOFTWARE PACKAGE; SOFTWARE.

applied overhead *See* ABSORBED OVERHEAD.

applied research *See* RESEARCH AND DEVELOPMENT COSTS.

apportionment (cost apportionment) Charging a proportion of a cost to a *cost centre or *cost unit because the cost centres or cost units are not directly incurring those costs although they share in incurring them. A *basis of apportionment is always required. *See also* COST ALLOCATION.

appraisal The assessment of alternative courses of action with a view to establishing which action should be taken. Appraisals may be financial, economic, or technical in emphasis. *See* DECISION MAKING.

appraisal costs *See* COST OF QUALITY. *See also* ENVIRONMENTAL COSTS.

appraisal definition A method of *depreciation that values an asset at the beginning of an *accounting period and again at the end. Any diminution in value is charged as an expense to the *profit and loss account.

appreciation 1. An increase in the value of an *asset through inflation, a rise in market price, or interest earned. The directors of a company have an obligation to adjust the nominal value of land and buildings and other assets in balance sheets to take account of appreciation. *See* ASSET STRIPPING. 2. An increase in the value of a currency with a *floating exchange rate relative to another currency. *Compare* DEPRECIATION; DEVALUATION.

appropriation The allocation of the *net profits of an organization in its accounts. For example, in a company appropriations are usually in the form of cash *dividends or *scrip dividends to shareholders, transfers to reserves, and amounts for taxation. In a partnership appropriations tend to be in the form of salaries, interest on capital, and profit.

appropriation account 1. *See* PROFIT AND LOSS APPROPRIATION ACCOUNT. 2. A financial statement prepared by a government department to show its expenditure and receipts for a financial year.

APR Abbreviation for *annual percentage rate.

a priori theories of accounting Theories used in measurement and valuation systems of accounting that are based on deductive reasoning from certain axioms or assumptions rather than experience. The 1960s was a particularly fruitful period for a priori research in financial accounting. *See also* NORMATIVE THEORIES OF ACCOUNTING; POSITIVE ACCOUNTING THEORY.

APS Abbreviation for *Asset Protection Scheme.

APT Abbreviation for *arbitrage pricing theory.

arbitrage The entering into a set of financial obligations to obtain profits with no risk, usually by taking advantage of differences in interest rates, exchange rates, or commodity prices between one market and another. Arbitrage is non-speculative because an arbitrageur will only switch from one market to another if the rates or prices in both markets are known and if the profit to be gained outweighs the costs of the operation. Thus, a large stock of a commodity in a user country may force its price below that in a producing country; if the difference is greater than the cost of shipping the goods back to the producing country, this could provide a profitable opportunity for arbitrage. Similar opportunities arise with *bills of exchange and foreign currencies. A person or firm that engages in arbitrage is known as an **arbitrageur**.

arbitrage pricing theory (APT) A model proposed by Stephen Ross in 1976 for calculating returns on securities. It is an alternative to the *capital asset pricing model (CAPM). APT assumes a number of different systematic risk factors without, however, definitely identifying the various types of risk. In setting *discount rates for decisions or valuations, companies therefore generally prefer to base their calculations on the CAPM.

arbitrary allocation A *cost allocation in which the *allocation base used is not likely to give accurate costs. For example, the cost of a lecture is not significantly dependent on the number of students: a class of 10 students requires one lecturer for (say) one hour as does a class of 200 students. Therefore using the number of students as an allocation base would result in an arbitrary allocation. The system of *activity-based costing is based on the idea that arbitrary allocations should be avoided and replaced with *cause-and-effect allocations.

arbitration The determination of a dispute by an arbitrator or arbitrators rather than by a court of law. Any civil (i.e. noncriminal) matter may be settled in this way; commercial contracts often contain **arbitration clauses** providing for this to be done in a specified way. Various industries and chambers of commerce have set up tribunals for dealing with disputes in their particular trades or business. The judgment of the arbitrator may be either binding or indicative. The current legal framework for arbitration is provided by the Arbitration Act 1996, which repealed part of the Arbitration Act 1950 and the whole of the Arbitration Acts of 1976 and 1979.

ARD Abbreviation for *accounting reference date.

Argenti's failure model *See* CORPORATE FAILURE PREDICTION.

arithmetic mean (arithmetic average) An average obtained by adding together the individual quantities and dividing the total by their number. For example, the average of 6, 7, and 107 is $(6 + 7 + 107)/3 = 40$. This value, however, gives no idea of the spread of numbers. *Compare* GEOMETRIC MEAN; WEIGHTED AVERAGE.

arm's length **1.** Denoting a transaction entered into by unrelated parties, each acting in their own best interests in paying or charging prices based on fair market values. In the preparation of financial statements it is normally assumed that all transactions are conducted at arm's length, although it is appreciated that this may not be the case with companies belonging to the same group, who make special arrangements between themselves for taxation or other reasons. Because of the possibility of transactions being carried out at other than arm's length and the reader of financial statements being unaware of this fact, *Financial Reporting Standard 8, Related Party Disclosures, was issued in 1995. From 1 January 2005 this was superseded for listed companies by *International Accounting Standard 24. *See* RELATED PARTIES; RELATED PARTY TRANSACTIONS. **2.** Denoting an investment portfolio in which the owner is not aware of the asset composition or the transactions entered into. *See* BLIND TRUST.

ARR Abbreviation for *accounting rate of return.

arrangement **1.** *See* DEED OF ARRANGEMENT; SCHEME OF ARRANGEMENT; VOLUNTARY ARRANGEMENT. **2.** A transaction or sale arranged by an intermediary, as in the case of an estate agent selling a mortgage as an agent for a bank.

arrears A liability that has not been settled by the due date. For example, *cumulative preference shares entitle the shareholders to receive an annual fixed dividend. If this is not paid, the dividend is said to be in arrears and this fact must be disclosed in the notes to the financial statements.

articles of association The document that governs the running of a registered company. It sets out voting rights of shareholders, conduct of shareholders' and directors' meetings, powers of the management, etc. Either the articles are submitted with a *memorandum of association when application is made for incorporation or the relevant model articles contained in the Companies Regulations 2008 are adopted. The articles constitute a contract between the company and its members but this applies only to the rights of shareholders in their capacity as members. Therefore directors or company solicitors (for example) cannot use the articles to enforce their rights. The articles of a public company may be altered by a *special resolution of the members in a general meeting; since 2007 it has been possible to change the articles of a private company by *written resolution.

articles of incorporation (corporate charter) In the USA, the official document that details a company's existence. It is similar to the *memorandum of association formerly required in the UK (now subsumed within the *articles of association).

articles of partnership *See* PARTNERSHIP AGREEMENT.

articulated accounts Accounts prepared under the *double-entry book-keeping system, in which the retained earnings figure on the *profit and loss account equals the increase in net worth of the business on the *balance sheet, subject to any other increases, such as an injection of new capital.

artificial person An entity that is recognized by the law as a **legal person**, i.e. one having legal rights and duties distinct from the individuals who comprise it. For example, a company is a person in the sense that it can sue and be sued, hold property, etc., in its own name. It is not, however, an individual or natural person. *See* CORPORATION.

ASB **1.** Abbreviation for *Accounting Standards Board. **2.** Abbreviation for *asset-backed security.

ASC Abbreviation for *Accounting Standards Committee.

A shares In the USA, the most important class of *ordinary shares. A shares usually have greater voting power than *B shares and may carry various other privileges.

ASOBAT Acronym for *A Statement of Basic Accounting Theory*, an influential publication by the *American Accounting Association. It argued for a user-friendly approach to financial statements and considered the *qualitative characteristics of accounting information.

as per advice Words written on a *bill of exchange to indicate that the drawee has been informed that the bill is being drawn on him or her.

assented stock A security, usually an ordinary share, the owner of which has agreed to the terms of a *takeover bid. During the takeover negotiations, different prices may be quoted for assented and **non-assented stock**.

assessable capital stocks In the USA: **1.** Capital stock of banks, subjecting stockholders to liabilities in excess of the sum originally subscribed **2.** Capital stock not fully paid and therefore subject to calls.

asset In common terms any object, tangible or intangible, that is of value to its possessor. In most cases it either is cash or can be turned into cash; exceptions include prepayments, which may represent payments made for rent, rates, or motor licences, in cases in which the time paid for has not yet expired. Most accounting bodies throughout the world would now define an asset as a source of future economic benefits obtained or controlled as a result of past transactions or events. *Tangible assets include land and buildings, plant and machinery, fixtures and fittings, trading stock, investments, debtors, and cash; *intangible assets include *goodwill, patents, copyrights, and trademarks. *See also* DEFERRED DEBIT.

For *capital gains tax purposes, an asset consists of all forms of property, whether situated in the UK or abroad, including options, debts, incorporeal property, currency (other than sterling), and any form of property either created by the person disposing of it or owned without being acquired (*see* CHARGEABLE ASSETS). It must, however, consist of some form of property for which a value can be ascertained. Some assets are, however, exempt from capital gains tax.

asset-backed commercial paper (ABCP) *See* COMMERCIAL PAPER.

asset-backed fund A fund in which the money is invested in tangible or corporate assets, such as property or shares, rather than being treated as savings loaned to a bank or other institution. Asset-backed funds can be expected to grow with inflation in a way that bank savings cannot.

asset-backed medium-term note (ABMTN) *See* MEDIUM-TERM NOTE.

asset-backed security (ASB) A bond or note whose *collateral is the cash flows from a pool of financial obligations such as mortgages, car loans, or credit-card receivables. *See* SECURITIZATION. *See also* STRUCTURED FINANCE.

asset classification The classification of assets as required by law on a *balance sheet. Assets must be classified as fixed (i.e. held for use on a continuing basis) or current (i.e. not intended for continuing use but held on a short-term basis). Fixed assets are further classified as intangible (e.g. *goodwill) or tangible (e.g. land and buildings). *Fixed assets must be depreciated (*see* DEPRECIATION) over their useful economic life to comply with the Companies Act and *Financial Reporting Standard 15. *Current assets include stock, debtors, prepayments, cash at bank, and cash in hand. Fixed assets may be shown at *historical cost less accumulated depreciation, or under the *alternative accounting rules. Current assets must be shown at the lower of historical cost (or *current cost under the alternative accounting rules) and *net realizable value. *International Financial Reporting Standard 5 introduced a new classification of non-current assets *held for sale.

asset cover A ratio that provides a measure of the solvency of a company; it consists of its *net assets divided by its *debt. Those companies with high asset cover are considered the more solvent.

asset deficiency The condition of a company when its *liabilities exceed its *assets. Although each particular circumstance must be interpreted in its own context, the financial viability of an organization with an asset deficiency must be in question.

asset management 1. The management of the financial assets of a company in order to maximize the return on the investments. 2. An investment service offered by banks and some other financial institutions. In the UK some private banks offer an asset management service for wealthy customers. *See also* PORTFOLIO.

Asset Protection Scheme (APS) A UK government initiative, launched in February 2009, designed to revive bank lending in the wake of the global financial crisis. Under the scheme, banks holding *toxic assets such as mortgage-backed securities and *collateralized debt obligations can insure themselves against further losses from these assets by paying a fee to HM Treasury. *Compare* TARP.

asset revaluation reserve *See* REVALUATION RESERVE ACCOUNT.

assets register *See* FIXED-ASSETS REGISTER.

asset stripping The acquisition or takeover of a company whose shares are valued below their *asset value, and the subsequent sale of the company's assets. Having identified a suitable company, an entrepreneur or investment company acquires a controlling interest in it by buying its shares; after revaluation, properties or other assets held can be sold for cash, which is distributed to shareholders (now including the entrepreneur). Subsequently, the entrepreneur can either revitalize the management of the company and later sell off the acquired shareholding at a profit or, in some cases, close the business down. Because the asset stripper is heedless of the welfare of the other shareholders, the employees, the suppliers, or creditors of the stripped company, the practice is generally deprecated. *See also* PRIVATE EQUITY FIRM.

asset turnover *See* CAPITAL TURNOVER.

asset valuation 1. An assessment of the value at which the *assets of an organization, usually the *fixed assets, should be entered into its balance sheet. The valuation may be arrived at in a number of ways; for example, a revaluation of land and buildings would often involve taking professional advice. 2. The assessment of the value of assets, most usually by a *present value calculation.

asset value (per share) (break-up value) The total value of the assets of a company less its liabilities, divided by the number of ordinary shares in issue. This represents in theory, although probably not in practice, the amount attributable to each share if the company was wound up. The true value of the assets may well not be the total of the values shown by a company's balance sheet, since it is not the function of balance sheets to value assets. It may, therefore, be necessary to substitute the best estimate that can be made of the market values of the assets (including goodwill) for the values shown in the balance sheet. If there is more than one class of share, it may be necessary to deduct amounts due to shareholders with a priority on winding up before arriving at the amounts attributable to shareholders with a lower priority. If a company goes into liquidation or receivership, the break-up value of the assets may well be below their book value, especially if the assets include obsolete technology saleable only for its scrap value. The asset value per share is also known as the **net asset value** (**NAV**). *See also* BALANCE-SHEET ASSET VALUE; BOOK VALUE.

assignment **1.** The act of transferring, or a document (a **deed of assignment**) transferring, property to some other person. Examples of assignment include the transfer of rights under a contract or benefits under a trust to another person. *See also* ASSIGNMENT OF LEASE. **2.** The transfer of a bank loan from the lending bank to another bank in order to reduce the credit risk of the lending bank. This practice is contrary to the principles of *relationship banking.

assignment of lease The transfer of a *lease by the tenant (assignor) to some other person (assignee). Leases are freely transferable at common law although it is common practice to restrict assignment by conditions (*covenants) in the lease. An assignment that takes place in breach of such a covenant is valid but it may entitle the landlord to put an end to the lease and re-enter the premises. An assignment transfers the assignor's whole estate to the assignee, unlike a sub-lease (*see* HEAD LEASE).

assignment of life policies Transfer of the legal right under a *life-assurance policy to collect the proceeds. Assignment is only valid if the life insurer is advised and agrees; life assurance is the only form of insurance in which the assignee need not possess an insurable interest. In recent years policy auctions have become a popular alternative to surrendering endowment assurances. In these auctions, a policy is sold to the highest bidder and then assigned to him or her by the original policyholder.

associated undertaking (**associate**) An *undertaking that is not defined as a *subsidiary undertaking but is nevertheless one in which another company or group has a *participating interest and exercises a *significant influence. Accounting for associates is regulated by *Financial Reporting Standard 9, Associates and Joint Ventures. The relevant *International Accounting Standard is IAS28, Investments in Associates.

Association for Payment Clearing Services (**APACS**) An association set up by the UK banks in 1985 to manage payment clearing and overseas money transmission in the UK. The Association has four main Interest Groups: the Card Payments Group, the Cash Services Group, the Electronic Commerce Group, and the Liquidity Managers Group (formed in 2002 from a merger of the Treasurers Group and the City Markets Group). APACS also has four operating companies under its aegis: **BACS Payment Schemes Ltd**, which is responsible for automated interbank clearing, payment, and settlement services in the UK; **VocaLink**, which physically processes direct debit and direct credit payments; Cheque and Credit Clearing Co. Ltd, which operates a bulk clearing system for interbank cheques and paper credits; and **CHAPS**, which provides electronic funds transfer in sterling and euros.

Association of Accounting Technicians (**AAT**) An association set up in 1980 by the *Consultative Committee of Accountancy Bodies (CCAB) to provide a second-tier accounting qualification. This qualification can enable an individual to obtain subsequently a full CCAB qualification.

 SEE WEB LINKS

• AAT website

Association of Authorized Public Accountants (AAPA) A UK professional body for qualified accountants who have been authorized to carry out *audits of companies. Fellows of the Association are designated FAPA and Associates are designated AAPA. In 1996 the Association became a subsidiary of the *Association of Chartered Certified Accountants.

Association of Chartered Certified Accountants (ACCA) The professional association for *chartered certified accountants. It was formed in 1938 as the Association of Certified and Corporate Accountants and known as the **Chartered Association of Certified Accountants** from 1984 until 1996, when it adopted its present name. With over 120,000 members in 170 countries, it is one of the largest professional accountancy bodies in the world.

(⊕) SEE WEB LINKS

• ACCA website: includes information on training and careers as well as industry news

Association of Corporate Treasurers (ACT) An organization set up to encourage and promote the study and practice of treasury management in companies. Although a small organization in relation to the professional accounting bodies, it has become influential in the field of corporate treasurership. Fellows of the Association are designated FCT and members as MCT.

(⊕) SEE WEB LINKS

• Website of the ACT

Association of Independent Financial Advisers (AIFA) The trade body for *independent financial advisers in the UK, established in 1994. It represents the views of the profession to the *Financial Services Authority, parliament, and other policy makers, and promotes the benefits of financial advice to the public.

Association of International Accountants (AIA) A professional body for accountants that is dedicated to the idea of 'international accounting.' It was founded in the UK in 1928 and now has members in over 85 countries. Full members may be associates (AAIA) or fellows (FAIA) and are known as international accountants. The AIA is a *Recognized Qualifying Body.

(⊕) SEE WEB LINKS

• AIA website

assurance Insurance against an eventuality (especially death) that must occur. *See* LIFE ASSURANCE.

assured The person named in a *life-assurance policy to receive the proceeds in the event of maturity or the death of the life assured. As a result of the policy, the person's financial future is 'assured'.

ATM Abbreviation for *automated teller machine.

at par *See* PAR VALUE.

at sight The words used on a *bill of exchange to indicate that payment is due on presentation. *Compare* AFTER DATE; AFTER SIGHT.

ATT Abbreviation for Associate of the Association of Tax Technicians, a qualification undertaken by employees working in taxation at a level below that of members of the *Chartered Institute of Taxation. The Association was set up in 1989 under the sponsorship of the Institute.

attachment A procedure enabling a creditor, who has obtained judgment in the courts (the judgment creditor), to secure payment of the amount due from the debtor. The judgment creditor obtains a further court order to the effect that money or property due from a third party to the debtor must be frozen and paid instead to the judgment creditor to satisfy the amount due. For instance, a judgment creditor may, through a *third-party debt order, attach the salary due to the debtor from the debtor's employer.

attainable standard In *standard costing, a cost or income standard set at a level that is attainable by the operators under the conditions applicable during the relevant cost period. *Compare* EXPECTED STANDARD; IDEAL STANDARD.

attest To bear witness to an act or event. The law requires that some documents are only valid and binding if the signatures on them have been attested to by a third party. This also requires the third party's signature on the document.

attest function The function performed by a qualified auditor who provides an *audit opinion as to the truth and fairness of the *financial statements of an organization.

at the money Describing a call or put *option in which the exercise price is the same (or very nearly the same) as the current market price of the *underlying. *See also* IN THE MONEY.

attributable profit The part of the total estimated profit earned on a *long-term contract, after allowing for estimated remedial and maintenance costs and any other non-recoverable costs, that fairly reflects the profit attributable to that part of the work completed at a specified accounting date.

attribute A characteristic that each member of a population either has or does not have. For example, if an auditor is examining the invoices of a company to establish whether each document has been signed and approved, the population will be the invoices and the attribute is the signature.

attributes sampling An examination of less than 100% of a population to determine the proportion of the population that has a specified *attribute. Attributes sampling is used by auditors in *compliance tests, where the characteristic being sought is a deviation from required control procedures. *See* SAMPLE.

auction market preferred stock (**AMPS**) A type of US *preference share the dividend of which is variable and set by means of an auction process between investors.

audit An independent examination of, and the subsequent expression of opinion on, the financial statements of an organization. This involves the auditor in collecting evidence by means of *compliance tests (tests of control) and *substantive tests (tests of detail). *External audits (i.e. audits performed by an auditor external to the organization) are required under statute for limited companies by the Companies Act and for various other undertakings, such as housing associations and building societies, by other Acts of Parliament.

*Internal audits are performed by auditors within an organization, usually an independent department, such as an internal-audit department. Internal auditors examine various areas, including financial and non-financial concerns, with emphasis on ensuring that internal controls are working effectively. Internal auditors may assist the external auditor of an organization. Non-statutory audits can be performed at the request of the owners, members, or trustees of an undertaking, for example. Financial statements other than the annual accounts may also be audited; for example, summaries of sales made by an organization. *See also* AUDIT OPINION; AUDITOR; AUDITORS REPORT; INDEPENDENCE OF AUDITORS; STATUTORY AUDIT.

Audit Commission An independent public body, named in full the Audit Commission for Local Authorities and the National Health Service in England and Wales, which is responsible for ensuring that public money is spent economically and effectively in the areas of local government, housing, health, criminal law, justice, and the fire and rescue services. It was established by the Local Government Finance Act 1982. A similar body for Scotland, Audit Scotland, was created in 2000.

(((()))) SEE WEB LINKS

• Website of the Audit Commission: now includes reports on all audited organizations
• Website of Audit Scotland

audit committee In public companies, a committee of *non-executive directors that is responsible for oversight of financial reporting, internal and external audit, compliance with regulatory codes, and *risk management. The UK's *Combined Code on Corporate Governance now recommends that all public companies establish audit committees to encourage accountability and public confidence. Such committees enhance the independence of auditors by enabling them to report to a body that is independent of the executive directors. In the USA the role of audit committees was strengthened by the *Sarbanes–Oxley Act 2002, passed in the wake of the Enron scandal. *See also* REMUNERATION COMMITTEE.

audit completion checklist A list of items to be checked by audit staff to ensure that the *financial statements being audited give a *true and fair view. The list will include all statutory disclosures and accounting standard requirements; for example, 'Have all the accounting policies been disclosed as required by *Financial Reporting Standard 18, Accounting Policies?' The checklist may be used throughout the audit but is more specifically designed to be used as a final check before handing the files to the reporting partner of the audit firm for signature.

audit evidence The evidence required by an auditor on which to base an *audit opinion on the *financial statements of the company whose accounts are being audited. Sources of information include the accounting systems and the underlying documentation of the enterprise, its tangible assets, management and employees, its customers, suppliers, and any other third parties who have dealings with, or knowledge of, the enterprise or its business. The evidence will be obtained by means of *compliance tests (tests of controls) and *substantive tests (tests of details and *analytical review). Techniques involved in gathering the evidence include inspection, observation, enquiry, analysis, and *computer-assisted audit techniques.

audit exemption The exemption from *statutory audit by a registered auditor that can be claimed by certain *small companies. Companies with a turnover of not more than £1 million and a balance-sheet total of not more than £1.4 million may be totally exempt from audit. Companies with a turnover in the range £1 million to £5.6 million (and a balance-sheet total of not more than £2.8 million) may claim exemption from the audit requirement but still need a *reporting accountant's report. The **audit exemption report** must state that the accounts are, in the opinion of the accountant, in agreement with the accounting records kept by the company and that the accounts have been drawn up in a manner consistent with the provisions of the Companies Act. Also, the accountant must report that, on the basis of the information contained in the accounting records, the company is entitled to the exemption on the basis of size. The audit exemption report was formerly known as a **compilation report**.

audit expectations gap The gap between the role of an auditor, as perceived by the auditor, and the expectations of the users of *financial statements. It may be subdivided into a gap in communications and a gap in performance. The **communications gap** is caused by public expectations being unreasonable; for example, users of accounts may expect all fraud to have been discovered by a statutory audit, whereas the auditor is only expected to plan the audit to prevent and detect fraud to comply with *Statement of Auditing Standards 110, Fraud and Error. The communications gap could be closed by ensuring that the users of accounts understand what an audit is and what its limitations are. The **performance gap** occurs when public expectations are reasonable but the auditor's performance does not fulfil them, i.e. there is a shortfall in the auditor's performance. This can only be overcome by improving the quality of the auditor's work.

audit fee (**auditors' remuneration**) The amount payable to an auditor for an audit; this has to be approved at the *annual general meeting of a company. In the *financial statements, audit fees must be distinguished from fees payable to the auditor for non-audit work.

auditing guidelines Documents issued by the former *Auditing Practices Committee (APC) and subsequently adopted by the *Auditing Practices Board (APB), which now has the responsibility for issuing all auditing pronouncements. Guidelines are not prescriptive, but they give guidance as to the methods of applying *auditing standards. Auditors could be asked to explain any departures from the guidelines if their failure to follow auditing standards is being investigated. Guidelines are generally grouped into three areas: industry-specific, detailed operational, and reporting guidelines.

Auditing Practices Board (APB) A body constituted in 1991 to replace the *Auditing Practices Committee (APC). Intended to be more independent of the auditing profession than the APC, the APB has half of its members drawn from outside practice, for example from universities and the legal profession. The Board was reconstituted in 2002–03 under the chairmanship of Richard Fleck, a specialist in corporate and regulatory law. Its objective is to establish the highest standards of auditing practice in the UK and the Republic of Ireland in such a way that the developing needs of users of financial information are met and public confidence in the auditing process is maintained. It is no longer empowered to issue *Statements of Auditing Standards in its own right but continues to publish Practice Notes (PN) and Bulletins (see AUDITING STANDARDS). The APB is part of the *Financial Reporting Council.

(⊕) SEE WEB LINKS

• Website of the APB

Auditing Practices Committee (APC) A committee of the *Consultative Committee of Accountancy Bodies set up in 1976 and replaced by the *Auditing Practices Board in 1991. During the period 1980 to 1991 it was responsible for issuing two *auditing standards, The Auditor's Operational Standard (April 1980) and The Audit Report (March 1989; now superseded), and 38 auditing guidelines.

auditing standards Basic principles and essential procedures with which auditors are required to comply in the conduct of any audit of financial statements. The *Auditing Practices Committee issued a series of Auditing Standards between 1980 and 1991. The standards issued by its successor body, the *Auditing Practices Board (APB), were known as *Statements of Auditing Standards (SAS); these have now been superseded by the *International Standards in Auditing issued by the *International Auditing and Assurance Standards Board. The APB continues to issue *Practice Notes (to assist the auditor in applying auditing standards of general application to particular circumstances and industries) and Bulletins (designed for issue when guidance is required on new or emerging issues). Practice Notes and Bulletins are not prescriptive; they are an indication of current good practice. *See also* GENERALLY ACCEPTED AUDITING STANDARDS; STATEMENT ON AUDITING STANDARDS; STATEMENT ON INTERNAL AUDITING STANDARDS.

Auditing Standards Board In the USA, the organization responsible for the issue of *Statements of Auditing Standards. It is part of the *American Institute of Certified Public Accountants.

audit manual A written document that explains the auditing policies and procedures of a firm.

audit opinion An opinion contained in an *auditors' report. It expresses a view as to whether or not the *financial statements audited have been prepared consistently using appropriate accounting policies, in accordance with relevant legislation, regulations, or applicable accounting standards. The opinion also has to state that there is adequate disclosure of information relevant to the proper understanding of the financial statements. If the auditors are satisfied on these points, and if any departure from legislation, regulations, or applicable accounting standards has been justified and adequately explained in the financial statements, an unqualified opinion will be given. If the scope of the auditors' examination has been limited, or the auditors disagree materially with the treatment or disclosure of a matter in the financial statements, or they do not comply with relevant accounting or other requirements, a *qualified audit report or *adverse opinion will be issued. *See also* DISCLAIMER OF OPINION; EXCEPT FOR.

auditor A person or firm appointed to carry out an *audit of an organization. In the UK an external auditor must be a registered auditor or a member of a

*Recognized Supervisory Body and be eligible for appointment under the rules of that body. The supervisory bodies are required to have rules designed to ensure that persons eligible for appointment as company auditors are either individuals who hold the appropriate qualification or firms controlled by properly qualified persons. These bodies must also ensure that eligible persons continue to maintain the appropriate level of competence and must monitor and enforce compliance with their rules. These rules do not apply to internal auditors. *See also* INDEPENDENCE OF AUDITORS.

auditors' remuneration *See* AUDIT FEE.

auditors' report (audit report) A report by the auditors appointed to audit the accounts of a company or other organization. Auditors' reports may take many forms depending on who has appointed the auditors and for what purposes. Some auditors are engaged in an internal audit while others are appointed for various statutory purposes. The auditors of a limited company are required to form an opinion as to whether the annual accounts of the company give a *true and fair view of its profit or loss for the period under review and of its state of affairs at the end of the period; they are also required to certify that the accounts are prepared in accordance with the requirements of the Companies Act. The auditors' report is technically a report to the members of the company and it must be filed together with the accounts with the Registrar of Companies. The report must also include an audit of the directors' report with respect to consistency. The Companies Act 2006 creates a new criminal offence of knowingly or recklessly supplying false or deceptive information in an auditors' report.

audit plan (audit planning memorandum; audit strategy) A document outlining the strategy to be applied to each manageable area of the accounting system and *financial statements of an audit client. The plan would take into account the assessed levels of inherent risk (i.e. the susceptibility of account balances or classes of transactions to material misstatement) and control risk (the risk that material misstatements are not prevented or detected by the internal control system); it would also outline the nature, timing, and extent of the *substantive tests to be employed.

audit programme A document listing the individual audit tests to be performed to achieve an *audit plan. The tests will check that the accounting system operates in the manner recorded. For example, a credit sales transaction will be traced through to payment. *Compliance tests will be made to check that the internal control system is working. *Substantive tests of details (e.g. account balances and transactions) and an *analytical review (an overall analysis of the *financial statements) will also be outlined. The audit programme gives guidance to the audit staff involved and provides a record of work done and the conclusions drawn; it therefore provides a basis for effective quality control and meeting *audit evidence requirements.

audit report *See* AUDITORS REPORT.

audit risk The risk that an auditor fails to qualify the *auditors' report when the *financial statements are materially misleading, i.e. do not give a true and fair view. The audit risk consists of three components:

- the inherent risk, i.e. the likelihood of misstatements occurring in the absence of controls;
- the *control risk, i.e. the risk that misstatements may not be prevented or detected on a timely basis by the *internal control system;
- the *detection risk, i.e. the risk that the auditor's *substantive tests will not detect a misstatement that exists on an account balance or class of transactions.

A quantification of each of these elements, when multiplied together, gives a measure of the audit risk. *See also* ALPHA RISK AND BETA RISK.

audit rotation The practice of appointing an audit firm for a set period, such as five years, after which it must give up the position. The aim is to reduce the effective control of the auditor by directors, who may threaten to remove the auditors if they do not comply with their requirements. However, the practice is generally criticized on the grounds of cost, disruption, and the consequent reduced quality of the audit work.

audit software Computer programs used by an auditor to examine an enterprise's computer files. Utility programs may be used, for example, for sorting and printing data files. Package or tailor-made programs may be used to interrogate the computer-based accounting system of a client. The auditor may also use more sophisticated audit software for *compliance tests and *substantive tests. *Computer-assisted audit techniques (CAATs) include the use of *embedded audit facilities, enabling program codes and additional data to be incorporated into the client's computerized accounting system to facilitate a continuous review of the system. There are two main examples of embedded audit facilities: *integrated test facilities (ITF), which involve the creation of a fictitious entity to which transactions are posted for checking purposes; and *systems control and review files (SCARF), which collect certain predefined transactions for further examination.

audit strategy *See* AUDIT PLAN.

audit tests *See* COMPLIANCE TESTS; SUBSTANTIVE TESTS.

audit trail (paper trail) The sequence of documents, computer files, and other records examined during an *audit, showing how a transaction has been dealt with by an organization from start to finish. Documents will require cross-referencing so the trail is not broken. For example, a sales transaction can be traced from the item of stock sold, to the invoice, through the sales day book, to the sales account, and finally to the bank account. *See also* COMPUTER-ASSISTED AUDIT TECHNIQUES.

audit working papers Files that contain the detailed evidence and information gathered during an audit. Typical contents include information of continuing importance (e.g. the organizational plan of a company), planning information, assessment of the client's accounting and *internal control systems, details of work carried out and by whom, financial information and summaries, evidence of work having been appropriately reviewed, and the conclusions reached. These files provide the reporting partner of the audit firm with the evidence necessary to form an opinion; they are also useful for future reference.

authorized auditor An individual granted special authorization to act as the auditor of a company under the Companies Act 1967. Authorizations were granted to individuals not otherwise eligible to act as auditors on the basis of their experience. The power to grant authorizations ended in 1978; since 1989 an authorized auditor is not eligible for appointment as an auditor of a listed company.

authorized investments Formerly, certain legally authorized investments considered suitable for trust funds, as set out in the Trustees Investment Act 1961. A much wider *general power of investment for trustees was introduced in 2000.

authorized minimum share capital In the UK, the statutory minimum of £50,000 for the share capital of a public company. There is no minimum share capital for private companies.

authorized share capital (nominal share capital; nominal capital; registered capital) Formerly, the maximum amount of *share capital that a company was authorized to issue, as detailed in the company's *memorandum of association. The authorized share capital also had to be disclosed on the face of the *balance sheet or alternatively in the notes to the accounts. The requirement for a company to specify its maximum authorized share capital was abolished as part of the implementation of the Companies Act 2006. Instead, companies registered under the new Act are required to submit a statement of capital and initial holdings. A company's *articles of association may still include provisions limiting the number of shares to be issued. *See also* ISSUED SHARE CAPITAL.

automated teller machine (ATM) A computerized machine usually attached to the outside wall of a high-street bank or building society that enables customers to withdraw cash from their *current accounts at any hour of the day. The machines may also be used to effect transfers and obtain statements. They are operated by *cash cards or *multifunctional cards in conjunction with a *personal identification number. ATMs are often known colloquially as **cash dispensers**.

available hours 1. The number of hours available to complete a job, task, or process. 2. The number of working hours available during an accounting period expressed as either machine hours, direct labour hours, or production hours.

aval A guarantee of payment by a third party, often a bank, on a *bill of exchange or promissory note.

AVC Abbreviation for *additional voluntary contribution.

AVCO Abbreviation for *average cost.

average collection period *See* DEBTOR COLLECTION PERIOD.

average cost 1. The average cost per unit of output calculated by dividing the *total costs, both *fixed costs and *variable costs, by the total units of output. 2. **(AVCO; weighted-average cost)** A method of valuing units of *raw material or *finished goods issued from stock; it involves recalculating the unit value to be used for pricing the issues after each new consignment of raw materials or finished goods has been added to the stock. The average cost is obtained by dividing the total stock value by the number of units in stock. Because the issues are at an average cost, it follows that the valuation of the closing stock should be made on the same average cost basis. The method may also be used in *process costing to value the work in process at the end of an accounting period.

average costing A method of obtaining unit costs sometimes used when the items produced have a high degree of homogeneity. The unit cost is obtained by dividing the total production cost by the number of items produced. *See also* CONTINUOUS-OPERATION COSTING; PROCESS COSTING.

average life A somewhat artificial measure sometimes used to compare bonds of different duration and different repayment schedules. It is calculated as the average of the periods for which funds are available, weighted by the amounts available in each of these periods.

avoidable costs Costs that are not incurred if a particular course of action is taken or an alternative decision is made. For example, if a specific product is not produced, material and labour costs may not be incurred. In this instance material and labour costs are avoidable costs. *Variable costs are often avoidable costs, whereas *fixed costs, such as business rates, are not avoidable in the short term. *See also* RELEVANT COST.

BAA Abbreviation for *British Accounting Association.

baby bond 1. *See* CHILD TRUST FUND. 2. In the USA, any bond having a denomination of less than $1000.

backdate 1. To agree that salary increases, especially those settled in a pay award, should apply from a specified date in the recent past. 2. *See* ANTEDATE.

back duty An amount of tax that should have been paid in previous years but was not assessed because the taxpayer failed to disclose full income details to HM Revenue. A back duty case may arise when a source of income has been omitted totally from a tax return or when the level of business profits has been understated. If an Inspector of Taxes believes that back duty is payable, an enquiry will be instigated. If back duty is found to be payable it is likely that there will be interest and *penalties added to the tax charge.

back-end load The final charge made by a *unit trust or *investment trust when an investor sells shares in the fund. *Compare* FRONT-END LOAD.

backflush accounting A method of costing a product based on a management philosophy that includes having the minimum levels of stock available; in these circumstances, the valuation of stocks becomes less important, making the complex use of *absorption costing techniques unnecessary. Backflush accounting works backwards; after the actual costs have been determined they are allocated between *stocks and *cost of sales to establish profitability. There is no separate accounting for *work in progress.

backlog depreciation A *depreciation charge that occurs when an asset is revalued. The additional depreciation that arises as a consequence of the increase in the value of the asset also increases the *accumulated depreciation; this increase is known as backlog depreciation.

back-to-back credit **(countervailing credit)** A method used to conceal the identity of the seller from the buyer in a credit arrangement. When the credit is arranged by a British finance house, the foreign seller provides the relevant documentation. The finance house, acting as an intermediary, issues its own documents to the buyer, omitting the seller's name and so concealing the seller's identity.

back-up copy A copy of information held in a computer taken in case the original is lost or destroyed. If the original information is on disk, the back-up copy should be on a completely different disk, or tape, and stored in a separate location from the original. Any sensible business will have back-up copies of all information held on its computer. How frequently the copies are made will depend upon how rapidly the information changes, its difficulty of replacement, and its importance.

BACS Payment Schemes Ltd *See* ASSOCIATION FOR PAYMENT CLEARING SERVICES.

bad debt An amount owed by a debtor that is unlikely to be paid; for example, due to a company going into liquidation. The full amount should be written off to the *profit and loss account of the period or to a *provision for bad debts as soon as it is foreseen, on the grounds of prudence. *See also* DOUBTFUL DEBT.

bad debts recovered Debts originally classed as *bad debts and written off to the *profit and loss account (or to a provision for bad and *doubtful debts) but subsequently recovered either in part or in full. Bad debts recovered should be written back to the profit and loss account of the period (or to a provision for bad and doubtful debts).

bailment A delivery of goods from the **bailor** (the owner of the goods) to the **bailee** (the recipient of the goods), on the condition that the goods will ultimately be returned to the bailor. The goods may thus be hired, lent, pledged, or deposited for safe custody. A delivery of this nature is usually also the subject of a contract; for example, a contract with a bank for the deposit of valuables for safekeeping. Nonetheless, in English law a bailment retains its distinguishing characteristic of a business relationship that arises outside the law of contract and is therefore not governed by it.

balance The amount representing the difference between the debit and credit sides of an account. It is included on the side of the lesser total, to ensure it equals the greater total. A balance is brought down on to the opposite side of the account. For example, if the total credits on an account exceed the total debits, a balance is inserted on the debit side and then brought down on to the credit side. *See also* TRIAL BALANCE.

balanced scorecard (BSC) An approach to management that integrates both financial and non-financial *performance measures in a framework proposed by Professors Kaplan and Norton. The BSC was first reported in the *Harvard Business Review* in 1992 and has since been adopted by a wide range of organizations. It is considered one of the most significant recent developments in management accounting. The approach looks at performance from four interrelated dimensions:

- the **financial perspective** – how do we measure financial performance? Possible performance measures include *operating profits, *return on capital employed, and *unit costs.
- the **customer perspective** – how do we measure customer satisfaction? Possible performance measures include customer profitability, customer satisfaction, and market share.
- the **internal business-process perspective** – what must we excel at? Possible measures include time to develop new products, defect rates, and product returns.
- the **learning and growth perspective** – how can we continue to improve and create value? Possible measures include employee satisfaction and employee productivity.

The balanced scorecard approach requires managers to identify both lagging and leading measures. **Lagging measures** are financial measures that show the impact of decisions made in the past, whereas **leading measures** are non-financial measures relating to the customer, internal business-process, and learning and growth perspectives. The latter are the drivers of future financial performance.

balance off The practice of totalling the debit and credit sides of an account and inserting a *balance to make them equal at the end of a financial accounting period. For example, on the *debtors' ledger control account amounts owed will be debited, amounts settled will be credited. When balancing off the account the balance inserted will be on the credit side, representing amounts owed that have still not been settled. On the first day of the next accounting period, the balance will be brought forward from the credit side to the debit side, representing the opening amount of debtors.

balance of payments The accounts setting out a country's transactions with the outside world. They are divided into various sub-accounts, notably the *current account and the *capital account. The former includes the trade account, which records the balance of imports and exports (the **balance of trade**). The conventions used for presenting balance-of-payments statistics are those recommended by the *International Monetary Fund.

balance sheet (statement of financial position) A statement of the total assets and liabilities of an organization at a particular date, usually the last day of the *accounting period. The first part of the statement lists the fixed and current assets and the liabilities, whereas the second part shows how they have been financed; the totals for each part must be equal. Under the UK Companies Act the balance sheet is one of the primary statements to be included in the *annual accounts of a company. The Companies Act requires that the balance sheet of a company must give a *true and fair view of its state of affairs at the end of its financial year, and must comply with statute as to its form and content. In theory, the balance sheet represents the amount that would be available for the benefit of members if the company were immediately wound up and liabilities were discharged out of the proceeds of selling its assets. In practice, however, a balance sheet may not accurately value a company, as some assets may be given an unrealistic value and important *intangible assets may be omitted altogether (*see* ASSET VALUE (PER SHARE); BOOK VALUE). It can be difficult to compare the balance sheets of companies from different countries as they may disclose different information. *See also* BALANCE-SHEET FORMATS.

balance-sheet asset value The value of an asset as represented on the *balance sheet. For tangible fixed assets this is the cost less accumulated depreciation (although freehold land is generally not subject to depreciation). *Intangible assets are shown at cost less *amortization. Current assets are valued at the lower of cost and *net realizable value. Under the *alternative accounting rules, the historical cost of certain assets (for example, buildings and stocks) may be replaced by current cost. *See also* NET BOOK VALUE.

balance-sheet audit An *audit limited to *verification of the existence, ownership, valuation, and presentation of the assets and liabilities in a balance sheet. For example, the existence of a building would be satisfied by an inspection and an examination of the deeds would provide evidence of ownership. The valuation of the building could be based on historical cost, in which case the original purchase contract would be examined; alternatively it may have been revalued, in which case the documentation for the revaluation would need to be examined; this may need to be supported by further enquiry. The balance-sheet presentation and disclosures for the building would be checked against the Companies Act and requirements of *accounting standards.

balance-sheet equation *See* ACCOUNTING EQUATION.

balance-sheet formats Methods of presenting a *balance sheet, as set out in the Companies Act. There are two formats: one vertical (format 1) and one horizontal (format 2). Both formats give the same basic disclosures, but format 1 also requires the calculation and disclosure of the net current assets and liabilities. The items are classified under letters, Roman numerals, and Arabic numbers. Items preceded by letters and Roman numerals must be shown on the face of the balance sheet, while those preceded by Arabic numbers may be shown in the notes to the accounts. Unless the directors believe there are valid arguments for a change, a company must adhere to the format it has chosen. Details of any changes and the reasons for making them must be disclosed in the notes to the accounts.

balance-sheet total The total *net worth of an organization as shown at the bottom of the *balance sheet, i.e. the fixed assets plus net current assets less long-term liabilities. In the qualification conditions for *small company and *medium-sized company exemptions, the balance-sheet total is the total of fixed and current assets before deduction of current and long-term liabilities.

balancing allowance The allowance available on disposal of an asset when the proceeds are less than the *written-down value for tax purposes. For example, if the written-down value of an asset is £23,000 and on disposal the proceeds totalled £15,000, there would be a balancing allowance of the difference of £8000. *Compare* BALANCING CHARGE.

balancing charge The charge that may be assessable to *corporation tax on the disposal of an asset when the proceeds realized on the sale of the asset exceed the *written-down value, for tax purposes. The balancing charge amounts to the difference between the proceeds and the written-down value. For example, if the written-down value is £23,000 and the proceeds on disposal were £30,000, there would be a balancing charge of the difference of £7000. The balancing charge is deducted from the other allowances for the period. If the charge exceeds the allowances available, the net amount is added to the profit for the period and assessed to tax.

balancing figure A figure that is inserted to make one total equal another. *See* BALANCE; BALANCE OFF.

balloon **1.** A large sum repaid as an irregular instalment of a loan repayment. **2.** In the USA, the final loan repayment, when this amount is significantly more than the prior repayments.

bancassurance (Allfinanz) The combination of traditional loan and savings bank products with such assurance products as *life assurance and pensions. It is now common for major UK banks to provide this combined service and the practice is spreading worldwide.

bank A commercial institution that takes deposits and extends loans. Banks are concerned mainly with making and receiving payments on behalf of their customers, accepting deposits, and making short-term loans to private individuals, companies, and other organizations. However, they also provide money transmission services and in recent years have diversified into many areas of financial services. In the UK, the banking system comprises the *Bank of England (the central bank), the *commercial banks, *merchant banks, branches of foreign and Commonwealth banks, the *National Savings Bank, and the National Girobank (*see* GIRO). The first (1990) *building society to become a bank in the UK was the Abbey National (now Abbey, part of the Santander Group), after its public *flotation; many other building societies have now followed this precedent. In other countries banks are also usually supervised by a central bank.

bank certificate A certificate, signed by a bank manager, stating the balance held to a company's credit on a specified date. It may be asked for during the course of an audit.

bank charge The amount charged to a customer by a bank, usually for a specific transaction, such as paying in a sum of money by means of a cheque or withdrawing a sum by means of an automated teller machine. However, modern practice is to provide periods of commission-free banking by waiving most charges on personal current accounts. Business customers invariably pay tariffs in one form or another.

bank confirmation A request made by an auditor to a bank to confirm details of an audit client's bank accounts, together with any other assets held by the bank, and any other financial information.

bank deposit A sum of money placed by a customer with a bank. The deposit may or may not attract interest and may be instantly accessible or accessible at a time agreed by the two parties. Banks may use a percentage of their customers' deposits to lend on to other customers; thus most deposits may only exist on paper in the bank's books. Money on deposit at a bank is usually held in a *savings account, a *deposit account, or a *current account.

bank draft (banker's cheque; banker's draft) A cheque drawn by a bank on itself or its agent. A person who owes money to another buys the draft from a bank for cash and hands it to the creditor who need have no fear that it might be dishonoured. A bank draft is used if the creditor is unwilling to accept an ordinary cheque.

banker's cheque *See* BANK DRAFT.

banker's discount The discount calculated by a bank when purchasing a *bill of exchange.

banker's draft *See* BANK DRAFT.

banker's order An order to a bank by a customer to pay a specified amount at specified times (e.g. monthly or quarterly), until the order is cancelled, from a specific bank account of the customer to another named bank account.

banker's payment A *bank draft drawn in favour of another bank, as settlement of business between the two banks.

banker's reference (status enquiry) A report on the creditworthiness of an individual supplied by a bank to a third party, such as another financial institution or a bank customer. References and status enquiries are often supplied by specialist credit-reference agencies, who keep lists of defaulters, bad payers, and people who have infringed credit agreements. References must be very general and recent legislation has given new rights to the subjects of such reports, which restrict their value even further.

bank float The time spent by a remittance in the banking system, during which the sum of money is available to neither the payer nor the payee.

Bank for International Settlements (BIS) An international bank that fosters cooperation among central banks and other agencies in pursuit of monetary and financial stability. The BIS was originally established in 1930 as a financial institution to coordinate the payment of war reparations between European central banks. It was hoped that the BIS, with headquarters in Basle, would develop into a European central bank but many of its functions were taken over by the *International Monetary Fund (IMF) after World War II. Since then the BIS has fulfilled several roles including acting as a trustee and agent for such international groups as the OECD, the European Monetary System, and the IMF. The frequent meetings of the BIS directors have been a useful means of cooperation between central banks, especially in combating short-term speculative monetary movements. The BIS also sets *capital adequacy ratios for banks in European countries. The original members were France, Belgium, West Germany, Italy, and the UK. There are now 55 members worldwide including most European central banks (notably the ECB), as well as the monetary authorities of the USA, Japan, Russia, and China. The London agent is the Bank of England, whose governor is a member of the board of directors of the BIS.

bank giro credit *See* BANK TRANSFER; GIRO.

banking directives Directives on various aspects of banking practice issued by the EU parliament and Council of Ministers; they include directives on solvency ratios, large exposures, and money laundering. The most important is the Second Banking Directive, which concerns the licensing of banks in EU countries other than their domicile. The Investment Services Directive and *Markets in Financial Instruments Directive applied the principles outlined in the Second Directive to investment products.

bank interest The interest charge made by a bank to a person or company, based on the daily cleared overdraft balance or a committed loan. The *interest rate will usually be the *base rate plus between 1% and 5%.

bank loan (bank advance) A specified sum of money lent by a bank to a customer, usually for a specified time, at a specified rate of interest. In most cases banks require some form of security for loans, especially if the loan is to a commercial enterprise, although if a bank regards a company as a good credit risk, loans may not be secured. *See also* OVERDRAFT.

bank mandate A document given by a customer of a bank to the bank, requesting that the bank should open an account in the customer's name and honour cheques and other orders for payment drawn on the account. The mandate specifies the signatures that the bank should accept for transactions on the account and also contains specimens of the signatures.

Bank of England The central bank of the UK. It was established in 1694 and came under public ownership in 1946. The Bank of England acts as the government's bank by providing loans and arranging borrowing through the issue of *gilt-edged securities. The bank helps to implement financial and monetary policy as directed by the Treasury. In 1997 the Bank took over sole responsibility for setting the *base rate, which had previously been a joint responsibility with the Chancellor of the Exchequer. The Bank formerly had wide powers to supervise the banking system, but these passed to the *Financial Services Authority in 1997.

(((🌐))) SEE WEB LINKS

• Bank of England website

bank overdraft *See* OVERDRAFT.

bank rate *See* BASE RATE.

bank reconciliation statement A statement that reconciles the bank balance in the books of an organization with the *bank statement. Differences may be due to cheques drawn by the organization but not yet presented to the bank, bank charges deducted from the account not yet notified to the organization, and payments made to the bank but not yet recorded by the organization. Bank reconciliations are usually performed weekly or monthly and are a form of internal control check. *See* ACCOUNT RECONCILIATION.

bank report A report made by a bank at the request of an auditor of a business, giving details of the business's dealings with the bank during a specified period.

bankruptcy The state of an individual who is unable to pay his or her debts and against whom a **bankruptcy order** has been made by a court. Such orders deprive bankrupts of their property, which is then used to pay their debts. See feature BANKRUPTCY LAW on p. 52.

bank statement A regular record, issued by a bank or building society, showing the credit and debit entries in a customer's account, together with the current balance. The frequency of issue will vary with the customer's needs and the volume of transactions going through the account. Cash dispensers enable customers to ask for a statement whenever one is required.

bank transfer (bank giro credit) A method of making payments in which the payer may make a payment at any branch of any bank for the account of a payee with an account at any branch of the same or another bank.

bar chart (bar diagram) A chart that presents statistical data by means of rectangles (i.e. bars) of differing heights. For example, the sales figures for a range of products for an accounting period may be presented in this way, the different sizes of the bars enabling the users to see at a glance how each product has performed during the period.

bargain purchase The purchase of assets or other goods for substantially less

BANKRUPTCY LAW

Bankruptcy proceedings are started by a **bankruptcy petition**, which may be presented to the court by
(1) a creditor or creditors;
(2) a person affected by a *voluntary arrangement to pay debts set up by the debtor under the Insolvency Act 1986;
(3) the Director of Public Prosecutions;
(4) the debtor himself.
The grounds for a creditors' petition are that the debtor appears to be unable to pay a debt for which a statutory demand has been made or that a court has ordered him or her to pay. The debt must amount to at least £750. The grounds for a petition by a person bound by a voluntary arrangement are that the debtor has not complied with the terms of the arrangement or has withheld material information. The Director of Public Prosecutions may present a petition in the public interest under the Powers of Criminal Courts Act 1973. The debtor may also present a petition on the grounds of being unable to pay his debts.

Once a petition has been presented, the debtor may not dispose of any property. The court may halt any other legal proceedings against the debtor. An interim receiver may be appointed. This will usually be the *official receiver, who will take any necessary action to protect the debtor's estate. A special manager may be appointed if the nature of the debtor's business requires it.

The court may make a **bankruptcy order** at its discretion. Once this has happened, the debtor is an *undischarged bankrupt, who is deprived of the ownership of all property and must assist the official receiver in listing it, recovering it, protecting it, etc. The official receiver becomes manager and receiver of the estate until the appointment of a **trustee in bankruptcy**. The bankrupt must prepare a statement of affairs for the official receiver within 21 days of the bankruptcy order. A *public examination of the bankrupt may be ordered on the application of the official receiver or the creditors, in which the bankrupt will be required to answer questions about his or her affairs in court.

Within 12 weeks the official receiver must decide whether to call a **meeting of creditors** to appoint a trustee in bankruptcy. The trustee's duties are to collect, realize, and distribute the bankrupt's estate. The trustee may be appointed by the creditors, the court, or the Secretary of State and must be a qualified *insolvency practitioner or the official receiver. All the property of the bankrupt is available to pay the creditors, except for the following:

- equipment necessary for him to continue in employment or business;
- necessary domestic equipment;
- income required for the reasonable domestic needs of the bankrupt and his family.

The court has discretion whether to order sale of a house in which a spouse or children are living.

All creditors must prove their claims to the trustee. Only unsecured claims can be proved in bankruptcy. When all expenses have been paid, the trustee will divide the estate. The Insolvency Act 1986 sets out the order in which creditors will be paid (*see* PREFERENTIAL CREDITOR).

The bankruptcy may end automatically after one year, but in some cases a court order is required. The bankrupt is discharged and receives a certificate of discharge from the court.

See also INSOLVENCY SERVICE.

than the fair market value. A bargain purchase can be made when the vendor is in liquidation or is otherwise financially distressed.

bargain purchase option *See* CAPITAL LEASE.

bargain renewal option *See* CAPITAL LEASE.

barometer stock A *security whose performance is regarded as an indication of the way in which the market is moving. In the USA such a stock is often called a **bellwether security**.

barter A method of trading in which goods or services are exchanged without the use of *money. It is a cumbersome system, which severely limits the scope for trade. Means of exchange, such as money, enable individuals to trade with each other at much greater distance and through whole chains of intermediaries, which are inconceivable in a barter system.

BAS Abbreviation for *Board for Actuarial Standards.

base currency The currency used as the basis for an exchange rate, i.e. a foreign currency rate of exchange is quoted per single unit of the base currency, usually US dollars.

base rate **1.** The rate of interest used as a basis by banks for the rates they charge their customers. In practice most customers will pay a premium over base rate on loans and will receive below the base rate on deposits with banks. **2.** An informal name for the rate at which a country's central bank lends to the banking system, which effectively controls the lending rate throughout the system. In the UK sole responsibility for setting the base rate was given to the Bank of England in 1997. The base rate is more formally known as the **bank rate**.

base stock A certain volume of stock, assumed to be constant in that stock levels are not allowed to fall below this level. When the stock is valued, this proportion of the stock is valued at its original cost. This method is not normally acceptable under Statement of Standard Accounting Practice 9 for financial accounting purposes.

basic costing method The major *costing method adopted by an organization.

basic earnings per share A company's *earnings per share for a financial period calculated without taking into account any obligations that the company has outstanding that would lead to dilution. *Compare* FULLY DILUTED EARNINGS PER SHARE.

basic rate of income tax In the UK, a rate of income tax below the higher rate. It is currently 20%, which is applied to the first £37,400 of *taxable income (2009–10). *See also* HIGHER RATE OF INCOME TAX.

basic standard A cost or income standard set in *standard costing to form the basis upon which other standards are set. For example, the number of labour minutes allowed per unit of product produced would be a basic standard to which the current wage rates can be applied in order to produce a *current standard.

basic wage rate The wage rate paid to an operator for a specified time period worked; it excludes any payments for incentive bonus, shift premium, overtime, working conditions, and other premium payments that, when added to the basic wage rate, make up the final gross pay.

basis of apportionment The basis used for the *apportionment of costs between a number of *cost centres when the costs are to be shared between them equitably. This occurs when an overhead cannot be directly assigned to one particular cost centre. For example, rent and business rates are seldom incurred by individual cost centres, therefore floor area is often used as a basis of apportionment to share the costs between appropriate cost centres. *See also* ALLOCATION BASE.

basis of assessment The basis upon which personal income or business profits are assessed in the UK for each *fiscal year. The individual rules for each income-tax *schedule identify the profits or income to be assessed in that year. These rules are complex and the advice of a tax expert should be sought. The basis of assessment does not necessarily equate to the actual tax year. In the case of a partnership that has been trading for many years, the profits for the year to 30 April 2010, i.e. those arising during the period 1 May 2009 to 30 April 2010, will form the basis of the assessment for the tax year 2010–11. This is known as the *current-year basis of assessment. Other income received during the year, e.g. building society interest received, is assessed on an actual basis and so for 2010–11 the basis of assessment will be the tax year, i.e. the interest received during the year 6 April 2010 to 5 April 2011.

basis period The period, usually a year, during which profits earned or income generated form the *basis of assessment for the tax year.

basis point One hundredth of one per cent; this unit is often used in finance when prices involve fine margins.

batch A measure of production often used if the individual units of production are small or homogeneous. In this case the costs of production are best expressed per batch, by combining a specified number of units together to form a batch. This method of production is known as **batch processing**.

batch costing A form of costing in which the unit costs are expressed on the basis of a *batch produced. This is particularly appropriate where the cost per unit of production would result in an infinitesimal unit cost and where homogeneous units of production can conveniently be collected together to form discrete batches.

batch-level activities *See* ACTIVITY.

B2B Abbreviation for business-to-business; denoting direct trading between commercial organizations, especially via the Internet.

BCG matrix *See* BOSTON MATRIX.

b/d Abbreviation for *brought down.

bean counters A derogatory name for accountants.

bear A dealer on a stock exchange, currency market, or commodity market who expects prices to fall. A **bear market** is one in which a dealer is more likely to sell securities, currency, or goods than to buy them. A bear may even sell securities, currency, or goods without having them. This is known as selling short or establishing a **bear position**. The bear hopes to close (or cover) a short position by buying in at a lower price the securities, currency, or goods previously sold. The difference between the purchase price and the original sale price represents the successful bear's profit. A concerted attempt to force prices down by one or more bears by sustained selling is called a **bear raid**. In a **bear squeeze**, sellers force prices up against someone known to have a bear position to cover. *Compare* BULL.

bearer A person who presents for payment a cheque or *bill of exchange marked 'pay bearer'. As a bearer cheque or bill does not require endorsement it is considered a high-risk form of transfer.

bearer security (bearer bond) A security for which proof of ownership is possession of the security certificate; this enables such bonds to be transferred from one person to another without registration. No register of ownership is kept by the company in whose name it is issued. This is unusual as most securities are registered, so that proof of ownership is the presence of the owner's name on the security register. *Eurobonds are bearer securities, enabling their owners to preserve their anonymity, which can have taxation advantages. Bearer bonds are usually kept under lock and key, often deposited in a bank. Dividends are usually claimed by submitting coupons attached to the certificate.

bed and breakfasting Formerly, an operation in which a shareholder sold a holding one evening and made an agreement with the broker to buy the same holding back again when the market opened the next morning. The object was generally to establish a loss, which could be set against other profits for calculating capital gains tax. Tax changes have made this set of transactions obsolete, as the time elapsed between the sale and repurchase of shares must now be above 30 days for the holder to benefit in this way. However, other assets (e.g. works of art) are still sometimes bed-and-breakfasted for tax purposes.

behavioural accounting An approach to accounting that considers the psychological and social aspects of accounting in addition to the technical aspects. The operation of *budgetary control systems is an area in which behavioural accounting is very important. *See also* PERFORMANCE MEASUREMENT.

behavioural finance The study of the role played by psychological factors in financial decision making and hence their effect on overall market outcomes. In particular, behavioural finance studies the ways in which individual and group behaviour deviates from the rational pursuit of self-interest posited by classical economic theory (*see* BOUNDED RATIONALITY). A range of cognitive and emotional biases affecting decision making in conditions of uncertainty have been identified.

bellwether security *See* BAROMETER STOCK.

below-the-line Denoting those entries printed below the horizontal line on a company's *profit and loss account that show how the profit is distributed or where the funds to finance the loss have come from. *Compare* ABOVE-THE-LINE.

benchmarking A technique for measuring an organization's products, services, or activities against other best-performing organizations. Benchmarking is a continuous process and helps an organization focus on being competitive. Most of the early work in this area was carried out in manufacturing but the technique is now applied in a wide range of organizations. Typical areas in which benchmarking can be expected to bring benefits to an organization include:

- **customer satisfaction**. An organization wishing to improve some aspect of its performance (e.g., its website) might ask customers how this compares with that of competitors. By identifying and making improvements the company can expect to improve sales in the long run.
- **cost reduction**. The benchmarking exercise may identify an area in which the organization has higher costs than competitors. Potential savings may be identified, such as reducing the number of suppliers or making better use of technology. Benchmarking can be applied to all departments.
- **increased efficiency and effectiveness**. Benchmarking can help to streamline processes and identify ways of delivering a better service.

Before introducing benchmarking an organization will have to identify the costs of the exercise and the potential benefits and cost savings. The most significant cost will be the management time.

beneficiary **1.** A person for whose benefit a *trust exists. **2.** A person who benefits under a will. **3.** A person who receives money from the proceeds of a *letter of credit. **4.** A person who receives payment at the conclusion of a transaction, e.g. a retailer who has been paid by a customer by means of a credit card.

benefit–cost ratio The evaluation of a proposed activity by determining the value of the anticipated benefits likely to accrue compared to the costs that will be incurred. If the benefits exceed the costs the activity is financially attractive, although there may be many non-financial factors to take into account before making a final decision. The benefits, some of which may be of a qualitative nature, may be enjoyed by some groups and the costs borne by others, which may make the analysis more complex.

benefits in kind Benefits other than cash arising from employment. The UK tax legislation seeks to assess all earnings to tax, whether they be in the form of cash or in kind. The treatment of benefits depends on the level of total earnings, including the value of any benefits, and whether the employee is a director of a company. The general rule is to value benefits at their cash equivalent although some specific benefits (e.g. company cars) are subject to specific valuation rules. For employees earning less than £8500, the benefits are only assessable if they are living accommodation or if they are capable of being turned into cash, such as credit tokens. For all *directors or higher-paid employees (i.e. employees with total earnings, including benefits, in excess of £8500) the benefits must be reported on form P11D by the employer at the end of the *fiscal year. This form will include details of company cars and associated fuel provided by the employer, beneficial loans, mobile telephones or laptop computers, medical insurance provided by the employer, subscriptions paid, and any costs paid on the employee's behalf. These benefits will be assessed to tax. This often takes the form of a restriction to the *income tax code. *See also* FRINGE BENEFITS.

bequest A gift made by a *will.

BERR Abbreviation for the former Department for Business, Enterprise and Regulatory Reform. *See* DEPARTMENT FOR BUSINESS, INNOVATION AND SKILLS.

beta coefficient A measure of the volatility of a share. A share with a high beta coefficient is likely to respond to stock market movements by rising or falling in value by more than the market average. *See also* ALPHA COEFFICIENT; CAPITAL ASSET PRICING MODEL.

betterment In the USA, the replacement of a major item of plant or machinery by one that will provide better performance; betterment thus involves capital expenditure.

b/f Abbreviation for *brought forward.

BGC Abbreviation for bank giro credit. *See* BANK TRANSFER.

bid **1.** The price or yield at which a buyer indicates that he or she is willing to buy a financial obligation. *See* BID PRICE. **2.** An approach by one company to buy the share capital of another. *See* TAKEOVER BID.

bid price The price at which a *market maker will buy shares: the lower of the two figures quoted on the screens of the *Stock Exchange Automated Quotations System, the higher being the *offer price. Some dealers prefer to rely on the figure quoted, others prefer to haggle over the price.

Big Bang The upheaval on the *London Stock Exchange (LSE) when major changes in operation were introduced on 27 October 1986. The major changes enacted on that date were: (a) the abolition of LSE rules enforcing a rigid distinction between jobbers and brokers; (b) the abolition of fixed commission rates charged by *stockbrokers to their clients. The measures were introduced by the LSE in return for an undertaking by the government (given in 1983) that they would not prosecute the LSE under the Restrictive Practices Act. The term is sometimes used more generally to mean the *globalization and modernization of the London securities market at this time.

Big Four **1.** The four largest firms of accountants in the world, i.e. Deloitte, Ernst and Young, KPMG, and Price WaterhouseCooper. These four firms carry out the great majority of audits for public companies worldwide; they are also the world's biggest suppliers of management consultancy services. **2.** The major high-street or *commercial banks in the UK: Barclays (now incorporating Woolwich), Lloyds, HSBC (formerly Midland), and NatWest (now part of the Royal Bank of Scotland Group). In terms of market capitalization the four were joined in the 1990s by Abbey National (subsequently Abbey, now part of the Santander group) and the Halifax (subsequently HBOS, now part of the Lloyds Banking Group), which changed their status from *building societies to banks.

big GAAP The *generally accepted accounting principles applied to large entities. *Compare* LITTLE GAAP.

bilateral bank facility A *facility provided by a bank to a corporate customer. The agreement is restricted to the two parties, which enables a relationship to develop between the bank and the customer (*see* RELATIONSHIP BANKING). *Compare* SYNDICATED BANK FACILITY.

bilateral netting A method of reducing bank charges in which two related

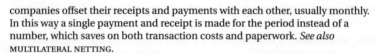

companies offset their receipts and payments with each other, usually monthly. In this way a single payment and receipt is made for the period instead of a number, which saves on both transaction costs and paperwork. *See also* MULTILATERAL NETTING.

bill 1. Short for *bill of exchange. 2. A colloquial name for a *sales invoice.

bill broker (discount broker) A broker who buys *bills of exchange (especially Treasury bills) from traders and sells them to banks and *discount houses or holds them to maturity.

billion Formerly, one thousand million (10^9) in the USA and one million million ($10^{1}2$) in the UK; now it is almost universally taken to be one thousand million.

bill of entry A detailed statement of the nature and value of a consignment of goods prepared by the shipper of the consignment for customs entry.

bill of exchange An unconditional order in writing, addressed by one person (the drawer) to another (the drawee) and signed by the person giving it, requiring the drawee to pay on demand or at a fixed or determinable future time a specified sum of money to or to the order of a specified person (the payee) or to the bearer. If the bill is payable at a future time the drawee signifies acceptance, which makes the drawee the party primarily liable upon the bill; the drawer and endorsers may also be liable upon a bill. The use of bills of exchange enables one person to transfer to another an enforceable right to a sum of money. A bill of exchange is not only transferable but also negotiable, since if a person without an enforceable right to the money transfers a bill to a holder in due course, the latter obtains a good title to it. *See* ACCOMMODATION BILL; DISHONOUR.

bill of quantities (bill of materials) A document drawn up by a quantity surveyor showing in detail the materials and parts required to build a structure (e.g. factory, house, office block), together with the price of each component and the labour costs. The bill of quantities is one of the tender documents that goes out to contractors who wish to quote for carrying out the work.

bill of sale 1. A document by which a person transfers the ownership of goods to another. Commonly the goods are transferred conditionally, as security for a debt, and a **conditional bill of sale** is thus a mortgage of goods. The mortgagor has a right to redeem the goods on repayment of the debt and usually remains in possession of them; the mortgagor may thus obtain false credit by appearing to own them. An **absolute bill of sale** transfers ownership of the goods absolutely. The Bills of Sale Acts 1878 and 1882 regulate the registration and form of bills of sale. **2.** A document recording the change of ownership when a ship is sold; it is regarded internationally as legal proof of ownership.

bill rate (discount rate) The rate on the *discount market at which *bills of exchange are discounted (i.e. purchased for less than they are worth when they mature). The rate will depend on the quality of the bill and the risk the purchaser takes. First-class bills, i.e. those backed by banks or well-respected finance houses, will be discounted at a lower rate than bills involving greater risk.

bills payable An item that may appear in a firm's accounts under current liabilities, summarizing the *bills of exchange being held, which will have to be paid when they mature.

bills receivable An item that may appear in a firm's accounts under current assets, summarizing the *bills of exchange being held until the funds become available when they mature.

BIMBO *Acronym for* buy-in management buy-out: a form of *management buy-out in which management invests in the venture together with outsider venture capitalists (such as a *private equity firm), who have more managerial control than is usual with a management buy-out.

bin card (store card) A card attached to each site or bin in which individual items of *stock are stored to record the receipts, issues, and balances of each item of stock in units. The bin card balance should indicate the physical stock available at any time; regular reconciliations with the physical quantities should be made to ensure accuracy.

biological assets *Assets that are living plants or animals, such as trees in a plantation or orchard, cultivated plants, sheep and cattle, etc. The term was introduced in *International Accounting Standard 41, Agriculture, which became operative for annual financial statements covering periods beginning on or after 1 January 2003.

BIS Abbreviation for *Bank for International Settlements.

black knight A person or firm that makes an unwelcome *takeover bid for a company. *Compare* GREY KNIGHT; WHITE KNIGHT.

black market An illegal market for a particular good or service. It can occur when regulations control a particular trade (as in arms dealing) or a particular period (as in wartime). *Compare* GREY MARKET.

black swan In *risk management, a high-impact event that should not be regarded as impossible just because it is highly improbable.

Black Wednesday Wednesday, 16 September 1992, when sterling was forced out of the Exchange Rate Mechanism, leading to a 15% fall in its value against the Deutschmark. See feature EUROPEAN ECONOMIC AND MONETARY UNION on p. 175.

blank bill A *bill of exchange in which the name of the payee is left blank.

blank cheque *See* CHEQUE.

blank endorsed *See* ENDORSEMENT.

blanket rate A production overhead *absorption rate used for a factory as a whole; it is sometimes used as an alternative to calculating a rate for each individual *cost centre.

blank transfer A share transfer form in which the name of the transferee and the transfer date are left blank. The form is signed by the registered holder of the shares so that the holder of the blank transfer has only to fill in the missing details to become the registered owner of the shares. Blank transfers can be deposited with a bank, when shares are being used as a security for a loan. A blank transfer can also be used when shares are held by *nominees, the beneficial owner holding the blank transfer.

blind trust A trust that administers the private financial affairs of a person in public office without informing him or her of the transactions entered into, so that there can be no conflict of interest. *See also* ARM S LENGTH.

blocked funds Money that cannot be transferred to another country because of *exchange controls.

block grant A grant made to an organization in the public sector, in which the organization is allowed to decide by its own procedures how to spend the grant.

blue chip Colloquial name for any of the ordinary shares in the most highly regarded companies traded on a stock market. Originating in the USA, the name comes from the colour of the highest value chip used in poker. Blue-chip companies have a well-known name, a good growth record, and large assets. The main part of an institution's equity portfolio will consist of blue chips.

blue-sky law In the USA, a law providing for state regulation and supervision for issuing investment securities in that state. It includes broker licensing and the registration of new issues.

Board for Actuarial Standards (BAS) An organization established in 2005 with a remit to set technical standards for the actuarial profession. It is part of the *Financial Reporting Council.

body corporate A *corporation consisting of a body of persons legally authorized to act as one person, while being distinct from that person. For example, the shareholders of a company are separate from the company. *See* ARTIFICIAL PERSON.

boilerplate A copy intended for use in making other copies. The term is sometimes used to mean a group of instructions that is incorporated in several different places in a computer program or the detailed standard form of words used in a contract, guarantee, etc.

boiler room A colloquial name for a *bucket shop that specializes in selling securities over the telephone. So-called **boiler-room scams** involve the selling of worthless shares to gullible investors, usually by cold calling.

Bombay Stock Exchange (BSE) India's leading stock exchange, listing nearly 5000 companies. The main index is the BSE Sensex of 30 representative stocks.

bona fide In good faith, honestly, without collusion or fraud. A bona fide purchaser for value without notice is a person who has bought property in good faith, without being aware of prior claims to it (for example, that it is subject to a trust). The purchaser will not be bound by those claims, unless (if the property is land) they were registered.

bona vacantia Goods without an apparent owner. An example could be the possessions of a person with no living relatives who has died intestate. The Crown is entitled to any personal property without an apparent owner. The prerogative may also be extended to real estate by the doctrine of **escheat**, the return of ownerless land to the superior landowner.

bond An IOU issued by a borrower to a lender. Bonds usually take the form of fixed-interest securities issued by governments, local authorities, or companies. However, bonds come in many forms: with fixed or variable rates of interest, redeemable or irredeemable, short- or long-term, secured or unsecured, and marketable or unmarketable. Fixed-interest payments are usually made twice a year but may alternatively be credited at the end of the agreement (typically 5 to 10 years). The borrower repays a specific sum of money plus the face value (par) of the bond. Most bonds are unsecured and do not grant shares in an organization (*see* DEBENTURE). Bonds are usually sold against loans, mortgages, credit-card income, etc., as marketable securities. A discount bond is one sold below its face value; a premium bond is one sold above par. *Compare* NOTE.

bonus dividend A *dividend issued to a shareholder in addition to those expected. Typically, two dividends are issued each year. If an additional dividend is paid to shareholders, perhaps because of a takeover, this is known as a bonus dividend.

bonus issue *See* SCRIP ISSUE.

bonus shares Shares issued to the existing shareholders of a company following a *scrip issue. The number of shares received depends on the level of the shareholding prior to the bonus issue. The number of bonus shares is usually one share for a specified number of shares held before the issue. For example, if the specified number is four this would be denoted as a 1:4 bonus issue. It is also possible to have a 2:1 bonus, when two shares are issued for every one held.

book-keeper A person employed to keep the *books of account for a business. Such a person may be a member of the *Association of Accounting Technicians.

book-keeping The keeping of the *books of account of a business. The records kept enable a *profit and loss account and the *balance sheet to be compiled. Most firms now use *business software packages of programs to enable the books to be kept by computer.

book of prime entry A book or record in which certain types of transaction are recorded before becoming part of the *double-entry book-keeping system. The most common books of prime entry are the *day book, the *cash book, and the *journal.

books of account The *ledgers, *journals, and other accounting records in which a business records its transactions. If the business is a limited company the accounting records must show in sufficient detail the position of the company at any time. *See* STATUTORY BOOKS.

book value **1.** *See* NET BOOK VALUE. **2.** (net asset value) The value of a company calculated as that of its total assets less *intangible assets and *liabilities. The information required to calculate the book value is all in the *balance sheet. However, it can be very misleading to measure value on this basis, as assets (stocks, buildings, land) are historical accounting figures. The book value of a company is often compared to its *market value, particularly as a means of valuing intangible assets (*see* INTELLECTUAL CAPITAL). Coca-Cola and Dell Computers are examples of companies whose book value is 10% or less of the market value. The **market-to-book ratio** is calculated by taking current market price per share and dividing by the book value per share. This ratio indicates management's success in creating value for its shareholders, with a high ratio being preferred. The ratio can be compared over time and against other companies. *See also* BALANCE-SHEET TOTAL; NET ASSETS; NET WORTH.

EXAMPLE

A company has the following figures on its balance sheet:

fixed assets		£300,000
goodwill		£100,000
current assets	£150,000	
current liabilities	(£100,000)	
		£50,000
		£450,000
10% debentures		£100,000
		£350,000
ordinary shares of £1		£100,000
reserves		£200,000
5% preference shares		£50,000
		£350,000

From these figures the book value of the company and the book value per share can be calculated as follows:

total value of net assets		£450,000
less intangible assets (goodwill)		£100,000
cpp		£350,000
less: preference shares	£50,000	
debentures	£100,000	
		£150,000
book value		£200,000

$$\text{book value per share} = \frac{£200,000}{100,000 \text{ shares}} = £2 \text{ per share}$$

If the market price per share is £10 then the market-to-book ratio is:

$$\frac{\text{current market price}}{\text{book value per share}} = \frac{£10}{£2} = 5$$

bootstrap **1.** A *leveraged buyout of the kind now mainly associated with *private equity firms. **2.** A company that is started up with very little capital, the intention being that costs will be met out of operating revenues.

borrowed capital *See* LOAN CAPITAL.

borrowing costs Costs that are incurred when an organization borrows money. Interest payments are an example of borrowing costs. Borrowing costs may be recognized as an expense when incurred or capitalized as part of the cost of an asset. For listed companies in the EU, the treatment of borrowing costs is now governed by *International Accounting Standard 23, Capitalization of Borrowing Costs.

Boston matrix (BCG matrix) A technique for analysing the potential of a business or business unit by reference to market share and growth rate. The matrix was developed by the Boston Consulting Group (BCG) in the 1970s. It is used to help large diversified firms identify those business units or products that generate cash and those that use it, so that an overall strategy can be developed. It can also be used as a tool of *portfolio management. Four main categories are displayed in a two-dimensional matrix:

- a **star** is a high-growth business competing in a market where it is relatively strong compared with the competition. Although such businesses generate large cash flows, high investment will be necessary to meet increasing demand.
- a **cash cow** is a low-growth business with a relatively high market share. As these are mature, successful businesses with relatively little need for investment they generate substantial cash flows that can be used to develop other businesses or products.
- a **question mark** (or **problem child**) is a business with low market share but which operates in higher growth markets. Such businesses are usually unable to sustain the level of investment necessary to turn them into stars.
- a **dog** is a business with a low market share in a low-growth market. Firms frequently face strategic decisions whether to continue to support dogs. *See also* GE MATRIX.

		Market Share	
		High	Low
Market Growth Rate	High	STAR	QUESTION MARK
	Low	CASH COW	DOG

bottom line A colloquial expression for *net profit after tax. This is the earnings figure used in the *earnings-per-share calculation of a company.

The introduction of *Financial Reporting Standard (FRS) 3, Reporting Financial Performance, in October 1992 amended the regulations in *Statement of Standard Accounting Practice 3, Earnings per Share, to include *extraordinary items in the bottom-line earnings figure. Further changes to the calculation and disclosure of earnings per share were introduced by FRS 14, Earnings per Share, and its successor FRS 22, Earnings Per Share. These have reduced the significance of the concept. The relevant *International Accounting Standard is IAS 33. *See also* ABOVE-THE-LINE.

bought day book A US term for the *purchase day book.

bought deal A method of raising capital for acquisitions or other purposes, used by listed companies as an alternative to a *rights issue or *placing. The company invites market makers or banks to bid for new shares, selling them to the highest bidder, who then sells them to the rest of the market in the expectation of making a profit. Bought deals originated in the USA and are becoming increasingly popular in the UK, although they remain controversial as they violate the principle of *pre-emption rights. *Compare* COMPETITIVE BOUGHT DEAL; PLACED DEAL. *See also* VENDOR PLACING.

bought ledger *See* CREDITORS LEDGER.

bounded rationality The type of rationality that most people (or organizations) resort to when faced with complex decisions in fast-moving, real-life situations where perfect information is unavailable. Given these constraints, decision makers will be content to find an alternative that gives satisfactory profits rather than one that maximizes profits. The concept of bounded rationality is thus a corrective to the assumption of many economic theories that economic agents make ideally rational decisions to optimize their self-interest. Similarly, some theorists have introduced the concepts of **bounded willpower** and **bounded self-interest** to explain decision making that appears to deviate from this model. *See* BEHAVIOURAL FINANCE.

BPR 1. Abbreviation for *business process re-engineering. **2.** Abbreviation for *business property relief.

branch accounting An accounting system in which each department or branch of a business is established as a separate *cost centre or *budget centre. The net profit per branch may be added together to arrive at the profit for the whole business. **Branch accounts** may be prepared to show the performance of both a main trading centre (i.e. the head office) and subsidiary trading centres (i.e. branches) but with all the accounting records being maintained by head office. Alternatively, **separate entity branch accounts** are prepared in which branches maintain their own records, which are later combined with head-office records to prepare accounts for the whole business.

brands *Intangible assets, such as a product or company name, sign, symbol, design, or reputation, which if operated in combination will lead to greater benefits from the sales or service through brand differentiation. The accounting treatment for brands is closely linked to the controversy surrounding accounting for *goodwill. Some companies, neither wishing to write off an amount representing goodwill immediately to their reserves nor to amortize it, have shown an amount for brands on their balance sheets. These amounts may remain on the balance sheet without amortization. Some companies have also chosen to place on their balance sheets internally created brands, as well as those acquired. Although there is general agreement that the existence of brands can have a beneficial impact on the earnings of a company, there is less agreement on the reliability of valuing brands in the balance sheet. In the UK this debate has been largely resolved by the introduction of *Financial Reporting Standard 10, Goodwill and Intangible Assets. *International Accounting Standard 38, Intangible Assets, requires a similar treatment. In the USA it has been standard practice to capitalize and amortize goodwill and all intangibles are treated in the same fashion; thus in the USA brands have not been an important accounting issue.

breach of contract A failure by a party to a *contract to perform obligations under that contract or an indication of an intention not to do so. An indication that a contract will be breached in the future is called **repudiation** or an **anticipatory breach**; it may be either expressed in words or implied from conduct. Such an implication arises when the only reasonable inference from a person's acts is an intention not to fulfil his or her part of the bargain. For example, an anticipatory breach occurs if a person contracts to sell a car to A but sells and delivers it to B before the delivery date agreed with A. The repudiation of a contract entitles the injured party to treat the contract as discharged and to sue immediately for *damages for the loss sustained. The same procedure only applies to an actual breach if it constitutes a **fundamental breach**, i.e. a breach of a major term of the contract. In either an anticipatory or an actual breach, the injured party may, however, decide to affirm the contract instead. When an actual breach relates only to a minor term of the contract (a warranty) the injured party may sue for damages but has no right to treat the contract as discharged. The process of treating a contract as discharged by reason of repudiation or actual breach is sometimes referred to as rescission. Other remedies available under certain circumstances for breach of contract are an injunction and specific performance.

breach of trust The contravention by a *trustee of the duties imposed by a *trust. If one of several trustees agrees to a breach of trust by a co-trustee, this also constitutes a breach of trust.

breakeven analysis (cost-volume-profit analysis; CVP analysis) The technique used in *management accounting in which costs are analysed according to *cost behaviour characteristics into *fixed costs and *variable costs and compared to sales revenue in order to determine the level of sales volume, sales value, or production at which the business makes neither a profit nor a loss (*see* BREAKEVEN POINT). The technique is also used in decision-making to assist management to determine such questions as the profit or loss likely to arise from any given level of production or sales, the impact on profitability of changes in the fixed or variable costs, and the levels of activity required to generate a desired profit. Breakeven analysis may either be carried out by drawing a *breakeven chart or by calculation. For example, the formula for determining the level of activity required to generate a desired profit is:

(total fixed costs + desired level of profit)/contribution per unit of production.

See also CONTRIBUTION.

breakeven chart (breakeven graph) A graph on which an organization's total costs, analysed into *fixed costs and *variable costs, are drawn over a given range of activity, together with the sales revenue for the same range of activity. The point at which the sales-revenue curve crosses the total-cost curve is known as the *breakeven point (expressed either as sales revenue or production/sales volume). The breakeven chart, like *breakeven analysis, may also be used to determine the profit or loss likely to arise from any given level of production or sales, the impact on profitability of changes in the fixed or variable costs, and the levels of activity required to generate a required profit.

breakeven point The level of production, sales volume, percentage of capacity, or sales revenue at which an organization makes neither a profit nor a loss. The breakeven point may either be determined by the construction of a *breakeven chart or by calculation. The formulae are:

breakeven point (units) = total fixed costs/contribution per unit;

breakeven point (sales) = (total fixed cost × selling price per unit)/
contribution per unit.

See also CONTRIBUTION.

break-up value 1. The value of an asset on the assumption that an organization will not continue in business. On this assumption the assets are likely to be sold piecemeal and probably in haste. 2. The *asset value per share of a company.

bribery and corruption Offences relating to the improper influencing of people in positions of trust. The offences commonly grouped under this expression are now statutory. Under the Public Bodies Corrupt Practices Act 1889, amended by the Prevention of Corruption Act 1916, it is an offence corruptly to offer to a member, officer, or servant of a public body any reward or advantage to do anything in relation to any matter with which that body is concerned; it is also an offence for a public servant or officer to corruptly receive or solicit such a reward. The Prevention of Corruption Act 1906 amended by the 1916 Act is wider in scope. Under this Act it is an offence corruptly to give or offer any valuable consideration to an agent to do any act or show any favour in relation to a principal's affairs.

BRIC Denoting the economies of Brazil, Russia, India, and China, which experienced fast growth in the 2000s and are predicted to overtake many Western economies by 2050. The acronyms **BRICET** (including Eastern Europe and Turkey) and **BRIMC** (including Mexico) are also sometimes used. Funds investing in these countries are known as **BRIC funds**.

bricks-and-clicks *See* CLICKS-AND-MORTAR.

bridging loan A loan taken on a short-term basis to bridge the gap between the purchase of one asset and the sale of another. It is particularly common in the property and housing market.

British Accounting Association (BAA) The major body of accounting academics in the UK, originally founded as the Association of University Teachers in Accounting. It has approximately 800 members, a significant number of whom are either from or based overseas, and issues a quarterly journal, the *British Accounting Review*.

(⊕) SEE WEB LINKS
• Website of the BAA

broker An agent who brings two parties together, enabling them to enter into a contract to which the broker is not a principal. The broker's remuneration consists of a **brokerage**, which is usually calculated as a percentage of the sum involved in the contract but may be fixed according to a tariff. Brokers are used because they have specialized knowledge of certain markets or to conceal the identity of a principal, in addition to introducing buyers to sellers. *See* BILL BROKER; STOCKBROKER.

brought down (b/d) In book-keeping, describing an opening balance that has been transferred from the previous period.

brought forward (b/f) In book-keeping, describing an amount that is the total of the corresponding column on the previous page.

BSC Abbreviation for *balanced scorecard.

BSE Abbreviation for *Bombay Stock Exchange.

B shares In the USA, a category of less important *ordinary shares. B shares are usually distinguished from *A shares by their limited voting power.

bubble A situation in which asset prices are seriously inflated. The unstable boom thus created may lead to a market crash. The most infamous example of this was the South Sea Bubble of 1720, which led to the collapse of the British share market and the bankruptcy of many investors. More recent examples include the so-called 'dot.com bubble' of 1999–2000 and the house-price bubble of the mid 2000s.

bucket shop A derogatory term for a firm of brokers, dealers, agents, etc., of questionable standing and frail resources, that is unlikely to be a member of an established trade organization. *See also* BOILER ROOM.

budget **1.** A financial or quantitative statement, prepared prior to a specified accounting period, containing the plans and policies to be pursued during that period. It is used as the basis for *budgetary control. Generally a *functional budget is drawn up for each functional area within an organization, but in addition it is also usual to produce a *capital budget, a *cash-flow budget, stock budgets, and a *master budget, which includes a budgeted profit and loss account and balance sheet. **2. (the Budget)** In the UK, the government's annual budget, which is presented to parliament by the Chancellor of the Exchequer (traditionally, but not always, on a Tuesday in March). It contains estimates for the government's income and expenditure, together with the tax rates and the fiscal policies designed to meet the government's financial goals for the succeeding fiscal year. *See also* PRE-BUDGET REPORT.

budgetary control The process by which *financial control is exercised within an organization. *Budgets for income and expenditure for each *function of the organization are prepared in advance of an accounting period and are then compared with actual performance to establish any *variances. Individual function managers are made responsible for the *controllable costs within their budgets, and are expected to take remedial action if the *adverse variances are regarded as excessive.

budget centre A section or area of an organization under the responsibility of a manager for which *budgets are prepared; these budgets are compared with actual performance as part of the *budgetary control process. A budget centre may be a *function, department, section, individual, *cost centre, or any combination of these that the management wishes to treat as a budget centre. It is usual to produce regular financial statements on the basis of each budget centre so that each budget-centre manager is aware of its budgeted and actual performance and any *variances that arise.

budget committee The committee responsible for the operation of the *budgetary control process within an organization. The membership and responsibilities of the committee vary between organizations, but a typical committee might comprise a chief executive as chairman, the functional managers as members, and a financial manager as committee secretary or *budget director. The committee is responsible for ensuring the formulation of the budgets according to the directives and policies communicated by the board of *directors, scrutinizing the various budgets for coordination and acceptability, and ultimately submitting the budgets (or budget revisions) to the board of directors for approval.

budget cost allowance The amount of budgeted expenditure that a *cost centre or *budget centre is allowed to spend according to its budget, having regard to the level of *activity (or other basis of cost incurrence) actually achieved during the *budget period. The budget cost allowance is usually based on the level of activity achieved and whether the *cost item is classified as a *fixed cost or a *variable cost.

budget director The member of a *budget committee who is responsible for the administration of the *budgetary control process. The precise responsibilities vary between organizations, but the budget director acts as secretary to the budget committee and in this capacity coordinates the flow of information from the managers of the *budget centres to the budget committee and from the budget committee to the board of directors.

budgeted capacity (normal capacity) The productive *capacity available in an organization for a budget period as expressed in the *budget for that period. It may be expressed in terms of *direct labour hours, *machine hours, or *standard hours.

budgeted cost A cost included in a *budget representing the cost expected to be incurred by a *budget centre, *cost centre, *cost unit, product, process, or job.

budgeted revenue The income level included in a *budget representing the income that is expected to be achieved during that budget period.

budget expenditure head A way of analysing a budget and presenting financial statements under major headings, each budget heading being the responsibility of a particular manager. Under some circumstances a manager may be responsible for more than one budget expenditure head.

budget manual A manual setting out the administrative procedures and operations that should be applied in the operation of the *budgetary control system. It covers guidelines for the operation of the *budget committee and the *budget centres and includes such information as levels of responsibility, budget timetable, budget preparation, and budget-revision procedures.

budget period A period for which a *budget is prepared and during which it is intended to apply. It is usual for the budget period to be a year, but it is often broken down into shorter control periods, such as a month or a quarter. The budget periods should coincide with the *accounting periods adopted by the organization.

budget slack The surplus that arises when managers preparing a budget overestimate costs or underestimate revenues. Most organizations would want to eliminate budget slack but some managers may be motivated to create it to improve their performance evaluations. In certain cases, slack may be deliberately created by organizations to protect against uncertainty in the environment: for example, a company may hold excess stocks of a product to make sure that customers can always order the quantities they need. However, managers who create excessive slack in this way can be seen as inefficient. *Participative budgeting may be one way of reducing budget slack.

building society Traditionally, a financial institution that accepts deposits, upon which it pays interest, and makes loans for house purchase or house improvement secured by *mortgages. They developed from the *Friendly Society movement in the late 17th century and were non-profit-making with mutual status. These institutions can be found in the UK, Australia, South Africa, Ireland, and New Zealand. The US *savings and loan associations are broadly similar organizations.

In the UK, the Building Societies Act 1986 greatly widened the range of services they are permitted to offer; this has enabled them to compete with the commercial banks in many areas. They offer cheque accounts, which pay interest on all credit balances, cash cards, credit cards, loans, money transmission, foreign exchange, and valuation and conveyancing services. The distinction between banks and building societies is fast disappearing; indeed many building societies have obtained the sanction of their members to become *public limited companies. This means that they become profit-making banks, owned by their shareholders, instead of non-profit-making societies owned by subscribing members. These changes have led to the merger of many building societies to provide a national network that can compete with the *Big Four banks. Competition is well illustrated in the close relationship of interest rates between banks and building societies as they both compete for the market's funds. Moreover, the competition provided by the building societies has forced the banks into offering free banking services, paying interest on current accounts, and Saturday opening. Similar changes have taken place in all the other countries that have building societies. The UK building societies are now regulated by the *Financial Services Authority.

built-to-flip Describing a start-up company, typically in the IT field, that is designed to be sold to an acquirer at the earliest opportunity rather than built up into an enduring concern. Such a company is designed to sell itself, or the idea on which it is based, rather than a product or service.

bulk discount *See* DISCOUNT.

bull A dealer on a financial market who expects prices to rise. A **bull market** is one in which prices are rising or expected to do so, i.e. one in which a dealer is more likely to be a buyer than a seller, even to the extent of buying without having made a corresponding sale, thus establishing a **bull position** or a **long position**. A bull with a long position hopes to sell these purchases at a higher price after the market has risen. *Compare* BEAR.

bulldog bond An unsecured or secured *bond issued in the UK domestic market by a non-UK borrower.

bullet loan A loan in which the whole of the principal is repaid in a single final payment known as a **bullet**, although interest may be paid in interim payments. *Compare* AMORTIZING LOAN.

bunny bond A bond that gives the holder the option of receiving interest or additional bonds.

burden In the USA, another word for *overheads.

burn-out turnaround The process of restructuring a company that is in trouble by producing new finance to save it from liquidation, at the cost of diluting the shareholding of existing investors.

business For *value-added tax purposes, an activity is a business (and, hence, potentially liable to VAT) if it amounts to an 'economic activity' within the meaning of the EU VAT Directive. Elsewhere in the UK Taxes Acts, the meaning of the term 'business' seems to derive from the context. A 'property business' is the aggregate of all lettings carried on by one taxpayer, income tax on property income being levied on the profits of the taxpayer's single 'property business'. The courts have generally considered that every company carries on a business, that being the essential nature of a company. Sometimes, the business is merely holding shares in other companies (*see* INVESTMENT TRUST). When computing profits on which an income tax charge is imposed, deductions are made for expenditure with a business purpose. No deductions are made for expenditure with a domestic purpose, nor (generally) where there is *duality of purpose.

business asset When calculating that part of a capital gain that is chargeable to *capital gains tax, *entrepreneurs' relief is available where the gain arises on the disposal of business assets. (Prior to its abolition in 2008, taper relief was similarly available on the disposal of business assets.) For entrepreneurs' relief, the following are treated as business assets:
• shares and securities in a trading company (listed or unlisted), where 5% or more of the shares have been held;
• an asset used for the purposes of trade carried on by an unlisted trading company;
• an asset held for the purposes of trade carried on by the taxpayer, either alone or in partnership.
Assets held by trustees are treated as business assets if they fulfil the requirements outlined above for individuals.

business combination The bringing together of separate economic entities as a result of one entity uniting with, or obtaining control over, the *net assets and operations of another.

business entity *See* ACCOUNTING ENTITY.

Business Link A UK government website for business people that provides guidance on such matters as tax, payroll, employment law, health and safety, etc. It also offers practical advice on finance, marketing, budgeting, information technology, and many other areas of general business practice.

((⊕)) SEE WEB LINKS
• Business Link home page: includes a section for accountants and tax advisers

business name (registered name) The name under which a sole trader, partnership, limited liability partnership, or company carries on business. The choice of a business name is restricted by the Companies Act, so that (for example) a misleading name may not be used. In the case of an individual or partnership, the names and addresses of the individuals concerned must be disclosed in documents issuing from the business (including e-mails) and upon business premises.

business plan 1. A detailed plan setting out the objectives of a business over a stated period, often three, five, or ten years. A business plan is drawn up by many businesses, especially if the business has passed through a bad period or if it has had a major change of policy. For new businesses it is an essential document for raising capital or loans. The plan should quantify as many of the objectives as possible, providing monthly *cash flows and production figures for at least the first two years, with diminishing detail in subsequent years; it must also outline its strategy and the tactics it intends to use in achieving its objectives. Anticipated *profit and loss accounts should form part of the business plan on a quarterly basis for at least two years, and an annual basis thereafter. For a group of companies the business plan is often called a **corporate plan**. **2.** A forecast of the activity volumes and cash flows relating to a specific project within an organization.

business process re-engineering (BPR; process innovation) An approach to the restructuring of business organizations that aims to achieve lower costs and improved quality of output through a radical reassessment of the organization's working methods. It involves the analysis of an organization in terms of its core processes, followed by a fundamental redesign of these processes through the application of enhanced information technology. However, radical BPR can be difficult to implement in practice, not least because of employee resistance. Employees may be concerned about losing their jobs, which will affect morale.

business property relief An *inheritance tax relief available on certain types of business property. For an interest in an unlisted business, including a partnership share, the relief is 100%. Land or buildings owned and used in a company under the control of the donor, or a partnership in which the donor was a partner, attract 50% relief. A majority controlling interest in a listed company also attracts 50% relief.

business rates The local tax paid in the UK by businesses. It is based on a local valuation of the property occupied by the business and the **Uniform Business Rate** (**UBR**) set by central government. *Compare* COUNCIL TAX.

business segments Separately identifiable parts of the business operations of a company or group whose activities, assets, risks, and returns can be clearly identified. Companies are obliged to disclose in their annual report and accounts certain financial information relating to business segments (*see* SEGMENTAL REPORTING). Although *Statement of Standard Accounting Practice 25 provides guidance as to what comprises a business segment, many inconsistencies appear in the information provided by companies. Standard setters have recognized that companies are not keen to improve segmental reporting because they fear they could suffer some competitive disadvantage. *International Financial Reporting Standard 8, Operating Segments, which became effective from January 2009, extends the requirement for segmental reporting.

business software package (office suite) One of a wide range of *software programs sold in packages to enable computers to be used for a variety of business uses. They range in complexity and expense from those suitable for an individual PC to large systems operated on a mainframe or a network. A typical package would include one or more of: book-keeping programs, which provide facilities for keeping sales, purchase, and nominal ledgers; accounting packages, enabling balance sheets, budgetary control, and sale and purchase analysis to be undertaken automatically (*see* SPREADSHEET); payroll packages, dealing with wages, salaries, PAYE, National Insurance, pensions, etc.; and *database management systems to maintain company records. Business software packages may also include more general software, such as a spreadsheet program and a word-processing application. The programs comprising the package are designed to work together and use each other's data. *See also* AUDIT SOFTWARE.

buy-in The purchase of a holding of more than 50% in a company by (or on behalf of) a group of executives from outside the company, who wish to run the company.

buy-out The purchase of a substantial holding in a company by its existing managers. *See* MANAGEMENT BUY-OUT.

by-product A product from a process that has secondary economic significance compared to the *main product of the process. For example, while the primary reason for cracking oil is to produce petroleum, other products produced as a result of the process, such as lubricating oil, paraffin, and other distillates, are by-products. *See also* JOINT PRODUCTS; PROCESS COSTING.

CAATs Abbreviation for *computer-assisted audit techniques.

Cadbury Report A report on the financial aspects of *corporate governance in the UK issued in 1992 by a committee under Sir Adrian Cadbury. The so-called **Cadbury Code** of best practice recommended that *non-executive directors should be appointed for specified terms and reappointment should not be automatic, that such directors should be selected through a formal process, and that both their selection and their appointment should be a matter for the board as a whole. Together with the recommendations of the *Greenbury Report and the *Hampel Report, the Cadbury Code laid the foundations of the *Combined Code on Corporate Governance, first issued in 1998.

cafeteria plan In the USA, an agreement that permits employees to select a fringe benefit from a variety of such benefits (including cash); under the tax code, the benefit is not included in the gross income of the participants solely because the participants are required to choose from a variety of benefits.

CAFR Abbreviation for *comprehensive annual financial report.

callable bonds Fixed-rate bonds, usually *convertibles, in which the issuer has the right, but not the obligation, to redeem (call) the bond at par during the life of the bond. The call exercise price may be at par, although it is usually set at a premium. A **grace period** during which the borrower is unable to call the bond will usually be included in the terms of the agreement; conversion after the grace period will only be possible if certain conditions are met, usually related to the price of the underlying share.

called-up share capital When the *issued share capital of a company consists of *partly paid shares, that part of the share capital that has been paid for by subscribers. *Compare* PAID-UP SHARE CAPITAL.

call option *See* OPTION.

Canadian Institute of Chartered Accountants (CICA) The professional body of practising accountants in Canada; it was originally founded in 1902 as the Dominion Association of Chartered Accountants.

cap A ceiling on a charge; for example, an interest-rate cap would set a maximum interest rate to be charged on a loan, regardless of prevailing general interest-rate levels. A lender would charge a fee for including a cap at the outset to offset this risk. Caps may also limit annual increases to a certain level. *Compare* FLOOR. *See also* COLLAR.

CAPA Abbreviation for *Confederation of Asian and Pacific Accountants.

capacity The level of productive capacity that an organization can attain under particular circumstances. It may be expressed in terms of *direct labour hours, *machine hours, or *standard hours. *See also* BUDGETED CAPACITY; IDLE CAPACITY.

capacity usage variance   *See* FIXED OVERHEAD CAPACITY VARIANCE.

Caparo case   The landmark case of *Caparo Industries plc v Dickman and others* (1990), in which the House of Lords ruled that auditors owe a duty of care to existing shareholders as a body rather than to individual shareholders.

capital   **1.** The total value of the assets of a person less liabilities.   **2.** The amount of the proprietors' interests in the assets of an organization, less its liabilities.   **3.** The money contributed by the proprietors to an organization to enable it to function; thus *share capital is the amount provided by way of shares and the *loan capital is the amount provided by way of loans. However, the capital of the proprietors of companies not only consists of the share and loan capital, it also includes *retained earnings, which accrues to the holders of the ordinary shares.   **4.** In economic theory, a factor of production, usually either machinery and plant (**physical capital**) or money (**financial capital**). However, the concept can be applied to a variety of other assets (e.g., *human capital or *intellectual capital). Capital is generally used to enhance the productivity of other factors of production (e.g. combine harvesters enhance the productivity of land; tools enhance the value of labour) and its return is the reward following from this enhancement. In general, the rate of return on capital is called *profit.

capital account   **1.** An account in the financial records of a limited company showing the total amounts for each class of share capital, for example the *preference share capital and the *ordinary share capital.   **2.** An account or series of accounts showing the interests of each partner in the net assets of a partnership. This account records the partners' capital contributions, goodwill valuation, and revaluations. In sole tradership accounts, the capital account records the interest the sole trader holds in the net assets of the business.   **3.** An account recording *capital expenditure on such items as land and buildings, plant and machinery, etc.   **4.** A budgeted amount that can only be spent on major items, especially in public-sector budgeting.   **5.** That part of the *balance of payments account that shows flows of money between currencies for investment purposes.

capital adequacy ratio (solvency ratio)   The proportion of a bank's total assets that is held in the form of *shareholders' equity and certain other defined classes of capital. It is a measure of the bank's ability to meet the needs of its depositors and other creditors. The minimum international requirement is 8% but some countries may require banks to have a higher ratio.

capital allocation   The allocation of investment capital to particular units within an organization on the basis of possible losses, which are calculated by *value-at-risk techniques. This is particularly common in financial institutions. Capital allocation may also be related to the funding structure of units and is often used as a basis for the calculation of *shareholder value or *Economic Value Added.

capital allowances   Allowances against UK income tax or corporation tax available to a business, sole trader, partnership, or limited company that has spent capital on *plant and machinery used in the business. Capital allowances are also given on industrial buildings and some agricultural and commercial buildings. The level of allowance varies according to the different categories of asset. Plant and machinery qualifies for a standard 20% *writing-down allowance. Certain *first-year allowances were previously available to smaller businesses that invested in specified assets but these were replaced by an all-purpose *Annual Investment Allowance from April 2008. An allowance of 2% calculated by the *straight-line method is currently available on industrial buildings; this is to be phased out by April 2011. An allowance of 10% is also available for certain long-life assets expected to last for 25 years or more. The allowances are treated as an expense in the computation of taxable profit and the capital allowance period reflects the period during which the accounts are prepared. If a business's capital allowances exceed its profit, it may obtain relief for the loss this generates by applying the usual loss relief rules.

(((( )))) SEE WEB LINKS
• Details of capital allowances from the HMRC website

capital asset *See* FIXED ASSET.

capital asset pricing model (CAPM) A model that can be used to calculate the expected or average return on an investment. It assumes that this return will be composed of the *risk-free rate of return and a *risk premium. Formally, the CAPM is based on the equation:

$$E(R_i) = R_f + \beta_i[E(R_m) - R_f],$$

where $E(R_i)$ is the expected/average return on the asset or portfolio i, R_f is the risk-free rate of return, $E(R_m)$ is the expected/average return on all assets, and β_i is the *beta coefficient of the asset or portfolio i. The beta is the percentage that the return on i will change with a 1% change in R_m. The CAPM is a measure of the risk in the asset or the portfolio. It is the basis for calculating the required return on an investment and is frequently used to calculate the discount rate for a *net present value calculation.

capital at risk A measure of possible worst-case losses in excess of the average that is used in banking to calculate both capital requirements and certain performance measures, such as *risk-adjusted return on capital (RAROC). It is usually based on the *value-at-risk methodology.

capital budget (capital expenditure budget; capital investment budget) The section of the *master budget that covers the amount of *capital expenditure an organization expects to undertake within a given *budget period.

capital budgeting (capital investment appraisal; investment appraisal) The process by which an organization appraises a range of different investment projects with a view to determining which is likely to give the highest financial return. The approaches adopted include *net present value, the *internal rate of return, the *profitability index, the *accounting rate of return, and the *payback period method. *See also* COST-BENEFIT ANALYSIS; DISCOUNTED CASH FLOW; ECONOMIC APPRAISAL.

capital costs *See* CAPITAL EXPENDITURE.

capital cover The capital value of a *portfolio, often a portfolio of property, divided by the capital sum to be financed. The lower the capital cover, the higher the risk.

capital distribution *See* DISTRIBUTION.

capital duty A duty imposed by the European Community in 1973 to replace certain elements of the UK's stamp duty. Capital duty was abolished with effect from 16 March 1988.

capital employed Either the sum of the *shareholders' equity in a company and its long-term debt or the *fixed assets of a company plus its *net current assets. Although this term is neither legally defined nor required to be disclosed in a *balance sheet, it is an important element of *ratio analysis, particularly in the calculation of *return on capital employed.

capital expenditure (capital costs; capital investment; investment costs; investment expenditure) The *expenditure by an organization of an appreciable sum for the purchase or improvement of a *fixed asset; the amount expended would warrant the item being depreciated over an estimated useful life of a reasonably extended period. Capital expenditure is not charged against the profits of the organization when it takes place, but is regarded as an investment to be capitalized in the *balance sheet as a fixed asset and subsequently charged against profits by depreciating the asset over its estimated useful life. Relief against taxation is available through *capital allowances.

capital expenditure budget *See* CAPITAL BUDGET.

capital fund *See* ACCUMULATED FUND.

capital gain The gain on the disposal of an asset calculated by deducting the cost of the asset from the proceeds received on its disposal. Under *capital gains tax legislation the *chargeable gain may be reduced by various exemptions and reliefs. Capital gains by companies are adjusted by *indexation and are chargeable to *corporation tax.

capital gains tax (CGT) A UK tax on *capital gains. Most countries have a form of income tax under which they tax the profits from trading and a different tax to tax substantial disposals of assets either by traders for whom the assets are not trading stock (e.g. a trader's factory) or by individuals who do not trade (e.g. sales of shares by an investor). The latter type of tax is a capital gains tax. In the UK, capital gains tax is charged on the total amount of *chargeable gains accruing to a person in a fiscal year after deducting any allowable *capital losses. Since April 2008 the tax has been levied at a single rate of 18%. The use of *taper relief and *indexation to reduce a chargeable gain was also abolished from April 2008, when a new system of *entrepreneurs' relief was introduced.

(⊕) SEE WEB LINKS

• A guide to capital gains tax from the Gov.uk website

capital gearing *See* GEARING.

capital instruments The means used by companies to raise finance, including *shares, *debentures, and loans; it also includes *options and *warrants that give the holder the right to subscribe for or to obtain capital instruments. In company accounts it is essential to distinguish between capital instruments and *equity; the regulations in *Financial Reporting Standard (FRS) 4, Capital Instruments, have now been superseded by those in FRS 25, Financial Instruments: Disclosure and Presentation, which closely follow *International Accounting Standard 32.

capital intensive Denoting a company with significant funds invested in *fixed assets, such as plant and machinery. These companies are regarded as high-risk investments, particularly in times of recession, because a small reduction in sales would cause a sharp reduction in profits, as a substantial part of the company's costs are fixed in the short term. *Compare* LABOUR INTENSIVE.

capital investment *See* CAPITAL EXPENDITURE.

capital investment appraisal *See* CAPITAL BUDGETING.

capital investment budget *See* CAPITAL BUDGET.

capitalization **1.** The act of providing *capital for a company or other organization. **2.** The structure of the capital of a company or other organization, i.e. the extent to which its capital is divided into share or loan capital and the extent to which share capital is divided into ordinary and preference shares. *See also* THIN CAPITALIZATION. **3.** The conversion of the reserves of a company into capital by means of a *scrip issue. **4.** The accounting practice of treating *capital expenditure as a fixed asset on the balance sheet rather than charging it against profits when it occurs.

capitalization issue *See* SCRIP ISSUE.

capitalization of borrowing costs *See* BORROWING COSTS.

capitalized value **1.** The value at which an asset has been recorded in the balance sheet of a company or other organization, usually before the deduction of *depreciation. **2.** The capital equivalent of an asset that yields a regular income, calculated at the prevailing rate of interest. For example, a piece of land bringing in an annual income of £1000, when the prevailing interest rate is 10%, would have a notional capitalized value of £10,000 (i.e. £1000/0.1). This may not reflect its true value.

capital lease In the USA, a lease that does not legally constitute a purchase although the leased asset should be recorded as an asset on the lessee's books if any one of the following four criteria is met:
- the lease transfers ownership of the property to the lessee at the end of the lease term;
- a **bargain purchase option** exists; i.e. an option exists enabling the lessee to buy the leased property at the end of the lease for a minimal amount or to renew the lease for a nominal rental (a **bargain renewal option**);
- the lease term is 75% or more of the life of the property;
- the *present value of minimum lease payments equals or exceeds 90% of the fair value of the property. *See also* FINANCE LEASE.

capital loss (allowable capital loss) The excess of the cost of an asset over the proceeds received on its disposal. Both individuals and companies may set capital losses against *capital gains to establish tax liability. Since 1994 *indexation is no longer permitted to create or increase a capital loss.

capital maintenance concept **1.** The **financial capital maintenance concept** is that the capital of a company is only maintained if the financial or monetary amount of its *net assets at the end of a financial period is equal to or exceeds the financial or monetary amount of its net assets at the beginning of the period, excluding any distributions to, or contributions from, the owners. **2.** The **physical capital maintenance concept** is that the physical capital is only maintained if the physical productive or operating capacity, or the funds or resources required to achieve this capacity, is equal to or exceeds the physical productive capacity at the beginning of the period, after excluding any distributions to, or contributions from, owners during the financial period.

capital market A market in which long-term *capital is raised by industry and commerce, the government, and local authorities. The money comes from private investors, insurance companies, pension funds, and banks and is usually arranged by issuing houses and *merchant banks. *Stock exchanges are also part of the capital market in that they provide a market for the shares and loan stocks that represent the capital once it has been raised. It is the sophistication of their capital markets that distinguishes the industrial countries from the developing countries, in that this facility for raising industrial and commercial capital is either absent or undeveloped in the latter.

capital rationing The situation that arises when managers have insufficient money to invest in all projects with a positive *net present value. The term **soft capital rationing** is used of situations in which a company sets its own limits on the amount of money available for investment in projects; if there are external constraints on money available for investments, the term **hard capital rationing** is used. Whenever capital rationing exists, managers need to rank potential investments so that net present value can be maximised (*see* PROFITABILITY INDEX).

capital redemption reserve A reserve created if a company purchases its own shares in circumstances that result in a reduction of share capital. It is a reserve that cannot be distributed to the shareholders and thus ensures the maintenance of the capital base of the company and protects the *creditors' buffer. *See also* PERMISSIBLE CAPITAL PAYMENT.

capital reduction *See* REDUCTION OF CAPITAL.

capital reserve *See* UNDISTRIBUTABLE RESERVES.

capital risk The risk, in a lending operation, that the capital amount of the investment may be less than its *par value, even at maturity.

capital stock In the USA, the equity shares in a corporation. The two basic types of capital stock are *common stock and *preferred stock.

capital structure (financial structure) **1.** The balance between the assets and liabilities of a company, the nature of its assets, and the composition of its borrowings. The assets may be fixed (tangible or intangible) or current (stock, debtors, or creditors); the borrowings may be long- or short-term, fixed or floating, secured or unsecured. Ideally the assets and liabilities should be matched. *See also* GEARING. **2.** The mix of differently rated classes of debt in a *structured finance instrument. *See* TRANCHE.

capital surplus In the USA, the difference between the *par value of a share and its *issue price. It is the equivalent of a *share premium in the UK.

capital transactions Transactions relating to share capital and reserves, long-term debt capital, or fixed assets of a company, as opposed to *revenue transactions. For example, the purchase of a building is a capital transaction, while the maintenance of a building is a revenue transaction.

capital turnover (asset turnover) The ratio of the sales of a company or other organization to its *capital employed (i.e. its assets less current liabilities). It is presumed that the higher this ratio, the better the use that is being made of the assets in generating sales. *See also* RATE OF TURNOVER.

CAPM Abbreviation for *capital asset pricing model.

capped floating-rate note (capped FRN) *See* FLOATING-RATE NOTE.

captive finance company A finance company controlled by an industrial or commercial company.

captive insurance company An insurance company set up by one or more commercial or industrial companies with the object of insuring their risks.

carousel fraud *See* MISSING TRADER INTRA-COMMUNITY FRAUD.

carriage inwards Delivery costs of goods purchased. If the costs relate to *fixed assets, they may be capitalized with the cost of the fixed asset on the *balance sheet.

carriage outwards Delivery costs of goods sold. This is a business expense, which is written off to the *profit and loss account for the period.

carried down (c/d) In book-keeping, describing an amount that is to be transferred as the opening balance in the next period.

carried forward (c/f) In book-keeping, describing the total of a column of figures that is to be the first item in the corresponding column on the next page.

carrying amount The balance-sheet value of an asset or liability. For example, a *fixed asset, such as a building, will be shown at the historical cost less the accumulated *depreciation to date, using the *historical-cost convention. Under *alternative accounting rules it can be shown at the revalued amount less the accumulated depreciation to date.

carrying costs (cost of carry; holding costs) 1. The costs of maintaining an inventory, including any *opportunity costs, protective measures, wastage, etc. **2.** The costs of holding a particular financial position; these may include funding costs and *opportunity costs (often calculated at the prevailing *risk-free rate of return).

CASE Acronym for *Committee on Accounting for Smaller Entities.

cash *Legal tender in the form of banknotes and coins that are readily acceptable for the settlement of debts.

cash accounting 1. An accounting scheme for *value added tax enabling a *taxable person to account for VAT on the basis of amounts paid and received during the period of the VAT return. Relief for bad debts is automatically available under this scheme. In order to qualify for the scheme, expected turnover should not exceed £1.35M in the next 12 months. A business already in the scheme is allowed a 25% tolerance limit above this threshold. **2. (cash-flow accounting)** A system of accounting that records only the cash payments and receipts relating to transactions made by a business, rather than when the money is earned or when expenses are incurred, as in *accrual accounting. UK legislation does not permit this system of accounting to be used for *published accounts.

cash at bank The total amount of money held at the bank by a person or company, either in current or deposit accounts. It is included in the *balance sheet under *current assets.

cash basis of accounting (receipts and payments basis) Accounting based on the cash concept rather than the *accruals concept. Transactions are recorded on the date that cash is received or paid out and are included in the *profit and loss account in which these payments occur. Under this system there is no accounting for debtors, prepayments, creditors, accruals, stocks, and fixed assets.

cash book A book or record in which bank cash transactions are recorded. These include receipts (from customers) and payments (to suppliers) as well as bank charges, interest received, etc. A cash book is a type of *day book, recording transactions in date order; the balance will be included in the *trial balance. The cash book is regularly reconciled with the *bank statement as an internal control check. Cash transactions not made through the bank are generally recorded in a petty-cash book.

cash budget *See* CASH-FLOW BUDGET.

cash card A plastic card enabling customers of retail banks to obtain cash from *automated teller machines, in conjunction with a *personal identification number. Many cash cards also function as *cheque cards and *debit cards.

cash cow *See* BOSTON MATRIX.

cash crop A crop that is sold for money as opposed to one that is consumed by the producer (a **subsistence crop**). In tropical and subtropical areas, cocoa, coffee, sugar and bananas are common cash crops. In cooler areas cash crops include grain and some vegetables.

cash cycle In manufacturing industry, the interval between an outlay of cash to buy raw materials and the receipt of payment for the manufactured goods produced from them.

cash discount *See* DISCOUNT.

cash dispenser *See* AUTOMATED TELLER MACHINE.

cash dividend A *dividend paid in cash rather than shares. Cash dividends are paid net of income tax, credit being given to the shareholder for the tax deducted.

cash equivalents Highly liquid investments that are capable of being converted into known amounts of cash without notice and that were within three months of maturity when acquired; from this total must be deducted bank advances that are repayable within three months from the date of the advance. Cash equivalents are an important element of a *cash-flow statement as required by *Financial Reporting Standard 1 and *International Accounting Standard 7. There has been some controversy regarding the requirement for three months maturity, which is an issue to be reconsidered when the standard is reviewed.

cash float Notes and coins held for the purpose of being able to give change to customers.

cash flow **1.** The movement of cash into and out of a business, as recorded in the *cash-flow statement or projected in a *cash-flow budget. **2.** The net income from a particular transaction after all cash expenses have been met (non-cash expenses such as depreciation being specifically excluded from the calculation).

cash-flow accounting *See* CASH ACCOUNTING.

cash flow at risk A measure of the risks to a firm's cash flows, calculated by applying the concept of *value-at-risk.

cash-flow budget (cash budget; cash-flow forecast; cash-flow projection; financial budget) A *budget that summarizes the expected cash inflows and the expected cash outflows of an organization over a *budget period, usually prepared on a monthly basis. It is the result of the analysis in cash-flow terms of the *functional budgets and the *capital budget, adjusted by other cash-flow items, such as interest, tax, and dividend payments. It is used as a planning aid to determine when cash surpluses are likely to be available for investment or when cash deficits are likely to arise requiring additional finance.

cash-flow statement (statement of cash flows) A statement showing the inflows and outflows of cash and *cash equivalents for a business over a financial period. The inflows and outflows are classified under the headings of operating activities, dividends from joint ventures and associated returns on investments, and servicing of finance, taxation, capital expenditure, and financial investment, acquisitions and disposals, equity dividends paid, management of liquid resources, and financing. In the UK, *Financial Reporting Standard 1 requires certain companies to publish a cash-flow statement in their annual report and accounts. The corresponding *International Accounting Standard is IAS 7, Cash-Flow Statements. In the USA the term **statement of changes in financial position** is generally preferred.

cash flow to capital expenditure ratio A ratio calculated by dividing a company's *cash flows from operations less *dividends by the expenditures for plant and equipment. It demonstrates a company's ability to maintain its plant and equipment from its own resources, rather than from borrowing.

cash flow to total debt ratio A ratio for assessing the solvency of a company, calculated by dividing the *cash flow from operations by the total *liabilities. It indicates a company's ability to satisfy its debts.

cash inflows The cash receipts of a business. Cash inflows arise from transactions such as sales of trading stock, receipts from debtors for credit sales, and disposals of *fixed assets.

cashless society A society in which modern electronic credit and debit cards can be substituted for cash in all or nearly all purchases. *See* ELECTRONIC FUNDS TRANSFER AT POINT OF SALE.

cash management The planning, monitoring, and execution of a firm's policy regarding *liquidity.

cash outflows The cash payments made by a business. Cash outflows arise from transactions such as purchase of materials, *direct labour costs, *overheads, and payment of taxes and dividends.

cash-payments journal A *day book recording payments of cash from an organization's bank account. This journal may be combined with a *cash-receipts journal to form a *cash book.

cash ratio (liquidity ratio) The ratio of the cash reserve that a bank keeps in coin, banknotes, etc., to its total liabilities to its customers, i.e. the amount deposited with it in current accounts and deposit accounts. Because cash reserves earn no interest, bankers try to keep them to a minimum, consistent with legal reserve requirements.

cash-receipts journal A *day book recording receipts of cash into an organization's bank account. This journal may be combined with a *cash-payments journal to form a *cash book.

cash sale A sale made for cash, rather than on credit terms. Cash sales should be entered in the *cash book rather than the *sales day book.

cash to current liabilities ratio A ratio calculated by dividing a company's cash and marketable *securities by its *current liabilities. It demonstrates the company's ability to satisfy short-term financial obligations.

CAT Abbreviation for *Certified Accounting Technician.

cause-and-effect allocation A *cost allocation in which the *allocation base is a significant determinant of the cost. To ensure that *indirect costs are accurately assigned to *cost objects, managers need to use cause-and-effect allocations rather than the *arbitrary allocations sometimes used in *traditional costing systems. *See* ACTIVITY-BASED COSTING.

CBI *See* CONFEDERATION OF BRITISH INDUSTRY.

CBO Abbreviation for collateralized bond obligation. *See* COLLATERALIZED DEBT OBLIGATION.

CCA Abbreviation for *current-cost accounting.

CCAB Abbreviation for *Consultative Committee of Accountancy Bodies.

c.c.c. Abbreviation for *cwmni cyfyngedig cyhoeddus: the Welsh equivalent of plc.

CCE Abbreviation for *current cash equivalent.

CD Abbreviation for *certificate of deposit.

c/d Abbreviation for *carried down.

CDO **1.** Abbreviation for *collateralized debt obligation. **2.** Abbreviation for *credit default option.

CDS Abbreviation for *credit default swap.

ceiling In the USA, an amount equal to the *net realizable value of an asset. The market cannot exceed the ceiling (upper limit) when employing the lower of cost or market method of *inventory valuation. If market is greater than the ceiling, the latter is chosen.

central bank A bank that provides financial and banking services for the government of a country and its commercial banking system as well as implementing the government's monetary policy. The main functions of a central bank are: to manage the government's accounts; to accept deposits and grant loans to the commercial banks; to control the issue of banknotes; to manage the public debt; to help manage the exchange rate when necessary; to influence the interest rate structure and control the money supply; to hold the country's reserves of gold and foreign currency; to manage dealings with other central banks; and to act as lender of last resort to the banking system. Examples of major central banks include the Bank of England in the UK, the *Federal Reserve System of the USA, and the *European Central Bank.

centralization The process or situation in which decision making is confined to the top managers of an organization. *Compare* DECENTRALIZATION.

certainty equivalent method In *capital budgeting, a method of risk analysis in which a particularly risky return is expressed in terms of the *risk-free rate of return that would be its equivalent.

certificate of deposit (CD) A negotiable certificate issued by a bank in return for a term deposit of up to five years. They originated in the USA in the 1960s. From 1968, a sterling CD was issued by UK banks. They were intended to enable the *merchant banks to attract funds away from the clearing banks with the offer of competitive interest rates. However, in 1971 the clearing banks also began to issue CDs as their negotiability and higher average yield had made them increasingly popular with the larger investors.

A secondary market in CDs has developed, made up of the *discount houses and the banks in the interbank market. They are issued in various amounts between £10,000 and £50,000, although they may be subdivided into units of the lower figure to facilitate negotiation of part holdings.

certificate of incorporation The certificate that brings a company into existence; it is issued to the shareholders by the Registrar of Companies when the company's constitutional documents have been received and approved. Until the certificate is issued, the company has no legal existence. *Compare* CERTIFICATE TO COMMENCE BUSINESS. *See also* ARTICLES OF ASSOCIATION.

certificate of insurance A certificate giving abbreviated details of the cover provided by an insurance policy. In a motor-insurance policy or an employers' liability policy, the information that must be shown on the certificate of insurance is laid down by law and in both cases the policy cover does not come into force until the certificate has been delivered to the policyholder.

certificate of origin A document that states the country from which a particular parcel of goods originated. In international trade it is one of the shipping documents and will often determine whether or not an import duty has to be paid on the goods and, if it has, on what tariff. Such certificates are usually issued by a chamber of commerce in the country of origin.

certificate of value A statement made in a document certifying that the transaction concerned is not part of a transaction (or series of transactions) for which the amount involved exceeds a certain value. The statement is made in relation to stamp duty, denoting that either it is not payable or it is payable at a reduced rate.

certificate to commence business A document issued by the Registrar of Companies to a public company on incorporation; it certifies that the nominal value of the company's share capital is at least equal to the authorized minimum of £50,000. Until the certificate has been issued, the company cannot do business or exercise its borrowing powers.

certified accountant *See* CHARTERED CERTIFIED ACCOUNTANT.

Certified Accounting Technician (CAT) A second-tier accounting qualification offered by the *Association of Chartered Certified Accountants. It provides an alternative to the CCAB qualification offered by the *Association of Accounting Technicians.

certified check In the USA, a depositor's cheque (check), which a bank guarantees to pay.

certified public accountant (CPA) A member of the *American Institute of Certified Public Accountants. The title is conferred by state authorities; a certified public accountant is licensed to give an *audit opinion on a company's financial statements.

cessation In the context of a business, the ceasing of trading.

c/f Abbreviation for *carried forward.

CFD Abbreviation for *contract for differences.

CGT Abbreviation for *capital gains tax.

chairman (chairwoman; chairperson; chair) The most senior officer in a company, who presides at the *annual general meeting of the company and usually also at meetings of the board of directors. This officer may combine the roles of chairman and managing director, especially in a small company of which he is the majority shareholder, or he may be a figurehead, without executive participation in the day-to-day running of the company. He is often a retired managing director. In the USA the person who performs this function is often called the president.

chairman's report (chairperson's report; chairwoman's report) A report by the chair of a company in the annual report and accounts (*see* ANNUAL ACCOUNTS), addressed to the *members of the company, giving an overview of the company's activities during the financial period. These statements are not prescribed by regulation and often present a favourable view of the activities and prospects of an organization. The report often also gives a survey of what can be expected in the coming year. It is signed by the chairperson, who usually reads it at the *annual general meeting.

CHAPS *Acronym for* Clearing House Automated Payment System. *See* ASSOCIATION FOR PAYMENT CLEARING SERVICES.

chapter 7 In the USA, the statute of the Bankruptcy Reform Act 1978 that refers to liquidation proceedings. It provides for a trustee appointed by the court to make a management charge, secure additional financing, and operate the business in order to prevent further loss. The intention of the statute, which is based on fairness and public policy, is to accept that honest debtors may not always be able to discharge their debts fully and to give them an opportunity to make a fresh start both in their business and personal lives. In an attempt to prevent opportunistic bankruptcies, the Bankruptcy Abuse Prevention and Consumer Protection Act 2005 has made it more difficult for debtors to file under Chapter 7. *Compare* CHAPTER 11; CHAPTER 13.

chapter 11 In the USA, the statute of the Bankruptcy Reform Act 1978 that refers to the reorganization of partnerships, corporations, and municipalities, as well as sole traders, who are in financial difficulties. Unless the court rules otherwise, the debtor remains in control of the business and its operations. By allowing activities to continue, debtors and creditors can enter into arrangements, such as the restructuring of debt, rescheduling of payments, and the granting of loans. *Compare* CHAPTER 7; CHAPTER 13.

chapter 13 In the USA, the statute of the Bankruptcy Reform Act 1978 that refers to debt restructuring and provides for individuals to repay creditors over time. *Compare* CHAPTER 7; CHAPTER 11.

charge **1.** A legal or equitable interest in land, securing the payment of money. It gives the creditor in whose favour the charge is created (the **chargee**) the right to payment from the income or proceeds of sale of the land charged, in priority to claims against the debtor by unsecured creditors. **2.** An interest in company property created in favour of a creditor (e.g. as a *debenture holder) to secure the amount owing. Most charges must be registered by the *Registrar of Companies (*see also* REGISTER OF CHARGES). A **fixed charge** is attached to specific fixed assets (e.g. premises, plant and machinery) and while in force prevents the company from dealing freely in those assets without the consent of the lender. A **floating charge** is not immediately attached to any specific asset but 'floats' over all the company's assets, to which it will not attach until **crystallization**, i.e. until some event (typically winding-up) causes it to become fixed. Before crystallization, the company may deal freely with such assets; this type of charge is suitable for *current assets, whose values must necessarily fluctuate. If the company goes into liquidation, fixed-charge holders are paid before *preferential creditors, who are paid before floating-charge holders.

   A charge can also be created upon shares. For example, the articles of association usually give the company a lien in respect of unpaid calls, and company members may, in order to secure a debt owed to a third party, charge their shares, either by a full transfer of shares coupled with an agreement to retransfer upon repayment of the debt or by a deposit of the share certificate.

chargeable account period *See* ACCOUNTING PERIOD.

chargeable assets All forms of property, wherever situated, that are not specifically designated as exempt from tax on *capital gains. **Exempt assets** include motor cars, National Savings Certificates, foreign currency for private use, betting winnings, life-insurance policies for those who are the original beneficial owners, works of art of national importance given for national purposes, principal private residences, *gilt-edged securities, certain low-value items (*see* CHATTEL EXEMPTION), and investments under *personal equity plans and *Individual Savings Accounts.

chargeable event Any transaction or event that gives rise to a liability to *income tax or to *capital gains tax.

chargeable gain In the UK, that part of a *capital gain arising as a result of the disposal of an asset that is subject to taxation. Non-chargeable gains include:
- gains resulting from proceeds that are taxable under *income tax;
- gains from exempt assets (*see* CHARGEABLE ASSETS);
- gains covered by other exemptions and reliefs (e.g. personal exemption from capital gains tax of £10,100 for 2009–10);
- gains not charged in full or at all owing to the new system of *entrepreneurs' relief.

chargeable person Any person resident, or ordinarily resident, in the UK during the year in which a *chargeable gain assessable to *capital gains tax was made as the result of that person disposing of an asset.

chargeable transfer A lifetime gift that is not covered by any of the exemptions and is therefore liable to *inheritance tax. A *potentially exempt transfer becomes a chargeable transfer where the death of the donor occurs within seven years of the transfer being made. A **chargeable lifetime transfer** is one that is neither an *exempt transfer nor potentially exempt; in practice, this applies only to payment into a *discretionary trust. Such a transfer is liable to inheritance tax at the lifetime rate of 20%, payable at the time of the transfer.

charge and discharge accounting A form of accounting used in the manorial system of the Middle Ages, in which individuals charge themselves with sums or estate they should receive and credit themselves with sums paid out.

charge card A plastic card entitling the holder to purchase goods or services either up to a prescribed limit or (in some cases) without limit, provided that payment in full is made at regular intervals (usually monthly). Some charge cards are issued by retailers and may only be used in that retailer's outlets. However, most charge cards are issued by financial services companies (e.g. American Express, Diners' Club) and these have a wide acceptability similar to *credit cards. The main difference between a charge card and a credit card is that the former does not allow the customer to roll over credit from month to month (although some cards now allow for large purchases to be paid off over a longer period). Charge card users therefore pay a fixed annual fee rather than interest. Because charge cards were formerly issued very selectively, they are more prestigious than other forms of credit card.

charges forward An instruction to the effect that all carriage charges on a consignment of goods will be paid by the consignee after he receives them.

charges register *See* REGISTER OF CHARGES.

charitable contributions *See* POLITICAL AND CHARITABLE CONTRIBUTIONS.

charity accounts The accounts of a charitable organization showing receipts (such as donations, grants, and fund-raising amounts received) and payments made (such as expenses, grants, and donations given). The specific regulations the charity will be required to conform to depend upon its legal form and its size. The Charities Act 1993 introduced a new accounting regime for charities.

Charity Commission The government department that acts as both an adviser to, and an investigator of, charities. It is responsible to the Home Secretary and is governed by the Charities Act 1993.

((⊕)) SEE WEB LINKS
- Website of the Charity Commission: includes guidance on charitable status and financial reporting for charities

chartered accountant (CA) In the UK, a qualified member of the *Institute of Chartered Accountants in England and Wales, the *Institute of Chartered Accountants of Scotland, or the *Institute of Chartered Accountants in Ireland. These were the original bodies to be granted royal charters. Other bodies of accountants now have charters (the Association of Chartered Certified Accountants, the Chartered Institute of Management Accountants, and the Chartered Institute of Public Finance and Accountancy) but their members are not known as chartered accountants. Most firms of chartered accountants are engaged in public practice concerned with auditing, taxation, and other financial advice; however, many trained chartered accountants fulfil management roles in industry.

Chartered Association of Certified Accountants *See* ASSOCIATION OF CHARTERED CERTIFIED ACCOUNTANTS.

chartered certified accountant (CCA) A member of the *Association of Chartered Certified Accountants. The Association's members are trained in industry, in the public sector, and in the offices of practising accountants. Membership is granted on the basis of completion of the Association's examinations and of sufficient relevant work experience. Members are recognized by the UK Department for Business, Innovation and Skills as qualified to audit the accounts of companies. They may be associates (ACCA) or fellows (FCCA) of the Association and, although they are not *chartered accountants, they fulfil much the same role. Chartered certified accountants were known as **certified accountants** until 1996. In the USA the equivalent is a *certified public accountant (CPA).

chartered company A *company incorporated by Royal Charter rather than by the Companies Act or by a private Act of Parliament.

Chartered Institute of Management Accountants (CIMA) The professional association that was founded in 1919 as the Institute of Cost and Works Accountants (ICWA). Its members work mainly in industry and commerce. *See also* MANAGEMENT ACCOUNTING.

((⊕)) SEE WEB LINKS
- CIMA website

Chartered Institute of Public Finance and Accountancy (CIPFA) The professional association that was founded in 1885 as the Corporate Treasurers' and Accountants' Institute. Its members work principally in public-sector accounting.

 SEE WEB LINKS

• CIPFA website

Chartered Institute of Purchasing and Supply (CIPS) A professional organization, based in the UK, for those working in purchasing, supply-chain management, and related areas. It offers training, qualifications, and a range of professional support services.

Chartered Institute of Taxation (CIOT) A professional institute for those working within the taxation field, in accountancy practices, legal firms, banks, and commerce, as well as in HM Revenue and Customs. Members are designated CTA (Chartered Trust Advisor) or, for those qualifying before 1994, ATII or FTII (Associate or Fellow of the Taxation Institute Incorporated).

SEE WEB LINKS

• Website of the CIOT: includes general and technical tax information and guidance on professional standards

chartist An *investment analyst who uses charts of prices and volumes in an attempt to predict what will happen in financial markets. Most chartist analysis is based on the assumption that history repeats itself and that the movements of share prices conform to a small number of repetitive patterns.

chart of accounts A detailed listing of all the accounts used by an organization, showing classifications and subclassifications. For example, each letter or number in an *account code will indicate a feature, such as transaction type and the department responsible.

chattel exemption The exemption from *capital gains tax that applies to gains from the disposal of chattels (i.e., items of moveable personal property) of less than £6000. It does not apply to *wasting assets.

cheque A preprinted form on which instructions are given to an account provider (a bank or building society) to pay a stated sum to a named recipient. It is a common form of payment of debts of all kinds (*see also* CURRENT ACCOUNT).

In a **crossed cheque** two parallel lines across the face of the cheque indicate that it must be paid into a bank account and not cashed over the counter (a **general crossing**). A **special crossing** may be used in order to further restrict the negotiability of the cheque, for example by adding the name of the payee's bank. Under the Cheques Act 1992 legal force is given to the words *account payee only on cheques, making them non-transferable and thus preventing fraudulent conversion of cheques intercepted by a third party. An **open cheque** is an uncrossed cheque that can be cashed at the bank of origin. An **order cheque** is one made payable to a named recipient 'or order', enabling the payee to either deposit it in an account or endorse it to a third party, i.e. transfer the rights to the cheque by signing it on the reverse. In a **blank cheque** the amount is not stated; it is often used if the exact debt is not known and the payee is left to complete it. However, the drawer may impose a maximum by writing 'under £…' on the cheque. A **rubber cheque** is one that is 'bounced' back to the drawer because of insufficient funds in the writer's account. In the USA the word is spelled **check**. *See also* BANK DRAFT; STALE CHEQUE.

cheque account An account with a bank or building society on which cheques can be drawn. The US name for such an account is a **checking account**. *See* CURRENT ACCOUNT.

cheque card A plastic card issued by a retail bank to its customers to guarantee cheques drawn on the customer's current account up to a specified limit. The card carries the account number, the name of the customer, and has to be signed by the customer. The card number must be written on the reverse of the cheque that it is guaranteeing. Many cheque cards have now been replaced by *multifunctional cards, which also function as *cash cards and *debit cards.

cheque-in facility A machine that will print on a cheque the amount of the cheque in machine-readable form. These machines are used mainly by banks to assist them in processing cheques, although companies are being encouraged to use them in order to reduce their bank charges.

cherry picking 1. Any accounting practice that is designed to highlight a company's most profitable transactions while as far as possible excluding loss-making transactions from the balance sheet (*see* OFF-BALANCE-SHEET). It is thus a form of *window dressing or *creative accounting. **2.** Any business policy that involves identifying a minority of the most profitable customers and concentrating on these to the exclusion of any other customers. *See* CUSTOMER PROFITABILITY ANALYSIS.

Chicago Mercantile Exchange (CME) The prime US futures and options market. It trades in financial and commodity contracts. It was started in 1919 as a commodity futures market but in 1972 opened the **International Monetary Market**, the world's first market for *financial futures. CME acquired the Chicago Board of Trade in 2007 and the *New York Mercantile Exchange in 2008.

Child Trust Fund (baby bond) A UK government-backed savings scheme for children introduced from 6 April 2005. On that date, the UK government provided every child born on or after 1 September 2002 with £250 (£500 for the poorest families) to invest in an approved scheme; children born after 6 April 2005 receive this sum at birth. A further government payment will be made on the child's seventh birthday and parents and others will be allowed to top up the funds to a maximum of £1200 a year tax free. The funds will mature when the child is 18.

Chinese wall A notional information barrier between the separate divisions, departments, or teams of a business to ensure that no improper or price-sensitive unpublished information passes between them.

CHIPS Abbreviation for *Clearing House Interbank Payments System.

CICA Abbreviation for *Canadian Institute of Chartered Accountants.

CIMA Abbreviation for *Chartered Institute of Management Accountants.

CIOT Abbreviation for *Chartered Institute of Taxation.

CIPFA Abbreviation for *Chartered Institute of Public Finance and Accountancy.

CIPS Abbreviation for *Chartered Institute of Purchasing and Supply.

circularization of debtors A technique used by an auditor in which all *debtors to a company are asked to confirm the amounts outstanding (**positive circularization**) or to reply if the amount stated is incorrect or in dispute (**negative circularization**). The object is to ensure that the debts do exist and are correctly valued in the financial statements of a company.

circulating assets *See* CURRENT ASSETS.

CIS Abbreviation for *Construction Industry Scheme.

City The financial district of London in which are situated the head offices of many banks, the money markets, the foreign exchange markets, the commodity and metal exchanges, the insurance market (including Lloyd's), the *London Stock Exchange, and the offices of the representatives of foreign financial institutions. Occupying the so-called **Square Mile** on the north side of the River Thames between Waterloo Bridge and Tower Bridge, the City has been an international merchanting centre since medieval times. Although many institutions remain in the Square Mile, others have migrated east along the river to new offices in the Docklands area.

City Code on Takeovers and Mergers A code first laid down in 1968, and subsequently modified, giving the practices to be observed in company takeovers (*see* TAKEOVER BID) and *mergers. It is administered by a panel (the **Takeover Panel**) including representatives from major financial and business institutions. The code does not have the force of law but the panel can admonish offenders and refer them to their own professional bodies for disciplinary action. It can also request the *Financial Services Authority to enforce its decisions.

The code attempts to ensure that all shareholders, including minority shareholders, are treated equally, are kept advised of the terms of all bids and counterbids, and are advised fairly by the directors of the company receiving the bid on the likely outcome if the bid succeeds. Its many other recommendations are aimed at preventing directors from acting in their own interests rather than those of their shareholders, ensuring that the negotiations are conducted openly and honestly, and preventing a spurious market arising in the shares of either side.

Under the Companies Act 2006 the Takeover Panel will be required to issue new rules to replace the City Code. These will incorporate articles of the EU's Takeover Directive (2005) and will have statutory authority.

class action A legal action in which a person sues as a representative of a class of persons who share a common claim.

clearance An indication from a taxing authority that a certain provision does not apply to a particular transaction. The procedure is only available when specified by statute, as, for example, on the reorganization of a company's share capital and on the demerger of a company's trade. Exceptionally, the Revenue grants a clearance under the extra-statutory concessional treatment whereby a dividend paid on the liquidation of a company is subject to capital gains tax and not to income tax.

cleared balance A balance on a bank account, excluding any receipts that have not yet been *cleared for value.

cleared for fate Denoting the date on which the payer's bank has confirmed that funds are available to provide value for a transfer in accordance with the instructions given in a cheque, etc. This may be up to four working days after the cheque has *cleared for value. Once a cheque has cleared for fate the funds transferred to the payee cannot be reclaimed unless there is evidence of deliberate fraud. *See* CLEARING CYCLE.

cleared for value Denoting the time at which a credit to a customer's bank account is used for calculating interest and for establishing the undrawn balance of an agreed overdraft facility. *See* CLEARING CYCLE.

clearing cycle The process by which a payment made by cheque, etc., through the banking system is transferred from the payer's to the payee's account. In the UK the average time for a cheque to be *cleared for value is two working days. However, it may be another two working days before the cheque is **cleared for withdrawal** (i.e. before the payee can withdraw money against the funds transferred) and six working days in all before the cheque is *cleared for fate.

clearing house A centralized and computerized system for settling indebtedness between members. The best known in the UK is the *Association for Payment Clearing Services (APACS), which enables the member banks to offset claims against one another for cheques and orders paid into banks other than those upon which they were drawn. Similar arrangements exist in financial exchanges, in which sales and purchases are registered with the clearing house for settlement at the end of the accounting period. *See also* CLEARSTREAM; CREST; EUROCLEAR; LONDON CLEARING HOUSE.

Clearing House Interbank Payments System (CHIPS) A US bank *clearing house for large-value dollar transactions. It is owned by financial institutions and operated by the **Clearing House Payments Company**. Any bank may participate providing that it has a regulated US presence.

Clearing Houses Automated Payment System (CHAPS) *See* ASSOCIATION FOR PAYMENT CLEARING SERVICES.

Clearstream A pan-European facility for the clearing and settlement of *eurobonds, based in Luxembourg. It was founded (as Clearstream International) in 2000, when *Deutsche Börse Clearing merged with the clearing company Centrale de Livraison de Valeurs Mobilès (Cedel International). It is now a wholly owned subsidiary of Deutsche Börse.

clickable Denoting a company or organization that operates on the *Internet. *See* E-COMMERCE.

clicks-and-mortar (bricks-and-clicks) Denoting a business that combines *e-commerce ('clicks') with the use of physical premises such as retail outlets or warehouses.

climate change levy A UK tax charged on the supply of electricity, gas, coal, and coke, as they are supplies that are regarded as leading to global warming. The levy is imposed by the Finance Act 2000 on any supply made on or after 1 April 2001.

CLO Abbreviation for collateralized loan obligation. *See* COLLATERALIZED DEBT OBLIGATION.

clock card *See* TIME CARD.

close company A company resident in the UK that is under the control of five or fewer participators or any number of participators who are also directors. There is also an alternative asset-based test, which applies if five or fewer participators, or any number who are directors, would be entitled to more than 50% of the company's assets on a winding-up. The principal consequences of being a close company are that the provision of certain *benefits in kind to shareholders can be treated by HM Revenue as a *distribution, as can loans or quasi-loans. There are a number of other consequences. In the USA close companies are known as **closed companies**. *See also* CLOSE INVESTMENT HOLDING COMPANY.

closed-end funds Funds in which the capital is fixed, such as those held by investment companies, rather than open-ended, such as unit trusts.

close family The family members of an individual, or members of the individual's household, who may be expected to influence, or be influenced by, that person in their dealings with an *accounting entity, thus leading to *related party transactions.

close investment holding company A *close company that does not exist wholly or mainly as a trading company, a property company letting to third parties, or a holding company of a trading company. Such a company is subject to *corporation tax at the full rate on its profits; it cannot benefit from the lower rates and reliefs available to other companies.

closely held corporation In the USA, a public corporation that has only a limited number of *stockholders and consequently few of its shares are traded.

closing balance The debit or credit balance on a ledger at the end of an *accounting period, which will appear on the *balance sheet at that date and be carried forward to the next accounting period. A debit closing balance (such as an *accrual) will be carried forward to the credit side of a ledger and a credit closing balance (such as a prepayment) will be carried forward to the debit side.

closing entries Final entries made at the end of an *accounting period to close off the income and expense ledgers to the *profit and loss account.

closing-rate method (net-investment method) A method of restating the figures in a balance sheet in another currency using the closing rate of exchange for all assets and *liabilities, i.e. the rate of exchange quoted at the close of business on the balance-sheet date.

closing stock The *stock remaining within an organization at the end of an *accounting period as *raw materials, *work in progress, or *finished goods. It is necessary to establish the level of closing stocks so that the cost of their creation is not charged against the profits of the period (*see* OPENING STOCK). Closing stocks are therefore valued and deducted from the costs of the period and appear as *current assets in the *balance sheet.

club deal *See* SYNDICATED BANK FACILITY.

cluster sampling A method of selecting a *sample in which the population is divided into clusters (groups) from each of which a random sample is taken. This technique is often used in auditing. For example, groups of, say, invoices are chosen at random by the auditor and then each item in each group is examined in detail.

CoCoA *See* CONTINUOUSLY CONTEMPORARY ACCOUNTING.

COGS Abbreviation for cost of goods sold. *See* COST OF SALES.

cold calling A method of selling a product or service in which a sales representative makes calls, door-to-door, by post, or by telephone, to people who have not previously shown any interest in the product or service. In the UK, the selling of investments by cold calling is regulated by the *Financial Services Act 1986.

collar An arrangement in which both the maximum (*cap) and minimum (*floor) rate of interest payable on a loan are fixed in advance.

collateral A form of *security, especially an impersonal form of security, such as life-assurance policies or shares, used to secure a bank loan. In some senses such impersonal securities are referred to as a secondary collateral, rather than a primary security, such as a guarantee.

collateralize In the USA, to pledge assets to secure a debt. If the borrower defaults on the terms and conditions of the agreement the assets will be forfeited.

collateralized debt obligation (CDO) A *structured finance instrument consisting of a bond or note backed by a pool of fixed-income assets. Rights to the cash flows from this pool, along with different levels of credit risk, are allocated to different classes (*tranches) of note. Some specific types of CDO include **collateralized bond obligations** (**CBO**s), **collateralized loan obligations** (**CLO**s), and **collateralized mortgage obligations** (**CMO**s). A *structured investment vehicle is a specialized form of CDO. The collapse in the value of CDOs exposed to *subprime mortgage loans was a major factor in the financial crisis of 2008–09; such instruments became *toxic assets with no market.

collectibles Items, such as art, stamps, and antiques, that are acquired not only for their aesthetic merits but because they are a potential source of *capital gains and of *inflation protection.

collecting bank (remitting bank) The bank to which a person who requires payment of a cheque (or similar financial document) has presented it for payment.

collection account A bank account opened for the specific purpose of reducing *bank float for remittances from specific customers or groups of customers, usually those that are abroad or who pay in a foreign currency.

collection period The time, expressed in days, weeks, or months, that it takes to obtain payment of a debt by a customer.

collective bargaining Bargaining between employers and employees over wages, terms of employment, etc., when the employees are represented by a trade union or some other collective body.

Collector of Taxes A civil servant responsible for the collection of taxes for which assessments have been raised by *Inspectors of Taxes and for the collection of tax under pay as you earn (PAYE).

collusion **1.** An agreement between two or more parties in order to prejudice a third party, or for any improper purpose. Collusion to carry out an illegal, not merely improper, purpose is punishable as a conspiracy. **2.** In legal proceedings, a secret agreement between two parties as a result of which one of them agrees to bring an action against the other in order to obtain a judicial decision for an improper purpose. **3.** A secret agreement between the parties to a legal action to do or to refrain from doing something in order to influence the judicial decision. For instance, an agreement between the plaintiff and the defendant to suppress certain evidence would amount to collusion. Any judgment obtained by collusion is a nullity and may be set aside.

columnar accounts Accounts set out in several columns; it is common to present a trial balance in this way. By adding across the columns adjustments are automatically fed into the financial statements.

co-managers Banks that rank after *lead managers in marketing a new issue, usually a *eurobond. They are usually chosen for their ability to place a large portion of the issue with their customers.

Combined Code on Corporate Governance A code of best practice in the field of *corporate governance, first issued with the *Hampel Report of 1998. The Code, which incorporated the earlier recommendations of the *Cadbury Report and the *Greenbury Report, concerns such matters as the role of *non-executive directors, directors' remuneration, and general issues of audit, accountability, and relations with shareholders. UK listed companies are required to disclose whether or not they have complied with the Code, and to explain any departures from it. Revised versions of the Code were issued in 2003 and 2006. *See also* HIGGS REPORT; SMITH REPORT; TURNBULL REPORT.

(⊕) SEE WEB LINKS

• Full text of the Combined Code (2008) from the FRC website

combined financial statement In the USA, the aggregation of the *financial statements of a related group of entities in order to present the financial information as if the group was a single entity. Intercompany transactions are eliminated from combined financial statements.

comfort letter *See* LETTER OF COMFORT.

commercial bank A privately owned bank that provides a wide range of financial services, both to the general public and to firms. The principal activities are operating cheque current accounts, receiving deposits, taking in and paying out notes and coin, and making loans. Additional services include trustee and executor facilities, the supply of foreign currency, the purchase and sale of securities, insurance, a credit-card system, and personal pensions. They also compete with the *finance houses and *merchant banks by providing venture capital and with *building societies by providing mortgages.

The main banks with national networks of branches in the UK are the so-called *Big Four – the Royal Bank of Scotland Group (now including NatWest), Barclays, Lloyds (now including HBOS), and HSBC – together with Abbey, and Alliance and Leicester (both now part of the Santander Group). Following the banking and financial crisis of 2008–09, the UK government now holds a major stake in Lloyds and the Royal Bank of Scotland (*see* UK FINANCIAL INVESTMENTS). The commercial banks are also known as **high-street banks**, **joint-stock banks**, or **retail banks**.

commercial collection agency *See* DEBT COLLECTION AGENCY.

commercial paper (CP) A relatively low-risk short-term (maturing at 60 days or less in the US but longer in the UK) form of borrowing. Commercial paper is often regarded as a reasonable substitute for Treasury bills, certificates of deposit, etc. The main issuers have traditionally been large creditworthy institutions, such as insurance companies, bank trust departments, and pension funds. Although commercial paper was traditionally unsecured, recent years have seen a major growth in **asset-backed commercial paper** (**ABCP**), in which the CP is secured against assets held by a *structured investment vehicle (usually longer-term debt). From 2007 the market in ABCP was severely affected by the *subprime lending crisis.

commission A payment made to an intermediary, such as an agent, salesman, broker, etc., usually calculated as a percentage of the value of the goods sold. Sometimes the whole of the commission is paid by the seller (e.g. an estate agent's commission in the UK) but in other cases (e.g. some commodity markets) it is shared equally between buyer and seller. In advertising, the commission is the discount (usually between 10% and 15%) allowed to an advertising agency by owners of the advertising medium for the space or time purchased on behalf of their clients. A **commission agent** is an agent specializing in buying or selling goods for a principal in another country for a commission.

commissions paid account An account used to record commissions paid by an organization to agents and others. In a double-entry system, the commissions paid account is debited and the bank account (or the creditors' account until it is paid) is credited. This account may be combined with the *commissions received account.

commissions received account An account used to record commissions received by an organization. In a double-entry system, the commissions received account will be credited and the bank account (or the debtors' account until it is received) is debited. This account may be combined with the *commissions paid account.

commitment fee A fee charged by a bank to keep open a line of credit or to continue to make available unused loan facilities. Usually the annual charge is made by the lender on the daily undrawn balance of the facility and is often expressed in *basis points.

commitments for capital expenditure Expenditure on fixed assets to which a company is committed for the future. The aggregate amounts of contracts for *capital expenditure not provided for in the accounts for the year and the aggregate amount of capital expenditure authorized by the directors but not yet accounted for should be disclosed in the *notes to the accounts. These disclosures will usually be made in the directors' report.

committed costs Costs, usually *fixed costs, that the management of an organization have a long-term responsibility to pay. Examples include rent on a long-term lease and depreciation on an asset with an extended life.

committed facility An agreement between a bank and a customer to provide funds up to a specified maximum at a specified *interest rate (in the UK this usually based upon an agreed margin over the *London Inter Bank Offered Rate) for a certain period. The total cost will be the interest rate plus the *mandatory liquid asset cost. The agreement will include the conditions that must be adhered to by the borrower for the facility to remain in place. *Compare* UNCOMMITTED FACILITY. *See also* REVOLVING BANK FACILITY.

Committee on Accounting for Smaller Entities (CASE) A specialist committee established by the *Accounting Standards Board to advise it on the application of accounting standards to smaller entities. It was instrumental in the development of the *Financial Reporting Standard for smaller entities (FRSSE). The most recent version of the FRSSE was issued in December 2008.

commodity **1.** A raw material traded on a commodity market, such as grain, coffee, cocoa, wool, cotton, jute, rubber, pork bellies, or orange juice (sometimes known as **soft commodities**) or base metals and other solid raw materials (known as **hard commodities**). In some contexts soft commodities are referred to as **produce**. **2.** A good regarded in economics as the basis of production and exchange.

commodity code Codes applied to each classification of direct material and other products used or produced by an organization. The codes facilitate recording in the material and finished goods control systems.

commodity contract A contract for settlement by receipt or delivery of a *commodity.

common costs **1.** In *process costing, those costs incurred by a process before the point at which the *joint products or *by-products are subjected to separate treatment. The common costs, therefore, must be borne by all the output, i.e. by the *main product, the joint products, and the by-products. *See also* JOINT COSTS. **2.** Costs regarded as unchanged as a result of a managerial decision. For example, if an increase in production is being considered, the total rent payable would be described as a cost common to both the situations before and after the production increase as the rent did not change as a result of the decision to increase production. *Compare* RELEVANT COST. **3.** Costs that are common to a number of processes or products and are therefore shared by them. Common costs are usually *fixed costs and require allocation to the appropriate *cost objects. *See* COST ALLOCATION.

common-size financial statements A method of analysing and comparing *financial statements by expressing the individual elements as percentages of the total. For example, with *profit and loss accounts all the costs could be expressed as a percentage of the sales figure. It is then possible to compare these percentages with those for another company or the industry average, enabling conclusions to be drawn on the performance of the company. *See* ACCOUNTING RATIO; FINANCIAL STATEMENT ANALYSIS; RATIO ANALYSIS.

common stock In the USA, the equivalent of the ordinary shares in a public company or privately held firm that give the holders voting and dividend rights.

Common stock holders are paid after bondholders and the holders of *preferred stock in the event of corporate bankruptcy.

commorientes Persons who die at the same time. If two people die simultaneously, or if it is uncertain who died first, it is assumed that the older person died first in so far as the devolution of their property is concerned. Thus, if two people are killed in a car crash, a bequest from the younger to the elder is treated as having lapsed.

community interest company A *limited company registered under the Companies (Audit, Investigations and Community Enterprise) Act 2004. Registration requires the approval of the Regulator of Community Interest Companies who must be satisfied that the company satisfies the 'community interest test', namely, that a reasonable person would consider that the company's activities are being carried on for the benefit of the community. A company formed for a political purpose cannot be registered as a community interest company. There are limitations as to the amount of dividends such a company can pay to its members.

Companies Acts Legislation governing the activities of companies. In the UK, the first Companies Act was passed in 1844. More recently, the Companies Act 1985 contained comprehensive legislation and the Companies Act 1989 incorporated various EC directives into UK law. A new Companies Act, replacing almost all the previous legislation, received the Royal Assent in 2006; its provisions were not fully implemented until late 2009.

(⊕) SEE WEB LINKS
- FAQs relating to the 2006 Act provided by the Department for Business, Innovation and Skills
- Full text of the Companies Act 2006

Companies House The office of the *Registrar of Companies. Companies with a registered office in England or Wales are served by the registry at Cardiff; those in Scotland by the registry in Edinburgh. Certain documents lodged there are open to inspection. These documents include the *accounts of limited companies, the *annual return, any *prospectus, the *memorandum and *articles of association, and particulars of the directors, the secretary, the *registered office, some types of company *charge, and notices of liquidation.

(⊕) SEE WEB LINKS
- Companies House website: includes guidance on incorporating and winding up a company

company A corporate enterprise that has a legal identity separate from that of its members; it operates as one single unit, in the success of which all the members participate. An **incorporated company** is a legal person in its own right, able to own property and to sue and be sued in its own name. A company may have limited liability (a *limited company), so that the liability of the members for the company's debts is limited. An *unlimited company is one in which the liability of the members is not limited in any way.

A **registered company**, i.e. one registered under the Companies Acts, is much the most common type of company. A company may be registered either as a *public limited company or a private company. A public limited company must have a name ending with the initials 'plc' and share capital of at least £50,000, of which at least £12,500 must be paid up. A private company is any registered company that is not a public company. The shares of a private company may not be offered to the public for sale. Unregistered companies include *joint-stock companies, in which the members pool their stock, **chartered companies**, formed under Royal Charter, and **statutory companies**, formed by special Act of Parliament (e.g. the privatized utilities).

There are legal requirements placed on companies to make certain financial information regarding their activities public. Such information normally comprises a *profit and loss account and *balance sheet and is included with other financial and non-financial information in an annual report and accounts (*see* ANNUAL ACCOUNTS). The term company is often used more widely to refer to any association of persons, such as a *partnership, joined together for the purpose of conducting a business, although legally there are significant differences. *See also* ARTIFICIAL PERSON; CORPORATION.

company auditor A person appointed as an *auditor of a company under the Companies Act, which requires that a company's annual *financial statements must be audited. Since 1989 only *registered auditors are eligible for appointment.

company doctor A businessperson or an accountant with wide commercial experience, who specializes in analysing and rectifying the problems of ailing companies. The company doctor may either act as a consultant or may recommend policies and be given executive powers to implement them.

company formation The procedure to be adopted for forming a company in the UK. The subscribers to the company must send to the *Registrar of Companies a statement giving details of the registered address of the new company together with the names and addresses of the first directors and secretary (if one has been appointed), with their written consent to act in these capacities. They must also give a declaration (**declaration of compliance**) that the provisions of the Companies Act have been complied with and provide the *articles of association (sometimes accompanied by a memorandum of association). Provided all these documents are in order the Registrar will issue a *certificate of incorporation and, in the case of a public company, a certificate enabling it to start business. In the latter case additional information is required.

Measures designed to simplify the process of company formation were enacted in the Companies Act 2006 and came into force in late 2009.

company limited by guarantee An incorporated organization in which the liability of members is limited by the constitutional documents to the amount they agree to pay in the event of a *liquidation. Such a company does not issue shares to its members. *See* LIMITED COMPANY.

company limited by shares An incorporated organization in which the liability of members is limited by the constitutional documents to the amounts paid, or due to be paid, for shares. In the UK this is the most popular form of company. *See* LIMITED COMPANY.

company officers *See* OFFICERS OF A COMPANY.

Company Reporting Directive An EU directive (2006) designed to enhance public confidence in financial reporting within the EU, chiefly by increasing the transparency of financial statements and reports. Listed companies are also required to publish information regarding their *corporate governance. Together with the *Statutory Audit Directive, this directive is often seen as the European equivalent to the US *Sarbanes–Oxley Act (Sox); as such, the two directives are often referred to jointly as **Eurosox**.

company seal A seal with the company's name engraved on it in legible characters, often used to authenticate share certificates and other important documents issued by the company or affixed to contracts. Until recent reforms in English company law, certain types of contract were not binding unless made under seal.

company secretary An *officer of a company. The appointment is usually made by the directors. The secretary's duties are mainly administrative, including preparation of the agenda for directors' meetings. However, the modern company secretary has an increasingly important role, which may include managing the office and entering into contracts on behalf of the company. Duties imposed by law include the submission of the annual return and the keeping of minutes. The secretary of a public company is required to have certain qualifications, as set out in the Companies Acts. Under the Companies Act 2006 a private company is no longer required to appoint a company secretary. *See* INSTITUTE OF CHARTERED SECRETARIES AND ADMINISTRATORS.

company voluntary arrangement *See* VOLUNTARY ARRANGEMENT.

comparability The accounting principle that financial information for a company should be comparable with financial information for other similar companies. Comparability is one of the most important characteristics of useful financial information. The concept is defined in the Accounting Standards Board's *Statement of Principles and in *Financial Reporting Standard 18, Accounting Policies. It is also recognized in the International Accounting Standards Board's *Framework for the Preparation and Presentation of Financial Statements.

comparative advantage The relative efficiency in a particular economic activity of an individual or group of individuals over another economic activity, compared to another individual or group. One of the fundamental propositions of economics is that if individuals or groups specialize in activities in which their comparative advantage lies, then there are gains from trade. This proposition, first outlined by David Ricardo (1772–1823), is one of the main arguments for free trade and against such restrictions as tariffs and quotas.

comparative amount *See* CORRESPONDING AMOUNT.

comparative figures Figures given for previous years in the *financial statements of an organization for the purpose of comparison. Corresponding figures for the previous financial year are required by law. If accounting policies have changed or a prior-year adjustment has been made, comparative figures may need to be adjusted to make them meaningful.

compensating balance A sum of money deposited at a bank by a customer as a condition for the bank to lend money to the customer.

compensating error An error that is not revealed in a *trial balance because one error is cancelled out by another error or errors.

compensation for loss of office A lump-sum ex gratia payment made to an employee or director as compensation for the termination of a *service contract. The payment can be wholly or partly tax free provided that the employee is not entitled to the compensation under the service contract. *See* GOLDEN HANDSHAKE.

Competition Commission A commission established in 1948 as the Monopolies and Restrictive Practices Commission, renamed the **Monopolies and Mergers Commission** in 1973, and given its present title in 1999 under the Competition Act 1998. It investigates questions referred to it on monopolies and mergers and its Appeals Tribunal hears appeals against decisions by the *Office of Fair Trading and utility regulators relating to anticompetitive trade practices.

( ) SEE WEB LINKS
• Website of the Competition Commission

competitive bought deal A form of underwriting agreement, generally similar to a straightforward *bought deal, in which the borrower seeks simultaneous competitive quotations from a number of banks for the purchase of an entire new issue of bonds, or similar securities, at a fixed price.

competitor analysis The gathering of data about a competitor's products and prices in order to identify actual or future sources of competitive advantage. An understanding of a competitor's strengths and weaknesses will help an organization to develop its own strategy. *See* BENCHMARKING.

compilation report *See* AUDIT EXEMPTION.

completion risk The inherent risk in *project financing that the project will not be completed. *Compare* TECHNOLOGICAL RISK; SUPPLY RISK.

compliance audit An *audit of *internal control procedures to evaluate how well they operate in practice. For example, a *sample of invoices could be checked to ensure that they have been properly authorized (indicated by a signature or stamp). *See also* COMPLIANCE TESTS.

compliance tests Tests used during an audit to determine the effectiveness of a company's control procedures. The extent of compliance testing will depend upon the extent to which specific controls are relied upon. Results of compliance testing will indicate the necessary level of *substantive testing (tests of transactions, balances, etc.). If controls are found to be working well, substantive testing may be reduced to some extent. *See also* COMPLIANCE AUDIT.

composition An agreement between a debtor and his or her creditors discharging the debts in exchange for a proportion of what is due. The agreement may be registered as a *deed of arrangement or form part of an individual *voluntary arrangement. *See also* SCHEME OF ARRANGEMENT.

compound discount The difference between the value of an amount in the future and its present discounted value. For example, if £100 in five years' time is worth £88 now, the compound discount will be £12. The compound discount will depend upon the *discount rate applied.

compound interest   *See* INTEREST.

comprehensive annual financial report (CAFR) In the USA, the official annual report of the government.

comprehensive auditing   *See* VALUE FOR MONEY AUDIT.

comprehensive income   The total of the *operating profits and the *holding gains of a company for an accounting period. The operating profit is the difference between the operating income and expenditure. The holding gains result from any increases in the value of assets between their dates of purchase and their dates of sale. In *historical-cost accounting no distinction is made between operating profits and holding gains. One criticism of this form of accounting is that, by not recognizing holding gains, profits can be overstated and distributed; this could affect the running of the company. *Current-cost accounting is based on the maintenance of physical operating capacity and isolates holding gains.

comprehensive income statement   The standard *International Financial Reporting Standard term for the *profit and loss account.

comptroller   The title of the financial director in some companies or the chief financial officer of a group of companies. The title is more widely used in the USA than in the UK. *See also* CONTROLLER.

compulsory liquidation (compulsory winding-up)   The *liquidation of a company by a court. A petition must be presented both at the court and the registered office of the company. Those by whom it may be presented include: the company, the directors, a creditor, an official receiver, and the Secretary of State for Business, Innovation and Skills. The grounds on which a company may be wound up by the court include: a special resolution of the company that it be wound up by the court; that the company is unable to pay its debts; that the number of members is reduced below two; or that the court is of the opinion that it would be just and equitable for the company to be wound up. The court may appoint a provisional *liquidator after the winding-up petition has been presented; it may also appoint a special manager to manage the company's property. On the grant of the order for winding-up, the official receiver becomes the liquidator and continues in office until some other person is appointed, either by the creditors or the members. *Compare* CREDITORS VOLUNTARY LIQUIDATION; MEMBERS VOLUNTARY LIQUIDATION.

computer-assisted audit techniques (CAATs) Techniques developed by auditors for performing *compliance tests and *substantive tests on computer systems for firms in which the data being audited is processed by computers and held on computer files. There are two main categories of technique.
(1) The auditor creates a set of input data to be processed by the computer programs; the results are then checked against the expected results.
(2) Computer audit software is used by the auditor to select data from a number of files. Various operations are then performed on the data and the results are transferred to a special audit file to be printed out in a required format. *See also* EMBEDDED AUDIT FACILITY; INTEGRATED TEST FACILITY.

conceptual framework A statement of theoretical principles that provides guidance for financial accounting and reporting. In the UK the conceptual framework is the *Statement of Principles issued by the *Accounting Standards Board. In the USA the *Financial Accounting Standards Board issues Statements of Financial Accounting Concepts under its conceptual framework project. The *International Accounting Standards Board has also published a Framework for the Preparation and Presentation of Financial Statements. *See also* ACCOUNTING CONCEPTS.

Confederation of Asian and Pacific Accountants (CAPA) A regional accountancy organization in the Asia–Pacific region. CAPA has a membership of 34 accountancy organizations in 24 countries and is by far the world's largest regional accountancy organization. The mission of CAPA is to provide leadership in the development, enhancement, and coordination of the accountancy profession in the Asia–Pacific region, thus enabling the profession to provide services of consistently high quality in the public interest.

( ) SEE WEB LINKS
• CAPA website

Confederation of British Industry (CBI) An organization that lobbies for British business on matters of concern, chiefly to the UK government but also to the European Union and other international bodies. Its objective is to help create and sustain the conditions in which British business can compete and prosper. The CBI was formed from a merger of several other employers' organizations in 1965 and now represents some 250 000 UK companies. Its ruling body is the CBI Council, which meets on a quarterly basis in London. There are also 12 regional councils.

( ) SEE WEB LINKS
• CBI website

confidence level (confidence coefficient) The probability that a range of numbers calculated from a *sample of a population includes the value of the population parameter being estimated.

confirmation A technique used by an auditor to obtain third-party evidence in support of information supplied by a client. For example, confirmation may be sought from a bank of balances held by a client (*see* BANK CONFIRMATION). *See also* CIRCULARIZATION OF DEBTORS.

confirmation note A document confirming the main facts and figures of a deal between two parties, usually a deal that has been agreed verbally or by telephone. The *London code of conduct recommends that the dealer records the telephone calls and that both parties send confirmation notes.

confirmed irrevocable letter of credit *See* LETTER OF CREDIT.

confirming house An organization that purchases goods from local exporters on behalf of overseas buyers. It may act as a principal or an agent, invariably pays for the goods in the exporters' own currency, and purchases on a contract that is enforceable in the exporters' own country. The overseas buyer, who usually pays the confirming house a commission or its equivalent, regards the confirming house as a local buying agent, who will negotiate the best prices on its behalf, arrange for the shipment and insurance of the goods, and provide information regarding the goods being sold and the status of the various exporters.

confiscation risk The risk that assets in a foreign country may be confiscated, expropriated, or nationalized; a non-resident owner's control over the assets may also be interfered with.

conglomerate A group of companies merged into one entity, although they are active in totally different fields. A conglomerate is usually formed by a company wishing to diversify so that it is not totally dependent on one industry.

connected person In the context of the Companies Act (disclosure requirements for directors and connected persons), a director's spouse, child, or stepchild (under 18 years of age), a body corporate with which a director is associated, a trustee for a trust that benefits a director or connected person, or a partner of a director.

consent letter A letter contained in a *prospectus in which an expert (e.g. a *reporting accountant) consents to the issue of the prospectus, together with the inclusion of any report written by that expert or any references made to that expert.

consideration **1.** A promise by one party to a *contract that constitutes the price for buying a promise from the other party to the contract. A consideration is essential if a contract, other than a deed, is to be valid. It usually consists of a promise to do or not to do something or to pay a sum of money. **2.** The money value of a contract for the purchase or sale of securities on the London Stock Exchange, before commissions, charges, stamp duty, and any other expenses have been deducted. **3.** For *capital gains tax purposes, the actual amount received on the disposal of an asset, in money or money's worth. Any receipt is potentially liable to be treated as consideration. For VAT, a consideration in something other than money must be capable of being expressed in money.

consignee **1.** Any person or organization to whom goods are sent. **2.** An agent who sells goods, usually in a foreign country, on *consignment on behalf of a principal (consignor).

consignment **1.** A shipment or delivery of goods sent at one time. **2.** Goods sent **on consignment** by a principal (consignor) to an agent (consignee), usually in a foreign country, for sale either at an agreed price or at the best market price. The agent, who usually works for a commission, does not normally pay for the goods until they are sold and does not own them, although usually having possession of them. The final settlement, often called a **consignment account**, details the cost of the goods, the expenses incurred, the agent's commission, and the proceeds of the sale.

consignment note A document accompanying a consignment of goods in transit. It is signed by the *consignee on delivery and acts as evidence that the goods have received. It gives the names and addresses of both consignor and consignee, details the goods, usually gives their gross weight, and states who has responsibility for insuring them while in transit. It is not a negotiable document and in some circumstances is called a **way bill**.

consignment stock Stock held by one party (the dealer) but legally owned by another; the dealer has the right to sell the stock or to return it unsold to its legal owner. It is sometimes difficult to distinguish between the commercial realities of the transaction and the legal agreement. In accounting it is important that the concept of *substance over form is applied and that the *financial statements reflect the commercial reality. The *Accounting Standards Board issued *Financial Reporting Standard 5, Reporting the Substance of Transactions, to resolve these issues.

consignor 1. Any person or organization that sends goods to a *consignee. 2. A principal who sells goods on *consignment through an agent (consignee), usually in a foreign country.

consistency concept One of the four fundamental *accounting concepts laid down in *Statement of Standard Accounting Practice (SSAP) 2, Disclosure of Accounting Policies; it is also recognized in the Companies Act and the EU's *Fourth Company Law Directive. The concept requires consistency of treatment of like items within each accounting period and from one period to the next; it also requires that *accounting policies are consistently applied. Under *Financial Reporting Standard 18, Accounting Policies, which has now replaced SSAP 2, the consistency concept is no longer recognized as a fundamental principle. Rather, an entity is required to implement those policies that are judged most appropriate to its circumstances for the purpose of giving a *true and fair view. *Comparability is therefore held to be a more important characteristic of financial statements than consistency.

consolidated accounts *See* CONSOLIDATED FINANCIAL STATEMENTS.

consolidated balance sheet The *balance sheet of a group providing the financial information contained in the individual financial statements of the parent company of the group and its subsidiary undertakings, combined subject to any necessary *consolidation adjustments. It must give a *true and fair view of the state of affairs of a group as at the end of the financial year, and its form and content should comply with the Companies Act. If the balance sheet formats require the disclosure of the balances attributable to group undertakings (creditors, debtors, investments), the information should be analysed to show the amounts attributable to parent and fellow subsidiary undertakings of the parent company, and amounts attributable to unconsolidated subsidiaries.

consolidated cash-flow statement The information contained in the individual cash-flow statements of a group of undertakings combined by *consolidation, subject to any *consolidation adjustments. Cash-flow statements are regulated by *Financial Reporting Standard 1 and *International Accounting Standard 7.

consolidated financial statements (consolidated accounts; group accounts; group financial statements) The financial statements of a group of companies obtained by *consolidation. These are required by the Companies Act and *Financial Reporting Standard 2, Accounting for Subsidiary Undertakings. The information contained in the individual financial statements of a group of undertakings is combined into consolidated financial statements, subject to any *consolidation adjustments. The consolidated accounts must give a *true and fair view of the profit or loss for the period and the state of affairs as at the last day of the period of the undertakings included in the consolidation. Subsidiary undertakings within the group may be excluded from consolidation (*see* EXCLUSION OF SUBSIDIARIES FROM CONSOLIDATION), and the parent company itself may be exempt from preparing consolidated accounts (*see* EXEMPTIONS FROM PREPARING CONSOLIDATED FINANCIAL STATEMENTS).

Accountants also need to be aware of *International Accounting Standard 27, Consolidated and Separate Financial Statements (revised 2003), and *International Financial Reporting Standard 3, Business Combinations. The UK *Accounting Standards Board and the *International Accounting Standards Board disagree on many issues relating to consolidated financial statements.

consolidated goodwill The difference between the fair value of the consideration given by an acquiring company when buying a business and the aggregate of the fair values of the separable net assets acquired. *Goodwill is generally a positive amount. Under *Financial Reporting Standard 10, Goodwill and Intangible Assets, goodwill should normally be capitalized on the *balance sheet and *amortized to the *profit and loss account over a period not exceeding 20 years. The international accounting standards relevant to the treatment of consolidated goodwill are *International Financial Reporting Standard 3, Business Combinations, *International Accounting Standard (IAS) 36, Impairment of Assets, and IAS 38, Intangible Assets.

consolidated income and expenditure account The information contained in the individual income and expenditure accounts of a *group of organizations combined by *consolidation into a single document for the group. This is subject to any necessary *consolidation adjustments.

consolidated profit The combined profit of a *group of organizations presented in the *consolidated profit and loss account. Any intra-group items should be eliminated by *consolidation.

consolidated profit and loss account A combination of the individual *profit and loss accounts of the members of a *group of organizations, subject to any consolidation adjustments. The consolidated profit and loss account must give a *true and fair view of the profit and loss of the undertakings included in the consolidation. A parent company may be exempted, under the Companies Act, from publishing its own profit and loss account if it prepares group accounts. The individual profit and loss account must be approved by the directors, but may be omitted from the company's annual accounts. In such a case, the company must disclose its profit or loss for the financial year and also state in its notes that it has taken advantage of this exemption.

consolidation The process of combining and adjusting financial information from the individual financial statements of a parent undertaking and its subsidiaries to prepare *consolidated financial statements. These statements should present financial information for the group as a single economic entity. *See* CONSOLIDATION ADJUSTMENTS.

consolidation adjustments Adjustments that need to be made in the process of the *consolidation of the accounts of a group of organizations. If there have been intra-group transactions, such as sales from one subsidiary company to another, any profits or losses resulting from these transactions should be eliminated from the *consolidated financial statements. For example, if one group undertaking has sold a fixed asset to another at a profit, the profit should be eliminated from both the profit and loss account and the consolidated balance sheet.

consortium A combination of two or more businesses formed on a temporary basis, often to quote for and carry out a single large project. The purpose of forming a consortium may be to eliminate competition between the members or to pool skills, not all of which may be available to the individual companies. Consortia often involve the setting up of a *special purpose vehicle or a *joint venture. *See also* CONSORTIUM RELIEF.

consortium relief A modified form of *group relief applying to consortia. A consortium is held to exist if 20 or fewer companies each own at least 5% of the ordinary share capital of the consortium company and together the consortium members hold at least 75% of the ordinary shares of the consortium company. Losses can be surrendered between the consortium members and the consortium company. The loss that can be surrendered is restricted to the proportion of the claimant's profits that corresponds with the surrendering company's interest in the consortium. From 1 April 2000 members of a consortium no longer have to be resident in the UK to qualify for relief.

constant dollar *See* CURRENT COST.

constant purchasing power accounting *See* CURRENT PURCHASING POWER ACCOUNTING.

constraint A circumstance that prevents an organization achieving higher levels of performance. A constraint results from the impact of a limiting factor (or principal budget factor), which must be eliminated or reduced before the constraint is removed. For example, at various times a shortage of skilled labour, materials, production capacity, or sales volume may constitute a limiting factor. Constraints are also brought into the statement of problems in *linear programming.

Construction Industry Scheme (CIS) A set of statutory provisions that require a person making a payment to a subcontractor in (usually) the building industry to deduct tax at basic rate from all payments made, unless the recipient produces a certificate provided by the Revenue permitting payment to be made without deduction of tax. The current CIS commenced on 6 April 2007.

Consultative Committee of Accountancy Bodies (CCAB) A committee set up in 1970 by the six *accountancy bodies to foster closer cooperation. At the time of the *Accounting Standards Committee it was a valuable part of the process of setting standards but has lost that role with the establishment of the *Accounting Standards Board. It still plays an active part in many financial accounting and reporting issues.

consumable materials Materials that are used in a production process although, unlike *direct materials, they do not form part of the *direct cost of sales. Examples are cooling fluid for production machinery, lubricating oil, and sanding discs. In circumstances in which direct materials of small value are used, such as cotton or nylon thread or nails and screws, they are sometimes treated in the same way as consumable materials.

Consumer Price Index (**CPI**) **1.** In the UK, the usual name for the **Harmonized Index of Consumer Prices** (**HICP**), a measure of price level introduced in 1997 to enable comparisons within the EU. In the UK government inflation targets are now based on the CPI rather than the *Retail Price Index. **2.** In the USA, the measure of price level calculated monthly by the Bureau of Labor Statistics. It is commonly known as the cost-of-living index and gives the cost of specific consumer items compared to the base year of 1967. Since 2000 the Federal Reserve Board has preferred to base its inflation forecasts on the Personal Consumption Expenditure Price Index (PCEPI), which is regarded as a more sophisticated measure.

(⊕) SEE WEB LINKS
• HICP data from the UK National Statistics website

contingencies Potential gains and losses known to exist at the balance-sheet date although the actual outcomes will only be known after one or more events have occurred (or not occurred). Depending on the nature of a particular contingency, it may be appropriate to include it in the financial statements or to show it as a *note to the accounts; *Financial Reporting Standard 12 provides guidance on the appropriate accounting treatment. Generally, accountants apply the *prudence concept and will disclose information on *contingent losses more readily than on *contingent gains.

contingency theory of management accounting The view that there is no single *management accounting system acceptable to all organizations or any system that is satisfactory in all circumstances in a single organization. Consequently, accounting systems are contingent upon the circumstances that prevail at any time; they must be capable of development in order to take into consideration such factors as changes in the environment, competition, organizational structures, and technology.

contingent agreement *See* EARN-OUT AGREEMENT.

contingent asset A possible asset that arises from past events and whose existence will be confirmed only by the occurrence of one or more uncertain future events, which are not wholly in the control of the accounting entity. Under *Financial Reporting Standard 12, an entity should not recognize a contingent asset unless the appropriate economic events can be expected. In these circumstances a brief description of the nature of the contingent asset should be given together with, where practicable, an estimate of its financial effects. The relevant *International Accounting Standard is IAS 37. *Compare* CONTINGENT LIABILITY.

contingent consideration A payment that is contingent on a particular factor or factors occurring. The concept is often used in relation to *earn-out agreements.

contingent contract *See* EARN-OUT AGREEMENT.

contingent gain A gain that depends upon the outcome of some contingency. For example, if a company is making a substantial legal claim against another organization, the company has a contingent gain (depending upon the successful outcome of the claim). *Compare* CONTINGENT LOSS. *See also* CONTINGENT ASSET.

contingent liability **1.** A possible obligation that arises from past events, whose existence will be confirmed only by the occurrence of one or more uncertain future events not wholly within an entity's control. **2.** A present obligation that arises from past events in which either the amount of the obligation cannot be measured reliably or it is not probable that a transfer of economic benefits will be required to settle the obligation. Under *Financial Reporting Standard 12, an entity should not recognize a contingent liability. The relevant *International Accounting Standard is IAS 37. *Compare* CONTINGENT ASSET. *See also* CONTINGENT LOSS.

contingent loss A loss that depends upon the outcome of some contingency. For example, if there is a substantial legal claim for damages against a company, there is a contingent loss (depending on the outcome of the claim). *Compare* CONTINGENT GAIN. *See also* CONTINGENT LIABILITY.

continuous budget A budget for a future month or a quarter, which is added to an organization's budget as the latest month or quarter is dropped. The budget for the entire period is revised and updated as necessary, which encourages management to consider continuously short-range plans of the organization.

continuous improvement The ongoing process of improving an organization's goods or services, with the aim of increasing customer satisfaction. In a highly competitive environment, organizations need to search actively for ways of reducing costs, improving quality, and eliminating waste. *See also* KAIZEN COSTING; TOTAL QUALITY MANAGEMENT.

continuously contemporary accounting (CoCoA) A method of accounting that defines a company's financial position as the ability of that enterprise to adapt to a changing environment; it permits the recognition of general price level changes. Although favoured by some academics, practitioners have shown little interest.

continuous-operation costing A system of costing applied to industries in which the method of production is in continuous operation; examples include electricity generation and bottling. Because the product is homogeneous, this costing system is essentially a form of *average costing in which the unit cost is obtained by dividing the total production cost by the number of items produced. *Compare* PROCESS COSTING.

continuous stocktaking (continuous inventory; continuous stock-checking; perpetual audit) A system of stocktaking designed to ensure that all the items of stock are physically counted and reconciled with the accounting records shown on the *bin cards and the *stock ledger within a specified period. For example, a stocktaking team may be working continuously so that all items of stock are checked four times a year, when adjustments are made to the accounting records to adjust them to the physical stock. Continuous stocktaking is useful for determining the availability of each item of stock and establishing when stock levels reach *reorder levels.

contra A book-keeping entry on the opposite side of an account to an earlier entry, with the object of cancelling the effect of the earlier entry.

contra accounts Accounts that can be offset, one against the other. For example, if Company A owes money to Company B and Company B also owes money to Company A, the accounts can be offset against each other, enabling both debts to be settled by one payment.

contract A legally binding agreement. Agreement arises as a result of an *offer and acceptance, but a number of other requirements must be satisfied for an agreement to be legally binding:

- there must be a *consideration (unless the contract is by deed);
- the parties must have an intention to create legal relations;
- the parties must have capacity to contract (i.e. they must be competent to enter a legal obligation, by not being a minor, mentally disordered, or drunk);
- the agreement must comply with any formal legal requirements;
- the agreement must be legal;
- the agreement must not be rendered void either by some common-law or statutory rule or by some inherent defect.

In general, no particular formality is required for the creation of a valid contract. It may be oral, written, partly oral and partly written, or even implied from conduct. However, certain contracts are valid only if made by deed (e.g. transfers of shares in statutory companies, transfers of shares in British ships, legal *mortgages, certain types of *lease) or in writing (e.g. *hire-purchase agreements, *bills of exchange, *promissory notes, contracts for the sale of land made after 21 September 1989), and certain others, though valid, can only be enforced if evidenced in writing (e.g. guarantees, contracts for the sale of land made before 21 September 1989). *See also* SERVICE CONTRACT.

Certain contracts, though valid, may be liable to be set aside by one of the parties on such grounds as misrepresentation or the exercise of undue influence. *See also* BREACH OF CONTRACT.

contract cost The total cost of a *long-term contract, obtained by using *contract costing techniques.

contract costing A costing technique applied to *long-term contracts, such as civil-engineering projects, in which the costs are collected by contract. A particular problem of long-term projects is the determination of annual profits to be taken to the profit and loss account when the contract is incomplete. This requires the valuation of work in progress at the end of the financial year.

contract for differences (CFD) A *derivative contract in which one party (the issuer) agrees to pay another (the buyer) the difference between the current value of an *underlying (e.g. an equity, bond, or index) and the value at the time the contract was made: if the difference is negative, the buyer pays the issuer. Settlement is on a daily basis for as long as the contract remains open. Exchange-traded CFDs went on sale for the first time in August 2007, on the Australian Stock Exchange.

contract for services A contract undertaken by a self-employed individual. The distinction between a contract for services (self-employed) and a *contract of employment or service (employee) is fundamental in establishing the tax position. With a contract for services the person may hire and pay others to carry out the work, will be responsible for correcting unsatisfactory work at their own expense, and may make losses as well as profits.

contract of employment (contract of service) A contract by which an employee agrees to undertake certain duties under the direction and control of the employer in return for a specified wage or salary. The contract need not be in writing, but under the Employment Rights Act 1996 the employee must be given a written statement of terms of employment. Implied in every contract are the employer's duty to protect the employee from danger and risks to health, and the employee's duty to do the work to the best of his or her ability. Employees who have been continuously employed in the same business for certain minimum periods have statutory rights, relating for example to unfair dismissal and *redundancy, that do not apply to the self-employed. A self-employed person is engaged under a *contract for services and owes his employer or customer no other duty than to complete the specified work in accordance with the terms of the individual contract. Termination of a contract of employment in breach of the terms of the contract is wrongful dismissal and may be remedied at law.

contribution (contribution margin) In *marginal-costing systems, the additional profit that will be earned by an organization when the *breakeven-point production has been exceeded. The **unit contribution** is the difference between the unit selling price of a product and its *marginal cost of production. The **total contribution** is the product of the unit contribution and the number of units produced. This is based on the assumptions that the marginal cost and the sales value will be constant.

contribution income statement The presentation of an *income statement or *profit and loss account using the *marginal costing layout. In such a treatment the *fixed costs are not charged to the individual products produced (as in *absorption costing) but are treated as a deduction from the total *contribution of all the products.

EXAMPLE

A company manufactures two products, A and B. The simplified contribution income statement below shows the combined contribution of these products, from which total fixed costs can be deducted to show total profit.

	Product A	Product B	Total
Sales revenue	2000	5000	7000
Variable costs	1400	2900	4300
Contribution	1600	2100	2700
Total fixed costs			1200
Total profit			1500

---

contribution margin ratio (contribution-to-sales ratio; production–volume ratio; profit–volume ratio) The ratio of the *contribution per product to the sales value, often expressed as a percentage. It is a way of ranking a range of products in terms of their relative profitability, the highest percentage indicating the highest contribution per pound of sales. *See also* LIMITING FACTOR.

contributory pension A pension in which the employee, as well as the employer, contributes to the pension fund. *Compare* NON-CONTRIBUTORY PENSION SCHEME.

control **1.** The ability to direct the financial and operating policies of an undertaking with the intention of gaining economic benefits from its activities. **2.** The ability to obtain the economic benefits that flow from an asset.

control accounts Accounts in which the balances are designed to equal the aggregate of the balances on a substantial number of subsidiary accounts. Examples are the sales ledger control account (or total debtors account), in which the balance equals the aggregate of all the individual debtors' accounts, the purchase ledger control account (or total creditors account), which performs the same function for creditors, and the stock control account, whose balance should equal the aggregate of the balances on the stock accounts for each item of stock. This is achieved by entering in the control accounts the totals of all the individual entries made in the subsidiary accounts. The purpose is twofold: to obtain total figures of debtors, creditors, stock, etc., at any given time, without adding up all the balances on the individual records, and to have a crosscheck on the accuracy of the subsidiary records.

controllability concept The principle that managers should only be held responsible for *controllable costs and *controllable investment. This concept is often difficult to apply in practice. Many costs are not easily classified as either controllable or uncontrollable and others are clearly only partially controllable. For example, the manager at a building society branch is not responsible for advertising costs, staff salaries, or interest rates on savings or loans. *See* CONTROLLABLE CONTRIBUTION.

controllable contribution The sales revenue of a division less those costs that are controllable by the divisional manager (*see* CONTROLLABLE COSTS). Controllable contribution is the most appropriate measure of a divisional manager's performance. In practice, however, it can be difficult to distinguish between controllable costs and *uncontrollable costs. Where a division is a *profit centre, *depreciation is not a controllable cost, as the manager is not responsible for investment decisions. However, the manager of an investment centre is responsible for investments and therefore depreciation is a controllable cost.

controllable costs Costs identified as being controllable and therefore able to be influenced by a particular level of management. Information about those costs is therefore directed to the correct management personnel in the appropriate *operating statements. In any system of *responsibility accounting, managers can only be regarded as responsible for those costs over which they have some control.

controllable investment The *capital employed that is controllable by a divisional manager. When calculating *performance measures for a division it is important to ensure that only those assets and liabilities that a manager can influence are included. *See* CONTROLLABLE CONTRIBUTION.

controllable variance In *standard costing or *budgetary control, a *variance that is regarded as controllable by the manager responsible for that area of an organization. The variance occurs as a result of the difference between the *budget cost allowance and the actual cost incurred for the period. *See also* CONTROLLABLE COSTS.

controlled foreign company A foreign company in which a UK-resident company or individual has a 40% stake or more. The UK resident can be charged to UK tax in respect of profits from the controlled foreign company if the rate of tax paid by the foreign company is significantly less than the rate that would be payable in the UK. The tax rules applying to controlled foreign companies are very complex and are currently being reexamined as it has been argued that they contravene EU law.

controller In the USA, the chief accounting executive of an organization. The controller will normally be concerned with financial reporting, taxation, and auditing but will leave the planning and control of finances to the *treasurer. *See also* COMPTROLLER.

controlling interest An interest in a company that gives a person or another company control of it. To have a controlling interest in a company, a shareholder would normally need to own or control more than half the voting shares. However, in practice, a shareholder might control the company with considerably less than half the shares, if the other shares were divided among a large number of different holders. For legal purposes, a director is said to have a controlling interest in a company if he or she alone, or together with his or her spouse, minor children, and the trustees of any settlement in which he or she has an interest, owns more than 20% of the voting shares in a company or in a company that controls that company. *See also* MINORITY INTEREST; PARTICIPATING INTEREST.

control period The span of time for which budgeted figures are compared with actual results. Splitting up the financial year into control periods makes control of the figures more manageable.

control risk (internal control risk) The risk that misstatements in the *financial statements of a company will not be prevented or detected on a timely basis by the internal control system of a business. It is a part of the *audit risk; an assessment of the control risk must be made for each audit objective. In assessing the control risk, an auditor will need to be familiar with the accounting and internal control system and test its effectiveness in operation by means of *compliance tests.

convenience store A store that trades primarily on the convenience it offers to customers. The products stocked may be influenced by local tastes or ethnic groups and the stores are often open long hours as well as being conveniently placed for customers in residential areas. They are often members of a multiple chain.

convention A general agreement or customary practice.

conversion The tort (civil wrong) equivalent to the crime of theft. It is possible to bring an action in respect of conversion to recover damages, but this is uncommon.

conversion cost The costs incurred in a production process as a result of which raw material is converted into finished goods. The conversion costs usually include *direct labour and *manufacturing overheads but exclude the costs of *direct material itself.

conversion right The right given under the terms of a debenture trust deed enabling the investor to convert *debt to *equity. *See also* CONVERTIBLE.

convertible **1.** A *bond or stock that can be converted into other securities, usually equity, on predetermined conditions. **2.** A government security in which the holder has the right to convert a holding into new stock instead of obtaining repayment.

conveyancing The transfer of ownership of land from the person currently holding title to a new owner.

cook the books To falsify financial records or statements with the intention of misleading others on the financial performance or financial position of an accounting entity.

core inflation The rate of inflation calculated to exclude certain items that are subject to sudden and shortlived price movements, mainly food and energy. Core inflation is considered a better indicator of overall long-term trends than unadjusted **headline inflation**.

corporate charter *See* ARTICLES OF INCORPORATION.

corporate failure prediction The use of various techniques to assess whether or not a company is likely to go into *liquidation. One model, devised by Edward Altman, uses multivariate analysis based on the *financial statements of a company to arrive at a *Z score. An Altman's Z score of 1.8 or less is taken as an indication that the company may fail. Another technique is **Argenti's failure model**, which is used to calculate scores for a company based on defects of the company, management mistakes, and the symptoms of failure.

corporate governance The manner in which organizations, particularly limited companies, are managed and the nature of *accountability of the managers to the owners. This topic has been of increased importance since the publication of the *Cadbury Report in 1992, which set out a code of practice later incorporated into the *Combined Code on Corporate Governance. There is a stock-exchange requirement for listed companies to state their compliance with this Code or to explain any departure from it.

corporate modelling The use of simulation models to assist the management of an organization in carrying out planning and decision making. A budget is an example of a corporate model.

corporate report **1.** A comprehensive package of information that describes the economic activities of an organization; for *limited companies it is in the form of the annual report and accounts (*see* ANNUAL ACCOUNTS). **2.** A discussion document issued by the Accounting Standards Steering Committee in 1975, which proposed various improvements for financial reporting. The document attracted considerable academic attention, although it is hard to see that it made any significant impact on company practice.

corporate social reporting *See* SOCIAL RESPONSIBILITY REPORTING.

Corporate Venturing Scheme (CVS) A scheme designed to encourage established companies to invest in the full-risk ordinary shares of companies of the same kind as those qualifying under the *Enterprise Investment Scheme; the scheme encourages the investing and qualifying companies to form mutually beneficial corporate venturing relationships. Companies investing through the CVS may obtain *corporation tax relief (at 20%) on the amount invested provided that the shares are held for at least three years after issue or, if later, three years after the trade for which the money was raised begins. Investing companies also obtain relief for most allowable losses on the shares and deferral of corporation tax when a chargeable gain from the disposal of CVS shares is reinvested in a new CVS investment.

(⊕) SEE WEB LINKS
• Introduction to the CVS from the HMRC website

corporation A succession of persons or body of persons authorized by law to act as one person and having rights and liabilities distinct from the individuals forming the corporation. The *artificial person may be created by Royal Charter, statute, or common law. The most important type is the registered *company formed under the Companies Act. **Corporations sole** are those having only one individual forming them; for example, a bishop, the sovereign, the Treasury Solicitor. **Corporations aggregate** are composed of more than one individual, e.g. a limited company. They may be formed for special purposes by statute; the BBC is an example. Corporations can hold property, carry on business, bring legal actions, etc., in their own name. *See also* DOMESTIC CORPORATION.

corporation tax (CT) Tax charged on the total profits of a company *resident in the UK arising in each *accounting period. The rate of corporation tax depends on the level of profits of the company. From April 2009 the small companies rate of 22% applies to companies with total profits of £300,000 or less. Full-rate corporation tax of 28% currently applies to companies with total profits of over £1.5 million. There is a *marginal relief for those companies with total profits between £300,000 and £1.5 million. Large companies pay corporation tax in instalments: other companies pay CT nine months after the end of the company's chargeable accounting period. Certain *capital allowances are deductible for corporation tax purposes, as are losses carried forward from previous years. Any *chargeable gains from the disposal of fixed assets are included in the total profits for corporation tax purposes.

(⊕) SEE WEB LINKS
• Corporation Tax area of the HMRC website: includes information about making a return online

correcting entry An entry made in an accounting system to correct an error.

correspondent bank A bank in a foreign country that offers banking facilities to the customers of a bank in another country. These arrangements are usually the result of agreements, often reciprocal, between the two banks. The most frequent correspondent banking facilities used are those of money transmission.

corresponding amount (comparative amount) An amount in the published financial accounts of a limited company that relates to the previous financial year. For example, the accounts will show the total sales for the current year and a corresponding amount for the previous year. Corresponding amounts are required by the Companies Act to provide a comparison. However, if the corresponding amounts are not comparable (e.g. as a result of a change of accounting policy), they should be restated; particulars of the adjustment and reasons for it should be disclosed in the notes to the accounts.

COSA   Abbreviation for *cost of sales adjustment.

cost   The expenditure on goods and services required to carry out the operations of an organization. There are a number of different ways of defining cost, the major ones being *average cost, *first-in-first-out cost, *historical cost, *last-in-first-out cost, and *replacement cost. *See also* FIXED COST; MARGINAL COST; OPPORTUNITY COST.

cost absorption   *See* ABSORPTION.

cost accounting   The techniques used in collecting, processing, and presenting financial and quantitative data within an organization to ascertain the cost of the *cost centres, the *cost units, and the various operations. Cost accounting is now regarded as a division of *management accounting, which also incorporates the techniques of planning, decision making, and control.

Cost Accounting Standards Board   A board established in the USA in 1970 by Congress to promote consistency in cost-accounting practices and to assist in the reporting of actual costs of government contracts. The board's responsibilities were taken over in 1980 by the Government Accounting Office (now the Government Accountability Office).

cost accumulation   The process of collecting costs as a product progresses through the production system, enabling the total cost of manufacture to be built up in a sequential fashion.

cost allocation   The process of assigning costs to one or more *cost objects when it is not possible to trace a cost directly. *Indirect costs (overheads) always have to be assigned to cost objects using cost allocations. The basis on which costs are assigned to cost objects is called the *allocation base or *cost driver. The purposes of cost allocation can be briefly summarised as follows:
- to provide information for decisions: an example would be deciding whether or not to replace a machine;
- to set selling prices;
- to measure profits accurately (product profitability and customer profitability);
- to motivate management or employees.

Two types of systems can be used to assign indirect costs to cost objects: *traditional costing systems and *activity-based costing. Traditional costing systems focus on product costs and are often criticized for relying on *arbitrary allocations. Activity-based costing systems use *cause-and-effect allocations.

cost apportionment   *See* APPORTIONMENT.

cost ascertainment   The process of determining the costs of the operations, processes, *cost centres, and *cost units within an organization.

cost assignment (cost attribution)   The procedures by which direct or indirect costs are charged to or made the responsibility of particular *cost centres, and ultimately charged to the products manufactured or services provided by the organization. Procedures used to achieve cost attribution include *absorption costing, *activity-based costing, *marginal costing, and *process costing. *See also* COST ALLOCATION; COST TRACING.

cost behaviour The changes that occur to total costs as a result of changes in activity levels within an organization. The total of the *fixed costs tends to remain unaltered by changes in activity levels in the short term, whereas the total of the *variable costs tends to increase or decrease in proportion to activity. There are also some costs that demonstrate *semi-variable cost behaviour, i.e. they have both fixed and variable elements. The study of cost behaviour is important for *breakeven analysis and also when considering decision-making techniques.

cost-benefit analysis A technique used in *capital budgeting that takes into account the estimated costs to be incurred by a proposed investment and the estimated benefits likely to arise from it. In a *financial appraisal the benefits may arise from an increase in the revenue from a product or service, from saved costs, or from other cash inflows, but in an *economic appraisal the economic benefits, such as the value of time saved or of fewer accidents resulting from a road improvement, often require to be valued.

cost centre The area of an organization for which costs are collected for the purposes of *cost ascertainment, planning, decision making, and control. Cost centres are determined by individual organizations; they may be based on a function, department, section, individual, or any group of these. Cost centres are of two main types: **production cost centres** in an organization are those concerned with making a product, while **service cost centres** provide a service (such as stores, boilerhouse, or canteen) to other parts of the organization.

cost classification The process of grouping expenditure according to common characteristics. Costs are initially divided into *capital expenditure and *revenue expenditure. In a production organization the revenue expenditure is classified sequentially to enable a product cost to build up in the order in which these costs tend to be incurred. Revenue costs would normally include:
- direct material,
- direct labour,
- direct expenses,
- manufacturing overheads,
- administration overheads,
- selling overheads,
- distribution overheads,
- research overheads.

cost code *See* ACCOUNTING CODE.

cost control The techniques used by various levels of management within an organization to ensure that the costs incurred fall within acceptable levels. Cost control is assisted by the provision of financial information to management by the accountant and by the use of such techniques as *budgetary control and *standard costing, which highlight and analyse any variances.

cost control account *See* COST LEDGER CONTROL ACCOUNT.

cost convention The custom used as a basis for recording the costs to be charged against the profit for an accounting period. The cost convention used may be based on *historical cost, *current cost, or *replacement cost.

cost driver In a system of *activity-based costing, any factor such as number of units, number of transactions, or duration of transactions that drives the costs arising from a particular *activity. When such factors can be clearly identified and measured, they will be used as a basis for allocating costs to cost objects. The term cost driver is therefore effectively synonymous with both *activity measure and *allocation base and the literature often uses them interchangeably. *See also* ACTIVITY COST POOL; COST ALLOCATION.

cost estimation The procedure that uses estimated unit costs for both *direct costs and *overheads in order to build up the estimated costs of products, services, and processes for the purposes of planning, control, and pricing.

cost function A formula or equation that represents the way in which particular costs behave when plotted on a graph. For example, the most common cost function represents the total cost as the sum of the *fixed costs and the *variable costs in the equation $y = a + bx$, where y is the total cost, a is the total fixed cost, b is the variable cost per unit of production or sales, and x is the number of units produced or sold.

costing methods The techniques and procedures used in *cost accounting and *management accounting to obtain the costs of services, products, processes, and *cost centres to provide the information required to undertake *performance measures, decision making, planning, and control. These techniques include *absorption costing, *activity-based costing, *marginal costing, and *process costing.

costing principles In *management accounting, the rules that provide an acceptable treatment of the costs incurred by an organization. Examples include the principles used in valuing stocks and the principle that in establishing product costs an allowance for any *normal loss must be included.

cost item A category of costs incurred by an organization that are of a similar nature; they are collected together both for the purposes of reporting and because they can be subjected to similar treatment by the costing system. Examples of cost items are rent, consumable materials, and sundry selling expenses.

cost ledger The *books of account in which the *cost accounting records are contained. These records may be kept manually or be computer-based and may be either separate or integrated with the financial records.

cost ledger control account (**cost control account**) The *control account that appears in the financial accounting ledger in an accounting system in which separate books are maintained for the financial and costing records. The balance on the cost ledger control account agrees with the net total of the entries made in the *cost ledger. Including the cost ledger control account in the financial accounting ledger makes the latter a self-balancing record from which a *trial balance can be extracted.

cost object Any item for which a separate measurement of *costs is desired. This may be a product, a service, a customer, or a specific operation associated with any of these (e.g., designing a new product, processing a mortgage application, making a telephone call to a customer). The number of cost objects identified and the frequency of measuring the costs will vary between organizations; a product cost will normally be calculated on a weekly or monthly basis, whereas the cost of processing a mortgage application may only be calculated on an annual basis.

cost of capital The return, expressed in terms of an interest rate, that an organization is required to pay for the capital used in financing its activities. This will vary according to the type or types of capital employed (e.g., *equity share capital, *loan capital, or some mixture of the two). One approach to establishing the cost of capital is therefore to compute a unique *weighted average cost of capital for each organization, based on its particular mix of capital sources. The cost of capital is often used as a *hurdle rate in *discounted cash flow calculations.

cost of carry *See* CARRYING COSTS.

cost of goods manufactured (manufacturing cost of finished goods) The total production cost of the finished goods transferred from the production facility of an organization during an accounting period. It is made up of the total expenditure for the period on *direct materials, *direct labour, *direct expenses, and *manufacturing overheads adjusted by the opening and closing stocks of raw materials and the *work in progress at the beginning and end of the period. The cost of goods manufactured is often computed in the *manufacturing account or in a **cost of goods manufactured statement** for a period.

cost of goods sold (COGS) *See* COST OF SALES.

cost of quality The total costs of ensuring good quality or rectifying poor quality. Ultimately, by improving quality managers will reduce costs and improve profits. Four categories of costs are useful for this analysis:
- **prevention costs**. These are the costs incurred in preventing mistakes. Examples include training, quality planning, process controls, and market research. Expenditure in this area is seen as an investment.
- **appraisal costs**. These include the costs of inspecting parts from suppliers, inspecting and testing products in manufacture, and performing quality audits.
- **internal failure costs**. These are the costs incurred when a product does not conform to quality standards. Examples include the costs of scrap, repairs to defective products, and downtime. They are incurred before the customer receives the product.
- **external failure costs**. These are the costs incurred when the customer receives a poor quality product. Examples include the costs of investigating complaints, of replacing products returned by the customer, and warranty charges. If the customer is dissatisfied and finds a new supplier, the total cost will be much higher. *See also* ENVIRONMENTAL COSTS.

cost of sales (cost of goods sold; COGS) A figure representing the cost to an organization of supplying goods or services for sale, excluding administration and other general overheads. In a sales organization, it is the *opening stock at the beginning of an accounting period plus the purchases for the period, less the closing stock at the end of the period. In a manufacturing organization, the purchases for the period would be replaced by the *production cost of finished goods for the period. In a service providing organization, the cost of sales would be calculated as *direct costs adjusted by the opening and closing values of *work in progress. The cost of sales figure is deducted from the *sales revenue to obtain the *gross profit for the period. *See also* DIRECT COST OF SALES.

cost of sales adjustment (COSA) An adjustment to the trading profit of an organization as a result of a *holding gain on the *cost of sales. This occurs in *current-cost accounting.

cost-plus contract A contract entered into by a supplier in which the goods or services provided to the customer are charged at cost plus an agreed percentage markup. This method of pricing is very common if the cost of producing the commodity is unknown or if its production will involve significant research work. However, because simple cost-plus contracts do not encourage suppliers to minimize their costs, there has been a move away from this type of contract in UK government orders with private industry.

cost-plus pricing An approach to establishing the selling price of a product or service in a commercial organization, in which the total cost of the product or service is estimated and a percentage *mark-up is added in order to obtain a profitable selling price. A variation to this approach is to estimate the costs to a particular stage, say the costs of production only, and then to add a percentage mark-up to cover both the other overheads (including administration, selling, and distribution costs) and the profit margin. This approach to costing is very different from *target costing. *Compare* FULL COST PRICING; MARGINAL COST PRICING.

cost-plus transfer prices *Transfer prices set by *cost-plus pricing, which include a mark-up to provide a profit for the supplying division. When *variable costs rather than full costs are used in this calculation, the mark-up will need to be higher to cover both the *fixed costs and a profit margin. This method involves a problem for managers, as cost-plus transfer pricing does not identify the output levels that will maximize prices.

cost pool *See* ACTIVITY COST POOL.

cost prediction The estimation of future cost levels based on historical *cost behaviour characteristics, using such statistical techniques as *linear regression.

cost sheet A form used in costing to collect together all the costs of a service, product, process, or *cost centre, for presentation to the management or for use in the costing system.

cost standard A predetermined level of cost expected to be incurred by a *cost item used in the supply, production, or operation of a service, product, process, or *cost centre. A cost standard is often applied to a *performance standard in order to calculate *standard overhead costs.

cost tracing The process of assigning *direct costs to the relevant *cost objects. *Compare* COST ALLOCATION.

cost unit A unit of production for which the management of an organization wishes to collect the costs incurred. In some cases the cost unit may be the final item produced, for example a chair or a light bulb, but in other more complex products the cost unit may be a sub-assembly, for example an aircraft wing or a gear box. Cost units may also be expressed as batches of items, particularly when the unit cost of the individual product would be very small; for example, the cost unit for a manufacturer of pens might be the cost per thousand pens. *See also* COST OBJECT.

cost-volume-profit analysis *See* BREAKEVEN ANALYSIS.

council tax A UK local-government tax raised according to property valuation. It replaced the community charge (or poll tax) in 1993–94. The tax is charged on the value of a domestic property as defined by a series of bands, with different bands applying to different regions of the UK. Council tax assumes that two people live at the address, with rebates for single occupancy and a scale of exemptions for those on lower earnings. *Compare* BUSINESS RATES.

countervailing credit *See* BACK-TO-BACK CREDIT.

country cheques *See* TOWN CLEARING.

country risk The risk of conducting transactions with, or holding assets in, a particular foreign country arising from political or economic events within that country. *See* POLITICAL CREDIT RISK; TRANSFER CREDIT RISK.

coupon 1. One of several dated slips attached to a bond, which must be presented to the agents of the issuer or the company to obtain an interest payment or dividend. Coupons are mainly used with *bearer securities. **2.** The rate of interest paid by a fixed-interest bond. **3.** A general name for bonds and notes on US Treasury markets.

coupon stripping A financial process in which the *coupons are stripped off a *bearer security and then sold separately as a source of cash, with no capital repayment; the bond, bereft of its coupons, becomes a *zero coupon bond and is also sold separately.

covenant 1. A promise made in a deed. Such a promise can be enforced by the parties to it as a contract, even if the promise is gratuitous: for example, if A covenants to pay B £100 per month, B can enforce this promise even without having done anything in return. Covenants were formerly used to minimize income tax, by transferring income from taxpayers to non-taxpayers (such as children or charities). However, since the Finance Act 1988 and the introduction of the *gift aid system, covenants can no longer be used for tax planning in this way.

Covenants may be entered into concerning the use of land, frequently to restrict the activities of a new owner or tenant (e.g. a covenant not to sell alcohol or run a fish-and-chip shop). Such covenants may be enforceable by persons deriving title from the original parties. This is an exception to the general rule that a contract cannot bind persons who are not parties to it.

2. An undertaking in a loan agreement the breaching of which will make the loan repayable immediately. *See also* EVENT OF DEFAULT; RATIO COVENANT.

covering An action taken to reduce or eliminate the risk involved in having an *open position in a financial, commodity, or currency market.

CPA 1. Abbreviation for *certified public accountant. **2.** Abbreviation for *critical-path analysis. **3.** Abbreviation for *customer profitability analysis.

CPI *See* Consumer Price Index.

CPM Abbreviation for critical-path method. *See* critical-path analysis.

CPP accounting *See* current purchasing power accounting.

C2 Principles A code of best practice, established by Thomas Dunfee and David Hess of the University of Pennsylvania, describing how a company and its employees should deal with any attempt to make or solicit improper payments.

creative accounting Misleadingly optimistic, though not illegal, forms of accounting. This can occur because there are a number of accounting transactions that are not subject to regulations or the regulations are ambiguous. Companies sometimes make use of these ambiguities in order to present their financial results in the best light possible. In particular, companies often wish to demonstrate increasing *accounting profits and a strong balance sheet. Examples of transactions in which creative accounting has taken place concern *consignment stocks and *sale and repurchase agreements. In these contexts, creative accounting will involve the separation of legal title from the risks and rewards of the activities, the linking of several transactions to make it difficult to determine the commercial effect of each transaction, or the inclusion in an agreement of options, which are likely to be exercised. Such policies are often referred to as *cherry picking or *window dressing. In the 1990s and 2000s a series of scandals raised the profile of issues such as *corporate governance and the responsibilities of auditors, leading governments and standard-setting bodies to address some of the worst abuses. However, the banking crisis of 2008 revealed the extent to which financial institutions had used *securitizations, *special purpose vehicles, and other complex *off-balance sheet arrangements to present accounts that many would consider highly misleading.

credit **1.** The reputation and financial standing of a person or organization. **2.** The sum of money that a trader or company allows a customer before requiring payment. **3.** The funding of members of the public to purchase goods and services with money borrowed from finance companies, banks, and other money lenders. **4.** An entry on the right-hand side of an account in *double-entry book-keeping, usually showing a sale or a liability. *See* credit entry. **5.** A payment into an account.

credit balance A balancing amount of an account in which the total of credit entries exceeds the total of debit entries. Credit balances represent revenue, liabilities, or capital.

credit card A plastic card issued by a bank or finance organization to enable holders to obtain credit in shops, hotels, restaurants, petrol stations, etc. The retailer or trader receives monthly payments from the credit-card company equal to its total sales in the month by means of that credit card, less a service charge. Customers also receive monthly statements from the credit-card company, which may be paid in full within a certain number of days with no interest charged; alternatively, they may make a specified minimum payment and pay interest on the outstanding balance. Credit cards may be used to obtain cash at a bank or its ATMs.

credit control Any system used by an organization to ensure that its outstanding debts are paid within a reasonable period. It involves establishing a **credit policy**, *credit rating of clients, and chasing accounts that become overdue. *See also* FACTORING.

credit crunch A period during which lenders are unwilling to extend credit to borrowers. The term is particularly associated with the period beginning in late 2007, when the previous era of 'easy credit' came to a sudden end in the wake of the *subprime lending fiasco.

credit default option (CDO) An *option to enter into a *credit default swap at a particular price on a particular date. It is thus a form of *swaption. *See also* CREDIT DERIVATIVE.

credit default swap (CDS) A *credit derivative in which a buyer agrees to pay premiums to a seller, who in return contracts to pay the buyer a much larger sum if a specified loan or bond etc. defaults. It thus resembles a form of insurance, the difference being that the buyer need have no insurable interest in the asset concerned. CDSs can therefore be used for pure speculation as well as for *hedging. The lack of regulation and transparency in the vast CDS market has been widely identified as a factor in the global financial meltdown of 2008.

credit derivative A *derivative in which the payoff is related to the credit rating or payment performance of the *underlying. There are two main types. An **unfunded credit derivative** is a contract between two parties, one of whom (the protection seller) assumes the credit risk associated with the underlying in return for payments from the other (the protection buyer). A **funded credit derivative** is a *structured finance product in which the risk associated with the performance of the underlying is packaged in the form of tradable instruments (securities). A *credit default swap is an example of the first type and a *collateralized debt obligation of the second. *See* SECURITIZATION.

credit enhancement The use of various techniques to raise the credit rating of *asset-backed securities. This is known as **internal enhancement** when it is carried out by the issuer of the security and **external enhancement** when it is done by a third party, such as a *monoline insurer.

credit entry An entry made on the right hand side of an account, representing an increase in a liability, revenue, or equity item or a decrease in an asset or expense. For example, when a supplier is paid there will be a credit to the bank as cash is spent and a corresponding debit to the creditors' control account. *Compare* DEBIT ENTRY.

credit note A document expressing the indebtedness of the organization issuing it, usually to a customer. When goods are supplied to a customer an invoice is issued; if the customer returns all or part of the goods the invoice is wholly or partially cancelled by a credit note.

creditor–days ratio A ratio that gives an estimate of the average number of days' credit taken by an organization before the creditors are paid. It is calculated by the formula:

(trade creditors × 365)/annual purchases on credit.

creditors Those to whom an organization or an individual owes money, for example unpaid suppliers of raw materials. The balance on the *creditors' ledger control account is included in the balance sheet: creditors whose payments are due in less than one year are classed as *current liabilities; creditors whose payments are due after more than one year are *long-term liabilities. The payment of creditors should be tightly controlled to ensure that full credit periods are taken and that any prompt-payment discounts are received.

creditors' buffer The fixed capital of a company, which cannot be reduced or distributed (except with special permission). The knowledge that there is this fixed capital base gives creditors the confidence to invest in the company in the short term (for example as suppliers) or in the longer term (for example as debenture holders).

creditors' ledger (bought ledger; purchases ledger) A memorandum *ledger account in which individual creditors' accounts are recorded; it is additional to the *nominal ledger and forms part of the internal control system. In each individual creditor's account there is a record of the purchases made (credit), payments made (debit), discounts received (debit), and returns outwards (debit). The total sum of all the creditors' ledger accounts is periodically extracted and compared to the total on the *creditors' ledger control account as part of the internal control system. The total of the individual creditors' ledger accounts should always equal the creditors' ledger control accounts; any differences that do occur must be investigated.

creditors' ledger control account (purchases ledger control account) The nominal (or general) ledger control account recording the totals of the entries made to the individual *creditors' ledgers from the purchases journal and the cash payments journal. The total on the creditors' ledger control account is periodically compared to the sum total of individual creditors' ledger accounts as part of the internal control system. The creditors' ledger control account should always equal the total of the individual creditors' ledger amounts; any differences that do occur must be investigated.

creditors' voluntary liquidation (CVL) The winding-up of a company by special resolution of the members when it is insolvent. A **meeting of creditors** must be held within 14 days of such a resolution and the creditors must be given seven days' notice of the meeting. The creditors also have certain rights to information before the meeting. A *liquidator may be appointed by the members before the meeting of creditors or at the meeting by the creditors. If two different liquidators are appointed, the creditors' nominee is usually preferred. CVLs, also known as **creditors' voluntary winding-ups**, are the most common form of liquidation in use in the UK. *Compare* MEMBERS VOLUNTARY LIQUIDATION.

credit rating An assessment of the creditworthiness of an individual or a firm, i.e. the extent to which they can safely be granted credit. Traditionally, banks have provided confidential trade references (*see* BANKER S REFERENCE), but recently **credit-reference agencies** (also known as **rating agencies**) have grown up, which gather information from a wide range of sources, including the county courts, bankruptcy proceedings, hire-purchase companies, and professional debt collectors. This information is then provided as a **credit reference**, for a fee, to interested parties. The consumer was given some protection from such activities in the Consumer Credit Act 1974, which allows an individual to obtain a copy of all the information held by such agencies relating to that individual, as well as the right to correct any discrepancies. There are also agencies that specialize in the corporate sector, giving details of a company's long-term and short-term debt. This can be extremely important to the price of the company's shares on the market, its ability to borrow, and its general standing in the business community. Credit ratings for the debt instruments of large corporations are provided by such organizations as Moody's Investor Service and Standard and Poor. *See also* ANCILLARY CREDIT BUSINESS.

credit risk **1.** The risk taken when a loan is made that the borrower will default on or delay repayment of the principal or payments of interest. *See also* POLITICAL CREDIT RISK; TRANSFER CREDIT RISK. **2.** The risk that the flow of payments from a *credit derivative will decline owing to an adverse movement in the credit rating of the *underlying.

credit sale A sale made on terms in which cash is to be paid at an agreed future date. As the debtors, who are customers to whom credit sales have been made, pay, the debtors' control account balance will be reduced.

creditworthiness An assessment of a person's or a business's ability to pay for goods purchased or services received. Creditworthiness may be presented in the form of a *credit rating.

CREST An electronic share settlement system created by the Bank of England for the securities industry that began operation in 1996. Using CREST, shares are registered electronically, purchases and sales are settled instantaneously on the due date, and the dividends can be paid electronically direct to the shareholder's bank. Paper certificates and associated paperwork have been abolished for those who join CREST. As with paper shares, the company register of shareholders provides proof of ownership. Those wishing to retain paper certificates are able to do so. Since September 2002 CREST has been wholly owned by *Euroclear.

critical-path analysis (CPA; critical-path method; CPM; network analysis; programme evaluation and review technique; PERT) A decision-making technique to determine the minimum time needed to complete a project by establishing the time taken to complete the longest path (i.e. the **critical path**) through a network of activities. The network diagram is drawn up by arranging each activity sequentially, bounded by the **critical events** that record the start and/or completion of each activity. Estimated activity times allow the earliest and latest start times for each event to be established, and from this information the critical path can be determined.

crore *See* LAKH.

cross-default clause The most onerous clause in a loan agreement, stating that if the borrower defaults on one loan, any other loans may become repayable. The cross-default clause is activated when another lender is in a position to call a default on its loan or an event occurs which, with the passage of time, is capable of giving any lender the right to call a default. *See* EVENT OF DEFAULT.

crossed cheque *See* CHEQUE.

cross rate An exchange rate between two currencies based upon the rate of each of them with a third currency, often the US dollar.

cross-sectional analysis The comparison of the *accounting ratios of one company with those of another in order to assess the profitability, *liquidity, and *capital structure of the company.

crown jewel option A form of *poison pill in which a company, defending itself against an unwanted *takeover bid, writes an *option that would allow a partner or other friendly company to acquire one or more of its best businesses at an advantageous price if control of the defending company were lost to the unwelcome predator. The granting of such an option may not always be in the best interests of the shareholders of the defending company.

CT Abbreviation for *corporation tax.

cum rights *See* EX-.

cumulative preference share A type of *preference share that entitles the owner to receive any dividends not paid in previous years. Companies are not obliged to pay dividends on preference shares if there are insufficient earnings in any particular year. Cumulative preference shares guarantee the eventual payment of these dividends in arears before the payment of dividends on ordinary shares, provided that the company returns to profit in subsequent years. In the USA, such shares are known as **cumulative preferred stocks**.

currency **1.** Any kind of money that is in circulation in an economy. **2.** Anything that functions as a medium of exchange, including coins, banknotes, cheques, *bills of exchange, promissory notes, etc. **3.** The money in official use in a particular country. *See* FOREIGN EXCHANGE. **4.** The time that has to elapse before a bill of exchange matures.

currency risk *See* EXCHANGE-RATE EXPOSURE.

current account **1.** An active account at a bank or building society into which deposits can be paid and from which withdrawals can be made by cheque (*see* CHEQUE ACCOUNT), ATM, debit card, standing order, and direct debit. **2.** An account in which intercompany or interdepartmental balances are recorded. **3.** An account recording the transactions of a partner in a partnership that do not related directly to that partner's capital in the partnership (*see* CAPITAL ACCOUNT). **4.** The part of the *balance of payments account that records non-capital transactions, such as the sale of goods or services.

current-asset investment An investment (e.g. shares) intended to be held for less than one year. *See also* FIXED-ASSET INVESTMENT.

current assets (circulating assets; circulating capital; floating assets) Those assets of an organization that are constantly changing their form as they circulate from cash to goods and back to cash again. Cash is used to purchase raw materials, which become work in progress when issued to a production department. The work in progress becomes finished goods, which once they are sold, become debtors or cash from an accounting point of view. Debtors are ultimately changed into cash when they pay, thus completing the cycle. *Compare* FIXED ASSET.

current cash equivalent (CCE) In *continuously contemporary accounting, the measure of assets and liabilities.

current cost 1. A cost calculated to take into consideration current circumstances of cost and performance levels. **2.** The sum that would be required at current prices to purchase or manufacture an asset. This may be the replacement cost or the historical cost adjusted for inflation by means of an appropriate price index. **3. (constant dollar)** In the USA, the method of converting historical cost to current cost and then adjusting to constant purchasing power by using the average *Consumer Price Index for the current year.

current-cost accounting (CCA) A form of accounting in which the approach to *capital maintenance is based on maintaining the operating capability of a business. Assets are valued at their **deprival value**, which is the loss that a business would suffer if it were to be deprived of the use of the asset. This may be the *replacement cost of the asset, its *net realizable value, or its *economic value to the business. Current-cost accounting ensures that a business maintains its operating capacity by separating *holding gains from *operating profits, thereby preventing them being distributed to shareholders. The current-cost accounting profit figure is derived by making a number of adjustments to the *historical-cost accounting profit and loss account: these are the *cost of sales adjustment, *depreciation adjustment, monetary *working-capital adjustment, and the *gearing adjustment. The current-cost reserve in the balance sheet is used to 'collect' the current cost adjustments. This method of accounting was used widely in the UK in the late 1970s and early 1980s, when inflation was high; it was not popular, however, and as inflation has reduced it has been largely abandoned. *Statement of Standard Accounting Practice 16, Current Cost Accounting, was issued in March 1980 but withdrawn in April 1988.

current-cost depreciation A *depreciation charge that is calculated on the *current cost of assets.

current-cost operating profit Using *current-cost accounting, the amount remaining after the *cost of sales adjustment, depreciation adjustment, and *working-capital adjustment have been made to the conventional *accounting profit.

current liabilities Amounts owed by a business to other organizations and individuals that should be paid within one year from the balance-sheet date. These generally consist of trade creditors, *bills of exchange payable, amounts owed to group and related companies, taxation, social-security creditors, proposed dividends, *accruals, *deferred credit, payments received on account, bank overdrafts, and short-term loans. Any long-term loans repayable within one year from the balance-sheet date should also be included. Current liabilities are distinguished from long-term liabilities on the balance sheet.

current purchasing power accounting (constant purchasing power accounting; CPP accounting) A form of accounting that measures profit after

allowing for the maintenance of the *purchasing power of the shareholders'
capital. The *Retail Price Index is used to adjust for general price changes to
ensure that the shareholders' capital maintains the same monetary purchasing
power. There is no requirement to allow for the maintenance of the purchasing
power of the loan creditors' capital. Current purchasing power accounting was
covered by the provisional *Statement of Standard Accounting Practice 7, issued
in May 1974 and withdrawn in October 1978.

current ratio (working-capital ratio) The ratio of the *current assets of a
business to the *current liabilities, expressed as x:1 and used as a test of liquidity.
For example, if the current assets are £250,000 and the current liabilities are
£125,000 the current ratio is 2:1. There is no simple rule of thumb, but a low
ratio, e.g. under 1:1, would usually raise concern over the liquidity of the
company. Too high a ratio, e.g. in excess of 2:1, may indicate poor management
of *working capital; this would be established by calculating the *inventory
turnover ratio and *debtor collection period ratio. Care must be taken when
making comparisons between companies to ensure that any industry
differences are recognized. The *liquid ratio is regarded as a more rigorous test
of liquidity.

current replacement cost The cost of replacing an asset, or the services
provided by the asset, estimated at the balance-sheet date. Current replacement
costs may be difficult to establish if, for example, the asset cannot be replaced as
a result of obsolescence.

current standard In *standard costing, a cost, income, or *performance
standard based on current operating conditions and established for use over a
short period of time. *Compare* BASIC STANDARD; NORMAL STANDARD. *See also*
OPERATIONAL VARIANCE; REVISION VARIANCE.

current-value accounting An accounting method that takes account of
changes in specific prices rather than changes in the general price level. Assets
can be valued at their *net realizable value, *current replacement cost, or *net
present value – or a combination of these.

current-year basis The *basis of assessment of profits for tax purposes in the
UK, in which tax is charged in a *fiscal year on profits arising in the accounts for
the period ending in that tax year. *Compare* PRECEDING-YEAR BASIS.

curvilinear cost function Any cost relationship that results in a curved line
when plotted on a graph.

customer capital *See* INTELLECTUAL CAPITAL.

customer-level activities *See* ACTIVITY.

customer perspective *See* BALANCED SCORECARD.

customer profitability analysis (CPA) The analysis of profits by customer.
In the past, management accounting reports focused exclusively on product
profitability, but in more recent years it has become clear that managers need to
understand both product and customer profitability. Typically, organizations
that introduce CPA discover that a small number of customers account for most
of the profit; identifying profitable customers can therefore be very important.
See also LIFETIME VALUE.

EXAMPLE

A company has a number of different *activities. The managers want to compare two activities to see how they affect the cost of each customer.

Activity	Cost
sales visits	£100 per sales visit
sales order processing	£80 per sales order

Customer	A	B
annual sales	£10,000	£10,000
number of sales visits	5	20
number of sales orders	5	40

Customer-related costs

	A	B
sales visits	£500	£2000
	(5 visits @ £100)	(20 visits @ £100)
sales order processing	£400	£3200
	(5 orders @ £80)	(40 orders @ £80)

The sales visits and order processing costs for Customer A are £900 (£500 + £400). For Customer B the same costs are £5200 (£2000 + £3200). The two customers have the same sales value (£10,000) and therefore the managers need to ask why the costs incurred by Customer B are so much higher. To improve profits, the managers should (i) consider making fewer visits to Customer B, and (ii) look at how they can reduce the cost of processing orders. The analysis above would not be possible if the company had a *traditional costing system as opposed to an *activity-based costing system.

A management accountant will be interested to see how the analysis above changes the behaviour of managers. One possibility is that they will react by stopping all visits to customers. This would reduce costs immediately, but could result in a future loss of customers.

Customs and Excise *See* REVENUE AND CUSTOMS, HM.

customs duty A levy on the importation of certain goods and on some goods manufactured from the imported goods. Customs duties are also charged on some exports. Membership of the EU has required the abolition of import duties between member states and the establishment of a Common External Tariff. *Compare* EXCISE DUTY.

customs invoice An invoice for goods imported or exported, which is prepared especially for the customs authorities.

cut-off date The date on which an accounting period ends and the accounts of a business are ruled off. It is important that this should happen on the correct date to ensure that a true and fair view of the performance and position of a business is given. An *auditor will pay particular attention to the cut-off date as accounts can be manipulated for purposes of *window dressing.

CVA Abbreviation for company *voluntary arrangement.

CVL Abbreviation for *creditors' voluntary liquidation.

CVP analysis *See* BREAKEVEN ANALYSIS.

CVS Abbreviation for *Corporate Venturing Scheme.

***cwmni cyfyngedig cyhoeddus* (c.c.c.)** Welsh for *public limited company.

cycle billing The method sometimes adopted in large organizations for invoicing their customers at different time intervals. Often using the alphabet as a basis, customers starting with the letter A may be invoiced on the first day, B on the second day, and so on. This method has the advantage of spreading the work load in the organization and ensuring a steady inflow of cash – providing that there are many customers with comparable accounts.

cycle time The length of time required from the placing of an order by a customer to the delivery of the product or service. In companies using *just-in-time techniques, this should be equivalent to the time taken from start to finish of the manufacturing process. Reducing cycle times is very important for just-in-time companies; some ways in which this can be done include reducing set-up times, improving quality to reduce time spent on inspection and replacing faulty parts, and preventative maintenance to reduce machine downtime.

DA Abbreviation for *deposit account.

daisy chain The buying and selling of the same items several times over, for example stocks and shares. This may be done to 'inflate' trading activity (that is, the sale of the same items are being included in the sales figure more than once).

damages Compensation, in monetary form, for a loss or injury, breach of contract, tort, or infringement of a right. Damages refers to the compensation awarded, as opposed to damage, which refers to the actual injury or loss suffered. The legal principle is that the award of damages is an attempt, as far as money can, to restore the position of the injured party to what it was before the event in question took place; i.e. the object is to provide restitution rather than profit. See feature ASSESSMENT OF DAMAGES on p. 131.

dangling debit A practice in which companies wrote off *goodwill to *reserves and created a goodwill account, which was deducted from the total of shareholders' funds. This treatment is no longer possible under *Financial Reporting Standard 10.

data The information that is processed, stored, or produced by a computer. The distinction between program (instructions) and data is a fundamental one in computing.

database An organized collection of information held on a computer. A special computer program, called a **database management system** (*DBMS), is used to organize the information held in the database according to a specified schema, to update the information, and to help users find the information they seek. There are two kinds of DBMS: simple DBMS, which are the electronic equivalents of a card index; and programmable DBMS, which provide a programming language that allows the user to analyse the data held in the database. On large computer systems, other programs can generally communicate with the DBMS and use its facilities. The term **data bank** is used for a collection of databases. *See also* DATA WAREHOUSE; MANAGEMENT INFORMATION SYSTEM.

data capture The insertion of information into a computerized system. For example, information about the sale of an item (the item sold, the sales price, and discount given, date and location of sale, etc.) is taken into the accounting system either at the point of sale in a retail organization by an electronic till or by keyboarding into the system when the invoice is prepared. This information is then readily available and up-to-date; it can also be used to adjust stock levels.

data flow chart (data flow diagram) A chart that illustrates the way in which specified data is handled by a computer program. Its purpose is to specify the data, to show where it is used or changed, where it is stored, and which reports use it.

ASSESSMENT OF DAMAGES

Damages are not assessed in an arbitrary fashion but are subject to various judicial guidelines. The general principle is that the claimant is entitled to full compensation for his or her losses. The purpose of damages in tort is to put the claimant in the position that he or she would have been in had the tort not been committed. The purpose of damages in contract is to put the claimant in the position that he or she would have been in had the contract been performed. In either case the claimant must take all reasonable steps to mitigate his or her losses. Damages can be further classified as liquidated or unliquidated, general or specific, and substantial, nominal, or exemplary.

Liquidated and unliquidated damages
Damages capable of being quantified in monetary terms are known as **liquidated damages**. In particular, liquidated damages include instances in which a genuine pre-estimate can be given of the loss that will be caused to one party if a contract is broken by the other party. If the anticipated breach of contract occurs this will be the amount, no more and no less, that is recoverable for the breach. Liquidated damages must be distinguished from any penalties specified in a contract as payable on its breach (which do not usually constitute a genuine estimate of the likely loss). Another form of liquidated damages is that expressly made recoverable under a statute. These may also be known as **statutory damages** if they involve a breach of statutory duty or are regulated or limited by statute. **Unliquidated damages** are those fixed by a court rather than those that have been estimated in advance.

General and specific damages
General damages represent compensation for general damage, which is the kind of damage the law presumes to exist in any given situation. They are recoverable even without being specifically claimed and are awarded for the usual or probable consequences of the wrongful act complained of. For example, in an action for medical negligence, pain and suffering is presumed to exist, therefore if the action is successful, general damages would be awarded as compensation even though not specifically claimed or proved. Loss of earnings by the injured party, however, must be specifically claimed and proved, in which case they are known as **specific damages**.

   Prospective damages are awarded to a plaintiff, not as compensation for any loss suffered at the time of a legal action but in respect of a loss it is reasonably anticipated will be suffered at some future time. Such an injury or loss may sometimes be considered to be too remote and therefore not recoverable.

Substantial, nominal, and exemplary damages
Substantial damages are awarded to provide compensation when actual damage has been caused. By contrast, **nominal** and **contemptuous damages** are awarded for trifling amounts – usually when the court is of the opinion that although the plaintiff's rights have been infringed no real loss has been suffered, or, that although actual loss has resulted, the loss has been caused in part by the conduct of the plaintiff. The prospect of receiving only nominal or contemptuous damages prevents frivolous actions being brought. The award is usually accompanied by an order that each party bears their own legal costs.

   Exemplary damages, on the other hand, are punitive damages awarded not merely as a means of compensation but also to punish the party responsible for the loss or injury. This usually occurs when the party causing the damage has done so wilfully or has received financial gain from the wrongful conduct. Exemplary damages will be greater than the amount that would have been payable purely as compensation.

data mining The process of extracting useful knowledge from the huge volumes of data kept in modern computer databases. Sophisticated algorithms and statistical techniques are used to identify significant trends or patterns within complex data and to form predictive models.

data processing (DP) The class of computing operations that manipulate large quantities of information. In business, these operations include book-keeping, printing invoices, payroll calculations, and general record keeping. Data processing forms a major use of computers in business, and many firms have full-time data-processing departments.

data protection Safeguards relating to personal data, i.e. personal information about individuals that is stored on a computer or 'relevant manual filing systems'. Legislation to prevent the potential misuse of such data has now been enacted in many countries. See feature DATA PROTECTION ACT 1998 on p. 175.

data warehouse A computer *database in which data from multiple operational processing systems can be stored, accessed, and interrogated. It is a facility specifically designed to give decision makers instant access to relevant information through the use of query and reporting tools. *See* DECISION SUPPORT SYSTEM; EXPERT SYSTEM; MANAGEMENT INFORMATION SYSTEM.

dawn raid An attempt by one company or investor to acquire a significant holding in the equity of another company by instructing brokers to buy all the shares available in that company as soon as the stock exchange opens, usually before the target company knows that it is, in fact, a target. The dawn raid may provide a significant stake from which to launch a *takeover bid. The conduct of dawn raids is restricted by the *City Code on Takeovers and Mergers.

day book A specialized *book of prime entry recording specific transactions. For example, the *sales day book records invoices for sales, the *purchase day book records invoices received from suppliers. Day-book entries are transferred to memorandum *ledgers, such as the *debtors' ledger and the *creditors' ledger, while totals of entries are transferred to the *nominal ledger control accounts, such as the *debtors' ledger control account and the *creditors' ledger control account.

days' sales in inventory The amount of inventory (stock) expressed in days of sales. For example, if 2 items a day are sold and 20 items are held in inventory, this represents 10 days' (20/2) sales in inventory.

days' sales in receivables The amount of *receivables (i.e. debtors) expressed in days of sales. For example, if £5000 worth of sales are made each day and the total debtors' balance outstanding is £500,000, this represents 100 (£500,000/£5000) days' sales.

days' sales outstanding The amount of sales outstanding expressed in days. For example, if £5000 worth of sales were made per day and £50,000 worth of sales were outstanding, this would represent 10 days' (£50,000/£5000) of sales outstanding.

DBMS Abbreviation for database management system. *See* DATABASE.

DB scheme Abbreviation for *defined-benefit pension scheme.

DATA PROTECTION ACT 1998

In the UK the principles of data protection, the responsibilities of data controllers, and the rights of data subjects are now governed by the Data Protection Act 1998, which came into force on 1 March 2000. As compared to the Data Protection Act 1984, the 1998 Act extends the operation of protection beyond computer storage, replaces the system of registration with one of notification, and demands that the level of description by data controllers under the new Act is more general than the detailed coding system previously required. Under the 1998 Act, the eight principles of data protection are:

(1) The information to be contained in personal data shall be obtained, and personal data shall be processed, fairly and lawfully.

(2) Personal data shall be held only for specified and lawful purposes and shall not be used or disclosed in any manner incompatible with those purposes.

(3) Personal data held for any purpose shall be relevant to that purpose and not excessive in relation to the purpose(s) for which it is used.

(4) Personal data shall be accurate and, where necessary, kept up to date.

(5) Personal data held for any purpose shall not be kept longer than necessary for that purpose.

(6) Personal data shall be processed in accordance with the rights of data subjects.

(7) Appropriate technical and organizational measure shall be taken against unauthorized and unlawful processing of personal data and against accidental loss or destruction of, or damage to, personal data.

(8) Personal data shall not be transferred to a country or territory outside the European Union unless that country or territory ensures an adequate level of protection for the rights and freedoms of data subjects in relation to the processing of personal data.

Data controllers must now notify their processing of data (unless they are exempt) with the **Information Commissioner** by completing and returning a notification form (this can now be done online). Notification is renewable annually; a data controller who fails to notify his or her processing of data, or any changes that have been made since notification, commits a criminal offence.

The Information Commissioner can seek information from and ultimately take enforcement action against data controllers for noncompliance with their full obligations under the 1998 Act. Appeals against decisions of the Commissioner may be made to the **Data Protection Tribunal**. Apart from non-notification, strict liability criminal offences under the 1998 Act include:

- obtaining, disclosing (or bringing about the disclosure), or selling (or advertising for sale) personal data, without consent of the data controller;
- obtaining unauthorized access to data;
- asking another person to obtain access to data;
- failing to respond to an information and/or enforcement notice.

Data subjects have considerable rights conferred on them under the 1998 Act. They include:

- the right to find out what information is held about them;
- the right to seek a court order to rectify, block, erase, and destroy personal details if these are inaccurate, contain expressions of opinion, or are based on inaccurate data;
- the right to prevent processing where such processing would cause substantial unwarranted damage or substantial distress to themselves or anyone else;
- the right to prevent the processing of data for direct marketing;
- the right to compensation from a data controller for damage or damage and distress caused by any breach of the 1998 Act.

DCF Abbreviation for *discounted cash flow.

DC scheme Abbreviation for *defined-contribution pension scheme.

DCV Abbreviation for *direct charge voucher.

Dearing Report The report of a committee set up under the chairmanship of Sir Ronald Dearing to examine the setting of accountancy standards in the UK. The report, *The Making of Accounting Standards*, was published in 1988; this led to the replacement of the *Accounting Standards Committee by the *Accounting Standards Board and to the establishment of the *Financial Reporting Council, the *Financial Reporting Review Panel, and the *Urgent Issues Task Force.

death duty (estate duty) A tax levied on the estate of a person who has died; the amount of the tax is calculated by assessing the estate of the deceased person in accordance with the appropriate tax regulations. In the UK, *inheritance tax is a tax of this kind.

debenture 1. The most common form of long-term loan taken by a company. It is usually a loan repayable at a fixed date, although some debentures are irredeemable securities; these are sometimes called perpetual debentures. Most debentures also pay a fixed rate of interest, and this interest must be paid before a dividend is paid to shareholders. Most debentures are also secured on the borrower's assets, although some, known as **naked debentures** or unsecured debentures, are not. In the USA debentures are usually unsecured, relying only on the reputation of the borrower. In a secured debenture, the bond may have a fixed *charge (i.e. a charge over a particular asset) or a floating charge. If debentures are issued to a large number of people (for example in the form of **debenture stock** or **loan stock**) trustees may be appointed to act on behalf of the debenture holders. There may be a premium on redemption and some debentures are *convertible, i.e. they can be converted into ordinary shares on a specified date, usually at a specified price. The advantage of debentures to companies is that they carry lower interest rates than, say, overdrafts and are usually repayable a long time into the future. For an investor, they are usually saleable on a stock exchange and involve less risk than *equities. 2. A deed under seal setting out the main terms of such a loan.

debenture redemption reserve A capital reserve into which amounts are transferred from the *profit and loss account for *debentures that are redeemable at a future date. The aim is to limit the profits available for distribution, although the reserve does not provide the actual funds for redeeming the debentures. To provide these funds a periodic *sinking-fund payment needs to be made to a debenture-redemption reserve fund, matched with investments earmarked for the fund.

debenture trust deed An agreement specifying the rights of *debenture holders, for example, the power to appoint a receiver in specified circumstances of default by a company.

debit An entry on the left-hand side of an account in *double-entry book-keeping that increases either the assets or the recorded expenditure of the organization keeping the book. In the case of a bank account, a debit shows an outflow of funds from the account.

debit and credit rules The rules to be followed under the method of *double-entry book-keeping. The rules are:
- any *asset account is increased by making a *debit entry and decreased by making a *credit entry;
- any *expense account is increased by making a debit entry and decreased by making a credit entry;
- any *liability account is decreased by making a debit entry and increased by making a credit entry;
- any *revenue account is decreased by making a debit entry and increased by making a credit entry;
- any *capital account is decreased by making a debit entry and increased by making a credit entry.

debit balance The balance of an account whose total *debit entries exceed the total of the *credit entries. Debit balances represent expenditure and *assets.

debit card A plastic card issued by a bank or building society to enable its customers to pay for goods or services at retail outlets by using the telephone network to debit their cheque accounts directly. It is also known as a **payment card**. The retail outlets need to have the necessary computerized input device, into which the card is inserted; the customer may be required to tap in a *personal identification number. Most debit cards also function as *cheque cards and *cash cards. In the USA these cards are sometimes called **asset cards**.

debit entry An entry made in *double-entry book-keeping on the left-hand side of an account. It records either an increase in an asset or expense or a decrease in a liability, revenue, or equity item. For example, cash paid into the bank from a debtor will increase the asset of cash. The entries to be made are debiting the bank and crediting the *debtors' ledger control account. *Compare* CREDIT ENTRY.

debit note A document sent by an organization to a person showing that the recipient is indebted to the organization for the amount shown in the debit note. Debit notes are rare as invoices are more regularly used; however, a debit note might be used when an invoice would not be appropriate, e.g. for some form of inter-company transfer other than a sale of goods or services.

debt **1.** A sum owed by one person or organization to another. In commerce, it is usual for debts to be required to be settled within one month of receiving an invoice, after which *interest may be incurred. A long-term debt may be covered by a *bill of exchange, which can be a *negotiable instrument. *See also* DEBENTURE. **2.** Any funding instrument other than equity, such as a *bond or a promissory note. *See* LOAN CAPITAL.

debt administration *See* ADMINISTRATOR; ANCILLARY CREDIT BUSINESS.

debt capital *See* LOAN CAPITAL.

debt collection agency An organization that specializes in collecting the outstanding debts of its clients, charging a commission for doing so. Such agencies now often prefer to be called **commercial collection agencies**. *See* ANCILLARY CREDIT BUSINESS.

debt–equity ratio A ratio used to examine the financial structure or *gearing (leverage) of a business. The long-term debt, normally including *preference shares, of a business is expressed as a percentage of its equity. A business may have entered into an agreement with a bank that it will maintain a certain debt–equity ratio; if it breaches this agreement the loan may have to be repaid. A highly geared company is one in which the debt is higher than the equity, compared to companies in a similar industry. A highly geared company offers higher returns to shareholders when it is performing well but should be regarded as a speculative investment. The debt–equity ratio is now sometimes expressed as the ratio of the debt to the sum of the debt and the equity.

debt instrument A document used to raise non-equity finance consisting of a *promissory note, *bill of exchange, or any other legally binding bond.

debtor collection period (average collection period) The period, on average, that a business takes to collect the money owed to it by its trade debtors. If a company gives one month's credit then, on average, it should collect its debts within 45 days. The **debtor collection period ratio** is calculated by dividing the amount owed by trade debtors by the annual sales on credit and multiplying by 365. For example if debtors are £25,000 and sales are £200,000, the debtors collection period ratio will be:

$$(£25,000 \times 365)/£200,000 = 46 \text{ days approximately.}$$

debtors Those who owe money to an organization, for example for sales of goods. The balance on the *debtors' ledger control account is included in the balance sheet (subject to any *provision for bad debts) under *current assets. Amounts due from debtors in more than one year should be disclosed separately. A memorandum listing of the individual account of each debtor is also kept, this is known as the *debtors' ledger. The total of the debtors' ledger is periodically checked with the total on the debtors' control account as a form of internal control.

debtors' ledger (sales ledger; sold ledger) A memorandum *ledger account in which individual debtors' accounts are recorded. Each account records sales made (debit), payments received (credit), discounts given (credit), and *returns inwards (credit). The total sum of all individual debtors' ledgers is periodically extracted and compared to the total on the *debtors' ledger control account as part of the internal control system. The total of the individual debtors' ledger accounts should always equal the debtors' ledger control account.

debtors' ledger control account (sales ledger control account) A *nominal ledger (or general ledger) control account that records the totals of entries made to the individual *debtors' ledgers from the *sales day book and the cash receipts journal. The total on the *debtors' ledger control account is periodically compared with the sum total of individual debtors' ledger accounts as part of the internal control system. The debtors' ledger control account should always equal the total of the individual debtors' ledger amounts.

debt restructuring The adjustment of a debt, either as a result of legal action or by agreement between the interested parties, to give the debtor a more feasible arrangement with the creditors for meeting the financial obligations. The management may also voluntarily restructure debt, for example by replacing long-term debt with short-term debt.

decentralization The delegation of decision-making responsibilities to the subunits of an organization. The advantages claimed for decentralization are that local managers are more aware of immediate problems, are better motivated, and have greater control over local circumstances. The disadvantages of decentralization are the possibility of wasteful competition between subunits, the duplication of certain services and functions, and the loss of central control and access to information.

decision making The act of deciding between alternative courses of action. In the running of a business, accounting information and techniques are used to facilitate decision making, especially by the provision of decision models, such as *discounted cash flow, *critical-path analysis, *marginal costing, and *breakeven analysis. *See also* RELEVANT COST.

decision model A model that simulates the elements or variables inherent in a business decision, together with their relationships to each other and the constraints under which they operate; the purpose of the model is to enable a solution to be arrived at in keeping with the objectives of the organization. For example, a *linear programming decision model may arrive at a particular production mix that, having regard to the constraints that exist, either minimizes costs or maximizes the contribution. Other decision models include *decision trees, *discounted cash flow, and the *payback period method.

decision support system (DSS) A computer system specifically designed to assist managers in making unstructured or semistructured decisions, i.e. the nature of the problem requiring a decision is not known in advance. A language subsystem has to be included in the DSS to allow users to communicate easily with the system and a problem processing subsystem, such as a *spreadsheet, is also required. Typically, a system of this type has a store of internal data and is able to access external data. A **group decision support system** (**GDSS**) is designed to facilitate group decision making. *See also* DATA WAREHOUSE; EXPERT SYSTEM; MANAGEMENT INFORMATION SYSTEM.

decision table A table used to aid decision making. The table shows the problems requiring actions to be considered and estimated probabilities of outcomes. Where probabilities are difficult to estimate, the maximax and maximin criteria are often used, the former leading to the selection of the option with the greatest maximum outcome, the latter to the selection of the action with the greatest minimum outcome.

decision trees Diagrams that illustrate the choices available to a decision maker and the estimated outcomes of each possible decision. Each possible decision is shown as a separate branch of the tree, together with each estimated outcome for each decision and the subjective *probabilities of these outcomes actually occurring. From this information the *expected values for each outcome can be determined, which can provide valuable information in decision making.

declaration of dividend A statement in which the directors of a company announce that a *dividend of a certain amount is recommended to be paid to the shareholders. The *liability should be recognized as soon as the declaration has been made and the appropriate amount is included under *current liabilities on the *balance sheet. The company pays the dividend net of income tax to the shareholders.

declining balance method *See* DIMINISHING-BALANCE METHOD.

decommissioning costs The costs incurred in ceasing an operation or activity. An example might be the removal of an oil rig and the restoration of the seabed. Under *Financial Reporting Standard 12, a provision should be made for decommissioning costs relating to damage already done, e.g. the damage caused by the installation of a rig. The relevant *International Accounting Standard is IAS 37.

deductions at source A method of tax collection in which a person paying income to another deducts the tax on the income and is responsible for paying it to the authorities. Tax authorities have found that, in general, it is easier to collect tax from the payer rather than the recipient of income, especially if paying the tax is made a condition of the payer's obtaining tax relief for the payment. The payee receives a credit against any tax liability for the tax already suffered. Examples of this in the UK system are *PAYE, share dividends, interest on government securities, trust income, and subcontractors in the building industry.

deed of arrangement A written agreement between a debtor and his or her creditors that has been registered as such with the Insolvency Service. The agreement may take the form of a *composition of debts or a *scheme of arrangement of the debtor's affairs. Unlike an individual *voluntary arrangement, a deed of arrangement can only be entered into when no bankruptcy order has been made.

deed of covenant A former legal document enabling a person to obtain tax relief on regular annual payments to a charity. From 2000 it was replaced by the *gift aid system.

deed of partnership A *partnership agreement drawn up in the form of a deed. It covers the respective *capital contributions of the partners, their entitlement to interest on their capital, their profit-sharing percentages, agreed salary, etc.

deed of variation A deed by which the beneficiary under a will or an intestacy redirects the gift to some other person (who may or may not be a beneficiary of the estate). Provided this is done within two years of the deceased's death and statutory requirements are complied with, the redirection is not treated as a gift for inheritance tax or capital gains tax purposes.

deeply discounted security A loan stock or government security issued on such terms that the amount payable on maturity or any other redemption exceeds or may exceed the issue price by more than 15% or, if less, by more than 1/2% for each completed year between issue and redemption. For example, a **deep discount bond** might be a four-year loan stock issued at £95 for every £100 nominal (the discount exceeds 1/2% per annum) or a 25-year loan stock issued at £75 for every £100 nominal (the discount exceeds 15% in total). Under the current tax rules, as set out in the Income Tax (Trading and Other Income) Act 2005, profits on any disposal of such securities are charged to income tax.

deep market A market for a security, commodity, currency, etc. in which there are currently a large number of transactions. In such a market the *spread between bid and offer prices will be narrow and sizable transactions can take place without moving the price of the security etc. A deep market is highly liquid. *Compare* THIN MARKET.

deep pocket A description of a person or company who appears to have an apparently endless supply of money and would, therefore, be worth suing. The big accountancy firms are protected by professional-liability insurance and can therefore be said to have deep pockets.

defalcation Embezzlement of property belonging to another party.

default A failure to fulfil a contractual or other legal obligation. Defaults include failure to settle a debt, failure to defend legal proceedings, failure to submit a *value added tax (VAT) return on time or to make a VAT payment on the appropriate date. In the case of a VAT default, a *surcharge liability notice is served on the *taxable person.

defeasance Irrevocably committing specific assets to meet long-term obligations. It provides a method of eliminating from a company's balance sheet liabilities that carry no appropriate right of early repayment. *See* SINKING FUND.

defective accounts Accounts that do not comply with legislation or *accounting standards. By the terms of the Companies Act a company producing such accounts may be called on to issue revised accounts. Although an apparently modest legislative change, it has done much to enhance the authority of the *Financial Reporting Review Panel.

defended takeover bid A *takeover bid for a company in which the directors of the target company oppose the bid.

defensive interval ratio A ratio that demonstrates the ability of a business to satisfy its current debts by calculating the time for which it can operate on current liquid assets, without needing revenue from the next period's sales. Current assets less stock is divided by the projected daily operational expenditure less non-cash charges. Projected daily operational expenditure is calculated by dividing by 365 the total of the *cost of sales, operating expenses, and other cash expenses.

deferred annuity An *annuity in which payments do not start at once but either at a specified later date or when the policyholder reaches a specified age.

deferred asset *See* DEFERRED DEBIT.

deferred consideration agreement An agreement in which payment of the consideration is delayed either until a certain date or until a specified and certain event has occurred.

deferred credit (deferred income; deferred liability) Income received or recorded before it is earned, under the *accruals concept. The income will not be included in the *profit and loss account of the period but will be carried forward on the *balance sheet until it is matched with the period in which it is earned. A common example of a deferred credit is a government grant. The grant is shown as a separate item or under *creditors in the balance sheet, and an annual amount is transferred to the profit and loss account until the deferred credit balance is brought to nil.

deferred debit (deferred asset; deferred expense) An item of expenditure incurred in an accounting period but, under the *accruals concept, not matched with the income it will generate. Instead of being treated as an operating cost for that period, it is treated as an *asset with the intention of treating it as an operating cost to be charged against the income it will generate in a future period. An example is rent paid for a period beyond the end of the accounting period.

deferred income *See* DEFERRED CREDIT.

deferred liability *See* DEFERRED CREDIT.

deferred ordinary share **1.** A type of ordinary share, formerly often issued to founder members of a company, in which dividends are paid only after all other types of ordinary share have been paid. Such shares often entitle their owners to a large share of the profit. **2.** A type of share on which little or no dividend is paid for a fixed number of years, after which it ranks with other ordinary shares for dividend.

deferred taxation A sum set aside for tax in the accounts of an organization that will become payable in a period other than that under review. It arises because of timing differences between tax rules and accounting conventions. The principle of **deferred-tax accounting** is to reallocate a tax payment to the same period as that in which the relevant amount of income or expenditure is shown. Historically, the most common reason for this timing difference is because the percentages used for the calculation of *capital allowances have differed from those used for *depreciation.

deficit A loss that results when expenditure exceeds income.

defined-benefit pension scheme (DB scheme) An occupational pension scheme in which the rules specify the benefits to be received on retirement and the scheme is funded accordingly. The benefits are normally calculated on a formula incorporating years of service and salary levels (*see* FINAL SALARY SCHEME). Accounting for pension costs poses a number of difficulties for accountants; the basic regulations are set out in *Statement of Standard Accounting Practice 24, although *Financial Reporting Standard 17, Retirement Benefits, and *International Accounting Standard 19, Employee Benefits, should also be consulted.

   In recent years rising costs have led many companies to close their existing DB schemes to new employees, who are obliged to join *defined-contribution pension schemes.

defined-contribution pension scheme (DC scheme) A pension scheme in which the benefits are based on the value of the contributions paid in by each member. The rate of contribution is normally specified; the amount of pension an individual will receive will depend on the size of the fund accumulated and the annuity that can be obtained from it at the date of retirement. *Compare* DEFINED-BENEFIT PENSION SCHEME.

deflation The situation in which there is a general decrease in prices, especially when this is accompanied by falling levels of output, employment, and trade. Because of these associations, advocates of anti-inflationary policies usually now prefer the term *disinflation. *Compare* INFLATION.

defunct company A company that has been wound up and has therefore ceased to exist.

delivery lead time The delay between the time at which an order is placed to replenish an item of *stock and the receipt of the item ordered.

Delphi technique A technique for predicting a future event or outcome, in which a group of experts are asked to make their forecasts, initially independently, and subsequently by consensus in order to discard any extreme views. In some circumstances subjective *probabilities can be assigned to the possible future outcomes in order to arrive at a conclusion.

demerger A business strategy in which a large company or group of companies splits up so that its activities are carried on by two or more independent companies. Alternatively, subsidiaries of a group are sold off. Demerging was popular in the late 1980s when large conglomerates became unfashionable.

demutualization The act by which a *mutual, such as a *building society, changes its status to that of a public limited company. In the 1980s and 1990s this was seen in the retail financial services industry worldwide.

department A discrete section of an organization under the responsibility of a **department manager**; separate costs and, where appropriate, income are allocated or apportioned to the department for the purposes of costing, performance appraisal, and control.

departmental accounting The process of providing accounting information analysed by department, so that each department of an organization can be treated as a separate *cost centre, *revenue centre, or *profit centre (as appropriate) and the department manager can have access to the department's performance.

departmental budget A budget for a particular department of an organization for a budget period. Ideally, it will be produced either by, or in consultation with, the department manager concerned in accordance with the procedures set out in the *budget manual; coordinated with other budgets on which it may have an impact; and agreed with the *budget committee for integration into the master budget, which is submitted to the board of directors for approval.

Department for Business, Innovation and Skills The UK government department responsible for consumer and competition policy, company legislation, employment law, science and research, higher education, and adult learning. It was formed in 2009 from a merger of the **Department for Business, Enterprise and Regulatory Reform** (**BERR**) and the Department for Innovation, Universities and Skills (DIUS).

 SEE WEB LINKS

• BIS website

depletion The using up of an *asset, especially a mineral asset. For example, a quarry is depleted by the extraction of stone. *See also* DEPLETION ACCOUNTING; WASTING ASSET.

depletion accounting A method of calculating the *depreciation of a *wasting asset, based on the rate at which it is being used. For example, a coal mine could be depreciated on the basis of the rate at which coal is extracted from it.

deposit **1.** A sum of money paid by a buyer as part of the sale price of something in order to reserve it. Depending on the terms agreed, the deposit may or may not be returned if the sale is not completed. **2.** A sum of money left with an organization, such as a bank, for safekeeping or to earn interest or with a broker, dealer, etc., as a security to cover any trading losses incurred. **3.** A sum of money paid as the first instalment on a *hire-purchase agreement. It is usually paid when the buyer takes possession of the goods.

deposit account (DA) An *account with a bank or building society from which money cannot be withdrawn without notice and on which interest is paid. *See also* SAVINGS ACCOUNT.

depository receipt A certificate issued by a depository, bank, or other company stating what has been deposited for safekeeping.

deposits in transit Cash receipts that have arrived at a company's bank too late in the current month to be credited to the depositor's bank statement. An adjustment will therefore be required to the *bank reconciliation statement.

depreciable amount The value of a *fixed asset used as the basis for calculating the *depreciation charge for the period. When using the *diminishing-balance method of depreciation, the depreciable amount is the book value of the asset at the end of the previous financial period. However, when the *straight-line method of depreciation is used, the depreciable amount is based on cost, or alternatively on valuation, if the asset has been subject to revaluation at some prior stage.

depreciable asset A fixed asset that is to be the subject of *depreciation.

depreciated cost (depreciated value) *See* NET BOOK VALUE.

depreciation **1.** The measure of the cost or revalued amount (*see* REVALUATION) of the economic benefits of a tangible fixed asset that have been consumed during an *accounting period. This includes the wearing out, using up, or other reduction in the *useful economic life of a tangible fixed asset. A **provision for depreciation** can be computed by means of a number of generally accepted techniques, including the *straight-line method, the *diminishing-balance method, the *sum-of-the-digits method, the *production-unit method, and the *revaluation method. The depreciation reduces the book value of the asset and is charged against income of an organization in the income statement or *profit and loss account. In the UK, *Financial Reporting Standard 15 deals with the subject of depreciation in the accounts. The relevant *International Accounting Standard is IAS 16, Property, Plant and Equipment. **2.** A fall in the value of a currency with a *floating exchange rate relative to other currencies. Depreciation can refer both to day-to-day movements and to long-term realignments in value. For currencies with a *fixed exchange rate a *devaluation or *revaluation of currency is required to change the relative value. *Compare* APPRECIATION.

depreciation rate The percentage rate used in the *straight-line method and *diminishing-balance method of *depreciation in order to determine the amount of depreciation that should be written off a *fixed asset and charged against income or the profit and loss account.

deprival value *See* CURRENT-COST ACCOUNTING; VALUE TO THE BUSINESS.

depth of market *See* DEEP MARKET; THIN MARKET.

depth tests Tests of the different control features of an internal-control system, which are linked together to become a *walk-through test. Depth tests differ from walk-through tests in that the *sample tested must be representative of the population in order to achieve the compliance objectives. *See* COMPLIANCE TESTS.

derecognition The removal from the *balance sheet of *assets and *liabilities that had previously been recognized in the *financial statements of a company. Derecognition is a key aspect of *off-balance-sheet finance. *Financial Reporting Standard 5 sets out the following outcomes in relation to assets: complete derecognition; no derecognition; partial derecognition. For UK listed companies *International Accounting Standard 39 and *International Financial Reporting Standard 7 now apply.

deregistration Ceasing to be registered for *value added tax. When a *taxable person ceases to make *taxable supplies, deregistration is compulsory and notification is required within 30 days. Failure to give the required notification may result in a penalty being charged.

deregulation The removal of controls imposed by governments on the operation of markets. Many economists and politicians believe that during the mid-20th century governments imposed controls over markets that had little or no justification in economic theory. Since the 1980s many governments have followed a deliberate policy of deregulation. However, most economists still argue that certain markets should be regulated, particularly if market failure is involved.

derivative A financial instrument, the price of which has a strong correlation with an *underlying commodity, currency, economic variable, or financial instrument. The main types of derivatives are *futures contracts, forwards (*see* FORWARD DEALING), *swaps, and *options. They are traded on derivatives markets or over the counter (OTC). The market-traded derivatives are standard, while the OTC trades are specific and customized. The 1990s and 2000s saw a huge growth in the market for complex derivatives products and the lack of transparency associated with these instruments is widely seen as a factor in the global financial collapse of 2008 (*see* COLLATERALIZED DEBT OBLIGATION; CREDIT DEFAULT SWAP). *Financial Reporting Standard 13 requires that the current market value of derivatives is disclosed in financial statements; *International Accounting Standard 39 also states that this value may be recognized in the profit and loss account (*see* FAIR VALUE ACCOUNTING). *See also* CREDIT DERIVATIVE; STRUCTURED FINANCE.

derivative claim A legal action brought by a shareholder on behalf of a company for a wrong done to it. A company will usually sue in its own name but if those against whom it has a cause of action are in control of the company (i.e.

directors or majority shareholders) a shareholder may bring a derivative action. The company will appear as defendant so that it will be bound by, and able to benefit from, the decision. The need to bring such an action must be proved to the court before it can proceed.

Designated Professional Body (DPB) A professional body registered with the *Financial Services Authority as having statutory responsibility for regulating its profession. There are now 10 DPBs: the Association of Chartered Certified Accountants, the Council for Licensed Conveyancers, the Institute of Actuaries, the Institute of Chartered Accountants in England and Wales, the Institute of Chartered Accountants in Ireland, the Institute of Chartered Accountants of Scotland, the Law Society, the Law Society of Northern Ireland, the Law Society of Scotland, and the Royal Institution of Chartered Surveyors. The DPBs were formerly known as **Recognized Professional Bodies (RPBs)**.

detection risk The risk that an auditor will fail to detect any misstatements that have occurred. Unlike the *control risk and the inherent risk, the level of the detection risk can be directly controlled by the auditor, who can modify his or her programme of testing. *See* AUDIT RISK.

Deutsche Börse An international market place organizer for trading in securities, commodities, and derivatives, with its headquarters in Frankfurt, Germany. Established as a holiday company in 1992, Deutsche Börse AG owns and operates the *Frankfurt Stock Exchange and (since 2000) the clearing and settlement facility *Clearstream. It is also joint owner of the electronic derivatives exchange Eurex, which acquired the US-based International Securities Exchange in 2007.

devaluation A fall in the value of a currency relative to gold or to other currencies. Governments engage in devaluation when they feel that their currency has become overvalued, for example through high rates of inflation making exports uncompetitive or because of a substantially adverse balance of trade. The intention is that devaluation will make exports cheaper and imports dearer, although the loss of confidence in an economy forced to devalue invariably has an adverse effect. Devaluation is a measure that need only concern governments with a *fixed exchange rate for their currency. With a *floating exchange rate, devaluation or revaluation takes place continuously and automatically (*see* DEPRECIATION; REVALUATION OF CURRENCY).

development costs *See* RESEARCH AND DEVELOPMENT COSTS.

development-state enterprise In the USA, a business that is employing all its resources to establish itself. Either the planned sales phase has not commenced or no significant revenues have yet been generated.

different costs for different purposes In *management accounting, the principle that the management of an organization is likely to need different information, and thus different costs, for the various activities it carries out, especially when making decisions. For example, when calculating the price of a product on a *cost-plus basis, management would need to ensure that all costs, both fixed and variable, are charged to the product. On the other hand, in determining whether or not additional units of a product should be produced, only the variable costs would be relevant to that decision.

differential analysis (incremental analysis) An assessment of the impact on costs and revenues of specific management decisions. Such an analysis will focus on identifying the **differential** (or **incremental**) **cash flows**, i.e. those costs or revenues that will change as a result of a specific decision. In *decision making, the **differential costs** are the only *relevant costs.

differential pricing A method of pricing a product in which the same product is supplied to different customers, or different market segments, at different prices. This approach is based on the principle that to achieve maximum market penetration the price charged should be what a particular market will bear. *See* REVENUE MANAGEMENT.

differentiated marketing Marketing in which provision is made to meet the special needs of consumers. For example, weight watchers require diet drinks and left-handed people require left-handed scissors.

dilapidations Disrepair of leasehold premises. The landlord may be liable to repair certain parts of domestic premises (e.g. the structure and exterior, and the sanitary appliances) under the Landlord and Tenant Act 1985 if the lease is for less than seven years. Otherwise, the lease will usually contain a covenant by either the landlord or the tenant obliging them to keep the premises in repair. Under the Landlord and Tenant Act 1985, a landlord cannot enforce a repairing covenant against a tenant by ending the lease prematurely unless a notice is first served specifying the disrepair and giving time for the repairs to be carried out. If there is no covenant in the lease, the tenant is under a common-law duty not to damage the premises and must keep them from falling down.

diluted earnings per share *See* FULLY DILUTED EARNINGS PER SHARE.

diminishing-balance method (reducing-balance method) A method of computing the *depreciation of a *fixed asset in an accounting period, in which the percentage to be charged against income is based on the depreciated value at the beginning of the period (*see* NET BOOK VALUE). This has the effect of reducing the annual depreciation charge against profits year by year. The annual percentage to be applied to the annual depreciated value is determined by the formula:

$$\text{rate of depreciation} = 1 - (S/C)^{1/N},$$

where N is the estimated life in years, S is the estimated scrap value at the end of its useful life, and C is the original cost.

direct charge voucher (DCV) A *prime document that records the purchases of parts and material directly chargeable to a job or process, without passing through the organization's stores. The document gives a description of the items, the commodity codes, the value of the items, and the accounting or cost code to which the items are chargeable.

direct costing *See* MARGINAL COSTING.

direct cost of sales (prime cost) The *cost of sales, expressed as *direct materials, *direct labour, and *direct expenses only. The direct cost of sales excludes any *overhead.

direct costs **1.** Product costs that can be directly traced to a product or *cost unit. They are usually made up of *direct materials costs (which can be charged directly to the product by means of *materials requisitions), *direct labour costs (charged by means of time sheets, time cards, or computer *direct data entries), and *direct expenses (which are subcontract costs charged by means of an invoice from the subcontractor). The total of direct materials, direct labour, and direct expenses is known as the *direct cost of sales. **2.** Departmental or *cost centre overhead costs that can be traced directly to the appropriate parts of an organization, without the necessity of cost *apportionment. For example, the costs of a maintenance section that serves only one particular cost centre should be charged directly to that cost centre. *Compare* INDIRECT COSTS.

direct data entry The process of recording accounting and other transactions directly onto a computer system from individual department terminals. For example, direct labour times spent on jobs or processes can be entered directly into the computer system through a terminal in the operating department. Usually the entry is subjected to tests and constraints to ensure that it complies with certain parameters and to ensure that the system is not corrupted by the inputs from a remote terminal.

direct expense Expenditure that would not be incurred unless a particular *cost unit were produced (excluding the costs of direct labour and materials). Direct expenses are included in the *direct cost of an item.

direct financing lease In the USA, a method used by lessors in *capital leases, in which the lessor has purchased the asset solely for the purpose of leasing it. The minimum lease payments must be collectable and no significant uncertainties should attach to the amount of unreimbursable costs yet to be incurred.

direct hour An hour spent working on a product, service, or *cost unit of an organization. It is usually expressed as a *direct labour hour, *machine hour, or *standard hour.

direct labour Workers directly concerned with the production of a product, service, or *cost unit, such as machine operators, assembly and finishing operators, etc. *Compare* INDIRECT LABOUR.

direct labour cost (direct wages) Expenditure on wages paid to those operators who are directly concerned with the production of a product, service, or *cost unit. It is one of the *cost classifications making up the *direct cost of sales of a cost unit; it is quantified as the product of the time spent on each activity (collected by means of time sheets or job cards) and the rate of pay of each operator concerned. A percentage of the direct labour cost is sometimes used as a basis for absorbing production overheads to the cost unit in *absorption costing.

direct labour efficiency variance In a *standard costing system, a *variance arising as part of the *direct labour total cost variance. It compares the actual labour time taken to carry out an activity with the standard time allowed and values the difference at the *standard direct labour rate per hour. The resultant adverse or favourable variance is the amount by which the budgeted profit is affected by virtue of labour efficiency. The formula for this variance is:

(standard hours allowed for production − actual hours taken) × standard rate per *direct labour hour.

direct labour hour An hour spent working on a product, service, or *cost unit produced by an organization by those operators whose time can be directly traced to the production. The direct labour hour is sometimes used as a basis for absorbing *manufacturing overheads to the cost unit in *absorption costing.

direct labour hour rate (labour hour rate) **1.** The individual rate of pay per hour paid to operators categorized as *direct labour. **2.** An *absorption rate used in *absorption costing. It is obtained by the following formula:

(budgeted cost centre overheads)/(budgeted direct labour hours).

direct labour rate of pay variance In a *standard costing system, a *variance arising as part of the *direct labour total cost variance. It compares the actual rate paid to direct labour for an activity with the *standard rate of pay allowed for that activity for the actual hours worked. The resultant adverse or favourable variance is the amount by which the budgeted profit is affected by differences in direct labour rates of pay. The formulae for this variance are:

(standard rate per hour – actual rate per hour) × actual hours worked,

or alternatively:

(standard rate per hour × actual hours worked) – actual wages paid.

direct labour total cost variance The combination of the *direct labour rate of pay variance and the *direct labour efficiency variance; it compares the actual cost and the standard cost of the direct labour incurred in carrying out the actual production. The formula for this variance is:

(standard rate per hour × actual hours worked) – actual labour cost.

direct materials Materials that are directly incorporated in the final product or *cost unit of an organization. For example, in the production of furniture, direct materials would include wood, glue, and paint. *Compare* INDIRECT MATERIALS.

direct materials cost Expenditure on *direct materials. It is one of the *cost classifications that make up the *direct cost of sales of a *cost unit and is ascertained by collecting together the quantities of each material used on each product by means of *materials requisitions and multiplying the quantities by the cost per unit of each material. A percentage on direct materials cost is sometimes used as a basis for absorbing production overheads to the cost unit in *absorption costing.

direct materials inventory *See* DIRECT MATERIALS STOCKS.

direct materials mix variance In *standard costing systems, part of the *direct materials usage variance; it is the difference between the total material used in standard proportions (*see* STANDARD MIX) and the material used in actual proportions, valued at standard prices (*see* STANDARD PURCHASE PRICE; STANDARD SELLING PRICE).

direct materials price variance In a *standard costing system, a *variance arising as part of the *direct materials total cost variance. There are two alternative points at which the materials price variance may be established: when the material is purchased or when it is issued to production. When established on issue to production, the variance compares the actual price paid for direct material used in a product with the *standard purchase price of the material consumed. When established on purchase, it compares the actual price paid for the direct material purchased with the standard price allowed for the purchased material. The resultant adverse or favourable variance is the amount by which the budgeted profit is affected by differences in direct material prices. The formulae for this variance are:

(standard price per unit of material – actual price per unit of material) × actual units consumed or purchased,

or alternatively:

(standard price per unit of material × actual units consumed or purchased) – actual material cost.

direct materials quantity variance *See* DIRECT MATERIALS YIELD VARIANCE.

direct materials stocks (direct materials inventory) The list of *raw materials in store awaiting transfer to production, after which the materials are incorporated into *work in progress.

direct materials total cost variance A combination of the *direct materials price variance and the *direct materials usage variance; it compares the actual cost and the standard cost of the direct material consumed in carrying out the actual production. The formula for this variance is:

(standard price per unit of material × actual units of material consumed) – actual material cost.

direct materials usage variance In a *standard costing system, a *variance arising as part of the *direct materials total cost variance. It compares the actual quantity of material used to carry out production with the standard quantity allowed, and values the difference at the standard material price per unit. The resultant adverse or favourable variance is the amount by which the budgeted profit is affected by virtue of material usage. The formula for this variance is:

(standard quantity of material allowed for production – actual quantity used) × standard price per unit of material.

See also DIRECT MATERIALS MIX VARIANCE; DIRECT MATERIALS YIELD VARIANCE.

direct materials yield variance (direct materials quantity variance) In *standard costing systems, part of the *direct materials usage variance; it is the difference between the total standard quantity of material allowed for a process in standard proportions (*see* STANDARD MIX) and the total actual material used, also in standard proportions, valued at standard prices (*see* STANDARD PURCHASE PRICE; STANDARD SELLING PRICE).

direct method A method of preparing a *cash-flow statement under *Financial Reporting Standard 1 and *International Accounting Standard 7: operating cash receipts and payments are aggregated to show the net cash flow from operating activities.

director A person appointed to carry out the day-to-day management of a company. A public company must have at least two directors, a private company at least one. The directors of a company, collectively known as the **board of directors**, usually act together, although power may be conferred (by the *articles of association) on one or more directors to exercise executive powers; in particular there is often a managing director with considerable executive power.

The first directors of a company are usually named in its articles of association or are appointed by the subscribers; they are required to give a signed undertaking to act in that capacity, which must be sent to the *Registrar of Companies. Subsequent directors are appointed by the company at a general meeting, although in practice they may be appointed by the other directors for ratification by the general meeting. Directors may be discharged from office by an *ordinary resolution with special notice at a general meeting, whether or not they have a *service contract in force. They may be disqualified for *fraudulent trading or *wrongful trading or for any conduct that makes them unfit to manage the company.

Directors owe general duties of honesty and loyalty to the company (fiduciary duties) and a duty of care; their liability in *negligence depends upon their personal qualifications (e.g. a chartered accountant must exercise more skill than an unqualified person). For the first time, the Companies Act 2006 sets out seven specified duties of directors:

- the duty to act within the powers of the company's constitution and to exercise the powers for the purposes for which they are conferred;
- the duty to act in good faith to promote the success of the company for the benefit of its members as whole;
- the duty to exercise independent judgment;
- the duty to exercise reasonable care, skill, and diligence;
- the duty to avoid conflicts of interest;
- the duty not to accept benefits from third parties;
- the duty to declare an interest in any proposed transaction or arrangement with the company.

Directors' remuneration consists of a salary and in some cases directors' fees, paid to them for being a director, and an expense allowance to cover their expenses incurred in the service of the company. Directors' remuneration must be disclosed in the company's accounts and shown separately from any pension payments or *compensation for loss of office. *See also* EXECUTIVE DIRECTOR; NON-EXECUTIVE DIRECTOR; SHADOW DIRECTOR.

directors' interests The interests held by *directors in the shares and debentures of the company of which they are a director. The directors' interests can also include options on shares and debentures of the company. These interests must be disclosed to comply with the Companies Acts.

directors or higher-paid employees Under UK tax law, a higher-paid employee is defined as one earning more than £8500 per annum. This amount, which has remained unaltered since it was set in 1979, includes remuneration together with benefits and reimbursed expenses. An employer must account to HM Revenue and Customs, on form P11D, for all benefits received by a higher-paid employee or director (for whom there is no earnings limit). These benefits are assessed at the cost to the employer, although special rules apply to certain benefits, e.g. company cars. *See* BENEFITS IN KIND.

directors' remuneration (directors' emoluments) The amounts received by directors from their office or employment, including all salaries, fees, wages, perquisites, and other profit as well as certain expenses and benefits paid or provided by the employer, which are deemed to be remuneration or emoluments.

directors' report An annual report by the directors of a company to its shareholders, which forms parts of the accounts required to be filed with the Registrar of Companies under the Companies Act. The information that must be given includes the principal activities of the company, a fair review of the developments and position of the business with likely future developments, details of research and development, significant issues on the sale, purchase, or valuation of assets, recommended dividends, transfers to reserves, names of the directors and their interests in the company during the period, employee statistics, and any political or charitable gifts made during the period. The government issued new regulations for the directors' report in 2005; these require a more comprehensive review of the company's performance and a description of the principal risks and uncertainties affecting its future. The scope of the directors' report was further expanded by the Companies Act 2006, which became fully operative in late 2009. *See also* OPERATING AND FINANCIAL REVIEW.

direct production cost of sales *See* DIRECT COST OF SALES.

direct taxation Taxation, the effect of which is intended to be borne by the person or organization that pays it. Economists distinguish between direct taxation and **indirect taxation**. The former is best illustrated by *income tax, in which the person who receives the income pays the tax and his or her income is thereby reduced. The latter is illustrated by *value added tax (VAT), in which the tax is paid by traders but the effects are borne by the consumers of the trader's goods or services. In practice these distinctions are rarely clear cut. For example, *corporation tax is a direct tax but its incidence can be shifted to consumers by higher prices or to employees by lower wages.

direct wages *See* DIRECT LABOUR COST.

direct worker An operator in an organization whose time is spent working on the product or *cost unit produced to such an extent that the operator's time is traceable to the product as a *direct cost. *See also* DIRECT LABOUR COST.

direct write-off method In the USA, the procedure of writing off bad debts as they occur instead of creating a provision for them. Although this practice is unacceptable for financial reporting purposes, it is the only method allowed for tax purposes.

disbursement A payment made by an agent, often a professional such as a solicitor or banker, on behalf of a client. This is claimed back when the client receives an account for the professional services.

discharge The release of a debtor from all provable debts (with minor exceptions) at the end of bankruptcy proceedings. In certain circumstances discharge is automatic. In other cases, the debtor or the official receiver may apply to the court for an **order of discharge**. This may be subject to conditions, such as further payments by the debtor to his creditors out of his future income, or it may be suspended until the creditors receive a higher proportion of the amount due to them. After discharge the debtor is freed from most of the disabilities to which he was subject as an *undischarged bankrupt. See feature BANKRUPTCY LAW on p. 52.

disclaimer of opinion A statement made by an auditor to the effect that a limitation on the scope of the audit report is so material that he or she has not been able to obtain sufficient evidence to support an opinion on the financial statements. *See* AUDIT OPINION; EXCEPT FOR; QUALIFIED AUDIT REPORT.

disclosure The provision of financial and non-financial information, on a regular basis, to those interested in the economic activities of an organization. The information is normally given in the annual report and accounts (*see* ANNUAL ACCOUNTS), which includes *financial statements and other financial and non-financial information. The annual report and accounts of a limited company is regulated by company legislation, *accounting standards, and, in the case of a quoted company, by stock exchange regulations.

discontinued operations The operations of a reporting entity that has been sold or permanently closed down in a period or before the earlier of three months after the commencement of the subsequent period and the date on which the financial statements are approved. According to *Financial Reporting Standard 3, if the sale or termination has a material effect on the reporting entity's operations and the assets, liabilities, and results are clearly distinguishable, the *profit and loss account should show the results of these operations separately. For UK listed companies *International Financial Reporting Standard 5, Non-current Assets Held for Sale and Discontinued Operations now applies.

discount **1.** A deduction from a *bill of exchange when it is purchased before its maturity date. The party that purchases (discounts) the bill pays less than its face value and therefore makes a profit when it matures. The amount of the discount consists of interest calculated at the *bill rate for the length of time that the bill has to run. **2.** A reduction in the price of goods below list price, for buyers who pay cash (**cash discount**), for members of the trade (**trade discount**), for buying in bulk (**bulk** or **quantity discount**), etc. *See* DISCOUNT ALLOWED; DISCOUNT RECEIVED. **3.** To convert a *future value into a *present value, as by the *discounted cash flow method. **4.** The amount by which the market price of a security is below its *par value. A £100 par value loan stock with a market price of £95 is said to be at a 5% discount.

discount allowed A discount granted by a company to a client, for example for a bulk purchase or a prompt payment. It is shown as an expense in the *profit and loss account.

discounted cash flow (DCF) A method used in *capital budgeting, *capital expenditure appraisal, and decision appraisal that predicts the stream of cash flows, both inflows and outflows, over time and discounts them, using a *cost of capital or *hurdle rate, to *present values in order to determine whether the project or decision is likely to be financially feasible. A number of appraisal approaches use the DCF principle, namely *net present value, *internal rate of return, and the *profitability index. Most computer spreadsheet programs now include a DCF appraisal routine.

discounted payback method A method of *capital budgeting in which managers calculate the time required before the forecast discounted cash inflows from an investment will equal the initial investment expenditure (*see* DISCOUNTED CASH FLOW). This method is similar to the *payback period method but makes some allowance for the *time value of money. Despite theoretical problems, it is widely used in practice.

discounted value *See* PRESENT VALUE.

discount factor (present-value factor) A factor that, when multiplied by a particular year's predicted cash flow, brings the cash flow to a *present value. The factor takes into consideration the number of years from the inception of the project and the *hurdle rate that the project is expected to earn before it can be regarded as feasible. The factor is computed using the formula:

discount factor $= 1/(1 + r)^t$,

where r is the hurdle rate required and t is the number of years from project inception. In practice there is little necessity to compute discount factors when carrying out appraisal calculations as they are readily available in discount tables. Most computer spreadsheet programs now include a *discounted cash flow routine, which also obviates the need for using discount factors.

discount house A company or bank on the *discount market that specializes in discounting *bills of exchange, especially Treasury bills.

discounting **1.** The application of *discount factors to each year's cash flow projections in a *discounted cash flow appraisal calculation. **2.** The process of selling a *bill of exchange before its maturity at a price below its face value.

discount market In the UK, the part of the *money market consisting of banks, *discount houses, and *bill brokers. By borrowing money at short notice from commercial banks or discount houses, bill brokers are able to discount bills of exchange, especially Treasury bills, and make a profit.

discount rate The *hurdle rate of interest or *cost of capital rate applied to the *discount factors used in a *discounted cash flow appraisal calculation. The discount rate may be based on the cost-of-capital rate adjusted by a risk factor based on the risk characteristics of the proposed investment in order to create a hurdle rate that the project must earn before being worthy of consideration. Alternatively, the discount rate may be the interest rate that the funds used for the project could earn elsewhere.

discount received A discount granted to a supplier, for example for a bulk purchase or a prompt payment. It is shown as a credit in the *profit and loss account.

discovery value accounting In the USA, the method of accounting used for extractive enterprises, such as oil and gas.

discretionary costs (managed costs) Costs incurred as a result of a managerial decision; the extent of these costs is consequently subject to managerial discretion. A characteristic of such costs is that they are often for a specified amount or subject to a specific formula, such as a percentage of sales revenue. Examples include advertising and research expenditure.

discretionary trust **1.** A *trust in which the shares of each beneficiary are not fixed by the settlor in the trust deed but may be varied at the discretion of some person or persons (often the trustees). Such trusts may be particularly useful when the needs of the beneficiaries are likely to change, as in the case of children. Formerly, many discretionary trusts took the form of **accumulation and maintenance (A & M) trusts**, in which income could be carried forward from one year to the next with no distributions to the beneficiaries being required. Apart from their other advantages, such trusts were widely used to avoid liability to *inheritance tax, leading to a series of changes to the law. Most discretionary trusts are now *relevant property trusts for tax purposes; from April 2008 all existing A & M trusts were reclassified as either *18-25 trusts or relevant property trusts, thereby losing their remaining tax advantages. **2.** In the USA, an *investment trust in which the managers can decide what investments to make.

discussion memorandum In the USA, a document published by the *Financial Accounting Standards Board before issuing a *Statement of Financial Accounting Standards. The document specifies the topic under consideration, describes the alternative accounting treatments, and explains the perceived advantages and disadvantages of each treatment.

dishonour 1. To fail to pay a cheque when the account of the drawer does not have sufficient funds to cover it. When a bank dishonours a cheque it marks it 'refer to drawer' and returns it to the payee through his or her bank. **2.** To fail to accept a *bill of exchange (**dishonour by non-acceptance**) or to fail to pay a bill of exchange (**dishonour by non-payment**). **3.** To fail to honour any other financial obligation.

disinflation A fall in the rate of *inflation, especially one that is not accompanied by falls in output and employment. *See* DEFLATION.

disintermediation The elimination of such middlemen as brokers and bankers from financial transactions. Disintermediation has been a consequence of new technology, deregulation, and *globalization. Although it enables both parties to a transaction to save costs on commissions and fees, these savings have to be offset by the increase in the *credit risk.

disinvestment The reducing of investment in an activity, asset, company, or location.

disposals account An account used to record the disposal of a fixed *asset. The original cost (a debit entry), *accumulated depreciation (a credit entry), and the amount received (credit entry) are transferred to the account, the balancing figure being any profit (debit entry) or loss (credit entry) on disposal.

disposal value *See* NET RESIDUAL VALUE.

disproportionate expense and undue delay A reason for excluding an individual subsidiary undertaking from the *consolidated financial statements of a group. It concerns a situation in which there would be a relatively high cost and an excessive time lag in obtaining the information necessary for the preparation of the consolidated accounts. *Financial Reporting Standard 2, Accounting for Subsidiary Undertakings, seeks to narrow this exclusion by stating that disproportionate expense and undue delay cannot justify the exclusion from consolidation of subsidiary undertakings that are individually or collectively material in the context of the group. *See also* EXCLUSION OF SUBSIDIARIES FROM CONSOLIDATION.

dissimilar activities A situation in which the activities of one undertaking in a group are so different from those of the other group undertakings that its inclusion in *consolidated financial statements would be incompatible with the obligation to give a *true and fair view of the activities of the group. This exclusion may not be used merely because some of the undertakings are industrial, some commercial, and some provide services, for example. Nor is exclusion permitted merely because the industrial or commercial activities involve different products or provide different services. *Financial Reporting Standard 2, Accounting for Subsidiary Undertakings, states that it would be unusual for activities to be so different that the exclusion of the subsidiary undertakings would be appropriate. In the unlikely case that it were appropriate to use this exclusion, the excluded subsidiary should be recorded in the consolidated financial statements, using the *equity method of accounting. UK listed companies must now comply with *International Accounting Standard 27, which does not permit any exclusion on these grounds. *See also* EXCLUSION OF SUBSIDIARIES FROM CONSOLIDATION.

dissolution The ending of a business entity, for example the breaking up of a *partnership on the death of one of the partners. In the case of a registered company this may be achieved on the completion of a *liquidation or by the Registrar of Companies striking it off the companies register as 'defunct'. The latter will occur generally because there is reason to believe that the company is no longer carrying on business or it has failed to file accounts. Directors of a company can likewise apply to the Registrar of Companies to have it struck off. The company can be restored to the register on application by petition and payment of the relevant fee.

distress The seizure of goods as security for the performance of an obligation. The two principal situations covered by the remedy of distress are (1) between landlord and tenant when the rent is in arrears; and (2) when goods are unlawfully on an occupier's land and have done or are doing damage.

distributable profits (distributable reserves) The profits of a company that are legally available for distribution as *dividends. They consist of a company's accumulated *realized profits after deducting all realized losses, except for any part of these net realized profits that have been previously distributed or capitalized. *Public limited companies, however, may not distribute profits to such an extent that their net assets are reduced to less than the sum of their *paid-up or *called-up share capital and their *undistributable reserves.

distribution 1. A payment by a company from its *distributable profits, usually by means of a *dividend. 2. (**capital distribution**) A final payment made on the winding up of a company, which may include the repayment of share capital. A capital distribution to an individual is usually subject to capital gains tax, rather than income tax. 3. The division of a person's property and assets according to law, e.g. in cases of bankruptcy or after death. 4. The allocation of goods to consumers by means of wholesalers and retailers.

distribution centre A warehouse, usually owned by a manufacturer, that receives goods in bulk and despatches them to retailers.

distribution channel The network of firms necessary to distribute goods or services from the manufacturers to the consumers; it therefore primarily consists of wholesalers and retailers.

distribution overhead (**distribution cost; distribution expense**) The *cost classification that includes the costs incurred in delivering a product to the customers. Examples include postage, transport, packaging, and insurance.

distribution to owners In the USA, a payment of a *dividend to shareholders (stockholders).

distributor An intermediary, or one of a chain of intermediaries (*see* DISTRIBUTION CHANNEL), that specializes in transferring a manufacturer's goods or services to the consumers.

diversification **1.** Movement by a manufacturer or trader into a wider field of products. This may be achieved by buying firms already serving the target markets or by expanding existing facilities. It is often undertaken to reduce reliance on one market, which may be diminishing (e.g. tobacco), to balance a seasonal market (e.g. ice cream), or to provide scope for general growth. **2.** The spreading of an investment *portfolio over a wide range of companies to avoid serious losses if a recession is localized to one sector of the market.

divestment **1.** The act of realizing the value of an asset by selling or exchanging it. It is the opposite of investment. **2.** The selling of or closing down of one or more of a business's operating activities.

dividend The *distribution of part of the earnings of a company to its shareholders. The dividend is normally expressed as an amount per share on the *par value of the share. Thus a 15% dividend on a £1 share will pay 15p. However, investors are usually more interested in the **dividend yield**, i.e. the dividend expressed as a percentage of the share value; thus if the market value of these £1 shares is now £5, the dividend yield would be $1/5 \times 15\% = 3\%$. The size of the dividend payment is determined by the board of directors of a company, who must decide how much to pay out to shareholders and how much to retain in the business; these amounts may vary from year to year. In the UK it is usual for companies to pay a dividend every six months, the largest portion (the *final dividend) being announced at the company's AGM together with the annual financial results. A smaller *interim dividend usually accompanies the interim statement of the company's affairs, six months before the AGM. Dividends are paid by *dividend warrant in the UK. In the USA dividends are usually paid quarterly by **dividend check**. *See also* DIVIDEND COVER; YIELD.

Interest payments on *gilt-edged securities are also sometimes called dividends although they are fixed.

dividend cover The number of times a company's *dividends to ordinary shareholders could be paid out of its *net profits after tax in the same period. For example, a net dividend of £400,000 paid by a company showing a net profit of £1M is said to be covered 2½ times. Dividend cover is a measure of the probability that dividend payments will be sustained (low cover might make it difficult to pay the same level of dividends in a bad year's trading) and of a company's commitment to investment and growth (high cover implies that the company retains its earnings for investment in the business). Negative dividend cover is unusual, and may be a sign that a company is in difficulties. In the USA, the dividend cover is expressed as the **pay-out ratio**, the total dividends paid as a percentage of the net profit. *See also* PRICE–DIVIDEND RATIO.

dividend-growth model A method for calculating the *cost of capital for a company, using the dividends paid and likely to be paid by the company.

dividend in specie A dividend paid other than in cash.

dividend policy A company's policy on the extent to which *profits should be distributed by way of *dividends to shareholders and on the extent to which profits should be retained in the business.

dividends in arrears Dividends that are due but have not been paid. Dividends in arrears must be disclosed in the notes to the *financial statements of a company. *See* PREFERENCE DIVIDEND.

dividends payable Any *dividends that have been declared by a company but not yet paid. They are shown as an *appropriation in the *profit and loss account and a *current liability in the *balance sheet.

dividend waiver A decision by a major shareholder in a company not to take a dividend, usually because the company cannot afford to pay it.

dividend warrant The cheque issued by a UK company to its shareholders when paying *dividends. It states the tax deducted and the net amount paid. This document must be sent by non-taxpayers to the Inland Revenue when claiming back the tax.

dividend yield *See* DIVIDEND.

division A part of an organization, usually an *investment centre or *profit centre, which, although ultimately responsible to head office, enjoys a degree of autonomy in terms of decisions. Divisions usually operate in clearly defined product, market, or geographical areas, and are formed to facilitate decision making and control in large organizations.

divisional performance measurement The way in which the central management of an organization measures the performance of each of the individual divisions in a divisionalized structure. Methods used include *return on capital employed, *residual income, and profit-to-sales ratio. *See* PERFORMANCE MEASUREMENT.

DJIA Abbreviation for *Dow Jones Industrial Average.

documentary credit *See* LETTER OF CREDIT.

documentary draft Any order in writing requiring the recipient to pay the amount specified on the face of the document, either on presentation of the document (**sight draft**) or at a fixed future date (**time draft**).

dog *See* BOSTON MATRIX.

dollarization The adoption by a country of the US dollar in place of its own currency, usually as a means of controlling inflation and interest-rate volatility. Partial dollarization is said to occur when a country gives the US dollar equal status to its own currency or pegs its currency one-to-one with the dollar.

dollar value LIFO In the USA, a method of expressing the value of an *inventory in monetary values rather than units. Each homogeneous group of inventory items is converted into base-year prices by using the appropriate price indices. The difference between opening and closing inventories is a measure in monetary terms of the change in the accounting period. *See* LAST-IN-FIRST-OUT COST.

domestic corporation A *corporation (company) established in the USA under federal or state law.

domicile (domicil) 1. The country or place of a person's permanent home, which may differ from that person's nationality or place where they are a *resident. Domicile is determined by both the physical fact of residence and the continued intention of remaining there. For example, a citizen of a foreign country who is resident in the UK is not necessarily domiciled there unless there is a clear intention to make the UK a permanent home. In order to prove that the **domicile of origin** has been relinquished in favour of the **domicile of choice**, tangible changes have to be made. Links with the domicile of origin must be severed and active steps taken to become involved with the country that is the domicile of choice, e.g. by making a will under its laws. Under the common law, it is domicile and not residence or nationality that determines a person's civil status. Whether a person is domiciled in the UK may affect their liability to UK taxation (*see* NON-DOMICILED). A corporation may also have a domicile, which is determined by its place of registration. **2.** In banking, an account is said to be domiciled at a particular branch and the customer will usually treat that branch as his or her main banking contact. Computer technology, however, now allows customers to use other branches exactly as if their account was domiciled there.

dominant influence An influence that can be exercised over a company to achieve the operating and financial policies desired by the holder of the influence, notwithstanding the rights or influence of any other party. If one organization exerts such a dominant influence over a company, this company should be treated as a subsidiary of the organization and consolidated into the group accounts of the organization. This principle is made clear in *Financial Reporting Standard 2, Accounting for Subsidiary Undertakings. The relevant *International Accounting Standard is IAS 27.

donated capital In the USA, a gift of an asset to a company. The value is credited to a donated-capital account, which is a stockholders' equity account.

dormant company A company that has had no significant accounting transactions for the accounting period in question. Such a company need not appoint auditors.

double account system A now outdated way of presenting *financial statements, used by railways and public utilities prior to privatization.

double declining balance method A method of *depreciation in which the historical cost (or revalued amount) of an *asset less its estimated residual value (*see* NET RESIDUAL VALUE) is divided by the number of years of its estimated useful life and the resulting amount is multiplied by two to give the depreciation figure. For example, in the first year an asset costing £12,000 with an estimated residual value of £2000 and an estimated useful life of 10 years would have a depreciation charge of £2000, i.e. $2 \times [(£12,000 - £2000)/10]$.

double-entry book-keeping A method of recording the transactions of a business in a set of *accounts, such that every transaction has a dual aspect and therefore needs to be recorded in at least two accounts. For example, when a person (debtor) pays cash to a business for goods he has purchased, the cash held by the business is increased and the amount due from the debtor is decreased by the same amount; similarly, when a purchase is made on credit, the stock is decreased and the amount owing to creditors is increased by the same amount. This double aspect enables the business to be controlled because all the *books of account must balance.

double-entry cost accounting The maintenance of *cost accounting records using the principles of *double-entry book-keeping.

double taxation agreement An agreement made between two countries identifying the relief available to companies or individuals that are subject to tax in both countries. As a result of such agreements several different types of **double taxation relief** are available:
(1) relief by agreement, providing for exemption, in whole or in part, of certain categories of income;
(2) credit agreement, in which tax charged in one country is allowed as a credit in the other;
(3) deduction agreement, in which the overseas income is reduced by the foreign tax paid on it;
(4) if there is no agreement the UK tax authorities will allow the foreign tax paid as a credit up to the amount of the corresponding UK liability.

doubtful debt An amount owed to an organization by a debtor that it might well not receive. A provision for doubtful debts may be created, which may be based on specific debts or on the general assumption that a certain percentage of debtors' amounts are doubtful. As the doubtful debt becomes a *bad debt, it may be written off to the provision for doubtful debts or alternatively charged to the *profit and loss account if there is no provision. *See* PROVISION FOR BAD DEBTS.

Dow Jones Industrial Average (DJIA) An index of *security prices based on 30 companies used on the *New York Stock Exchange. Dow Jones also publishes other indices and the DJIA is now just one of a number of US stock price indices.

( ) SEE WEB LINKS
• Dow Jones Indexes website

downsizing A reduction in the size of an organization, especially by cutting the number of direct employees. The main purpose of downsizing is to improve profitability by reducing costs, although there may also be gains in both focus and flexibility. Apart from the damage to staff morale, the main dangers are that the loss of experienced employees will lead to loss of customers and 'business memory'. *Compare* RIGHTSIZING.

DP Abbreviation for *data processing.

DPB *See* DESIGNATED PROFESSIONAL BODY.

draft 1. *See* BANK DRAFT. 2. Any order in writing to pay a specified sum, e.g. a *bill of exchange. 3. A preliminary version of a document, before it has been finalized.

dragon bond A foreign *bond issued in the Asian bond markets.

drawback The refund of import duty by HM Revenue and Customs when imported goods are re-exported. Payment of the import duty and claiming the drawback can be avoided if the goods are stored in a bonded warehouse immediately after unloading from the incoming ship or aircraft until re-export.

drawdown The drawing of funds against a bank loan or other credit facility.

drawee 1. The person on whom a *bill of exchange is drawn (i.e. to whom it is addressed). The drawee will accept it and pay it on maturity. 2. The bank on whom a cheque is drawn, i.e. the bank holding the account of the individual or company that wrote it. 3. The bank named in a *bank draft. *Compare* DRAWER.

drawer 1. A person who signs a *bill of exchange ordering the *drawee to pay the specified sum at the specified time. 2. A person who signs a cheque ordering the drawee bank to pay a specified sum of money on demand.

drawings *Assets (cash or goods) withdrawn from an unincorporated business by its owner. If a business is incorporated, drawings are usually in the form of *dividends or *scrip dividends. Drawings are shown in a **drawings account**, which is used, for example, by the partners in a *partnership.

drop lock A bond initially issued with a variable rate of interest that becomes a fixed-rate bond if the index or rate falls below a predetermined trigger level.

DSS Abbreviation for *decision support system.

dual aspect The principle that every financial event has an aspect that gives rise to a *debit entry and an aspect that gives rise to a *credit entry.

dual-capacity system A system of trading on a stock exchange in which the functions of *stockbroker and stockjobber are carried out by separate firms. In a **single-capacity system** the two functions can be combined by firms known as *market makers. Dual capacity existed on the *London Stock Exchange prior to October 1986 (*see* BIG BANG), when a single-capacity system was introduced.

duality A principle of UK income tax and corporation tax under which expenditure is not deductible in computing the profits subject to tax if the expenditure has a dual purpose. A deduction in computing trading profits is therefore denied for any expense not incurred wholly and exclusively for the purposes of the trade. The duality principle refuses relief by apportionment of a payment but permits relief where a wholly business expenditure can be identified by dissection of a payment.

dual-rate transfer prices *Transfer prices that are set at different levels for the supplying and receiving divisions of an organization. The dual prices method charges a low price, say a price based on the *marginal cost, to the buying division, while at the same time crediting a high price, say a price based on *full cost pricing, to the selling division. The idea is that this will encourage a buying division to buy within the organization without penalizing the selling division. However, this is only likely to be beneficial to the organization as a whole if the selling division has sufficient spare capacity to supply the buying division's needs. A compensating entry to eliminate unrealized profits is required in the books of the head office when *consolidation of the divisional results takes place. Managers rarely use this method in practice as it can easily lead to confusion.

due diligence **1.** An analysis, normally conducted by an independent accountant, of the current financial position and future prospects of a company prior to a *stock exchange flotation or a major investment of capital. **2.** An internal analysis by a lender, such as a bank, of existing debts owed by a borrower in order to identify or re-evaluate the risks involved.

Du Pont formula A formula for breaking down return on investment into two parts: margin and turnover (*see* RETURN ON CAPITAL EMPLOYED). The return on investment = net income/invested capital. This can be restated as:

(net income/sales) × (sales/invested capital),

i.e. margin × turnover.

duration The average life of the discounted values of the cash flows associated with a *bond.

duration driver A measure of the amount of time required to perform an *activity when this is a significant *cost driver. Duration drivers provide a more accurate basis for allocating costs than the number of transactions when there is a significant variation in the time required to complete an activity. For example, if all deliveries are completed in 10 minutes then it is simple (and accurate) to use the number of deliveries as a cost driver. If one delivery requires 10 minutes and another two hours, then using time for deliveries as the cost driver will improve the accuracy of the costing system. However, duration drivers are often seen as more expensive to measure and record than transaction drivers.

early repayment tax clause A clause in a loan agreement that allows the loan to be repaid if changes occur to any relevant tax legislation that would have the effect of increasing the amount of interest payable.

earned income For tax purposes, the following types of income are treated as earned income:
• income from employment;
• income from trades, professions, and vocations;
• foreign business profits;
• patent and copyright income received by the creator;
• a proportion of the annuity paid to a retired partner.
There is now little difference in the tax treatment of earned and *unearned income under the UK taxation system.

earnings The net income or *profit of a business. Because of the importance of earnings in calculating the *earnings per share, there has been considerable debate as to its definition. Under *Statement of Standard Accounting Practice (SSAP) 6, earnings excluded *extraordinary items; this permitted some companies to use *creative accounting to ensure that they reported a high earnings figure. The introduction of *Financial Reporting Standard 3 removed SSAP 6 and amended SSAP 3, also concerned with earnings, so that any extraordinary items are now included in the calculation. This has led to a greater volatility in the earnings per share figure. The relevant *International Accounting Standard is IAS 33.

earnings available for ordinary shareholders The *profit of a company that is available for distribution in the form of a *dividend to the holders of ordinary shares.

earnings before interest and tax *See* EBIT; EBITDA.

earnings per share (eps) The *profit in pence attributable to each *ordinary share in a company, based on the *consolidated profit for the period, after deducting *minority interests and *preference share dividends. This profit figure is divided by the weighted average number of equity shares in issue during the period. The eps may be calculated on a **net basis** or a **nil basis**. Using the net basis, the tax charge includes any variable elements of tax, such as unrelieved overseas tax arising from the payment or proposed payment of dividends (*see* OVERSEAS-INCOME TAXATION). The nil basis excludes such items from the tax charge. The eps should be shown on the face of the *profit and loss account, both for the period under review and for the corresponding previous period. The basis of calculating the earnings per share should be disclosed on the face of the profit and loss account or in the notes to the accounts.
  Earnings per share was seen as an important measure of performance in the 1950s and 1960s but its significance has since declined. In recent years the UK and international standard setters have worked together to agree a common

approach to eps. This resulted in the issuing of a revised *International Accounting Standard 33, Earnings Per Share, and *Financial Reporting Standard (FRS) 22, Earnings Per Share, in 2004. These require the disclosure of both basic eps and *fully diluted earnings per share on the profit and loss account. *See also* BOTTOM LINE; HEADLINE EARNINGS PER SHARE.

earnings retained *See* RETAINED EARNINGS.

earnings yield The ratio of the *earnings per share of a company to the market price of the share, expressed as a percentage. *See also* PRICE–EARNINGS RATIO.

earn-out agreement (contingent contract) An agreement to purchase a company in which the purchaser pays a lump sum at the time of the acquisition, with a promise to pay more (a *contingent consideration) if certain criteria, usually specified earnings levels, are met for a specified number of years. This method of acquisition has been popular in 'people' businesses, in particular advertising agencies.

e-banking *See* HOME BANKING.

EBIT Abbreviation for earnings before interest and tax, the *profit of a company as shown on the *profit and loss account, before deducting the variables of interest and tax. This figure, which is used in calculating many ratios, enables better comparisons to be made with other companies.

EBITDA Abbreviation for earnings before interest, taxation, depreciation, and amortization. This figure is frequently cited by investment analysts since it represents a *cash-flow vision of shareholders' return.

e-business A company that engages in *e-commerce.

ECB Abbreviation for *European Central Bank.

ECGD Abbreviation for *Export Credits Guarantee Department.

e-commerce The use of the *Internet to buy and sell goods and services. At the simplest level, a company will probably have a website that provides details of products and contacts.

Economic and Monetary Union See feature EUROPEAN ECONOMIC AND MONETARY UNION on p. 175.

economic appraisal A method of *capital budgeting that makes use of *discounted cash flow techniques to determine a preferred investment. However, instead of using annual projected cash flows in the analysis, the technique discounts over the project's life the expected annual *economic costs and *economic benefits. It is mainly used in the assessment of governmental or quasi-governmental projects, such as road, railway, and port developments.

economic batch quantity A refinement of the *economic order quantity to take into account circumstances in which the goods are produced in batches. The formula is:

$$Q = [2cdr/h(r-d)]^{\frac{1}{2}},$$

where Q is the quantity to be purchased or manufactured, c is the cost of processing an order for delivery, d is the demand in the period for that stock item, h is the cost of holding a unit of stock, and r is the rate of production.

economic benefits The projected benefits revealed by an *economic appraisal. Economic benefits are usually gains that can be expressed in financial terms as the result of an improvement in facilities provided by a government, local authority, etc. For example, the economic benefits arising from the construction of a new or improved road might include lower vehicle operating costs, time savings for the road users, and lower accident costs as a result of fewer accidents. In each case the savings would be in economic terms, that is, excluding the effect of taxes and subsidies within the economy. *See* ECONOMIC COSTS.

economic costs The projected costs revealed by an *economic appraisal. Economic costs differ from financial costs in that they exclude the transfer payments within the economy, which arise when an investment is made. In the construction of a road, for example, the economic costs exclude taxes and import duties on the materials and plant used in its construction, while any subsidies made are added back to the costs. *See* ECONOMIC BENEFITS.

economic exposure 1. The possible impact on the value of a business of macroeconomic variables. **2.** The exposure of a business selling goods abroad or buying goods from abroad to the risks resulting from changes in exchange rates. *See* EXCHANGE-RATE EXPOSURE.

economic income Income calculated by comparing the *net present value of future *cash flows at the beginning and end of a period.

economic order quantity (EOQ) A decision model, based on differential calculus, that determines the optimum order size for purchasing (sometimes called the **economic purchase quantity**) or manufacturing (**economic manufacturing quantity**) an item of stock. The optimum order quantity is that which equates the total ordering and total holding costs. The formula used is:

$Q = \sqrt{(2cd/h)}$,

where Q is the quantity to be purchased or manufactured, c is the cost of processing an order for delivery, d is the demand in the period for that stock item, and h is the cost of holding a unit of stock. *See also* ECONOMIC BATCH QUANTITY.

economic value The *present value of expected future *cash flows. For example, the economic value of a *fixed asset would be the present value of any future revenues it is expected to generate, less the present value of any future costs related to it.

Economic Value Added (EVA) A performance measure used to evaluate a company's **economic profit** (i.e., the value added to a company by its activities in a given time period). It is the calculation of a company's net *operating profit after taxes, minus a *cost of capital charge for the investment or capital employed in the business. The Stern Stewart consulting organization registered EVA as a tradename in the 1990s.

economies of scale (scale effect) Reductions in the average cost of production, and hence in the unit costs, when output is increased. If the average costs of production rise with output, this is known as **diseconomies of scale**. Economies of scale can enable a producer to offer his product at more competitive prices and thus to capture a larger share of the market. **Internal economies of scale** occur when better use is made of the factors of production and by using the increased output to pay for a higher proportion of the costs of marketing, financing, and development, etc. Internal diseconomies can occur when a plant exceeds its optimum size, e.g. requiring a disproportionate unwieldy administrative staff. **External economies** and diseconomies arise from the effects of a firm's expansion on market conditions and on technological advance.

economies of scope *See* SCOPE ECONOMIES.

ECP Abbreviation for *euro-commercial paper.

ECU Abbreviation for *European Currency Unit.

EDI Abbreviation for *electronic data interchange.

EDX London An exchange for equity derivatives established in 2003 by the *London Stock Exchange. It uses technology supplied by the *OMX group and took over the markets of the London Securities and Derivatives Exchange (OMLX). EDX is a *Recognized Investment Exchange.

effective annual rate The total interest paid or earned in a year expressed as a percentage of the principal amount at the beginning of the year.

effective interest method A method for accounting for *bond premiums or discounts. The interest expense is calculated by multiplying the *carrying amount of the bond at the beginning of an *accounting period by the effective interest rate. This is the real rate of interest on a loan calculated by dividing the nominal interest by the proceeds of the loan.

effective units *See* EQUIVALENT UNITS.

effective yield *See* GROSS REDEMPTION YIELD.

efficiency A measure of the ability of an organization to produce and distribute its product. In accounting terms it is quantified by a comparison of the *standard hours allowed for a given level of production and the actual hours taken. This represents the gain or loss due to efficiency, which is usually expressed as a *direct labour efficiency variance or *overhead efficiency variance. *See also* EFFICIENCY RATIO.

efficiency ratio A ratio that measures the efficiency of labour or an activity over a period by dividing the *standard hours allowed for the production by the actual hours taken. It is usually expressed as a percentage, using the formula:

(standard hours allowed × 100)/actual hours worked.

efficiency variances *See* DIRECT LABOUR EFFICIENCY VARIANCE; OVERHEAD EFFICIENCY VARIANCE.

efficient markets hypothesis A theory holding that transactors in financial markets cannot make abnormal returns on the basis of exploiting information, since market prices incorporate all available information. The economist Eugene Fama has defined three categories of market efficiency: **weak-form**

efficiency, in which only historical information is incorporated into the market prices; **semi-strong-form efficiency**, in which all publicly available information, past or present, is incorporated; and **strong-form efficiency**, in which all public or private information is incorporated.

EFRAG Abbreviation for *European Financial Reporting Advisory Group.

EFTPOS Abbreviation for *electronic funds transfer at point of sale.

18–25 trust A *trust established for the benefit of a young person, who becomes absolutely entitled to the trust property on or before his or her 25th birthday. An 18-25 trust can now only be created by the will of the young person's parent or step-parent (until April 2008 it could also be created by converting an existing accumulation and maintenance trust; *see* DISCRETIONARY TRUST). The trust is charged to *inheritance tax (i) on settlement; (ii) when any distribution is made to the beneficiary, he or she being over 18 years old; and (iii) when the beneficiary becomes absolutely entitled, he or she being over 18 years old.

Eighth Company Law Directive An EU directive (1984) concerning the role and regulation of auditors. Its provisions were incorporated into UK law in the Companies Act 1989. In 2006 it was superseded by a revised and expanded version, the *Statutory Audit Directive.

EIS Abbreviation for *Enterprise Investment Scheme.

EITF Abbreviation for *Emerging Issues Task Force.

election to waive exemption *See* OPTION TO TAX.

elective resolution Formerly, a decision by all the members of a *private limited company to dispense with certain provisions of the Companies Act 1985, for example the holding of an *annual general meeting. The requirement for such a resolution was abolished by the Companies Act 2006.

electronic banking *See* HOME BANKING.

electronic data interchange (EDI) The use of electronic data-transmission networks to move information. For example, EDI can be used for orders, invoices, and payments to suppliers, customers, banks, etc., without recourse to hard copy. EDI is dependent on users having compatible technology and systems that are transparent to the other members of the network.

electronic funds transfer at point of sale (EFTPOS) The automatic debiting of a purchase price from the customer's bank or credit-card account by a computer link between the checkout till and the bank or credit-card company. The system can only work when the customer has a *debit card or *credit card recognized by the retailer. In the now dominant **chip and pin** system the transaction is ratified by use of the customer's *personal identification number (PIN), rather than by signature of a printed voucher.

electronic mail *See* E-MAIL.

electronic transfer of funds (ETF) The transfer of money from one bank account to another by means of computers and communications links. Banks routinely transfer funds between accounts using computers; ETF is also used in *home banking services. *See also* ELECTRONIC FUNDS TRANSFER AT POINT OF SALE.

elements of cost In a production process, the three primary cost elements of material, labour, and expenses. *See* COST CLASSIFICATION.

eligible paper 1. Treasury bills, short-dated gilts, and any first-class security, accepted by a British bank or an accepting house and thus acceptable by the Bank of England for rediscounting, or as security for loans to discount houses. The Bank of England's classification of eligible paper influences portfolios because of the ability to turn them into quick cash, and thus reinforces the Bank's role as lender of last resort. 2. Acceptances by US banks available for rediscounting by the Federal Reserve System.

e-mail (electronic mail) Software that enables messages (e.g. letters, memos, documents) between individuals or from individuals to groups to be exchanged by computer. Its operation can be restricted to a *local area network or it can be open to a wide area network, such as the *Internet, by means of telephone lines. Messages are held in a **mailbox**, access to which is usually controlled by a user identification and password. Some systems now support the composition and delivery of **multimedia mail**, which can combine text, graphics, voice, fax, and other forms of information in a single message.

embedded audit facility A *computer-assisted audit technique in which the program and additional data are provided by the auditor and incorporated into the computerized accounting system of the client. This facility enables a continuous review of a client's computerized accounting system to be made. The two most common types of embedded audit facility are an *integrated test facility and the use of a *systems control and review file.

emergency tax code An income tax code issued by the Inland Revenue in the event of an employee not having the correct code available for the employer to apply to earnings under pay as you earn. The code gives the basic *personal allowance, but does not allow for any further allowance. This code is used until the correct code has been notified to the employer by HM Revenue.

Emerging Issues Task Force (EITF) In the USA, the body responsible to the *Financial Accounting Standards Board for suggesting appropriate treatment for new accounting problems and practices, without the delays involved in issuing a *Statement of Financial Accounting Standards. The comparable body in the UK is the *Urgent Issues Task Force.

EMIs Abbreviation for *Enterprise Management Incentives.

emoluments Amounts received from an office or employment including all salaries, fees, wages, perquisites, and other profits as well as certain expenses and benefits paid or provided by the employer, which are deemed to be emoluments. They are subject to *income tax. *See also* DIRECTORS REMUNERATION.

emphasis of matter An optional paragraph in an auditor's report referred to by the *Auditing Practices Committee in their standard 'The Audit Report' issued in April 1980. This paragraph was to be used if the auditor considered that information was adequately disclosed in the *financial statements but that the reader's attention should be drawn to important matters in these statements to ensure that they were not overlooked. The use of such a paragraph was intended to be rare. In May 1993 the *Auditing Practices Board issued a new *Statement of

Auditing Standards, Auditors' Reports on Financial Statements, which does not include the option of an emphasis-of-matter paragraph.

employee empowerment The practice of giving employees more responsibility and autonomy in decision making. This can lead to better decision making as well as to higher levels of training, motivation, and productivity among employees.

employee report A simplified version of the statutory annual report and accounts of a company prepared for the employees of the company (*see* ANNUAL ACCOUNTS). Although this is a voluntary practice, such documents should comply with the provisions of the Companies Act relating to *non-statutory accounts. Employee reports were particularly popular in the 1930s and the 1970s.

employee share ownership plan (ESOP) A method of providing the employees of a company with shares in the company. The ESOP buys shares in its sponsoring company, usually with assistance from the company concerned. The shares are then allocated to the employees, often on the basis of relative pay but sometimes more equally. The advantage claimed for ESOPs is that they do not require dilution of the sponsoring company's share capital by the creation of new shares. In the USA they are known as **employee stock option plans**. *See also* EMPLOYEE SHARE OWNERSHIP TRUST; SHARE INCENTIVE SCHEME; SHARE OPTION.

employee share ownership trust (ESOT) A trust set up by a UK company, under the provisions introduced in 1989, to acquire shares in the company and distribute them to the employees. The company's payments to the trust are tax-deductible. The trust deed sets out the specified period of employment and all those employees who fulfil the requirements must be included in the class of beneficiaries of the trust. *See also* EMPLOYEE SHARE OWNERSHIP PLAN; SHARE INCENTIVE PLAN; SHARE INCENTIVE SCHEME.

employment costs The expenditure incurred in employing personnel. It includes salaries, wages, bonuses, incentive payments, employer's National Insurance contributions, and employer's pension scheme contributions.

EMS Abbreviation for European Monetary System. See feature EUROPEAN ECONOMIC AND MONETARY UNION on p. 175.

EMV Abbreviation for *expected monetary value.

encryption The encoding of electronic data so that it can be transmitted without interception. With the growing use of the *Internet for commercial purposes, there has been an ongoing need for secure encryption methods, notably in the transmission of credit card details.

ending inventory In the USA, the stock held at the end of a financial period. It appears on the *profit and loss account in the calculation of *cost of sales and on the *balance sheet.

end-of-day sweep An automatic transfer of funds from one bank account held by a company to another of its bank accounts, usually one that pays interest on deposits. The sweep takes place at the end of every day, or at the end of the day when certain conditions are met.

endorsement (indorsement) **1.** A signature on the back of a *bill of exchange or cheque, making it payable to the person who signed it. A bill can be endorsed any number of times, the presumption being that the endorsements were made in the order in which they appear, the last named being the holder to receive payment. If the bill is **blank endorsed**, i.e. no endorsee is named, it is payable to the bearer. In the case of a **restrictive endorsement** of the form 'Pay X only', it ceases to be a *negotiable instrument. A **special endorsement**, when the endorsee is specified, becomes payable **to order**, which is short for 'in obedience to the order of'. **2.** A signature required on a document to make it valid in law. **3.** An amendment to an insurance policy or cover note, recording a change in the conditions of the insurance.

energy cost The expenditure on all the sources of energy required by an organization; these can include electricity, gas, solid fuels, oil, and steam.

engagement letter (letter of engagement) A letter used by an auditor to define clearly the scope of the auditors' responsibilities in an engagement. It provides written confirmation of the auditors' acceptance of the appointment, the scope of the audit, the form of the report, and details of any non-audit services to be provided. It is usual to discuss the contents of the letter with the management of the business to be audited before sending it.

engineered costs The building up of the levels of costs likely to be incurred by a production process by means of constructing synthetic costs, based on a logical consideration of the make-up of each cost item. For example, the expected labour cost for a particular product may be obtained by using time studies to determine the labour times likely to be required and multiplying the result by the expected rates of pay. The method is used for *standard costing, budgeting, and planning purposes in which estimated unit costs are likely to be required before production takes place.

enrolled agents In the USA, agents recognized by the Treasury Department for representing the taxpayer when dealing with the *Internal Revenue Service.

enterprise fund In the USA, an organization, such as a government-owned utility, that provides goods or services to the public for a fee that makes the organization self-supporting.

Enterprise Investment Scheme (EIS) An investment scheme in the UK that replaced the Business Expansion Scheme (BES) on 1 January 1994. Its purpose is to help certain types of small higher-risk unlisted trading companies to raise capital. Individuals who invest between £500 and £500,000 in eligible shares are entitled to a tax relief of 20% of the amount subscribed. Gains on the sales of shares issued under the scheme are exempt from capital gains tax. *See also* CORPORATE VENTURING SCHEME; VENTURE CAPITAL TRUST.

(⊕) SEE WEB LINKS
• A guide to the EIS from the Gov.uk website

Enterprise Management Incentives (EMIs) An approved *share option scheme designed to help small high-risk unlisted companies attract and retain employees. Under the scheme, an employee of a qualifying company (broadly, an independent trading company with gross assets of no more than £30M) may receive share options of a value up to £100,000 free of tax.

entity *See* ACCOUNTING ENTITY.

entity view The view of an *accounting entity that emphasizes the importance of the business or the organization and its separateness from its owners. It is based on the *accounting equation, in which the sum of the assets is equal to the claims on these assets by owners and others. *Compare* PROPRIETARY VIEW; RESIDUAL EQUITY THEORY.

entrepreneurs' relief A *capital gains tax relief introduced from 6 April 2008, when it replaced *taper relief and *indexation allowance. Under the new relief, gains arising from the disposal of *business assets are taxed as if reduced by $4/9$ths this means the gain is charged at an effective rate of 10%, rather than the standard rate of 18%. The relief can be claimed more than once, up to a lifetime total of £1M of gains qualifying for relief.

entry A record made in a book of account, register, or computer file of a financial transaction, event, proceeding, etc. *See also* DOUBLE-ENTRY BOOK-KEEPING.

entry value The current *replacement cost of an asset. This value may be used in *current-value accounting. *Compare* EXIT VALUE.

environmental accounting *See* GREEN REPORTING; SOCIAL RESPONSIBILITY REPORTING.

environmental audit (green audit) An *audit of the impact of the activities of an organization on the environment. Its purpose is usually to ensure that the organization has clear environmental policies, that its operations comply with the stated environmental policies, and that its policies are subject to regular review. Environmental audits may be conducted internally or externally by environmental consultants. *See also* GREEN REPORTING; SOCIAL AUDIT; SOCIAL RESPONSIBILITY REPORTING.

environmental costs The *costs of making sure that a company's activities do not damage the environment or that any such damage is put right. There are many types of environmental costs and these are often difficult to identify as they are hidden in *overheads. Measuring environmental costs is now an important issue for many companies, as national regulations become more stringent and penalties or fines more severe. It is useful to classify environmental costs into four categories:

- **environmental appraisal costs**. These are the costs of activities performed to monitor environmental effects that a firm is responsible for. Examples include the costs arising from inspection of products and contamination testing.
- **environmental prevention costs**. These are the costs of activities performed to prevent the production of waste that could cause damage to the environment. Examples include the costs of recycling products, training staff, and carrying out environmental studies.
- **environmental internal failure costs**. These are the costs of activities that have to be performed when contaminants and waste have been produced by a company but not discharged into the environment. Examples include treating toxic waste and maintaining pollution equipment.
- **environmental external failure costs**. These are the costs incurred by a company if it discharges waste into the environment. Examples include the

costs of cleaning up oil spills or cleaning a polluted river. A company may also incur fines or other penalties or lose sales if it acquires a poor environmental reputation.

See also COST OF QUALITY.

EONIA Acronym for Euro Overnight Index Average, the overnight *reference rate for the eurozone *interbank market, as computed by the European Central Bank. *Compare* EURONIA. *See also* EURO INTER BANK OFFERED RATE.

EOQ Abbreviation for *economic order quantity.

eps Abbreviation for *earnings per share.

equal-instalment depreciation *See* STRAIGHT-LINE METHOD.

equipment trust certificate In the USA, a document setting out the details of a loan used to fund the purchase of equipment. The holder of the certificate has a secured interest in the asset in the event of a corporate default.

equitable apportionment The process of sharing common costs between *cost centres in a fair manner, using a *basis of apportionment that reflects the way in which the costs are incurred by the cost centres.

equity **1.** A beneficial interest in an asset. For example, a person having a house worth £250,000 with a mortgage of £100,000 may be said to have an equity of £150,000 in the house. *See also* NEGATIVE EQUITY. **2.** The amount of money returned to a borrower in a mortgage or hire-purchase agreement, after the sale of the specified asset and the full repayment of the lender of the money. **3.** The net assets of a company after all creditors (including the holders of *preference shares) have been paid off. **4.** The ordinary share capital of a company. **5.** The market value of a company's issued *ordinary shares.

equity accounting The practice of showing in a company's accounts a share of the undistributed profits and a share of the net assets of another company in which it holds a share of the *equity. *See* EQUITY METHOD; GROSS EQUITY METHOD.

equity dilution A reduction in the percentage of the *equity owned by a shareholder as a result of a new issue of shares in the company, which rank equally with the existing voting shares.

equity dividend cover A ratio that shows how many times the *dividend to ordinary shareholders can be paid out of the profits of a company available for distribution. The higher the cover, the greater the certainty that dividends will be paid in the future.

equity finance Finance raised from shareholders in the form of *ordinary shares and reserves, as opposed to *non-equity shares and to *debt finance.

equity gearing *See* GEARING.

equity instrument Any instrument, including a *non-equity share, *warrant, or *option, that provides evidence of an ownership interest in an entity.

equity method A method of accounting for *associated undertakings in which the investor initially discloses in its financial statements the amount of the investment at its cost, identifying any *goodwill arising. In subsequent periods the *carrying amount is adjusted by:

(1) the investor's share of the results of the associate, less any goodwill, *amortization, or write off;

(2) the investor's share of any relevant gains or losses and any other changes in the investee's *net assets.

The share of the associates' results is included immediately after the group operating profit in the consolidated profit and loss account. This method is required by *Financial Reporting Standard 9. The relevant *International Accounting Standard is IAS 28, Investments in Associates. *See also* GROSS EQUITY METHOD.

equity share　Any *share in a company, other than a *non-equity share.

equity share capital　The *share capital of a company that consists of its equity shares as opposed to any *non-equity shares.

equivalent units (effective units)　Unfinished units of production that remain in a process at the end of a period as *work in progress (or process). Degrees of completion are assigned to each cost classification, which, when applied to the number of units in work in progress, give an equivalent number of completed units. The equivalent units have an impact on the valuation of opening and closing work in progress.

EXAMPLE

A company has 3000 units of work in progress: expenditure on direct materials is 100% complete but expenditure on direct labour and overheads is judged to be only 50% complete. The equivalent units are given in the table.

equivalent units	cost classification	work in progress (units)	degrees of completion (%)
3000	direct materials	3000	100
1500	direct labour	3000	50
1500	overheads	3000	50

ERM　Abbreviation for Exchange Rate Mechanism. See feature EUROPEAN ECONOMIC AND MONETARY UNION on p. 175.

error or mistake　A claim by the taxpayer that there has been an overpayment of tax. A formal claim has to be made within six years against the over-assessment to income tax or capital gains tax resulting from an error or mistake in, or omission from, any return or statement.

ESOP　Abbreviation for *employee share ownership plan (or, in the USA, employee stock option plan).

ESOT　Abbreviation for *employee share ownership trust.

estate duty　*See* INHERITANCE TAX.

estimated assessment　A *tax assessment raised by HM Revenue based on the estimated profits or income of a taxpayer. The level of profits from the assessment of the previous period is often used as a rough indication of the expected profits for the assessment under consideration. The taxpayer has 30 days to appeal against the assessment. An estimated assessment will be revised once the actual profits or income for the *fiscal year in question are known. Under *self-assessment, estimated assessments are not normally raised.

ETF Abbreviation for *electronic transfer of funds.

ethical investment (socially responsible investment) An investment made in a company not engaged in an activity that the investor considers to be unethical, such as armaments or tobacco, or an investment in a company of which the investor approves on ethical grounds, e.g. one having a good environmental or employment record.

Euribor Acronym for *Euro Inter Bank Offered Rate.

euro The currency unit of the European Union's *eurozone, divided into 100 cents. In January 1999 it was adopted for all purposes except cash transactions by Austria, Belgium, Finland, France, Germany, Ireland, Italy, Luxembourg, The Netherlands, Portugal, and Spain; Greece followed suit in 2001. Euro-denominated notes and coins were issued in January 2002 and the national currencies were withdrawn after a short period of dual circulation. Slovenia adopted the euro in 2007, as did Cyprus and Malta on 1 January 2008. The euro is also legal tender in Andorra, French Guiana, Guadeloupe, Kosovo, Madeira, Martinique, Mayotte, Monaco, Montenegro, Réunion, San Marino, and the Vatican City. See feature EUROPEAN ECONOMIC AND MONETARY UNION on p. 175.

Eurobanks Financial intermediaries that deal in the *eurocurrency market.

eurobond A *bond issued in a *eurocurrency. The eurobond market is now one of the largest markets for raising money (it is much larger than the UK stock exchange). The reason for this popularity is that *secondary market investors can remain anonymous, usually for the purpose of avoiding tax. For this reason it is difficult to ascertain the exact size and scope of operation of the market. Issues of new eurobonds normally take place in London, largely through syndicates of US and Japanese investment banks; they are *bearer securities, unlike the shares registered in most stock exchanges, and interest payments are free of any *withholding taxes. There are various kinds of eurobonds. An ordinary bond, called a **straight**, is a fixed-interest loan of 3 to 8 years duration; others include **floating-rate notes**, which carry a variable interest rate based on the *London Inter Bank Offered Rate; and **perpetuals**, which are never redeemed. Some carry *warrants and some are *convertible. Eurobonds in British pounds are referred to as **eurosterling bonds**.

Euroclear A pan-European provider of clearing, settlement, and related services for bond, equity, and investment-fund transactions. Based in Brussels, it was set up in 1968 by the US bank J. P. Morgan. With *Clearstream, it is one of the two main clearing systems for *eurobonds. *See also* CREST.

euro-commercial paper (ECP) *Commercial paper issued in a *eurocurrency, the market for which is centred in London. It provides a quick way of obtaining same-day funds by the issue of unsecured notes, for example in Europe for use in New York.

eurocurrency A foreign currency deposit at a bank located outside the country where the currency is issued as a legal tender. For example, dollars deposited in a bank in Switzerland are *eurodollars, yen deposited at a US bank are **euroyen**, etc. The deposit need not be held at a European bank in Europe. Eurocurrency is used for lending and borrowing; the **eurocurrency market** often provides a cheap and convenient form of liquidity for the financing of international trade and investment. The main borrowers and lenders are the commercial banks, large companies, and the central banks. By raising funds in eurocurrencies it is possible to secure more favourable terms and rates of interest, and sometimes to avoid domestic regulations and taxation. The deposits and loans were initially on a short-term basis but increasing use is being made of medium-term and long-term loans, particularly through the raising of *eurobonds. This has to some extent replaced the syndicated loan market, in which banks lent money as a group in order to share the risk.

eurodollars Dollars deposited in financial institutions outside the USA. The eurodollar market evolved in London in the late 1950s when the growing demand for dollars to finance international trade and investment coincided with a greater supply of dollars. The prefix 'euro' indicates the origin of the practice but it now refers to all dollar deposits made anywhere outside the USA. *See also* EUROCURRENCY.

Eurofirst 300 Index See feature THE FTSE INDEXES on p. 175.

Euro Inter Bank Offered Rate (Euribor) The rate of interest charged on interbank loans within the eurozone. *See* INTERBANK MARKET. *See also* EONIA; EURONIA.

euromarket 1. A market that emerged in the 1950s for financing international trade. Its principal participants are *commercial banks, large companies, the European Central Bank, and the central banks of member states of the EU. Its main business is in *eurobonds, *euro-commercial paper, *euronotes, and euroequities issued in *eurocurrencies. The largest euromarket is in London, but there are smaller ones in Paris, Brussels, and Frankfurt. **2.** The European Union, regarded as one large market for goods.

Euronext.liffe *See* LIFFE. *See also* EURONEXT NV.

Euronext NV A market and clearing system for equities and traded derivatives, established in September 2000 with the merger of the Amsterdam, Brussels, and Paris stock exchanges. It acquired the London futures exchange *LIFFE (now Euronext.liffe) in 2001 and the Lisbon Stock Exchange (now Euronext Lisbon) in 2002. A merger with NYSE Group, the owner of the *New York Stock Exchange, was approved in December 2006, leading to the creation of **NYSE Euronext** – the world's first global stock market.

(⊕) SEE WEB LINKS
• NYSE Euronext website

EURONIA Acronym for Euro Overnight Index Average, a *reference rate computed as a weighted average of euro overnight funding rates in the London interbank market. *Compare* EONIA; SONIA. *See* OVERNIGHT RATE.

euronote A form of *euro-commercial paper consisting of short-term negotiable *bearer notes. They may be in any currency but are usually in dollars or euros. The **euronote facility** is a form of *note issuance facility set up by a syndicate of banks, which underwrites the notes.

European Central Bank (ECB) The central bank of the European Union, which was established in 1998 and became fully operational on 1 January 1999. From that date it superseded the European Monetary Institute and the European Monetary Cooperation Fund. It is responsible for *eurozone monetary policy and in particular the setting of interest rates. It is independent of national governments but works with the central banks of the individual eurozone countries through the **European System of Central Banks** (**ESCB**). It is based in Frankfurt-am-Main, Germany. See feature EUROPEAN ECONOMIC AND MONETARY UNION on p. 175.

(((⊕))) SEE WEB LINKS
• Website of the ECB

European Court of Auditors The EU institution responsible for auditing all revenue and spending by the European Communities or any body set up by the Communities. Its mission is to promote sound financial management while ensuring openness and accountability in the Communities' use of public funds.

European Currency Unit (ECU) A former currency medium and unit of account created in 1979 to act as the reserve asset and accounting unit of the European Monetary System (EMS). The value of the ECU was calculated as a weighted average of a basket of specified amounts of European Union currencies. Fluctuations in the value of the ECU in terms of the currencies of the member states were controlled by the EMS. The ECU also acted as the unit of account for all EU transactions. ECU reserves were not allocated to individual countries but held in the European Monetary Cooperation Fund. With the introduction of the *euro in January 1999 the ECU ceased to exist. The initial value of the euro against other currencies was set at one ECU. See feature EUROPEAN ECONOMIC AND MONETARY UNION on p. 175

European Economic and Monetary Union (EMU) The EU policy that culminated in the creation of the *European Central Bank (1999) and a single European currency for participating states. See feature ECONOMIC AND MONETARY UNION on p. 175.

European Financial Reporting Advisory Group (EFRAG) A group set up in 2001 to advise the European Commission on the use of *International Accounting Standards within the EU. It coordinates the views of preparers and users of financial statements as well as accounting professionals and represents these to both the Commission and the *International Accounting Standards Board.

European Monetary System (EMS) The former system of exchange-rate stabilization involving the countries of the European Union. See feature EUROPEAN ECONOMIC AND MONETARY UNION on p. 175.

European option An *option that can only be exercised on its expiry date. *Compare* AMERICAN OPTION.

European System of Central Banks *See* EUROPEAN CENTRAL BANK.

Eurosox *See* COMPANY REPORTING DIRECTIVE; STATUTORY AUDIT DIRECTIVE.

EUROPEAN ECONOMIC AND MONETARY UNION

Monetary cooperation between the member states of the European Union began in 1979, with the establishment of the **European Monetary System** (**EMS**), a system of exchange-rate stabilization.

The EMS consisted of two main elements: the **Exchange Rate Mechanism** (**ERM**), under which participating countries committed themselves to maintaining the values of their currencies within agreed limits, and a *balance of payments support mechanism, organized through the European Monetary Cooperation Fund. The ERM operated by giving each currency a value in *European Currency Units (ECUs) and drawing up a parity grid giving exchange values in ECUs for each pair of currencies. If market rates differed from the agreed parity by more than a permitted percentage (2.25% or 6% depending on the currency), the relevant governments were required to take action to correct the disparity.

The EMS suffered a major crisis in September 1992, when two currencies, the UK pound and the Italian lira, were effectively forced out of the ERM by speculative pressure (*see* BLACK WEDNESDAY). The lira subsequently rejoined but the pound did not. From 1993 the currencies in the system were allowed wider (plus or minus 15%) fluctuations.

Although some participants had seen the EMS as no more than a means of stabilizing exchange rates, the view that its ultimate goal should be **Economic and Monetary Union** (**EMU**), with a single currency and a single monetary policy directed by a European central bank, became official EU policy in 1989. The decision to create a common currency was enshrined in the Maastricht Treaty of 1991, which created the European Monetary Institute to coordinate the process of convergence.

In June 1998 11 EU countries – all the then member states except Denmark, Greece, Sweden, and the UK – committed themselves to monetary union. Their currencies were locked together irrevocably and the *European Central Bank (ECB) was established to direct the single monetary policy essential for EMU. A common currency, the *euro, was launched for all purposes except cash transactions in January 1999. Euro bank notes and coins came into circulation from January 2002 and the national currencies were withdrawn after a short transitional period.

A new exchange-rate mechanism, known as **ERM II**, was established in January 1999 to enable those EU states remaining outside the *eurozone to link their currencies to the euro if they so wished (with fluctuation rates of plus or minus 15% as the basic rule). Its initial members were Denmark and Greece (the latter of which adopted the euro in 2001).

With the single currency established, all countries subsequently joining the EU are required to participate in ERM II as soon as this is judged economically practicable and to adopt the euro in due course. Countries must participate in ERM II for a minimum of two years before adopting the euro. Of the 12 states that have joined the EU since 2004, Slovenia joined the eurozone in 2007 and Cyprus and Malta in 2008. Of the established members, only Sweden and the UK remain outside the European Monetary System.

Euro-Top 100 Index See feature THE FTSE INDEXES on p. 175.

eurozone The 15 member countries of the European Union that have adopted the *euro as their currency, namely Austria, Belgium, Cyprus, Finland, France, Germany, Greece, Ireland, Italy, Luxembourg, Malta, The Netherlands, Portugal, Slovenia, and Spain. See feature EUROPEAN ECONOMIC AND MONETARY UNION on p. 175.

EV Abbreviation for *expected value.

EVA Abbreviation for *Economic Value Added.

event of default A critical clause in a loan agreement, the breaching of which will make the loan repayable immediately. The breaching of any *covenant clause will be an event of default. Events of default also include failure to pay, failure to perform other duties and obligations, false *representation and warranty, *material adverse change, bankruptcy, and *alienation of assets. *See also* CROSS-DEFAULT CLAUSE.

events accounting A method of accounting in which data is stored and reported in respect of particular events rather than being classified chronologically or in any other way.

ex- (Latin: without) A prefix used to exclude specified benefits when a security is quoted. A share is described as **ex-dividend** (xd or ex-div) when a potential purchaser will no longer be entitled to receive the company's current dividend, the right to which remains with the vendor. Government stocks go ex-dividend 36 days before the interest payment. Similarly, **ex-rights**, **ex-scrip**, **ex-coupon**, **ex-capitalization** (**ex-cap**), and **ex-bonus** mean that each of these benefits belongs to the vendor rather than the buyer. **Ex-all** means that all benefits belong to the vendor. **Cum-** (Latin: with) has exactly the opposite sense, meaning that the dividend or other benefits belong to the buyer rather than the seller. The price of a share that has gone ex-dividend will usually fall by the amount of the dividend, while one that is **cum-dividend** will usually rise by this amount. However, in practice market forces usually mean that these falls and rises are often slightly less than expected.

ex ante (Latin) Short for *ex ante facto*: before the event. The phrase is used, for example, of a budget that is prepared as an estimate and subsequently compared with actual figures. *Compare* EX POST.

Excel *Trademark* A widely used *spreadsheet program supplied by Microsoft.

except for (with the exception of) A qualification by an auditor stating that the *financial statements of the company audited give a *true and fair view 'except for' the effects of any adjustments that might have been found necessary, had a **limitation of scope** not affected the evidence available. This limitation is not so significant that a *disclaimer of opinion is required.
   The auditor may also use the 'except for' opinion if he or she disagrees with the treatment or disclosure of a matter in the financial statements but concludes that the effect of the disagreement is not so significant that an *adverse opinion is required. An opinion is expressed, which is qualified by stating that the financial statements give a true and fair view except for the effects of the matter giving rise to the disagreement. *See also* QUALIFIED AUDIT REPORT.

exceptional items Costs or income affecting a company's *profit and loss account that fall within the ordinary activities of the reporting entity, but need to be disclosed because of their exceptional size or incidence if the *financial statements are to give a *true and fair view. Unlike *extraordinary items they are included in the calculation of the normal trading profit or loss. The current rules are set out in *Financial Reporting Standard 3, Reporting Financial Performance, which redefined virtually all previously extraordinary items as exceptional. Neither exceptional nor extraordinary items are recognized under *International Financial Reporting Standards.

exchange control Restrictions on the purchase and sale of foreign exchange. It is operated in various forms by many countries, in particular those who experience shortages of *hard currencies; sometimes different regulations apply to transactions that would come under the capital account of the *balance of payments. Recent decades have seen a gradual movement towards dismantling exchange controls by developed countries. The UK abolished all forms of exchange control in 1979.

exchange gain or loss A gain or loss resulting from an exchange-rate fluctuation arising from the conversion of other currencies into the domestic currency.

exchange rate The number of units of one currency, usually the home currency, expressed in terms of a unit of another currency. The UK is exceptional in expressing exchange rates as the number of units of a foreign currency that £1 sterling will buy.

exchange-rate exposure (exchange-rate risk; foreign-exchange rate risk) The risk associated with uncertain exchange rates. The three types of risk are *transaction exposure, *translation exposure, and *economic exposure.

Exchange Rate Mechanism (ERM) See feature EUROPEAN ECONOMIC AND MONETARY UNION on p. 175.

excise duty A duty or tax levied on certain goods consumed within a country, such as alcoholic drinks and tobacco products, unlike customs duty, which is levied on imports. In the UK, both excise and customs duties are collected by HM Revenue and Customs.

exclusion of subsidiaries from consolidation Subsidiary undertakings may be excluded from *consolidation on the following grounds:
(1) an individual subsidiary may be excluded from consolidation if its inclusion is not *material for the purpose of giving a *true and fair view;
(2) an individual subsidiary may be excluded from consolidation for reasons of disproportionate expense in respect of its value (*see* DISPROPORTIONATE EXPENSE AND UNDUE DELAY);
(3) if *severe long-term restrictions substantially hinder the exercise of the rights of a parent company over the assets or the management of an undertaking, it may be excluded from consolidation;
(4) if the interest in a subsidiary undertaking is held with a view to resale, and has not previously been included in the consolidated accounts prepared by the parent company, that subsidiary may be excluded from consolidation;
(5) a subsidiary undertaking may be excluded from consolidation if its activities

are so different from those of the other group undertakings that its inclusion would be incompatible with the obligation to give a *true and fair view. Such exclusion does not arise merely because some of the undertakings are industrial, some commercial, and some provide different services (*see* DISSIMILAR ACTIVITIES).

executive director A *director of a company who has management responsibilities for the day-to-day activities of the business. *Compare* NON-EXECUTIVE DIRECTOR.

executive share option scheme An approved *share option scheme that entitles a specified class of directors or employees to purchase shares in the company in which they are employed. *See* SAVINGS RELATED SHARE OPTION SCHEME.

executor A person named in a will of another person to gather in the assets of that person's estate, paying any outstanding liabilities and distributing any residue to the beneficiaries in accordance with the instructions contained in the will.

exemptions from preparing consolidated financial statements Under the Companies Act a parent company is not required to prepare *consolidated financial statements for a financial year in which the group headed by that company qualifies as a *small group or a *medium-sized group. A group is not eligible for exemption if any member of the group is a public company or a body corporate that has power under its constitution to offer its shares or debentures to the public and may lawfully exercise that power; an authorized institution under the Banking Act 1987; an insurance company; or an authorized person under the Financial Services Act 1986. Under the Companies Act and *Financial Reporting Standard 2, Accounting for Subsidiary Undertakings, a parent undertaking is exempt from preparing group accounts when it is itself a subsidiary of a parent company in the European Union and consolidated financial statements are prepared at the highest level. Also, a parent undertaking is exempt from preparing group accounts when all of its subsidiaries are excluded. *See* EXCLUSION OF SUBSIDIARIES FROM CONSOLIDATION.

exempt supplies Supplies of goods or services in the categories of items that are identified as exempt from *value added tax, as given in the Value Added Tax Act 1994. The main categories are: land (including rent), insurance and financial services, postal services, betting, sport, charities (except on their business activities), education (non-profitmaking), health services, and burial and cremation.

exempt transfers Transfers resulting in no liability to *inheritance tax. These are:
• the first £3000 transferred in any tax year;
• gifts to a spouse or civil partner;
• normal expenditure out of income;
• small gifts, up to £250, to any number of individuals;
• marriage gifts, up to £5000 for each parent and £2500 for grandparents of the parties to the marriage, but limited to £1000 for other gifts;
• gifts to charities;

- gifts for national purposes;
- gifts for public benefit;
- gifts to political parties;
- certain transfers to employee trusts.

See also POTENTIALLY EXEMPT TRANSFER.

exercise price (strike price; striking price) The price per share at which a traded *option entitles the owner to buy the *underlying in a call option or to sell it in a put option.

ex gratia pensions A pension paid by an employer although there is no legal, contractual, or implied commitment to provide it.

existing use value The price at which a property can be sold on the open market assuming that it can only be used for the existing use and that there is vacant possession.

exit charge The charge to *inheritance tax made when an asset is taken out of a *discretionary trust.

exit value The *net realizable value of an asset, i.e. its market price at the date of a balance sheet less the selling expenses. Exit values are effectively *break-up values and are not consistent with the *going-concern concept, which assumes that a business is continuing to trade. *Compare* ENTRY VALUE.

expectations gap *See* AUDIT EXPECTATIONS GAP.

expected deviations rate The extent of non-compliance with recognized control procedures that an auditor expects to find when performing *compliance tests on a population or a *sample of it.

expected error The extent of the errors that an auditor expects to find when performing *substantive tests on a population or a sample of it.

expected monetary value (EMV) In decision making, the sum of the products of the outcomes in monetary terms and the probabilities of these outcomes arising. In *decision trees subjective probability estimates are assigned to each possible outcome. In the EMV, the outcomes are expressed in terms of money. *Compare* EXPECTED VALUE.

> **EXAMPLE**
>
> A manager calculates that a project has three possible monetary outcomes, each of which is assigned a different subjective probability. The EMV can then be calculated as follows:
>
> | possible outcomes (£) | subjective probability (p) | product (£ × p) |
> | --- | --- | --- |
> | 3000 | 0.5 | 1500 |
> | 4000 | 0.3 | 1200 |
> | 6000 | 0.2 | 1200 |
> | | 1.0 | EMV = 3900 |
>
> The figure of 3900 can then be compared with the EMVs of alternative projects as a guide to decision making.

expected standard In *standard costing, a cost, income, or performance standard set at a level that is expected to be achieved by the actual result. *Compare* ATTAINABLE STANDARD; IDEAL STANDARD.

expected value (EV) In decision making, the sum of the products of the outcomes in quantitative terms, such as units of output or sales, weights, or volumes, and the probabilities of these outcomes arising. *Compare* EXPECTED MONETARY VALUE.

expenditure The costs or expenses incurred by an organization. They may be *capital expenditure or *revenue expenditure. Although expenditure is usually incurred by an outlay of money, expenditure may also arise in accounting by the acknowledgment of a liability, for example rent accrued due, which is regarded as expenditure in the period accrued although it will not be paid until a later date.

expenditure code *See* ACCOUNTING CODE.

expenditure variance *See* OVERHEAD EXPENDITURE VARIANCE.

expense account **1.** An account, opened in either the cost ledger or the nominal ledger, for each *expenditure heading in which the costs of an organization are recorded before being totalled and transferred to the *profit and loss account at the end of an accounting period. **2.** The amount of money that certain staff members are allowed to spend on personal expenses in carrying out their activities for an organization.

expert system A computer application used to solve problems in a particular area of knowledge. The system uses the computer's ability to store, organize, and retrieve large amounts of information and is programmed to make decisions of the type that would be made by an expert in the field. Typically, an expert-system program asks questions of the user, who chooses one of several possible answers. This leads to other questions, and eventually to a conclusion. A common successful use is in basic medical diagnosis, but expert systems can also be designed for analysis of company results, review of loan applications, buying stocks and shares, and other financial purposes.

Export Credits Guarantee Department (ECGD) A UK government department that now operates under the name UK Export Finance. It encourages exports from the UK by making export credit insurance available to exporters and guaranteeing repayment to UK banks that provide finance for exports on credit terms of two years or more. It also insures British private investment overseas against war risk, expropriation, and restrictions on the making of remittances. Some sections of the ECGD were privatized in 1991, including short-term credit insurance.

ex post (Latin) Short for *ex post facto*: after the event. This abbreviation is used, for example, to refer to the collection of financial data for transactions after they have been effected. *Compare* EX ANTE.

exposure draft Generally, a draft issued as a discussion document prior to the release of a final document. Specifically, it refers to a draft issued for discussion by the *Accounting Standards Committee before issuing an *accounting standard.

ex rights *See* EX-.

extended trial balance A *trial balance that gives a vertical listing of all the *ledger account balances with three additional columns for adjustments, *accruals, and *prepayments, and a final two columns (each containing a debit and a credit side) that show the entries in the *profit and loss account and the *balance sheet.

extendible bond issue A *bond, the maturity of which can be extended at the option of all the parties.

external audit An *audit of an organization carried out by an auditor who is external to, and independent of, the organization. An example would be a *statutory audit carried out on behalf of the shareholders of a limited company. *Compare* INTERNAL AUDIT.

external failure costs *See* COST OF QUALITY. *See also* ENVIRONMENTAL COSTS.

extraordinary general meeting *See* GENERAL MEETING.

extraordinary items Costs or income affecting a company's *profit and loss account that do not derive from the *ordinary activities of the company, are not expected to recur, and, if undisclosed, would distort the normal trend of profits. Such items are therefore disclosed after the normal trading profit or loss has been shown. This requirement and a wider definition of ordinary activities were introduced by *Financial Reporting Standard 3, Reporting Financial Performance, with the result that virtually all previously extraordinary items are now treated as *exceptional items. The concepts of extraordinary and exceptional items are not recognized under *International Financial Reporting Standards.

extraordinary resolution A *resolution submitted to a general meeting of a company; 14 days' notice of such a resolution is required, and the notice should state that it is an extraordinary resolution. 75% of those voting must approve the resolution for it to be passed.

extrapolation Estimating unknown quantities that lie outside a series of known values. *Compare* INTERPOLATION.

extra-statutory concession A concession made by HM Revenue and Customs to taxpayers, which is usually followed in practice but which is not specified in the tax legislation.

face value *See* PAR VALUE.

facility An agreement between a bank and a company that grants the company a line of credit with the bank. This can either be a *committed facility or an *uncommitted facility.

facility fee *See* AGENCY FEE.

facility-sustaining activity In *activity-based costing, an *activity that is performed to sustain the organization as a whole. Examples include security, safety, maintenance, and plant management. It is not possible to identify these costs with particular products.

factoring The buying of the trade debts of a manufacturer, assuming the task of debt collection and accepting the credit risk, thus providing the manufacturer with working capital. A firm that engages in factoring is called a **factor**. **With service factoring** involves collecting the debts, assuming the credit risk, and passing on the funds as they are paid by the buyer. **With service plus finance factoring** involves paying the manufacturer up to 90% of the invoice value immediately after delivery of the goods, with the balance paid after the money has been collected. This form of factoring is clearly more expensive than with service factoring. In either case the factor, which may be a bank or finance house, has the right to select its debtors.

factors of production The resources required to produce economic goods. They are land (including all natural resources), labour (including all human work and skill), capital (including all money, assets, machinery, raw materials, etc.), and entrepreneurial ability (including organizational and management skills, inventiveness, and the willingness to take risks). For each of these factors there is a price, i.e. rent for land, wages for labour, interest for capital, and profit for the entrepreneur.

factory costs (factory expenses) The expenditure incurred by the manufacturing section of an organization. Factory costs include *direct materials, *direct labour, *direct expenses, and *manufacturing overheads but not mark-up or profit.

factory overhead (indirect manufacturing costs) Those manufacturing costs of an organization that cannot be traced directly to the product. Examples are factory rent, maintenance wages, and depreciation of general production machinery. In the USA factory overhead is known as **factory burden**.

fair presentation The requirement that financial statements should not be misleading. 'Fair presentation' is the US and *International Accounting Standards equivalent of the British requirement that financial statements give a *true and fair view.

fair value (fair market value) The amount of money for which it is assumed an asset or liability could be exchanged in an *arm's length transaction between informed and willing parties. If there is no active market for an asset, then a price may have to be estimated. The concept is essential in *acquisition accounting and is covered in *Financial Reporting Standard 7, Fair Value in Acquisition Accounting, and *International Financial Reporting Standard 3, Business Combinations. It is also important, if controversial, in derivatives accounting (*see* FAIR VALUE ACCOUNTING).

fair value accounting (FVA; mark-to-market accounting) A form of accounting in which financial instruments are valued according to their current market price (or an estimate of that price). FVA developed in the 1980s and 1990s with the growth in the derivatives trade and the practice of marking these products to market (*see* MARKING TO MARKET); it is now enshrined in *International Financial Reporting Standards. This form of accounting differs from traditional *historical-cost accounting in that it allows for the recording of unrealized gains where the market price of assets has risen above their historical cost. Owing to the nature of the derivatives market, fair value accounting can therefore introduce a high degree of volatility to the profit and loss account (*see* HEDGE ACCOUNTING). Critics of FVA argue that it exacerbated the banking crisis of 2008, as mark-to-market rules helped to create a downward price spiral in which complex derivatives products held by the banks rapidly became *toxic assets.

FAPA Abbreviation for Fellow of the *Association of Authorized Public Accountants.

farming As defined by the Income Tax (Trading and Other Income) Act 2005, the occupation of land wholly or mainly for the purpose of husbandry (which is declared not to include market gardening). Special tax provisions apply for farming. For income tax, profits can be averaged. Inheritance tax relief at 100% may be available against the value of farm land and machinery used for farming (*see* AGRICULTURAL PROPERTY RELIEF).

FASAC Abbreviation for *Financial Accounting Standards Advisory Council.

FASB Abbreviation for *Financial Accounting Standards Board.

FATFML Abbreviation for *Financial Action Task Force on Money Laundering.

favourable variance In *standard costing and *budgetary control, any difference between the actual and budgeted performance of an organization where this creates an addition to the budgeted profit. For example, this may occur if the actual sales revenue is greater than that budgeted or if actual costs are less than budgeted costs. *Compare* ADVERSE VARIANCE. *See* ANALYSIS OF VARIANCE; VARIANCE.

FCA Abbreviation for Fellow of the *Institute of Chartered Accountants in England and Wales.

FCCA Abbreviation for Fellow of the *Association of Chartered Certified Accountants.

FCIS Abbreviation for Fellow of the *Institute of Chartered Secretaries and Administrators.

FCMA Abbreviation for Fellow of the *Chartered Institute of Management Accountants.

FCPA Abbreviation for the *Foreign Corrupt Practices Act 1977.

FCT Abbreviation for Fellow of the *Association of Corporate Treasurers.

feasibility study An investigation to determine which of a range of decisions is likely to give a satisfactory return in a *financial appraisal or *economic appraisal of the alternatives.

Federal funds (Fed funds) Non-interest-bearing deposits held at the US *Federal Reserve System that are traded between member banks. The **Federal funds rate** or **Fed funds rate** is the *overnight rate paid on these funds.

Federal Reserve System (Fed) The organization, consisting of the 12 Federal Reserve Banks, that functions as the *central bank of the USA. Created by the Federal Reserve Act 1913, the system controls monetary policy, regulates the cost of money and the money supply to local banks, and supervises international banking by means of its agreement with the central banks of other countries. The system is administered centrally by the **Federal Reserve Board**, based in Washington DC.

(()) SEE WEB LINKS

• Website of the Board of Governors of the Federal Reserve System: includes information on monetary policy, banking regulation, and consumer concerns

feedback control An approach to *financial control in which managers monitor outputs achieved against a budget or desired output. Problems are only identified after they have occurred. Compare *feedforward control.

feedforward control An approach to *financial control in which managers try to anticipate problems in the future and take action before they occur. Compare *feedback control.

fellow subsidiary One of two or more of the *subsidiary undertakings in a group of companies that consists of a parent company and at least two subsidiaries.

FIAB Abbreviation for Fellow of the *International Association of Book-keepers.

fictitious asset An *asset shown in a balance sheet that does not exist. The asset may have been inadvertently left on the books despite having ceased to exist or no longer having any value (as with *goodwill); alternatively, it may be shown as part of a deliberate fraud.

fidelity bond An insurance policy that provides cover against specified losses occurring from the dishonest acts or defalcations by an employee.

FIFO cost Abbreviation for *first-in-first-out cost.

filing of accounts The lodging of the *financial statements of a company with the *Registrar of Companies. There are penalties for late filing. Companies that meet the statutory definition of a *small company or a *medium-sized company are permitted to file *abbreviated accounts.

final accounts The *annual accounts produced at the end of a company's financial year as opposed to any interim accounts produced during the year.

final dividend A *dividend recommended by the directors of a company to be paid to the shareholders, subject to the shareholders giving approval at the *annual general meeting. It is an *appropriation of profits in the *profit and loss account and, until paid, is shown as a current liability in the *balance sheet. *See also* INTERIM DIVIDEND.

final salary scheme An occupational pension scheme in which payments are determined by the employee's final salary. *See* DEFINED-BENEFIT PENSION SCHEME.

finance 1. The practice of manipulating and managing money. 2. The capital involved in a project, especially the capital that has to be raised to start a new business. 3. A loan of money for a particular purpose, especially by a *finance house.

Finance Act The annual UK Act of Parliament that changes the law relating to taxation, implementing the rates of income tax, corporation tax, etc., proposed in the preceding *Budget.

finance charge A charge levied for the benefit of being able to delay payment of a sum due.

finance company A company that provides finance, normally in the form of loans. As it tends to finance ventures with a high risk factor, the cost of borrowing is likely to be higher than that made by a clearing bank.

finance house An organization, many of which are owned by *commercial banks, that provides finance for *hire-purchase or leasing agreements. A consumer, who buys an expensive item (such as a car) from a trader and does not wish to pay cash, enters into a hire-purchase contract with the finance house, who collects the deposit and instalments. The finance house pays the trader the cash price in full, borrowing from the commercial banks in order to do so. The finance house's profit is the difference between the low rate of interest it pays to the commercial banks to borrow and the high rate it charges the consumer. Most finance houses are members of the Finance Houses Association.

finance lease A lease that transfers substantially all the risks and rewards of ownership of an *asset to the lessee. In accounting, it is as if the lessee owned the asset in question. Under *Statement of Standard Accounting Practice (SSAP) 21, Accounting for Leases and Hire Purchase Contracts, the lessee should record the finance lease as an asset in the *balance sheet. *International Accounting Standard 17, Leases, is similar to SSAP 21 but has different disclosure requirements. *Compare* OPERATING LEASE.

finance vehicle An entity set up by a company to obtain some financial benefit. The setting up of overseas companies to lower tax liabilities is a prime example of a finance vehicle.

financial accounting The branch of *accounting concerned with classifying, measuring, and recording the transactions of a business. At the end of a period, usually a year but sometimes less, a *profit and loss account and a *balance sheet are prepared to show the performance and position of the business.

Financial accounting is primarily concerned with providing a *true and fair view of the activities of a business to parties external to it. To ensure that this is done correctly, considerable attention will be paid to *accounting concepts and to any requirements of legislation, *accounting standards, and (where appropriate) the regulations of the *stock exchange. Financial accounting can be separated into a number of specific activities, such as conducting *audits, taxation, *bookkeeping, and *insolvency. **Financial accountants** need not be qualified, in that they need not belong to an *accountancy body, although the majority of those working in public practice will be. *Compare* MANAGEMENT ACCOUNTING.

Financial Accounting Foundation In the USA, the funding body of the *Financial Accounting Standards Board; it appoints its members and reviews the process of setting standards and accounting principles.

Financial Accounting Standards Advisory Council (FASAC) In the USA, a council that advises the *Financial Accounting Standards Board as to its agenda and accounting standards.

Financial Accounting Standards Board (FASB) In the USA, a nongovernment body founded in 1973 with the responsibility of promulgating *generally accepted accounting principles (GAAP). This is achieved by the issue of *Statements of Financial Accounting Standards, which practising *certified public accountants are expected to follow. Owing to the FASB's close relationship with the *Securities and Exchange Commission, US companies that desire a market listing have to comply with the standards it issues.

((⊕)) SEE WEB LINKS
• Website of the FASB

Financial Action Task Force on Money Laundering (FATFML) An organization founded in 1989 by the *Organization for Economic Cooperation and Development to curtail the practice of *money laundering, chiefly by persuading individual governments to legislate against it. Its policies have been codified in the Forty Recommendations on money laundering and, more recently, in the Nine Special Recommendations on terrorist financing.

financial adaptability The ability of an accounting entity to take effective action to alter the amounts and timing of *cash flows so that it can respond to unexpected needs or opportunities.

financial appraisal The use of financial evaluation techniques to determine which of a range of possible alternatives is preferred. Financial appraisal usually refers to the use of *discounted cash flow techniques but it may also be applied to any other approaches used to assess a business problem in financial terms, such as *ratio analysis, *profitability index, or the *payback period method. *Compare* ECONOMIC APPRAISAL.

financial asset An *asset that is either cash, a contractual right to receive cash, the right to exchange a *financial instrument with another *accounting entity under potentially favourable terms, or an *equity instrument of another entity.

financial budget *See* CASH-FLOW BUDGET.

financial capital maintenance *See* CAPITAL MAINTENANCE CONCEPT.

financial control (**financial management**) The actions of the management of an organization taken to ensure that the costs incurred and revenue generated are at acceptable levels. Financial control is assisted by the provision of financial information to management by the accountant and by the use of such techniques as *budgetary control and *standard costing, which highlight and analyse any *variances.

financial distress The situation in which the activity of a business is influenced by the possibility of impending insolvency. The costs of distress can be divided into those related to bankruptcy and those incurred without bankruptcy. The costs of bankruptcy are those directly incurred in winding up or restructuring the business. The costs short of bankruptcy are those arising from a sudden change in suppliers' and customers' behaviour, prompted by their concerns over dealing with a potentially insolvent firm. They also include costs engendered by the diversion of managerial focus and conflicts between stakeholders, notably managers, debt holders, and shareholders. As a firm increases the level of its debt or *gearing, so the costs of financial distress will rise (and hence the cost of funding). The costs of financial distress are an important factor in determining the firm's level of gearing.

financial expense An item of expenditure recorded in the financial records rather than the cost records. Examples include interest paid and directors' fees.

financial futures A *futures contract in currencies, interest rates, or other financial assets. The contract is a standard one, which is exchange-traded. In the UK financial futures and options are traded on the *LIFFE (now Euronext.liffe). *See also* HEDGE; PORTFOLIO INSURANCE.

financial gearing *See* GEARING; DEBT–EQUITY RATIO.

Financial Industry Regulatory Authority (**FINRA**) In the USA, a self-regulatory organization established in 2007 from a merger of the National Association of Securities Dealers (NASD) and the regulatory arm of the New York Stock Exchange. A private corporation rather than a government agency, it acts as a professional association for brokers and dealers on the securities market, with responsibility for training, arbitration, and the enforcement of a written code of practice. It also advises the US *Securities and Exchange Commission and acts as regulator to the New York Stock Exchange, NASDAQ, and other leading US markets.

((⊕)) SEE WEB LINKS

• FINRA website: includes a wide range of resources for both professionals and private investors

financial institution Any organization whose core activity is to provide financial services or advice in relation to financial products. Financial institutions include state bodies, such as central banks, and private companies, such as banks, building societies, and financial markets. At one time there was a clear distinction and regulatory division between deposit-taking institutions, such as banks, and non-deposit-taking institutions, such as brokers. This is no longer the case; brokers and other companies now often invest funds for their clients with banks and in the money markets.

financial instrument A contract involving a financial obligation. Examples include stocks, bonds, loans, and derivatives. *See also* CAPITAL INSTRUMENTS; NEGOTIABLE INSTRUMENT.

financial leverage *See* GEARING.

financial liability A contractual obligation to either deliver cash or another *financial asset to another *accounting entity or to exchange financial instruments with another entity on potentially unfavourable terms.

financial management 1. The branch of financial economics that is concerned with questions of business funding and the management of a business in the interests of shareholders. 2. *See* FINANCIAL CONTROL.

financial modelling The construction and use of planning and decision models based on financial data to simulate actual circumstances in order to facilitate decision making within an organization. The financial models used include *discounted cash flow, *economic order quantity, *decision trees, *learning curves, and *budgetary control.

Financial Ombudsman Service (FOS) A UK body set up to deal with complaints in relation to financial services and products. It was established by the *Financial Services and Markets Act 2000 to replace a number of separate complaint schemes: the Banking Ombudsman; Building Societies Ombudsman; Insurance Ombudsman; Investment Ombudsman; and Pensions Ombudsman.

(⊕) SEE WEB LINKS
• Website of the Financial Ombudsman Service

financial period *See* ACCOUNTING PERIOD.

financial perspective *See* BALANCED SCORECARD.

financial planning The formulation of short-term and long-term plans in financial terms for the purposes of establishing goals for an organization to achieve, against which its actual performance can be measured.

financial ratio *See* ACCOUNTING RATIO.

financial report The *financial statements of a company. *See also* ANNUAL ACCOUNTS.

Financial Reporting Council (FRC) A UK body set up in 1990, following the recommendation of the *Dearing Report, to promote confidence in financial reporting. There are six operating bodies: the *Financial Reporting Review Panel, the *Accounting Standards Board, the *Auditing Practices Board, the Board for Actuarial Standards, the *Professional Oversight Board, and the *Accountancy and Actuarial Discipline Board. The FRC also maintains and promotes the *Combined Code on Corporate Governance. Its members are appointed by the Secretary of State for Business, Enterprise and Regulatory Reform.

(⊕) SEE WEB LINKS
• Website of the FRC

Financial Reporting Exposure Draft (FRED) A document issued by the

*Accounting Standards Board for discussion and debate prior to the issue of a
*Financial Reporting Standard.

Financial Reporting Release (FRR) In the USA, a pronouncement on
financial reporting policy made by the *Securities and Exchange Commission.

Financial Reporting Review Panel (FRRP) An operating body of the UK
*Financial Reporting Council, which acts as its sole director. The panel
investigates departures from the accounting requirements of the Companies
Acts and is empowered to take legal action to remedy any such departures. Its
remit covers the financial reports of public companies and large private
companies. All other companies are subject to scrutiny by the Department for
Business, Innovation and Skills. The panel does not look at all company
accounts but has doubtful cases drawn to its attention.

(⊕) SEE WEB LINKS
• FRRP website: includes findings in particular investigations

Financial Reporting Standard (FRS) Any of a series of standards issued
by the UK *Accounting Standards Board. Many of the more recent FRSs have
the aim of harmonizing UK practice with the standards published by the
*International Accounting Standards Board.

(⊕) SEE WEB LINKS
• Summaries of all FRSs in issue from the Accounting Standards Board website

Financial Reporting Standard for smaller entities (FRSSE) An
*accounting standard issued by the Accounting Standards Board (ASB) that
collects in one document, in simplified and appropriate form, the requirements
from other accounting standards and *Urgent Issues Task Force (UITF) abstracts
that are applicable to smaller entities. First issued in March 1999, it can be
adopted by entities qualifying as *small companies under company legislation
and other analogous bodies. Small entities choosing to comply with these
reporting standards are exempt from applying all other accounting standards
and UITF abstracts. Smaller entities that do not adopt these standards remain
subject to the full range of accounting standards and UITF abstracts. Revised
versions of the FRSSE were issued in January 2005, January 2007, and June 2008.
See also LITTLE GAAP.

(⊕) SEE WEB LINKS
• Downloadable pdf of the current FRSSE from the ASB website

Financial Services Act 1986 A UK act of parliament that came into force in
April 1988. Its purpose was to regulate investment business in the UK by means
of the *Securities and Investment Board and its *Self-Regulating Organizations.
It provided legislation for many of the recommendations of the *Gower Report.
In 2000 the Act was replaced by the *Financial Services and Markets Act.

Financial Services Action Plan (FSAP) A communication published by the
European Commission in 1999, consisting of 42 proposed measures designed to
complete the integration of EU financial markets by 2005. The legislative phase
of FSAP was largely completed by 2007, with the approval of such key measures
as the *Markets in Financial Instruments Directive (MiFID), the Capital
Requirements Directive, and the expanded *Eighth Company Law Directive.

FINANCIAL REPORTING STANDARDS

1. Cash Flow Statements, issued 1991, revised 1996
2. Accounting for Subsidiary Undertakings, issued 1992, amended 2004
3. Reporting Financial Performance, issued 1992
4. Capital Instruments, issued 1993, now superseded by FRS 25 below
5. Reporting the Substance of Transactions, issued 1994, amended 1994, 1998, 2003
6. Acquisitions and Mergers, issued 1994
7. Fair Values in Acquisition Accounting, issued 1994
8. Related Party Transactions, issued 1995
9. Associates and Joint Ventures, issued 1997
10. Goodwill and Intangible Assets, issued 1997
11. Impairment of Fixed Assets and Goodwill, issued 1998
12. Provisions, Contingent Liabilities and Contingent Assets, issued 1998
13. Derivatives and Other Financial Instruments: Disclosures, issued 1998
14. Earnings Per Share, issued 1998, now superseded by FRS 22 below
15. Tangible Fixed Assets, issued 1999
16. Current Tax, issued 1999
17. Retirement Benefits, issued 2000, revised 2002
18. Accounting Policies, issued 2000
19. Deferred Tax, issued 2000
20. Share-based Payment, issued 2004
21. Events After the Balance Sheet Date, issued 2004
22. Earnings Per Share, issued 2004
23. The Effects of Change in Foreign Exchange Rates, issued 2004
24. Financial Reporting in Hyperinflationary Economies, issued 2004
25. Financial Instruments: Disclosure and Presentation, issued 2004
26. Financial Instruments: Measurement, issued 2004
27. Life Assurance, issued 2004.
28. Corresponding Amounts, issued 2005
29. Financial Instruments: Disclosures, issued 2005
30. Heritage Assets, issued 2009

Financial Services and Markets Act 2000 Legislation, implemented in November 2001, establishing a regulatory framework for UK banking, insurance, and investment. Under the terms of the Act, the *Financial Services Authority became the key regulator, taking over functions from the Bank of England, the Building Societies Commission, and the Treasury. However, the Bank of England still retains a regulatory interest where systemic risk to the UK financial system is concerned. *See also* FINANCIAL OMBUDSMAN SERVICE.

Financial Services Authority (FSA) An independent, nongovernmental body that regulates the financial services industry in the UK. It was set up in 1997 and given statutory powers by the Financial Services and Markets Act 2000. The FSA is financed by the industry and its board, which consists of a chairman, a chief executive officer, three managing directors, and 11 nonexecutive directors (including the deputy chairman), is appointed by the Treasury. The Financial Services and Markets Act specifies four statutory objectives for the FSA:

- to maintain market confidence;
- to promote public understanding of the financial system;
- to ensure a satisfactory degree of consumer protection;
- to reduce the extent to which it is possible for a business carried on by a regulated person to be used for a purpose connected with financial crime.

(⊕) SEE WEB LINKS
- Website of the FSA

Financial Services Compensation Scheme A body established under the UK *Financial Services and Markets Act 2000 to provide compensation to customers of insolvent businesses or to those who have incurred losses as a result of bad financial advice.

financial stability measures Quantitative measures that help to determine whether a company or group is likely to be able to meet its financial obligations, including interest, dividends, and capital repayments. The measures include the *gearing ratio and *interest cover.

financial statement analysis An analysis of the *financial statements of a business to assess its performance and position. Ratios are normally calculated from the financial statements to assess the profitability, solvency, *working capital management, liquidity, and *capital structure of an organization. They may also be calculated over a period to enable an analysis of trends to be formulated or compared to other similar companies or industry averages. In conducting the analysis, regard will need to be paid to the *accounting policies of the company and the extent to which any *creative accounting may have taken place. *See* ACCOUNTING RATIO; COMMON-SIZE FINANCIAL STATEMENTS; RATIO ANALYSIS.

financial statements The annual statements summarizing a company's activities over the last year. They consist of the *profit and loss account, *balance sheet, *statement of total recognized gains and losses, and, if required, the *cash-flow statement, together with supporting notes. *See also* GENERAL PURPOSE FINANCIAL STATEMENTS; SIMPLIFIED FINANCIAL STATEMENTS; SUMMARY FINANCIAL STATEMENT.

financial structure *See* CAPITAL STRUCTURE.

Financial Times–Stock Exchange Share Indexes See feature THE FTSE INDEXES on p. 203.

financial year **1.** Any year connected with finance, such as a company's *accounting period or a year for which budgets are made up. **2.** In the UK, a specific period relating to *corporation tax, i.e. the 12 months beginning on 1 April in one year and ending on 31 March in the next year. Corporation-tax rates are fixed for specific financial years by the Chancellor in the Budget; if a company's accounting period falls into two financial years the profits have to be apportioned to the relevant financial years to find the rates of tax applicable. *Compare* FISCAL YEAR.

finished goods Products that have completed the manufacturing process and are available for distribution to customers.

finished goods stock (finished goods inventory) The value of goods that have completed the manufacturing process and are available for distribution to customers. In any accounting period there will be *opening stock of finished goods at the beginning of the period and *closing stock of finished goods at the end of the period. Methods of valuing finished goods stock are covered by *Statement of Standard Accounting Practice 9 and may include *first-in-first-out cost or *average cost methods.

finished goods stocks budget A budget that expresses in both financial and quantitative terms the planned levels of *finished goods at various times during the budget period.

FINRA *See* Financial Industry Regulatory Authority.

firewall In a conglomerate, a barrier created between the organization, funding, and ownership of one business entity and those of other entities in the group, so that problems experienced by the one do not affect others.

firm 1. Any business organization. 2. A business *partnership.

firm offer An offer to sell goods that remains in force for a stated period. For example, an 'offer firm for 24 hours' binds the seller to sell if the buyer accepts the offer within 24 hours. If the buyer makes a lower bid during the period that the offer is firm, the offer ceases to be valid. An offer that is not firm is usually called a quotation in commercial terms.

firm order An order to a broker (for securities, commodities, currencies, etc.) that remains firm for a stated period or until cancelled. A broker who has a firm order from a principal does not have to refer back if that broker can execute the terms of the order in the stated period.

first-in-first-out cost (FIFO cost) A method of valuing units of *raw material or *finished goods issued from stock based on using the earliest unit value for pricing the issues until all the stock received at that price has been used up. The next latest price is then used for pricing the issues, and so on. Because the issues are based on a FIFO cost, the valuation of closing stocks is described as being on the same FIFO basis. The method may also be used in *process costing to value the work in process at the end of an accounting period. *Compare* last-in-first-out cost; next-in-first-out cost.

first mortgage debenture A *debenture with the first charge over property owned by a company. Such debentures are most commonly issued by property companies.

first-tier market The main market on which the equity of large companies is traded. There is customarily a high level of regulation and supervision in such markets. *Compare* second-tier market.

first-year allowance In the UK, a special *capital allowance against *corporation tax that is granted in the year of purchase of an asset in place of the standard *writing-down allowance of 25%. Various first-year allowances, often targeted at smaller businesses wishing to invest in new technology, have been made available at various times. From April 2008 all existing first-year allowances were replaced by an *Annual Investment Allowance of £50,000.

fiscal policy The use of government spending and taxation to influence macroeconomic conditions. Fiscal policy was actively pursued to sustain full employment in the post-war years; however, monetarists and others have claimed that this set off the inflation of the 1970s. Thereafter fiscal policy remained generally 'tight' in most Western countries until the economic downturn of the late 2000s. *Compare* MONETARY POLICY.

fiscal year In the UK, the 12-month period beginning on 6 April in one year and ending on 5 April in the next (the fiscal year 2015–16 runs from 6 April 2015 to 5 April 2016). Income tax, capital gains tax, and annual allowances for inheritance tax are all calculated for fiscal years, and the UK Budget estimates refer to the fiscal year. In the USA the fiscal year now runs from 1 October to the following 30 September. The fiscal year is sometimes called the **tax year** or the **year of assessment**. *Compare* FINANCIAL YEAR.

fixed asset (capital asset) An asset of a business intended for continuing use, rather than a short-term *current asset (such as stock). Fixed assets must be classified in a company's *balance sheet as intangible, tangible, or investments. Examples of *intangible assets include *goodwill, *patents, and *trademarks. Examples of tangible fixed assets include land and buildings, plant and machinery, fixtures and fittings. Fixed assets must be written off to the *profit and loss account over their useful economic life; this is effected by the *amortization of intangible fixed assets and the *depreciation of tangible fixed assets. An investment included as a fixed asset is shown at its purchase price, market value, or directors' valuation, or using the equity method of accounting (*see* EQUITY ACCOUNTING).

fixed-asset investment Expenditure on tangible assets that are likely to have a life of more than one year.

fixed-assets register (assets register; plant register) A listing of the *fixed assets of a company. It records a description of the asset, its location, cost, revaluation, estimated net value, estimated *useful economic life, *depreciation method, accumulated provision for depreciation, and *net book value.

fixed-asset to equity-capital ratio A ratio used to calculate a business's ability to satisfy long-term debt. The value of the fixed assets is divided by the equity capital; a ratio greater than 1 means that some of the fixed assets are financed by debt.

fixed-asset–turnover ratio A ratio that measures an organization's activity over a period by calculating the number of times the sales are a multiple of the balance-sheet value of the *fixed assets. The fixed-asset values may be taken either at the beginning or the end of the period or an average of the two.

fixed budget (static budget) A budget that does not take into account any circumstances resulting in the actual levels of activity achieved being different from those on which the original budget was based. Consequently, in a fixed budget the *budget cost allowances for each cost item are not changed for the variable items. *Compare* FLEXIBLE BUDGET.

fixed capital The amount of an organization's *capital that is tied up in its *fixed assets.

fixed charge 1. *See* CHARGE. 2. The part of an expense that remains unchanged, irrespective of the amount of the commodity or service used or consumed. For example, in the UK both the electricity and gas industries operate tariffs consisting of a fixed charge, which remains unchanged irrespective of the consumption of energy, and a variable charge, based on the energy consumed.

fixed-charge–coverage ratio *See* INTEREST COVER.

fixed cost (fixed expense) An item of expenditure that remains unchanged, in total, irrespective of changes in the levels of production or sales. Examples are business rates, rent, and some salaries. *Compare* SEMI-VARIABLE COST; VARIABLE COST.

fixed exchange rate A rate of exchange between one currency and another that is fixed by government and maintained by that government's economic policy and its buying or selling its currency to support or depress it. *Compare* FLOATING EXCHANGE RATE.

fixed-interest security Any *security that gives a fixed stated interest payment. They include *gilt-edged securities, *bonds, *preference shares, and *debentures; as they entail less risk than *equities they offer less scope for capital appreciation. They do, however, often give a better yield than equities.

fixed overhead absorption rate The budgeted fixed overheads divided by the budgeted *standard hours, budgeted production in units, or other budgeted production measure. *See* ABSORPTION RATE.

fixed overhead capacity variance (capacity usage variance; idle capacity variance) In a system of *standard costing, the difference arising between the actual hours worked and the *budgeted capacity available, valued at the standard fixed overhead absorption rate per hour. It can be measured in machine hours or labour hours. *See* CAPACITY; IDLE CAPACITY; IDLE CAPACITY RATIO.

fixed overhead cost The elements of the *indirect costs of an organization's product that, in total, remain unchanged irrespective of changes in the levels of production or sales. Examples include administrative salaries, sales personnel salaries, and factory rent.

fixed overhead efficiency variance In a system of *standard costing, the difference arising between the actual labour hours worked and the standard time allowed for the quantity actually produced, valued at the standard fixed overhead absorption rate per hour. *See* OVERHEAD EFFICIENCY VARIANCE.

fixed overhead expenditure variance In a system of *standard costing, the difference arising between the fixed overhead budgeted and the fixed overhead incurred. *See* OVERHEAD EXPENDITURE VARIANCE.

fixed overhead total variance In a system of *standard costing, the total difference arising between the standard fixed overhead absorbed for the actual units produced and the actual fixed overhead expenditure incurred. *See* OVERHEAD TOTAL VARIANCE.

fixed overhead volume variance (overhead volume variance; volume variance) In a *standard costing system, the difference arising between the actual production in units and the budgeted production, valued at the standard fixed overhead absorption rate per unit. It measures the over- or under-recovery of fixed overheads as a result of the level of activity actually achieved differing from the level of activity budgeted.

fixed production overhead The elements of an organization's *factory overheads that, in total, remain unchanged irrespective of changes in the level of production or sales. Examples include factory rent, depreciation of machinery using the *straight-line method, and the factory manager's salary.

fixed-rate loan A loan on which the interest rate is fixed at the start of the loan.

flash report In the USA, a management report that highlights key data for corrective action.

flat tax (proportional tax) A tax with a single rate (as opposed to one in which the rate of tax increases with the size of the *tax base) and with no reliefs or exemptions apart from a standard personal allowance. In recent years a flat rate of income tax has been introduced in Russia and a number of Eastern European economies. The advantages claimed for such a system are that it is very simple to understand and operate, thereby reducing administrative costs for both government and business, that it eliminates many forms of tax avoidance, that the abolition of the higher-rate tax bands encourages enterprise and wealth creation, and that the raising of the threshold at which people begin to pay tax benefits the lowest earners (who also gain from the elimination of poverty traps). Opponents argue that it denies governments flexibility in setting tax policy and offends against the *ability-to-pay principle by shifting the burden of tax from the wealthiest to those on middle incomes. *Compare* PROGRESSIVE TAX; REGRESSIVE TAX.

flexed allowance (flexed budget allowance) The budgeted expenditure level for each of the variable cost items adjusted to the level of activity actually achieved. *See* BUDGET COST ALLOWANCE; FLEXIBLE BUDGET.

flexible budget A budget that takes into account the fact that values for income and expenditure on some items will change with changing circumstances. Consequently, in a flexible budget the *budget cost allowances for each variable cost item will change to allow for the actual levels of activity achieved. A budget that has been adjusted in this way is known as a **flexed budget**. *Compare* FIXED BUDGET. *See also* OPERATIONAL VARIANCE; REVISION VARIANCE.

flexible manufacturing system An automated production line that can be adapted to produce more than one product line. Use of a flexible manufacturing system enables companies to lower costs and vary production quickly in response to changes in consumer demand.

float 1. In the USA, the proportion of a corporation's stocks that are held by the public rather than the corporation or institutional investors. 2. Money created as a result of a delay in processing cheques, e.g. when one account is credited before the paying bank's account has been debited. *See* BANK FLOAT. 3. Money set aside as a contingency fund or an advance to be reimbursed. 4. *See* CASH FLOAT. 5. *See* FLOTATION.

floating assets *See* CURRENT ASSETS.

floating charge *See* CHARGE.

floating exchange rate A rate of exchange between one currency and others that is permitted to float according to market forces. Most major currencies and countries now have floating exchange rates but governments and central banks intervene, buying or selling currencies when rates become too high or too low. *Compare* FIXED EXCHANGE RATE.

floating-rate loan A loan that does not have a fixed interest rate throughout its life. Floating-rate loans can take various forms but they are all tied to a short-term market indicator; in the UK this is usually the *London Inter Bank Offered Rate.

floating-rate note (FRN) A *eurobond with a floating-rate interest, usually based on the *London Inter Bank Offered Rate. They first appeared in the 1970s and are usually issued as negotiable *bearer bonds. A **perpetual FRN** has no *redemption. A **capped FRN** is one with a maximum rate of interest. *Compare* VARIABLE-RATE NOTE.

floor The minimum interest rate on a loan or other obligation, as set in advance by the lender. *Compare* CAP. *See also* COLLAR.

flotation The process of launching a public company for the first time by inviting the public to subscribe for its shares (also known as 'going public'). It applies both to private and to previously nationalized share issues, and can be carried out by means of an *introduction, *issue by tender, *offer for sale, *placing, or *public issue. After flotation the shares can be traded on a stock exchange. Flotation allows the owners of the business to raise new capital or to realize their investments.

flotation costs Costs arising on the *flotation of a company.

flowchart A diagram representing the sequence of logical steps required to solve a problem. There are a number of conventional symbols used. The important ones are the process box, which indicates a process taking place, and the decision lozenge, which indicates where a decision is needed.

FMCG Abbreviation for fast-moving consumer goods.

footnote Explanatory narrative and numerical data that follows the *financial statements of a company and is integrally related to them.

forbearance The position taken by a lender who chooses not to exercise his or her legal right of *foreclosure when a borrower defaults. Instead, the lender may renegotiate the terms of the loan.

forecast reporting The inclusion of projected figures in the *annual accounts and report of a company. For example, forecast sales figures may be included.

foreclosure The legal right of a lender of money if the borrower fails to repay the money or part of it on the due date. The lender must apply to a court to be permitted to sell the property that has been held as security for the debt. The court will order a new date for payment in an order called a **foreclosure nisi**. If the borrower again fails to pay, the lender may sell the property. This procedure can occur when the security is the house in which the mortgagor lives and the mortgagor fails to pay the mortgagee (bank, building society, etc.) the mortgage instalments. The bank, etc., then forecloses the mortgage, dispossessing the mortgagor.

foreign company (oversea company) A company incorporated outside the UK but having a subsidiary or established place of business within the UK. Foreign companies are subject to provisions of the Companies Act 2006 relating to registration, accounts, constitution, directors, name, etc.

Foreign Corrupt Practices Act 1977 (FCPA) Legislation enacted in the USA outlawing bribery and corruption by US companies in their overseas operations. A 1998 amendment extended the scope of the Act to include actions by foreign citizens and companies while on US territory.

foreign currency The currency of another country, which is not used in the preparation of an organization's domestic accounts. However, the existence of foreign subsidiaries or branches or overseas transactions may mean that an organization must translate these foreign currencies into the domestic currency to prepare its *financial statements. The rules for doing so are contained in *Statement of Standard Accounting Practice 20, Foreign Currency Translation.

foreign currency cross-rate A mechanism whereby an exchange rate can be calculated between two currencies for which no direct rate of exchange exists. The US dollar, which is customarily used as the vehicle currency in foreign-exchange trading, is the common denominator of such calculations. Thus, there may not be a direct rate between, say, the Barbados dollar and the Argentine peso. A cross-rate is calculated by divided the $US rate for the peso by the $US rate for the Barbados dollar, showing how many Barbados dollars are needed to purchase one peso.

foreign emoluments Earnings received by a person domiciled outside the UK (*see* DOMICILE), who is employed by a *non-resident employer.

foreign exchange (FOREX; FX) The currencies of foreign countries, as bought and sold on a **foreign-exchange market**. The foreign-exchange *spot market caters for transactions in which the two currencies are exchanged usually within two business days. The *forward-exchange market caters for situations in which the exchange does not take place until a specified date in the future.

foreign-exchange dealer A person who buys and sells *foreign exchange on a foreign-exchange market, usually as an employee of a *commercial bank. Banks charge fees or commissions for buying and selling foreign exchange on behalf of their customers; dealers may also be authorized to speculate in forward exchange rates.

forensic accounting **1.** Accounting undertaken in relation to proceedings in a court of law. In such circumstances accountants may be called on to provide expert investigations and evidence. **2.** Accounting that set out to determine the nature of past business activity, often on the basis of incomplete documentation.

FOREX *See* FOREIGN EXCHANGE.

forfaiting A form of *debt discounting for exporters in which a forfaiter accepts at a discount, and without recourse, a *promissory note, *bill of exchange, *letter of credit, etc., received from a foreign buyer by an exporter.

Maturities are normally from one to three years. Thus the exporter receives payment without risk at the cost of the discount.

forfeited share A *partly paid share in a company that the shareholder has to forfeit because of a failure to pay a subsequent or final payment. Such shares must be sold or cancelled by a public company but a private company is not regulated in this respect.

forgery The legal offence of making a false instrument in order that it may be accepted as genuine, thereby causing harm to others. Under the Forgery and Counterfeiting Act 1981, an instrument may be a document or any device (e.g. magnetic tape) on which information is recorded. An instrument is considered false, for example, if it purports to have been made or altered by someone who did not do so, on a date or at a place when it was not, or by someone who does not exist.

for information only Denoting a quotation given to provide a client with a guide to current market prices. It cannot be treated as a firm offer either to buy or to sell at the quoted price.

Form 20-F In the USA, the form required by the *Securities and Exchange Commission for the filing of annual results by non-US companies.

Form 10-K In the USA, the form filed annually with the *Securities and Exchange Commission by public traded companies. Audited financial statements and supporting detail are included; it normally provides more information than the annual report to stockholders. In most cases, the report must be filed within 90 days of the end of a company's financial year (larger companies now have a shorter deadline of 60–75 days).

Form 10-Q In the USA, the form filed quarterly with the *Securities and Exchange Commission by public traded companies. The form contains interim financial statements and may be for a single quarter or may be cumulative. Comparative figures are provided for the same period in the previous year. The information provided is less detailed than on *Form 10-K and does not have to be audited.

format The method of presenting financial statements chosen by an organization. Incorporated bodies must use the formats prescribed by the Companies Act for their *balance sheet and *profit and loss account. The profit and loss format is also regulated by *Financial Reporting Standard 3, Reporting Financial Performance, and *International Accounting Standard 1, Presentation of Financial Statements. *See* BALANCE-SHEET FORMATS; PROFIT AND LOSS ACCOUNT FORMATS.

formation expenses The expenses incurred on setting up a company. According to the Companies Act, these expenses must not be treated as an asset of the company.

forward dealing Dealing in commodities, securities, currencies, freight, etc., for delivery at some future date at a price agreed at the time the contract (called a **forward contract**) is made. This form of trading enables dealers and manufacturers to cover their future requirements by hedging their more immediate purchases (*see* HEDGE). Strictly, a forward contract differs from a

*futures contract in that the former cannot be closed out by a matching transaction, whereas a futures contract can, and often is. However, this distinction is not always adhered to and the terms are sometimes used synonymously.

forward differential *See* FORWARD POINTS.

forward-exchange market A *foreign-exchange market in which currencies are traded for exchange at a future date. If an importer has an obligation to pay for goods in a foreign currency at some time in the future and does not wish to accept the risk that a currency fluctuation may lead to that obligation increasing, the importer can cover the risk by buying the foreign currency for delivery at a future date. Rates for standard periods for one, two, three, six, and twelve months can be obtained, while for other forward periods the price may have to be negotiated.

forward forward rate The rate of interest that will apply to a loan or deposit beginning on a future date and maturing on a second future date.

forward margin *See* FORWARD POINTS.

forward points (forward differential; forward margin) The amount to be added to or deducted from the spot foreign-exchange rate to calculate the forward exchange rate.

forward-rate agreement (FRA) **1.** A contract between two parties that determines the rate of interest that will apply to a future loan or a deposit, which may or may not materialize. **2.** A specified amount of a specified currency to be exchanged on an agreed future date at a specified rate of exchange.

founders' shares The shares issued to the founders of a company. These shares sometimes carry special *dividend rights and voting rights.

Fourth Company Law Directive (Fourth Accounting Directive) An EU directive (1978) concerning the harmonization of company law and accounting practices in member states. It recognized five *accounting concepts as fundamental: the *accounting entity concept, the *accruals concept, the *consistency concept, the *going-concern concept, and the *prudence concept. In 2006 the Fourth Directive was superseded by the *Company Reporting Directive and the *Statutory Audit Directive.

FRA Abbreviation for *forward-rate agreement.

fragmentation A situation that arises when two transactions, especially foreign-exchange transactions, offset each other commercially but not in terms of taxation.

Framework for the Preparation and Presentation of Financial Statements A document setting out the basic *accounting concepts informing *International Accounting Standards and *International Financial Reporting Standards. It was issued by the International Accounting Standards Committee in 1989 and adopted by its successor body, the *International Accounting Standards Board (IASB), in 2001. The Framework defines the objectives of financial statements; identifies the qualitative characteristics that make information in financial statements useful; defines the basic elements of financial statements and the concepts for recognizing and measuring them; and provides concepts of *capital maintenance. It serves as a guide to the IASB in developing new Standards and as a guide to management in resolving issues that are not addressed directly in a Standard or Interpretation issued by the Board.

franked investment income Formerly, dividends and other distributions from UK companies received by other companies. The principle of the *imputation system of taxation was that once one company had paid corporation tax, any dividends it paid could pass through any number of other companies without carrying a further corporation-tax charge.

franked SORPs *See* STATEMENT OF RECOMMENDED PRACTICE.

Frankfurt Stock Exchange (Frankfurt Wertpapierbörse) The oldest and largest of eight regional stock exchanges in Germany, accounting for more than 75% of equity trading in Germany. It first recorded trading in 1820 and is now owned by *Deutsche Börse. The main market indicator is the Deutsche Aktienindex (DAX index).

fraudulent conveyance The transfer of property to another person with the aim of putting it beyond the reach of creditors. For example, if a man transfers his house into the name of his wife because he realizes that his business is about to become insolvent, the transaction may be set aside by the court under the provisions of the Insolvency Act 1986.

fraudulent trading Carrying on business with intent to defraud creditors or for any other fraudulent purpose. This includes accepting money from customers when the company is unable to pay its debts and cannot meet its obligations under the contract. Such conduct is a criminal offence. The liquidator of a company may apply to the court for an order against any person who has been a party to fraudulent trading to make such contributions to the assets of the company as the court thinks fit. 'Fraudulent' in this context implies actual dishonesty or real moral blame. *Compare* WRONGFUL TRADING.

FRC Abbreviation for *Financial Reporting Council.

FRED Abbreviation for *Financial Reporting Exposure Draft.

free asset ratio The ratio of the market value of an insurance company's assets to its liabilities.

free cash flow A measure of the cash that a company is generating or consuming. Free cash flow is often defined as after-tax *operating profit less net *capital expenditure:

free cash flow = revenues – operating expenses + depreciation – taxes – capital
    expenditure costs

However, there is no precise definition of free cash flow: another equation might include changes in *working capital. Making comparisons between companies on this basis is not very useful if they are using different definitions. Free cash flow is not determined in accordance with *generally accepted accounting principles (GAAP) and should be considered in addition to, not as a substitute for, financial measures determined in accordance with GAAP.

Free cash flow is important for managers as a positive cash flow can be used to pay dividends, acquire other companies, or invest in new opportunities. It is also an important measure of a company's ability to reduce debt. The value of a company can be calculated as the sum of the future discounted free cash flows (*see* DISCOUNTED CASH FLOW).

free depreciation A method of granting tax relief to organizations by allowing them to charge the cost of *fixed assets against taxable profits in whatever proportions and over whatever period they choose. This gives businesses considerable flexibility, enabling them to choose the best method of *depreciation depending on their anticipated cash flow, profit estimates, and taxation expectations.

freehold An estate in land that is now usually held in fee simple. Land that is not freehold will be *leasehold.

free in and out Denoting a selling price that includes all costs of loading goods (into a container, road vehicle, ship, etc.) and unloading them (out of the transport).

free issue *See* SCRIP ISSUE.

freezing injunction A court order preventing a defendant from dealing with specified assets. Such an order will be granted in cases in which the plaintiff can show that there will be a substantial risk that any judgment given against the defendant will be worthless, because the defendant will sell assets to avoid paying it. It is usually granted to prevent assets leaving the jurisdiction of the English courts, but may in exceptional circumstances extend to assets abroad. It was formerly called a **Mareva injunction**, after the 1975 case *Mareva Compania Naviera SA* v *International Bulkcarriers SA*.

Friendly Society A non-profitmaking *mutual company registered as such under the Friendly Society Acts (1896–1955). Mutual insurance societies were formerly widespread but many closed after the introduction of National Insurance in 1946. Those that remain offer a range of personal assurance and insurance benefits relating to sickness, pensions, and unemployment.

fringe benefits **1.** Non-monetary benefits offered to the employees of a company in addition to their wages or salaries. They include company cars, expense accounts, the opportunity to buy company products at reduced prices, private health plans, canteens with subsidized meals, luncheon vouchers, cheap loans, social clubs, etc. Some of these benefits, such as company cars, do not escape the tax net. *See* BENEFITS IN KIND. **2.** Benefits, other than dividends, provided by a company for its shareholders. They often include reduced prices for the company's products or services, Christmas gifts, and special travel facilities. *See* SHAREHOLDERS PERKS.

FRN Abbreviation for *floating-rate note.

front-end fee A charge levied by a lender when a loan is set up or when the first payment of the loan is taken.

front-end load The initial charge made by a unit trust, life-assurance company, or other investment fund to pay for administration and commission for any introducing agent. The investment made on behalf of the investor is, therefore, the total initial payment less the front-end load. *Compare* BACK-END LOAD.

frozen assets Assets that for one reason or another cannot be used or realized. This may happen when a government refuses to allow certain assets to be exported. *See* FREEZING INJUNCTION.

FRR Abbreviation for *Financial Reporting Release.

FRRP Abbreviation for *Financial Reporting Review Panel.

FRS Abbreviation for *Financial Reporting Standard.

FRSSE Abbreviation for *Financial Reporting Standard for smaller entities.

frustration of contract The termination of a contract as a result of an unforeseen event that makes its performance impossible or illegal. A contract to sell an aircraft could be frustrated if it crashed before the contract was due to be implemented. Similarly an export contract could be frustrated if the importer was in a country that declared war on the country of the exporter.

FSA Abbreviation for *Financial Services Authority.

FSAP Abbreviation for *Financial Services Action Plan.

FTSE Share Indexes See feature THE FTSE INDEXES on p. 203.

(⊕) SEE WEB LINKS
• Website of the FTSE Group

full absorption costing *See* ABSORPTION COSTING.

full consolidation The method of *consolidation in which 100% of each item of all subsidiary undertakings is brought into the *consolidated financial statements of a group. This will include *assets, *liabilities, income, and expenses. If a subsidiary undertaking is less than 100% owned, the percentage pertaining to the *minority interest must be adjusted for. This method of consolidation is generally adopted in the UK. *Compare* PROPORTIONAL CONSOLIDATION.

full costing method (full costs) A method of costing a product or service that charges all the costs of an organization, both *direct costs and *overheads, to the *cost unit. The full costing method usually takes the *absorption approach to the costing of products and services. *Compare* MARGINAL COSTING.

full cost pricing A method of setting the selling prices of a product or service that ensures the price is based on all the costs likely to be incurred in its supply. *Compare* COST-PLUS PRICING; MARGINAL COST PRICING.

full-cost transfer prices *Transfer prices that are set by *full cost pricing but do not include a profit margin for the supplying division. This method is widely used in practice. However, there can be problems for managers if they do not have accurate cost information, which may lead to poor decision making.

fully diluted earnings per share The *earnings per share (eps) for a company that takes into account not only the number of shares in issue but also those that may be issued as a result of such factors as convertible loans and options or warranties. *Financial Reporting Standard 22, issued in 2004, requires

THE FTSE INDEXES

The FTSE Share Indexes are compiled by the FTSE Group, an independent company owned jointly by the *Financial Times* and the London Stock Exchange. They consist of weighted arithmetic averages for 10 broad sectors of the market (general industrial, cyclical consumer goods, etc.), which are further divided into 38 industry subsectors. They are widely used by investors and portfolio managers.

The widest measure of the market is provided by the **FTSE All-Share Index** of over 700 shares and fixed-interest stocks, which includes a selection from the financial sector. Calculated after the end of daily business, it covers over 98% of the market and some 90% of turnover by value.

For many years the **Financial Times Ordinary Share Index** (**FT 30**) was the main day-to-day market barometer. It records the movements of 30 leading industrial and commercial shares, chosen to be representative of British industry rather than of the Stock Exchange as a whole; it therefore excludes banks, insurance companies, and government stocks. The index, which started from a base of 100 in 1935, is an unweighted geometric average, calculated hourly during the day and closing at 4.30 pm.

The FT 30 has been superseded as the main indicator of market activity by the **FTSE 100 Index** (**Footsie**), a weighted index representing the price of 100 securities with a base of 1000 on 3 January 1984. This is calculated minute-by-minute and its constituents – the 100 largest UK companies on the LSE – are reviewed quarterly.

In 1992 the UK index series was extended to create two further real-time indexes, the **FTSE 250**, comprising companies capitalized between £150 million and £1 billion, and the **FTSE 350**, which aggregates the FTSE 100 and the FTSE 250. They are calculated both inclusive and exclusive of investment companies. The FTSE 350 is the source for the **FTSE 350 Supersectors**, a series of 18 indexes based on industry baskets that provide an instant view of industry performance across the market.

There are also several indexes for smaller companies. The **FTSE SmallCap Index** covers over 300 companies capitalized between £20 million and £150 million; it is calculated at the end of the day's business, both including and excluding investment trusts. The **FTSE Fledgling Index** covers all those companies that are too small to be included in the SmallCap Index but meet the other criteria for inclusion in the UK Index series. The mainly smaller companies on the London Stock Exchange's *Alternative Investment Market are covered by the **FTSE AIM Index Series**.

The **Financial Times Government Securities Index** measures the movements of government stocks (gilts).

Several indexes now measure the performance of companies resident and incorporated in the European Union. These include the **Euro-Top 100 Index** of the 100 most highly capitalized EU companies, the **FTSE Euro 100 Index** of *eurozone companies, and the **FTSE New EU Index**, which covers the markets of the ten countries that joined the EU in May 2004. In 2003 FTSE Ltd launched the Eurofirst Index series in conjunction with the cross-border derivatives exchange Euronext NV; the most important of these is the **FTSE Eurofirst 300 Index** of blue-chip European companies.

The **FTSE World Index Series** was launched in 1987 and now covers over 2700 share prices from 48 countries. With sectors for the developed world and the emerging economies, it is calculated daily and published in sterling, euros, US dollars, and yen.

that diluted earnings per share be disclosed on the face of the profit and loss account as well as *basic earnings per share. The US equivalent is **primary earnings per share**.

fully paid share A *share on which the full nominal or *par value has been paid by the shareholder (plus any premium). *Compare* PARTLY PAID SHARE. *See also* PAID-UP SHARE CAPITAL.

function A section or department of an organization that carries out a discrete activity, under the control of a manager or director. It is the section of the business for which *functional budgets are produced. Examples of separate functions are production, sales, finance, and personnel.

functional budget A financial or quantitative statement prepared for a *function of an organization; it summarizes the policies and the level of performance expected to be achieved by that function for a *budget period.

functional currency The currency of the economic environment in which a business operates. It is usually, although not necessarily, the currency in which the business will produce its audited accounts.

function costing The technique of collecting the costs of an organization by *function and presenting them to the functional management in operating statements on a regular basis.

fund 1. A resource managed on behalf of a client by a *financial institution. 2. A separate pool of monetary and other resources used to support designated activities.

fundamental accounting concepts *See* ACCOUNTING CONCEPTS.

fundamental analysis 1. A detailed analysis of the annual reports and accounts, as well as other information pertaining to a company, to assess whether its shares are incorrectly valued on the market. 2. *See* INVESTMENT ANALYST.

fundamental error A material mistake in, or omission from, the accounts of a business; it is not a recurring adjustment or the correction of an accounting estimate made in a prior period. When a fundamental error is discovered applying to a prior period, a *prior-period adjustment should be made.

funded pension scheme A pension scheme that pays benefits to retired people from a pension fund invested in securities. The profits produced by such a fund are paid out as pensions to the members of the scheme. *Compare* PAY-AS-YOU-GO PENSION SYSTEM.

funds flow statement *See* SOURCE AND APPLICATION OF FUNDS.

fungible issue 1. A *bond issued on the same terms and conditions as a bond previously issued by the same company. It has the advantage of having paperwork consistent with the previous bond and of increasing the depth of the market of that particular bond (*see* DEEP MARKET; THIN MARKET). The *gross redemption yield on the fungible issue will probably be different from that of the original issue, which is achieved by issuing the bond at a discount or a premium. 2. A security that is interchangeable with another of the same class.

fungibles **1.** Interchangeable goods, securities, etc., that allow one to be replaced by another without loss of value. Bearer bonds and banknotes are examples. **2.** Perishable goods the quantity of which can be estimated by number or weight.

furnished holiday accommodation Domestic accommodation available for letting for at least 140 days each year and actually let for at least 70 days. Each letting during a seven-month period of the year must also be for less than 31 days. When this arithmetical definition is satisfied, the income arising is treated as if it were trading income. Loss relief is available, pension contributions can be made on the basis of the letting income, and the income qualifies as earned income.

Futures and Options Exchange (London FOX) *See* LIFFE.

futures contract An agreement to buy or sell a fixed quantity of a particular commodity, currency, or security for delivery at a fixed date in the future at a fixed price. Unlike an *option, a futures contract involves a definite purchase or sale and not an option to buy or sell; it therefore may entail a potentially unlimited loss. However, **futures** provide an opportunity for those who must purchase goods regularly to *hedge against changes in price and for speculators to make large profits. In London, futures are traded in a variety of markets. *Financial futures are traded on the *LIFFE (now Euronext.liffe), whose commodity department deals with shipping and with cocoa, coffee, and other foodstuffs; the London Metal Exchange deals with metals; and the International Petroleum Exchange (ICE Futures Europe) with oil. In many cases actual goods (*see* ACTUALS) do not pass between dealers in these **futures markets**, a bought contract being cancelled out by an equivalent sale contract, and vice versa; money differences arising as a result are usually settled through a *clearing house. In some futures markets only brokers are allowed to trade; in others, both dealers and brokers are permitted to do so. *See also* FORWARD DEALING.

future value The value that a sum of money (the *present value) invested at compound interest will have in the future. If the future value is F, and the present value is P, at an annual rate of interest r, compounded annually for n years, $F = P(1 + r)^n$. Thus a sum with a present value of £1000 will have a future value of £1973.82 at 12% p.a., after six years.

FVA Abbreviation for *fair value accounting.

FX Abbreviation for *foreign exchange.

GAAP **1.** Abbreviation for *generally accepted accounting practice.
2. Abbreviation for *generally accepted accounting principles.

GAAS Abbreviation for *generally accepted auditing standards.

gaming duty A tax levied on the profits of a gaming company in addition to corporation tax. The tax (currently at rates ranging from 15% to 50%) is imposed by the Betting and Gaming Duties Act 1981 on the profits of companies registered under the Gambling Act 2005. The Finance Act 2007 extends the charge to 'remote gaming winnings', which are defined as gaming on the Internet, by telephone, by television, by radio, or equivalent media.

Gantt chart A chart presenting a planned activity as a series of horizontal bands against a series of vertical lines representing dates. It can be used to measure progress or to compare planned production in a period to actual production. The technique was devised by Henry A. Gantt in 1917.

GAO Abbreviation for *Government Accountability Office.

garage To transfer assets and liabilities internationally in order to benefit from tax advantages.

Garner v Murray A case (1904) cited in the determination of the dissolution of a *partnership. If any partners have a debit balance on their capital accounts at the end of the dissolution of a partnership, they must make the necessary contribution to the partnership. However, if a partner is insolvent, the other partners will have to bear the loss (*see* INSOLVENCY). In the event of the insolvency of a partner any losses should be shared in the ratio of the last agreed capital balances before the dissolution took place. This is known as the *Garner v Murray* rule. Many *partnership agreements specifically exclude this rule, however, and agree instead that any such deficit will be borne in the *profit-sharing ratio.

garnishee order The former name for a *third-party debt order.

GASB Abbreviation for *Governmental Accounting Standards Board.

GATT Abbreviation for *General Agreement on Tariffs and Trade.

GDP Abbreviation for *gross domestic product.

gearing (capital gearing; equity gearing; financial gearing; leverage)
The relationship between the funds provided to a company by *ordinary shareholders and the long-term funds with a fixed interest charge, such as *debentures and *preference shares. A company is said to be highly geared when its fixed charges on debt are significantly higher than those for other companies. A highly geared company is considered to be a speculative investment for the ordinary shareholder and will be expected to show good returns when the

company is doing well. The US word **leverage** is increasingly used in the UK. *See also* FINANCIAL DISTRESS.

gearing adjustment In *current-cost accounting, an adjustment that reduces the charge to the owners for the effect of price changes on *depreciation, *stock, and *working capital. It is justified on the grounds that a proportion of the extra financing is supplied by the *loan capital of the business.

gearing ratios (leverage ratios) Ratios that express a company's capital *gearing. There are a number of different ratios that can be calculated from either the *balance sheet or the *profit and loss account. Ratios based on the balance sheet usually express *debt as a percentage of *equity, or as a percentage of debt plus equity. **Income gearing** is normally calculated by dividing the *profit before interest and tax by the gross interest payable to give the *interest cover.

GE matrix (McKinsey Matrix) A tool for analysing the relative strengths of brands or business units within a large diversified corporation. A range of measures are used to score items on each of two dimensions: (i) the attractiveness of the industry or market; and (ii) the strength of the product or business. On this basis, each item is assigned to one of nine cells on a two-dimensional grid:

The corporation should invest in items that appear towards the top left-hand corner of the grid and consider disinvesting from those towards the bottom right-hand corner. Those that appear between these extremes require the most careful appraisal.

To add further dimensions, individual items are usually shown on the grid as pie charts of varying size; the diameter of the pie indicates the size of the relevant market and the size of the 'slice' indicates the market share.

The GE matrix is essentially a more sophisticated development of the *Boston matrix. It is so-called because it was first used by the management consultants McKinsey in their work for General Electric (GE).

General Accounting Office (GAO) *See* GOVERNMENT ACCOUNTABILITY OFFICE.

General Agreement on Tariffs and Trade (GATT) A trade treaty that operated from 1948 until 1995, when it was replaced by the *World Trade

Organization (WTO). GATT was supported by 95 nations and a further 28 nations applied its rules de facto. Its objectives were to expand world trade and to provide a permanent forum for international trade problems. GATT was especially interested in extending free trade, which it achieved in eight 'rounds': Geneva (1947), Annecy (1948), Torquay (1950), Geneva (1956), Dillon (1960–61), Kennedy (1964–67), Tokyo (1973–79), and Uruguay (1986–94).

General Commissioners An unpaid local body of persons of good standing appointed to hear appeals against income tax, corporation tax, and capital gains tax assessments or matters of dispute arising from them. General Commissioners can appoint their own clerk, often a lawyer, who can advise them on procedure and legal matters. *Compare* SPECIAL COMMISSIONERS.

general controls Controls, other than *application controls, that relate to the environment within which computer-based accounting systems are developed, maintained, and operated; they are therefore applicable to all the applications. The objectives are to ensure the proper development and implementation of applications and the integrity of program and data files.

general expenses Those expenses of an organization that cannot easily be placed in any other *cost classification.

general insurance Insurance cover against the occurrence of certain specified events. The most common examples of general insurance relate to the risks of fire, automobile damage or loss, and theft.

general ledger *See* NOMINAL LEDGER.

generally accepted accounting practice (GAAP) In the UK, the practices generally followed by accountants in preparing company accounts. These are defined chiefly by officially issued *accounting standards but also by theoretical *accounting concepts and the requirements of company law and the stock exchange.

Increasingly, UK tax law has taken accounting practice as the rule to determine the amount of profit on which tax is imposed. In the Finance Act 2000, statute, for the first time, used the concept of 'normal accounting practice' to enact anti-avoidance legislation (in this case, to prohibit a company from obtaining a tax advantage by triggering a capital gain on the sale of its future rents). Intriguingly, the way in which the statute is worded has the effect that future pronouncements by the Accounting Standards Board (or the International Accounting Standards Board) in this area are automatically given statutory effect. Thus, a manner of measuring profit for tax purposes that is permitted in one year may be outlawed the following year, without there being any statutory change.

generally accepted accounting principles (GAAP) In the USA, the rules, *accounting standards, and *accounting concepts followed by accountants in measuring, recording, and reporting transactions. There is also a requirement to state whether *financial statements conform with GAAP. The equivalent UK term, which has a less precise significance, is *generally accepted accounting practice. *See* FINANCIAL REPORTING STANDARD; INTERNATIONAL ACCOUNTING STANDARD; INTERNATIONAL FINANCIAL REPORTING STANDARD; STATEMENT OF

FINANCIAL ACCOUNTING STANDARDS; STATEMENT OF PRINCIPLES; STATEMENT OF STANDARD ACCOUNTING PRACTICE.

generally accepted auditing standards (GAAS) In the USA, the ten broad guidelines set down by the *Auditing Standards Board of the *American Institute of Certified Public Accountants (AICPA). There are currently three General Standards, three Field Work Standards, and four Standards of Reporting. In carrying out audit work for a client, a certified public accountant is also obliged to apply *generally accepted accounting principles. *See also* AUDITING STANDARDS; INTERNATIONAL STANDARD ON AUDITING; STATEMENT OF AUDITING STANDARDS; STATEMENT ON AUDITING STANDARDS; STATEMENT ON INTERNAL AUDITING STANDARDS.

general meeting Under the Companies Act 2006, a meeting of company members that is not an *annual general meeting. Such a meeting was formerly known as an **extraordinary general meeting**. The Companies Act requires adequate notice to be given of a general meeting, in hard copy form, in electronic form, or by means of a website. A private company is now exempted from holding general meetings. However, the Act enables 10% of members of a private company to requisition a general meeting (5% where more than 12 months has elapsed since the last general meeting). Under the 2006 Act many decisions that could formerly only be made at a general meeting can now be made by *written resolution.

general obligation bond In the USA, a security in which the government department with the authority to levy taxes has unconditionally promised payment.

general partner A member of a *partnership who has unlimited liability for any debts of that partnership. *Compare* LIMITED PARTNER.

general power of investment A power, introduced by the Trustee Act 2000, that allows trustees to make any kind of investment that they could make if they were absolutely entitled to the assets of the trust fund. Previously, trustees were only permitted to make certain *authorized investments. There are still some restrictions on investments in land.

general price level An index that gives a measure of the purchasing power of money. In the UK, the best-known measure is the *Retail Price Index; in the USA it is the *Consumer Price Index.

general purpose financial statements The *annual accounts and report prepared by companies; they are intended to serve the needs of many users and are therefore regarded as general purpose documents. **Specific purpose statements** are sometimes prepared to meet the needs of a particular group of users. However, as many annual report and accounts are over 80 pages in length it would not be practical to extend them further in an attempt to meet more closely the needs of the special groups of users. Therefore general purpose financial statements are often regarded as compromise documents designed to satisfy to a large extent the information needs of a number of different groups. Recent changes in legislation and the increasing complexity of *accounting standards have resulted in statements that are likely to be understood only by the financially sophisticated. In the USA the usual term is **all-purpose financial**

statements. *See also* INFORMATION OVERLOAD; SIMPLIFIED FINANCIAL STATEMENTS; UNDERSTANDABILITY.

genuine commercial reasons In tax law, a number of *anti-avoidance provisions include a let-out whereby a transaction is not caught under the provisions if it can be shown that it was carried out for 'genuine commercial reasons'. Such a let-out is found, for example, in the legislation on transactions in securities, which imposes an income tax charge in place of a charge to capital gains tax: the Income Tax Act 2007 removes the income tax charge if the taxpayer shows that the transaction is carried out for genuine commercial reasons. A genuine commercial reason can include a non-financial reason. Thus, a view that it is important for the future prosperity of a company to maintain family control of that company can be a genuine commercial reason.

geographic segment A geographical area consisting of an individual country or group of countries in which a company or group operates. Under *Statement of Standard Accounting Practice 25, Segmental Reporting, companies are required to disclose certain financial information in respect of the geographic segments in which they operate or to which they supply products or services. The information is normally given in the notes to the financial statements in the *annual accounts and report. Although segmental information should be of benefit to users, companies are allowed a good deal of discretion as to how they present this information, which can reduce the benefit considerably in practice. *See* ORIGIN OF TURNOVER; SEGMENTAL REPORTING.

geometric mean An average obtained by calculating the nth root of a set of n numbers. For example the geometric mean of 7, 100, and 107 is $\sqrt[3]{74\,900} = 42.15$, which is considerably less than the *arithmetic mean of 71.3.

gift aid A system enabling individuals and companies to donate money to charities and for the charities to recover the tax paid on these donations. The taxpayer must make a **gift aid declaration** to the charity, stating that the payment is to be treated as gift aid. This system was first introduced in 1990, but tax relief was subject to the donation being of a minimum value. From April 2000, however, the system was extended to gifts of any value, including regular and one-off payments. It replaced the *deed of covenant in favour of charities from that date, although existing covenants remain valid. There are equivalent arrangements whereby tax relief can be obtained on gifts of land, stocks and shares, or plant and machinery.

gifts *inter vivos* Gifts made during an individual's lifetime. The treatment of such gifts, for *inheritance tax purposes, depends on the amount of the gift, the occasion of the gift, and the recipient of the gift. Small gifts can be covered by the small gifts exemption (if less than £250) or by the individual's annual exemption (if less than £3000). Additional gifts are exempt if they are given on the occasion of marriage. Any gift from one individual to another individual is a *potentially exempt transfer and only becomes liable to tax if the donor dies within seven years of making the gift. Gifts to some *discretionary trusts are chargeable to inheritance tax at lifetime rates, which is half the death rate. The level of charge is dependent on the size of the transfer to the discretionary trust and the amount of previous *chargeable transfers within the preceding seven years. *See also* EXEMPT TRANSFERS.

gift with reservation A gift in which the donor retains some benefit from the asset given away. Examples include:

- shares given away from which the donor continues to receive the dividends;
- property given by a parent to a child, although the parent continues to live in the property, rent-free.

HM Revenue and Customs has detailed rules to cover gifts with reservation to ensure that such gifts are not used as a means of avoiding tax.

gilt-edged security (gilt) A fixed-interest security or stock issued by the British government in the form of **Exchequer stocks** or **Treasury stocks**. Gilts are among the safest of all investments, as the government is unlikely to default on interest or on principal repayments. They may be irredeemable or redeemable. **Redeemable gilts** are classified as: **long-dated gilts** or **longs** (not redeemable for 15 years or more), **medium-dated gilts** or **mediums** (redeemable in 5 to 15 years), or **short-dated gilts** or **shorts** (redeemable in less than 5 years).

Like most fixed-interest securities, gilts are sensitive not only to interest rates but also inflation rates. This led the government to introduce *index-linked gilts in the 1970s, with interest payments moving in a specified way relative to inflation.

Most gilts are issued in units of £100. If they pay a high rate of interest (i.e. higher than the current rate) a £100 unit may be worth more than £100 for a period of its life, even though it will only pay £100 on *redemption.

gilt repo market A market in the sale and repurchase of *gilt-edged securities set up by the Bank of England in 1996. Its size relative to the money market has made it an attractive market for the implementation of monetary policy with regard to the liquidity of the banking system.

gilt strip A discount UK government stock that has been issued by the Bank of England since 1996. A bond can be divided into a set of payments, which are made by the state and sold at a discount.

giro **1.** A banking arrangement for clearing and settling small payments that has been used in Europe for many years. In 1968 the Post Office set up the UK National Girobank (now **Girobank plc**) based on a central office in Bootle, Merseyside. Originally a system for settling debts between people who did not have bank accounts, it now offers many of the services provided by *commercial banks, with the advantage that there are more post offices, at which Girobank services are provided, than there are bank branches. Also the post offices are open for longer hours than banks. Girobank also offers banking services to businesses, including an **automatic debit transfer** system, enabling businesses to collect money from a large number of customers at regular intervals for a small charge.

Bank Giro is a giro system operated in the UK, independently of Girobank, by the clearing banks. It has no central organization, being run by bank branches. The service enables customers to make payments from their accounts by credit transfer to others who may or may not have bank accounts.

Bancogiro is a giro system in operation in Europe, enabling customers of the same bank to make payments to each other by immediate book entry.

2. A colloquial name for a social security payment made by the UK Department for Work and Pensions to a person in need of financial support.

global bond **1.** A single bond for the total amount of a new issue of bonds, issued on a temporary basis to the bank (normally the *paying agent) that has responsibility for distributing the actual bonds to investors. In due course the global bond, sometimes referred to as a **global bearer bond**, is exchanged for the actual bonds. **2.** A bond traded in a number of different markets.

global custody Safekeeping, usually by banks, of securities held on behalf of clients. It can include full portfolio services, with valuation and reporting, settlement of trades, registration of ownership, use of specialized nominee companies, collection of domestic and foreign income, and tax accounting. These services span markets and securities in a number of different countries.

globalization **1.** The process that has enabled investment in financial markets to be carried out on an international basis. It has come about as a result of improvements in technology and *deregulation; with globalization, for example, investors in London can buy shares or bonds directly from Japanese brokers in Tokyo rather than passing through intermediaries. *See also* DISINTERMEDIATION. **2.** The process by which the world economy has become dominated by powerful *multinational enterprises operating across national and geographical barriers. The emergence since the 1980s of a single world market in which companies can easily move their operations from one country to another to take advantage of factors such as lower labour costs has affected the ability of national governments to order their own economic affairs. The benefits and drawbacks of this process, and the extent to which it may be controlled or influenced, are the subject of much controversy. **3.** The internationalization of products and services by large firms, so that the same product can be marketed in many different countries, usually with the same brand name and imagery.

GNP Abbreviation for *gross national product.

goal congruency The situation in which the objectives of agents coincide with those of principals, so that e.g. the goals of individual managers coincide with those of the organization as a whole and its shareholders. The creation and maintenance of goal congruency is a major concern of agency theory (*see* AGENCY RELATIONSHIP).

going-concern concept One of four fundamental *accounting concepts recognized in *Statement of Standard Accounting Practice (SSAP) 2, Disclosure of Accounting Policies; it is also referred to in the Companies Acts and the EU's *Fourth Company Law Directive. It is the assumption that an enterprise will continue in operation for the foreseeable future, i.e. that there is no intention or necessity to liquidate or significantly curtail the scale of the enterprise's operation. The implication of this principle is that assets are shown at cost, or at cost less depreciation, and not at their *break-up values; it also assumes that liabilities applicable only on liquidation are not shown. The **going-concern value** of a business is higher than the value that would be achieved by disposing of its individual assets, since it is assumed that the business has a continuing potential to earn profits. This assumption will underlie the preparation of *financial statements. If an auditor thinks that a business may not be a going concern, the *auditors' report should be qualified.

Under the terms of *Financial Reporting Standard 18, Accounting Policies, which replaced SSAP 2 in December 2000, users of financial statements may

goodwill

assume that the going-concern concept has been applied unless there is clear warning to the contrary. *International Accounting Standard 1, Presentation of Financial Statements, contains a similar requirement.

golden handcuffs Financial incentives offered to key staff to persuade them to remain with an organization.

golden handshake (golden good-bye) An ex gratia payment or payment for loss of office made by an employer to an employee if the contract of employment is terminated; for example, in the case of a takeover. It is possible, under certain circumstances, for the compensation payment to be paid wholly or partly tax-free. The payment must not be made as a result of a contractual obligation to make such a payment nor should the employee be entitled to the payment. If it can be shown that the payment complies with the regulations then the first £30,000 is tax-free, with only the balance chargeable to tax.

golden hello A payment made to induce an employee to take up employment. The tax treatment depends on the nature of the payment; in some cases the taxpayer has successfully argued that the payment should be tax-free. However, in 1991 the House of Lords ruled that a payment made to a well-known footballer, as an inducement to join a new club, was taxable.

golden key The key that unlocks the *golden handcuffs; it usually consists of a single payment to an employee who has not lived up to expectations or who is no longer considered worth retaining.

golden parachute A clause in an employment contract, usually of a senior executive, that provides for financial and other benefits if this person is sacked or decides to leave as the result of a takeover or change of ownership.

golden share A share in a company that controls at least 51% of the voting rights. A golden share has been retained by the UK government in some *privatization issues to ensure that the company does not fall into foreign or other unacceptable hands.

Goldilocks economy A colloquial term for an economy that combines low inflation with steady economic growth. Such an economy is 'not too hot, not too cold, but just right' – like the porridge in the story of *Goldilocks and the Three Bears*.

good output In *process costing, the sound and flawless output from a process either to a succeeding process or to finished goods stock, the *normal loss and the *abnormal loss having been accounted for in the process costing procedures.

goods received note (GRN) A form completed by the recipient of ordered goods confirming the specification of the goods received. The form includes a description of the goods, the quantity, the *commodity code, the date received, and the order number.

goodwill An *intangible asset reflecting a business's customer connections, reputation, and similar factors. It can be valued as the difference between the value of the separable net assets of a business and the total value of the business. *Purchased goodwill is the difference between the *fair value of the price paid for a business and the aggregate of the fair values of its separable net assets. It may be written off to *reserves or recognized as an *intangible asset in the balance sheet and written off by *amortization to the *profit and loss account over its useful economic life. Internally generated or *inherent goodwill should not be recognized in the financial statements of an organization. The treatment of goodwill is governed by *Financial Reporting Standard 10. The relevant *International Accounting Standards are IAS 22, Business Combinations; IAS 36, Impairment of Assets; and IAS 38, Intangible Assets.

goodwill write-off reserve A special *reserve against which to place a goodwill write-off. The reserve has a debit balance and is referred to as the *dangling debit.

Government Accountability Office (GAO) The investigation and audit department of the US Congress, established (as the **General Accounting Office**) in 1921.

Governmental Accounting Standards Board (GASB) In the USA, the organization responsible for *accounting standards for government units. It is under the control of the *Financial Accounting Foundation.

government grant An amount paid to an organization to assist it to pursue activities considered socially or economically desirable. Grants may be revenue-based, i.e. made by reference to a specified category of revenue expenditure. Revenue-based grants should be credited to the *profit and loss account in the same period as the revenue expenditure to which they relate. Capital-based grants are made by reference to specified categories of capital expenditure and should be credited to the profit and loss account over the *useful economic life of the asset to which they relate. *Statement of Standard Accounting Practice 4, Accounting for Government Grants, provides guidance with respect to the treatment of grants.

Gower Report A report on the protection of investors delivered to the UK government in 1984 by Professor Jim Gower. Many of its recommendations were adopted in the subsequent *Financial Services Act 1986.

grace and notice provision The provision in a loan agreement that a borrower who fails on the due date to meet either an interest obligation or capital repayment obligation or who fails to comply with an undertaking is not initially in default. This prevents the *cross-default clause being invoked. The grace and notice provision is inserted into a loan agreement to avoid problems arising because of administrative mistakes, such as payments not being made on the correct day.

grace period *See* DAYS OF GRACE.

green audit *See* ENVIRONMENTAL AUDIT.

Greenbury Report A report on *corporate governance issued in 1995 by a committee under the chairmanship of Sir Richard Greenbury. Developing a number of recommendations of the *Cadbury Report, it stressed the importance of a *remuneration committee of *non-executive directors, the provision of information on remuneration policy in the annual report and accounts, and the restriction of notice and contract periods to less than one year. Many of its recommendations were incorporated in the *Combined Code on Corporate Governance. *See also* HAMPEL REPORT.

greenmail The purchase of a large block of shares in a company, which are then sold back to the company at a premium over the market price in return for a promise not to launch a bid for the company. This practice is not uncommon in the USA, where companies are much freer than in the UK to buy their own shares. Although the morality of greenmail is dubious, it can be extremely profitable.

green reporting (**environmental accounting**) A report by the directors of a company that attempts to quantify the costs and benefits of that company's operations in relation to the environment. At present relatively few companies disclose such information in their *annual accounts and report. This is, however, a growing practice and reflects the concerns of many investors, consumers, and other stakeholders. New Zealand is one of several countries that have recently introduced legislation on green reporting. The European Union's *Accounts Modernization Directive, which is binding on publicly listed companies from 1 January 2005, states that company information should disclose the environmental impact of a business's activities 'where appropriate'. *See also* ENVIRONMENTAL AUDIT; ENVIRONMENTAL COSTS; SOCIAL RESPONSIBILITY REPORTING.

grey knight In a takeover battle, a counterbidder whose ultimate intentions are undeclared. The original unwelcome bidder is the *black knight, the welcome counterbidder for the target company is the *white knight. The grey knight is an ambiguous intervener whose appearance is unwelcome to all.

grey market **1.** Any market for goods that are in short supply. It differs from a black market in being legal. **2.** A market in shares that have not been issued, although they are due to be issued in a short time. Market makers will often deal with investors or speculators who are willing to trade in anticipation of receiving an allotment of these shares or are willing to cover their deals after flotation. This type of grey market provides an indication of the market price (and premium, if any) after flotation. An investor who does not receive the anticipated allocation has to buy the shares on the open market, often at a loss.

GRN Abbreviation for *goods received note.

gross corporation tax The total *corporation tax payable on the profits chargeable to corporation tax for an accounting period, before deduction of any income tax suffered on investment income.

gross dividend The amount of a *dividend prior to the deduction of tax. Gross dividend is therefore equal to the dividend payable plus the *tax credit. *See* ADVANCE CORPORATION TAX.

gross dividend per share The total of the *gross dividends paid by a company in a year divided by the total number of ordinary shares on which the dividend is paid.

gross dividend yield *See* DIVIDEND.

gross domestic product (**GDP**) The monetary value of all the goods and services produced by an economy over a specified period. It is measured in three ways:

(1) on the basis of expenditure, i.e. the value of all goods and services bought, including consumption, capital expenditure, increase in the value of stocks, government expenditure, and exports less imports;

(2) on the basis of income, i.e. income arising from employment, self-employment, rent, company profits (public and private), and stock appreciation;

(3) on the basis of the value added by industry, i.e. the value of sales less the costs of raw materials.

In the UK, statistics for GDP are published monthly by the government on all three bases, although there are large discrepancies between each measure. Economists are usually interested in the real rate of change of GDP to measure the performance of an economy, rather than the absolute level of GDP. *See also* GROSS NATIONAL PRODUCT.

gross equity method A method of accounting for *associated undertakings in which the investor shows on the face of the *balance sheet its share of the net amount of the investee's aggregate gross assets and liabilities; in the *profit and loss account, the share of the *turnover is noted. *See also* EQUITY METHOD.

gross margin *See* GROSS PROFIT.

gross margin ratio *See* GROSS PROFIT PERCENTAGE.

gross national product (GNP) The *gross domestic product (GDP) with the addition of interest, profits, and dividends received from abroad by UK residents and with those payments made from the UK to overseas residents deducted. The GNP better reflects the welfare of the population in monetary terms, although it is not as accurate a guide to the productive performance of the economy as the GDP.

gross profit (gross margin; gross profit margin) The difference between the sales revenue of a business and the *cost of sales. It does not include the costs of finance, administration, or distribution. *Compare* NET PROFIT.

gross profit percentage (gross margin ratio) A ratio of financial performance calculated by expressing the *gross profit as a percentage of sales. With retailing companies in particular, it is regarded as a prime measure of their trading success. The only ways in which a company can improve its gross margin ratio are to increase selling prices and/or reduce its *cost of sales.

gross redemption yield (effective yield; yield to maturity) The internal rate of return of a bond bought at a specified price and held until maturity; it therefore includes all the income and all the capital payments due on the bond. The tax payable on the interest and the capital repayments is ignored.

gross up To convert a net amount into its equivalent gross amount. For example, an amount payable net of 17.5% *value added tax would be grossed up to the amount payable including 17.5% value added tax, i.e. by multiplying the net amount by 1.175.

group A parent undertaking and its subsidiary or subsidiaries. In UK tax law, two or more companies constitute a group where one company holds more than 50% of the shares in the other(s). This test is usually applied to the voting share capital only. Where there is a group of companies, the availability of the lower rates of corporation tax is restricted. Where the links between companies are made by share ownership of 75% or over, assets can be passed among the companies without a tax charge in respect of *capital gains. *See* CONSOLIDATED FINANCIAL STATEMENTS; GROUP RELIEF. *See also* MEDIUM-SIZED GROUP; SMALL GROUP.

group accounts (group financial statements) *See* CONSOLIDATED FINANCIAL STATEMENTS.

group company A company that is a *subsidiary undertaking or a *holding company.

group income A *dividend paid by one *group company to another. The dividends received are not subject to *corporation tax.

group registration Registration for *value added tax for a group of companies under common control. The business carried on by any group member is treated as that of the *representative member. VAT is not charged on supplies between group members.

group relief Relief available to companies within a 75% group as a result of which *qualifying losses can be transferred to other group companies. The losses transferred are available to set against the other group members' profits chargeable to corporation tax, thus reducing the overall tax liability for the group. A 75% group, for group relief, exists if one company holds 75% or more of:
- the ordinary share capital, and
- the distributable income rights, and
- the rights to the net assets in a winding-up.

From 1 April 2000 members of a group no longer have to be resident in the UK to qualify for relief. *See also* CONSORTIUM RELIEF.

group undertaking *See* SUBSIDIARY UNDERTAKING.

growth rate The amount of change over a period in some of the financial characteristics of a company, such as sales revenue or profits. It is normally measured in percentage terms and can be compared to the *Retail Price Index, or some other measure of inflation, to assess the real performance of the company.

guarantee A promise made by a third party (**guarantor**), who is not a party to a contract between two others, that the guarantor will be liable if one of the parties fails to fulfil the contractual obligations. For example, a bank may make a loan to a person, provided that a guarantor is prepared to repay the loan if the borrower fails to do so. The banker may require the guarantor to provide some *security to support the guarantee.

guaranteed bond In the USA, a *bond issued by one party with payment guaranteed by another party. A common example is a bond issued by a *subsidiary undertaking, which is guaranteed by the *holding company.

hacker A person who uses a computer system without authorization, generally gaining access by means of a telephone connection.

halal Acceptable under Islamic law. The term is applied to those forms of banking and finance that avoid the religious prohibition against taking interest payments. *Compare* HARAAM. *See* ISLAMIC FINANCE.

Hampel Report A report issued in 1998 by a committee under the chairmanship of Sir Ronald Hampel. It reviewed the implementation of the Cadbury Code (*see* CADBURY REPORT) and the Greenbury Code (*see* GREENBURY REPORT) and incorporated these into a *Combined Code on Corporate Governance.

Hang Seng Index An arithmetically weighted index based on the capital value of selected stocks on the *Hong Kong Stock Exchange. The number of stocks was initially 33, because this is a lucky number in Chinese astrology. There are now 42 constituent stocks, with plans to increase this to 50.

haraam Forbidden by Islamic law. In financial contexts, this applies chiefly to lending or borrowing money at interest. Various schemes enable Muslims to take out loans, notably mortgages, without violating this principle of faith. *Compare* HALAL. *See* ISLAMIC FINANCE.

hard commodity *See* COMMODITY.

hard currency A currency that is commonly accepted throughout the world; they are usually those of the Western industrialized countries although other currencies have achieved this status, especially within regional trading blocs. Holdings of hard currency are valued because of their universal purchasing power. Countries with *soft currencies go to great lengths to obtain and maintain stocks of hard currencies, often imposing strict restrictions on their use by the private citizen.

hardware The electronic and mechanical parts of a computer system; for example, the central processing unit, disk drive, screen, and printer. *Compare* SOFTWARE.

harmonization **1.** The harmonization of financial reporting internationally, especially as a result of the activities of the *International Accounting Standards Board (IASB). **2.** The harmonization of practices and regulations in the member states of the European Union. **3.** *See* TAX HARMONIZATION.

harvesting strategy Making a short-term profit from a particular product shortly before withdrawing it from the market. This is often achieved by reducing the marketing support it enjoys, such as advertising, on the assumption that the effects of earlier advertising will still be felt and the product will continue to sell.

haulage The charge made by a **haulier** (**haulage contractor**) for transporting goods, especially by road. If the goods consist of a large number of packages (e.g. 100 tonnes of cattlefood packed in 2000 bags each weighing 50 kilograms) there will be a separate charge for loading and unloading the vehicle.

head lease The main or first *lease, out of which **sub-leases** may be created. For example, if A grants a 99-year lease to B and B then grants a 12-year lease of the same property to C, the 99-year lease is the head lease and the 12-year lease is a sub-lease.

headline earnings per share A form of *earnings per share information provided by the Chartered Financial Analyst Society (formerly the Institute of Investment Management and Research). The figure includes all the trading profits and losses for the year, including interest and profits and losses from operations discontinued or acquired at any point during the year. Excluded from the figure are profits or losses from the sale or termination of a discontinued operation, from the sale of *fixed assets or businesses, or from any permanent diminution in their value or write off. Abnormal trading items should be included in the figure but prominently displayed in a note if they are significant. Many companies disclose the headline earnings per share in addition to those required by *Financial Reporting Standard 22 or *International Accounting Standard 33, and the *Financial Times* uses the method for calculating the *price–earnings ratio.

headline inflation *See* CORE INFLATION.

Health and Safety Executive (HSE) A UK government body appointed to look after the health, safety, and welfare of people at work; to protect the public from risks arising from work activities; and to control the use and storage of dangerous substances. It is composed of representatives from trade unions, employers, and local authorities with a full-time chairman. The HSE enforces its policies through inspection of industrial and other premises.

hedge A financial transaction or position designed to mitigate the risk of other financial exposures. For example, a manufacturer may contract to sell a large quantity of a product for delivery over the next six months. If the product depends on a raw material that fluctuates in price, and if the manufacturer does not have sufficient raw material in stock, an *open position will result. This open position can be hedged by buying the raw material required on a *futures contract; if it has to be paid for in a foreign currency the manufacturer's currency needs can be hedged by buying that foreign currency forward or on an *option. Operations of this type do not offer total protection because the prices of spot goods and futures do not always move together, but it is possible to reduce the vulnerability of an open position substantially by hedging.

Buying futures, options, or other *derivatives products as a hedge is only one kind of hedging; it is known as **long hedging**. In **short hedging**, something is sold to cover a risk. For example, a fund manager may have a large holding of long-term fixed income investments and is worried that an anticipated rise in interest rates will reduce the value of the *portfolio. This risk can be hedged by selling interest-rate futures on a *financial futures market. If interest rates rise the loss in the value of the portfolio will be offset by the profit made in covering the futures sale at a lower price.

hedge accounting Certain accounting treatments that may be followed when an entity uses financial *derivatives to *hedge against risk. Their purpose is to offset the extreme movements that may appear in a company's profit and loss account when a volatile derivative is *marked to market (*see* FAIR VALUE ACCOUNTING). The various options are set out in *International Accounting Standard 39, Financial Instrument: Recognition and Measurement.

hedge fund A *unit trust that is subject to minimum regulation, typically a partnership or mutual fund that attempts to achieve large gains by exploiting market anomalies. These funds are often high-return and are regarded as speculative. Typically, they accept only accredited investors, require a high minimum level of investment (£500,000 or more), and pay high performance-related fees to managers. Many are domiciled in offshore financial centres.

held-for-sale A classification of non-current assets introduced by *International Accounting Standard 5, Non-current Assets Held for Sale and Discontinued Operations. An asset, or group of assets, is to be classified in this way if it is available for sale in its present condition and its sale is expected to be completed within one year. Assets classified as held-for-sale are to be valued at the lower of the *carrying amount and *fair value less any direct selling costs (i.e. the *net realizable value). They must be disclosed separately from other assets on the balance sheet. *See also* VIEW TO RESALE.

herd basis An election to treat a *production herd as a capital asset. The election is irrevocable and must be made within two years from the end of the first year of assessment or company accounting period for which the tax liability will be affected by the purchase of the herd. *See also* BIOLOGICAL ASSETS.

hidden reserve Funds held in reserve but not disclosed on the balance sheet (they are also known as **off-balance-sheet reserves** or **secret reserves**). They arise when an asset is deliberately either undisclosed or undervalued. Such hidden reserves were formerly permitted for some UK banking institutions but are now effectively prohibited as they can be used to manipulate earnings figures and undermine the principle of transparency. *Financial Reporting Standard 5, Reporting the Substance of Transactions, is aimed at such *off-balance-sheet finance.

hidden tax *See* STEALTH TAX.

Higgs Report A report on the role and effectiveness of *non-executive directors produced by a committee under Sir Derek Higgs; it was published with the *Smith Report on *audit committees in 2003. The findings of both reports led to revisions in the *Combined Code on Corporate Governance.

higher rate of income tax A rate of *income tax that is higher than the *basic rate of income tax. For 2009–10 higher rate tax is payable on taxable income, after *personal allowances and other allowances, of over £37,400. The rate of tax is 40%. From April 2010 taxable income above £150,000 will be subject to a new **top rate of income tax** of 50%.

highlights Brief summaries of financial information often given some prominence in the *annual accounts and report of a company. As there are no regulations covering their form and content there is considerable variety in the information they disclose. However, it is normal practice to show at the least the sales revenue, *profits, *earnings per share, and *dividend for the current and previous financial year.

high–low method A method used to predict *cost behaviour in which the observations of the cost levels for various activity levels are plotted on a graph; a straight line is drawn through the plots recording costs at the highest and lowest activity levels. This line then purports to represent the cost behaviour characteristics of that cost item. The method suffers from the major drawback that the line drawn has no particular mathematical characteristics, making the technique weak at cost prediction.

high-street bank *See* COMMERCIAL BANK.

HIP Abbreviation for *human-information processing.

hire purchase (HP) A method of buying goods in which the purchaser takes possession of them as soon as an initial instalment of the price (a **deposit**) has been paid and obtains ownership of the goods when all the agreed number of subsequent instalments have been paid. A **hire-purchase agreement** differs from a **credit-sale agreement** and **sale by instalments** (or a **deferred payment agreement**) because in these transactions ownership passes when the contract is signed. It also differs from a contract of hire, because in this case ownership never passes. Hire-purchase agreements were formerly controlled by government regulations stipulating the minimum deposit and the length of the repayment period. These controls were removed in 1982. Hire-purchase agreements were also formerly controlled by the Hire Purchase Act 1965, but most are now regulated by the Consumer Credit Act 1974. In this Act a hire-purchase agreement is regarded as one in which goods are bailed in return for periodical payments by the bailee; ownership passes to the bailee if the terms of the agreement are complied with and the option to purchase is exercised.

A hire-purchase agreement often involves a *finance company as a third party. The seller of the goods sells them outright to the finance company, which enters into a hire-purchase agreement with the hirer.

historical cost A method of valuing units of stock or other assets based on the *original cost incurred by the organization. For example, the issue of stock using *first-in-first-out cost or *average cost charge the original cost against profits. Similarly, the charging of depreciation to the *profit and loss account, based on the original cost of an asset, is writing off the historical cost of the asset against profits.

historical-cost accounting A system of accounting based primarily on the original costs incurred in a transaction. It is relaxed to some extent by such practices as the valuation of stock at the lower of cost and *net realizable value and, in the UK, *revaluation of fixed assets. The advantages of historical-cost accounting are that it is relatively objective, easy to apply, difficult to falsely manipulate, suitable for audit verification, and fulfils the *stewardship function. In times of high inflation, however, the results of historical-cost accounting can be misleading as profit can be overstated, assets understated in terms of current values, and *capital maintenance is only concerned with the nominal amount of the capital invested rather than its purchasing power. Because of these defects it is argued that historical-cost accounting is of little use for decision making, but attempts to replace it with such other methods as *current-cost accounting have failed.

Company legislation sets out the rules for the application of historical-cost accounting to *financial statements. Companies may also choose to use *alternative accounting rules based on the *modified historical-cost convention. *See also* FAIR VALUE ACCOUNTING.

historical-cost convention The convention under which *assets are carried in the *books of account at their historical cost. *See also* MODIFIED HISTORICAL-COST CONVENTION.

historical summary A voluntary statement appearing in the *annual accounts and report of some companies in which the main financial results are given for the previous five to ten years.

HMRC Abbreviation for HM *Revenue and Customs.

holding company (parent company) A company that holds shares in other companies in a *group (usually, but not necessarily, its subsidiaries).

holding gain A gain that results from the length of time an asset has been held rather than its use in the operations of a business. A holding gain is realized when the asset is sold but remains unrealized when the asset is still held. *See also* CURRENT-COST ACCOUNTING; COST OF SALES ADJUSTMENT.

home banking Carrying out banking transactions by means of a home computer linked to a bank's computer via the Internet (**e-banking**) or by means of a telephone link to a call centre or a computerized system (**telephone banking**). This enables the account-holder to carry out certain operations – most commonly checking the balance held or transferring sums between accounts – at any time of the day or night without leaving the home or office. Although regular transfers, such as direct debits, can be arranged, paying in or drawing cheques is not possible in home banking (although it is using a *postal account). In the UK these services are now offered by all the high-street banks but only a minority of account-holders make regular use of them. Home banking is, however, a growing trend among business customers.

Hong Kong Stock Exchange (SEHK) The main market for listed securities in Hong Kong, first established in 1947. The leading market indicator is the *Hang Seng Index.

horizontal form The presentation of a *financial statement in which the debits are given on one side of the statement and the credits on the other. In the case of a *balance sheet, the *fixed assets and *current assets would be shown on the left-hand side of the statement and the *capital and *liabilities on the right-hand side. *Compare* VERTICAL FORM. *See also* BALANCE-SHEET FORMATS; PROFIT AND LOSS ACCOUNT FORMATS.

horizontal integration The combination of two or more companies in the same business, carrying out the same process or production, usually to reduce competition and gain *economies of scale. *Compare* VERTICAL INTEGRATION.

hostile bid *See* AGREED BID.

hot money **1.** Money that moves at short notice from one financial centre to another in search of the highest short-term interest rates, for the purposes of *arbitrage, or because its owners are apprehensive of some political intervention in the money market, such as a *devaluation. Hot money can influence a country's *balance of payments. **2.** Money that has been acquired dishonestly and must therefore be untraceable.

HP Abbreviation for *hire purchase.

human capital The skills, general or specific, acquired by an individual in the course of training and work experience. The concept was introduced by Gary Becker (1930–2014) in the 1960s in order to point out that wages reflect in part a return on human capital. This theory has been used to explain large variations in wages for apparently similar jobs and why even in a recession a firm may retain its workers on relatively high wages, despite high levels of involuntary unemployment. *See also* INTELLECTUAL CAPITAL.

human-information processing (HIP) The cognitive processes involved in thinking, remembering, interpreting, and *decision making. The importance to the accountant is that an understanding of the way in which people use information in the decision-making process should make it possible to determine the most appropriate information to be provided and the most suitable form.

human-resource accounting (human-asset accounting) An attempt to recognize the human resources of an organization, quantify them in monetary terms, and show them on the *balance sheet. A value is placed on such factors as the age and experience of employees as well as their future earnings power for the company. Although this approach has aroused some interest, in practice considerable difficulty has been met in quantifying the value of human resources.

hurdle rate The rate of interest in a *capital budgeting study that a proposed project must exceed before it can be regarded as worthy of consideration. The hurdle rate is often based on the *cost of capital or the *weighted average cost of capital, adjusted by a factor to represent the risk characteristics of the projects under consideration.

hybrid A synthetic financial instrument formed by combining two or more individual financial instruments, such as a bond with a warrant attached.

hyperinflation A situation in which levels of *inflation are so high that money becomes virtually worthless and monetary exchange breaks down. For accounting purposes, hyperinflation is defined in *International Accounting Standard 29; the appropriate accounting treatment in the UK is set out in *Financial Reporting Standard 24 and in the USA by *Statement of Financial Accounting Standard 52.

hyperlink A word, phrase, or image on a web page that is clickable and enables navigation to another page on the site or another site on the World Wide Web. *See* INTERNET.

hypothecation **1.** An authority given to a banker, usually as a **letter of hypothecation**, to enable the bank to sell goods that have been pledged to them as security for a loan. It applies when the bank is unable to obtain the goods themselves. The goods have often been pledged as security in relation to a documentary bill, the banker being entitled to sell the goods if the bill is dishonoured by non-acceptance or non-payment. **2.** A mortgage granted by a ship's master to secure the repayment with interest, on the safe arrival of the ship at her destination, of money borrowed during a voyage as a matter of necessity (e.g. to pay for urgent repairs). The hypothecation of a ship itself, with or without cargo, is called **bottomry** and is effected by a **bottomry bond**; that of its cargo alone is **respondentia** and requires a **respondentia bond**. The bondholder is entitled to a maritime lien. **3.** The practice of reserving the revenue from a particular tax or duty for spending on a particular stated purpose: for example, dedicating revenues received from the tax on tobacco products to health spending.

h

IAASB Abbreviation for *International Auditing and Assurance Standards Board.

IAB Abbreviation for *International Association of Book-keepers.

IAPC Abbreviation for International Auditing Practices Committee. *See* INTERNATIONAL AUDITING AND ASSURANCE STANDARDS BOARD.

IAS Abbreviation for *International Accounting Standard.

IASB Abbreviation for *International Accounting Standards Board.

IASC Abbreviation for *International Accounting Standards Committee.

IASC Foundation Abbreviation for *International Accounting Standards Committee Foundation.

IBOR Abbreviation for Inter Bank Offered Rate. *See* INTERBANK MARKET.

IBRD Abbreviation for *International Bank for Reconstruction and Development.

ICAEW Abbreviation for *Institute of Chartered Accountants in England and Wales.

ICAI Abbreviation for *Institute of Chartered Accountants in Ireland.

ICAS Abbreviation for *Institute of Chartered Accountants of Scotland.

ICE Abbreviation for *IntercontinentalExchange.

ICE Futures *See* INTERCONTINENTALEXCHANGE.

ICMA Abbreviation for *International Capital Markets Association.

ICQ Abbreviation for *internal control questionnaire.

ICSA Abbreviation for *Institute of Chartered Secretaries and Administrators.

ideal standard In *standard costing, a cost, income, or performance standard set at such a level that it is only likely to be achieved under the most favourable conditions possible. *Compare* EXPECTED STANDARD.

identifiable assets and liabilities (separable assets and liabilities) The *assets and *liabilities of a business that can be disposed of without disposing of the entire business.

idle capacity The part of the *budgeted capacity within an organization that is unused. It is measured in hours using the same measure as production. Idle capacity can arise as a result of a number of causes in all of which the actual hours worked is less than the budgeted hours available. The reasons can include non-delivery of raw materials, shortage of skilled labour, or lack of sales demand.

idle capacity ratio The ratio, sometimes expressed as a percentage, of the production capacity idle during a specified period to the capacity as expressed in the budget. Capacity can be measured in machine hours or labour hours and idle capacity is measured in the same way. The formula is:

(budgeted hours − actual hours worked × 100)/budgeted hours.

idle capacity variance *See* FIXED OVERHEAD CAPACITY VARIANCE.

idle time The time, usually measured in labour hours or machine hours, during which a production facility is unable to operate. *See also* IDLE CAPACITY; WAITING TIME.

IFA Abbreviation for *independent financial adviser.

IFAC Abbreviation for *International Federation of Accountants.

if-converted method In the USA, the method used for determining the dilution of *convertible securities that are not *common stock equivalents in the calculation of *fully diluted earnings per share. The assumption is made that the securities are converted at the beginning of the year or the issue date if later.

IFRIC Abbreviation for *International Financial Reporting Interpretations Committee.

IFRS Abbreviation for *International Financial Reporting Standard.

IHT Abbreviation for *inheritance tax.

IIA Abbreviation for *Institute of Internal Auditors.

IIB Abbreviation for *Institute of Insurance Brokers.

ijarah *See* ISLAMIC FINANCE.

ijarawa-iktina *See* ISLAMIC FINANCE.

illiquid Denoting the position of a company lacking sufficient cash, or assets that can be quickly converted into cash, to meet the demands of creditors. *See also* LIQUID RATIO.

IMA Abbreviation for *Institute of Management Accountants.

IMF Abbreviation for *International Monetary Fund.

immediate holding company A company that has a *controlling interest in another company, even though it is itself controlled by a third company, which is the *holding company of both companies. *Compare* INTERMEDIATE HOLDING COMPANY.

impairment A reduction in the *recoverable amount of a fixed asset or *goodwill below its *carrying amount. This may be owing to obsolescence, damage, or a fall in the market value of such assets. *Financial Reporting Standard 11 sets out the regulations for accounting for impairments by the process of conducting an *impairment review. The relevant international standards are *International Accounting Standard 36, Impairment of Assets, and *International Financial Reporting Standard 5, Disposal of Non-current Assets and Presentation of Discontinued Operations.

impairment review A review, which under *Financial Reporting Standard 11, should be conducted by entities if events or changes in circumstances indicate that the *carrying amount of a *fixed asset or *goodwill may not be recoverable. If *intangible assets or *goodwill are not *amortized over a period of 20 years or less, impairment reviews must be conducted annually.

impersonal account A *ledger account that does not bear the name of a person, such as a *nominal account or *real account.

imprest account A means of controlling *petty-cash expenditure in which a person is given a certain sum of money (float or imprest). When some of it has been spent, that person provides appropriate vouchers for the amounts spent and is then reimbursed so that the float is restored. Thus at any given time the person should have either vouchers or cash to a total of the amount of the float.

imputation system Formerly, the UK system in which the *advance corporation tax (ACT) paid by a company making a *qualifying distribution could be set against the *gross corporation tax for the company. The shareholder receiving the dividend was treated as having suffered tax on the dividend. ACT was abolished with effect from 1 April 1999.

imputed cost A cost that is not actually incurred by an organization but is introduced into the management accounting records in order to ensure that the costs incurred by dissimilar operations are comparable. For example, if rent is not payable by an operation it will be introduced as an imputed cost so that the costs may be compared with an operation that does pay rent.

IMRO Abbreviation for *Investment Management Regulatory Organization.

income and expenditure account An account, similar to a *profit and loss account, prepared by an organization whose main purpose is not the generation of profit. It records the income and expenditure of the organization and results in either a surplus of income over expenditure or of expenditure over income. Such an organization's accounts do not use the *accruals concept.

income code *See* ACCOUNTING CODE.

income gearing *See* GEARING RATIOS.

income generating unit A group of *assets, *liabilities, and associated *goodwill generating income that is largely independent of the reporting entity's other income strands.

income smoothing The manipulation by companies of certain items in their *financial statements so that they eliminate large movements in profit and are able to report a smooth trend over a number of years. The practice is pursued because of the belief that investors have greater confidence in companies that are reporting a steady increase in profits year by year. It is doubtful if any regulations can totally prevent this form of *creative accounting.

income standard In *standard costing, a predetermined level of income expected to be generated by an item to be sold. An income standard is often applied to a budgeted quantity in order to determine the *budgeted revenue.

income statement In the USA, the equivalent of a UK *profit and loss account.

income tax (IT) A direct tax on an individual's income. In general, individuals can earn income without paying tax up to a threshold, with subsequent income giving rise to tax liabilities, usually at increasing rates as income increases (*progressive taxation).

In UK tax legislation income is not defined; rather, amounts received are classified under various headings according to their source (*see* SCHEDULE). In order to be classed as income an amount received must fall under one of these headings. There are some specific occasions when the legislation requires capital receipts to be treated as income for taxation purposes, e.g. when a landlord receives a lump sum on the granting of a lease. In the UK the importance of the distinction between income and capital has diminished since income and capital gains are now charged at essentially the same rate. (Prior to 6 April 1988 capital was charged at 30%, whereas the top rate of income tax was 60%.) The tax is calculated on the taxpayer's taxable income, i.e. gross income less any *income tax allowances and deductions. If the allowances and deductions exceed the gross income in a *fiscal year, no income tax is payable. In the UK, there are currently (2009–10) two main tax-rate bands: a *basic rate of income tax of 20% on taxable earnings up to £37,400; and a *higher rate of income tax of 40% on taxable earnings over £37,400. From April 2010 a new top rate of income tax of 50% will be payable on taxable earnings above £150,000. The previous *starting rate of income tax of 10% was abolished from April 2008 for earned income but retained for income from savings. *See also* PAYE.

income tax allowances Allowances that may be deducted from a taxpayer's gross income before calculating the liability to *income tax. Every individual who is a UK resident is entitled to a *personal allowance, the level of which will depend on his or her age (*see* AGE ALLOWANCE). After 5 April 2000 the former married couple's allowance was discontinued for all couples in which the elder spouse was under 65 on that date; it has been replaced by tax credits for working families with children. If one spouse was born before 6 April 1935, the married couple's allowance is £6965 (2009–10). There is also a registered blind person's allowance of £1890.

income tax code A code number issued by HM Revenue and Customs that takes account of the *personal allowance available to the taxpayer together with any other additional allowances to which he or she is entitled. The code is used by the employer through the *PAYE scheme to calculate the taxable pay using tables supplied by the Revenue (now usually in the form of computer software). The income tax code can also be used to tax *benefits in kind, such as company cars, by reducing the code number and so collecting more tax each tax week or month. The code provides a means of ensuring that the tax due for the *fiscal year is deducted from the employee's earnings in equal weekly or monthly amounts.

income tax month *See* TAX MONTH.

income tax schedules *See* SCHEDULE.

incomplete records Accounting records from which some details are missing. For example, some transactions may not have been recorded at all or some may have been partially recorded. To complete the records the cash book must be examined and, with the other information available, the missing items deduced.

incorporated company *See* COMPANY.

incorporation The process by which a *company is registered under the Companies Act, by Act of Parliament, or by Royal Charter.

incorporation of audit firms The forming of a limited company by an audit *partnership to limit its liability against claims for *negligence. This is permitted under the Companies Act; a limited company can be established, which is owned by the partnership. Although partners directly involved in an audit can be sued, incorporation should prevent other partners from losing everything they own merely because they are members of the partnership. *See also* LIMITED LIABILITY PARTNERSHIP; PROFESSIONAL INDEMNITY INSURANCE.

incremental analysis *See* DIFFERENTIAL ANALYSIS.

incremental budget A budget prepared using a previous period's budget or actual performance as a basis, with incremental amounts added for the new budget period. This approach to budget preparation is not recommended as it often fails to take into account the changed operating conditions for the new budget period, which will not necessarily replicate those for the previous period. *Compare* ZERO-BASE BUDGET.

incremental cash flow *See* DIFFERENTIAL ANALYSIS.

incremental cost of capital The overall cost of raising extra finance. For example, if extra debt is incurred, this increases the risk to equity and debt funders, who will in turn demand a higher rate of return on their investment. The concept is also applied to funding raised to implement specific decisions, and should reflect the risks involved in the activity. *See* COST OF CAPITAL.

independence of auditors The fundamental principle that *auditors must be, and must be seen to be, independent to enable them to behave with integrity and make objective professional and business judgments. Specific threats to independence include:
- an overdependence upon the fees paid by an audit client, especially if fees are overdue;
- any family or personal relationship between auditor and client;
- any beneficial interest held by the auditor or the staff of the practice in shares or other investments or trusts involving the client;
- any loan between an auditor and the client;
- any services or hospitality offered by an audit client to the auditors;
- any services other than the audit provided by the auditor to the client; for example, an auditor may tender for audits by quoting a low audit fee with the intention of attracting more lucrative consultancy work (so-called *lowballing).

The independence of the auditor is strengthened by the Companies Act regulation of the qualification of auditors and by conferring certain rights on the auditor. The professional audit bodies give ethical guidance designed to deal with each of the above situations.

independent financial adviser (IFA) A person defined under the *Financial Services Act 1986 as an adviser on pensions, investments, or life assurance who is not committed to the products of any company or organization. Such a person is licensed to operate by the *Financial Services Authority (before 2000 by one of the *Self-Regulating Organizations or *Designated Professional Bodies). With no loyalties except to the customer, the IFA is bound legally to give impartial advice on products from the whole of the market and should give customers the option of paying for advice by a fee as opposed to commission. This distinguishes the IFA from both a **tied adviser**, who advises on products from a single provider, and a **multi-tied adviser**, who is committed to a selection of providers.

independent projects Projects that are independent of each other in a comparative *appraisal. Such projects are not *mutually exclusive projects, as it is possible to pursue all of them if circumstances permit.

independent taxation The system of personal taxation in which married women are treated as completely separate and independent taxpayers for both *income tax and *capital gains tax. Prior to April 1990 in the UK, the income of a married woman was added to the income of her husband and taxed accordingly.

indexation 1. The policy of connecting such economic variables as wages, taxes, social-security payments, annuities, or pensions to rises in the general price level (*see* INFLATION). This policy is often advocated by economists in the belief that it mitigates the effects of inflation. In practice, complete indexation is rarely possible, so that inflation usually leaves somebody worse off (e.g. lenders, savers) and somebody better off (borrowers). *See* RETAIL PRICE INDEX. 2. The practice of adjusting the *chargeable gain from the sale of an asset to take account of inflation over the period of ownership of the asset. In the UK *corporation tax system an indexation factor derived from the rise in the *Retail Price Index during the period of ownership is applied to the cost, or 31 March 1982 value, of an asset. The indexed cost or value is then deducted from the proceeds of sale on disposal of the asset, in order to establish the chargeable gain. Until the introduction of *taper relief in April 1998, indexation was also applied to gains chargeable to *capital gains tax. In the case of assets acquired before that date and disposed of before April 2008, the indexation allowance was calculated to 5 April 1998 and this figure was used to calculate the chargeable gain.

index-linked gilt A *gilt-edged security in which the UK government has an obligation to increase both interest and redemption payments pro rata to increases in the *Retail Price Index. Interest payments are calculated using the ratio of the RPI for the start date to RPI for the end date of the interest period.

indirect cost centre *See* SERVICE COST CENTRE.

indirect costs (indirect expenses) Expenses that cannot be traced directly to a *product or *cost unit and are therefore *overheads (*compare* DIRECT COSTS). As some indirect product costs may, however, be regarded as *cost centre direct costs, the indirect cost centre costs are usually those costs requiring *apportionment to cost centres in an *absorption costing system.

indirect labour Personnel not directly engaged in the production of a product or *cost unit manufactured by an organization. Examples of indirect labour include maintenance personnel, cleaning staff, and senior supervisors, such as foremen. *Compare* DIRECT LABOUR.

indirect labour cost The wages, bonuses, and other remuneration paid to *indirect labour.

indirect manufacturing costs *See* FACTORY OVERHEAD.

indirect materials Those materials that do not feature in the final product but are necessary to carry out the production, such as machine oil, cleaning materials, and consumable materials. *Compare* DIRECT MATERIALS.

indirect materials cost The expenses incurred in providing *indirect materials.

indirect method The method used for a *cash-flow statement in which the operating profit is adjusted for non-cash charges and credits to reconcile it with the net cash flow from operating activities.

indirect shareholder *See* NOMINEE SHAREHOLDING.

indirect taxation *See* DIRECT TAXATION.

Individual Savings Account (ISA) A savings portfolio for small investors introduced in the UK in 1999, replacing *personal equity plans (PEPs) and *Tax Exempt Special Savings Accounts (TESSAs). ISAs currently entitle individuals aged 50 or over to save up to £10,200 per year free of tax in the form of cash, stocks and shares, or a combination of the two: of this up to £5100 can be saved in cash with one provider (if this is transferred to a stocks-and-shares ISA within the same year, up to another £5100 cash can be saved that year). Under current rules, individuals aged less than 50 are entitled to save £7200 per year of which £3600 can be cash: these limits will be raised to the higher level enjoyed by older people in April 2010. ISAs were formerly available in two main forms: **maxi-ISAs**, which had to include shares and be supplied by a single provider; and **mini-ISAs**, in which each component could be supplied by different providers. This distinction was abolished from April 2008. ISAs can be cashed in at any time without loss of the tax relief, which includes exemption from personal income tax and capital gains tax. *See also* ISA MORTGAGE.

individual voluntary arrangement *See* VOLUNTARY ARRANGEMENT.

industrial buildings Factories and ancillary premises used for manufacturing a product or for carrying on a trade in which goods are subjected to any process. For qualifying buildings there is a special category of *capital allowance, known as **industrial-buildings allowance**. The *writing-down allowance of 4% is calculated using the *straight-line method. The allowance is based on the cost of the building including the cost of preparing the land, but excluding the cost of the land itself. The same allowance is available for certain agricultural and commercial buildings, including some hotels. An allowance of 100% of building cost is available for qualifying buildings in a designated enterprise zone.

industrial development bond In the USA, a *debt issued by a municipality to finance *assets, which are then leased to private industrial businesses in order to promote local economic development.

industry structure analysis The analysis of a particular industry in terms of the opportunities and threats presented to a firm by the immediately prevailing environment. This can be used: (i) to appraise the attractiveness of the industry to investors or new entrants; and (ii) to devise competitive strategies appropriate to the industry in question. The standard tool for such an analysis is *Porter's

Five Forces, which focuses on competition between existing firms, barriers to entry (i.e. factors that prevent competitors from entering the market), pressure from substitute products or services, the bargaining power of customers, and the bargaining power of suppliers.

ineligible group A *group of companies that does not qualify for an exemption (e.g. a *medium-sized company filing exemption) because a member of the group is a non-qualifying company for that particular exemption. For example, if a *public limited company or a bank is a member of a group all the companies in the group are ineligible for medium-sized company filing exemption.

inflation A general increase in prices in an economy and consequent fall in the purchasing value of money. *See also* CORE INFLATION; HYPERINFLATION; STAGFLATION.

inflation accounting A method of accounting that, unlike *historical-cost accounting, attempts to take account of the fact that a monetary unit (e.g. the pound sterling) does not have a constant value; because of the effects of inflation, successive accounts expressed in that unit do not necessarily give a fair view of the trend of profits. The principal methods of dealing with inflation have been *current-cost accounting and *current purchasing power accounting.

inflation targeting A policy in which the government or central bank announces a target rate for inflation in the medium term, as measured by a specified index, and then uses changes in interest rates or other tools of *monetary policy in an attempt to achieve this rate. The policy was pioneered in New Zealand from 1990 and has now been adopted by over 50 countries including the UK. In the USA the Federal Reserve operates a somewhat less strict regime in which a target range for inflation is announced.

information inductance The extent to which a person's behaviour is affected by the information they are required to communicate. For example, the directors of a company required to produce an annual report and accounts (*see* ANNUAL ACCOUNTS) may emphasize the favourable aspects of the *financial statements and may even adopt *creative accounting.

information intermediaries Individuals and groups who obtain, analyse, and interpret information, communicating their findings to others. An example is the analyst who uses the *financial statements and other information relating to a company to advise clients whether to buy, hold, or sell the company's shares. The information intermediary will make use of not only the *annual accounts and report, *preliminary announcements of profits, and *interim financial statements but also any other financial or non-financial information that is available, including that not on the public record, although this could lead to the accusation of *insider dealing.

information overload The increasing amount of financial information that companies are required to provide, some of which is beyond the user's ability to assimilate, analyse, and interpret. *See* GENERAL PURPOSE FINANCIAL STATEMENTS; SIMPLIFIED FINANCIAL STATEMENTS; SUMMARY FINANCIAL STATEMENT; UNDERSTANDABILITY.

information technology (IT) The use of computers and other electronic means to process and distribute information. Information can be transferred between computers using cables, satellite links, or telephone lines and the cellular network (mobile phones). Networks of connected computers can be used to send *e-mail, to interrogate remote *databases using the *Internet, and to transmit sound, pictures, and moving images. These systems also enable *electronic transfer of funds between banks, as well as *home banking, automated screen trading in stocks and shares, and the buying of goods and services on-line. In doing so, they have played a major role in the *globalization of financial and other markets since the 1980s. The entertainment industry has seen a similar convergence of the broadcast media with computers and telecommunications.

infrastructure (social overhead capital) The goods and services, usually requiring substantial investment, considered essential to the proper functioning of an economy. For example, roads, railways, sewerage, and electricity supply constitute essential elements of a community's infrastructure. Since the infrastructure often possesses many of the characteristics of public goods, it is often argued that they should be funded, partly if not wholly, by the government by means of taxation.

inherent goodwill (internally generated goodwill; non-purchased goodwill) The *goodwill presumed to be present in an existing business, although it has not been evidenced by a purchase transaction. Under *Financial Reporting Standard 10 and *International Accounting Standard 38, inherent goodwill should not be recognized on the *balance sheet.

inherent vice A defect or weakness of an item, especially of a cargo, that causes it to suffer some form of damage or destruction without the intervention of an outside cause. For example, certain substances, such as jute, when shipped in bales, can warm up spontaneously, causing damage to the fibre. Damage by this cause is excluded from most cargo insurance policies as an excepted peril.

inheritance tax (IHT) A tax introduced in the Budget of 1986. Inheritance tax is chargeable on the death of an individual domiciled in the UK on all property, wherever it is situated. A non-UK domiciled individual is charged on death to inheritance tax on all UK property. In order to prevent too obvious avoidance, inheritance tax is also charged retrospectively on certain lifetime gifts. Some classes of gifts, such as those between husbands and wives, are totally exempt (*see* EXEMPT TRANSFERS). Others are liable to tax if the transferor should die within seven years of making the gift; these are known as *potentially exempt transfers. The threshold at which inheritance tax takes effect was set at £325,000 for 2009–10; from April 2008 the allowance of the first spouse or civil partner to die can be transferred to the surviving partner, effectively raising the threshold to £650,000. No tax is payable if the cumulative total of all *chargeable transfers is less than the threshold. Above this amount, tax is payable on the excess at a single rate of 40%.

SEE WEB LINKS
- A guide to inheritance tax from the Gov.uk website

initial public offering (IPO) The first sale of shares by a *private limited company to the public. It can be difficult to set an *issue price that will be low enough to attract sufficient investors to take up the whole issue and yet high enough to give the company the maximum capital. An IPO is underpriced if the issue price is less than the market price and overpriced if the issue price is greater than the market price. *See* OFFER FOR SALE; PUBLIC ISSUE.

> **EXAMPLE**
>
> In August 2004 there was a highly publicized IPO from the Internet search engine Google – the largest technology IPO in history. The issue price was initially expected to be $135 but after much speculation it was set at $85. Two days after the IPO the share price was $100.34. The 18% increase represents shareholders' belief that Google would benefit from growth in the Internet advertising market over forthcoming years. In November 2004 the share price was over $180. Overall the IPO raised $1.7 billion for the company.

initial yield The gross initial annual income from an asset divided by the initial cost of that asset. *Compare* GROSS REDEMPTION YIELD.

input tax *Value added tax paid by a *taxable person on purchasing goods or services from a VAT-registered trader. The input tax, excluding *irrecoverable input VAT, is set against the *output tax in order to establish the amount of VAT to be paid to the tax authorities.

inside director In the USA, an employee of a company who has been appointed to the board of directors.

insider dealing (insider trading) Dealing in company securities with a view to making a profit or avoiding a loss while in possession of unpublished information that, if generally known, would affect their price. Under the Companies Securities (Insider Dealing) Act 1985 it is a criminal offence for those who are or have been connected with a company (e.g. the directors, the company secretary, employees, and professional advisers) to engage in such dealing on or, in certain circumstances, off the stock exchange. The prohibition extends to certain unconnected persons to whom confidential information has been conveyed. The *Financial Services Authority has the authority to undertake criminal prosecutions for insider dealing.

insolvency The inability to pay one's debts when they fall due. In the case of individuals this may lead to *bankruptcy and in the case of companies to *liquidation. In both of these cases the normal procedure is for a specialist, a trustee in bankruptcy or a liquidator, to be appointed to gather and dispose of the assets of the insolvent and to pay the creditors. Insolvency does not always lead to bankruptcy and liquidation, although it often does. An insolvent person may have valuable assets that are not immediately realizable.

insolvency administration order A court order for the administration of the insolvent estate of a deceased debtor in *bankruptcy.

insolvency practitioner A person authorized to undertake insolvency administration as a *liquidator, provisional liquidator, *administrator, *administrative receiver, or nominee or supervisor under a *voluntary arrangement. Insolvency practitioners must be members of an approved professional body, such as the Insolvency Practitioners Association or the Institute of Chartered Accountants.

Insolvency Service An executive agency of the *Department for Business,

Innovation, and Skills that investigates the affairs of bankrupts and of firms that have been liquidated by the court (*see* COMPULSORY LIQUIDATION). It can also act as a *liquidator and supervise *individual voluntary arrangements as well as performing various other administrative functions. See feature BANKRUPTCY LAW on p. 52.

inspector general In the USA, the federal office that performs audit and investigative activities on federal agencies, making periodic reports to Congress.

Inspector of Taxes A civil servant responsible to HM *Revenue and Customs for issuing tax returns and assessments, the conduct of appeals, and agreeing tax liabilities with taxpayers.

instability index of earnings A measure of the deviation between actual profits of a company and trend profit. The higher the index, the greater the instability of a company's profitability.

instalment sale In the USA, the equivalent of a UK retail sale by *hire purchase.

Institute of Certified Public Accountants A body of accountants established in 1903 and amalgamated in 1932 with the Central Association of Accountants; in 1941 this body amalgamated with the Chartered Association of Certified Accountants, now the *Association of Chartered Certified Accountants.

Institute of Chartered Accountants in England and Wales (ICAEW)
An institute formed in 1880 from the following five bodies: the Incorporated Society of Liverpool Accountants (1870); the Institute of Accountants in London (1870); the Manchester Institute of Accountants (1871); the Society of Accountants in England (1872); the Sheffield Institute of Accountants (1877). The ICAEW was established by Royal Charter in 1880 and merged with the Society of Incorporated Accountants and Auditors (1885) in 1957. The members of the ICAEW are prominent in public practice and tend to concentrate in areas of *financial accounting. *See also* ACCOUNTANCY BODIES; CHARTERED ACCOUNTANT.

(⊕) SEE WEB LINKS
• Website of the ICAEW: provides technical and business information as well as advice on training and careers

Institute of Chartered Accountants in Ireland (ICAI) An institute established in 1888 before the partition of Ireland. The Institute operates in both the Republic of Ireland and the province of Northern Ireland. *See also* ACCOUNTANCY BODIES; CHARTERED ACCOUNTANT.

(⊕) SEE WEB LINKS
• Website of the ICAI

Institute of Chartered Accountants of Scotland (ICAS) A body of accountants that originated with the Edinburgh Society of Accountants (1854), the Glasgow Institute of Accountants and Actuaries (1854), and the Aberdeen Society of Accountants (1867), which merged in 1951. It is the longest established professional accountancy body in the world. *See also* ACCOUNTANCY BODIES; CHARTERED ACCOUNTANT.

(⊕) SEE WEB LINKS
• Website of the ICAS

Institute of Chartered Secretaries and Administrators (ICSA) A professional body established in 1891 to represent the interests of company secretaries and administrators. It now has 36,000 members in over 70 countries and is regarded as the world's leading authority on questions of *corporate governance.

(⊕) SEE WEB LINKS

• ICSA website: includes a searchable knowledge bank on corporate governance issues

Institute of Directors (IoD) A nonpolitical organization for directors of companies, founded in London in 1903. There are approximately 55 000 members in the UK and more than 65 000 worldwide. Membership has increased more than 50% over the past five years and includes directors from many sectors of the economy. The Institute encourages members to improve their standards of performance and represents the views of business leaders to government and other organizations. Members receive a variety of benefits including information, advice, training, conferences, and publications.

(⊕) SEE WEB LINKS

• Website of the Institute of Directors

Institute of Insurance Brokers (IIB) The UK professional association for insurance broking firms, established in 1987. It represents the views of its members to the *Financial Services Authority, parliament, and other policy makers.

Institute of Internal Auditors (IIA) A professional body founded in 1945 in the USA; a British and Irish branch was established in 1948. Its journal is *The Internal Auditor*.

(⊕) SEE WEB LINKS

• Website of the IIA

Institute of Management Accountants (IMA) A US-based professional body established in 1919 as the National Association of Cost Accountants. There are now some 60,000 members worldwide.

(⊕) SEE WEB LINKS

• IMA website

institutional investor An organization, such as a bank, insurance company, or pension fund, that trades in very large volumes of securities. Institutional investors tend to dominate stock exchanges in many countries.

instrument *See* CAPITAL INSTRUMENTS; FINANCIAL INSTRUMENT; NEGOTIABLE INSTRUMENT.

insurance company A company that carries on an insurance business, or an insurance group, as defined in the Companies Act 2006 (s 1165).

intangible asset (invisible asset) An asset that can neither be seen nor touched. The most common of these are competencies, *goodwill, and *intellectual properties such as *patents, *trademarks, and copyrights. Goodwill is probably the most intangible and invisible of all assets as no document provides evidence of its existence and its commercial value is difficult to determine. However, it frequently does have very substantial value as the capitalized value of future profits, not attributable purely to the return on *tangible assets. While goodwill is called either an intangible asset or an invisible asset, such items as insurance policies and less tangible overseas investments are usually called invisible assets. Intangible assets are increasingly seen as the key to competitive advantage and the *market value of a firm (*see also* BOOK VALUE; INTELLECTUAL CAPITAL).

The accounting treatment for intangible assets has been a controversial topic. Items of intellectual property, such as *brands and publication titles, have appeared on the balance sheets of well-known companies identified as intangible assets, separate from goodwill. However, this was not in accordance with the requirements of *Statement of Standard Accounting Practice 22, which stated that goodwill has either to be written off immediately to *reserves or amortized over a period of years to the *profit and loss account. *Financial Reporting Standard 10, Goodwill and Intangible Assets, was issued in 1997 and resolved many of the controversies. Under the Companies Act intangible assets is a main heading that should appear on the face of the balance sheet. The following subheadings are required but may be shown either on the face of the balance sheet or in the notes: *research and development costs; concessions, patents, licences, trademarks, and similar rights and assets; goodwill; payments on account. The relevant *International Accounting Standards are IAS 22, Business Combinations; IAS 36, Impairment of Assets; and IAS 38, Intangible Assets.

integrated accounts A single set of accounting records containing both the financial accounts and the cost accounts of an organization in an integrated form (*see* FINANCIAL ACCOUNTING; MANAGEMENT ACCOUNTING). This avoids the necessity of reconciling separate financial and cost books and at the same time ensures that both records are based on the same data.

integrated office system (IOS) A program for use on a personal computer or small multiuser business computer that combines some of the functions otherwise performed by a series of single-purpose programs. A typical mix of functions in an integrated office system might be *spreadsheet, word processor, database management system, and graphics. The outputs of the various sections can usually be merged to form a final document containing pictorial, tabular, and textual material.

integrated test facility (ITF) An *embedded audit facility consisting of program, code, or additional data provided by the *auditor and incorporated into the computer element of the client's accounting system. Using ITF, a fictitious entity is created, for example a customer, within the context of the regular application. Transactions are then posted to the fictitious entity together with regular transactions and the results produced by the normal processing cycle are then compared with predetermined results. Such entries should be reversed at defined cut-off dates to ensure that they are not included in the financial reports. ITF enables an auditor and the client's management to check continuously on the internal processing functions. *See also* COMPUTER-ASSISTED AUDIT TECHNIQUES; SYSTEMS CONTROL AND REVIEW FILE.

intellectual capital A complex concept that includes human knowledge, information systems, brand names, and reputation. One popular definition is given by the equation:

intellectual capital = *human capital + structural capital + relationship capital

Here **human capital** includes knowledge, competences, and the experience and expertise of staff, **structural capital** includes information systems and databases, and **relationship** (or **customer**) **capital** includes customer relationships, *brands, and trademarks.

In accounting, intellectual capital is often treated as being synonymous with *intangible assets and valued in the same way, that is, by calculating the difference between the *market value of a company and its *book value. Measuring the intellectual capital is important if one is buying or selling a company or comparing the performance of one company with another.

EXAMPLE

In some companies the book value is only a small percentage of the market value. For example, in 2002 Microsoft had a market capitalization of $250 billion with tangible assets valued at less than $70 billion. The intellectual capital of Microsoft was therefore valued at over $180 billion.

Clearly, the balance sheet for Microsoft is not reporting the all-important intellectual capital of the company, which includes technology, patents, brands, and human knowledge.

---

intellectual property An *intangible asset, such as a copyright, *patent, *trademark, or design right. Intellectual property is an asset, and as such it can be bought, sold, licensed, or exchanged. Further, the intellectual property owner has the right to prevent the unauthorized use or sale of the property.

Examples of intellectual properties include inventions, literary and artistic works, names, images, designs used in commerce, and computer programs. *See also* ROYALTY.

interbank market The wholesale market for short-term money and foreign exchange in which banks, companies, and other organizations lend to use borrow from one another. The **Inter Bank Offered Rate** (**IBOR**) is the rate of interest charged on interbank loans in a particular financial centre. *See* LONDON INTER BANK OFFERED RATE.

intercompany transactions (**intragroup transactions**) Transactions between the companies in a *group. These may be in the form of charges or the transfer of goods or services. It is important in the preparation of *consolidated financial statements that such transactions are eliminated or suitable adjustments made as they do not reflect transactions between the group and external parties. *See also* CONSOLIDATION ADJUSTMENTS.

IntercontinentalExchange (**ICE**) The world's leading electronic market for energy and soft commodities contracts. It was established in 2000 and expanded into futures in 2001, when it acquired London's International Petroleum Exchange (now ICE Futures Europe). The ICE acquired the New York Board of Trade (now ICE Futures US) in 2007.

interest The charge made for borrowing a sum of money. The *interest rate is the charge made, expressed as a percentage of the total sum loaned, for a stated period of time (usually one year). Thus, a rate of interest of 15% per annum means that for every £100 borrowed for one year, the borrower has to pay a charge of £15, or a charge in proportion for longer or shorter periods. In **simple interest**, the charge is calculated on the sum loaned only, thus $I = Prt$, where I is the interest, P is the principal sum, r is the rate of interest, and t is the period. In **compound interest**, the charge is calculated on the sum loaned plus any interest that has accrued in previous periods. In this case $I = P[(1 + r)^n - 1]$, where n is the number of periods for which interest is separately calculated. Thus, if £500 is loaned for two years at a rate of 12% per annum, compounded quarterly, the value of n will be $4 \times 2 = 8$ and the value of r will be $12/4 = 3\%$. Thus, $I = 500[(1.03)^8 - 1] = £133.38$, whereas on a simple-interest basis it would be only £120. These calculations of interest apply equally to deposits that attract income in the form of interest.

In general, rates of interest depend on the money supply, the demand for loans, government policy, the risk of nonrepayment as assessed by the lender, the period of the loan, and relative levels of foreign-exchange rates into other currencies.

interest cover (fixed-charge–coverage ratio) A ratio showing the number of times interest charges are covered by earnings before interest and tax (*EBIT). For example, a company with interest charges of £12 million and earnings before interest and tax of £36 million would have its interest covered three times. The ratio is one way of analysing *gearing and reflects the vulnerability of a company to changes in interest rates or profit fluctuations. A highly geared company, which has a low interest cover, may find that an increase in the interest rate will mean that it has no earnings after interest charges with which to provide a dividend to shareholders. *Compare* FINANCIAL STABILITY MEASURES.

interest-in-possession trust A type of fixed-interest *trust in which there is an entitlement to the income generated by the trust assets. The *beneficiaries of an interest-in-possession trust, the life tenants, are entitled to the income arising for a fixed period or until their death. The capital in the trust then passes absolutely to a recipient known as the remainderman.

Formerly, any lifetime transfer into an interest-in-possession trust was a *potentially exempt transfer for purposes of *inheritance tax; from March 2006, however, such transfers are no longer possible unless the trust is for the benefit of a disabled person. *Compare* DISCRETIONARY TRUST.

interest rate The amount charged for a loan, usually expressed as a percentage of the sum borrowed. Conversely, the amount paid by a bank, building society, etc., to a depositor on funds deposited, again expressed as a percentage of the sum deposited. *See* ANNUAL PERCENTAGE RATE; BASE RATE; LONDON INTER BANK BID RATE; LONDON INTER BANK OFFERED RATE.

interest-rate guarantee An indemnity sold by a bank, or similar financial institution, that protects the purchaser against the effect of future movements in interest rates. It is similar to a *forward-rate agreement, but the terms are specified by the customer.

interest-rate risk (interest-rate exposure) The risk arising from changes in interest rates. In recent decades the different forms of interest-rate risk have been the subject of much analysis, monitoring, and scrutiny. In the 1980s, for example, the *savings and loan associations (S & L) in the USA faced a major crisis as a result of continuing to offer fixed-rate loans despite a steadily climbing interest rate; this meant that their interest revenues remained at a constant level while their interest costs rose. The main forms of interest-rate risk are: the risk that interest-rate changes will impact on the value of fixed-interest assets and liabilities; the risk of mismatches in terms of the repricing of interest on assets and liabilities (as illustrated by the S & L example); prepayment risk, in which a borrower repays an obligation, such as a mortgage, early; the risk that reinvestment may take place at lower rates; and the risk that, as rates rise, repayments will take longer than expected.

interest receivable account A ledger account that is credited with interest receivable (double entry to *debtors until received and then to the bank). It is credited to the *profit and loss account for the period.

interfirm comparison The process carried out by some independent bodies and trade associations in which the accounts and statistical data of comparable organizations are subjected to a *ratio analysis in order to compare the ranges of performance in various areas of operation of the different organizations.

interim accounts *See* INTERIM FINANCIAL STATEMENTS.

interim audit **1.** The conduct by auditors of certain phases of the *audit of a company during the course of a financial year, rather than leaving all the work until after the year has ended. **2.** An audit of the *interim financial statements of a company.

interim dividend A *dividend paid during a *financial year. *See also* DIVIDEND POLICY.

interim financial statements (interim accounts; interim report) *Financial statements issued for a period of less than a financial year. Although there are provisions under the Companies Act that refer to interim accounts in certain circumstances relating to the distribution of *dividends, there are no legal requirements obliging companies to produce interim accounts on a regular basis. However, *listed companies on the *London Stock Exchange are required to prepare a half-yearly report on their activities and *profit and loss during the first six months of each financial year. The interim financial statement must be either sent to the holders of the company's listed securities or advertised in at least one national newspaper not later than four months after the end of the period to which it relates. A copy of the interim financial statements must also be sent to the Company Announcements Office and to the competent authority of each other state in which the company's shares are listed. The vast majority of companies choose to send the interim statement to shareholders with a brief announcement of the headline figures reported in the press. There is no requirement for the interim statements to be audited. Although the stock-exchange regulations require mainly profit information, there is a trend for the larger companies to also provide *balance sheet and *cash-flow statements. In the UK, the requirements only call for six-monthly financial statements, but some of the larger companies with interests in the USA follow the US practice of issuing reports quarterly. The Accounting Standards Board has issued a guide to best practice for interim reports and *International Accounting Standard 34, Interim Financial Reporting, specifies their content.

interlocking accounts An accounting system that keeps *cost accounting and *financial accounting information separately, regularly reconciling the two by use of *control accounts.

intermediate holding company A company that is both a *holding company of one group and a *subsidiary undertaking of a larger group. It may qualify for exemption from publishing *consolidated financial statements as a holding company of the smaller group. *See* EXEMPTIONS FROM PREPARING CONSOLIDATED FINANCIAL STATEMENTS.

intermediation The activity of a bank, similar financial institution, broker, etc., in acting as an intermediary between the two parties to a transaction; the intermediary can accept all or part of the credit risk or the other commercial risks. *Compare* DISINTERMEDIATION.

internal audit An *audit that an organization carries out on its own behalf, normally to ensure that its own internal controls are operating satisfactorily. Whereas an external audit is almost always concerned with financial matters, this may not necessarily be the case with an internal audit; internal auditors may also concern themselves with such matters as the observation of the safety and health at work regulations or of the equal opportunities legislation. It may also be used to detect any theft or fraud (*see also* INTERNAL CONTROL).

internal auditor An auditor who is a member of an *internal audit department of a company.

internal business-process perspective *See* BALANCED SCORECARD.

internal control The measures an organization employs to ensure that opportunities for fraud or misfeasance are minimized. Examples range from requiring more than one signature on certain documents, security arrangements for stock-handling, division of tasks, keeping of *control accounts, use of special passwords, handling of computer files, etc. It is one of the principal concerns of an *internal audit to ensure that internal controls are working properly so that the external auditors can have faith in the accounts produced by the organization. Internal control should also reassure management of the integrity of its operations.

internal control questionnaire (ICQ) A document used by an auditor to assess the *internal control system of an organization. Questions will be tailored to the cycle being audited; for example, the sales or revenue cycle will check that sales are authorized, goods are invoiced, invoices are properly prepared, recorded, and supported, and payment is received at the correct time. The questionnaire will be used by the auditor to identify strengths and weaknesses in the system, which can be used to predict the errors or irregularities that could occur. These predictions enable the auditors to design *substantive tests to discover and quantify errors.

internal control risk *See* CONTROL RISK. *See also* AUDIT RISK.

internal control system A system of controls, both financial and non-financial, set up by the management of a company to carry out the business of the company in an orderly and efficient manner. The system should ensure that management policies are adhered to, assets are safeguarded, and the records of the company's activities are both complete and accurate. The individual components of an internal control system are the individual internal controls.

internal failure costs *See* COST OF QUALITY. *See also* ENVIRONMENTAL COSTS.

internally generated goodwill *See* INHERENT GOODWILL.

internal rate of return (IRR) An interest rate that gives a *net present value of zero when applied to a projected cash flow of an asset, liability, or financial decision. This interest rate, where the *present values of the cash inflows and outflows are equal, is the internal rate of return for a project under consideration, and the decision to adopt the project would depend on its size compared with the *cost of capital. The approximate IRR can be computed manually by *linear interpolation but most computer *spreadsheet programs now include a routine enabling the IRR to be computed quickly and accurately. The IRR technique suffers from the possibility of *multiple solution rates in some circumstances. If it suggests a different decision to that obtained from *net present value (NPV) then more weight should be given to the latter, as NPV is a superior decision tool.

Internal Revenue Code (IRC) The federal tax law of the USA, which comprises the regulations applied to taxpayers.

Internal Revenue Service (IRS) In the USA, the branch of federal government responsible for collecting most types of taxes. The IRS administers the *Internal Revenue Code, investigates tax abuses, and makes criminal prosecution for tax fraud through the US tax court.

International Accounting Standard (IAS) Any of the accounting standards issued by the board of the *International Accounting Standards Committee (IASC) between 1973 and 2001. In 2001 the IASC was replaced by the *International Accounting Standards Board (IASB), which announced that its accounting standards would be designated *International Financial Reporting Standards (IFRS). The IASB stated that all of the International Accounting Standards issued by the IASC would continue to be applicable unless and until they were amended or withdrawn by the new body. For years starting on or after 1 January 2005, listed companies in the EU are required to use adopted IASs in their consolidated accounts.

International Accounting Standards Board (IASB) An independent, privately funded body responsible for establishing and improving international accounting standards. It superseded the *International Accounting Standards Committee (IASC) in 2001. According to the mission statement of the IASB, its objectives are:

- to develop, in the public interest, a single set of high-quality, understandable, and enforceable global accounting standards that require high-quality, transparent, and comparable information in financial statements and other financial reporting, thereby helping participants in the world's capital markets and other users make economic decisions;
- to promote the use and rigorous application of those standards;

INTERNATIONAL ACCOUNTING STANDARDS

1. Presentation of Financial Statements (revised 2003)
2. Inventories (revised 2003)
7. Cash Flow Statements
8. Accounting Policies, Changes in Accounting Estimates, and Errors (revised 2003)
10. Events After the Balance Sheet Date (revised 2003)
11. Construction Contracts
12. Income Taxes
14. Segment Reporting (revised 2003)
16. Property, Plant and Equipment (revised 2003)
17. Leases (revised 2003)
18. Revenue
19. Employee Benefits
20. Accounting for Government Grants and Disclosure of Government Assistance
21. The Effects of Changes in Foreign Exchange Rates (revised 2003)
23. Capitalization of Borrowing Costs
24. Related Party Disclosures (revised 2003)
26. Accounting and Reporting by Retirement Benefit Plans
27. Consolidated and Separate Financial Statements (revised 2003)
28. Investments in Associates (revised 2003)
29. Financial Reporting in Hyperinflationary Economies
30. Disclosures in the Financial Statements of Banks and Similar Financial Institutions
31. Interests In Joint Ventures (revised 2003)
32. Financial Instruments: Disclosure and Presentation
33. Earnings Per Share (revised 2003)
34. Interim Financial Reporting
36. Impairment of Assets
37. Provisions, Contingent Liabilities and Contingent Assets
38. Intangible Assets
39. Financial Instruments: Recognition and Measurement
40. Investment Property (revised 2003)
41. Agriculture

As indicated, 14 IASs were issued in revised form under the International
Accounting Standards Board's Improvements Project in December 2003.

- to bring about convergence of national accounting standards with
  *International Accounting Standards and *International Financial Reporting
  Standards.
  The IASB has no authority to require compliance with its accounting
standards. However, many countries (including the USA and member states of

the EU) now require that statements of publicly traded companies are prepared in accordance with IASB standards. The organization is based in London. See feature INTERNATIONAL STANDARD SETTERS on p. 248.

(( )) SEE WEB LINKS

• Website of the IASB: includes summaries of standards in issue

International Accounting Standards Committee (IASC) A committee that came into existence in 1973 as a result of an agreement by accounting bodies in a number of countries. Its objectives were the formulation and publication of accounting standards, the promotion of their worldwide acceptance, and the harmonization of regulations, accounting standards, and procedures relating to the presentation of *financial statements. The IASC published some 29 *International Accounting Standards before it was superseded by the *International Accounting Standards Board in 2001.

International Accounting Standards Committee Foundation (IASC Foundation) The parent entity of the *International Accounting Standards Board (IASB), whose members it is responsible for appointing. It is funded by contributions from the major accounting firms, private financial institutions, and industrial companies, banks, and other international and professional organizations. The IASC Foundation was formed as a not-for-profit corporation in March 2001, its constitution having been approved by the board of the former *International Accounting Standards Committee (IASC) in 2000. See feature INTERNATIONAL STANDARD SETTERS on p. 248.

International Association of Book-keepers (IAB) A professional association of book-keepers. Members must have passed, or be exempt from, the Association's exams and have completed a period working in a book-keeping position. The Association offers qualifications in book-keeping, accounting, management, personal finance, and business.

(( )) SEE WEB LINKS

• Website of the IAB

International Auditing and Assurance Standards Board (IAASB) A standing committee of the *International Federation of Accountants (IFAC) with a specific responsibility to issue exposure drafts and guidelines on auditing and related services. It also issues *International Standards on Auditing (ISA). The IAASB assumed these responsibilities from the former **International Auditing Practices Committee (IAPC)** in 2002. Its members are nominated by IFAC member bodies, the Transnational Auditors Committee (TAC), and, in the case of public members, other organizations or interested parties.

(( )) SEE WEB LINKS

• Website of the IAASB: a pdf version of the latest Handbook of International Standards on Auditing and Quality Control can be downloaded free of charge

International Bank for Reconstruction and Development (IBRD) A specialized agency established by the Bretton Woods Conference of 1944 to help finance post-war reconstruction and raise standards of living in developing countries by making loans to governments or guaranteeing outside loans. It lends on broadly commercial terms, either for specific projects or for more general social purposes; funds are raised on the international capital markets.

The Bank and its affiliates, the International Development Association and the International Finance Corporation, are often known as the **World Bank**; it is owned by the governments of 186 (2009) countries. Members must also be members of the *International Monetary Fund. The headquarters of the Bank are in Washington, with a European office in Paris and a Tokyo office.

(⊕) SEE WEB LINKS
• Website of the World Bank Group

international banking facility (IBF) A banking facility in the USA that is authorized by the *Federal Reserve System to participate in *eurocurrency lending. Such facilities are exempt from reserve requirement and may have many other advantages usually associated with offshore banking.

International Capital Markets Association (ICMA) A trade association and self-regulatory organization for European participants in the international capital markets. It was formed in 2005 by a merger of the **International Securities Market Association** (**ISMA**) and the International Primary Market Association. ICMA is based in Zürich.

International Federation of Accountants (IFAC) A body formed in 1977 with the objective of developing an international accountancy profession with high-quality harmonized standards. The IFAC is a global organization and works with 157 member organizations in 123 countries. It does not issue standards. *See also* WORLD CONGRESS OF ACCOUNTANTS.

(⊕) SEE WEB LINKS
• IFAC website

International Financial Reporting Interpretations Committee (IFRIC)
A committee that assists the *International Accounting Standards Board (IASB) by providing guidance on the application and interpretation of *International Financial Reporting Standards. Its members are appointed by the trustees of the *International Accounting Standards Committee Foundation. The committee assists the IASB by working with similar interpretative groups sponsored by national standard-setters. Before December 2001, the **Standard Interpretations Committee (SIC)** was the IASB's interpretative body. In that month the SIC was reconstituted as IFRIC with the following specified duties:
• to interpret the application of International Accounting Standards (IASs) and International Financial Reporting Standards (IFRSs), to provide timely guidance on financial reporting issues not specifically addressed in IASs and IFRSs, and to undertake other tasks at the request of the IASB;
• to carry out these duties with regard to the IASB's objective of working actively with national standard setters to bring about convergence of national accounting standards;
• publish, after clearance by the IASB, draft Interpretations for public comment and consider comments made within a reasonable period before finalising an Interpretation;
• report to the IASB and obtain its approval for final Interpretations.
See feature INTERNATIONAL STANDARD SETTERS on p. 248.

(⊕) SEE WEB LINKS
• IFRIC section of the IASB website

INTERNATIONAL FINANCIAL REPORTING STANDARDS

There are currently seven IRFRs:

1. First-time Adoption of International Financial Reporting Standards
2. Share-based Payment
3. Business Combinations
4. Insurance Contracts
5. Non-current Assets Held for Sale and Discontinued Operations
6. Exploration for and Evaluation of Mineral Assets
7. Financial Instruments: Disclosures
8. Operating Segments

International Financial Reporting Standard (IFRS) Any of the accounting standards issued by the *International Accounting Standards Board (IASB) since its institution in 2001. For financial years starting on or after 1 January 2005 listed companies in the EU are required to follow IFRSs in their published accounts. See box above. *See also* INTERNATIONAL ACCOUNTING STANDARD.

International Monetary Fund (IMF) A specialized agency of the United Nations established in 1947 to promote stability and convertibility in the international monetary system. The Fund assists any member experiencing short-term balance of payments difficulties by supplying the amount of foreign currency it wishes to purchase in exchange for the equivalent amount of its own currency. The member repays this amount by buying back its own currency in a currency acceptable to the Fund, usually within three to five years. High levels of borrowing are conditional on the implementation of IMF suggested policies for a country. The Fund is financed by subscriptions from its members, the amount determined by an estimate of their means. The organization has a weighted voting system in which the larger countries have more votes. The day-to-day working of the IMF is carried on by an executive board representing the Fund's 185 members; this is based in Washington.

(((⊕))) SEE WEB LINKS
• Website of the IMF

International Organization for Securities Commissions (IOSCO) A body formed in 1987 with the objective of establishing internationally agreed standards of regulation for the world's securities and futures markets. IOSCO also favours internationally agreed accounting standards to aid in multinational share offering by companies. In May 2000 IOSCO recommended that its members accept *International Accounting Standards.

International Securities Market Association *See* INTERNATIONAL CAPITAL MARKETS ASSOCIATION.

International Standard on Auditing (ISA) Any of the statements on basic principles and essential procedures in auditing issued by the *International Auditing and Assurance Standards Board. In the UK, auditors are required to comply with ISAs (UK and Ireland) for any audit of *financial statements for periods commencing on or after 15 December 2004. Revised ISAs were issued in October 2009 and apply to audits for periods ending on or after 15 December 2010.

((⊕)) SEE WEB LINKS
• Free downloadable pdf of the latest Handbook of International Standards on Auditing and Quality Control from the IFAC online bookstore

International Valuation Standards Council (IVSC) An independent not-for-profit organization dedicated to the development of international standards for the valuation of assets. Founded in 1981, it was originally concerned with real-estate valuation but now produces standards for many types of assets, including *intangible assets. The Council, which is based in London, works in close collaboration with the *International Accounting Standards Board.

((⊕)) SEE WEB LINKS
• IVSC website

Internet An international network of computers connected by modems, dedicated lines, telephone cables, and satellite links, with associated software controlling the movement of data. It offers facilities for accessing remote databases, transfer of data between computers, and *e-mail. In addition, there are high-level services, the most important of these being the **World Wide Web**, a multimedia facility allowing pictures, sound, and video to be displayed. A particular feature of the Web is the use of *hyperlinks between pages and documents. The wider availability of personal computers has led to an enormous growth in the number of Internet users. This has resulted in increasing commercial exploitation in such areas as electronic shopping, *home banking, advertising, and marketing research. Most businesses now have their own websites and companies are increasingly using the Internet to publish their *annual accounts and other financial information. It is also possible for individuals and companies to file their tax returns on line. *See also* INFORMATION TECHNOLOGY.

interpolation Estimating unknown quantities that lie between two of a series of known values. *Compare* EXTRAPOLATION.

intestate A person who dies without having made a will. The estate, in these circumstances, is divided according to the rules of **intestacy**. The division depends on the personal circumstances of the deceased. If there is a spouse or civil partner then there is a fixed statutory legacy, with the remainder being split between an *interest-in-possession trust for the surviving partner and the children's absolute entitlement to the other half, if they are over 18. Where there is no surviving spouse the estate is divided between the children or their issue. Where there are no children then the split is rather more complicated and can include parents, brothers and sisters, grandparents, uncles, and aunts.

in the money Describing an *option that would generate a gain if currently exercised. An option that would not generate a gain is described as being **out of the money**, whereas one that would generate neither a gain nor a loss is *at the money.

intragroup transactions *See* INTERCOMPANY TRANSACTIONS.

INTERNATIONAL STANDARD SETTERS

In April 2001 the *International Accounting Standards Board (IASB) assumed standard-setting responsibilities from its predecessor body, the International Accounting Standards Committee (IASC). The structure, functions, and composition of the IASB and associated bodies had been unanimously approved by the IASC a year earlier.

Structure

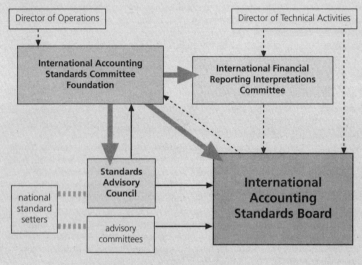

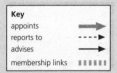

The IASB has sole responsibility for setting accounting standards.

The *International Accounting Standards Committee (IASC) Foundation trustees appoint IASB members.

The *Standards Advisory Council (SAC) provides a formal vehicle for groups and individuals to contribute to the formulation of accounting standards.

The *International Financial Reporting Interpretations Committee (IFRIC) provides guidance on the application and interpretation of *International Financial Reporting Standards (IFRSs).

Membership

The IASB consists of 15 members, due to rise to 16 by 2012. It is required that at least five members have a background as practising auditors, at least three have a background as users of financial statements, and at least one has an academic background. The current chairman is Sir David Tweedie.

Seven of the full-time members have a defined responsibility for liaison with one or more national standard-setters; these members are also non-voting members of the national standard-setting bodies in question. The national bodies are:

Australia and New Zealand	Australian Accounting Standards Board (AASB)
	Financial Reporting Standards Board (FRSB)
Canada	Accounting Standards Board (AcSB)
France	Conseil Nationale de la Comptabilité (CNC)
Germany	German Accounting Standards Committee (DRSC)
Japan	Accounting Standards Board (ASBJ)
United Kingdom	Accounting Standards Board (ASB)
United States	Financial Accounting Standards Board (FASB)

The publication of an IASB Exposure Draft, International Financial Reporting Standard, or final Interpretation of the International Financial Reporting Interpretations Committee is dependent on at least eight of the Board's 14 members voting for approval. Although the IASB claims that it is not dominated by any regional or professional interest, there is criticism that there are too many members from the US and the UK.

The IASC Foundation consists of 22 trustees from diverse geographical and functional backgrounds: six from North America, six from Europe, four from the Asia–Pacific region, and five from any other area. Trustees are normally appointed for a term of three years, renewable once.

The SAC currently comprises about 50 members who normally meet at least three times a year. The membership includes chief financial and accounting officers from international organizations, leading financial analysts and academics, regulators, accounting standard setters, and partners from leading accounting firms. Members are not paid. There are plans to reduce the membership to about 35, the majority of whom should be active users of financial statements.

Recent developments

Recent years have seen considerable progress in the planned convergence of national and international standards.

United States. Publicly traded companies in the USA are currently required to prepare their financial statements in accordance with IASB standards and to include a reconciliation to domestic *generally accepted accounting principles. In November 2004 the IASB announced the membership of a new international working group established jointly with the US *Financial Accounting Standards Board (FASB) with the aim of improving international accounting standards. Previously, the IASB and FASB had conducted separate projects on this topic.

Japan. The position of publicly traded companies in Japan is the same as that of US companies. In October 2004 the IASB and the Accounting Standards Board of Japan (ASBJ) started talks about a joint project to resolve all differences between IFRSs and Japanese standards.

Australia. Australia adopted IFRSs and IASs as its national accounting standards from 1 January 2005.

Europe. All EU listed companies are required to prepare their financial statements in accordance with IASB standards from 1 January 2005. There is no similar requirement for non-listed companies. However, member states of the EU can require all companies in important sectors, such as banking or insurance, to conform to IASs or IFRSs whether they are listed or not.

in transit Denoting goods or cash that have been sent by one part of an entity to another. Funds or goods in transit need to be accounted for. For example, if a branch of a company has remitted a cheque to its head office, which has not been received by the end of the accounting year, the accounts will need to be adjusted for cash in transit to ensure that they balance.

introduction A method of issuing new securities in which a broker or issuing house takes small quantities of the company's shares and issues them to clients at opportune moments. It is also used by existing public companies that wish to issue additional shares. *Compare* OFFER FOR SALE; PLACING.

inventoriable costs Costs that can be included in the valuation of *stocks, *work in progress, or *inventories according to *Statement of Standard Accounting Practice 9. Stocks should be valued at the lower of cost or *net realizable value and the costs incurred up to the stage of production reached. This effectively means that inventoriable costs for finished goods and work in progress include both fixed and variable production costs but exclude the selling and distribution costs.

inventory (stock; stock-in-trade) The products or supplies of an organization on hand or in transit at any time. For a manufacturing company the types of inventory are raw materials, work in progress, and finished goods. An inventory count usually takes place at the end of the *financial year to confirm that the actual quantities support the figures given in the *books of account. The differences between the inventories at the beginning and the end of a period are used in the calculation of *cost of sales for the *profit and loss account and the end inventory is shown on the *balance sheet as a *current asset.

inventory accounting The accounting records and systems used for the ordering, receipt, issuing, and valuation of materials bought by an organization for stock. It includes the recording of the entries on *bin cards and in the stock ledger as well as the procedures adopted to carry out an effective *stocktaking.

inventory control (stock control) A control system to ensure that adequate but not excessive levels of stocks are maintained by an organization, having regard to consumption levels, delivery lead times, reorder levels, and reorder quantities of each commodity.

inventory turnover (stock turnover) A ratio that measures the number of times items of stock are used annually. To obtain an accurate measure of stock turnover the following formula is used for each commodity:

number of units used per annum/number of units in stock.

The number of units in stock may be taken at the start or the end of the year or may be the average of both. Because the information required for this ratio is only likely to be available from the internal management accounts, a different formula using final accounts figures is often used as an overall measure of inventory turnover (*see* RATE OF TURNOVER).

inventory valuation (stock valuation) The valuation of stocks of raw material, work in progress, and finished goods. According to *Statement of Standard Accounting Practice 9, stocks should be valued at the lower of cost or *net realizable value and the costs incurred up to the stage of production reached. This effectively means that finished goods and work in progress should include both fixed and variable production costs but exclude the selling and distribution costs. In the UK valuing stocks at cost, the *first-in-first-out cost, or the *average cost may be used, but not the *last-in-first-out cost or the *next-in-first-out cost. *Marginal cost may be used as a basis of stock valuation for *management accounting purposes but is unacceptable by Statement of Standard Accounting Practice 9 for *financial accounting.

investing activities A heading required in the cash-flow statement of an organization by *Financial Reporting Standard 1, Cash Flow Statements, which shows the cash flows related to the acquisition or disposal of any asset held by the organization as a *fixed asset or as a *current-asset investment, other than assets included within *cash equivalents.

investment analyst A person employed by stockbrokers, banks, insurance companies, unit trusts, pension funds, etc., to give advice on the making of investments, especially investments in securities, commodities, etc. Many pay special attention to the study of *equities in the hope of being able to advise their employers to make profitable purchases of ordinary shares. To do this they use a variety of techniques, including a comparison of a company's present profits with its future trading prospects; this enables the analyst to single out the companies likely to outperform the general level of the market. This form of **technical analysis** is often contrasted with **fundamental analysis**, in which predicted future market movements are related to the underlying state of an economy and its expected trends. Analysts who rely on past movements to predict the future are called *chartists.

investment appraisal *See* CAPITAL BUDGETING.

investment bank A US bank that fulfils many of the functions of a UK *merchant bank. It is usually one that advises on mergers and acquisitions and provides finance for industrial corporations by buying shares in a company and selling them in relatively small lots to investors. Capital provided to companies is usually long-term and based on fixed assets. In the USA, commercial banks were excluded from selling securities for many years but the law was relaxed in the late 1980s and most of the remaining restrictions were removed in 1999. The financial crisis of 2008 saw the demise of several leading investment banks, notably Lehman Brothers, Bear Sterns, and Merrill Lynch.

investment centre A section of an organization in which *capital expenditure is made under the instructions of the management controlling that investment centre. The size and nature of investment centres are determined by individual organizations; they may be a *division, *subsidiary undertaking, *function, *department, or section, or any group of these.

investment company *See* INVESTMENT TRUST.

investment costs *See* CAPITAL EXPENDITURE.

investment expenditure *See* CAPITAL EXPENDITURE.

Investment Management Regulatory Organization (IMRO) A former *Self-Regulating Organization set up in 1986 to regulate institutions offering investment management. It was absorbed into the *Financial Services Authority in 2001.

investment properties Properties owned by a company that holds investments as part of its business, such as an *investment trust or a property-investment company. Investment properties may also include properties owned by a company whose main business is not the holding of investments. Such properties are strictly defined by *Statement of Standard Accounting Practice 19, Accounting for Investment Properties, as being an interest in land and/or buildings:

(1) in respect of which construction work and development have been completed; and

(2) that is held for its investment potential, any rental income being negotiated at arm's length.

However, a property owned and occupied by a company for its own purposes is not an investment property, and a property let to and occupied by another company in the same group is not an investment property for the purposes of its own accounts or the *consolidated financial statements. Investment properties should not be depreciated annually unless they are held on a lease. If they are leased they should be depreciated on the basis set out in Statement of Standard Accounting Practice 12, Accounting for Depreciation, at least over the period, when the unexpired term is 20 years or less. Investment properties should be included in the *balance sheet at their open-market value, movements being taken to the *investment revaluation reserve unless it is insufficient to cover a deficit, in which case it should be taken to the *profit and loss account.

investment revaluation reserve A *reserve created by a company with *investment properties, if these properties are included in the *balance sheet at open-market value. Changes in the value of investment properties should be disclosed as movements on the investment revaluation reserve, unless the total of the investment revaluation reserve is insufficient to cover a deficit, in which case the amount by which the deficit exceeds the amount in the investment revaluation reserve should be charged to the *profit and loss account. In the case of *investment trust companies and property *unit trusts it may not be appropriate to deal with these deficits in the profit and loss account; in these circumstances they should be shown prominently in the financial statements.

Investment Services Directive (ISD) An EU directive (1993) providing a regulatory framework for securities dealing. It enshrined the principle that securities firms admitted by their domestic regulator should be allowed to operate at a European level. From 2007 the ISD was superseded by the *Markets in Financial Instruments Directive (MiFID), which greatly strengthens the single market for financial services.

investment tax credit In the USA, an incentive to investment in which part of the cost of an asset subject to depreciation is used to offset income tax falling due in the year of purchase.

investment trust (investment company) A company that invests the funds provided by shareholders in a wide variety of securities. It makes its profits from the income and capital gains provided by these securities. The investments made are usually restricted to securities quoted on a stock exchange, but some will invest in unlisted companies. The advantages for shareholders are much the same as those with *unit trusts, i.e. spreading the risk of investment and making use of professional managers. Investment trusts, which are not generally *trusts in the usual sense, but private or public limited companies, differ from unit trusts in that in the latter the investors buy units in the fund but are not shareholders. Some investment trusts aim for high capital growth (**capital shares**), others for high income (**income shares**).

The profits of an investment trust are subject to *corporation tax at the full rate; the lower rates of tax applied to trading companies are not available. They are also subject to special provisions in relation to dividends. *See also* VENTURE CAPITAL TRUST.

invisible asset *See* INTANGIBLE ASSET.

invisible earnings Earnings from international transactions involving such services as insurance, banking, shipping, tourism, and accountancy.

invoice *See* SALES INVOICE.

invoice discounting A form of debt discounting in which a business sells its invoices to a *factoring house at a discount for immediate cash. The service does not usually include sales accounting and debt collecting.

involuntary unemployment Unemployment in which workers who would be willing to work for lower wages than those in employment are still unable to find work. J M Keynes (1883–1946) argued that recessions are characterized by involuntary unemployment because firms may be unwilling or unable to cut the wages of workers they employ. Although neoclassical economists have found difficulty accepting this concept, a number of theories have been suggested to explain it (*see* HUMAN CAPITAL).

IoD Abbreviation for *Institute of Directors.

IOS Abbreviation for *integrated office system.

IOSCO Abbreviation for *International Organization for Securities Commissions.

IPO Abbreviation for *initial public offering.

IR35 A rule introduced in the Finance Act 2000 that requires an individual who provides services to an employer through an intermediary (such as a limited company) to be taxed on the basis that he or she is an employee rather than self-employed. This requires deduction of tax at source under the *PAYE rules, imposes Class 1 National Insurance contributions, and gives less favourable treatments for the deduction of expenses than formerly.

IRC Abbreviation for *Internal Revenue Code.

IRR Abbreviation for *internal rate of return.

irrecoverable input VAT VAT *input tax paid on items acquired in order to produce *exempt supplies.

irrevocable letter of credit *See* LETTER OF CREDIT.

IRS Abbreviation for *Internal Revenue Service.

ISA **1.** Abbreviation for *International Standard on Auditing. **2.** Abbreviation for *Individual Savings Account.

ISA mortgage A *mortgage in which the borrower repays only the interest on the loan to the lender, but at the same time puts regular sums into an *Individual Savings Account (ISA). When the ISA matures it is used to repay the capital. An ISA mortgage is similar to an endowment mortgage, except that it does not provide any life-assurance cover and that ISA funds are untaxed.

ISD Abbreviation for *Investment Services Directive.

Islamic finance A system of finance that is bound by religious laws that prevent the taking of interest payments (*see* HALAL; HARAAM). Joint ventures in which the funder and the borrower share profits and risks are, however, acceptable. There are a number of different techniques by which this takes place. **Murabaha** is a good vehicle for temporary idle funds, which are used to purchase goods from a supplier for immediate sale and delivery to the buyer, who pays a predetermined margin over cost on a deferred payment date. The term can be as short as seven days. **Musharaka transactions** involve participation with other parties in trade financing, leasing, real estate, and industrial projects. Net profits are shared in proportions agreed at the outset. **Shirkah** is a partnership between a bank and a customer to share the risks and gains of a project. **Muqarada** is a joint venture by finance providers. **Ijarah** involves profit from rental income on real estate. **Ijarawa-iktina** is leasing of large capital items, such as property or plant and machinery. Leasing is achieved by the equivalent of monthly rental payments, and at the expiry the lessee purchases the equipment. The *Chartered Institute of Management Accountants now offers a certificate in Islamic finance. *See also* ALTERNATIVE FINANCE ARRANGEMENTS.

issue by tender (sale by tender) A type of *offer for sale in which an issuing house asks investors to tender for a new issue of shares or other securities, which are then allocated to the highest bidders. It is usual for the tender documents to state the lowest price acceptable. This method is not frequently employed. *Compare* PUBLIC ISSUE.

issued share capital (subscribed share capital) The amount of the *authorized share capital of a company for which shareholders have subscribed. *See also* CALLED-UP SHARE CAPITAL; PAID-UP SHARE CAPITAL; SHARES OUTSTANDING.

issue price (offering price) The price at which a new issue of shares is sold to the public. Once the issue has been made the securities will have a market price, which may be above (at a premium on) or below (at a discount on) the issue price (*see also* STAG). In an *introduction or *public issue, the issue price is fixed by the company on the advice of its stockbrokers and bankers; in an *issue by tender the issue price is fixed by the highest price that can be obtained for the whole issue; in a *placing the issue price is negotiated by the issuing house or broker involved. *See also* INITIAL PUBLIC OFFERING; OFFER FOR SALE.

IT **1.** Abbreviation for *income tax. **2.** *Abbreviation for* *information technology.

ITF Abbreviation for *integrated test facility.

IVA Abbreviation for individual *voluntary arrangement.

IVSC Abbreviation for *International Valuation Standards Council.

JDS Abbreviation for Joint Disciplinary Scheme. *See* ACCOUNTANCY AND ACTUARIAL DISCIPLINE BOARD.

JIT techniques Abbreviation for *just-in-time techniques.

job An identifiable discrete piece of work carried out by an organization. For costing purposes a job is usually given a *job number.

job card (job ticket) Traditionally, a card containing the written instructions for the operations to be carried out for the completion of a job. The instructions are now likely to be in the form of a computer printout.

job cost The costs incurred in carrying out a *job. These are usually analysed into the constituent costs, for example *direct materials costs, *direct labour costs, and *overheads.

job costing (job order costing; specific order costing) A costing process to assess the individual costs of performing each *job. This is important in organizations that produce a range of different products and also in service organizations.

job number A number assigned to each job where *job costing is in operation; it enables the costs to be charged to this number so that all the individual costs for a job can be collected.

job ticket *See* JOB CARD.

joint account A bank or building-society account held in the names or two or more people, often husband and wife. On the death of one party the balance in the account goes to the survivor(s), except in the case of partnerships, executors' accounts, or trustees' accounts. It is usual for any of the holders of a joint account to operate it alone.

joint and several liability A liability that is entered into by a group, on the understanding that if any of the group fail in their undertaking the liability must be shared by the remainder. Thus, if two people enter into a joint and several guarantee for a bank loan, if one becomes bankrupt the other is liable for repayment of the whole loan.

joint audit An *audit carried out by two or more firms, who prepare the *auditors' report jointly.

joint costs In *process costing, the costs incurred prior to the separation point after which the *joint products are treated individually. The joint costs are therefore common to the joint products; in order to determine individual product costs, the joint costs need to be apportioned between the joint products. The joint costs may be apportioned on the basis of the number of units, weights, or volumes of each product or their *sales values at the *separation point. *See also* COMMON COSTS.

Joint Disciplinary Scheme (JDS) *See* Accountancy and Actuarial Discipline Board.

joint products The output of a process in which there is more than one product and all the products have similar or equal economic importance. *Compare* main product; by-product.

joint-stock company A *company in which the members pool their stock and trade on the basis of their joint stock. This differs from the earliest type of company, the merchant corporations or regulated companies of the 14th century, in which members traded with their own stock, subject to the rules of the company. Joint-stock companies originated in the 17th century; some still exist, although they are now rare.

joint venture A commercial undertaking entered into jointly by two or more entities. Joint ventures are generally governed by the Partnership Act 1890 but they differ from *partnerships in that they are limited by time or by activity. Separate books are not usually kept and the joint venturers will have a profit- or loss-sharing ratio for the purpose of the joint venture only. In its financial statements each reporting entity accounts for its own share of the assets, liabilities, and cash flows of the venture. Joint ventures have become increasingly common as companies cooperate with each other in international markets, in order to share costs, exploit new technologies, or gain access to new markets.

journal **1.** A *book of prime entry in which transfers to be made from one *account to another are recorded. It is used for transfers not recorded in any other of the books of prime entry, such as the *sales day book or the *cash book. **2.** Any *day book.

judgment debtor A person against whom a court judgment has been entered, ordering payment of money that he or she owes to another person (the **judgment creditor**).

judgmental sampling (non-statistical sampling) A form of sampling in which the auditor selects a *sample from a population on the basis of his or her own experience and assessment of the situation, rather than using *statistical sampling techniques.

junk bond A *bond that offers a high rate of interest because it carries a higher than usual probability of default. The issuing of junk bonds to finance the takeover of large companies in the USA is a practice that has developed rapidly over recent decades and has spread elsewhere. *See* leveraged buyout.

just-in-time (JIT) An approach to manufacturing designed to match production to demand by only supplying goods to order. This has the effect of reducing stocks of raw material and finished goods, encouraging those production activities that add value to the output, and minimizing levels of scrap and defective units. Just-in-time techniques are often associated with *continuous improvement and *Kaizen costing in the approach known as *Total Quality Management.

kaizen costing A technique for reducing and managing costs during the manufacturing process. _Kaizen_ is the Japanese term for making *continuous improvements to a process through small incremental changes. Managers will start with the previous year's actual costs and set a target cost-reduction ratio for the current year. All employees are expected to contribute to improving processes and reducing costs. For _kaizen_ costing to succeed, a degree of *employee empowerment is therefore required.

Keogh plan A US savings scheme to create a pension plan for self-employed people or employees of small and unincorporated businesses, in which tax is deferred until withdrawals are made. It can be held at the same time as a corporate pension or individual retirement account. Keogh plans originated with the Self-Employment Individuals Retirement Act 1982.

key management Those employees in senior positions in an organization who have authority for directing or controlling its major activities and resources.

kickback A colloquial term for an illegal payment made to secure favourable treatment in the award of a contract.

killer bee An investment banker who helps a business to resist a predatory *takeover bid by devising strategies to make the target company appear a less attractive proposition. _See_ POISON PILL.

kite An informal name for an *accommodation bill. **Kite-flying** or **kiting** is the discounting of a kite (accommodation bill) at a bank, knowing that the person on whom it is drawn will dishonour it.

kiting **1.** _See_ KITE. **2.** An informal US name for the dishonest practice of improving the apparent cash position in a company's accounts by paying a large cheque on the last day of the accounting period from one of its current accounts into a second current account. Because the first account will not have been debited, but the second account will have been credited, the overall cash position is temporarily overstated. **3.** The act of changing a cheque illegally by altering the amount to be drawn.

know-how Industrial information and techniques that assist in manufacturing or processing goods or materials. *Capital expenditure incurred in the acquisition of know-how may qualify for allowances against *corporation tax.

knowledge management The creation and sharing of knowledge in an organization. Knowledge management is a relatively new concept and there are many different definitions. Successful knowledge management initiatives will typically lead to improved employee involvement, improved individual and organizational creativity, and enhanced intrapreneurship and innovation.

labour costs (wages costs) Expenditure on wages paid to those operators who are both directly and indirectly concerned with the production of the product, service, or *cost unit. *See also* DIRECT LABOUR COST; INDIRECT LABOUR COST.

labour hour rate *See* DIRECT LABOUR HOUR RATE.

labour intensive Denoting a company or industry in which *direct labour costs are more important than *capital expenditure. *Compare* CAPITAL INTENSIVE.

labour variances *See* DIRECT LABOUR EFFICIENCY VARIANCE; DIRECT LABOUR RATE OF PAY VARIANCE; DIRECT LABOUR TOTAL COST VARIANCE.

lagging measures *See* BALANCED SCORECARD.

lakh In the Indian subcontinent, a unit of 10^5 (100,000), often used in citing sums of money. For example, twenty lakh Indian rupees = IRS 2 million. A hundred lakh make one **crore** (10^7 or 10,000,000). Separators are often used to indicate the number of lakh rather than the number of millions, so that e.g. 4.5 million (45 lakh) is written 45,00,000.

landfill tax In the UK, a tax charge on the commercial disposal of waste by way of landfill. The current (2009–10) standard rate is £40 per tonne.

lapping In the USA, the fraudulent practice of concealing a shortage of cash by delaying the recording of cash receipts. In the UK it is referred to as **teeming and lading**. There are a number of variations, but essentially the cashier conceals the theft of cash received from the first customer by recording the cash received from the second customer as attributable to the first, and so on with subsequent customers. The cashier hopes to be in a position to replace the cash before the dishonesty is discovered. As such hopes are frequently based on attempts at gambling, the deception is often discovered.

last-in-first-out cost (LIFO cost) A method of valuing units of raw material or finished goods issued from stock by using the latest unit value for pricing the issues until all the quantity of stock received at that price is used up. The next earliest price is then used for pricing the issues, and so on. Because the issues are based on a LIFO cost, the valuation of closing stocks is described as being on the same LIFO basis. The method may also be used in *process costing to value the work in process at the end of an accounting period. This method of costing is not normally acceptable for stock valuation in the UK. *Compare* FIRST-IN-FIRST-OUT COST; NEXT-IN-FIRST-OUT COST.

LBO Abbreviation for *leveraged buyout.

leading and lagging Techniques often used at the end of a financial year to enhance a cash position and reduce borrowing. This is achieved by arranging for the settlement of outstanding obligations to be accelerated (leading) or delayed (lagging).

leading measures *See* BALANCED SCORECARD.

lead managers (lead banks) Banks that launch a new issue of bonds or *syndicated bank facility. They are usually chosen either because they have a close relationship with the borrower or because they have been successful in a *competitive bought deal contest. They are the main organizer of the transactions.

learning and growth perspective *See* BALANCED SCORECARD.

learning curve A technique that takes into account the reduction in time taken to carry out production as the cumulative output rises. The concept is based on a doubling of output, so that a 70% learning curve means that the cumulative average time taken per unit falls to 70% of the previous cumulative average time as the output doubles. The cumulative average time per unit is measured from the very first unit produced. The formula for the learning curve is:

$$y = ax^{-b},$$

where y is the cumulative average time per unit of production, a is the time taken to produce the first unit, x is the cumulative number of units manufactured to date, and b is the learning coefficient.

lease A contract between the owner of a specific asset, the **lessor**, and another party, the **lessee**, allowing the latter to hire the asset. The lessor retains the right of ownership but the lessee acquires the right to use the asset for a specific period of time in return for the payment of specific rentals or payments. *Statement of Standard Accounting Practice 21, Accounting for Leases and Hire Purchase Contracts, classifies leases into *operating leases and *finance leases with differing accounting treatments.

leaseback (renting back) An arrangement in which the owner of an *asset (such as land or buildings) sells it to another party but immediately enters into a *lease agreement with the purchaser to obtain the right to use the asset. Such a transaction is a method for raising funds and can affect the *financial statements of a company, depending on whether a *finance lease or an *operating lease is entered into.

leasehold The right acquired under a *lease to use land and buildings for a specified period in return for the payment of a specific rental.

least squares method A method of estimating *cost behaviour in which observed cost levels for various activity levels are plotted on a graph and the line of best fit is calculated (*see* LINEAR REGRESSION). The regression line can then be used to forecast the total costs incurred for different levels of activity. Because this method uses all the observations and determines the line of best fit mathematically, it is seen as a better predictor than the *high–low method.

ledger A collection of *accounts of a similar type. Traditionally, a ledger was a large book with separate pages for each account; in modern systems they will usually consist of computer records. The most common ledgers are the *nominal ledger containing the *impersonal accounts, the *debtors' ledger containing the accounts of an organization's customers, and the *creditors' ledger containing the accounts of an organization's suppliers.

ledger account An *account in a ledger that holds the records for all the transactions relating to that particular person (e.g. a *debtor), thing (e.g. *stock item), or activity (e.g. sales).

legal capital In the USA, the amount of *stockholders' equity, which cannot be reduced by the payment of dividends. This is the value of a company's shares in the balance sheet.

legal person *See* ARTIFICIAL PERSON.

legal tender Money that must be accepted in discharge of a debt. It may be **limited legal tender**, i.e. it must be accepted but only up to specified limits of payment; or **unlimited legal tender**, i.e. acceptable in settlement of debts of any amount. Bank of England notes and the £2 and £1 coins are unlimited legal tender in the UK. Other Royal Mint coins are limited legal tender; i.e. debts up to £10 can be paid in 50p and 20p coins; up to £5 by 10p and 5p coins; and up to 20p by bronze coins.

lessee *See* LEASE.

lessor *See* LEASE.

letter of awareness A formal letter written by a parent company to a lender, acknowledging its relationship with another group company and its awareness of a loan being made to that company. It is the weakest form of a *letter of comfort.

letter of comfort A letter to a bank from the parent company of a subsidiary that is trying to borrow money from the bank. The letter gives no guarantee for the repayment of the projected loan but offers the bank the comfort of knowing that the subsidiary has made the parent company aware of its intention to borrow; the parent also usually supports the application, giving, at least, an assurance that it intends that the subsidiary should remain in business and that it will give notice of any relevant change of ownership. *See also* LETTER OF AWARENESS.

letter of credit (documentary credit) A letter from one banker to another authorizing the payment of a specified sum to the person named in the letter on certain specified conditions. Commercially, letters of credit are widely used in the international import and export trade as a means of payment. In an export contract, the exporter may require the foreign importer to open a letter of credit at the importer's local bank (the issuing bank) for the amount of the goods. This will state that it is to be negotiable at a bank (the negotiating bank) in the exporter's country in favour of the exporter; often, the exporter (who is called the beneficiary of the credit) will give the name of the negotiating bank. On presentation of the shipping documents (which are listed in the letter of credit) the beneficiary will receive payment from the negotiating bank.

An **irrevocable letter of credit** cannot be cancelled by the person who opens it or by the issuing bank without the beneficiary's consent, whereas a **revocable letter of credit** can. In a **confirmed letter of credit** the negotiating bank guarantees to pay the beneficiary, even if the issuing bank fails to honour its commitments (in an **unconfirmed letter of credit** this guarantee is not given). A confirmed irrevocable letter of credit therefore provides the most reliable means of being paid for exported goods. However, all letters of credit have an expiry date, after which they can only be negotiated by the consent of all the parties.

A **circular letter of credit** is an instruction from a bank to its correspondent banks to pay the beneficiary a stated sum on presentation of a means of identification. It has now been replaced by traveller's cheques.

Although the International Chamber of Commerce recommended **documentary credit** as the preferred term for these instruments in 1983, 'letter of credit' is still the more generally used term.

letter of engagement *See* ENGAGEMENT LETTER.

letter of intent (memorandum of understanding) A document that sets out the main terms of an agreement between two or more parties and their intention to enter into a binding *contract once certain details have been finalized. A letter of intent is not itself a formal contract but certain of its provisions (e.g. concerning payment for any work completed) may nevertheless be enforceable. Letters of intent are widely used in the UK construction industry, where their usual purpose is to encourage a contractor to begin work on a time-sensitive project before legal formalities have been completed.

letter of representation A formal written record of representations made by the management of an organization to the auditors. The letter is prepared by the auditor and signed by management on a date as near as possible to the date of the *auditors' report and after all audit work has been completed, including the review of events occurring after the *balance sheet date, for example. The information referred to in the letter is material to the *financial statements for which the auditor is unable to obtain independent corroborative evidence. These matters might include any future legal claims and *adjusting events.

leverage 1. The US word for *gearing. 2. The use by a company of its limited assets to guarantee substantial loans to finance its business.

leveraged buyout (LBO) The acquisition of one company by another through the use of borrowed funds. The intention is that the loans will be repaid from the cash flow of the acquired company. In the 1980s many takeovers in the USA were financed by the issue of *junk bonds in highly leveraged buyouts. More recently, LBOs have become associated with the activities of *private equity firms.

leverage ratios *See* GEARING RATIOS.

LIAB Abbreviation for Licentiate of the *International Association of Book-keepers.

liability An obligation to transfer economic benefits (generally money) as a result of past transactions (e.g. the purchase of a *fixed asset or a *current asset). *See also* CONTINGENT LIABILITY; CURRENT LIABILITIES; DEFERRED CREDIT; LONG-TERM LIABILITY; SECURED LIABILITY.

LIBID Abbreviation for *London Inter Bank Bid Rate.

LIBOR Abbreviation for *London Inter Bank Offered Rate.

life assurance An insurance policy that pays a specified amount of money on the death of the life assured or, in the case of an endowment assurance policy, on the death of the life assured or at the end of an agreed period, whichever is the earlier. Life assurance grew from a humble means of providing funeral expenses to a means of saving for oneself or one's dependants, with certain tax advantages.

life-cycle costing The approach to determining the total costs of a *fixed asset that takes into account all the costs likely to be incurred both in acquiring it and in operating it over its effective life. For example, the initial cost to an airline of an aircraft is only part of the costs relevant to the decision to purchase it. The operating costs over its effective life are also relevant and would therefore be part of the decision-making data. This is an aspect of *terotechnology.

lifetime value The future long-term profitability of a particular customer. There is no clear agreement on how lifetime value can be measured. One technique is to forecast future cash flows for the customer, identify an appropriate *discount rate or *cost of capital, and then calculate the *net present value of the cash flows. This is a relatively simple calculation but it does involve managers making difficult assumptions. One key assumption is customer retention. Managers may not agree on how loyal a customer will be in the future and whether sales will increase or decrease. A company will always be looking at strategies for maximizing the lifetime value of customers. *See also* CUSTOMER PROFITABILITY ANALYSIS.

LIFFE The London International Financial Futures and Options Exchange. In 1982 a *financial futures market opened in London's Royal Exchange, to provide facilities within the European time zone for dealing in options and futures contracts, including those in government bonds, share indexes, foreign currencies, and interest rates. The London Financial Futures Exchange moved into its own premises in the City of London in 1991. The London Traded Options Market merged with LIFFE in 1992, when the words 'and Options' were added to its full name, although the familiar acronym (pronounced 'lifey') remained unchanged. Electronic trading via the LIFFE CONNECT system was introduced in 1989 but did not replace live pit trading until 1998. In 1996 LIFFE merged with the London Commodity Exchange, making it the first exchange to provide futures and options contracts on financial, equity, and commodity products and equity indices. Since 2002 it has been part of the pan-European exchange *Euronext NV, with markets in Amsterdam, Brussels, Lisbon, and Paris. The London exchange is now known as **Euronext.liffe**.

LIFO cost Abbreviation for *last-in-first-out cost.

lifting the veil The act of disregarding the veil of *incorporation that separates the personality of a corporation from the personalities of its members and directors. This exceptional course is occasionally sanctioned by statute, for example in relation to *wrongful trading or *fraudulent trading, when it may result in members or directors of a limited company incurring liability. It is also employed by the courts, for example if incorporation has been used to perpetrate fraud or gives rise to unreal distinctions between a company and its subsidiary companies.

LIMEAN Abbreviation for *London Inter Bank Mean Rate.

limitation of scope   *See* EXCEPT FOR.

limited company   A *company in which the liability of the members in respect of the company's debts is limited. It may be **limited by shares**, in which case the liability of the members on a winding-up is limited to the amount (if any) unpaid on their shares. This is by far the most common type of registered company. The liability of the members may alternatively be **limited by guarantee**; in this case the liability of members is limited by the memorandum to a certain amount, which the members undertake to contribute on winding-up. These are usually societies, clubs, or trade associations. Since 1980 it has not been possible for such a company to be formed with a share capital, or converted to a company limited by guarantee with a share capital. *See also* PUBLIC LIMITED COMPANY.

limited liability   *See* LIMITED COMPANY; LIMITED LIABILITY PARTNERSHIP.

limited liability partnership   A legally recognized entity under the Limited Liability Partnership Act 2000. This type of business organization is intended to combine the flexibility of a traditional *partnership with the corporate notion of limited liability. Persons intending to set up a limited liability partnership must register it with *Companies House. There are also several disclosure requirements that are similar in nature to those required by companies. Much of the pressure for this change in the law was led by accountancy and audit partnerships, wishing to limit the liability of partners against claims for *negligence. *See also* INCORPORATION OF AUDIT FIRMS; PROFESSIONAL INDEMNITY INSURANCE.

limited partner   A partner whose liability is limited to his or her investment in the *partnership. A partnership in which one or more (but not all) of the partners are limited partners is called a **limited partnership** and is governed by the Limited Partnership Act 1907. *Compare* GENERAL PARTNER. *See also* LIMITED LIABILITY PARTNERSHIP.

limited recourse financing   *See* PROJECT FINANCING.

limiting factor (principal budget factor)   A *constraint in budgetary control and decision making, the existence of which prevents an organization from achieving higher levels of performance and profitability. On identifying the limiting factor, resources are deployed in order to eliminate or reduce its effect, at which point it may be replaced by a different limiting factor. Examples of limiting factors are sales volume, skilled labour, and productive capacity.

linear cost function   *Cost behaviour that, when plotted on a graph against activity levels, results in a straight line. For example, total fixed cost levels and variable costs per unit of activity will both result in a straight line horizontal to the x-axis when activity, production, or sales is plotted on the x-axis. Total variable costs will also result in a straight line and is thus a linear cost function.

linear depreciation   *Depreciation charges that, when plotted on a graph against time on the x-axis, result in a straight line, as a constant amount per annum is written off the assets concerned. Both the *straight-line method of depreciation and the *rate per unit of production method, when the depreciation charge is plotted against production levels, result in linear depreciation.

linear interpolation A technique used in *discounted cash flow for calculating the approximate *internal rate of return of a project. The cash flows for the project are discounted at two *discount rates to obtain a small positive and a small negative *net present value. A linear relationship is assumed between the two results in order to calculate the discount rate that would give a net present value of zero.

linear programming A modelling technique that determines an optimal solution for attaining an objective by taking into consideration a number of *constraints. The *objective function, often to optimize profits or minimize costs, is expressed as an equation and the constraints are also expressed in mathematical terms. Where only two products and few constraints are involved a solution may be obtained graphically. More than two products requires the *simplex method to be used or alternatively a computer program.

linear regression The process of finding a **line of best fit** to a graph on which the values of two variables are plotted in pairs. The line of best fit, also known as the **least-squares line**, is computed mathematically, so that the squares of the divergence of the plots from the line are minimized. For example, a line of best fit through plots of cost levels incurred for levels of production can be used to determine the *cost behaviour characteristics of the selected cost. *See* LEAST SQUARES METHOD.

linked presentation The presentation in a balance sheet of an *asset that is in substance a financing; the item can be shown gross on the face of the balance sheet with the finance deducted from it within a single asset caption. To make a linked presentation there are a number of criteria to be met and it must be intended that the financing will be repaid from the proceeds of the asset and the company must not be able to keep the asset on repayment of the financing or be able to re-acquire it at any time. This is the procedure recommended in *Financial Reporting Standard 5, Reporting Financial Transactions. Note that the linked presentation approach is not possible under *International Financial Reporting Standards.

liquid assets (**liquid capital**; **quick assets**; **realizable assets**) Assets held in cash or in something that can be readily turned into cash with minimal capital loss (e.g. deposits in a bank current account, trade debts, marketable investments). The ratio of these assets to current liabilities provides an assessment of an organization's *liquidity or solvency. *See also* LIQUID RATIO; MANDATORY LIQUID ASSETS.

liquidation (**winding-up**) The distribution of a company's assets among its creditors and members prior to its dissolution. This brings the life of the company to an end. The liquidation may be voluntary (*see* CREDITORS VOLUNTARY LIQUIDATION; MEMBERS VOLUNTARY LIQUIDATION) or by the court (*see* COMPULSORY LIQUIDATION). *See also* LIQUIDATOR.

liquidator A person appointed by a court, or by the members of a company or its creditors, to regularize the company's affairs on a *liquidation (winding-up). In the case of a *members' voluntary liquidation, it is the members of the company who appoint the liquidator. In a *creditors' voluntary liquidation, the liquidator may be appointed by company members before the **meeting of creditors** or by the creditors themselves at the meeting; in the former case the liquidator can only exercise his or her powers with the consent of the court. If two liquidators are appointed, the court resolves which one is to act. In a *compulsory liquidation, the court appoints a provisional liquidator after the winding-up petition has been presented; after the order has been granted, the court appoints the *official receiver as liquidator, until or unless another officer is appointed.

   The liquidator is in a relationship of trust with the company and the creditors as a body; a liquidator appointed in a compulsory liquidation is an officer of the court, is under statutory obligations, and may not profit from the position. A liquidator must be a qualified *insolvency practitioner, according to the Insolvency Act 1986. On appointment, the liquidator assumes control of the company, collects the assets, pays the debts, and distributes any surplus to company members according to their rights. In the case of a compulsory liquidation, the liquidator is supervised by the court, a liquidation committee, and the Department for Business, Innovation and Skills. The liquidator receives a *statement of affairs from the company officers and must report on these to the court.

liquid instrument A *negotiable instrument that the purchaser is able to sell before maturity.

liquidity The extent to which an organization's assets are liquid (*see* LIQUID ASSETS), enabling it to pay its debts when they fall due and also to move into new investment opportunities.

liquidity index A measure of a company's liquidity assessed by calculating the number of days it would take for current assets to be converted into cash.

liquidity management A combination of day-to-day operations carried out by the financial management of an organization with the objective of optimizing its *liquidity so that it can make the best use of its liquid resources.

liquidity premium The relative advantage of holding assets in liquid form. Investors are prepared to receive lower returns on *liquid assets, because they can easily be transferred into cash with little capital loss. Liquid assets are thus to some extent a hedge against uncertainty.

liquidity risk The risk, in lending operations, that an investment cannot be liquidated during its life without significant costs.

liquid ratio (quick ratio) A ratio used for assessing the *liquidity of a company; it is the ratio of the *liquid assets (i.e. the *current assets less the *stock) to the *current liabilities. Although there is no rule of thumb, and there are industry differences, a liquid ratio significantly below 1:1 will give rise to concern. The liquid ratio is regarded as an acid test of a company's solvency and is therefore sometimes called the **acid-test ratio**.

EXAMPLE

A company has current assets of £250,000, including stock of £150,000, and liabilities of £120,000. This gives a liquid ratio of:

(£250,000 − £150,000)/£120,000 = 0.83,

i.e. 83% or 0.83:1. This may be interpreted as the company having 83 pence of liquid assets for every £1 of current liabilities. If, for some reason, the company was obliged to repay the current liabilities immediately there would be insufficient liquid assets to allow it to do so. The company might therefore be forced into a hurried sale of stock at a discount to raise finance.

listed company A company that has a listing agreement (*see* LISTING REQUIREMENTS) with a major stock exchange and whose shares have a quotation on that exchange. In the UK such companies were formerly called **quoted companies**.

listed security **1.** In general, a security that has a quotation on a recognized *stock exchange. **2.** On the *London Stock Exchange, a security that has a quotation in the Official List of Securities of the *main market, as opposed to the *Alternative Investment Market. *See also* FLOTATION; LISTING REQUIREMENTS.

listing requirements The conditions that must be satisfied before a security can be traded on a stock exchange. To achieve a quotation in the Official List of Securities of the *main market of the *London Stock Exchange, the requirements contained in a **listing agreement** must be signed by the company seeking quotation. The two main requirements of such a listing are usually:
• that the value of the company's assets should exceed a certain value;
• that the company publish specific financial and operating information, both at the time of *flotation and regularly thereafter.
Listing requirements are generally more stringent the larger the market. For example, the main market in London demands considerably more information from companies than the *Alternative Investment Market. The listing requirements are set out in the *Yellow Book.

little GAAP The *generally accepted accounting principles applied to *small companies. Some argue that with small companies, which are primarily owner-managed, compliance with GAAP imposes a heavy burden in relation to the value the owners receive from the information in the *annual accounts. There are difficulties in determining, however, the criteria that should be used to exempt companies as well as widespread concern that accounts that do not comply with accounting standards would not present a *true and fair view of a company's activities. *Compare* BIG GAAP. *See also* FINANCIAL REPORTING STANDARD FOR SMALLER ENTITIES.

LLP Abbreviation for *limited liability partnership.

LME Abbreviation for *London Metal Exchange.

loan capital (borrowed capital; debt capital) Capital used to finance an organization that is subject to payment of interest over the life of the loan, at the end of which the loan is normally repaid. There are different categories of loan capital: *mortgage debentures are secured on specific assets of the organization, while convertible debentures may be converted into equity according to the terms of the issue.

loan creditor A person or institution that has lent money to a business. For example, when a bank loan is obtained the bank becomes a loan creditor.

loan stock *See* DEBENTURE.

local area network (lan) A network of linked computers within a limited area or a common environment, such as an office building. A network operating system, network programs, and application programs are required.

local taxation A form of taxation levied by a local government authority rather than by central government. In the UK the *council tax and *business rates are the main local taxes.

lockbox In the USA, a Postal Service box used for the collection of customer payments. The recipient's bank will arrange collection from these boxes throughout the day, deposit the funds, and provide a computer listing of the payments with the daily total. This method is effective for small number of payments with a high value as the bank's charges per item are relatively high.

Lombard rate **1.** The rate of interest at which the German central bank, the Bundesbank, lends to German commercial banks, usually ½% above the *discount rate. **2.** The interest rate charged by a European commercial bank lending against security.

Lombard Street The street in the City of London that is the traditional centre of the *money market. Many commercial banks have offices in or near Lombard Street, as do many bill brokers and discount houses. The Bank of England is round the corner.

London approach The approach adopted by London banks to customers facing a cash-flow crisis. The key feature is that the banks remain supportive for as long as possible, decisions are made collectively, and all information and any money paid is shared between the lending banks on an equitable basis.

London Bullion Market The world's largest market for gold and silver trading. Market makers mainly quote prices in US dollars per troy ounce for spot and forward delivery. It is operated by the London Bullion Market Association (LBMA), whose primary task is to ensure that refiners of gold and silver meet the required standards of quality. The Association maintains close links with the Bank of England, which is responsible for the supervision of the market and for publishing its code of conduct.

London Clearing House (LCH) A *clearing house established in 1888 (known before 1991 as the International Commodities Clearing House). It provides futures and options markets with netting and settlement services as well as becoming a counterparty to every transaction between its members. In this capacity LCH takes the risk of its members defaulting; it also provides an independent guarantee from its shareholders and from the insurance market. In 2003 LCH merged with the Continental clearing house Clearnet to form **LCH.Clearnet**; the new group serves markets across Europe and is the sole clearer for *Euronext NV.

London code of conduct A code issued by the Bank of England, that is applicable to all wholesale dealings not regulated by the rules of a recognized exchange. It is considered the best practice for company treasurers by the *Association of Corporate Treasurers.

London Inter Bank Bid Rate (LIBID) The rate of interest at which banks bid for funds to borrow from one another on the London *interbank market. *See* LONDON INTER BANK OFFERED RATE.

London Inter Bank Mean Rate (LIMEAN) The median average between the London Inter Bank Offered Rate (LIBOR) and the London Inter Bank Bid Rate (LIBID).

London Inter Bank Offered Rate (LIBOR) The rate of interest at which banks offer to lend to each other on the London *interbank market. The loans are for a minimum of £250,000 for periods from overnight up to five years. LIBOR is the most significant interest rate for international banks. It is also used as a benchmark for lending to bank customers and as a reference rate for many derivatives. *See also* LONDON INTER BANK BID RATE.

London International Financial Futures and Options Exchange *See* LIFFE.

London Metal Exchange (LME) One of the world's largest non-ferrous metals exchanges, the total value of contracts each year being around $2000 billion. It is regulated by the UK Financial Services Authority. The range of metals traded includes copper, aluminium, nickel, zinc, and lead. Dealings include *futures and *options contracts.

London Stock Exchange The market in London that deals in securities. Dealings in securities began in London in the 17th century. The name Stock Exchange was first used for New Jonathan's Coffee House in 1773, although it was not formally constituted until 1802. The development of the industrial revolution encouraged many other share markets to flourish throughout the UK, all the remnants of which amalgamated in 1973 to form The Stock Exchange of Great Britain and Ireland. After the *Big Bang in 1986 this organization became the International Stock Exchange of the UK and Republic of Ireland Ltd (ISE) in an attempt to stress the international nature of the main UK securities market; it is now the London Stock Exchange plc. The reforms of 1986 included:

- allowing banks, insurance companies, and overseas securities houses to become members and to buy existing member firms;
- abolishing scales of commissions, allowing commissions to be negotiated;
- abolishing the division of members into jobbers and brokers, enabling a member firm to deal with the public, to buy and sell shares for their own account, and to act as *market makers;
- the introduction of the *Stock Exchange Automated Quotations System, a computerized dealing system that has virtually abolished face-to-face dealing on the floor of exchange.

The London Stock Exchange now has four core business areas:

- **equity markets**– the *main market for listed companies and the *Alternative Investment Market for unlisted securities;
- **trading services** – trading platforms that are used by broking firms around the world to buy and sell securities;
- **market information** – the provision of prices and news;

- **derivatives** – a recent diversification beyond the core equity markets. In collaboration with the Nordic exchange group *OMX, the London Stock Exchange created *EDX London in 2003.

( ) SEE WEB LINKS
- Website of the LSE: includes information for companies and traders as well as much educational material for private investors

long-form report A detailed report made by an *auditor on a client's financial statements.

long position A position held by a dealer in securities, commodities, currencies, or derivatives etc., in which holdings exceed sales, because the dealer expects prices to rise enabling a profit to be made by selling at the higher levels. *Compare* SHORT POSITION.

long-term contract A contract that falls into two or more accounting periods before being completed. Such a contract may be for the design, manufacture, or construction of a single substantial asset, for example in the construction or civil engineering industries. From an accounting point of view, there is a problem in determining how much profit can be reasonably allocated to each accounting period, although the contract is not complete. *Statement of Standard Accounting Practice (SSAP) 9, Stocks and Long Term Contracts, requires contracts to be assessed on an individual basis and shown in the *profit and loss account by recording turnover and related activity as the contract progresses (the **percentage-of-completion** method). Where the outcome of the contract can be assessed with reasonable certainty, even though it is not complete, the part of the profit that can be attributed to the work performed by an accounting date may be recognized in the profit and loss account. *Attributable profit is that part of the total profit currently estimated to arise over the duration of the contract, after allowing for estimated remedial costs, maintenance costs, and increases in costs not recoverable under the contract agreement. More recently, *Financial Reporting Exposure Draft 28 proposed the replacement of SSAP 9 with two international standards (IAS 11 and IAS 18), which likewise prescribe the percentage-of-completion method.

long-term debtors *Debtors who are not expected to pay what they owe in the near future. The debtors of an organization shown on the face of a *balance sheet under *current assets may be assumed by some readers to be expected to pay within 12 months, thus being comparable to *current liabilities. The legal definition of *fixed assets, however, means that current assets are merely those assets that an organization does not mean to keep in the business and there are no time implications. In some cases, possibly by mutual agreement, it may be many years before a company is able to recover money from certain debtors. The *Urgent Issues Task Force requires that if the size of the debt due after more than one year is material, the amounts should be disclosed on the face of the balance sheet.

long-term liability A sum owed that does not have to be repaid within the next accounting period of a business. In some contexts a long-term liability may be regarded as one not due for repayment within the next three, or possibly ten, years.

loss The amount by which the expenses of a transaction or operation exceed the income produced.

loss leader A product or service offered for sale by an organization at a loss in order to attract customers for other products or services.

loss reliefs Relief available to sole traders, partnerships, and companies making losses, as adjusted for tax purposes. *Capital allowances can create a trading loss or can enhance it. Trading losses can be carried forward to set against future trading profits.

For sole traders and partnerships, trading losses can be set against other income for the year of the loss and for the previous year. Partners can decide individually how to use their share of the losses. Special rules apply to trading losses in the early years of a trade. These losses can be carried back three years to a period before the trade commenced. It is possible to set trading losses against capital gains if the loss cannot be used first by setting against other income during the year.

For companies, a trading loss can be set off against the profits of the previous 12-month period provided the company was carrying on the same trade during that period. *Capital losses can be set against capital gains in the same period. Any surplus capital loss that cannot be utilized during the current year must be carried forward to set against future capital gains. Capital losses cannot be set against other income, unlike trading losses. *See also* TERMINAL-LOSS RELIEF.

Lotus 1-2-3 *Trademark* A *spreadsheet program for personal computers originated by Lotus Development Corp. (now part of IBM). It provides statistical, database, and graph-drawing facilities.

lowballing An alleged practice in which auditors compete for clients by reducing their fees for *statutory audits. The lower audit fees would be compensated by the auditor carrying out highly lucrative non-audit work, such as consultancy and tax advice, for the client. It is difficult to assess how widespread the practice is in an economic climate in which competition has pushed down audit fees, but a number of well-publicized examples suggest that it has been taking place since the 1980s. *See* INDEPENDENCE OF AUDITORS.

lower of cost and net realizable value rule The method of valuing *current assets and *work in progress required by *Statement of Standard Accounting Practice 9 and the Companies Act, in which they should be valued at the lower of either cost or *net realizable value for published accounts purposes.

machine hour A measurement of production in terms of the time taken for a machine operation to complete a given amount of production.

machine hour rate An *absorption rate used in *absorption costing, obtained by the formula:

budgeted *cost centre overheads/budgeted machine hours.

machinery and plant *See* PLANT AND MACHINERY.

macroeconomics The branch of economics that studies economies as a whole rather than the behaviour of particular economic agents. Modern macroeconomics is largely concerned with the relationships between such factors as money supply, employment, interest rates, government spending, investment, and consumption and with the role that government should play in a national economy. In recent economic thinking the distinction between macroeconomics and *microeconomics has become less clear cut than previously.

MACRS Abbreviation for modified *accelerated cost recovery system.

mad dog An informal name for a company with the potential to grow quickly, providing it can obtain substantial capital; risks are likely to be high. The information technology industry is an example of a sector that has included a number of mad dogs.

Madrid Stock Exchange (Bolsa de Madrid) The largest of the four stock exchanges in Spain, the others being at Barcelona, Bilbao, and Valencia. The exchanges now use a centralized settlement system.

main market The premier market for the trading of *equities on the *London Stock Exchange. The *listing requirements are more stringent, and the liquidity of the market is greater, than on the *Alternative Investment Market. A company wishing to enter this market must have audited trading figures covering at least five years and must place 25% of its shares in public hands. The main market currently deals in over 1600 securities.

main product The product of a process that has the greatest economic significance. Other products of secondary economic importance are regarded as *by-products; however, if all products have equal economic significance they are regarded as *joint products. *See also* PROCESS COSTING.

mainstream corporation tax (MCT) Formerly, the liability for *corporation tax of a company for an accounting period after the relevant *advance corporation tax was deducted. Advance corporation tax was abolished in 1999.

maintenance expense The costs incurred in carrying out the **maintenance function**. Factory maintenance would be classified as a *manufacturing overhead, office maintenance as an *administration overhead, salesmen's car maintenance as a *selling overhead, and distribution vehicle maintenance as a *distribution overhead.

make or buy decision A decision to make a product or component internally or to buy it in from a subcontractor. If the decision is based on cost terms alone, the *relevant costs of manufacture compared to purchase should be considered and if there is no spare capacity then *opportunity costs of manufacture may also be relevant. This decision often has to be made in the course of planning a manufacturing process.

malpractice insurance *See* PROFESSIONAL INDEMNITY INSURANCE.

managed costs *See* DISCRETIONARY COSTS.

managed service company A company whose business consists wholly or mainly of providing the services of an individual, who receives payments from the company in the form of dividends and payments for expenses rather than salary. From 2007 *PAYE is payable on (broadly) all payments made by a managed service company to an individual whose services are provided by that company.

management accounting The techniques used to collect, process, and present financial and quantitative data within an organization to help effective *performance measurement, *cost control, *planning, *pricing, and *decision making to take place. The major professional body of **management accountants** in the UK is the *Chartered Institute of Management Accountants (CIMA). *See also* COST ACCOUNTING.

management audit An independent review of the management of an organization, carried out by a firm of management consultants specializing in this type of review. The review will cover all aspects of running the organization, including the control of production, marketing, sales, finance, personnel, warehousing, etc.

management buy-in The acquisition of a company by an outside team of managers, usually specially formed for the purpose, often backed by a venture-capital organization. In the past a typical target might have been a small family-owned company, which the owners wished to sell, or an unwanted subsidiary of a public company. In recent years, however, *private equity firms have successfully targeted leading public companies.

management buy-out (MBO) The acquisition of a company by its managers, often in the face of closure, after the acquisition of the company by another group that wishes to dispose of it, or occasionally as a result of its owners wishing to dispose of the business through a trade sale. In some cases a management buyout occurs when a large corporate group of companies wishes to divest itself of an operating division. Financial backers tend to like managers who know the company's business intimately, staking their own assets and taking full control of the company with the aim of boosting its profitability. In a highly *leveraged buyout, funding will usually consist of a small amount of equity, allowing the management team to obtain and retain control, considerable straight debt, and a certain amount of *mezzanine finance. *See also* BIMBO.

management by exception **1.** A principle of management in which a management decision that cannot be made at one level is passed up to the next level for a decision; i.e. exceptional decisions are passed up the management tree. **2.** The principle used in *budgetary control in which items of income or expenditure that show no *variances or small variances require no action, whereas exceptional items showing *adverse variances to an unacceptable degree require action to be taken.

management by objectives (MBO) A management technique in which all levels of management are encouraged to specify quantitative and/or qualitative objectives to be achieved within a set period. Managers must then answer to higher levels of management for the actual performance achieved against these objectives.

management discussion and analysis (MD&A) In the USA, the section in the annual report to stockholders (*see* ANNUAL ACCOUNTS) and in *Form 10-K that is required by the *Securities and Exchange Commission. The purpose of the MD&A is to assist investors to understand the impact of changes in accounting and business activity that have affected comparisons with the results of previous years. Management should summarize and discuss, among other matters, the reasons for changes in the results of operations, capital resources, and liquidity.

management information system (MIS) An information system designed to provide financial and quantitative information to all the levels of management in an organization. Modern management information systems provide the data from an integrated computer *database, which is constantly updated from all areas of the organization in a structured way. Access to the data is usually restricted to the areas regarded as useful to particular managers, and access to confidential information is limited to top management. An MIS should run parallel to the configuration of the physical and organizational structures. The systematic application of *information technology has enabled MIS to drive these structures. *See also* DECISION SUPPORT SYSTEM.

management letter A letter written by an auditor to the management of a client company at the end of the annual audit to suggest any possible improvements that could be made to the company's accounting and *internal control system or to communicate any other such information that the auditor believes would be of benefit to the client.

mandate **1.** A written authority given by one person (the **mandator**) to another (the **mandatory**) giving the mandatory the power to act on behalf of the mandator. It is usually revocable until acted upon and comes to an end on the death, mental illness, or bankruptcy of the mandator. A cheque is a mandate from a customer to his or her bank. **2.** A document instructing a bank to open an account in the name of the mandator (customer), giving details of the way it is to be run, and providing specimen signatures of those authorized to sign cheques, etc.

mandatory liquid assets Certain *liquid assets, the structure and nature of which are defined by regulatory requirement, that a bank is required to maintain on its balance sheet. Such requirements may be implemented as an instrument of monetary control or as a protection against 'runs' on particular banks. The regulatory trend is away from this type of control, since it often gives a market advantage to short-term government debt, which is a major part of the specified assets.

manufacturing account (manufacturing statement) An accounting statement forming part of the internal final accounts of a manufacturing organization; for a particular period, it is constructed to show, inter alia, *direct cost of sales, *manufacturing overhead, total *production cost, and *cost of goods manufactured. In some cases a *manufacturing profit is also computed.

manufacturing cost of finished goods See COST OF GOODS MANUFACTURED.

manufacturing costs (manufacturing expenses) Items of expenditure incurred to carry out the manufacturing process in an organization. They include *direct materials, *direct labour, *direct expenses (such as subcontract costs), and *manufacturing overhead. See COST OF GOODS MANUFACTURED; COST OF SALES.

manufacturing lead time The elapsed time between placing a *production order and the receipt of the completed production.

manufacturing overhead (production overhead) The costs of production that cannot be traced directly to the product or *cost unit. Apart from the *direct costs, all other costs incurred in the manufacturing process are the manufacturing overhead; examples include depreciation of machinery, factory rent and business rates, cleaning materials, and maintenance expenses.

manufacturing profit/loss (production profit/loss) The difference between the value of the goods transferred from a *manufacturing account to a *trading account at a price other than the *cost of goods manufactured, and the cost of goods manufactured. This difference is measured in organizations wishing to submit the production department to market prices; it involves crediting production according to some formula, such as a price per unit.

manufacturing requisition See PRODUCTION ORDER.

manufacturing statement See MANUFACTURING ACCOUNT.

manufacturing time The time taken to produce a specified quantity of production.

Mareva injunction See FREEZING INJUNCTION.

margin 1. The *profit margin on sales of goods or services. It is often expressed as a percentage of revenue. See GROSS PROFIT; GROSS PROFIT PERCENTAGE; NET PROFIT; NET PROFIT PERCENTAGE. See also CONTRIBUTION; MARK-UP. 2. The difference between the prices at which a *market maker or commodity dealer will buy and sell. This is often known colloquially as a **haircut**. 3. In banking, the difference between the rate of interest on funds lent and funds borrowed by a bank. 4. Money or securities deposited with a stockbroker to cover any possible losses a client may make.

marginal cost The additional cost incurred as a result of the production of one additional unit of production. It usually equates to the *direct costs plus the *variable overhead costs.

marginal costing (**direct costing; variable costing**) A costing and decision-making technique that charges only the *marginal costs to the *cost units and treats the *fixed costs as a lump sum to be deducted from the total *contribution, in obtaining the profit or loss for the period. In some cases, *inventory valuation is also at marginal cost, although this approach does not conform to *Statement of Standard Accounting Practice 9 and is used for internal reporting purposes only. *Compare* ABSORPTION COSTING; FULL COSTING METHOD.

marginal cost pricing The setting of product selling prices based on the charging of *marginal costs only to the product. The approach is only likely to be used in exceptional circumstances, such as when competition is intensive, as its application to the complete range of products is likely to cause the business to make losses by its failure to cover its *fixed costs. *Compare* COST-PLUS PRICING; FULL COST PRICING.

marginal-cost transfer prices *Transfer prices set by *marginal cost pricing. When there is no market for the goods and services that are bought and sold between the divisions of an organization, the transfer price should be the marginal cost, which is normally assumed to be short-term *variable cost. Setting transfer prices equal to marginal costs helps managers to identify the output levels that will maximize profits. There can be problems if managers do not have accurate cost information.

marginal rate of tax The amount of extra tax that is incurred if a taxpayer earns £1 more than his or her current income. Under a *progressive tax regime, the marginal rate of tax rises as incomes rise. *See also* ABILITY-TO-PAY.

marginal relief (**small companies relief**) In the UK, relief available when the profits chargeable to *corporation tax of a company fall between the upper and lower limits for the *financial year (currently between £300,000 and £1,500,000).

marginal revenue The additional income that accrues to an organization as the result of selling an extra unit of sales.

margin of safety The difference between the level of activity at which an organization breaks even and a given level of activity greater than the *breakeven point, especially the forecast level in a *breakeven analysis. The margin of safety may be expressed in the same terms as the breakeven point, i.e. sales value, number of units, or percentage of capacity.

margin of safety ratio The *margin of safety expressed as a percentage of a given level of activity. For example, if the sales level achieved is £500,000 and the sales level breakeven point is £400,000, the margin of safety is £100,000 and the margin of safety ratio will be:

$(£100,000 \times 100)/£500,000 = 20\%.$

marker rate The base interest rate defined in the loan agreement, to which the spread is added in order to establish the interest rate payable on a variable-rate loan.

market-based transfer prices *Transfer prices that are based on market prices. When there is a perfectly competitive market for the goods and services that are bought and sold between divisions of an organization, the transfer price should be the market price. The transfer price may be slightly lower than the market price if the selling expenses are lower for interdivisional transfers, e.g. because there is no advertising cost for transfers between divisions. There is a problem for managers in that market prices may fluctuate.

market capitalization *See* MARKET VALUE.

marketing costs The costs incurred by an organization in carrying out its marketing activities. These would include sales promotion costs, salesmen's salaries, advertising, and point-of-sale promotional material, such as display stands.

marketing cost variance The adverse or favourable *variance between the budgeted *marketing cost for a period and the actual marketing cost incurred for the same period.

market maker A dealer in securities on the *London Stock Exchange who undertakes to buy and sell securities as a principal and is therefore obliged to announce buying and selling prices for a particular security at a particular time. Before October 1986 (*see* BIG BANG) this function was performed by a stockjobber, who was then obliged to deal with the public through a stockbroker. However, since the change in the rules at that time, market makers attempt to make a profit by dealing in securities as principals (selling at a higher price than that at which they buy; *see* MARGIN) as well as acting as agents, working for a commission. While this dual role may create a conflict of interest for market makers (*see* CHINESE WALL), it avoids the restrictive trade practice of the former system and reduces the cost of dealing in the market.

market price 1. The price of a raw material, product, service, security, etc., in an open market. In a formal market, such as a stock exchange, commodity market, foreign-exchange market, etc., there is often a *margin between the buying and selling price; there are, therefore, two market prices. In these circumstances the market prices often quoted are the average of the buying and selling price. **2.** The economic concept of the price at which commodities are exchanged in a market, either for money or for each other.

market price to book ratio *See* BOOK VALUE.

market report The report on the daily activities of the *stock exchange or – less commonly – of some other market.

market risk The risk inherent in dealing on a market where prices may change. The obvious market risks are buying on a market that subsequently falls and selling on a market that rises; these risks can be reduced by hedging (*see* HEDGE), especially by means of *futures contracts or *options, but they can never be eliminated. These forms of market risk are the obverse of the market opportunities that provide speculators with the chance of making a profit.

market-risk premium *See* RISK PREMIUM.

Markets in Financial Instruments Directive (MiFID) An EU directive

(2004) providing a comprehensive regulatory regime for financial services and markets throughout the European Economic Area. It superseded the *Investment Services Directive in November 2007. The main aims are to increase competition and enhance investor protection.

market-to-book ratio *See* BOOK VALUE.

market value 1. (market capitalization) The value of a company obtained by multiplying the number of its issued ordinary shares by their *market price. This may differ widely from the *book value of the company. **2. (open market value)** The value of an asset if it were to be sold on the open market at its current *market price. When land is involved it may be necessary to distinguish between the market value in its present use and that in some alternative use; for example, a factory site may have a market value as a factory site, and be so valued in the company's accounts, which may be less than its market value as building land. *See* FAIR VALUE.

marking to market The valuation of financial obligations according to current *market prices. In accounting, the practice of marking assets and liabilities to market is known as *fair value accounting. This is now required by *International Accounting Standards (notably IAS 39) but remains controversial. *See also* HEDGE ACCOUNTING.

marking to model The valuation of financial obligations according to pricing models. This occurs when there is not a current market price for the obligation, for example in relation to derivatives sold on the *over-the-counter market.

mark-up The amount by which the cost of a service or product has been increased to arrive at the selling price. It is calculated by expressing the *profit as a percentage of the cost of the good or service. For example, if a product cost £8 and is sold for £12, the mark-up would be:

$£4/£8 \times 100 = 50\%$.

Note that the *margin is calculated by expressing the profit as a percentage of the selling price; in this case it would be:

$£4/£12 \times 100 = 33.3\%$.

The mark-up is widely used in retailing, both for setting prices and as a ratio for control and decision making. *See* GROSS PROFIT PERCENTAGE; NET PROFIT PERCENTAGE.

marriage value The latent value released by the merger of two or more interests in land. Often the merger consists of the freehold and a long leasehold on the same property.

master budget The final coordinated overall *budget for an organization as a whole, which brings together the *functional budgets, the *capital budget, and the *cash-flow budget, as well as the budgeted profit and loss account and balance sheet for the period.

master file A computer file that holds *standing data, such as clients' names and addresses.

matched bargain A transaction in which a sale of a particular quantity of stock is matched with a purchase of the same quantity of the same stock. On the *London Stock Exchange transactions of this kind are now carried out electronically by the *Stock Exchange Trading System.

matching concept *See* ACCRUALS CONCEPT.

material **1.** The production supplies of an organization that feature as revenue expenditure purchased from a third party. Materials may be classed as either *direct materials, which feature in the final product produced (such as wood and metal in furniture), or *indirect materials, which are necessary to carry out production but do not feature in the final product (such as maintenance and cleaning materials). Materials are not necessarily *raw materials, but can include components and sub-assemblies used in the finished product. **2.** *See* MATERIALITY.

material adverse change A clause in a loan agreement or bank facility stating that the loan will become repayable if there should a material change in the borrower's credit standing. The clause can be contentious because it is not always clear what constitutes a material change.

material control The control of the materials required in a production process. It includes seeing that they are available in the required place, at the required time, and in the required quantities, as well as ensuring that the materials are properly accounted for. While it is clearly imperative that a production process should not be delayed by lack of materials, it is also important that overstocking of inventories should be avoided.

materiality The extent to which an item of accounting information is material. Information is considered material if its omission from or mis-statement in a *financial statement could influence the decision making of its users. Materiality is therefore not an absolute concept but is dependent on the size and nature of an item and the particular circumstances in which it arises.

materials cost The expenditure incurred by an organization on *direct materials or *indirect materials. The expenditure on direct materials is part of the *direct cost of sales and that on indirect materials is a *manufacturing overhead.

materials oncost *See* ONCOST.

materials requisition (stores issue note; stores requisition) A form requiring that a specified item be issued from an organization's stores for a specified use. Such a requisition is usually a *prime document, which must be properly completed and authorized. It will contain a description of the material, *commodity code, *job number or *accounting code, and the value of the material transferred from store to expenditure. The material requisition is used to credit stock and debit expenditure.

materials returns note (MRN; stores returns note; SRN) A form that records the return of material to store. A *prime document, it contains similar information to a *materials requisition and is used to debit stock and credit expenditure.

materials variances *See* DIRECT MATERIALS PRICE VARIANCE; DIRECT MATERIALS TOTAL COST VARIANCE; DIRECT MATERIALS USAGE VARIANCE.

material transfer note A form that records the transfer of material from one *accounting code to another. A *prime document, it will contain a description of the material, *commodity code, *job number or accounting code to be credited, job number or accounting code to be debited, and the value of material transferred.

matrix accounting The use of a matrix (an array of figures arranged in rows or columns) to record accounting transactions and events, rather than a *T account.

maturity date The date on which a document, such as a *bond, *bill of exchange, or insurance policy, becomes due for payment. In some cases, especially for redeemable government stocks, the maturity date is known as the **redemption date**. *See also* REDEMPTION.

maximum stock level The highest level of stock planned to be held; any amounts above the maximum would be considered excess stock.

MBO **1.** Abbreviation for *management buy-out. **2.** Abbreviation for *management by objectives.

MCT **1.** Abbreviation for Member of the *Association of Corporate Treasurers. **2.** Abbreviation for *mainstream corporation tax.

MD&A Abbreviation for *management discussion and analysis.

medium-sized company A company that is entitled to certain filing exemptions because it meets two out of three of the following criteria for the current and preceding year, or the two preceding financial years:
• the company's *net worth should not exceed £11.4 million;
• the *turnover should not exceed £22.8 million
• the average number of employees should not exceed 250.
 In a company's first *financial year it need only meet the conditions for that year; in its second financial year it may claim the filing exemptions of a medium-sized company if it met the conditions in its first financial year. A *public limited company, a banking or insurance company, an authorized person under the Financial Services Act 1986, or a member of an ineligible group may not claim medium-sized company filing exemptions.
 A medium-sized company must prepare full audited *financial statements for distribution to its shareholders but it may file *abbreviated accounts instead of full accounts with the *Registrar of Companies. *See also* SMALL COMPANY.

(🌐) SEE WEB LINKS
• Further details on filing exemptions for medium-sized companies

medium-sized group A *group that meets two out of three of the following criteria for the current and preceding year, or the two preceding financial years:
• the group's *net worth should not exceed £11.4 million net or £13.68 million gross;
• its *turnover should not exceed £22.8 million net or £27.36 million gross;
• the average number of employees should not exceed 250.
If a group is in its first financial year, it may still qualify if it falls within these limits.
 A group containing a public company, a banking or insurance company, or an

authorized person under the Financial Services Act 1986 is ineligible for the exemptions for medium-sized groups.

Under the Companies Act, a parent company is not required to prepare *consolidated financial statements for a financial year in which the group headed by that parent qualifies as a medium-sized group. *See also* SMALL GROUP.

medium-term note (MTN) A *note issued in a eurocurrency with a maturity of about three to six years. Although MTNs were traditionally unsecured, recent years have seen a growth in **asset-backed medium-term notes (ABMTN)**, in which the MTN is secured against assets held by a *structured investment vehicle.

member of a company A shareholder of a company whose name is entered in the *register of members. Founder members (*see* FOUNDERS SHARES) are those who sign the memorandum of association; anyone subsequently coming into possession of the company's shares becomes a member.

members' voluntary liquidation (members' voluntary winding-up)
The winding-up of a company by a special resolution of the members in circumstances in which the company is solvent. Before making the winding-up resolution, the directors must make a declaration of solvency. It is a criminal offence to make such a declaration without reasonable grounds for believing that it is true. When the resolution has been passed, a *liquidator is appointed; if, during the course of the winding-up, the liquidator believes that the company will not be able to pay its debts, a meeting of creditors must be called and the winding-up is treated as a members' *compulsory liquidation.

memorandum entry An entry in a *ledger that does not form part of the *double-entry book-keeping system. For example, individual debtors' ledgers are **memorandum ledgers**.

memorandum of association An official document setting out the details of a *company's existence. Until recently, a memorandum of association signed by the first subscribers had to be submitted to the Registrar of Companies when a new company was formed. The memorandum had to contain the following information:
- the company name;
- the address of the registered office;
- the objects of the company;
- the amount of *authorized share capital and its division;
- if applicable, a statement that the company is a public company;
- if applicable, a statement of limited liability;
- in the case of a *company limited by guarantee, the amount of the guarantee.

From late 2009, when the Companies Act 2006 became fully operational, the memorandum was replaced by a much shorter document stating simply that the members wish to form a company. *See also* ARTICLES OF ASSOCIATION.

memorandum of understanding *See* LETTER OF INTENT.

menu costs The costs incurred by a firm when it changes its prices. The term alludes to the case of a restaurant, which is obliged to reprint its menus every time it changes a price; this means that it will only make such changes when the costs of not doing so clearly outweigh the cost and inconvenience of reprinting. Menu costs are frequently cited as one explanation for the *stickiness of prices, i.e. their failure to respond immediately to shifts in supply and demand. Some analysts have argued that e-commerce will eradicate most traditional forms of menu costs.

merchant bank A bank that formerly specialized in financing foreign trade, an activity that often grew out of its own merchanting business. This led them into accepting *bills of exchange and functioning as accepting houses. More recently they have tended to diversify into the field of *hire-purchase finance, the granting of long-term loans (especially to companies), providing venture capital, advising companies on flotations and *takeover bids, underwriting new issues, and managing investment portfolios and unit trusts. Many of them are old-established and some offer a limited banking service. Their knowledge of international trade makes them specialists in dealing with the large multinational companies. Merchant banking has a long history in Europe. Several UK merchant banks were taken over in the 1990s either by the commercial banks or by large overseas banks. *See also* INVESTMENT BANK.

merger A combination of two or more businesses on a relatively equal footing that results in the creation of a new reporting entity. The shareholders of the combining entities mutually share the risks and rewards of the new entity and no one party to the merger obtains control over another. Under Financial Reporting Standard 6, 'Acquisitions and Mergers', to qualify as a merger a combination must satisfy four criteria:
• no party is the acquirer or acquired;
• all parties to the combination participate in establishing the management structure of the new entity;
• the combining entities are relatively equal in terms of size;
• the consideration received by the equity shareholders of each party consists primarily of equity shares in the combined entity, any other consideration received being relatively immaterial.
However, true mergers (as opposed to disguised takeovers) are very rare in the contemporary business environment. Owing to its widespread abuse, *merger accounting has been effectively banned by the recent *International Financial Reporting Standard 3, Business Combinations.

merger accounting A method of accounting that treats two or more businesses as combining on an equal footing. It is usually applied without any restatement of *net assets to fair value and includes the results of each of the combined entities for the whole of the *accounting period, as if they had always been combined. It does not reflect the issue of shares as an application of resources at fair value. The difference that arises on *consolidation does not represent *goodwill but is deducted from, or added to, *reserves. In the past merger accounting was often used to avoid recognizing goodwill in combinations that were essentially takeovers rather than true mergers. The recently issued *International Financial Reporting Standard 3, Business Combinations, prohibits merger accounting for all business combinations falling within its scope. *Compare* ACQUISITION ACCOUNTING.

merger relief Relief from adding to, or setting up, a *share premium account when issuing shares at a premium if an issuing company has secured at least a 90% equity holding in another company. This relief applies if the issuing company is providing for the allotment of equity shares in the issuing company in exchange for the equity shares (or non-equity shares) in the other company or by the cancellation of any such shares not held by the issuing company. *See* MERGER RESERVE.

merger reserve (merger capital reserve) A *reserve credited in place of a *share premium account when *merger relief is made use of. *Goodwill on consolidation may be written off against a merger reserve (unlike the share premium account).

mergers task force An office of the European Commission that oversees the regulation of *mergers.

mezzanine finance Finance, usually provided by specialist financial institutions, that is neither pure equity nor pure debt. It can take many different forms and can be secured or unsecured; it usually earns a higher rate of return than pure debt but less than equity. Conversely, it carries a higher risk than pure debt, although less than equity. It is often used in *management buy-outs.

MFR Abbreviation for *minimum funding requirement.

MICR Magnetic ink character recognition: a process in which ferromagnetic ink is used on cheques and other documents to enable them to be automatically sorted and the characters to be read and fed into a computer.

microcredit The lending of small sums of money on very low security, especially to small businesses or to small producers in the developing world.

microeconomics The analysis of economic behaviour at the level of individual market participants, mainly individual firms or consumers. For an individual or household microeconomics is concerned with the optimal allocation of a given budget, the labour supply choice, and the effects of taxation. For a business it is largely concerned with the production process, costs, and the marketing of output. *Compare* MACROECONOMICS.

MiFID Abbreviation for *Markets in Financial Instruments Directive.

minimum funding requirement (MFR) In the UK, the legal requirement that the assets of an occupational pension should represent at least 90% of its liabilities at any time. Since the liabilities and assets of a fund relate to future obligations and returns, both depend on certain actuarial assumptions about the future and thus may fluctuate from year to year. The MFR was introduced as a provision of the Pensions Act 1995 and came into force in 1997.

minimum premium value The minimum amount for a *share premium account. It is the amount by which the book value of the shares or the cost, whichever is the lower, exceeds the *par value of the shares issued.

minimum subscription The minimum sum of money, stated in the *prospectus of a new company, that the directors consider must be raised if the company is to be viable.

minimum wage The lowest rate of remuneration that an employer may legally pay. The minimum adult hourly rate (from October 2009) is £5.80. The youth rate for 18–21-year-olds is £4.83 per hour, and for 16–17 year olds £3.57. Special rules apply to apprentices.

minority interest The interest of individual shareholders in a company more than 50% of which is owned by a *holding company. For example, if 60% of the ordinary shares in a company are owned by a holding company, the remaining 40% will represent a minority interest. These **minority shareholders** will receive their full share of profits in the form of dividends although they will be unable to determine company policy as they will always be outvoted by the majority interest held by the holding company. *See* CONTROLLING INTEREST; PARTICIPATING INTEREST.

MIRAS Abbreviation for *mortgage interest relief at source.

MIS Abbreviation for *management information system.

misdeclaration penalty A penalty of up to 15% of the *value added tax lost in understating the VAT liability or overstating the VAT refund due on the VAT return, when the amounts involved are material. The penalty will apply if the inaccuracy equals the lesser of £1 million and 30% of the total amount of tax due for the period of the VAT return. The penalty can be avoided if the *taxable person can show that there was reasonable excuse, that there had been a voluntary disclosure, or that the taxable person had reason to believe that their VAT affairs were under investigation by HM Revenue and Customs. *See also* PERSISTENT MISDECLARATION PENALTY.

missing trader intra-community fraud (carousel fraud) A fraud in which a trader (commonly working in conjunction with others overseas) claims repayment of VAT on the export of goods to a fictitious purchaser in another EU country. Commonly the fraud involves a long chain of companies in different member states of the EU. An alternative to carousel fraud is **acquisition fraud**, in which a claim for input tax is made on the acquisition of fictitious goods or services. These two practices have been described by HM Revenue and Customs as 'a systematic criminal attack on the VAT system'. Specific statutory provisions to counter missing trader intra-community fraud are given in the Finance Act 2003.

mix variances *See* DIRECT MATERIALS MIX VARIANCE; SALES MARGIN MIX VARIANCE.

MLA Abbreviation for *mandatory liquid assets.

MNE Abbreviation for *multinational enterprise.

modified accelerated cost recovery system *See* ACCELERATED COST RECOVERY SYSTEM.

modified accounts The original name for what are now called *abbreviated accounts.

modified historical-cost convention A modification of the *historical-cost convention in which certain assets are included at revalued amounts rather than their original cost. Modified historical-cost accounting is permitted by the Companies Act. *See* ALTERNATIVE ACCOUNTING RULES.

monetary assets and liabilities Amounts receivable (assets) or payable (liabilities) that appear in a company's accounts as specific sums of money, e.g. cash and bank balances, loans, debtors, and creditors. These are to be distinguished from such non-monetary items as plant and machinery, stock in trade, or equity investments, which, although they are also expressed in accounts at a value (frequently cost), are not necessarily realizable at that value.

monetary measurement convention The accounting convention that transactions are only recognized in *financial statements if they can be measured in monetary terms. This means that some assets, such as a highly trained workforce or a sound customer base, will not be shown. It is also assumed, when preparing current statutory accounts, that money is a stable unit of measurement; in times of price changes, therefore, financial statements can be misleading. This is a major disadvantage of *historical-cost accounting.

monetary policy The procedures by which governments or central banks try to affect macroeconomic conditions by influencing the supply of money. Apart from simply printing more money, which is now rarely used in practice, there are four main options:

- using open-market operations (i.e., the sale or purchase of government debt) to expand or contract the money supply;
- raising or lowering reserve requirements (i.e. the percentage of their assets that banks must hold in cash) to affect liquidity;
- controlling the amount of money supplied to the banking system through short-term funds;
- changing the interest rate as a means of indirectly influencing the money supply.

A fifth option, which is generally only used as an extreme anti-recessionary measure, is so called *quantitative easing.

The traditional Keynesian view has been that monetary policy is at best a blunt instrument, while monetarism holds the opposite view. *Compare* FISCAL POLICY.

Monetary Policy Committee (MPC) The committee of *Bank of England officials and outside economic experts that has been responsible for setting interest rates in the UK since 1997. Prior to this date, interest rates were set by the Treasury.

monetary union A group of countries using a single currency. See feature EUROPEAN ECONOMIC AND MONETARY UNION on p. 175.

monetary working capital adjustment *See* WORKING-CAPITAL ADJUSTMENT.

money A medium of exchange that functions as a unit of account, a store of value, and a means for deferred payment. Originally money enhanced economic development by enabling goods to be bought and sold without the need for barter. However, throughout history money has been beset by the problem of its debasement as a store of value as a result of *inflation. Now that the supply of money is a monopoly of the state, most governments are committed in principle to stable prices. The word 'money' is derived from the Latin *moneta*, which was one of the names of Juno, the Roman goddess whose temple was used as a mint.

money laundering The practice of processing money from an illegal source, such as drug dealing, so that it appears to have come from a legitimate source. This may be achieved by paying the illegal cash into a foreign bank and transferring its equivalent to a bank with a good name in a hard-currency area. There are now stringent controls on this activity.

money market 1. The wholesale market for short-term loans and debt instruments. In the UK, money brokers arrange for loans between the banks, the government, the *discount houses, and the accepting houses, with the Bank of England acting as lender of last resort. The main items of exchange are *bills of exchange, Treasury bills, and trade bills. The market has traditionally taken place in and around *Lombard Street in the City of London. Private investors, through their banks, can place deposits in the money market at a higher rate of interest than bank deposit accounts. These are considered to be safe investments. *See also* INTERBANK MARKET. 2. The *foreign-exchange market and the bullion market in addition to the short-term loan market.

money-market line An agreement between a bank and a company that entitles the company to borrow up to a certain limit each day in the money markets, on a short-term basis (often overnight or in some cases up to one month). *See* UNCOMMITTED FACILITY.

monoline insurer A company that provides guarantees to bond issuers as a form of *credit enhancement. In the mid-2000s monoline insurers were very active in the markets for *collateralized debt obligations and other complex *structured finance instruments. The *subprime lending disaster of 2007 led to major losses for some monoline insurers.

Monte Carlo simulation A simulation in which random data are generated from specified distributions and used as an input into predictive or other models. In finance, such simulations are used to price complicated derivatives and portfolios and provide the basis for many *risk-management systems. Firms also employ them in their decision-making and capital-appraisal models.

moratorium 1. An agreement between a creditor and a debtor to allow additional time for the settlement of a debt. 2. A period during which one government permits a government of a foreign country to suspend repayments of a debt. 3. A period during which all the trading debts in a particular market are suspended as a result of some exceptional crisis in the market. In these circumstances, not to call a moratorium would probably lead to more insolvencies than the market could stand. The intention of such a moratorium is, first, that firms should be given a breathing space to find out exactly what their liabilities are and, secondly, that they should be given time to make the necessary financial arrangements to settle their liabilities.

mortgage An interest in property created as a security for a loan or payment of a debt and terminated on payment of the loan or debt. The borrower, who offers the security, is the **mortgagor**; the lender, who provides the money, is the **mortgagee**. *Building societies and banks are the usual mortgagees for house purchasers, although there are other providers. A mortgage is generally repaid by monthly instalments, usually over a period of 25 years. Repayments may consist of capital and interest (**repayment mortgage**) or of interest only, with arrangements being made to repay the capital, for example by means of an endowment assurance policy (**endowment mortgage**). Business uses of the mortgage include using property to secure a loan to start a business. Virtually any property may be mortgaged (though land is the most common). See feature MORTGAGE LAW on p. 287.

mortgage bond In the USA, a bond in which a debt is secured by a real asset (land or property). **Senior mortgage bonds** have first claim on assets and **junior mortgage bonds** are subordinate. A mortgage bond may have a closed-end provision, which prevents an organization issuing further bonds of a similar nature on the same asset or open-end provision, which permits further issues with the same status.

mortgage interest relief at source (MIRAS) Formerly, an arrangement allowing income tax relief to be given to a mortgagor on the first £30,000 of a loan taken out to purchase a main residence. MIRAS was progressively restricted from 1994 and abolished in 2000.

MPC *See* MONETARY POLICY COMMITTEE.

MRN Abbreviation for *materials returns note.

MTN Abbreviation for *medium-term note.

multicolumn reporting The presentation of financial information prepared on different bases (e.g. *historical-cost convention, *modified historical-cost convention, *replacement cost, etc.) in column form, each column representing a different basis. It is designed to facilitate understanding by the user.

multifunctional card A plastic card issued by a bank or building society to its customers to function as a *cheque card, *debit card, and *cash card. Multifunctional cards operate in conjunction with a *personal identification number.

multilateral netting **1.** A method of reducing bank charges in which the subsidiaries of a group offset their receipts and payments with each other, usually monthly, resulting in a single net intercompany payment or receipt made by each subsidiary to cover the period concerned. This saves both on transaction costs and paperwork. *See also* BILATERAL NETTING; NETTING **2.** The centralizing of international payments of a group of companies so that payments and receipts in different currencies can be offset, thus reducing transaction and hedging costs.

multimedia mail *See* E-MAIL.

multinational enterprise (MNE) A corporation that has production operations in more than one country for various reasons, including securing supplies of raw materials, utilizing cheap labour sources, servicing local markets taking advantage of tax differences, and bypassing protectionist barriers. Multinationals may be seen as an efficient form of organization, making effective use of the world's resources and transferring technology between countries. On the other hand, some have excessive power, are beyond the control of governments (especially weak governments), and are able to exploit host countries, especially in the developing world, where they are able to operate with low safety levels and inadequate control of pollution. *See* GLOBALIZATION.

multiple breakeven points Two or more activity levels at which an

MORTGAGE LAW

Types of mortgage

Under the Law of Property Act (1925), which governs mortgage regulations in the UK, there are two types of mortgage, legal and equitable.

A **legal mortgage** confers a legal estate on the mortgagee (lender). Under the 1925 Act, the only valid mortgages are:

(a) a lease granted for a stated number of years, which terminates on repayment of the loan at or before the end of that period; and

(b) a deed expressed to be a *charge by way of legal mortgage.

All other mortgages are **equitable mortgages**, in which the mortgagee obtains an equitable interest in the property only. Such a mortgage may arise in two ways:

(1) If the mortgagor (borrower) has only an equitable, as opposed to a legal, interest in the property (for example, because he or she is a beneficiary under a trust of the property) he or she can only grant an equitable mortgage. Provided that the mortgage is created by deed, the rights of the parties are very similar to those under a legal mortgage.

(2) An equitable mortgage can also be created of a legal or equitable interest by an informal written agreement, e.g. the mortgagor hands the title deeds to the mortgagee as security for a loan. The great majority of mortgages are now of this kind. Such a mortgagee has the remedies of repossession and foreclosure only (see below).

Second mortgages

A second or subsequent mortgage may be taken out on the same property, provided that the value of the property is greater than the amount of the previous mortgage(s). All mortgages of registered land are noted in the *register of charges on application by the mortgagee, and a charge certificate is issued. When mortgaged land is unregistered, a first legal mortgagee keeps the title deeds. A subsequent legal mortgagee and any equitable mortgagee who does not have the title deeds should protect their interests by registration.

Redemption

Under the so-called **equity of redemption**, the mortgagor is allowed to redeem the property at any time on payment of the loan together with interest and costs, which may include a penalty for early redemption; any provisions in a mortgage deed to prevent redemption (known as **clogs**) are void.

Repossession and foreclosure

In theory, the mortgagee always has the right to take possession of mortgaged property even if there has been no default. However, this right is usually excluded by building-society mortgages until default, and its exclusion may be implied in any instalment mortgage. Where residential property is concerned, the court has power to delay the recovery of possession if there is a realistic possibility that the default will be remedied in a reasonable time. In case of default, the mortgagee has a statutory right to sell the property, but this will normally be exercised after obtaining possession first. Any surplus left after the debt and the mortgagee's expenses have been met must be paid to the mortgagor. The mortgagee also has a statutory right to appoint a *receiver to manage mortgaged property in the event of default; this power is useful where business property is concerned. As a final resort, a mortgage may be brought to an end by *foreclosure, in which the court orders the transfer of the property to the mortgagee. This is not common in times of rising property prices, as the mortgagor would lose more than the value of the debt, so the court will not order foreclosure where a sale would be more appropriate.

organization breaks even. They can occur on *breakeven charts when the cost and revenue functions are not linear and the total cost curve and the total revenue curve cross each other more than once.

multiple solution rates The several rates of return that can in some circumstances be computed in an *appraisal based on *discounted cash flow using the *internal rate of return method. These circumstances may arise when the projected cash flows change from positive to negative and back to positive again, causing an internal rate of return at each change of sign in the stream of cash flows.

multi-tied adviser *See* INDEPENDENT FINANCIAL ADVISER.

muqarada *See* ISLAMIC FINANCE.

murabaha *See* ISLAMIC FINANCE.

musharaka *See* ISLAMIC FINANCE.

mutual A company that is owned by its members or depositors. In the UK *building societies used to have this structure, but most have now demutualized, becoming *public limited companies. Mutual life-assurance companies developed out of the *Friendly Societies. There are no shareholders and apart from benefits and running expenses there are no other withdrawals from the fund; thus any profits are distributed to policyholders.

mutually exclusive projects A number of alternative projects being considered for *appraisal, in which no one project can be pursued in conjunction with any of the other projects. For example, a parcel of land may be used to build a factory, an office block, or a mixture of the two. The alternatives are mutually exclusive because the choice of any one automatically excludes all the others. Mutually exclusive projects arise when there is a scarce resource, in this case land. *Compare* INDEPENDENT PROJECTS.

mutual trading The situation in which the income of a company arises solely from contributions by its members, the members being the owners of the company. The same provisions apply where the entity is an association and not a company. Historically, many insurance companies were created as *mutuals, as were the *building societies. The 'profits' of mutual trading are not subject to UK corporation tax as they are not, strictly speaking, profit but are more correctly regarded as a surplus of contributions.

naked position *See* OPEN POSITION.

NAO Abbreviation for *National Audit Office.

NASDAQ A US electronic market for securities that began operations in 1971, as the National Association of Securities Dealers Automated Quotations System. The first screen-based trading system to have no market floor, it is now the largest stock market in the USA, listing more than 3000 companies. **NASDAQ International** is an international system providing screen-based quotations for US-registered equities that came into operation in 1992. In 2008 NASDAQ acquired the Swedish exchange group *OMX.

(⊕) SEE WEB LINKS
• NASDAQ website

National Audit Office (NAO) A body set up in 1983 to audit the appropriation accounts of government departments and other public bodies and to examine the economy, efficiency, and effectiveness with which these bodies have used their resources. The NAO is headed by the Comptroller and Auditor General and reports to the Public Accounts Commission.

(⊕) SEE WEB LINKS
• Website of the NAO

National Insurance contributions (NIC) Payments made by those with earned income that contribute to the National Insurance Fund, from which benefits are paid. These benefits include retirement pensions, jobseekers' allowance, widow's benefits, incapacity benefit, and maternity benefits. There are six different classes of National Insurance contributions; the class applicable to a person depends on the type of earned income received by that person.

Class 1 is paid by those with earnings from employment. There are two parts to class 1, primary contributions paid by the employee and secondary contributions paid by the employer. The rates of contributions depend on the level of earnings and also whether or not the employee is a member of a contracted-out occupational, personal, or stakeholder pension scheme; for employees the standard rate is 11% on weekly earnings between £110 and £884 and 1% on weekly earnings thereafter (2009–10 figures).

Class 2 is a flat-rate contribution of £2.40 paid by the self-employed.

Class 3 is voluntary, and is also at a flat rate (£12.05 per week in 2009–10). It is paid by those wishing to maintain their contribution record even though they may be unemployed or their level of earnings is below that for mandatory contributions.

Class 4 is paid by the self-employed at a rate of 8% on income between a lower limit of £5471 per year and an upper limit of £43,875 per year and 1% on yearly income thereafter.

Class 1A is payable by employers who provide cars for private as well as business use for their employees. The level of payment depends on the cost and age of the car and the number of business miles travelled. It is based on the list price of the vehicle, on the day it was first registered as brand new.

Class 1B is payable by employers in value of any items included in a PAYE settlement with HM Revenue and Customs.

((⊕)) SEE WEB LINKS
• Guide to NICs from the Gov.uk website

nationalization The process of bringing the assets of a business into the ownership of the state. Examples of industries nationalized in the past in the UK include the National Coal Board and British Rail. Historically, nationalization has been achieved through compulsory purchase, although this need not necessarily be the case. Nationalization has often been pursued as much for political as economic ends and the economic justifications themselves are varied. One argument for nationalization is that if a company possesses a natural monopoly, then it should not be run for private profit; another is that certain industries are strategically important for the nation. In the 1980s and 1990s Conservative governments reversed the nationalizations of the post-war Labour governments with a series of *privatization measures, on the grounds that competition would increase efficiency and reduce prices. Labour administrations after 1997 proved reluctant to renationalize until the financial crisis of 2008, when several leading banks (notably the Royal Bank of Scotland) were partly nationalized to prevent their collapse.

National Savings A wide range of schemes for personal savers, administered by National Savings and Investments (NSI), a government agency established in 1969 as the Post Office Savings Department. They include premium bonds, guaranteed equity bonds, Children's Bonus Bonds, and inflation-linked savings certificates. The Department also offers *Individual Savings Accounts (ISAs) and (since January 2004) Easy Access Savings Accounts. The **National Savings Bank** (**NSB**; formerly the Post Office Savings Bank) was founded in 1861.

National Society of Accountants (NSA) In the USA, a professional association for accountants and tax practitioners. It was founded in 1945 as the National Society of Public Accountants (NSPA).

((⊕)) SEE WEB LINKS
• Website of the NSA

NAV Abbreviation for net asset value. *See* ASSET VALUE (PER SHARE); BOOK VALUE.

NBV Abbreviation for *net book value.

near money (quasi money) An asset that is immediately transferable and may be used to settle some but not all debts, although it is not as liquid as banknotes and coins. *Bills of exchange are examples of near money. Near money is not included in the money supply definitions.

negative cash flow 1. Any *cash outflow. 2. The difference between a company's cash inflows and cash outflows in a financial period when the latter is greater than the former. *See* NET CASH FLOW.

negative consolidation difference A *consolidation difference showing a credit balance. In *acquisition accounting this will represent negative *goodwill.

negative equity **1.** The difference between the value of a property (usually residential) and the outstanding amount borrowed against it where the latter is the greater. For example, if a property's current market value is £250,000 and the borrowing against it is £260,000, there is a negative *equity to the extent of £10,000. Negative equities occur chiefly when economic recession has an adverse effect on property prices. House owners who paid more for their houses than their current market value are unable to sell without realizing the loss. **2.** More generally, any asset that has a market value below the sum of money borrowed to purchase it.

negative goodwill on consolidation The *goodwill consolidation in which the price paid for an acquisition is less than the fair value of its net *tangible assets. According to *Financial Reporting Standard 10, negative goodwill should be recognized and separately disclosed on the *balance sheet, immediately below the goodwill heading. It should be recognized in the *profit and loss account in the periods in which the non-monetary assets acquired are depreciated or sold. Any negative goodwill in excess of the values of the non-monetary assets should be written back in the profit and loss account over the period expected to benefit from the negative goodwill. The relevant *International Financial Reporting Standard is IFRS 3, Business Combinations.

negative income tax (NIT) A means of targeting social security benefits to those most in need using the income-tax system. After submitting an income-tax return showing an income level below a set minimum, an individual would receive a direct subsidy from the tax authorities bringing income up to that level.

negative pledge A *covenant in a loan agreement in which a borrower promises that no secured borrowings will be made during the life of the loan or will ensure that the loan is secured equally and rateably with any new borrowings as specifically defined.

negative yield curve *See* YIELD CURVE.

negligence In law, a tort in which a breach of a duty of care results in damage to the person to whom the duty is owed. Such a duty is owed by manufacturers to the consumers who buy their products, by accountants, solicitors, doctors, and other professional persons to their clients, by a director of a company to its shareholders, etc. A person who has suffered loss or injury as a result of a breach of the duty of care can claim *damages in tort. The risk of being sued for negligence makes it essential for partners in accountancy firms that are not *limited liability partnerships to obtain *professional indemnity insurance.

negligible value Denoting an asset of little or no value. For *capital gains tax, if an asset is determined to have negligible value it can be treated as having been sold and immediately reacquired at the current negligible value (nil), resulting in an allowable *capital loss for capital gains tax purposes.

negotiability The ability of a document to change hands thereby entitling its owner to some benefit, so that legal ownership of the benefit passes by delivery or endorsement of the document. For a document to be negotiable it must also entitle the holder to bring an action in law if necessary. *See* NEGOTIABLE INSTRUMENT.

negotiable instrument A document of title that can be freely negotiated (*see* NEGOTIABILITY). Such documents are *cheques and *bills of exchange, in which the stated payee of the instrument can negotiate the instrument by either inserting the name of a different payee or by making the document 'open' by endorsing it (signing one's name), usually on the reverse. Holders of negotiable instruments cannot pass on a better title than they possess. Bills of exchange, including cheques, in which the payee is named or that bear a restrictive endorsement, such as 'not negotiable', are **non-negotiable instruments**.

negotiated transfer prices *Transfer prices set by negotiation between the supplying and receiving divisions of an organization. Negotiated transfer prices are appropriate when there is an imperfect market for the goods and services that are bought and sold between divisions. Negotiation may be seen as a way of reducing conflicts between managers. The relative bargaining power of the divisions is important; a mediator may be used to help the negotiations.

net Denoting an amount remaining after specific deductions have been made. For example, **net profit before taxation** is the profit made by an organization after the deduction of all business expenditure but before the deduction of the taxation charge.

net assets The assets of an organization less its *current liabilities. The resultant figure is equal to the *capital of the organization. Opinion varies as to whether long-term liabilities should be treated as part of the capital and are therefore not deductible in arriving at net assets, or whether they are part of the liabilities and therefore deductible. The latter view is probably technically preferable and is more common. A further practice is to split long-term liabilities and to treat those described as the 'finance element' as part of the capital. *Compare* NET CURRENT ASSETS. *See also* BOOK VALUE; NET WORTH.

net asset value (NAV) *See* ASSET VALUE (PER SHARE); BOOK VALUE.

net basis The basis upon which the *earnings per share of a company is calculated, taking into account both constant and variable elements in the company's tax charge. *Compare* NIL BASIS.

net book value (NBV; book value) The value at which an asset appears in the books of an organization (usually as at the date of the last balance sheet). This is the purchase cost or latest revaluation less any depreciation applied since purchase or revaluation. The net book value is also known as the **depreciated value** or **depreciated cost**. *See* BALANCE-SHEET ASSET VALUE.

net cash flow The difference between the cash coming into an organization (cash inflows) and that going out of it (cash outflows) in a financial period. The difference may be positive, in which case there is a surplus of cash, or negative, in which case there is a deficit.

net cash investment in a lease (net investment in a lease) The amount of funds invested in a lease by a lessor. It comprises the cost of the leased asset, together with grants received, rentals received, taxation payments and receipts, residual values, interest payments, interest received on cash surplus, and any profit taken out of the lease. *See* FINANCE LEASE.

net current assets *Current assets less *current liabilities. The resultant figure is also known as *working capital, as it represents the amount of the organization's capital that is constantly being turned over in the course of its trade. *See also* NET ASSETS.

net dividend The *dividend paid by a company to its shareholders, after excluding the *tax credit received by the shareholders.

net investment in a lease *See* NET CASH INVESTMENT IN A LEASE.

net-investment method *See* CLOSING-RATE METHOD.

net margin *See* NET PROFIT.

net margin ratio *See* NET PROFIT PERCENTAGE.

net present value (NPV) A method of *capital budgeting in which the value of an investment is calculated as the total *present value of all *cash inflows and *cash outflows minus the cost of the initial investment. If the net present value is positive, the return will be greater than that required by the capital markets and investment should be considered. A negative net present value indicates that the investment should be rejected. *See also* DISCOUNTED CASH FLOW.

EXAMPLE

A company is considering the purchase of a new computer system, which is expected to save £100,000 in cash operating costs each year. Its estimated useful life (how long it will last) is five years, at the end of which it will have no *net residual value.

The cash flows for the project are as follows:

Year 0:	cost of computer system £390,000
Year 1:	saving of £100,000
Year 2:	saving of £100,000
Year 3:	saving of £100,000
Year 4:	saving of £100,000
Year 5:	saving of £100,000

A simple analysis shows that the savings over five years are £500,000 (5 × £100,000) and the cost is £390,000, which gives a surplus of £110,000 (£500,000 − £390,000). However, such an analysis ignores the *time value of money: £1 received in the future is not equal to £1 received today. To calculate the present value of future cash flows it is necessary to calculate the *discount factor.

Assuming that the *cost of capital for the project is 8%, the discount factor is calculated as follows:

Year 1:	$£1/(1.08)^2 = 0.926$
Year 2:	$£1/(1.08)^2 = 0.857$
Year 3:	$£1/(1.08)^3 = 0.794$
Year 4:	$£1/(1.08)^4 = 0.735$
Year 5:	$£1/(1.08)^5 = 0.681$

(An alternative to calculating the discount factor in this way is the use of present value tables or spreadsheet routines.)

The net present value can then be calculated:

Year	Cash flow		Discount factor		Present value
Year 0:	(£390,000)	×	1.0000	=	(£390,000)
Year 1:	100,000	×	0.926	=	£92,600
Year 2:	100,000	×	0.857	=	£85,700
Year 3:	100,000	×	0.794	=	£79,400
Year 4:	100,000	×	0.735	=	£73,500
Year 5:	100,000	×	0.681	=	£68,100
		net present value			£9300

In this case, the net present value is positive and therefore it could be argued that managers should buy the new computer system. However, £9300 is quite a small amount and managers may not be confident that the savings will be the supposed £100,000 a year. Also, the new computer system may not last five years. The net present value calculation is very important as it highlights that this is a marginal decision.

net profit (net margin; net profit margin) The *gross profit less all the other costs of an organization in addition to those included in the *cost of sales. It is shown before and after taxation in the *profit and loss account.

net profit percentage (net margin ratio) A ratio of financial performance calculated by expressing the *net profit as a percentage of sales revenue. *Compare* GROSS PROFIT PERCENTAGE. *See also* MARGIN; MARK-UP.

net realizable value (NRV) 1. The sales value of the stock of an organization less the additional costs likely to be incurred in getting the stocks into the hands of the customer. It is the value placed on the closing stock according to the requirements of *Statement of Standard Accounting Practice 9, when the NRV is lower than cost. **2.** The amount at which any *asset could be disposed of, less any direct selling costs.

net residual value (disposal value) The expected proceeds from the sale of an asset, net of the costs of sale, at the end of its estimated useful life. It is used for computing the *straight-line method and *diminishing-balance method of depreciation, and also for inclusion in the final year's cash inflow in a *discounted cash flow appraisal.

netting The process of setting off matching sales and purchases against each other, especially sales and purchases of futures, options, and forward foreign exchange. This service is usually provided for an exchange or market by a *clearing house. It also provides a means by which a firm can deal with its risks, notably *exchange-rate exposure. *See* BILATERAL NETTING; MULTILATERAL NETTING. *See also* NOVATION.

netting off The deduction of one amount from another. For example, debtors are usually shown in a *balance sheet after netting off (deducting) a provision for *bad debts and *doubtful debts.

network analysis *See* CRITICAL-PATH ANALYSIS.

net worth The value of an organization when its liabilities have been deducted from the value of its assets. Often taken to be synonymous with *net assets, net worth so defined can be misleading in that balance sheets rarely show the real value of assets. *See* BOOK VALUE.

New York Mercantile Exchange (NYMEX) A futures exchange in New York dealing chiefly in oil products and metals. In 1994 it acquired the Commodity Exchange Inc. of New York (COMEX), becoming the world's largest market in commodity futures. It established a London trading floor, NYMEX Europe, in 2005. NYMEX was purchased by the *Chicago Mercantile Exchange in 2008.

New York Stock Exchange (NYSE) The main US stock exchange. It was founded in 1792 under the Buttonwood Agreement (the name of the tree under which 24 merchants agreed to give each other preference in their dealings); it moved to Wall Street in 1793. The New York Stock & Exchange Board was formally established in 1817; it was renamed the New York Stock Exchange in 1983. In 2006 the NYSE combined with the pan-European exchange *Euronext NV to create **NYSE Euronext**, the world's first global exchange. It acquired the electronic exchange Archipelago Holdings in 2006 and the American Stock Exchange in 2008.

(((⊕))) SEE WEB LINKS

• Information for traders, companies, and private investors from the NYSE Euronext website

next-in-first-out cost (NIFO cost) A method of valuing units of *raw material or *finished goods issued from stock by using the next unit price at which a consignment will be received for pricing the issues. It is effectively using *replacement cost as a stock valuation method, which is not normally acceptable as a stock valuation system in the UK when computing profits for taxation purposes. *Compare* FIRST-IN-FIRST-OUT COST; LAST-IN-FIRST-OUT COST.

NIC Abbreviation for *National Insurance contributions.

NIF Abbreviation for *note issuance facility.

NIFO cost Abbreviation for *next-in-first-out cost.

Nikkei Stock Average (Nikkei Index) The index of stock prices used on the *Tokyo Stock Exchange. It is a price-weighted index of 225 Japanese companies. It was restructured for the first time in its history in late 1991 by its administrator, the Nihon Keizai Shimbun financial newspaper group, in an attempt to reduce the impact of futures-related trading on the index. Membership of the index is now renewed annually.

nil basis The basis upon which the *earnings per share of a company is calculated taking into account only the constant elements in the company's tax charge. *Compare* NET BASIS.

nil paid shares *Shares issued without payment, usually as the result of a *rights issue.

nil-rate band The first slice of a *chargeable transfer or the estate on death that is subject to a nil rate of *inheritance tax. The nil rate band for 2009–10 is

£325,000. From April 2008 it became possible for spouses and civil partners to transfer their nil-rate band to the surviving partner on death, thereby effectively raising the threshold at which tax becomes payable to £650,000.

NIT Abbreviation for *negative income tax.

nominal account A *ledger account that is not a *personal account in that it bears the name of a concept, e.g. light and heat, bad debts, investments, etc., rather than the name of a person. These accounts are normally grouped in the *nominal ledger. *See also* REAL ACCOUNT.

nominal capital *See* AUTHORIZED SHARE CAPITAL.

nominal ledger (general ledger) The *ledger containing the *nominal accounts and *real accounts necessary to prepare the accounts of an organization. This ledger is distinguished from the personal ledgers, such as the *debtors' ledger and *creditors' ledger, which contain the accounts of customers and suppliers respectively.

nominal price **1.** A minimal price fixed for the sake of having some consideration for a transaction. It need bear no relation to the market value of the item. **2.** The price given to a security when it is issued, also called the **face value**, **nominal value**, or *par value. For example, XYZ plc 25p ordinary shares have a nominal price of 25p, although the market value may be quite different. The nominal value of a share is the maximum amount the holder can be required to contribute to the company.

nominal share capital *See* AUTHORIZED SHARE CAPITAL.

nominal value *See* PAR VALUE.

nominee A person named by another (the **nominator**) to act on his or her behalf, often to conceal the identity of the nominator. *See* NOMINEE SHAREHOLDING.

nominee shareholding A shareholding held in the name of a bank, stockbroker, company, individual, etc., that is not the name of the beneficial owner of the shares (the **indirect shareholder**). A shareholding may be in the name of nominees to facilitate dealing or to conceal the identity of the true owner. Although this cover was formerly used in the early stages of a takeover, to enable the bidder clandestinely to build up a substantial holding in the target company, this practice was prevented by the Companies Act 1985, which made it mandatory for anyone holding 5% or more of the shares in a public company to declare that interest to the company. The earlier Companies Act 1967 made it mandatory for directors to openly declare their holdings, and those of their families, in the companies of which they are directors. The Companies Act 2006 extends information and voting rights to indirect shareholders.

non-adjusting events Any events, either favourable or unfavourable, that occur between the *balance-sheet date and the date on which the *financial statements of an organization are approved by the board of directors, but which concern conditions that did not exist at the balance-sheet date. If they are sufficiently *material for their non-disclosure to affect a user's understanding of the financial statements, non-adjusting events should be disclosed in the notes to the accounts. If a non-adjusting event suggests that the *going-concern concept is no longer applicable to the whole, or a material part, of the company, changes in the amounts to be included in the financial statements should be made. For example, if serious industrial action has occurred, which if it continues could threaten the continued existence of the business, an appropriate provision should be made in the accounts. *Compare* ADJUSTING EVENTS.

non-contributory pension scheme An *occupational pension scheme in which all the contributions to the scheme are made by the employer.

non-controllable costs *See* UNCONTROLLABLE COSTS.

non-cumulative preference share A *preference share not having the right to *dividends that were not paid in previous years. *Compare* CUMULATIVE PREFERENCE SHARE.

non-domiciled Denoting a person whose country of *domicile is not the same as his or her country of residence for tax purposes. Before April 2008 a person resident but not domiciled in the UK paid no UK tax on foreign investment income unless this was remitted to the UK (*see* REMITTANCE BASIS). From that date so-called **non-doms** who have been resident in the UK for seven of the last ten years are required to pay a flat annual charge of £30,000 if they wish to avoid paying UK tax on foreign income and gains.

non-equity share A *share in a company having any of the following characteristics:
- any of the rights of the share to receive payments are for a limited amount that is not calculated by reference to the company's assets or profits or the dividends on any class of equity share;
- any of the rights of the share to participate in a surplus on *liquidation are limited to a specific amount that is not calculated by reference to the company's assets or profits;
- the share is redeemable either according to its terms or because the holder, or any party other than the issuer, can require its redemption.

This definition is based on that contained in *Financial Reporting Standard (FRS) 4, Capital Instruments. In January 2005 FRS 4 was replaced by FRS 25, Financial Instruments: Disclosure and Presentation, under which so called *preference shares are no longer classified as non-equity share capital (*see* PREFERENCE SHARE CAPITAL). The concept of non-equity shares is not recognized under *International Financial Reporting Standards.

non-executive director A director of a company who is not involved in the day-to-day management of the business but who is appointed to bring independent judgment on issues of strategy, performance, resources, and standards of conduct. In the UK the *Combined Code on Corporate Governance requires public listed companies to appoint non-executive directors or to explain why they have not done so. Apart from their watchdog role, such directors are often employed for their prestige, experience, contacts, or specialist knowledge.

non-participating preference share A *preference share that does not carry a right to participate in the profits of a company beyond a fixed rate of *dividend. This is the most common type of preference share.

non-production overhead costs The *indirect costs of an organization that are not classified as *manufacturing overhead. They include *administration overheads, *selling overhead, *distribution overhead, and (in some cases) *research and development costs.

non-purchased goodwill *See* INHERENT GOODWILL.

non-ratio covenant A form of *covenant in a loan agreement that includes conditions relating to the payment of dividends, the granting of guarantees, disposal of assets, change of ownership, and a *negative pledge. Breaching such a covenant will usually empower the lender to request repayment of any of the loan then outstanding, and the loan then becomes null and void. *Compare* RATIO COVENANT.

non-recourse finance A bank loan in which the lending bank is only entitled to repayment from the profits of the project the loan is funding and not from other resources of the borrower.

non-resident The status of an individual who has never lived in a particular country for fiscal purposes or who has moved to another country, either for employment or permanently. This person's liability to tax in the first country is restricted to income from sources within that country. Interest on all British government stocks is exempt from UK tax for non-residents. *See also* DOUBLE TAXATION AGREEMENT; RESIDENT. *Compare* NON-DOMICILED.

non-revolving bank facility A loan from a bank to a company in which the company has a period (often several years) in which to make its *drawdowns, as well as flexibility with regard to the amount and timing of the drawdowns, but once drawn an amount takes on the characteristics of a *term loan. *Compare* REVOLVING BANK FACILITY.

non-statistical sampling *See* JUDGMENTAL SAMPLING.

non-statutory accounts Any financial statement issued by a company that does not form part of the statutory *annual accounts. Such statements were formerly known as **abridged accounts**. Under the Companies Act a company has to make a statement on any non-statutory accounts it issues to the effect that they are not the statutory accounts. Such accounts are often reported in the media.

non-taxable income Income that is specifically exempt from tax. Examples of such income include:
- income received under a maintenance agreement or court order in cases of divorce or separation;
- statutory redundancy pay;
- income from National Savings Easy Access Savings Accounts;
- income from *Individual Savings Accounts (ISAs);
- up to £4250 annually from a 'rent-a-room' scheme;
- income from scholarships;
- winnings from betting (including the National Lottery) and competition prizes.

no par value capital stock In the USA and Canada, stock (shares) that have no *par value or assigned value printed on the stock certificate. An advantage of such stock is that it avoids a *contingent liability to stockholders in the event of a stock discount. For accounting purposes, on the issue of no par value capital stock, cash is debited and a capital stock account credited with the total proceeds received. No premium account is required. No par value shares are not permitted under UK law.

normal capacity *See* BUDGETED CAPACITY.

normal loss The loss arising from a manufacturing or chemical process through waste, seepage, shrinkage, or spoilage that can be expected, on the basis of historical studies, to be part of that process. It may be expressed as a weight or volume or in other units appropriate to the process. It is usually not valued but if it is, a notional scrap value is used. It is axiomatic in costing that normal losses are part of the normal *manufacturing costs, whereas the cost of *abnormal losses should not be borne by the good output. *See also* WASTE.

normal standard An average standard, used in *standard costing, set to be applied over a future period during which conditions are unlikely to change.

normal volume The volume of activity used to determine the overhead *absorption rate in a system of *absorption costing. It is usually the budgeted volume of production for a period.

normative theories of accounting Theories of accounting, often based on a priori concepts and deductive reasoning, that prescribe the accounting procedures and policies that should be followed rather than describing those that are followed in practice. *Compare* POSITIVE ACCOUNTING THEORY. *See also* A PRIORI THEORIES OF ACCOUNTING.

note A negotiable record of an unsecured loan. The word 'note' is now used in preference to *bond when the principal sum is repayable in less than five years.

note issuance facility (NIF; note purchase facility) A means of enabling short-term borrowers in the *eurocurrency markets to issue euronotes, with maturities of less than one year, when the need arises rather than having to arrange a separate issue of euronotes each time they need to borrow. A **revolving underwriting facility** (RUF) achieves the same objective.

note of historical cost profits and losses A memorandum item in the *annual accounts and report of a company giving an abbreviated restatement of the *profit and loss account, showing the reported profit or loss as if no *revaluations had been made. The statement need not be made where the difference is not material. *Financial Reporting Standard (FRS) 3, Reporting Financial Performance, states that such a note should be published. However, many accountants believe that the inclusion of such a note is questionable and *Financial Reporting Exposure Draft 22, Revision of FRS 3, would make the practice optional.

notes to the accounts (notes to financial statements) Information supporting that given on the face of a company's *financial statements. Many notes are required to be given by law, including those detailing *fixed assets, investments, *share capital, *debentures, and *reserves. Other information may be required by accounting standards or be given to facilitate the users' understanding of the company and its current and future performance.

not for profit organization (non-profit-making organization) An organization that provides goods or services with a policy that no individual or group will share in any profits or losses. Examples are government and charity organizations.

not negotiable Words marked on a *bill of exchange indicating that it ceases to be a *negotiable instrument, i.e. although it can still be negotiated, the holder cannot obtain a better title to it than the person from whom it was obtained, thus providing a safeguard if it is stolen. A cheque is the only form of bill that can be crossed 'not negotiable'; other forms must have it inscribed on their faces.

novation A cancellation of the rights and obligations under one loan agreement and their replacement by new ones under another agreement. The principal effect is to change the identity of the lender.

NPV Abbreviation for *net present value.

NRV Abbreviation for *net realizable value.

number of days' stock held A ratio that measures the average number of days' stock held by an organization. To obtain an accurate measure the following formula should be used for each commodity:

(number of units in stock × 365)/stock usage in units per annum.

The number of units in stock may be taken at the start or the end of the year or may be the average of both. Because the information required for the above ratio is only likely to be available from the internal management accounts, a different formula using final accounts figures is often used as an overall measure of stock levels:

(value of stocks × 365)/sales or *cost of sales per annum.

Again, the value of stocks may be taken at the start or the end of the period or may be an average of both. The second formula tends to be inaccurate and is an average of the turnover of all stocks. *See also* INVENTORY TURNOVER; RATE OF TURNOVER.

NYMEX Abbreviation for *New York Mercantile Exchange.

NYSE Abbreviation for *New York Stock Exchange.

NYSE Euronext *See* EURONEXT NV; NEW YORK STOCK EXCHANGE.

objective function In *linear programming, a statement that gives the aim of a decision in the form of an equation. For example, the objective function may be either to maximize the *contribution or to minimize the costs, based on a relationship between the factors of production.

objectives of financial statements The purposes for which the *financial statements in the *annual accounts and report have been made. It is essential to identify these purposes to determine (a) what information should be provided and (b) how it should be presented. The current thinking is that the objective is to provide information useful in economic decision making (*see* TRUEBLOOD REPORT). It is debatable how far present disclosures are appropriate for this purpose; there is some uncertainty as to the users of financial statements, the purposes they use them for, and how they process the information. In the UK the *Accounting Standards Board's *Statement of Principles attempted to address these issues but has been much criticized. The International Accounting Standards Board's *Framework for the Preparation and Presentation of Financial Statements also addresses the objectives of financial reporting. *See also* QUALITATIVE CHARACTERISTICS OF ACCOUNTING INFORMATION.

objectivity An *accounting concept attempting to ensure that any subjective actions taken by the preparer of accounts are minimized. The aim of the rules and regulations required to achieve objectivity is that users should be able to compare *financial statements for different companies over a period with some confidence that the statements have been prepared on the same basis. One of the major advantages claimed for *historical-cost accounting is that it is objective, but necessarily some subjective decisions will have been made.

objects clause A clause contained in the *articles of association of a company setting out the objects for which the company has been formed. The Companies Act 2006 removes the former requirement for a company to state its objects in this way. An act by a company that falls outside the scope of the objects clause is no longer voidable in law unless the company is a charity. *See* ULTRA VIRES.

obligation A commitment given to comply with the terms of a contract or to pay a debt.

OBS Abbreviation for *off-balance-sheet.

obsolescence A fall in the value of an asset as a result of its age or decline in its usefulness for other reasons. Obsolescence is an important factor both for *depreciation and *stock (inventory). In respect of depreciation, changes in technology or markets may mean a *fixed asset becomes obsolete before the end of its predicted useful life. In respect of stocks, obsolescence may mean that the total cost of outdated items held in stock have to be charged against the *profit and loss account immediately, as the rule is that stocks must be shown at the lower of cost or market value.

occupational pension scheme (superannuation) A *pension scheme open to employees within a certain trade or profession or working for a particular firm. An occupational pension scheme can either be insured or self-administered. If it is insured, an insurance company pays the benefits under the scheme in return for having the premiums to invest. In a self-administered scheme, the pension-fund trustees are responsible for investing the contributions themselves. In the UK, occupational and other work-related pensions are regulated by the *Pensions Regulator. *See also* DEFINED-BENEFIT PENSION SCHEME; DEFINED-CONTRIBUTION PENSION SCHEME.

((⊕)) SEE WEB LINKS
• Website of the Pensions Regulator: includes Codes of Practice and guidance for employers, trustees, and their advisers

off-balance-sheet (OBS) Denoting assets or liabilities that do not appear on the *balance sheet of a company. Various off-balance-sheet arrangements have been entered into by companies wishing to avoid full disclosure of their assets and liabilities: these include complex legal agreements, the use of *joint ventures or specially created subsidiaries, and *securitizations and other *structured finance arrangements. In **off-balance-sheet finance** (OBSF) a company removes some or all of its finance from the balance sheet, usually to enhance its *accounting ratios, such as the *gearing ratio and *return on capital employed, or to avoid breaking any agreements it has made with the banks in respect of the total amount it may borrow. Similarly, banks have used a variety of off-balance-sheet arrangements, typically involving securizations and *special purpose vehicles, to avoid their obligations under the *capital adequacy rules. The accounting profession has attempted to counter the most misleading of these practices by emphasizing that accounting should reflect the commercial reality of transactions and not simply their legal form. *Financial Reporting Standard 5, Reporting the Substance of Transactions, provides specific guidance for certain transactions, such as *factoring and *consignment stock, for which companies previously used off-balance-sheet finance. In the USA, the *Sarbanes–Oxley Act of 2002 introduced new regulations concerning the disclosure of off-balance-sheet arrangements in the wake of the Enron scandal of 2001. In the banking and financial sector, the lack of transparency arising from complex off-balance-sheet practices has been identified as a major factor in the financial meltdown of 2008. *See* CREATIVE ACCOUNTING; HIDDEN RESERVE.

offer The price at which a seller is willing to sell something. If there is an acceptance of the offer a legally binding *contract has been entered into. In law, an offer is distinguished from an **invitation to treat**, which is an invitation by one person or firm to others to make an offer. An example of an invitation to treat is to display goods in a shop window. *See also* OFFER PRICE.

offer by prospectus An offer to the public of a new issue of shares or debentures made directly by means of a *prospectus, a document giving a detailed account of the aims, objects, and capital structure of the company, as well as its past history. The prospectus must conform to the provisions of the Companies Act. *Compare* OFFER FOR SALE.

offer for sale An invitation to the general public to purchase the stock of a company through an intermediary, such as an issuing house or *merchant bank (*compare* OFFER BY PROSPECTUS); it is one of the most frequently used means of *flotation. An offer for sale can be in one of two forms: a *public issue (the more usual), in which stock is offered at a fixed price and some form of balloting or rationing is required if the demand for the shares exceeds supply; or an *issue by tender, in which individuals offer to purchase a fixed quantity of stock at or above some minimum price and the stock is allocated to the highest bidders. *Compare* INTRODUCTION; PLACING.

offer price The price at which a security is offered for sale by a *market maker and also the price at which an institution will sell units in a unit trust. *Compare* BID.

Office for National Statistics (ONS) The UK government's statistical unit, formed by a merger of the **Central Statistical Office** and the Office of Population Censuses and Surveys in 1996. It is an independent body responsible for collecting economic statistics for the government. Among its publications are *Financial Statistics* (monthly), *UK National Accounts* (the *Blue Book*; annual), *UK Balance of Payments* (the *Pink Book*; annual), and the *Annual Abstract of Statistics*.

(⊕) SEE WEB LINKS
• Free access to data produced by the Office for National Statistics

Office of Fair Trading (OFT) A government department that reviews commercial activities in the UK and aims to protect the consumer against unfair practices. It was established in 1973 and has three main operational areas: competition enforcement, consumer regulation enforcement, and markets and policies initiatives. It also runs advice and information services for both consumers and businesses and liaises with the relevant departments of the European Commission.

(⊕) SEE WEB LINKS
• Website of the OFT: includes advice for businesses and consumers

Office of Government Commerce (OGC) An office of HM Treasury established to help government departments and other public sector organizations deliver best value for money. It issues standards on best practice in procurement, project management, and service management and measures performance against these standards.

officers of a company The *directors of a company and the *company secretary. An officer of a company may not be appointed as the *auditor of that company.

office suite *See* BUSINESS SOFTWARE PACKAGE.

Official List **1.** A list of all the securities traded on the main market of the *London Stock Exchange. *See* LISTED SECURITY; LISTING REQUIREMENTS; YELLOW BOOK. **2.** A list prepared daily by the London Stock Exchange, recording all the bargains that have been transacted in listed securities during the day. It also gives dividend dates, rights issues, prices, and other information.

(⊕) SEE WEB LINKS
• Official List of securities on the LSE from the FCA website

official receiver (OR) A person appointed by the Secretary of State for Business, Enterprise and Regulatory Reform to act as a *receiver in *bankruptcy and winding-up cases. The High Court and each county court that has jurisdiction over insolvency matters has an official receiver, who is an officer of the court. Deputy official receivers may also be appointed. The official receiver commonly acts as the *liquidator of a company being wound up by the court.

offset account An account that reduces the gross amount of another account to derive a net balance. An example is a *fixed asset that remains in the *books of account at cost as a *debit balance and is offset by a provision for *depreciation account, which accumulates the annual charge for depreciation as a *credit balance.

offshore company **1.** A company not registered in the same country as that in which the persons investing in the company are resident. **2.** A company set up in a foreign country or *tax haven by a financial institution with the object of benefiting from tax laws or exchange control regulations in that country.

offshore financial centres Centres that provide advantageous deposit and lending rates to non-residents because of low taxation, liberal exchange controls, and low reserve requirements for banks. Some countries have made a lucrative business out of **offshore banking**; the Cayman Islands is currently one of the world's largest offshore centres. In Europe, Switzerland, the Channel Islands, and the Isle of Man are very popular. Such locations are often described as *tax havens because they can reduce customers' tax liabilities in entirely legal ways. The USA and Japan have both established domestic offshore facilities enabling non-residents to conduct their business under more liberal regulations than domestic transactions. Their objective is to stop funds moving outside the country.

OFR Abbreviation for *operating and financial review.

OFT Abbreviation for *Office of Fair Trading.

OGC Abbreviation for *Office of Government Commerce.

OMV Abbreviation for open market value. *See* MARKET VALUE.

OMX A company that owns and operates stock exchanges in Scandinavia and the Baltic States; it also markets advanced electronic trading systems for derivatives products that are used in many other exchanges worldwide. OMX acquired the Stockholm Stock Exchange in 1998, the Helsinki Exchange in 2003, and the Copenhagen Exchange in 2005. In 2008 it became a wholly owned subsidiary of *NASDAQ.

oncost **1.** The additional costs incurred as a consequence of employing personnel, i.e. **wages oncost**, or the additional costs incurred by storing and handling direct materials, i.e. **materials oncost** or **stores oncost**. **2.** A rarely used alternative name for *overheads.

onerous contract A *contract entered into in which the unavoidable costs of fulfilling the contract exceed any expected revenues and in which compensation has to be paid to the other party if the terms of the contract are not fulfilled.

opening balance The balance *brought forward at the beginning of an *accounting period. Opening balances may be on the *debit or the *credit side of a *ledger. *See also* BROUGHT DOWN.

opening entries *Journal entries made to open a business. All the *assets and *liabilities must be entered into the accounts, together with the owners' capital.

opening stock The stock held by an organization at the beginning of an accounting period as *raw materials, *work in progress, or *finished goods. The *closing stocks of one period become the opening stocks of the succeeding period and it is necessary to establish the level of closing stocks so that the cost of their creation is not charged against the profits of that period but brought forward as opening stocks to be charged against the profits of the succeeding period.

open market value (OMV) *See* MARKET VALUE.

open position (naked position) A trading position in which a dealer has commodities, *securities, or currencies bought but unsold or unhedged (*see* HEDGE), or sales that are neither covered nor hedged. In either case the dealer is vulnerable to market fluctuations until the position is closed or hedged.

operating and financial review (OFR) A statement published with a company's *annual accounts and *directors' report in which the directors interpret the *financial statements and discuss the business's performance, giving both positive and negative points. It is broadly similar to the *management discussion and analysis statement issued by US companies. For financial years beginning on or after 1 January 2005, listed companies have been required to prepare a statutory OFR; this should include key performance indicators and, where appropriate, information on employees and the company's environmental record. (The statement of best practice on the OFR issued by the Accounting Standards Board in 2003 was previously used by many companies). The requirement for a separate OFR has now been abolished under the Companies Act 2006; however, the same information is to be included in an expanded directors' report. *See* ACCOUNTS MODERNIZATION DIRECTIVE.

operating budget *See* PRODUCTION BUDGET.

operating costing The form of costing applied both to the provision of services within an organization and to the costing of continuous operating processes, such as electricity generation.

operating cycle The average time between acquiring *stock and receiving cash from its sale.

operating expenses and revenues The costs and revenues incurred or generated by an organization in the normal course of business, excluding any *extraordinary items.

operating lease A lease under which an asset is hired out to a lessee or lessees for a period that is substantially shorter than its useful economic life. Under an operating lease, some of the risks and rewards of the ownership of the leased asset remain with the lessor. *Statement of Standard Accounting Practice 21, Accounting for Leases and Hire Purchase Contracts, defines an operating lease as a lease other than a *finance lease.

operating performance ratios Various ratios used to analyse the financial performance of a company in terms of the return generated by the sales for an *accounting period. The higher the ratios, the higher the profitability of the organization. Examples are *net profit percentage and *gross profit percentage.

operating profit/loss The profit or loss made by a company as a result of its principal trading activity. This is arrived at by deducting its *operating expenses from its *trading profit, or adding its operating expenses to its trading loss; in either case this is before taking into account any *extraordinary items.

operating statement A financial and quantitative statement provided for the management of an organization to record the performance achieved by that area of the operation for which the management is responsible, for a selected budget period. An operating statement may include production levels, costs incurred, and (where appropriate) revenue generated, all compared with budgeted amounts and the performance in previous periods.

operational audit A review of an organization's activities to assess whether they are being carried out efficiently and effectively.

operational risk The risk of direct or indirect loss resulting from inadequate or failed internal processes and systems, or from a wide variety of external events. The control of operational risk has been the object of much attention in recent years, for example in the 2004 Basle Two accord concerning the *capital adequacy of banks and in the *Turnbull Report in the UK. It has also led to changes in the regulation of financial institutions and the requirements for the listing of public companies.

operational variance In *standard costing, a *variance that measures the difference between *current standards (i.e. standards adjusted to reflect the current operating conditions) and the actual performance achieved. *Compare* REVISION VARIANCE.

opinion shopping A colloquial name for the practice of seeking an *auditor who will approve a company's accounting policies.

opportunity cost The economic cost of an action measured in terms of the benefit foregone by not pursuing the best alternative course of action. The cost of funds, for example, must be measured in terms of the returns they could earn in the capital markets for taking the same degree of risk. Opportunity cost is an important factor in decision making (*see* COST-BENEFIT ANALYSIS), although it represents costs that are not recorded in the accounts of the relevant organization.

optimism bias The tendency for people to be optimistic about future events, especially those seen as following from their own plans and actions. Although optimism is no doubt a stimulus to enterprise, it has obvious dangers: these include increased risk taking, failure to estimate probabilities accurately, and inadequate contingency planning. In drawing up plans, schedules, and budgets there is a demonstrated tendency for managers to underestimate costs and duration and to overestimate benefits. This being so, there is now an explicit requirement for those managing government projects in the UK to include an adjustment for optimism bias.

option The right to buy or sell a fixed quantity of a commodity, currency, *security, etc., at a particular date at a particular price (the *exercise price). Unlike futures, the purchaser of an option is not obliged to buy or sell at the exercise price and will only do so if it is profitable; the purchaser may allow the option to lapse, in which case only the initial purchase price of the option (the option money or premium) is lost.

An option to buy is known as a **call option** and is usually purchased in the expectation of a rising price; an option to sell is called a **put option** and is bought in the expectation of a falling price or to protect a profit on an investment. Options, like futures, allow individuals and firms to *hedge against the risk of wide fluctuations in prices; they also allow dealers and speculators to gamble for large profits with limited initial payments.

Professional traders in options make use of a large range of potential strategies, often purchasing combinations of options that reflect particular expectations or cover several contingencies.

In a **European option** the buyer can only exercise the right to take up the option or let it lapse on the expiry date, whereas with an **American option** this right can be exercised at any time up to the expiry date. American options are generally worth more than European options because the option holder has more chance of buying or selling at a favourable price. American options are also more difficult to value. *See also* REAL OPTION.

option to tax (election to waive exemption) An irrevocable election made by a landlord to charge *value added tax on *exempt supplies of buildings (rents). This enables the otherwise *irrecoverable input VAT on costs relating to the property to be reclaimed by the landlord against the *output tax charged on the rents. In 2004 the Chancellor of the Exchequer announced that a consultation document would be published on the future of option to tax.

OR Abbreviation for *official receiver.

ordinarily resident In the UK *capital gains tax rules, an individual 'ordinarily resident' in the UK is subject to the tax even if not actually resident in the UK. Such a status might be held by an individual imprisoned in a foreign jail or a backpacker during the gap year between school and university. However, even a short period of not being resident in the UK is, for most individuals, likely to involve a period of not being ordinarily resident.

ordinary activities Any activities undertaken by an organization as part of its business and any related activities in which it engages in furtherance of, incidental to, or arising from, these activities. This definition is based on that given in *Financial Reporting Standard 3, Reporting Financial Performance. Ordinary activities include the effects on the reporting entity of any event in the various environments in which it operates, including the political, regulatory, economic, and geographical environments, irrespective of the frequency or unusual nature of the events. *See also* EXTRAORDINARY ITEMS.

ordinary resolution A *resolution that can be passed by a simple majority (i.e. of more than 50%) of company members voting in person or by proxy. It is appropriate where no other type of resolution is expressly required by the Companies Act 2006 or the *articles of association. *Compare* SPECIAL RESOLUTION.

ordinary share A *share in a company that carries the right to a share of the company's *profits without limit. Ordinary shares generally carry the right to vote. *See also* A SHARES; B SHARES; EQUITY SHARE; NON-EQUITY SHARE.

ordinary share capital The total *share capital of a company consisting of *ordinary shares.

ordinary shareholders' equity (ordinary shareholders' funds) The value of the *assets of a company net of its *liabilities and any amounts of capital due to holders of shares other than *ordinary shares (e.g. *preference shares). If the company were to go into liquidation this would be the equity available for distribution to the ordinary shareholders.

organization chart (organogram) A chart illustrating the structure of an organization; in particular it will show for which function of the business each manager is responsible and the chain of responsibility throughout the organization.

original cost The cost of an item at the time of purchase or creation. This applies particularly to *fixed assets in which depreciation by the *straight-line method uses the original cost as a basis for the calculation. *See also* HISTORICAL COST.

original entry error A mistake made in a *book of prime entry; for example, a purchase incorrectly entered in the purchase day book. Original entry errors are not revealed by the *trial balance.

originating timing difference A difference between profits or losses computed for tax purposes on a receipts-and-payments basis and profits presented in the *financial statements on an *accruals basis. These differences arise as a result of items of income and expenditure in tax computations being included in different periods from those in which they are included in financial statements. An originating timing difference is described as originating in the period in which it arises; it is capable of reversal in subsequent periods. These differences are dealt with in *Financial Reporting Standard (FRS) 19, Deferred Tax, which became mandatory in respect of accounting periods ending on or after 23 January 2002. *Compare* PERMANENT DIFFERENCE.

origin of turnover The *geographic segment from which products or services are supplied to a third party or another segment of the same organization, as defined by *Statement of Standard Accounting Practice 25, *Segmental Reporting. The standard requires certain companies to disclose this information in their *annual accounts and report.

OTC Bulletin Board (OTCBB) A regulated quotation service for equities sold on the US *over-the-counter market. It provides real-time quotes and last-sale prices for stocks that are not listed on one of the major US exchanges. The OTCBB was created by the National Association of Securities Dealers Inc. (NASD) in 1990.

OTC market Abbreviation for *over-the-counter market.

outlay cost The expenditure incurred as the initial cost of a project or activity. The outlay cost may include both *capital expenditure and expenditure on working capital, such as stocks of raw material.

out-of-pocket costs The additional costs that will be incurred as the result of a particular decision. In some circumstances, these costs will be more relevant to decision making than the total differential cash flows. For example, an organization with limited cash resources may make a decision to pursue an investment alternative that would not have been the first choice had it not offered the lowest level of out-of-pocket costs. *See also* RELEVANT COST.

output tax *Value added tax charged on total *taxable supplies by a trader registered for VAT. The standard rate is 17.5%.

outside director A US term for a *non-executive director.

outstanding shares *See* SHARES OUTSTANDING.

overabsorbed overhead In *absorption costing, the circumstance in which the *absorbed overhead is greater than the overhead costs incurred for a period. The *favourable variance represents an addition to the budgeted profits of the organization. *Compare* UNDERABSORBED OVERHEAD. *See also* OVERHEAD TOTAL VARIANCE.

overcapitalization A condition in which an organization has too much *capital for the needs of its business. If a business has more capital than it needs it is likely to be overburdened by interest charges or by the need to spread profits too thinly by way of dividends to shareholders. Businesses can now reduce overcapitalization by repaying long-term debts or by buying their own shares. *See also* THIN CAPITALIZATION; UNDERCAPITALIZATION.

overdraft A loan made to a customer with a cheque account at a bank or building society, in which the account is allowed to go into debit, usually up to a specified limit (the **overdraft limit**). Interest is charged on the daily debit balance. This is a less costly way of borrowing than taking a *bank loan (providing the interest rates are the same) as, with an overdraft, credits are taken into account.

overhang The surplus shares remaining with *underwriters when a new issue of shares has not been fully taken up by investors.

overhead (overhead cost) An *indirect cost of an organization. Overheads are usually classified as *manufacturing overheads, *administration overheads, *selling overheads, *distribution overheads, and *research and development costs.

overhead absorption *See* ABSORPTION.

overhead absorption rate *See* ABSORPTION RATE.

overhead analysis sheet (overhead distribution summary) A form on which the *manufacturing overhead is charged to the *cost centres of an organization by using appropriate allocation or apportionment techniques for each item of overhead cost.

overhead cost *See* OVERHEAD.

overhead cost absorbed (overhead cost recovered) The actual production for a period multiplied by the overhead *absorption rate budgeted for that period.

overhead distribution summary *See* OVERHEAD ANALYSIS SHEET.

overhead efficiency variance (overhead productivity variance; productivity variance) In a *standard costing system, that part of the *overhead total variance that arises from the more or less efficient use of the time available to carry out the actual production. It compares the actual time taken to carry out an activity with the standard time allowed and values the difference at the standard overhead *absorption rate per hour (fixed or variable). The resultant adverse or favourable variance is the amount by which the budgeted profit is affected by virtue of the overhead cost over- or under-recovered due to efficiency. The formula for this variance is:

(standard hours allowed for production – actual hours taken) × standard overhead absorption rate per hour (fixed or variable).

See also FIXED OVERHEAD EFFICIENCY VARIANCE; VARIABLE OVERHEAD EFFICIENCY VARIANCE.

overhead expenditure variance (expenditure variance) In a system of *standard costing, the *variance arising from the difference between the budgeted overhead allowance and the actual overhead incurred. This can be analysed into *fixed overhead expenditure variance and *variable overhead expenditure variance; it represents the amount by which the budgeted profits should be adjusted to account for the over- or under-spending on overheads.

overhead productivity variance *See* OVERHEAD EFFICIENCY VARIANCE.

overhead total variance In a system of *standard costing, the total variance that arises in respect of fixed and variable overheads; it represents the difference between the standard overhead recovered for the actual units produced and the actual overhead incurred for a period. Where the overhead recovered exceeds the overhead incurred an over-recovery or *overabsorbed overhead results. Where the overhead incurred exceeds that recovered then an under-recovery or *underabsorbed overhead results. *See* FIXED OVERHEAD TOTAL VARIANCE; VARIABLE OVERHEAD TOTAL VARIANCE.

overhead volume variance *See* FIXED OVERHEAD VOLUME VARIANCE.

overnight rate The interest rate at which major banks lend to one another on the overnight market (i.e. for repayment the next day). Indexes of the average overnight rate, such as *SONIA and *EONIA, provide an important *reference rate.

oversea company *See* FOREIGN COMPANY.

overseas-income taxation Income that has been subject to taxation outside the jurisdiction of the UK tax authorities. When the same income is subject to taxation in more than one country, relief for the double tax is given either under the provisions of the *double taxation agreement with the country concerned or unilaterally.

over-the-counter market (OTC market) A market in which financial obligations are bought and sold outside the jurisdiction of a recognized financial market; it was originally so named in the 1870s, from the practice of buying shares over bank counters in the USA. OTC markets are used for trading in specific tailor-made *derivative products. The world's largest OTC market is *NASDAQ.

overtrading   Trading in which a business has expanded too rapidly thus putting a strain on its financial resources. This can lead to *liquidity problems.

owners' equity   The beneficial interest in an organization held by its owners, i.e. the sum of its total assets less its total liabilities. The balance-sheet or *book value of the owners' equity is unlikely to be equal to its *market value. *See also* NET ASSETS; NET WORTH.

own shares purchase   The purchase or redemption of its own shares by a company; this is permitted subject to certain legal restrictions. For example, in the UK redeemable shares may only be redeemed if they are fully paid. If the redemption or purchase of a company's own shares would lead to a reduction of its capital, a *capital redemption reserve will need to be created. The Companies Act 2006 has made it easier for private companies to reduce their capital in this way. *See also* PERMISSIBLE CAPITAL PAYMENT.

O

package *See* BUSINESS SOFTWARE PACKAGE.

paid-in capital In the USA, the section of stockholders' equity on a company's *balance sheet, which shows the amount of stock issued, the premiums or discounts from selling the stock, stock received from donations, and the resale of treasury stock.

paid-up share capital The *issued share capital of a company when this consists of *fully paid shares, payment for which has been received. *Compare* CALLED-UP SHARE CAPITAL.

P & L account Abbreviation for *profit and loss account.

paper profit A profit shown by the books or accounts of an organization that is not a *realized profit. This is usually for one of three reasons:
- because the value of an asset has fallen below its book value;
- because the asset, although nominally showing a profit, has not actually been sold;
- because some technicality of book-keeping shows an activity to be profitable when it is not.

For example, a share that has risen in value since its purchase might show a paper profit but this would not be a real profit since the value of the share might fall again before it is sold.

paper trail *See* AUDIT TRAIL.

parallel hedge A *hedge in which exposure to fluctuation in one foreign currency is matched by a purchase or sale of another currency, which is expected to move in sympathy with the first currency.

parent undertaking (parent company) *See* HOLDING COMPANY.

***pari passu* clause** A *covenant in a loan agreement in which a borrower promises to ensure that the loan in question will rank *pari passu* (equally) with its other defined debts.

partial exemption A restriction in *value added tax legislation that can arise if a *taxable person makes a mixture of *taxable supplies and *exempt supplies. In these circumstances there is a restriction on the amount of *input tax that is available to set against *output tax.

partial intestacy The circumstances that arise if a will covers only part of the estate of the deceased. The part of the estate accounted for in the will is dealt with according to the wishes of the deceased as set out in the will, while the remainder is allocated in accordance with the rules of intestacy (*see* INTESTATE).

participated loan (participation financing) A large loan, exceeding the lending limit of an individual bank, that is shared among a group of lenders.

participating interest An interest held by an undertaking in the shares of another undertaking, which it holds on a long-term basis for the purpose of exercising some measure of control or influence over the activities of the second undertaking. This definition is based on that given in *Financial Reporting Standard (FRS) 2, Accounting for Subsidiary Undertakings. A holding of 20% or more of the shares of an undertaking is presumed to be a participating interest, unless the contrary is shown. FRS 2 is a lengthy and fairly complex standard; the Accounting Standards Board issued an amended version in December 2004. *See also* CONTROLLING INTEREST; MINORITY INTEREST; SIGNIFICANT INFLUENCE.

participating preference share A *preference share entitled to a fixed rate of *dividend and a further share in the profits of a company, for example after the *ordinary shares have received a certain percentage.

participative budgeting The setting of a budget in which various levels of management are involved in fixing the budgeted levels of performance against which their actual performance will ultimately be measured. Although there has been a lot of research in this area, the benefits of participative budgeting have proved hard to measure.

participator Any person having an interest in the capital or income of a company, e.g. a shareholder, loan creditor, or any person entitled to participate in the *distributions of the company.

partly paid share A share the full *par value of which has not been paid by the shareholder. Formerly, partly paid shares were issued by some banks and insurance companies to inspire confidence, in the knowledge that they could always call on their shareholders for further funds if necessary. Shareholders, however, did not like the liability of being called upon to pay out further sums on demand and the practice largely died out. It has been revived for large new share issues, especially in *privatizations, in which shareholders pay an initial sum for their shares and subsequently pay one or more calls on specified dates. *Compare* FULLY PAID SHARE. *See also* CALLED-UP SHARE CAPITAL; PAID-UP SHARE CAPITAL.

partnership An association of two or more people (**partners**) formed for the purpose of carrying on a business. Partnerships are governed by the Partnership Act 1890. Unlike an incorporated *company, a partnership does not have a legal personality of its own and therefore, as a general rule, partners are liable for the debts of the firm. **General partners** are fully liable for these debts, **limited partners** only to the extent of their investment. A **limited partnership** is one consisting of both general and limited partners and is governed by the Limited Partnership Act 1907. The *Limited Liability Partnership Act 2000 now enables some categories of business partnership to claim limited liability in a similar fashion to that enjoyed by *limited companies. A **partnership-at-will** is one for which no fixed term has been agreed. Any partner may end the partnership at any time provided that notice of the intention to do so is given to all the other partners. **Nominal partners** allow their names to be used for the benefit of the partnership, usually for a reward but not for a share of the profits. They are not legal partners. Partnerships are usually governed by a *partnership agreement.

partnership accounts The accounts kept by a *partnership. They include an *appropriation account in which the profit of a *partnership is shared between the partners in accordance with the *partnership agreement. This may be in the

form of salaries, interest on capital, and a share of the profit in the appropriate
*profit-sharing ratio. Each partner also has a *capital account and a *current
account. The former is used to account for capital contributions, *goodwill, and
revaluations; the latter for all other transactions, such as *appropriations of
profit and *drawings.

partnership agreement (articles of partnership) An agreement made
between the partners of a *partnership. In the absence of either an express or an
implied agreement the provisions of the Partnership Act 1890 apply. These
provisions are also applicable if an agreement is silent on a particular point. The
provisions are:

- partners share equally in the profits or losses of the partnership;
- partners are not entitled to receive salaries;
- partners are not entitled to interest on their capital;
- partners may receive interest at 5% per annum on any advances over and
  above their agreed capital;
- a new partner may not be introduced unless all the existing partners consent;
- a retiring partner is entitled to receive interest at 5% per annum on his or her
  share of the partnership assets retained in the partnership after his or her
  retirement;
- on dissolution of the partnership the assets of the firm must be used first to
  repay outside creditors, secondly to repay partners' advances, and thirdly to
  repay partners' capital. Any residue on dissolution should be distributed to the
  partners in the *profit-sharing ratio.

See also LIMITED LIABILITY PARTNERSHIP.

par value (face value; nominal value) The *nominal price of a share or other
security. If the market value of a security exceeds the nominal price it is said to
be **above par**; if it falls below the nominal price it is **below par**. Gilt-edged
securities are always repaid **at par** (usually £100), i.e. at the par value.

past-due loan A banking loan on which the interest is more than 90 days
overdue. After this grace period has elapsed, the borrower becomes liable for late
charges.

patent The grant of an exclusive right to exploit an invention. In the UK
patents are granted by the Crown through the Intellectual Property Office (IPO).
An applicant for a patent (usually the inventor or the inventor's employer) must
show that the invention is new, is not obvious, and is capable of industrial
application. An expert known as a **patent agent** often prepares the application,
which must describe the invention in considerable detail. The Intellectual
Property Office publishes these details if it grants a patent. A patent remains
valid for 20 years from the date of application (the **priority date**) provided that
the person to whom it has been granted (the **patentee**) continues to pay the
appropriate fees. During this time, the patentee may assign the patent or grant
licences to use it. Such transactions are registered in a public register at the IPO.
If anyone infringes the patentee's monopoly, the patentee may sue for an
injunction and *damages or an account of profits. However, a patent from the
IPO gives exclusive rights in the UK only: the inventor must obtain a patent from
the European Patent Office in Munich and patents in other foreign countries to
protect the invention elsewhere. For patents internationally the Patent Co-

operation Treaty procedure can be used. A patent is a form of *intellectual property and as such is an *intangible asset.

pathfinder prospectus An outline *prospectus designed to test the market reaction to the flotation of a new company.

payable to bearer Describing a *bill of exchange in which neither the payee or endorsee are named. A holder, by adding his or her name, can make the bill *payable to order.

payable to order Describing a *bill of exchange in which the payee is named and on which there are no restrictions or endorsements; it can therefore be paid to the endorsee.

pay and file A former procedure for paying *corporation tax introduced in the UK for accounting periods ended after 30 September 1993. Under the pay-and-file system, the company had to file a detailed return within twelve months of the end of the accounting period. For accounting periods ending after 1 July 1999 *self-assessment for companies replaced pay and file.

pay-as-you-earn *See* PAYE.

pay-as-you-go pension system (**unfunded pension system**) A system in which state retirement benefits are financed by contributions levied from current workers, as opposed to a funded system in which contributions are invested to pay for future benefits. The British *National Insurance system is a pay-as-you-go system.

payback period method A method of *capital budgeting in which the time required before the projected cash inflows for a project equal the investment expenditure is calculated; this time is compared to a required payback period to determine whether or not the project should be considered for approval. If the projected cash inflows are constant annual sums, after an initial capital investment the following formula may be used:

payback (years) = initial capital investment/annual cash inflow.

Otherwise, the annual cash inflows are accumulated and the year determined when the cumulative inflows equal the investment expenditure. The method is sometimes seen as a measure of the risk involved in the project.

The two major weaknesses of the payback method are:
- the *time value of money is not considered;
- the cash flows after the investment is recovered are not considered.

However, payback is a relatively simple technique for managers to use and for this reason it remains popular. Often managers use payback and *discounted cash flow techniques at the same time, even though they are very different methods of *capital budgeting (*see* DISCOUNTED PAYBACK METHOD).

EXAMPLE

A hospital is considering the purchase of a new X-ray machine for £50,000. The annual cash savings from the new machine are estimated at £20,000.

payback = initial capital investment/annual cash inflows
payback = £50,000/£20,000 = 2.5

The hospital will therefore recover its investment in 2.5 years. On this basis, it is difficult to say whether the hospital should buy the new machine. Most managers would see a payback period of less than 3 years as good.

PAYE Pay-as-you-earn. The UK scheme for collecting income tax and *National Insurance contributions, under which the onus is placed on employers to collect the tax from their employees as payments are made to them. There is an elaborate system of administration to ensure that broadly the correct amount of tax is deducted week by week or month by month and that the employer remits the tax collected to HM Revenue and Customs very quickly. The amount of tax due is calculated using *income tax codes and tax tables supplied to employers by the Revenue (now usually in the form of computer software). Although technically called pay-as-you-earn, the system would be better called 'pay-as-you-get-paid'.

(⊕) SEE WEB LINKS
• An introduction to PAYE for employers from the HMRC website

paying agent A bank or other organization that contracts under a **paying agency agreement** to pay, upon presentation to one of its designated offices, the interest and capital sums due on a *bearer security.

payment in advance *See* PREPAYMENT.

payment on account *See* PROGRESS PAYMENT.

PayPal A secure online system that enables account holders to pay for goods or services and arrange money transfers over the Internet. PayPal, which operates in 18 currencies worldwide, became a wholly owned subsidiary of eBay in 2002.

PBR Abbreviation for *pre-Budget report.

PCAOB Abbreviation for *Public Company Accounting Oversight Board.

PCP Abbreviation for *permissible capital payment.

PCTCT Abbreviation for profits chargeable to corporation tax. *See* TOTAL PROFITS.

PDF Abbreviation for portable document format. *See* ACROBAT.

PDR (P/D ratio) Abbreviation for *price–dividend ratio.

penalties Amounts demanded by the tax authorities in excess of the tax due when certain statutory requirements have not been satisfied. The penalty regime for *income tax and *corporation tax differs from that for *value added tax. For income tax and corporation tax the Inland Revenue has powers to impose penalties when it has been established that there has been a loss of tax as a result of the taxpayer's fraudulent or negligent conduct. Failure to submit a tax return attracts a fixed sum together with a daily penalty. The penalty for negligence or fraud depends on the amount of tax lost and can equal the tax lost. However, there is a mitigation procedure to reduce the penalty under certain circumstances. Value added tax penalties are more automatic without the same level of mitigation procedures. From 1 December 1993 the main VAT penalties are the *misdeclaration penalty and the *persistent misdeclaration penalty.

penalty for repeated errors *See* PERSISTENT MISDECLARATION PENALTY.

penny shares Securities with a very low market price (although they may not be as low as one penny) traded on a stock exchange. They are popular with small investors, who can acquire a significant holding in a company for a very low cost. Moreover, a rise of a few pence in a low-priced share can represent a high percentage profit. However, they are usually shares in companies that have fallen on hard times and may, indeed, be close to bankruptcy. The investor in this type of share is hoping for a rapid recovery or a takeover.

pension scheme Any arrangement the main purpose of which is to provide a defined class of individuals (called members of the scheme) with pensions. A pension scheme may include benefits other than a pension and may provide a pension for dependants of deceased members. *See also* OCCUPATIONAL PENSION SCHEME; PERSONAL PENSION SCHEME; STAKEHOLDER PENSION SCHEME.

Pensions Regulator The UK regulatory body responsible for protecting the benefits of those in work-based pension schemes; this includes all occupational schemes and any other schemes in which payments are made through the employer.

PEP Abbreviation for *personal equity plan.

P/E ratio Abbreviation for *price–earnings ratio.

percentage-of-completion *See* LONG-TERM CONTRACT.

percentage on direct labour cost A basis used in *absorption costing for absorbing the production overheads into the cost units produced. The formula used is:

(budgeted production overheads × 100)/budgeted direct labour cost.

percentage on direct material cost A basis used in *absorption costing for absorbing the *manufacturing overhead into the cost units produced. The formula used is:

(budgeted manufacturing overhead × 100)/budgeted direct material cost.

percentage on prime cost A basis used in *absorption costing for absorbing the *manufacturing overhead into the cost units produced. The formula used is:

(budgeted manufacturing overhead × 100)/budgeted prime cost.

performance bond A guarantee given to customers in some industries that goods will be delivered to a specific standard. The bond is normally given by a company's bankers, who are indemnified by the company.

performance measurement The process of (a) developing indicators to assess progress towards certain predefined goals and (b) reviewing performance against these measures. Performance measures can be applied to the whole organization or to particular departments, branches, or individuals. Many different measures can be used:
  financial measures
  • *return on capital employed
  • *residual income
  • *Economic Value Added

non-financial measures
- delivery time
- customer retention
- employee absenteeism
- staff turnover

Management accountants will be interested in identifying how different performance measures influence the behaviour of managers. For example, using return on capital employed as a measure will probably encourage managers to reduce investment; this may improve short-term performance figures but will damage the long-term performance of the company. Another problem may arise if managers improve delivery times to meet targets but significantly increase costs in the process. These two examples emphasize the importance of understanding the behavioural aspects of management accounting. Another issue is how to link non-financial and financial measures. The *balanced scorecard is a recent development that connects non-financial and financial performance measures to a company's overall strategy.

performance standard In *standard costing, the standard level of performance to be achieved during a period. For example, a standard performance for direct labour of two standard hours to complete a task would be combined with the *rate per standard hour for labour to create the *standard direct labour cost for the task.

period concept The accounting concept that the *financial statements of a company should be produced after regular periods. The *profit and loss account and *balance sheet are prepared at regular intervals, for example annually, instead of after each transaction or event. This provides comparability, consistency, and regular communications.

period costs Items of expenditure that tend to be incurred on a time basis, such as rent, insurance, and business rates. Because they are not related to a particular activity, they are usually treated as *fixed costs.

periodic stocktaking (periodic inventory) The counting or evaluating of the *stock held by an organization at the end of an *accounting period. Movement of stock is restricted during the period of *stocktaking.

period of account *See* ACCOUNTING PERIOD.

perks An informal word for **perquisites**, the benefits arising as a result of employment, in addition to regular renumeration. Perks are privileges that are expected mainly by senior employees (e.g. a company car, private health insurance, gym membership). *See* BENEFITS IN KIND; SHAREHOLDERS PERKS.

permanent difference A difference between profits or losses computed for tax purposes and profits presented in the *financial statements. For example, UK entertaining expenditure will be shown as an expense in the financial statements but will not be allowed as a deduction in deriving the profit or loss for tax purposes.

permanent diminution in value A fall in the value of an asset that is unlikely to be reversed. The *fixed asset must be shown in the *balance sheet at the reduced amount, which will be the estimated *recoverable amount. A provision has to be made through the *profit and loss account; if this is subsequently found to be no longer required, it should be written back to the profit and loss account. *Compare* TEMPORARY DIMINUTION IN VALUE.

permanent establishment Most tax treaties operate so that business profits are taxed in the country of the taxpayer's residence, unless the taxpayer has a 'permanent establishment' in the other territory. In the model *double taxation agreement drawn up by the Organization for Economic Cooperation and Development, a permanent establishment is defined as a 'fixed place of business through which the business of an enterprise is wholly or partly carried on'. The model agreement goes on to state specifically that the term 'permanent establishment' includes a place of management, branch, office, factory, workshop, mine, oil or gas well, quarry, or any other place of extraction of natural resources.

permanent interest bearing share (PIBS) A non-redeemable security, usually issued by a building society, that pays interest at a rate fixed at issue. This is often 10–13.5%, giving investors a high yield for perpetuity. However, these shares carry the risks associated with fixed-interest securities, being the last to be paid out should an issuing building society go into liquidation. Moreover, the second-hand market for PIBS is small (approximately £800 million), making it difficult to find a buyer at any particular price.

permissible capital payment (PCP) A payment made out of *capital when a company is redeeming or purchasing its own *shares and has used all available distributable profits as well as the proceeds of any new issue of shares. *See* OWN SHARES PURCHASE.

perpetual annuity The receipt or payment of a constant annual amount in perpetuity. Although the word annuity refers to an annual sum, in practice the constant sum may be for periods of less than a year. The *present value of a perpetual annuity is obtained from the formula:

$$P = a \times 100 / i,$$

where P is the present value, a is the annual sum, and i is the interest rate.

perpetual audit *See* CONTINUOUS STOCKTAKING.

perpetual debt A debt in respect of which the issuer has neither the right nor the obligation to repay the *principal amount of the debt. Usually *interest is paid at a constant rate, or at a fixed margin over a benchmark rate, such as the *London Inter Bank Offered Rate (LIBOR).

perpetual inventory The process of keeping records in a *stock ledger or on a *bin card in which the balance of the quantity in stock is entered after each receipt or issue of stock. In some systems the value of the stock balance is also entered after each transaction.

persistent misdeclaration penalty A penalty used in the collection of *value added tax. It applies when there has been a material inaccuracy in a VAT return, being the lower of £500,000 and 10% of the total true amount of VAT due for the quarter. The trader must also have received a *surcharge liability notice resulting from a previous error within the 15 months prior to the current VAT period. In these circumstances a penalty for repeated errors of 15% of the VAT lost will be charged.

personal accounts Accounts used to record transactions with persons, for example *debtors and *creditors.

personal allowance The allowance to which every individual resident in the UK is entitled in calculating their *taxable income for *income tax. The allowance depends on the age of the taxpayer. For 2009–10 the personal allowance for those under 65 is £6475, for those between 65 and 74 the allowance is £9490, and for those aged 75 and over it is £9640. *See also* INCOME TAX ALLOWANCES.

personal equity plan (PEP) A UK government scheme introduced in 1986 to encourage individuals to invest in company shares and equity-based unit and investment trusts. In April 1999 PEPs were superseded by *Individual Savings Accounts (ISAs); from that date no new subscriptions could be made to PEPs but existing plans were allowed to continue. Previously a maximum of £9000 a year could be invested. No income tax or capital gains tax was payable on income or gains generated by the PEP, unless interest of over £180 was withdrawn in any one year. In April 2008 all remaining PEPs were automatically converted into stocks-and-shares ISAs.

personal financial planning Financial planning for individuals, which involves analysing their current financial position, predicting their short-term and long-term needs, and recommending a financial strategy. This may involve advice on pensions, the provision of independent school fees, mortgages, life assurance, and investments.

personal identification number (PIN) A number memorized by the holder of a *cash card, *credit card, or *multifunctional card and used in *automated teller machines and *electronic funds transfer at point of sale to identify the card owner. The number is given to the cardholder in secret and is memorized so that if the card is stolen it cannot be used. The number is unique to the cardholder. *See* PHANTOM WITHDRAWALS.

Personal Investment Authority (PIA) A *Self-Regulating Organization that took over most of the responsibilities of the Financial Intermediaries, Managers and Brokers Regulatory Association (FIMBRA) and the Life Assurance and Unit Trust Regulatory Organization (LAUTRO) in 1994. Its remit was to regulate investment business carried out mainly with or for private investors. The PIA was absorbed into the *Financial Services Authority in December 2001.

personal ledger A *ledger containing *personal accounts, for example the debtors' ledger and the creditors' ledger.

personal pension scheme An arrangement in which an individual contributes part of his or her salary to a pension provider, such as an insurance company or a bank. The pension provider invests the funds so that at retirement a lump sum is available to the pensioner. This is used to purchase an *annuity to provide regular pension payments. In the UK the current system is that an employee who chooses a personal pension instead of the Second State Pension (SSP), or their employer's pension scheme, must pay National Insurance contributions at the full ordinary rate and the employer's share must be paid at the same rate. The state pays the difference between the lower contracted-out rate and the full ordinary rate direct to the personal pension scheme. From 2012 it will no longer be possible to contract out of the SSP through a personal pension scheme. The administration of pensions is scrutinized by the *Financial Ombudsman Service, which is empowered to deal with complaints relating to personal pension schemes. *See also* STAKEHOLDER PENSION SCHEME.

PERT Abbreviation for programme evaluation and review technique. *See* CRITICAL-PATH ANALYSIS.

PET Abbreviation for *potentially exempt transfer.

petroleum revenue tax (PRT) A tax on the profits from sales of oil and gas extracted in the UK or on the continental shelf. This tax was the principal means enabling the UK government to obtain a share in the profits made from oil in the North Sea. It has been abolished for oilfields getting development consent on or after 16 March 1993. The current rate of tax is 50%. Profits from oil extraction are also subject to a supplementary corporation tax charge of 20%.

petty cash The amount of cash that an organization keeps in notes or coins on its premises to pay small items of expense. This is to be distinguished from cash, which normally refers to amounts held at banks. Petty-cash transactions are normally recorded in a petty-cash book, the balance of which should agree with the amounts of petty cash held at any given time.

petty-cash book A book used to record *petty cash transactions. It is usually kept in an *imprest account.

PFI Abbreviation for private finance initiative. *See* PUBLIC–PRIVATE PARTNERSHIP.

phantom withdrawals The removal of funds from bank accounts through *automated teller machines (ATMs) by unauthorized means and without the knowledge or consent of the account holder. Until recently most banks maintained that such withdrawals were only possible where account holders had divulged their *personal identification numbers (PINs) to a third party. However, there is now firm evidence of ATM fraud perpetrated by technological means, including the use of 'skimming' devices to copy the details of inserted cards and miniature cameras to record PINs.

phishing A type of fraud in which victims are tricked into disclosing bank-account or credit-card details, passwords, or other sensitive information by bogus e-mails or text messages, usually purporting to be from a bank or other trustworthy source.

physical capital maintenance *See* CAPITAL MAINTENANCE CONCEPT.

physical inventory (physical stock check) The process of counting the physical balance of stock items at a particular time with a view to carrying out a stocktaking under a system of either *inventory control or *continuous stocktaking.

physical stock check *See* PHYSICAL INVENTORY.

PI *See* PROFITABILITY INDEX.

PIA Abbreviation for *Personal Investment Authority.

PIBS Abbreviation for *permanent interest bearing share.

PII Abbreviation for *professional indemnity insurance.

PIN Abbreviation for *personal identification number.

PINC Abbreviation for *property income certificate.

placed deal A transaction in which a bank, or group of banks, undertakes to market an entire new issue of bonds or similar securities. Unlike a *bought deal, the borrower is not guaranteed that the new issue will be successful. Such transactions are favoured by the smaller financial institutions, such as *merchant banks, who do not have large marketing departments.

placing The sale of shares by a company to a selected group of individuals or institutions. Placings can be used either as a means of *flotation or to raise additional capital for a listed company (*see also* PRE-EMPTION RIGHTS; RIGHTS ISSUE). Placings are usually the cheapest way of raising capital on a *stock exchange and they also allow the directors of a company to influence the selection of shareholders. The success of a placing usually depends on the placing power of the company's stockbroker. Placings of public companies are sometimes called **public placings**. In the USA a placing is called a **placement**. *Compare* INTRODUCTION; OFFER FOR SALE.

plain vanilla Describing a financial instrument in its simplest form (e.g. a straightforward *option with no exotic features). During the heyday of *structured finance, more traditional debt instruments were sometimes described as **vanilla finance**.

planning One of the functions of *management accounting in which plans for the future activities and operations of an organization are incorporated into its *budgets, etc.

planning, programming, budgeting system (PPBS) A budgeting system developed particularly for use in non-profitmaking organizations, such as national and local government. The system is based on the grouping together of activities with common objectives and a long-term plan relating to the objectives of the organization as a whole, which is subdivided into programmes. Conventional annual expenditure budgeting procedures are applied within this framework.

planning variance *See* REVISION VARIANCE.

plant and equipment A category of tangible *fixed assets that includes plant, machinery, fixtures and fittings, and other equipment.

plant and machinery The equipment required to operate a business. *Capital allowances are available for plant and machinery although neither is defined in the tax legislation. The working definition often used is that given in the taxation case *Yarmouth v France* (1887). This defines plant and machinery as 'whatever apparatus is used by a businessman for carrying on his business – not his stock in trade which he buys or makes for resale: but all goods and chattels, fixed or moveable, live or dead, which he keeps for permanent employment in the business'. Subsequent cases have been largely concerned with the distinction between plant actively used in a business, and so qualifying for capital allowances, and expenditure on items that relate to the setting up of the business, which do not so qualify. Items ruled to be plant and machinery range from a barrister's law books to sculptures and other decorative items intended to create ambience.

plant register   *See* FIXED-ASSETS REGISTER.

plc   Abbreviation for *public limited company.

ploughed-back profits   *See* RETAINED EARNINGS.

PLUS Markets   A stock exchange in London that offers both primary and secondary markets for shares in smaller companies. It developed from the Ofex trading facility in 2005–06 and is now a serious rival to the London Stock Exchange's *Alternative Investment Market. It became a UK *Recognized Investment Exchange in 2007.

POB   Abbreviation for *Professional Oversight Board.

point of sale (POS)   The place at which a consumer makes a purchase, usually a retail shop. It may, however, also be a doorstep (in door-to-door selling), a market stall, or a mail-order house.

poison pill   A tactic in which a company discourages unwanted *takeover bids by ensuring that a successful bid will trigger some event that substantially reduces the value of the company. Examples of such tactics include the sale of some prized asset to a friendly company or bank or the issue of securities with a conversion option enabling the bidder's shares to be bought at a reduced price if the bid is successful. *See also* STAGGERED DIRECTORSHIPS.

policy cost   An item of expenditure incurred as a consequence of a policy determined by the management of an organization. For example, the insurance premium determined by a key-man insurance policy taken out by an organization will be directly related to the sum assured.

political and charitable contributions   Donations for political or charitable purposes made by an organization. Under the Companies Act a disclosure of such a donation has to be made by companies that are not *wholly owned subsidiaries of another British company and which have on their own or with their subsidiaries given in the financial year in aggregate more than £200. Charitable purposes is taken to mean purposes that are exclusively charitable. A donation for political purposes is taken to mean the giving of money either directly or indirectly to a political party of the UK or any part of it, or to a person who is carrying on activities likely to affect support for a political party. The total amounts given for both political and charitable purposes must be separately disclosed. If the payments are for political purposes, where applicable, the following information must be provided: (a) the name of each person to whom money exceeding £200 in amount has been given for those purposes and the amount given; and (b) if more than £200 has been given as a donation or subscription to a political party, the identity of the party and the amount given must be disclosed.

political credit risk (sovereign risk)   The *credit risk that arises as a result of actions by a foreign government, which may affect the management of a foreign business, control of its assets, and its ability to make payments to its creditors. *Compare* TRANSFER CREDIT RISK. *See also* COUNTRY RISK.

pooling-of-interests method In the USA, a method of accounting formerly used in business combinations in which the acquiring company had issued voting common stock in exchange for voting common stock of the acquired company. In the pooling-of-interests method, the acquired company's net *assets were brought forward at book value, *retained earnings and *paid-in capital were brought forward, the net income was recognized for the full financial year regardless of the date of acquisition, and the expenses of pooling were immediately charged against earnings. In 2001 the US *Financial Accounting Standards Board ruled that the pooling-of-interests method should no longer be permitted.

Porter's Five Forces A framework for analysing the balance of power within a particular industry and hence its overall profitability. The frame identifies five forces in the microenvironment that drive competition and threaten a firm's ability to make profits: (1) rivalry between existing competitors (depending on e.g. their number, size, and relative market shares); (2) the threat of new entrants (i.e. the extent to which there are significant barriers to entering a market); (3) the threat of substitutes (i.e. products in another industry that the consumer may see as alternatives); (4) the strength of buyer power; and (5) the strength of supplier power. Forces (2), (3), (4), and (5) all feed back into force (1) by driving up competitive rivalry. The five-forces model is probably the most widely used tool in *industry structure analysis and is also a popular starting point in strategic management planning. It was developed by Michael E. Porter of Harvard Business School in the late 1970s.

portfolio **1.** The set of holdings in securities owned by an investor or institution. In building up an investment portfolio an institution will have its own investment analysts, while an individual may make use of the services of a *merchant bank that offers **portfolio management**. The choice of portfolio will depend on the mix of income and capital growth its owner expects, some investments providing good income prospects while others provide good prospects for capital growth. **2.** A list of the loans made by an organization. Banks, for example, attempt to balance their portfolio of loans to limit the risks.

portfolio insurance (portfolio protection) The use of a *financial futures and *options market to protect the value of a portfolio of investments. For example, a fund manager may expect the general level of prices to fall on the stock exchange. The manager could protect the portfolio by selling *futures contracts, which could then be bought back at a profit if the market falls. Alternatively, the manager could establish the value of the portfolio at current prices by buying put *options, which would provide the opportunity to benefit if there was a rise in the general level of prices.

portfolio theory The theory that rational investors are averse to taking increased risk unless they are compensated by an adequate increase in expected return. The theory also assumes that for any given expected return, most rational investors will prefer a lower level of risk and for any given level of risk they will prefer a higher return than a lower return. A set of efficient *portfolios can be calculated from which the investor will choose the one most appropriate for their risk profile. The practical conclusions of the theory are that investors should diversify widely and determine their levels of risk by lending a proportion of their assets or borrowing to buy more risky assets. *See also* PORTFOLIO INSURANCE.

POS Abbreviation for *point of sale.

positive accounting theory A theory that attempts to explain the nature of accounting, the role and activities of accountants, and relationships of accountancy to the economy. Unlike *normative theories of accounting, it does not set out to state what accounting procedures and policies should be, but rather to explain why they are what they are. *See also* A PRIORI THEORIES OF ACCOUNTING.

postal account A savings account with a bank or a building society that can only be operated by letter or (sometimes) by *automated teller machine (i.e. not over the counter or by telephone or over the Internet). Postal accounts usually pay a higher rate of interest than those that can be operated in person because of their cost structure.

post-balance-sheet events *See* ADJUSTING EVENTS; NON-ADJUSTING EVENTS.

post-cessation receipts Amounts accruing from a trading activity that are received after the trade has ceased. For tax purposes the receipts are treated as income in the year of receipt, from which any relevant trade expenses incurred can be deducted. An election can be made to treat post-cessation receipts as income in the year the trade ceased rather than the year of receipt.

post-completion audit A comparison of the actual cash flows and the forecast cash flows for an investment. Except for very large investments, it may be difficult to identify all the cash flows for an investment. A post-completion audit should identify bad investments made in the past and encourage managers to use more realistic forecasts for future investment projects.

post-date To insert a date on a document that is later than the date on which it is signed, thus making it effective only from the later date. A **post-dated** (or **forward-dated**) **cheque** cannot be negotiated before the date written on it, irrespective of when it was signed. *Compare* ANTEDATE.

post-retirement benefits Benefits provided by an employer to employees who have retired. For example, some employers provide health care and other benefits in addition to pensions, particularly in the USA. In the USA, *Statement of Financial Accounting Standards 106 requires that such benefits are dealt with on an *accruals basis and not a *cash basis. In 1992 the UK's *Urgent Issues Task Force stated that as a matter of principle such benefits should be recognized in *financial statements; this applied to all financial periods ending after 23 December 1994. The accounting treatment for retirement benefits is set out in *Financial Reporting Standard 17, Retirement Benefits, which was issued in 2000 and amended in November 2002. From 1 January 2005 listed companies are also required to comply with *International Accounting Standard 19, Employment Benefits. *See also* ACCRUED BENEFITS.

potentially exempt transfer (PET) A lifetime gift made by an individual that is neither an *exempt transfer for *inheritance tax purposes nor liable to an immediate charge (*see* CHARGEABLE TRANSFER). No charge occurs if the donor survives seven years after the date of the gift. If death occurs within seven years of the gift, the total lifetime gifts in the seven years preceding death are reviewed. The gifts are taken in chronological order with the first £325,000 (2009–10) worth of gifts being covered by the *nil-rate band. Gifts in excess of this sum are charged at a flat rate of 40% with graduated relief for gifts made between three and seven years before death.

PPBS Abbreviation for *planning, programming, budgeting system.

PPP *See* PUBLIC–PRIVATE PARTNERSHIP.

Practice Notes Notes issued by the *Auditing Practices Board to assist auditors when applying Statements of Auditing Standards of general application to particular circumstances and industries. These notes are intended to indicate good practice and to be persuasive rather than prescriptive. *See also* AUDITING STANDARDS.

pre-acquisition profits The *retained earnings of one company before it is taken over by another company. Preacquisition profits should not be distributed to the shareholders of the acquiring company by way of dividend, as such profits do not constitute income to the parent company but a partial repayment of its capital outlay on the acquisition of the shares.

pre-Budget report (PBR) In the UK, a statement made by the Chancellor of the Exchequer in October–December that reports on the state of the economy and points forward to the *Budget he will unveil in the spring. It is sometimes used to announce detailed policy initiatives.

preceding-year basis (PYB) A basis for assessing profits in which the assessment in any given *fiscal year is based on the accounts that ended during the previous tax year. In the UK, the PYB was replaced by the *current-year basis of assessment from 1997–98 onwards.

precept A command by the Commissioners of Inland Revenue to a taxpayer to make certain relevant documents available, usually by a specified date.

predetermined overhead rate An overhead *absorption rate computed in advance of operations. In practice, most absorption rates are computed from budgeted figures and are therefore predetermined overhead rates, which usually cover one year.

pre-emption rights The principle, established in UK company law, that existing shareholders should be offered a proportion of certain classes of newly issued securities before they are offered to anyone else and upon terms that are at least as favourable. To satisfy this principle a company must write to every shareholder (*see* RIGHTS ISSUE), involving an expensive and lengthy procedure. Newer methods of issuing shares, such as *vendor placings or *bought deals, are much cheaper and easier to effect, although they violate pre-emption rights. An issue of shares with no pre-emption rights can only be made if the shareholders have agreed to this in a *special resolution. In the USA pre-emption rights have now been largely abandoned but controversy over the principle is still widespread in the UK.

preference The favouring by an insolvent debtor of a particular creditor (e.g. by paying one creditor in full when there is no prospect of paying the others). If the debtor subsequently becomes bankrupt (in the case of an individual) or goes into insolvent liquidation (in the case of a company), and was motivated by a desire to improve the position of the creditor, the court can order that the position be restored to what it would have been had that creditor not been given preference. The court can also make orders when the debtor has given property away or sold it at an undervalue.

preference dividend A *dividend payable to the holders of *preference shares. Preference dividends not paid in previous periods will only be due to the holders of *cumulative preference shares.

preference share A share in a company that is entitled to a fixed percentage *dividend rather than a variable dividend; for example, a 6% preference share pays a dividend of 6% per annum. If the company goes into *liquidation, the preference shares are paid out after *loan capital, but before *ordinary share capital. *See also* PREFERENCE SHARE CAPITAL.

preference share capital *Share capital consisting of *preference shares. Under *Financial Reporting Standard (FRS) 4, Capital Instruments, preference share capital was classified as *non-equity share capital. However, FRS 4 has now been replaced by FRS 25 (International Accounting Standard 32), Financial Instruments: Disclosure and Presentation, which states that from 1 January 2005 preference shares should be classified as *liabilities rather than *shareholders' equity.

preferential creditor A creditor whose debt will be met in preference to those of other creditors and who thus has the best chance of being paid in full on the bankruptcy of an individual or the winding-up of a company. Preferential creditors, who are usually paid in full after *secured liabilities and before ordinary creditors, include the trustees of occupational pensions schemes and employees in respect of any remuneration outstanding. The status of the Crown (i.e. HM Revenue and Customs) as a preferential creditor was abolished from 2003.

preferential debt A debt that will be repaid in preference to other debts. *See* PREFERENTIAL CREDITOR.

preferred stock The US term for a *preference share.

prefinancing An arrangement in which a buyer (often an importer) finances the activities of a supplier by making an advance payment against delivery. This is sometimes used as a fair trade policy, in which Western importers pay farmers in the developing world for their crops some months in advance of harvest.

preliminary announcement An early announcement of their profit or loss for the year that *listed companies are required to make under *London Stock Exchange Regulations. The minimum information is a summarized *profit and loss account, although there has been a trend for companies to provide other information, such as *balance sheets. Companies must lodge their preliminary announcement with the Stock Exchange, but there is no requirement to send the information to shareholders. A number of companies publish some of the information in national newspapers and provide *investment analysts and journalists with substantial information, which receives considerable comment in the press. The *Accounting Standards Board has issued a guide to best practice in respect of preliminary announcements.

preliminary expenses Expenses incurred in the setting up of a *company, for example the cost of issuing shares. These expenses may be written off to the *share premium account.

premium **1.** The consideration payable for a contract of insurance or life assurance. **2.** An amount in excess of the nominal value of a share or other security. **3.** An amount in excess of the issue price of a share or other security. When dealings open for a new issue of shares it may be said that the market price will be at a premium over the issue price (*see* STAG).

premium on capital stock In the USA, the excess amount received from *stockholders over the *par value of the stock issued. The premium account is shown in the *balance sheet under the *paid-in-capital section of stockholders' *equity and should not be regarded as income.

prepayment (payment in advance) A payment made for goods or services before they are received. It is treated as *deferred debits under the *accruals concept, and is shown as a *debit balance under *debtors in the *current assets of the balance sheet.

present value (discounted value) The result arrived at in a *discounted cash flow calculation by multiplying a projected annual cash flow figure by a *discount factor derived from a *hurdle rate of interest and a time period.

present-value factor *See* DISCOUNT FACTOR.

prevention costs *See* COST OF QUALITY. *See also* ENVIRONMENTAL COSTS.

price–dividend ratio (PDR; P/D ratio) The current market price of a company share divided by the dividend per share for the previous year. It is a measure of the investment value of the share.

price–earnings ratio (P/E ratio) The current market price of a company share divided by the *earnings per share (eps) of the company. The P/E ratio usually refers to the annual eps and is expressed as a number (e.g. 5 or 10), often called the **multiple** of the company. Loosely, it can be thought of as the number of years it would take the company to earn an amount equal to its market value. High multiples, usually associated with low *yields, indicate that the company is growing rapidly, while a low multiple is associated with dull no-growth stocks. The P/E ratio is one of the main indicators used by fundamental analysts to decide whether the shares in a company are expensive or cheap, relative to the market.

price-level accounting A system of accounting that attempts to take into account changes in price levels, thus avoiding some of the criticisms of *historical-cost accounting. There have been many proposed methods but they have not been implemented, often because of the practical difficulties in operating them.

price-sensitive information Information (usually unpublished) about a company that is likely to cause its share prices to move. *See* INSIDER DEALING.

price variances *See* DIRECT MATERIALS PRICE VARIANCE; SALES MARGIN PRICE VARIANCE.

pricing The setting of selling prices for the products and services supplied by an organization. In many cases selling prices will be based on market prices but in other circumstances pricing will be based on costs, using information provided by the *management accounting system.

primary auditor The *auditor of the primary company, i.e. the *holding company, when *consolidated financial statements are being prepared. The primary auditor is responsible for the *audit opinion on the group's financial statement.

primary earnings per share *See* FULLY DILUTED EARNINGS PER SHARE.

primary market The market into which a new issue of securities is launched. *Compare* SECONDARY MARKET.

prime cost *See* DIRECT COST OF SALES.

prime documents The documents used to initiate and record the accounting entries in an accounting or management accounting system. Prime documents include *sales invoices, *materials requisitions, *materials returns notes, and *direct charge vouchers.

prime rate The rate of interest charged by US banks to their best borrowers. This is not the same as the UK *base rate, as even the best borrowers in the UK normally pay a margin over the base rate for an overdraft. The prime rate is therefore a lending rate, while the base rate is a yardstick.

principal 1. The sum on which interest is paid. **2.** A person who has given express or implied authority for another person to act as an agent on his or her behalf. *See* AGENCY RELATIONSHIP.

principal budget factor *See* LIMITING FACTOR; CONSTRAINT.

principal private residence The main private dwelling house of an individual. Gains arising on the disposal of this dwelling are exempt for *capital gains tax.

prior-period adjustments Material adjustments applicable to prior *accounting periods arising from changes in *accounting policies or from the correction of fundamental errors. They do not include normal recurring adjustments or corrections of accounting estimates made in prior periods. Under *Financial Reporting Standard 3, if prior-period adjustments fall within these definitions, the *financial statements for the current period should not be distorted, but the prior periods should be restated with an adjustment to the opening balance of the *retained earnings. The relevant *International Accounting Standard is IAS 8, Accounting Policies, Changes in Accounting Estimates, and Errors.

private equity firm An investment firm that seeks to make high returns by (i) obtaining a controlling interest in a target company (if this is a public company it is then taken private); (ii) subjecting it to radical financial and organizational restructuring over several years with the aim of maximizing profits; and (iii) selling the revitalized company or floating it on the stock exchange. Most private equity investment is funded by debt; acquisitions generally take the form of a highly leveraged *management buy-in (or *management buy-out; *see* BIMBO). Critics of the private equity industry, which saw spectacular growth in the early 2000s, have accused it of an *asset-stripping mentality; there have also been concerns about unfair tax advantages (*see* SHAREHOLDER DEBT; TAPER RELIEF) and exemptions from disclosure.

private finance initiative (PFI) *See* PUBLIC–PRIVATE PARTNERSHIP.

private ledger A *ledger containing confidential accounts. A *control account may be used to link it to the general ledger.

private limited company Any *limited company that is not a *public limited company. Such a company is not permitted to offer its shares for sale to the public and it is free from the rules that apply to public limited companies.

privatization (denationalization) The process of selling a publicly owned company or asset (*see* NATIONALIZATION) to the private sector. Privatization may be pursued for political as well as economic reasons. The economic justification for privatization is that a company will be more efficient under private ownership, although most economists would argue that privatization will only achieve this if it is accompanied by increased competition. Politically, privatization in the form of share offers to the general public has been seen as a means of widening the share-owning public and thus increasing the participation of individuals in the capitalist system.

probability The likelihood that a particular outcome will occur, on a scale of 0 (zero probability or certainty that it will not occur) to 1 (certainty that it will occur). Where probabilities are used in decision-making models they are usually subjective in nature. *See* EXPECTED VALUE; EXPECTED MONETARY VALUE.

probate value A valuation of all the assets included in the estate of a deceased person at the date of his or her death, taking account of any restrictions on the use of the assets. A probate value is agreed with HM Revenue and Customs for the purpose of calculating *inheritance tax.

problem child *See* BOSTON MATRIX.

process An operation in the production cycle of an organization that contributes to the completion of a product or *cost unit.

process costing A costing system sometimes applied to production carried out by a series of chemical or operational stages or processes. Its characteristics are that costs are accumulated for the whole production process and that average unit costs of production are computed at each stage (*see* AVERAGE COSTING). Special rules are applied in process costing to the valuation of *work in progress, *normal losses, and *abnormal losses. In process costing it is usual to distinguish between the *main product of the process, *by-products, and *joint products. *Compare* CONTINUOUS-OPERATION COSTING.

process innovation *See* BUSINESS PROCESS RE-ENGINEERING.

product An item, sub-assembly, part, or *cost unit manufactured or sold by an organization.

product costs The costs of production when charged to the *cost units and expressed as costs of individual products. Product costs may include both *direct costs and *indirect costs (overhead); many different costing methods, such as *absorption costing, *activity-based costing, and *process costing, are used in computing product costs.

production The *cost units manufactured by an organization. Production may be measured in units, *direct labour hours, *machine hours, or *direct labour cost.

production budget (operating budget) A budget set for the production function of an organization under a system of *budgetary control, which includes, inter alia, the production volumes and the *production cost to be incurred in a budget period. It will usually provide an analysis of the budgets by product and by accounting period.

production cost (total cost of production) The total of all the costs incurred in producing a product or *cost unit. In a *manufacturing account the production cost is represented by the total of the *direct cost of sales and the *manufacturing overhead. See COST OF GOODS MANUFACTURED.

production cost centre An area of an organization, such as a function, department, section, individual, or any group of these, in which production is carried out. See also COST CENTRE.

production cost variance In *standard costing, the *variance arising when the standard cost of the actual production is compared with the actual cost incurred. If the standard cost is higher than the actual cost a *favourable variance arises, while if the actual cost exceeds the standard cost an *adverse variance occurs. The production cost variance is usually analysed into the *direct materials total cost variance, the *direct labour total cost variance, and the *overhead total variance, each of which can be further analysed within such parameters as expenditure and efficiency. See ANALYSIS OF VARIANCE.

production department A section of an organization in which production is carried out.

production herd A group of living animals or other livestock kept for their products, such as milk or wool, or for their young. It can be treated as a capital asset (see HERD BASIS). See also BIOLOGICAL ASSETS.

production order (manufacturing requisition) A form issued to the production department of an organization specifying the production to be carried out by the department. A production order gives, inter alia, a description of the operations to be carried out, the quantities to be produced, the time allowed, and the completion times.

production overhead See MANUFACTURING OVERHEAD.

production planning The administrative operations ensuring that the material, labour, and other resources necessary to carry out production are available when and where they are required in the necessary quantities.

production profit/loss See MANUFACTURING PROFIT/LOSS.

production-unit method (units of production method of depreciation) A method of computing the *depreciation charge for a period on a piece of machinery in which the depreciation charge is based on the number of production units manufactured by the machine. When the machinery to be depreciated is purchased an estimate is made of the total number of units of production that will be made by the machine over its lifetime. A rate per production unit is then computed and applied to the production over the life of the machinery. The formula per production unit is as follows:

original cost – estimated residual value/estimated number of production units.

Unlike the *straight-line method of depreciation, which treats depreciation as a *fixed cost, the production-unit method treats it as a *variable cost.

production–volume ratio (PV ratio) *See* CONTRIBUTION MARGIN RATIO.

productivity variance *See* OVERHEAD EFFICIENCY VARIANCE.

product-sustaining-level activities *See* ACTIVITY.

profession Until 2005, profits from a profession were taxed under Schedule D Case II of the income tax legislation, whereas profits from a *trade were taxed under Schedule D Case I. Although there is no longer a separation of cases, profits of professions are taxed differently from those arising from a trade in a number of ways. Perhaps the most important distinction is that the value of goods gifted by a trader must be brought into the calculation of taxable profits, but there is no tax charge on the value of a professional service gifted.

The traditional approach of the courts is to say that a company cannot carry on a profession, as the profits of a profession must be dependent mainly upon the personal qualification of the person by whom it is practised, and that can only be an individual.

professional indemnity insurance (PII) A form of third-party insurance that covers a professional person, such as an accountant or auditor, against paying compensation in the event of being sued for *negligence. This can include giving defective advice if the person professes to be an expert in a given field. There have been a number of very high awards made to plaintiffs (especially in the USA where PII is known as **malpractice insurance**) and this has greatly increased the cost to the accountant of obtaining cover.

One solution is for accountants to form corporations rather than the traditional *partnerships, thus reducing their exposure to personal liability. In the UK the *Limited Liability Partnership Act 2000 now enables partnerships to claim the advantages of limited liability. *See also* INCORPORATION OF AUDIT FIRMS.

Professional Oversight Board (POB) An operating body of the *Financial Reporting Council (FRC). Its purpose is to provide independent oversight of the auditing profession through the *Recognized Supervisory Bodies and of the accounting profession through the *Designated Professional Bodies, with the ultimate aim of upholding public confidence in the governance of listed and other companies. It was formerly known as the **Professional Oversight Board for Accountancy** (**POBA**).

professional valuation An assessment of the value of an asset in the balance sheet or prospectus of a company by a person professionally qualified to give such a valuation. The professional qualification necessary will depend on the asset; for example, a qualified surveyor may be needed to value property, whereas unlisted shares might best be valued by a qualified accountant. *See also* INTERNATIONAL VALUATION STANDARDS COUNCIL.

profit 1. (margin; profit margin) For a single transaction or set of transactions, the excess of sales revenue over the costs of providing the goods or services sold.

See GROSS PROFIT; NET PROFIT. **2.** For a period of trading, the surplus of net assets at the end of a period over the net assets at the start of that period, adjusted where relevant for amounts of capital injected or withdrawn by the proprietors. As profit is notoriously hard to define, it is not always possible to derive one single figure of profit for an organization from an accepted set of data. The UK Taxes Acts do not provide a formulation of the measure of profit. In recent years the courts have tended to take the profits of a company for tax purposes as those shown in its accounts where these are drawn up in accordance with *generally accepted accounting practice. *See* ACCOUNTING PROFIT.

profitability index (PI) A method used in *discounted cash flow for ranking a range of projects under consideration in which *standard cash flow patterns are projected. It is based on the ratio:

total present values of cash inflows/initial investment,

the value of which is compared for each project.

The projects with a PI of less than 1 are not expected to earn the *required rate of return and are rejected. The projects with a PI in excess of 1 are ranked according to the magnitude of the PI.

profit and loss account (comprehensive income statement; P & L account)
1. An *account in the books of an organization showing the profits (or losses) made on its business activities with the deduction of the appropriate expenses.

2. A statement of the profit (or loss) of an organization over a financial period. It is one of the statutory accounts that, for most limited companies, has to be filed annually with the UK Registrar of Companies (*see* ANNUAL ACCOUNTS). The profit and loss account explains what has happened since the previous *balance sheet; the users of financial statements require information on the progress and future prospects of the company.

The P & L account typically consists of three parts. The first is a trading account, showing the total sales income less the costs of production, etc., and any changes in the value of stock or work in progress from the last accounting period. This gives the *gross profit (or loss). The second part gives any other income and lists administrative and other costs to arrive at a *net profit (or loss). From this net profit before taxation the appropriate corporation tax is deducted to give the net profit after taxation. In the third part, the net profit after tax is appropriated to dividends or to reserves (retained profit). The UK Companies Act gives a choice of four formats, one of which must be used to file a profit and loss account for a registered company.

profit and loss account formats The four formats given for *profit and loss accounts by the Companies Act:
- vertical format, analysing costs by type of operation and function;
- vertical format, analysing costs by items of expense;
- horizontal format, analysing costs by type of operation or function;
- horizontal format, analysing costs by items of expense.

The following three items must be disclosed on the face of the profit and loss account irrespective of which format is selected:
(1) profit or loss on ordinary activities before taxation;
(2) any amount set aside or proposed to be set aside to, or withdrawn or proposed to be withdrawn from, reserves;
(3) the aggregate amount of *dividends paid and proposed.

*Financial Reporting Standard 3, Reporting Financial Performance, issued in October 1992, developed the basic formats given in the Companies Act by adopting a layered format requiring the following additional components to be shown:

- the results of continuing operations, including the results of any acquisitions;
- the results of discontinued operations;
- profits and losses on the sale or termination of an operation, costs of fundamental reorganization or restructuring, and profits or losses on the disposal of *fixed assets;
- any extraordinary items.

Other countries allow different formats and this makes *comparability difficult. Even if all countries were to adopt the same format, there would probably still be problems with the precise definition of terms.

profit and loss account reserve A reserve that contains the balance of *retained earnings to carry forward. It is fully distributable and shown as part of shareholders' reserves on the *balance sheet.

profit and loss appropriation account A statement showing how the net profits or losses have been dealt with. In a company, the *retained earnings brought forward is added to the net profit for the year; from this total taxation and dividends paid and proposed are deducted; other transfers to and from reserves are deducted or added as appropriate. In *partnership accounts, the profit or loss available for appropriation is given at the beginning of the statement. Each partner's contribution of interest on *drawings and entitlement to salary and interest on capital, as appropriate, are deducted, leaving a balance to be shared between the partners in the *profit-sharing ratio.

profit centre A section or area of an organization to which revenue can be traced, together with the appropriate costs, so that profits can be ascribed to that area. Profit centres may be divisions, subsidiaries, or departments.

profit margin *See* PROFIT. *See also* MARGIN.

profit-related pay (PRP) **1.** The situation in which the pay of employees is related to the profit made by the employer. The purpose is to increase motivation, commitment, and effort by the workforce by ensuring that all staff have a positive stake in the commercial success of the company. For such a scheme to be a success it must be believed in, valued, and understood by all concerned. Staff must clearly understand that a bonus payment will be forthcoming if the organization has a good year but will not be if the organization does not make profits.

Profit-related rewards are usually offered in one of two ways. The simplest of these is to allocate an amount from the surplus generated by the organization and to share this out among employees. For maximum equality, this will be as a percentage increase in all employees' salaries. The other approach is to offer shares in the organization; the employees will thus become investors in their own future. *See also* PROFIT-SHARING SCHEME.

2. A former UK scheme enabling employees to be paid part of their salary tax-free; it was phased out in 2000–01. Payments to employees under a registered scheme could be tax-free up to the maximum for the year.

profits available for distribution *See* DISTRIBUTABLE PROFITS.

profit-sharing ratio (PSR) The ratio in which the profits or losses of a business are shared. For a partnership, the profit-sharing ratios will be set out in the *partnership agreement. This will show the amount, usually given as a percentage of the total profits, attributable to each partner. In some agreements there is a first charge on profits, which is an allocation of the first slice of the profits for the year. The remainder will then be split in the profit-sharing ratios as specified in the agreement. The profit-sharing ratios can also apply to the capital of the partnership, but this does not always follow. The partnership agreement can specify a different capital-sharing ratio. If no specific agreement has been made, profits and losses will be shared equally in accordance with the Partnership Act 1890.

profit-sharing scheme A scheme by which employees share in the profits of a business, usually through some type of share ownership. *See* EMPLOYEE SHARE OWNERSHIP PLAN; EMPLOYEE SHARE OWNERSHIP TRUST; SAVINGS RELATED SHARE OPTION SCHEME; SHARE OPTION.

profit variance In *standard costing, the variance consisting of the difference between the *standard operating profit budgeted to be made on the items sold and the actual profits made. The analysis of the profit variance into its constituent sales, direct labour, direct material, and overhead variances provides the management of the organization with information regarding the source of the gains and losses compared to the predetermined standard. *See* ANALYSIS OF VARIANCE.

profit–volume chart (PV chart) A graph showing the profits and losses to be made at each level of activity. The profit/loss line is usually plotted as a linear function, and the graph shows the total fixed cost level as the loss at zero activity, the *breakeven point activity level, and the profits or losses at each level of production or sales.

profit–volume ratio (PV ratio) *See* CONTRIBUTION MARGIN RATIO.

profit warning An announcement by a company that its future profits will be significantly lower than previously announced or forecast.

pro-forma financial statements *Financial statements for a period prepared before the end of the period, which therefore contain estimates.

proforma invoice An invoice sent in certain circumstances to a buyer, usually before some of the invoice details are known. For example, in commodity trading a proforma invoice may be sent to the buyer at the time of shipment, based on a notional weight, although the contract specifies that the buyer will only pay for the weight ascertained on landing the goods at the port of destination. When the missing facts are known, in this case the landed weight, a final invoice is sent.

programme evaluation and review technique (PERT) *See* CRITICAL-PATH ANALYSIS.

progressive tax A tax in which the rate of tax increases with increases in the *tax base. In the UK, the most obvious such tax is *income tax but progressive rates are also applied to *National Insurance contributions, *inheritance tax, and to a limited extent *corporation tax. Such taxes are generally justified on the *ability-to-pay principle. *Compare* FLAT TAX.

progress payment (payment on account) A stage payment made to a contractor based on the level of work completed at a specified date, as certified by an agreed authority. It is used in the costing of *long-term contracts, such as civil engineering, shipbuilding, or large items of plant and machinery.

project financing (limited recourse financing) An arrangement in which money or loans put up for a particular project (often a property development) are secured on that project and its foreseen earnings rather than forming part of the general borrowing of the company concerned. In case of default, the lender has no recourse to the other assets of the company.

project management software Software designed to facilitate and integrate key tasks in the management of a large project. These typically include scheduling, *critical-path analysis, budget control, and administrative support; the system may also include a collaborative *decision support system. A good system will be integrated and dynamic, so that the total knock-on effect of any departures from the original plan can be assessed in key areas (e.g. budgeting, scheduling) as the project evolves.

promissory note A document that is a *negotiable instrument and contains a promise to pay a certain sum of money to a named person, to that person's order, or to the bearer at a specified time in the future. It must be unconditional, signed by the maker, and delivered to the payee or bearer. They are widely used in the USA but are not in common use in the UK. A promissory note cannot be reissued, unless the promise is made by a banker and is payable to the bearer, i.e. unless it is a banknote.

proper accounting records Accounting records that are sufficient to show and explain an organization's transactions. For a company, the Companies Act requires that these records should be able to disclose with reasonable accuracy, at any time, the financial position of the company and enable the directors to ensure that the *balance sheet and *profit and loss account comply with the statutory regulations. In particular, the accounting records shall contain entries of all money received and spent and a record of the *assets and *liabilities of the company. If goods are being bought and sold, stock records must also be sufficient. In forming an *audit opinion an auditor performing a *statutory audit under the Companies Act will consider whether proper accounting records have been kept and proper returns adequate for audit have been received from branches not visited. Furthermore, the auditor will consider whether the accounts are in agreement with the accounting records and returns. *See also* STATUTORY BOOKS.

property income certificate (PINC) A certificate giving the bearer a share in the value of a particular property and a share of the income from it. PINCs can be bought and sold.

property tax A tax based on the value of property owned by a taxpayer. In the UK, *council tax and *business rates are charged on the value of a property, as defined by a series of value bands, which depend on the region of the UK in which the property is situated.

proportional consolidation A method of *consolidation used in group accounts in which subsidiaries are not fully owned; a proportionate share of each category of a joint venture's revenue, expenditure, assets, and liabilities is included line by line. This is a complex and controversial topic. The *Accounting Standards Board has rejected this method of consolidation, although it is accepted by the *International Accounting Standards Board. *Compare* FULL CONSOLIDATION.

proportional tax *See* FLAT TAX.

proposed dividend A *dividend that has been recommended by the directors of a company but not yet paid. *See* FINAL DIVIDEND.

proprietary company *See* PTY.

proprietary view The view of an *accounting entity that emphasizes the rights and interests of shareholders rather than the status of the enterprise as a separate entity. *Compare* ENTITY VIEW; RESIDUAL EQUITY THEORY. *See also* SHAREHOLDER VALUE.

proprietor An owner of property or of a business. The owners of a company are the *shareholders of the company.

prospectus A document that gives details about a new issue of shares and invites the public to buy shares or debentures in the company. A copy must be filed with the Registrar of Companies. The prospectus of a *listed company must comply with Stock Exchange regulations; that of an unlisted company must conform to the provisions of the Financial Services and Markets Act 2000. In either case, it will describe the aims, capital structure, and any past history of the venture, and may contain future profit forecasts. There are heavy penalties for knowingly making false statements in a prospectus. *See* OFFER BY PROSPECTUS.

provision An amount set aside out of profits in the accounts of an organization for a known liability (even though the specific amount might not be known) or for the diminution in value of an asset. Common examples include *provisions for bad debts, for *depreciation, and for *accruals. According to the UK Companies Act notes must be given to explain every material provision in the accounts of a limited company. Because of abuses in the use of provision, *Financial Reporting Standard 12 has defined a provision as a liability that is of uncertain timing or amount, to be settled by the transfer of economic benefits. The relevant *International Accounting Standard is IAS 37, Provisions, Contingent Liabilities and Contingent Assets.

provision for bad debts A provision calculated to cover the debts during an *accounting period that are not expected to be paid. A **general provision**, e.g. 2% of debtors, is not allowed as a deduction for tax purposes. A **specific provision**, in which specific debts are identified, is allowed if there is documentary evidence to indicate that these debts are unlikely to be paid. A **provision for doubtful debts** (or **allowance for doubtful accounts**) is treated in the same way for tax purposes.

provision for depreciation *See* DEPRECIATION.

proxy A person who acts in the place of a member of a company at a company meeting at which one or more votes are taken. The proxy need not be a member of the company but it is quite common for directors to offer themselves as proxies for shareholders who cannot attend a meeting. Notices calling meetings must state that a member may appoint a proxy and the appointment of a proxy is usually done on a form provided by the company with the notice of the meeting; it must be returned to the company not less than 48 hours before the meeting. A **two-way proxy form** is printed so that the member can state whether he wants the proxy to vote for or against a particular resolution. A **special proxy** is empowered to act at one specified meeting; a **general proxy** is authorized to vote at any meeting.

PRP Abbreviation for *profit-related pay.

PRT Abbreviation for *petroleum revenue tax.

prudence concept The *accounting concept that insists on a realistic view of business activity and stresses that anticipated revenues and profits have no place in a *profit and loss account until they have been realized in the form of cash or other assets for which the ultimate cash value can be assessed with reasonable certainty. However, provision should be made for all known expenses and losses whether the amount of these is known with certainty or is a best estimate in the context of the information available.

The prudence concept has been recognized as a fundamental accounting concept in *Statement of Standard Accounting Practice (SSAP) 2, Disclosure of Accounting Policies, and the EU's *Fourth Company Law Directive. However, *Financial Reporting Standard 18, which superseded SSAP 2 from 2000, recognized the prudence concept as a desirable rather than a fundamental quality of financial information.

PSBR Abbreviation for Public Sector Borrowing Requirement. *See* Public Sector Net Cash Requirement.

PSNCR Abbreviation for *Public Sector Net Cash Requirement.

PSR Abbreviation for *profit-sharing ratio.

Pty Abbreviation for proprietary company, the name given to a *private limited company in Australia and the Republic of South Africa. The abbreviation Pty is used after the name of the company as Ltd is used in the UK. It is also used in the USA for an insurance company owned by outside shareholders.

Public Company Accounting Oversight Board (PCAOB) In the USA, a non-profit organization charged with overseeing the conduct of auditors of public companies. It was established under the *Sarbanes–Oxley Act 2002 as one of a raft of measures designed to enhance the public's confidence in financial reporting after a series of high-profile accounting scandals. The Board is empowered to conduct investigations and disciplinary hearings and to impose sanctions.

 SEE WEB LINKS
• Website of the PCAOB

public examination In bankruptcy proceedings, an investigation into the affairs, dealings, and property of a debtor. It takes place in open court and the debtor is compelled to attend and answer questions on oath. See feature Bankruptcy Law on p. 52.

public finance accountant A member of the *Chartered Institute of Public Finance and Accountancy. The principal function of the members of this body is to prepare the financial accounts and act as management accountants for government agencies, local authorities, nationalized industries, and such bodies as publicly owned health and water authorities. As many of these bodies are non-profitmaking and are governed by special statutes, the skills required of public sector accountants differ from those required in the private sector.

public issue (public offering) An *offer for sale in which the public are invited, through advertisements in the national press, to apply for a new issue of shares or other securities at a price fixed by the company. *Compare* ISSUE BY TENDER. *See also* INITIAL PUBLIC OFFERING.

publicity costs Items of expenditure incurred in carrying out the publicity function in an organization. Such items might include the publicity manager's salary, the advertising costs, promotions, and point-of-sale material.

public limited company (plc) A company registered under the Companies Act as a public company. Its name must end with the initials 'plc' (or its Welsh equivalent, c.c.c.). It must have a share capital of at least £50,000 or the euro equivalent, of which at least 25% must be paid up. The company's constitutional documents must comply with the format given in the Companies (Model Articles) Regulations 2008. It may offer shares and securities to the public. The regulation of such companies is stricter than that of private companies. Most public companies are converted from private companies, under the re-registration procedure in the Companies Act.

public offering *See* PUBLIC ISSUE. *See also* INITIAL PUBLIC OFFERING.

public–private partnership (PPP) In the UK, any of various schemes devised to bring private-sector investment and expertise into the provision of public services. Examples include the **private-finance initiative** (**PFI**) hospital-building programme in the National Health Service, the sale of local authority housing stock to housing associations, and the controversial plan to modernize and refurbish the London Underground. Advocates of the policy claim that it results in better services and lower costs; sceptics argue that the real attraction to government is the fact that PPPs enable upfront borrowing costs to be passed to the private sector, thus improving the Treasury balance sheet.

Public Sector Net Cash Requirement (PSNCR) The borrowing required by the UK government if its expenditure exceeds its income.

published accounts Accounts of organizations published according to UK law. The most common are the accounts of *limited companies, which must be provided for their shareholders and filed with the Registrar of Companies at Companies House, Cardiff. Companies often include additional documents for shareholders that are not required by company law. *See* ANNUAL ACCOUNTS; ANNUAL RETURN; GENERAL PURPOSE FINANCIAL STATEMENTS.

purchase accounting The *International Financial Reporting Standards term for *acquisition accounting.

purchase day book (bought day book; purchases journal) The *book of prime entry in which invoice amounts for purchases are entered.

purchased goodwill *Goodwill acquired when an entity is purchased as opposed to that which has been internally generated. Positive goodwill arises where the purchase cost exceeds the aggregate *fair values of the *identifiable assets and liabilities. More details are provided by *Financial Reporting Standard 10, Goodwill and Intangible Assets. The relevant *International Accounting Standards are IAS 22, IAS 36, and IAS 38. *Compare* INHERENT GOODWILL.

purchase method In the USA, a method of accounting for business combinations in which cash and other assets are distributed or liabilities incurred. The purchase method is used if the criteria are not met for the *pooling-of-interests method. With the purchase method, the acquirer records the net assets acquired at the *fair value on the market. Any excess of the purchase price over fair market value is recorded as *goodwill. The net income of the acquired company is recognized from the date of acquisition.

purchase requisition A form, completed by a user department of an organization and issued to the purchasing department, requiring the latter to effect the purchase of the items specified in the requisition. The requisition usually includes the quantity and specification of the items required, the possible supplier, the date required, and the delivery point.

purchases account An *account in which records are kept of transactions involving the buying of goods, either on credit or for cash. The double entries involved will be: debit the purchases account with the amount purchased and credit the creditors' account for purchases on credit and the bank account for purchases for cash.

purchases budget A budget set for the purchasing function of an organization under a system of *budgetary control, which plans the volumes and cost of the purchases to be made in a budget period. It will usually provide an analysis of the budgets by material and by *accounting period.

purchases journal *See* PURCHASE DAY BOOK.

purchases ledger *See* CREDITORS LEDGER.

purchases ledger control account *See* CREDITORS LEDGER CONTROL ACCOUNT.

purchases returns Goods purchased from a supplier but returned to the supplier because they are faulty, are not exactly what was ordered, etc.

purchasing power The ability to purchase goods and services. In times of inflation a loss of purchasing power occurs when *monetary assets are held because of the decline in the purchasing power of the currency. If a company has monetary liabilities, a purchasing power gain will arise because the absolute sum of the loans will be repaid with currency with less purchasing power.

push down accounting The practice in the USA of incorporating the *fair value adjustments on acquisition, including *goodwill, made by the acquiring company into the *financial statements of the acquired subsidiary.

put option *See* OPTION.

PV chart *See* PROFIT–VOLUME CHART.

PYB Abbreviation for *preceding-year basis.

QE Abbreviation for *quantitative easing.

Q ratio (Tobin's Q) A ratio devised by the US economic analyst James Tobin to measure the impact of *intangible assets on business value. It is the ratio of the market value of a business to the *replacement cost of its assets.

qualified acceptance An acceptance of a *bill of exchange that varies the effect of the bill as drawn. If the holder refuses to take a qualified acceptance, the drawer and any endorsers must be notified or they will no longer be liable. If the holder takes a qualified acceptance, all previous signatories who did not assent from liability are released.

qualified audit report An *auditors' report in which some qualification of the *financial statements is required because (a) the auditor feels there is a limitation on the scope of the audit examination or (b) the auditor disagrees with the treatment or disclosure of a matter in the financial statements. The type of qualification used will depend upon the degree of *materiality of the limitation or disagreement. If the limitation of scope is very material, a *disclaimer of opinion will be issued; if it is less material the 'except for the limitation of scope' form of qualification will be issued in the report (*see* EXCEPT FOR). If the auditor disagrees with the accounting treatment or disclosure in the financial statements and feels the effect is material and potentially misleading, an *adverse opinion will be expressed. If the disagreement is not so material, a qualified opinion will be given using the 'except for the effects of the disagreement' form of qualification.

qualified stock option In the USA, an agreement giving employees the right to purchase company *stock at a later date at a specified option price, which is normally lower than the market price. This meets the requirements of the Internal Revenue Service (IRS).

qualifying distribution Formerly, a distribution from a company resulting in *advance corporation tax (ACT) being paid. Qualifying distributions included dividends and distributions from any company assets to shareholders (except for capital repayments). In the UK, the requirement for payment of ACT was abolished from 1 April 1999.

qualifying loss A trading loss arising in a current accounting period as a result of computing the profits and losses of an organization in accordance with accepted *corporation-tax principles.

qualitative characteristics of accounting information The characteristics that make information in financial reports as useful as possible. The US *Financial Accounting Standards Board, in its *Statement of Financial Accounting Concepts No. 2, identifies the qualities that are both useful to decision makers and make the documents understandable. Information must be both reliable and relevant; it must have predictive value, feedback value, timeliness, comparability, consistency, verifiability, neutrality, and representational faithfulness. The UK *Accounting Standards Board, in its *Statement of Principles, emphasises four qualities: *comparability, *relevance, *reliability, and *understandability. *See also* OBJECTIVES OF FINANCIAL STATEMENTS.

quality of earnings The degree to which the *net profit of an organization reflects accurately its operating performance; it is particularly important to ensure that *creative accounting has not taken place and that no events have occurred to distort the profit figure.

quango Acronym for quasi-autonomous non-governmental organization. Such bodies, some members of which are likely to be civil servants and some not, are appointed by a minister to perform some public function at the public expense. While not actually government agencies, they are not independent and are usually answerable to a government minister.

quantitative budgets Budgets that cover the non-financial aspects of *budgetary control, such as the number of units of product planned to be produced and the number of direct labour hours to be worked.

quantitative easing (QE; queasing) A form of *monetary policy that is sometimes used to stimulate the economy when interest rates have already been reduced close to zero; it is regarded as a policy of last resort when there is a serious risk of *deflation. Essentially, the central bank creates new money electronically by expanding its balance sheet and uses this to buy government bonds from financial institutions. The aim is to boost the amount of money in circulation and to increase the willingness of banks to lend. QE, which was introduced in the UK from March 2009, is regarded as a high-risk strategy because of the risk of hyperinflation. Economists disagree as to how far it differs from the older and discredited policy of simply printing extra money.

quarter days Four days traditionally taken as the beginning or end of the four quarters of the year, often for purposes of charging rent. In England, Wales, and Northern Ireland they are Lady Day (25 March), Midsummer Day (24 June), Michaelmas (29 September), and Christmas Day (25 December). In Scotland they are Candlemas (2 February), Whitsuntide (15 May), Lammas (1 August), and Martinmas (11 November).

quarterly report In the USA, a financial report issued by a company every three months. The usual contents are an *income statement, *balance sheet, statement of changes in financial position, and a narrative overview of business operations.

quasi-contract A legally binding obligation that one party has to another, as determined by a court, although no formal *contract exists between them. A *letter of intent may constitute a quasi-contract.

quasi-loan An arrangement in which a creditor agrees to meet some of the financial obligations of a borrower, on condition that the borrower reimburses the creditor.

quasi money *See* NEAR MONEY.

quasi-subsidiary A company, trust, partnership, or other arrangement that does not fulfil the definition of a *subsidiary undertaking but is directly or indirectly controlled by the reporting entity and gives rise to benefits for that entity that are in substance no different from those that would arise if it was a subsidiary. This definition is based on that given in *Financial Reporting Standard 5, Reporting on the Substance of Transactions. If a reporting entity has a quasi-subsidiary, the substance of the transactions entered into by the quasi-subsidiary should be reported in *consolidated financial statements.

Quattro Pro *Trademark* A widely used *spreadsheet supplied by Novell.

queasing *See* QUANTITATIVE EASING.

question mark *See* BOSTON MATRIX.

quick assets *See* LIQUID ASSETS.

quick ratio *See* LIQUID RATIO.

quick-succession relief Relief available when the same property is assessed for *inheritance-tax purposes in the estates of two separate individuals, the second of whom dies within 5 years of the first. For example, B inherits property from A, which was subject to inheritance tax on A's death of £X. If B dies within one year of the date of the gift, the inheritance tax, £X, that was paid on A's estate will be allowed in full against the inheritance-tax liability on B's estate. If B dies within 1–2 years after the date of A's death the relief is 80% of £X, within 2–3 years relief is 60% of £X, within 3–4 years relief is 40% of £X, and within 4–5 years relief is 20% of £X. The relief is deducted from the whole estate, not simply a particular part of it.

quoted company *See* LISTED COMPANY.

q

RAFT Abbreviation for *revolving acceptance facility by tender.

raider An organization or person that attempts to exploit a company with undervalued assets by making a hostile *takeover bid.

Ramsey principle In UK tax law, the principle that the court is entitled to look at a transaction or series of connected transactions as a whole in order to decide the taxpayer's liability to tax. It is named after the ruling in the case *Commissioners of Inland Revenue v W T Ramsey Ltd*, in which the House of Lords ruled against a company that had used certain self-cancelling transactions to create a non-taxable gain and a tax-relievable loss. The Ramsey principle can be seen as a limitation on the *Westminster doctrine; its scope has, however, been restricted by subsequent case law.

random-walk theory The theory that prices on a financial market move, for whatever reason, without any memory of past movements and that the movements therefore follow no pattern. This theory is used to dispute the predictions of *chartists, who do rely on past patterns of movements to predict present and future prices.

RAROC Abbreviation for *risk-adjusted return on capital.

ratchet effect An irreversible change to an economic variable, such as prices, wages, exchange rates, etc. For example, once a price or wage has been forced up by some temporary economic pressure, it is unlikely to fall back when the pressure is reduced (*see* STICKINESS). This rise may be reflected in parallel sympathetic rises throughout the economy, thus fuelling *inflation.

rate of interest *See* INTEREST; INTEREST RATE.

rate of return The annual income earned from the investment of resources in a commercial or economic activity, usually expressed as a percentage of the original investment. In a *discounted cash flow appraisal, for example, the rate of return may be expressed as an *internal rate of return, whereas investment in a division or subsidiary may be expressed as an *accounting rate of return or *return on capital employed. *See also* REQUIRED RATE OF RETURN.

rate of return pricing Setting the prices of a range of products so that they earn a predetermined *required rate of return or *return on capital employed.

rate of turnover (turnover ratio) The frequency, expressed in annual terms, with which some part of the assets of an organization is turned over (i.e. replaced by others of the same class). In order to calculate how frequently stock is turned over, the total sales revenue (or if a more accurate estimate is needed the *cost of sales) is divided by the average value of the stock. This provides a reasonable measure in terms of *current assets. Some accountants also divide the sales figure by the value of the *fixed assets to arrive at turnover of fixed assets. This is hardly realistic, although it does express the relationship of sales to the fixed assets of the organization, which in some organizations could be significant. *See also* CAPITAL TURNOVER; INVENTORY TURNOVER.

rate per direct labour hour A basis used in *absorption costing for absorbing the *manufacturing overhead into the *cost units produced. The formula is:

   budgeted manufacturing overhead/budgeted direct labour hours.

A different approach to *cost allocation is used in *activity-based costing systems.

rate per machine hour A basis used in *absorption costing for absorbing the *manufacturing overhead into the *cost units produced. The formula is:

   budgeted manufacturing overhead/budgeted machine hours.

This rate may not be very useful for managers if overheads do not increase or decrease as machine hours increase or decrease. *Activity-based costing systems can provide a more accurate *cause-and-effect allocation of costs.

rate per standard hour A basis used in *absorption costing for absorbing the *manufacturing overhead into the *cost units produced. The formula is:

   budgeted manufacturing overhead/budgeted standard hours.

A different basis of *cost allocation is used in *activity-based costing systems.

rate per unit A basis used in *absorption costing for absorbing the *manufacturing overhead into the *cost units produced. The formula is:

   budgeted manufacturing overhead/budgeted units.

A different basis of *cost allocation is used in *activity-based costing systems.

rates *See* BUSINESS RATES.

rating agency An organization that monitors the credit backing of bond issues and other forms of public borrowings. It may also give a rating of the risks involved in holding specific stocks. The two best known are Standard & Poor and Moody, both of which have been in existence for over 100 years. *See also* CREDIT RATING.

ratio analysis The use of *accounting ratios to evaluate a company's *operating performance and financial stability. Such ratios as *return on capital employed and *gross profit percentage can be used to assess profitability. The *liquid ratio can be used to examine solvency and *gearing ratios to examine the financial structure of the company. In conducting an analysis comparisons will be made with other companies and with industry averages over a period of time. The analysis of ratios can indicate how well a company is run, the risks of financial insolvency, and the financial returns provided. *See also* COMMON-SIZE FINANCIAL STATEMENTS; FINANCIAL STATEMENT ANALYSIS.

ratio covenant A form of *covenant in a loan agreement that includes conditions relating to such ratios as the *gearing ratio and *interest cover. Breaching such a covenant could indicate significant deterioration in the company's business or a major change in its nature; this will usually empower the lender to request repayment of any of the loan then outstanding, and the loan then becomes null and void.

rationalization A reorganization of a firm, group, or industry to increase its efficiency and profitability. This may include closing some units and expanding others (*horizontal integration), merging different stages of the production process (*vertical integration), merging support units, closing units that are duplicating effort of others, etc. A firm may also rationalize its product range to reflect changes in demand, concentrating its sales and marketing effort on its best sellers. *See also* DOWNSIZING; RIGHTSIZING.

raw materials *Direct materials used in a production process, which are at a low level of completion compared to the final product or *cost unit. Examples include steel plate, wood, and chemicals.

raw materials stock The inventory of *raw materials held at a specified time. The raw materials appear in the balance sheet under the heading of current assets. *See* INVENTORY VALUATION.

real account A *ledger account for certain types of property (e.g. land and buildings, plant, investments, stock) as opposed to a *nominal account for revenue or expense items (e.g. sales, motor expenses, discount received, etc.). This distinction is now largely obsolete and both sets of accounts are maintained in the same ledger, usually referred to as the *nominal ledger.

real estate In the USA, immovable property, especially land and buildings.

real-estate investment trust (REIT) A company that is resident in the UK, owns at least three properties that are let to third parties, and distributes at least 90% of its profits to its shareholders. A real-estate investment trust is exempt from UK corporation tax. The distributions made by an REIT are not treated as dividends, but are taxed in the hands of shareholders as if they were rent received directly by those shareholders.

real exchange rate An *exchange rate that has been adjusted for the effects of inflation.

realizable account An account drawn up on the dissolution of a *partnership. The account is debited with the assets of the partnership and any expenses on realization; it is credited with the proceeds of any sales made. The difference between the total debits and credits is either a profit or loss on realization and must be shared between the partners in the *profit-sharing ratio.

realizable assets *See* LIQUID ASSETS.

realization convention The general basis used in *financial statements prepared under *historical-cost accounting, in which increases or decreases in the market values of assets and liabilities are not recognized as gains or losses until the assets are sold or the liabilities paid.

realized profit/loss A profit or loss that has arisen from a completed transaction (usually the sale of goods or services or other assets). In accounting terms, a profit is normally regarded as having been realized when an asset has been legally disposed of and not when the cash is received, since if an asset is sold on credit the asset being disposed of is exchanged for another asset, a debtor. The debt may or may not prove good but that is regarded as a separate transaction. *Compare* PAPER PROFIT.

real option An *option that arises in the course of business activities rather than one purchased on a financial market. A common example of a real option is early investment in a technology, which will enable a firm to exploit the new technology should it prove successful.

real purchasing power The *purchasing power of a currency adjusted for inflation.

real rate of interest The rate of *interest charged for the use of financial resources adjusted for the effect of the inflation rate within an economy. For example, if the rate charged for borrowed funds is 8% and the inflation rate is 2% per annum, the real rate of interest is about 6%.

real terms A representation of the value of a good or service in terms of money, taking into account fluctuations in the price level. Economists are usually interested in the relationship between the prices of goods in real terms, i.e. by adjusting prices according to a price index or some other measure of inflation.

real terms accounting A system of *accounting in which the effects of changing prices are measured by their effect on a company's financial capital (i.e. *shareholders' equity) to see if its value is maintained in real terms. Assets are measured at *current cost. Profit is defined as any surplus remaining after the shareholders' funds (determined by reference to the current cost of *net assets) have been maintained in real terms. The unit of measurement may be either the nominal pound or the unit of constant purchasing power.

rebate 1. A discount offered on the price of a good or service, often one that is paid back to the payer, e.g. a tax rebate is a refund to the taxpayer. 2. A discount allowed on a *bill of exchange that is paid before it matures.

recapitalization In the USA, the process of changing the balance of the *debt and *equity financing of a company without changing the total amount of *capital. Recapitalization is often required as part of reorganization of a company under bankruptcy legislation.

receipts and payments basis *See* CASH BASIS OF ACCOUNTING.

receivables Claims held against customers and others for money, goods, or services. These will appear on the *balance sheet of a company.

receiver A person exercising any form of *receivership. In *bankruptcy, the *official receiver becomes receiver and manager of the bankrupt's estate. Where there is a floating *charge over the whole of a company's property, which was created before 16 September 2003, and a crystallizing event has occurred, an *administrative receiver may be appointed to manage the whole of the company's business. The administrative receiver will have wide powers to carry on the business of the company, take possession of its property, commence *liquidation, etc. A receiver appointed in respect of a *fixed charge can deal with the property covered by the charge only, and has no power to manage the company's business.

receivership A situation in which a lender holds a mortgage or charge (especially a floating *charge) over a company's property and, in consequence of a default by the company, a receiver is appointed to realize the assets charged in order to repay the debt.

reciprocal costs Costs apportioned from a *service cost centre to a *production cost centre that carries out work for the original service cost centre. Consequently, a proportion of the production cost centre costs should also be re-apportioned to the service cost centre. Cost *apportionment can be calculated either by the use of simultaneous equations or by a continuous apportionment method, until all the costs are charged to the production cost centre.

recognition The process of incorporating an accounting item into the *financial statements of an organization. Not only is the process essential for revenue and expenditure items, but it has become increasingly important in the proper treatment of *off-balance-sheet finance.

Recognized Investment Exchange (RIE) A body authorized in the UK under the Financial Services and Markets Act 2000 to sell financial instruments, with the approval of the *Financial Services Authority. There are currently eight RIEs in the UK: the *London Stock Exchange, Euronext.liffe (*see* LIFFE), ICE Futures (formerly the International Petroleum Exchange), the *London Metal Exchange, *EDX London, *SWX Europe, *PLUS Markets, and NYMEX Europe (*see* NEW YORK MERCANTILE EXCHANGE).

Recognized Professional Body (RPB) *See* DESIGNATED PROFESSIONAL BODY.

Recognized Qualifying Body (RQB) In the UK, a body recognized as issuing accounting qualifications. There are currently six such bodies: the *Institute of Chartered Accountants in England and Wales, the *Institute of Chartered Accountants of Scotland, the *Institute of Chartered Accountants in Ireland, the *Association of Chartered Certified Accountants, the *Chartered Institute of Public Finance and Accountancy, and the *Association of International Accountants. A *registered auditor must be approved by one of the RQBs.

Recognized Supervisory Body (RSB) In the UK, a body recognized as supervising and maintaining the conduct and technical standards of auditors performing *statutory audits. Currently the *Institute of Chartered Accountants in England and Wales, the *Institute of Chartered Accountants of Scotland, and the *Institute of Chartered Accountants in Ireland are recognized, together with the *Association of Chartered Certified Accountants; in principle, the *Association of Authorized Public Accountants is also recognized.

reconciliation *See* ACCOUNT RECONCILIATION; BANK RECONCILIATION STATEMENT.

reconciliation of movements in shareholders' funds (statement of changes in equity; statement of movements in shareholders' funds) A *financial statement bringing together the performance of an organization in a financial period, as shown in the *statement of total recognized gains and losses, with all other changes in *shareholders' equity in the period, including dividend payments or capital contributed by or repaid to shareholders. This statement is provided for in *Financial Reporting Standard 3, Reporting Financial Performance.

recontracting The renegotiation of contracts between a company in *financial distress and its creditors.

recourse The right of redress should the terms of a contract not be fulfilled. *See* WITHOUT RECOURSE.

recoverable advance corporation tax Formerly, *advance corporation tax (ACT) that could be set off in full against the current year's *gross corporation tax liability or set back against gross corporation tax for accounting periods beginning six years preceding the current accounting period. ACT was abolished with effect from 1 April 1999.

recoverable amount The value of an asset treated as the greater of its *net realizable value and its *value in use.

recovered overhead *See* ABSORBED OVERHEAD.

recovery rate *See* ABSORPTION RATE.

rectification note A form issued to the production department of an organization requiring a piece of work to be reworked or rectified. The form includes a specification of the work to be done, the number of units, the processes involved, and the date required.

redeemable shares *Shares (either *ordinary shares or *preference shares) in a company that the issuing company has the right to redeem, under terms specified on issue. Redemption may be funded from *distributable profits or from a fresh issue of shares. If the shares were issued at a premium and are to be redeemed at a premium and subject to a maximum amount, the premium may be funded from the *share premium account. If redemption reduces the total capital of the company, i.e. no fresh issue is made or the proceeds of the fresh issue do not fully replace the nominal value of the shares redeemed, a *capital redemption reserve will need to be credited, to ensure that the *creditors' buffer is maintained.

redemption The repayment of *shares, *stocks, *debentures, or *bonds. The amount payable on redemption is usually specified on issue. The **redemption date**, or dates, may or may not be specified on issue. *See also* GILT-EDGED SECURITY; MATURITY DATE.

redemption date *See* MATURITY DATE; REDEMPTION.

redemption premium (call premium) The amount over *par value that a bond issuer must pay an investor if the security is redeemed early.

redemption yield *See* GROSS REDEMPTION YIELD; YIELD.

reducing-balance method *See* DIMINISHING-BALANCE METHOD.

reduction of capital A reduction of a company's share *capital in accordance with the Companies Act 2006. The Act states that a private company can reduce its share capital provided that: (i) it passes a *special resolution to do so; (ii) the resolution is supported by a solvency statement; and (iii) the reduction is not restricted or prohibited by the company's articles. Alternatively, a private or public company can, subject to any restriction or prohibition in the articles, reduce its share capital on the passing of a special resolution confirmed by the court. A reduction of capital can also occur where there is a permitted redemption or repurchase of a private company's own shares out of capital.

redundancy payment The sum that an employee dismissed because of redundancy is entitled to receive from his or her employer under the Employment Rights Act 1996. The sum is the total of:
(1) one and a half weeks' pay for each year of the employee's continuous employment in which he was aged 41 or more;
(2) one week's pay for each year's service between the ages of 22 and 41; and
(3) half a week's pay for each year below the age of 22.
The sliding scale based on age has been retained despite the introduction of laws to combat age discrimination. However, the upper and lower age limits that previously applied have been abolished.

Continuous employment exceeding 20 years is ignored, and a maximum amount of weekly pay to be used in the calculation is prescribed by regulations made by the Secretary of State for Work and Pensions and reviewed annually. In 2009 the limit was £350. Redundancy costs are met entirely by the employer.

reference bank A bank nominated under the terms of a loan agreement to provide the marker rates for the purposes of fixing interest charges on a variable-rate loan.

reference rate **1.** An interest rate relative to which a bank prices its products, sometimes referred to as its *base rate. **2.** An interest rate relative to which financial markets price their products, for example the *London Inter Bank Offered Rate (LIBOR) or *Euro Inter Bank Offered Rate (EURIBOR).

refer to drawer Words written on a cheque that is being dishonoured by a bank, usually because the account of the person who drew it has insufficient funds to cover it and the manager of the bank is unwilling to allow the account to be overdrawn or further overdrawn. Other reasons for referring to the drawer are that the drawer has been made bankrupt, that there is a *third-party debt order against the drawer, that the drawer has stopped it, or that something in the cheque itself is incorrect (e.g. it is wrongly dated, words and figures don't agree, etc.). The words 'please re-present' may often be added, indicating that the bank may honour the cheque at a second attempt.

registered auditor An *auditor eligible to carry out *statutory audits in any member state of the European Union, in accordance with the *Eighth Company Law Directive. This was brought into UK law by the Companies Act 1989, which gave the *Recognized Qualifying Bodies power to approve such auditors. Registers of individuals and firms eligible to act as registered auditors are kept.

registered book-keeper A member of the *International Association of Book-keepers.

registered capital *See* AUTHORIZED SHARE CAPITAL.

registered company A *company incorporated in England and Wales or Scotland by registration with the *Registrar of Companies. It may be a *limited company or an *unlimited company, a private company or a public company.

registered name The name in which a UK company is registered. The name, without which a company cannot be incorporated, will be stated in the company's constitutional documents. Some names are prohibited by law and will not be registered; these include names already registered and names that in the opinion of the Secretary of State are offensive. The name may be changed by special resolution of the company and the Secretary of State may order a company to change a misleading name. The name must be displayed at each place of business, on stationery (including e-mails), and on bills of exchange, etc., or the company and its officers will be liable to a fine.

registered office The official address of a UK company, to which all correspondence can be sent. Statutory registers are kept at the registered office, the address of which must be disclosed on stationery (including e-mails) and in the company's annual return. Any change must be notified to the *Registrar of Companies within 14 days and published in the *London Gazette.*

registered trader A *taxable person who has complied with the *registration for value added tax regulations.

register of charges **1.** The register maintained by the Registrar of Companies on which certain *charges must be registered by companies. A charge is created when a company gives a creditor the right to recover a debt from specific assets. The types of charge that must be registered in this way, and the details that must be given, are set out in the Companies Act. Failure to register the charge within 21 days of its creation renders it void, so that it cannot be enforced against a liquidator or creditor of the company. The underlying debt remains valid, however, but ranks only as an unsecured debt. **2.** A list of charges that a company must maintain at its registered address or principal place of business. Failure to do so may render the directors and company officers liable to a fine. This register must be available for inspection by other persons during normal business hours.

register of debenture-holders A list of the holders of *debentures in a UK company. There is no legal requirement for such a register to be kept but if one exists it must be kept at the company's registered office or at a place notified to the *Registrar of Companies. It must be available for inspection, to debenture-holders and shareholders free of charge and to the public for a small fee.

register of directors and secretaries A register listing the directors and the secretary of a UK company, which must be kept at its *registered office. It must state the full names of the directors and the company secretary, an address for each, the nationality of directors, particulars of other directorships held, the occupation of directors, and in the case of a public company, their dates of birth. If the function of director or secretary is performed by another company, the name and registered office of that company must be given. The register must be available for inspection by members of the company free of charge and it may be inspected by the public for a small fee. Under the Companies Act 2006 directors may include a service address, rather than their residential address, in the register that is seen by the public.

register of directors' interests A *statutory book in which a company must detail the interests of its *directors in the *shares and *debentures of the company. The register must be available for inspection during the *annual general meeting of the company.

register of interests in shares A *statutory book required to be maintained by public companies. Interests in shares disclosed to the company by those persons knowingly interested in 3% or more of any class of the voting share capital must be disclosed in the register. Investments held by a spouse, children under 18 years, and corporate bodies over which the person has control are added to the person's own interests.

register of members (share register) A list of the *members of a company, which all UK companies must keep at their *registered office or some other address notified to the *Registrar of Companies. It contains the names and addresses of the members, the dates on which they were registered as members, and the dates on which any ceased to be members. If the company has a share capital, the register must state the number and class of the shares held by each member and the amount paid for the shares. Entry in the register constitutes evidence of ownership. Thus, a shareholder who loses a share certificate can obtain a replacement from the company provided proof of identity is supplied. However, as legal rather than beneficial ownership is registered, it is not always possible to discover from the register who controls the shares. Currently, the register must be available for inspection by members free of charge for at least two normal office hours per working day; others may inspect it on payment of a small fee. Under the Companies Act 2006 public access to the register will be limited. The register may be rectified by the court if it is incorrect.

Registrar of Companies An official charged with the duty of registering all the companies in the UK. There is one registrar for England and Wales and one for Scotland. The registrar is responsible for carrying out a wide variety of administrative duties connected with registered companies, including maintaining the **register of companies** and the *register of charges, issuing certificates of incorporation, and receiving annual returns.

registration for value added tax An obligation on a person making taxable supplies to register for *value added tax if at the end of any month the amount of taxable supplies in the period of 12 months ending in that month exceeds the **registration threshold** of £68,000 (2009).

registration statement In the USA, a lengthy document that has to be lodged with the *Securities and Exchange Commission. It contains all the information relevant to a new *securities issue that will enable an investor to make an informed decision whether or not to purchase the security.

regressive tax A tax in which the rate of tax decreases as income increases. Indirect taxes fall into this category. For example, the poor spend a higher proportion of their incomes on VAT than the rich. *Compare* PROGRESSIVE TAX. *See also* FLAT TAX.

Regulatory News Service (RNS) A screen-based service operated by the *London Stock Exchange for the rapid dissemination of information on *listed companies.

reinsurance An agreement by which one insurer indemnifies another insurer in part, or in total, for the risks of a policy issued by that other insurer.

reinvestment rate The interest rate at which an investor is able to reinvest income earned on an existing investment.

REIT *See* REAL-ESTATE INVESTMENT TRUST.

related parties Under *Financial Reporting Standard (FRS) 8, two or more parties are considered to be related parties when at any time during the relevant *accounting period:
• one party has direct or indirect control of the other party;
• the parties are under common control from the same source;
• one party has influence over the financial and operating policies of the other party to the extent that the other party might be inhibited from pursuing its own separate interest at all times, or the parties in entering a transaction are subject to influence from the same source to such an extent that one of the parties to the transaction has subordinated its own separate interests.
From 1 January 2005 listed companies are required to observe *International Accounting Standard 24, Related Party Disclosures.

related party transactions The transfer of assets, liabilities, or the performance of services by, to, or for a *related party irrespective of whether a price is charged. Under *Financial Reporting Standard 8, companies should disclose in their *annual accounts information on related party transactions. These should also give the name of the party controlling the reporting entity and, if different, that of the ultimate controlling party, whether or not any transactions have taken place.
From 1 January 2005 listed companies are required to observe *International Accounting Standard 24, Related Party Disclosures.

relationship banking The establishment of a long-term relationship between a bank and its corporate customers. The main advantage is that it enables the bank to develop in-depth knowledge of a company's business, which improves its ability to make informed decisions regarding loans to the company. The company expects to benefit by increased support during difficult times. *See also* BILATERAL BANK FACILITY; SYNDICATED BANK FACILITY.

relationship capital *See* INTELLECTUAL CAPITAL.

relevance 1. The accounting principle that the financial information provided by a company should (a) be of such a nature that it is capable of influencing the decisions of users of that information, and (b) be provided in time to influence those decisions. To be relevant, information must either have predictive value or act as confirmation or correction of earlier expectations. The concept is defined in the Accounting Standards Board's *Statement of Principles and in *Financial Reporting Standard 18, Accounting Policies. It is also recognized in the International Accounting Standards Board's *Framework for the Preparation and Presentation of Financial Statements. 2. In decision making, the principle that the impact of a particular decision on the performance of an organization can only be determined by identifying those elements of cost or revenue that are relevant to the decisions made. *See* RELEVANT COST; RELEVANT INCOME.

relevant accounts The *accounts that should be used to determine the amount of *distributable profit of a company. These accounts are the most recent audited *annual accounts of the company, prepared in compliance with the Companies Act. If the accounts are qualified by the auditors (*see* QUALIFIED AUDIT REPORT), the auditors must state in their report whether they consider that the proposed distribution would contravene the Companies Act.

relevant cost An expected future cost that varies with alternative courses of action. Decision making involves choosing between such alternatives and to make the best choice a manager needs to identify the future cash flows for each decision. Costs that have already been incurred as a result of past decisions (*sunk costs) are not relevant for decision making. Likewise, a future cost that will not be changed by a decision is irrelevant to that decision. *See* DIFFERENTIAL ANALYSIS.

An understanding of relevant costs is particularly important for the following types of decision:
- special selling-price decisions;
- product-mix decisions when capacity constraints exist;
- decisions on replacement of equipment;
- outsourcing (make or buy) decisions;
- decisions on whether to drop a product or close a department.

EXAMPLE

A company manufactures doors. It has 10 doors in stock that have been difficult to sell as the design is not popular with customers. The doors were completed last year and the following costs have been identified by a manager:
- material costs   £100
- labour cost   £200
- overheads   £200

All of these costs were incurred last year. A new customer has offered to purchase the doors for a total of £400 if they can be modified by the fitting of specialist locks. These locks will have to be purchased at a cost of £100 and the labour cost of fitting them will be £60. Finally, the delivery cost of the doors will be £50. Before deciding whether to accept the customer's offer, managers will have to identify the relevant costs of having the doors modified.

Irrelevant costs
The costs incurred last year (material, labour, and overheads) are not relevant to the decision. They are examples of past (sunk) costs. The original costs are not avoidable and are common to all alternatives.

Relevant costs
The cost of the locks, the labour cost of fitting them, and the cost of delivery are differential cash flows that will be incurred if the doors are modified. They are therefore relevant costs.

The position can be summarized in table form as follows:

	Costs incurred to date (past costs) (£)	Costs if doors modified (£)	Relevant costs (£)
material costs	100	100	0
labour costs	200	200	0
overhead costs	200	200	0
specialist locks		100	100
labour cost of fitting locks		60	60
delivery		50	50
total cost	500	710	210

The total cost of £710 includes past costs and future costs. It is confusing and illogical to include both costs together. The relevant costs are the differential cash flows. The customer's offer to pay £400 for the doors should therefore be accepted, as it is greater than the relevant costs of £210. It would be wrong to reject the order by saying that the £400 offered by the customer is less than the total cost of £710.

relevant income (**relevant revenue**) An item of revenue that changes as a result of a proposed decision. An item of revenue that remains unchanged as the result of a particular decision is irrelevant to that decision.

relevant property trust From March 2006, any trust that is not an *interest-in-possession trust, an age *18–25 trust, or a trust established for the benefit of a bereaved minor is a relevant property trust for *inheritance tax purposes. A relevant property trust is taxed (i) on creation, (ii) whenever there is a distribution to a beneficiary, and (iii) on each tenth anniversary of the settlement (*see* TEN-YEAR CHARGE). Trusts established for charitable purposes or as part of a superannuation scheme are generally exempt from these charges. *See also* DISCRETIONARY TRUST.

relevant range The range of levels of activity between which valid conclusions can be drawn from the *linear cost functions normally associated with a *breakeven analysis. Outside this range it is recognized that the linear relationships between fixed costs, variable costs, and revenue do not apply.

relevant revenue *See* RELEVANT INCOME.

releveraging Increasing the level of debt in the *capital structure of a business. *See* LEVERAGE.

reliability The accounting principle that the financial information provided by a company should have the characteristics of faithful representation, neutrality, completeness, freedom from material error, and caution when prepared in uncertain conditions. The concept is defined in the Accounting Standards Board's *Statement of Principles and in *Financial Reporting Standard 18, Accounting Policies. It is defined in similar terms in the US Financial Accounting Standards Board's *Statement of Financial Accounting Concepts No. 2 and the International Accounting Standards Board's *Framework for the Preparation and Presentation of Financial Statements.

remainderman The recipient of the remainder (residue) of an estate after the expenses, specific legacies, and *inheritance tax have been paid.

remittance basis An individual *resident, but not domiciled, in the UK is subject to UK income tax and capital gains tax on a remittance basis during the first six years in which he is so resident (*see* NON-DOMICILED). For later years, the remittance basis is applied if the individual so elects and he or she pays a fee of £30,000 for the tax year (Finance Act 2008). When the remittance basis applies, income arising from a foreign source is only subject to UK income tax if it is remitted to the UK and gains arising on the disposal of a foreign asset are only subject to UK capital gains tax insofar as they are remitted. In general, a remittance for this purpose is a transfer of money; the import of goods purchased abroad is not a remittance until the goods are sold. In *Slattery* *v Moore Stephens* (2003), the High Court awarded damages against an accountancy firm for failing to advise a client of the tax saving available to him from the application of the remittance basis.

remitting bank *See* COLLECTING BANK.

remuneration **1.** A sum of money paid for a service given. *See also* AUDIT FEE. **2.** A salary.

remuneration committee In UK public companies, a committee of *non-executive directors who decide the pay of executive directors. Many such bodies were set up as a result of the *Greenbury Report of 1995. Under the *Combined Code on Corporate Governance they are now recommended for all public listed companies. *See also* AUDIT COMMITTEE.

renewal notice An invitation from an insurer to continue an insurance policy that is about to expire by paying the **renewal premium**. The renewal premium is shown on the notice; it may differ from the previous premium, either because insurance rates have changed or because the insured value has changed. Many insurers increase the insured value of certain objects automatically, in line with inflation.

rent A payment made for the use of land or property usually, but not necessarily, based on a *lease.

rent-a-room A tax relief for individuals who receive payment for letting furnished accommodation in their only or main residence. Income of up to £4250 is exempt from tax. *See* NON-TAXABLE INCOME.

renting back *See* LEASEBACK.

reorder level The number of units of a particular item of stock to which the balance can fall before an order for replenishment is placed. A **reorder-level system** is a stock-control system based on the principle that orders for the replenishment of items of stock are only placed when the balance of stock for a particular item falls to a predetermined level. The **reorder quantity** is the quantity ordered to replenish stock when the stock level falls to the reorder level.

reorganization costs The costs of restructuring a business. *Financial Reporting Standard 3, Reporting Financial Performance, requires that reorganization costs, if they have a material effect on the nature and focus of a reporting entity's operations, should be shown separately as an *exceptional item on the face of the *profit and loss account after operating profit and before interest, under continuing operations or *discontinued operations as appropriate.

repackaged perpetual debt *Perpetual debt that carries a high rate of interest for a number of years and then bears no further interest (or only a nominal amount). The value of the debt is therefore negligible and the issuer will normally transfer it to a friendly third party so that it can be redeemed for a token amount.

repairs and maintenance The revenue expenditure incurred in maintaining the assets of an organization in their original condition (as far as this is possible).

Any expenditure incurred in improving the assets would normally be regarded as *capital expenditure and therefore not repairs and maintenance.

repayment claim A claim made by a taxpayer for repayment of tax overpaid in the *fiscal year. This can occur if *basic rate tax is deducted at source from all or most of the taxpayer's income without any relief for *personal allowances.

replacement cost The cost of replacing an asset, either in its present physical form or as the cost of obtaining equivalent services. If the latter is lower in amount than the former, the conclusion is that the assets currently used by the company are not those it would choose to acquire in the market place. Replacement cost may be used to value tangible fixed assets and in some circumstances such *current assets as stock.

replacement cycle The period over which a product or *fixed asset will need to be replaced owing to obsolescence.

repo *See* SALE AND REPURCHASE AGREEMENT.

reportable segment A *business segment for which information is required to be disclosed. *See* SEGMENTAL REPORTING.

report and accounts *See* ANNUAL ACCOUNTS.

reporting accountant 1. An accountant or firm of accountants who report on the financial information provided in a *prospectus. They may or may not be the company's own auditors. It is usual for reporting accountants to have had previous experience of new issues and the preparation of prospectuses. *See* ACCOUNTANTS REPORT. **2.** An accountant or firm of accountants who submit a report to accompany the *annual accounts of a *small company stating that (a) the accounts are consistent with the accounting records of the company and the provisions of the Companies Act and (b) that the company is exempt from *statutory audit on the basis of its size. The reporting accountant may not be an officer or employee of the company in question. *See* AUDIT EXEMPTION.

reporting currency The currency used by an organization in its *financial statements.

reporting partner The partner in a firm of auditors who forms an *audit opinion on the *financial statements of a client company and signs and dates the *auditors' report after the financial statements have been formally approved by the directors of the company.

report of the auditor(s) *See* AUDITORS REPORT.

representation and warranty A clause in a loan agreement in which the borrower gives a contractual undertaking confirming certain fundamental facts. These will include the borrower's power to borrow and to give guarantees, as well as confirmation that it is not involved in any major litigation.

representative member The company within a group of companies that must account for the *output tax and *input tax for *value added tax of all the companies in the group and be responsible for the quarterly VAT return for the group. All the companies within the group have *joint and several liability for any VAT due.

repurchase agreement *See* SALE AND REPURCHASE AGREEMENT.

repurchase of own debt The buying back by a company of its own *debt at an amount different from the amount of the *liability shown in the *balance sheet. *Urgent Issues Task Force (UITF) Abstract 8 ruled that any difference on repurchase should be taken to the *profit and loss account, except in specified exceptional circumstances. UITF 8 has been superseded by *Financial Reporting Standard 4, Financial Instruments: Disclosure and Presentation.

repurchase transaction A form of discounting in which a corporation raises funds from a bank by selling negotiable paper to it with an undertaking to buy the paper when it matures (*see* NEGOTIABLE INSTRUMENT).

required rate of return The *rate of return, usually expressed as a percentage, that an organization determines is necessary before an investment can be regarded as profitable and therefore justified. In a *discounted cash flow appraisal the required rate of return may be expressed as an *internal rate of return and in other circumstances the *return on capital employed or *accounting rate of return may be regarded as appropriate. In general, it is better to estimate a range rather than a precise figure.

requisition A form that requires the recipient department or organization to carry out a specified procedure. Examples are *purchase requisition, *materials requisition, and manufacturing requisition (*see* PRODUCTION ORDER).

research and development costs The costs to a company of its research and development. *Statement of Standard Accounting Practice 13, Accounting for Research and Development, distinguishes between pure research, applied research, and development.
- **Pure research** is original investigation undertaken to gain new scientific or technical knowledge and understanding, but without any specific applications.
- **Applied research** is original investigation undertaken to gain new scientific or technical knowledge with a specific practical aim or objective.
- **Development** is the use of scientific or technical knowledge to produce new or substantially improved materials, devices, products, processes, systems, or services prior to the commencement of commercial production.

Under this Statement the costs of pure and applied research should be written off in the year in which they were incurred. In the case of development expenditure, if there is reasonable expectation that the product or process involved is likely to create future income, then the company has the option of capitalizing the development costs, thereby creating an *intangible asset to be shown on the *balance sheet. In all other circumstances development expenditure must be written off to the profit and loss account as soon as it is incurred.

The relevant *International Accounting Standard is IAS 38, Accounting for Research and Development Activities.

reservation of title A sale of goods in which the seller retains title to the goods sold, or any products made from them, or the resulting sale proceeds, until the buyer pays for the goods. *See also* ROMALPA CLAUSE.

reserve Part of the *capital of a company, other than the share capital, largely arising from retained profit or from the issue of share capital at more than its nominal value. Reserves are distinguished from *provisions in that for the latter there is a known diminution in value of an asset or a known liability, whereas reserves are surpluses not yet distributed and, in some cases (e.g. *share premium account or *capital redemption reserve), not distributable. The directors of a company may choose to earmark part of these funds for a special purpose (e.g. a reserve for obsolescence of plant). However, reserves should not be seen as specific sums of money put aside for special purposes as they are represented by the general net assets of the company. Reserves are subdivided into *retained earnings (revenue reserves), which are available to be distributed to the shareholders by way of dividends, and *undistributable reserves, which for various reasons are not distributable as dividends, although they may be converted into permanent share capital by way of a bonus issue.

reserve accounting The transfer of items directly to *reserves, rather than through the *profit and loss account. In certain instances this may be permitted, for example in making *prior-period adjustments.

reserve asset cost *See* MANDATORY LIQUID ASSETS.

resident A person living or based in the UK to whom one of the following applies for a given tax year:
• the person is present in the UK for 183 days or more during that year;
• the person pays substantial visits to the UK, averaging 90 days or more for four or more consecutive years;
• the person has accommodation available for use in the UK and one visit is made during the year. This does not apply if the taxpayer is working abroad full-time nor to individuals who come to the UK for a temporary purpose only.

A UK resident or **resident company** is subject to UK tax on income or capital gains arising anywhere in the world (unless this is disapplied by a *double taxation agreement). From 15 March 1988 companies incorporated in the UK are regarded as resident in the UK for corporation-tax purposes, irrespective of where the management and control of the company is exercised. HM Revenue and Customs has an International Manual that provides more details. *Compare* DOMICILE.

residual equity theory A theory that emphasizes the rights and interests of *ordinary shareholders on the grounds that they are the real owners of a business. The theory is reflected in the *earnings per share figure, which assists ordinary shareholders in making investment decisions. Residual equity theory falls between the *proprietary view and the *entity view.

residual income (residual return) The net income that a *subsidiary undertaking or division of an organization generates after being charged a percentage return for the book value of the net assets or resources deemed to be under its control. The residual income approach by the headquarters or holding company of an organization is to require the subsidiary or division to maximize its profits after the charge for the use of those assets. This approach is very similar to the *Economic Value Added technique.

EXAMPLE

A company has two divisions. The managers of Division X have to decide whether or not to invest £1,000,000 in a project with a profit before interest and tax of

£200,000. The managers of Division Y have a similar decision: whether to invest £1,000,000 in a project with a profit before interest and tax of £100,000.

The position can be summarized in the following table:

	Division X (£)	Division Y (£)
proposed investment	1,000,000	1,000,000
profit before interest and tax	200,000	100,000
cost of capital	15%	15%

Residual income can then be calculated as follows:

	Division X (£)	Division Y (£)
profit before interest and tax	200,000	100,000
cost of capital charge (15% of £1,000,000)	150,000	150,000
residual income	150,000	(50,000)

The calculation indicates that the residual income of Division X will increase if the project is accepted. Managers should therefore accept the investment. By contrast, the residual income of Division Y will decrease if the project is accepted. Managers should therefore reject the investment.

Note that it is possible to have a different cost of capital percentage for each division. For example, if investments in Division Y are seen as having a higher risk than investments in Division X, the company can increase the cost of capital charge for Division Y. This is one reason why managers may choose residual income rather than *return on capital employed (ROCE) when measuring the performance of divisions. Recent surveys suggest that even though residual income can be regarded as theoretically superior to ROCE, the latter is preferred by managers.

residual value *See* NET RESIDUAL VALUE.

resolution A binding decision made by the members of a company. If a motion is put before the members of a company at a general meeting and the required majority vote in favour of it, the motion is passed and becomes a resolution. A resolution may also be passed by unanimous informal consent of the members.

UK company law recognizes several different types of resolution, each of which has different requirements in terms of the number of days' notice given to members and the required voting majority. The type of resolution required to make a particular decision may be prescribed by the Companies Act or by the company's articles. For example, an *extraordinary resolution is required to wind up a company voluntarily and a *special resolution is required to change the company's articles of association. *See also* ELECTIVE RESOLUTION; ORDINARY RESOLUTION; WRITTEN RESOLUTION.

responsibility accounting A *management accounting system designed to provide information to all levels of an organization, based on the responsibility of the individual managers for particular items of expenditure or income. *Budgetary control and *standard costing are both examples of responsibility accounting.

responsibility centre A section or area of an organization the costs or income of which can be assigned to be the responsibility of a particular manager. A responsibility centre may be a department, *cost centre, division, *profit centre, or *investment centre. Its size will vary from company to company: the number of employees in a centre may be as low as ten or in the high hundreds.

restricted stock (**restricted securities**) Shares in a company, usually held by selected employees, that are not owned outright by the holder until a stated condition is fulfilled. This may be a time limit (i.e. the employee must remain with the company for a specified number of years) or an individual or collective performance target. Restricted stock has become a popular alternative to *share option schemes. *See also* SHARE INCENTIVE SCHEME.

restricted surplus *See* UNDISTRIBUTABLE RESERVES.

restrictive covenant 1. A clause in a contract that restricts the freedom of one of the parties in some way. Employment contracts, for example, sometimes include a clause in which an employee agrees not to compete with the employer for a specified period after leaving the employment. Such clauses may not be enforceable in law. 2. A clause in a contract affecting the use of land. *See* COVENANT.

retailer schemes Twelve special schemes used by retailers to identify and allocate the total amount of *taxable supplies made into the *value added tax categories standard-rated, special-rated, zero-rated, and exempt.

Retail Price Index (**RPI**) An index of the prices of goods and services in retail shops purchased by average households, expressed in percentage terms relative to a base year, which is taken as 100. For example, if 1987 is taken as the base year for the UK (i.e. average prices in January 1987 = 100), then in June 1948 the RPI stood at 9.7, and in September 2009 at 215.3. The RPI is published by the Office for National Statistics on a monthly basis and includes the prices of some 650 goods and services in 11 groups. The prices of the goods are checked every month and individual items and groups are weighted to reflect their relative importance. Weightings are regularly updated by the Family Expenditure Survey. The RPI can be used to calculate the real change in earnings and expenditure by deflating financial data, and is one of the standard measures of the rate of *inflation. *Compare* CONSUMER PRICE INDEX.

(((🌐))) SEE WEB LINKS
• RPI data

retained earnings (**retained profits**; **ploughed-back profits**; **retentions**) The *net profit available for *distribution, less any distributions made, i.e. the amount kept within the company. Retained earnings are recorded in the profit and loss reserve.

retention of title *See* ROMALPA CLAUSE.

retentions *See* RETAINED EARNINGS.

retirement relief Formerly, a relief from *capital gains tax given to persons disposing of business assets at or over 50 years of age, or earlier if retiring due to ill-health. From 1999 it was phased out in favour of *taper relief, which was itself replaced by *entrepreneurs' relief in April 2008.

return on assets An *accounting ratio expressing the amount of *profit for an *accounting period as a percentage of the *assets of a company.

return on capital employed (ROCE) An *accounting ratio expressing the *profit of an organization for an *accounting period as a percentage of the capital employed. It is probably one of the most frequently used ratios for assessing the performance of organizations. In making the calculation, however, there are a number of differing definitions of the terms used. Profit is usually taken as profit before interest and tax, while capital employed refers to fixed assets plus *current assets minus *current liabilities. Sometimes the expression **return on investment** (ROI) is used, in which case even greater care must be used in understanding the calculation of the separate items. Management may consider that profit before interest and tax, expressed as a percentage of total assets, is a useful measure of performance. Shareholders, however, may be more interested in taking profit after interest and comparing this to total assets less all liabilities. The ratio can be further analysed by calculating profit margins and *capital turnover ratios.

EXAMPLE

A company has three divisions, whose performance can be summarized in the following table:

Division	Operating profit (£)	Capital employed	Return on capital employed
North	240,000	1,000,000	24%
South	300,000	2,000,000	15%
West	400,000	2,000,000	20%

On the basis of the ROCE figures, the North Division appears to make the best use of its capital employed. ROCE highlights the benefits that managers can obtain by reducing their investments in current or fixed assets. However, it is important to emphasize that relying on a single *performance measure is not desirable and managers should use ROCE in conjunction with other measures. For example, ROCE is often compared to *residual income.

return on equity (ROE) The net income of an organization expressed as a percentage of its equity capital.

return on investment (ROI) *See* RETURN ON CAPITAL EMPLOYED.

return period The quarterly *accounting period for tax payable by companies, to 31 March, 30 June, 30 September, and 31 December. Larger companies are required to pay corporation tax in instalments based on their estimated liability for each period. If the end of the accounting period does not coincide with one of these dates, there are five return periods in the year. The year end identifies the fifth return period; e.g. for an accounting period to 31 May, the return periods would be 31 March, 31 May, 30 June, 30 September, and 31 December.

returns inwards (sales returns) Goods returned to an organization by customers, usually because they are unsatisfactory.

returns inwards book (sales returns book) The *book of prime entry used to record any returns of goods sold. Returns are posted to the individual debtor's account in the *debtors' ledger and the total returns are posted to the *debtors' ledger control account and returns inwards accounts in the *nominal ledger.

returns on investments and servicing of finance A heading required on *cash-flow statements by *Financial Reporting Standard 1, Cash Flow Statements, to show receipts resulting from the ownership of investments and payments to the providers of finance. Cash inflows include interest and dividends received, while cash outflows include interest and dividends paid and the interest element of *finance lease rental payments. The equivalent heading is required by *International Accounting Standard 7.

returns outwards Goods returned by an organization to its suppliers, usually because they are unsatisfactory.

returns outwards book The *book of prime entry used to record any returns to suppliers of goods purchased. Returns are posted to the individual creditor's accounts in the *creditors' ledger and the total returns are posted to the *creditors' ledger control account and returns outwards accounts in the *nominal ledger.

revalorization of currency The replacement of one currency unit by another. A government often takes this step if a nation's currency has been devalued frequently or by a large amount. The practice is usually associated with high rates of inflation. *Compare* REVALUATION OF CURRENCY.

revaluation An increase in the value of an asset to reflect its current market value. The asset cost account is debited and the *revaluation reserve is credited. Under the *alternative accounting rules, certain assets may be revalued.

revaluation account In a *partnership to which a new partner is admitted or if an existing partner dies or retires, *assets and *liabilities must be revalued to their current market value. The differences between historical values and the revaluations are debited or credited to the revaluation account. The balance on the revaluation account will represent a profit or loss on revaluation, which must be shared between the partners in the *profit-sharing ratio.

revaluation method A method of determining the *depreciation charge on a *fixed asset against profits for an accounting period. The asset to be depreciated is revalued each year; the fall in the value is the amount of depreciation to be written off the asset and charged against the profit and loss account for the period. It is often used for such depreciating assets as loose tools or a mine from which materials are extracted.

revaluation of assets A revaluation of the assets of a company, either because they have increased in value since they were acquired or because *inflation has made the balance-sheet values unrealistic. The Companies Act makes it obligatory for the directors of a company to state in the directors' report if they believe the value of land differs materially from the value in the balance sheet. The Act also lays down the procedures to adopt when fixed assets are revalued. The difference between the net book value of a company's assets before and after revaluation is shown in a revaluation reserve account or, more commonly in the USA, an **appraisal-surplus account** (if the value of the assets has increased). *Financial Reporting Standard 15, Tangible Fixed Assets, contains a requirement that valuations are kept up to date. The relevant *International Accounting Standard is IAS 16, Property, Plant and Equipment.

revaluation of currency An increase in the value of a currency in terms of gold or other currencies. It is usually made by a government that has a persistent balance of payments surplus. It has the effect of making imports cheaper but exports become dearer and therefore less competitive in other countries; revaluation is therefore unpopular with governments. *Compare* DEVALUATION; REVALORIZATION OF CURRENCY.

revaluation reserve account (asset revaluation reserve) The reserve account to which the *unrealized profit or loss on *revaluation must be taken when the *alternative accounting rules are used for the valuation of an asset. Companies have the option of choosing another name for this reserve if they wish. The revaluation reserve should be reduced to the extent that the amounts transferred to it are no longer necessary for the purpose of the valuation method used. The treatment for *taxation purposes of any amounts credited or debited to the revaluation reserve must be disclosed in a note to the accounts.

revenue 1. Any form of income. 2. Cost and income items that are either charged or credited to the *profit and loss account for an accounting period.

Revenue and Customs, HM The UK government department responsible for the care, management, and collection of direct and indirect taxes, *National Insurance contributions, and customs and excise duties within the UK. Its other responsibilities include the payment of *tax credits and child benefit. It is governed by a small board known as the Commissioners of Revenue and Customs, but the day-to-day administration is carried out by civil servants. Inspectors of Taxes are responsible for assessing taxes, which are collected by Collectors of Taxes (*see also* SELF-ASSESSMENT). A taxpayer can appeal against an inspector's assessment. HM Revenue and Customs was formed from a merger of the Board of Inland Revenue and the Board of Customs and Excise in April 2005. A Revenue and Customs Prosecution Office, responsible for the prosecution of all revenue and customs cases, was established at the same time.

(⊕) SEE WEB LINKS

- Website of HMRC provides details of all UK tax rates, codes, and allowances and facilities for making returns online

revenue bonds Loans in which the *principal and *interest are payable from the earnings of the project financed by the loan. They are sometimes issued in the USA by municipalities, to finance such projects as toll bridges.

revenue centre An area of an organization for which income is collected. Revenue centres are determined by individual organizations and they may be a function, department, section, individual, or any group of these that generates income. *Compare* PROFIT CENTRE.

revenue expenditure Expenditure written off to the *profit and loss account in the *accounting period in which it is made. Such expenditure is deemed to have been incurred by the revenue generated within that financial period.

revenue function A formula or equation representing the way in which particular items of income behave when plotted on a graph. For example, the most common revenue function is that for total revenue in the equation $y = bx$, where y is the total revenue, b is the selling price per unit of sales, and x is the number of units sold.

revenue management (yield management) The use of sophisticated computer systems to analyse consumer behaviour, forecast demand, and adjust pricing in order to maximize revenues. Revenue management is mainly applicable to industries in which resources are fixed and perishable, such as the travel and hospitality industries. A seat on an aeroplane, for example, must be filled by the time of take off or contribute nil revenue; companies therefore need to know the optimum moment at which to maximize the yield from a flight by offering unfilled seats at a discount. At the same time, the company will want to encourage early rather than late booking as the general rule and may devise price incentives accordingly. Revenue management attempts to optimize overall yield through a complex process of market segmentation, price discrimination (e.g. charging a different price for an airline ticket depending on when, where, and by whom it is bought), and differentiating the product (e.g. charging more or less for a ticket depending on what travel restrictions apply).

revenue recognition The process of recording *revenue in the accounts of an organization in the appropriate *accounting period. Revenue could be recognized at various points; for example, when an order is placed, on delivery of the goods, or on receipt of payment. It is essential to recognize revenue correctly to be able to calculate the appropriate amount of *profit for a financial period. Normally, revenue is recognized when the buyer assumes the significant risks and rewards of ownership and the amount of revenue must be capable of reliable measurement. However, the complexity of some business transactions may make it difficult to determine in which financial period revenue should be recognized.

revenue reserve A reserve that is not an *undistributable reserve: i.e. a reserve that is distributable.

revenue support grant (RSG) In the UK, central government funding of local authorities to supplement income from local taxes. The grant helps local authorities to maintain services and taxes at levels comparable to other authorities. It was formerly known as the **rate support grant**.

revenue transaction A transaction that is generally of a short-term nature and is only expected to benefit the current period. Revenue transactions appear in the *profit and loss account of the period.

reverse premium A cash payment made to a lessee as an encouragement to enter into a *lease agreement. Under *Urgent Issues Task Force, Abstract 12, such payments received by a lessee should be spread on a *straight-line basis over the lease term or, if shorter than the full lease term, over the period to the review date on which the rent is first expected to be adjusted to the prevailing market rate.

reverse takeover 1. The buying of a larger company by a smaller company. 2. The purchasing of a public company by a private company. This may be the cheapest way that a private company can obtain a listing on a stock exchange, as it avoids the expenses of a *flotation and it may be that the assets of the public company can be purchased at a discount. The majority of reverse takeovers in the UK are now transacted on the *Alternative Investment Market.

reversionary bonus A sum added to the amount payable on death or maturity of a with-profits policy for life assurance. The bonus is added if the life-assurance company has a surplus or has a profit on the investment of its life funds. Once a reversionary bonus has been declared it cannot be withdrawn if the policy runs to maturity or to the death of the insured. However, if the policy is cashed, the bonus is usually reduced by an amount that depends on the length of time the policy has to run.

Review Panel *See* FINANCIAL REPORTING REVIEW PANEL.

revision variance (planning variance) In *standard costing, a *variance that is expected to arise from the difference between a standard as originally set and the standard as modified to reflect changed circumstances (the *current standard). An *operational variance can then be calculated to measure how far the changed circumstances have had the predicted effect on performance.

revolving acceptance facility by tender (RAFT) An underwritten facility from a bank to place sterling *acceptance credits through the medium of a tender panel of eligible banks.

revolving bank facility (standby revolving credit) A loan from a bank or group of banks to a company in which the company has flexibility with regard to the timing and the number of *drawdowns and repayments; any loan repaid can be reborrowed subject to fulfilment of the conditions of the *committed facility. The facility can be a *bilateral bank facility or a *syndicated bank facility.

rights issue A method by which listed companies on a stock exchange raise new capital, in exchange for new shares. The name arises from the principle of *pre-emption rights, according to which existing shareholders must be offered the new shares in proportion to their holding of old shares (a **rights offer**). For example in a 1 for 4 rights issue, shareholders would be asked to buy one new share for every four they already hold. As rights are usually issued at a discount to the market price of existing shares, those not wishing to take up their rights can sell them in the market. *Compare* BOUGHT DEAL; VENDOR PLACING; SCRIP ISSUE.

rightsizing The restructuring and *rationalization of an organization to improve effectiveness and cut costs, without involving a full *downsizing operation, which can often be overdone. Rightsizing could include increasing the size of an organization to meet increased demand, but it is more often used as a euphemism for moderate and controlled downsizing.

ring-fence **1.** To allow one part of a company or group to go into receivership or bankruptcy without affecting the viability of the rest of the company or group. **2.** To assign a sum of money to a particular purpose so that it does not become part of the general resources of an organization.

risk-adjusted discount rate In *capital budgeting and portfolio management, the *discount rate used in calculations of *present value; it will reflect the level of risk embodied in the cash flows being considered.

risk-adjusted return on capital (RAROC) A measure of the performance of units within a bank or financial organization, be they managerial units, products, distributional units, or such treasury-based units as trading desks. It was developed by Bankers' Trust and the Bank of America in the 1980s. In its most common form RAROC allocates *capital at risk to a unit and divides that into the return obtained from the unit. The capital is allocated in terms of a *value-at-risk methodology. A refinement of this system is known as **RAROC 2020**.

risk analysis The measurement and analysis of the risk associated with financial and investment decisions. It involves the identification of risk, the classification of risks in regard to their impact and likelihood, and a consideration of how they might best be managed. Risk analysis is particularly important with *capital-expenditure decisions because of the large amount of capital usually required and the long-term nature of the projects.

risk-based audit An auditing technique that assesses the levels of risk attached to different areas of an organization's system and uses the results to devise audit tests. The purpose is to focus the audit on the areas of highest risk in order to improve the chances of detecting errors. *See also* AUDIT RISK; SYSTEMS-BASED AUDIT.

risk capital (venture capital) Capital invested in a project in which there is a substantial element of risk, especially money invested in a new venture or an expanding business. It is also used in buyouts by *private equity firms and employee or *management buy-outs (*see* BIMBO). Risk capital is normally invested in the equity of the company in the hope of a high return; it is not a loan (but *see* SHAREHOLDER DEBT).

risk-free rate of return The *rate of return on an investment that has no risk. The return on US and UK Treasury bills is often regarded as a very close approximation to this rate. The risk-free rate is an important concept in the *capital asset pricing model.

risk management A process that aims to help organizations understand, evaluate, and take action on all their risks. A private-sector organization will need to identify and evaluate the trade-off between risk and expected return and to choose the course of action that will help it to maximize its value. Risk management is also relevant to the public sector. Common forms of risk management include taking out insurance against possible losses and the use of *derivatives to *hedge against changes in interest rates, exchange rates, or other economic variables. A bank will always try to manage the risks involved in lending by adjusting the level of charges and interest rates to compensate for a percentage of losses.

risk premium (market-risk premium) The difference between the expected *rate of return on an investment and the *risk-free rate of return (e.g. on a government stock) over the same period. If there is any risk element at all, the rate of return should be higher than if no risk is involved. *See* CAPITAL ASSET PRICING MODEL.

ROCE Abbreviation for *return on capital employed.

ROE Abbreviation for *return on equity.

ROI Abbreviation for return on investment. *See* RETURN ON CAPITAL EMPLOYED.

rolling budget A budget that is regularly updated by adding a further budget period, such as a month or a quarter, while at the same time dropping out the earliest month or quarter as appropriate.

rollover relief A relief that enables a charge to *capital gains tax or *corporation tax to be deferred when the proceeds from the disposal of an asset are reinvested in a new asset. Any gain arising from the disposal of the new asset will be correspondingly increased (unless the gain is once more 'rolled over'). The relief is only available for the following types of asset: a building for the purposes of trade; any land used only for the purposes of trade; fixed *plant and machinery; ships, aircraft, and hovercraft; *goodwill; satellites, space stations, and space vehicles; milk quotas and potato quotas; ewe and suckler cow premium quotas; fish quotas; rights of a member of a Lloyd's Syndicate; oil licences.

Romalpa clause (retention of title) A clause included in a contract of sale in which the seller retains the title of the goods sold until they have been paid for. This is of importance to accountants as it may affect the ownership of stocks; it is essential to determine whether the commercial substance of a transaction rests ownership of an asset in the purchaser, irrespective of any legal agreement. This clause derives its name from the case of *Aluminium Industrie Vasseen BV v Romalpa Aluminium Ltd* (1976), which was concerned with the practice of selling goods subject to *reservation of title.

rotation of directors Under the articles of association of most UK companies, the obligatory retirement of one third of the directors each year (normally at the annual general meeting), so that each director retires by rotation every three years. Retiring directors may be re-elected.

round tripping The use of a bank overdraft facility to deposit funds in the money market at rates that exceed the cost of the overdraft. The practice is frowned upon by banks because they may be having to use the money market to fund their customers' overdrafts. This accounts for the name 'round tripping'.

royalty A payment made for the right to use the property of another person for gain. This is usually an *intellectual property, such as a copyright (e.g. in a book) or a patent (e.g. in an invention). A royalty may also be paid to a landowner, who has granted mineral rights to someone else, on sales of minerals extracted from the land. A royalty is regarded as a *wasting asset as copyrights, patents, and mines have limited lives.

RPB Abbreviation for Recognized Professional Body. *See* Designated Professional Body.

RPI Abbreviation for *Retail Price Index.

RQB Abbreviation for *Recognized Qualifying Body.

RSB Abbreviation for *Recognized Supervisory Body.

RSG Abbreviation for *revenue support grant.

running costs The expenditure incurred in order to carry out the operations of a fixed asset. Examples are power, maintenance, and consumable materials for a machine or fuel, oil, tyres, and servicing for motor vehicles.

running yield *See* yield.

SAC Abbreviation for *Standards Advisory Council.

SAEF Abbreviation for *Stock Exchange Automatic Execution Facility.

Sage A range of *business software packages provided by The Sage Group Ltd. As well as accounting, book-keeping, and payroll functions, these typically include applications for financial control, operations management, project costing, and customer relationship management.

sale and leaseback A transaction in which the owner of an asset sells it and immediately purchases back from the buyer the right to use the asset under a *lease. The lease may be a *finance lease or an *operating lease.

sale and repurchase agreement (repurchase agreement; repo) An arrangement in which an *asset is sold by one party to another on terms that provide for the seller to repurchase the asset under certain circumstances. Sale and repurchase agreements, which are examples of *off-balance-sheet finance, are dealt with by *Financial Reporting Standard 5, Reporting the Substance of Transactions; for financial assets, the relevant *International Accounting Standard is IAS 39, Financial Instruments: Recognition and Measurement. In a number of cases the agreement will in substance be that of a secured loan in which the seller retains the risks and rewards of ownership of the asset. In these cases the seller should show the original asset on the balance sheet, together with a *liability for the amounts received from the buyer.

sale or return Terms of trade in which the seller agrees to take back from the buyer any goods that he has failed to sell, usually in a specified period. Some retail shops buy certain of their goods on sale or return.

sales account An *account used to record cash and credit sales transactions resulting from the sale of goods or services.

sales budget A budget set for the sales function of an organization under a system of *budgetary control; it includes, inter alia, the *sales volumes and the *sales revenue to be achieved in a budget period. It will usually provide an analysis of the budgets by product, market segment, and by accounting period.

sales cost budget A budget that determines the expenditure the *sales function is allowed to incur in achieving the *sales volumes and *sales revenue budgets during a budget period. It includes such costs as sales personnel salaries, advertising expenditure, and promotional costs.

sales credit note A credit note sent by a seller to a customer to cancel, or partly cancel, an invoiced charge.

sales day book (sales journal; sold day book) The *book of prime entry in which an organization records the invoices issued to its customers for goods or services supplied in the course of its trade. Postings are made from this book to the personal accounts of the customers, while the totals of the invoices are posted to the sales account in the *nominal ledger.

sales discount *See* DISCOUNT.

sales forecast An estimate of future sales volumes and revenue. It is usually based on past trends and takes into account current and future directions, such as government regulations, economic forecasts, and industry conditions.

sales function The section of an organization responsible for selling its products and services. *See* FUNCTION.

sales invoice A document sent by the seller of goods or services to the buyer, detailing the amounts due, discounts available, payment dates, and such administrative details as the account numbers and credit limits.

sales journal *See* SALES DAY BOOK.

sales ledger *See* DEBTORS LEDGER.

sales ledger control account *See* DEBTORS LEDGER CONTROL ACCOUNT.

sales margin mix variance (sales mix profit variance) In *standard costing, the adverse or favourable *variance arising as a result of a difference between the actual mix of sales achieved and the *standard mix of sales. It is the difference between the actual total sales volume based on the actual mix by product and the actual total sales volume based on the budgeted mix by product, valued at the standard margin per product.

sales margin price variance (selling price variance) In *standard costing, the adverse or favourable *variance arising as a result of the difference between the actual sales revenue achieved and the actual sales quantities at budgeted or *standard selling prices.

sales margin volume variance (sales volume variance) In *standard costing, the adverse or favourable *variance arising as a result of the difference between the actual number of units sold and those budgeted, valued at the standard profit margin.

sales margin yield variance (sales margin quantity variance) In *standard costing, the adverse or favourable *variance arising as a result of the difference between the budgeted sales quantity and the actual sales quantity in budgeted proportions (*see* STANDARD MIX), valued at the standard profit margin per product.

sales mix The relative proportions of individual products that make up the total units sold.

sales mix profit variance *See* SALES MARGIN MIX VARIANCE.

sales returns 1. *See* RETURNS INWARDS. 2. A report on sales made in a period.

sales returns book *See* RETURNS INWARDS BOOK.

sales revenue The income arising from the sales of products or services.

sales tax A tax based on the selling price of goods. Such taxes are not now generally favoured, since they have a cascade effect, i.e. if goods are sold on from one trader to another the amount of sales tax borne by the ultimate buyer becomes too great. *Value added tax was largely designed to meet this objection.

sales values 1. The prices charged for items when they are sold. 2. A method of apportioning the *joint costs between the *joint products in *process costing. From the *sales revenue of each independent product, the costs of the independent processes are deducted to give a sales value of each joint product at the *separation point. The joint costs are then apportioned between the joint products, in proportion to their relative sales values.

sales volume The number of units sold of each product.

sales volume variance *See* SALES MARGIN VOLUME VARIANCE.

salvage value (scrap value) The *net residual value of an asset at the end of its useful life, when it is no longer suitable for its original use. Fixed assets, stock, or waste arising from a production process can all have a salvage value.

sample 1. A small group of items selected from a larger group (population) to represent the characteristics of the larger group. Samples are often used in auditing because it is not feasible to inspect all the available documentation; however, conclusions drawn from a sample always contain a sampling error and must be used with caution. The larger the sample, in general, the more accurate will be the conclusions drawn from it. In **quota sampling** the composition of the sample reflects the known structure of the whole population. An alternative sampling procedure is **random** or **probability sampling**, which ensures that every item in a particular population has an equal chance of selection. Auditors often make use of the form of random sampling known as *cluster sampling. *See also* ATTRIBUTES SAMPLING; JUDGMENTAL SAMPLING; STATISTICAL SAMPLING. 2. A small quantity of a commodity, etc., selected to represent the bulk of a quantity of goods. 3. A small quantity of a product, given to potential buyers to enable them to test its suitability for their purposes.

samurai bond A bond issue, denominated in yen, made in the Japanese domestic market by a foreign (non-Japanese) issuer; it is thus the Japanese equivalent of a *Yankee bond.

Sandilands Committee A committee chaired by Sir Francis Sandilands, set up in 1975 by the UK government to consider the most appropriate way to account for the effects of inflation in the published accounts of companies. It recommended *current-cost accounting in preference to the *current purchasing power accounting favoured by the accountancy bodies. With the subsequent reduction in inflation, current-cost accounting was largely abandoned during the 1980s and 1990s.

sans recours *See* WITHOUT RECOURSE.

São Paulo Stock Exchange The most important of the stock exchanges in Brazil. Often known as **Bovespa** (an abbreviation of the full Portuguese name), it is now the largest exchange in Latin America.

Sarbanes–Oxley Act 2002 (Sarbox; Sox) Wide-ranging US legislation aiming to establish and enforce new standards in corporate governance, financial reporting, and auditing. The Act was passed in response to several high-profile corporate scandals, most notoriously the Enron scandal of 2001.

SAS **1.** Abbreviation for *Statement of Auditing Standards (UK). **2.** Abbreviation for *Statement on Auditing Standards (USA).

save-as-you-earn (SAYE) A method of making regular savings (not necessarily linked to earnings), which carries certain tax privileges. This method has been used to encourage tax-free savings in building societies or *National Savings and also to encourage employees to acquire shares in their own organizations.

savings account A bank or building-society account designed for the investment of personal savings. The rates tend to be higher than old-fashioned *deposit accounts and interest-bearing *current accounts. Some accounts offer instant access to funds, while others require that notice be given, typically 30, 60, or 90 days.

savings and loan association (S&L) The US equivalent of a UK *building society. It usually offers loans with a fixed rate of interest and has greater investment flexibility than a UK building society.

savings ratio The ratio of savings by individuals or households to disposable income, usually expressed as a percentage. Variations in the savings ratio reflect the changing preferences of individuals between present and future consumption. The ratio may be affected by cultural and demographic factors as well as by economic factors (most obviously, the rate of inflation).

savings related share option scheme An approved *share option scheme established by an employer for the benefit of executives or other employees. HM Customs and Revenue has detailed rules regarding the income tax and capital gains tax chargeable to individuals benefiting from such a scheme. *See also* EMPLOYEE SHARE OWNERSHIP PLAN; EMPLOYEE SHARE OWNERSHIP TRUST; SHARE INCENTIVE SCHEME.

SAYE Abbreviation for *save-as-you-earn.

scale effect *See* ECONOMIES OF SCALE.

scalpers Traders in financial markets who deal very frequently for small gains and may only hold a position for a few minutes.

SCARF Abbreviation for *systems control and review file.

scatter diagram A graph on which observations are plotted on the y-axis for events on the x-axis. For example, the wages incurred (y-axis) for each level of activity (x-axis) would produce a scatter graph from which a relationship can be established between the two variables, say by *linear regression, as an aid to predicting *cost behaviour.

schedule **1.** The part of legislation that is placed at the end of a UK Act of Parliament and contains subsidiary matter to the main sections of the act. **2.** In the UK, one of several schedules formerly used to classify various sources of income for *income-tax purposes and in some cases still applicable for *corporation tax. Before reform of the income-tax system in 2003–05 the broad classification was: Schedule A, rents from property in the UK; Schedule D, Case I, profits from trade; Case II, profits from professions or vocations; Case III, interest not otherwise taxed; Case IV, income from securities outside the UK;

Case V, income from possessions outside the UK; Case VI, other annual profits and gains; Schedule E, Cases I, II, and III, emoluments of offices or employments (the cases depending on the residential status of the taxpayer); Schedule F, dividends paid by UK companies. From April 2003 Schedule E was replaced by the three headings (i) employment income, (ii) pensions income, and (iii) social security income. From April 2005 the remaining schedules were replaced for income-tax purposes by the four headings (i) trading income, (ii) property income, (iii) savings and investment income, and (iv) miscellaneous income. Schedules A, D, and F were, however, retained for corporation tax purposes. **3.** Working papers submitted with tax returns or tax computations. **4.** A plan for undertaking some enterprise, especially one that details the timing of events.

scheme of arrangement **1.** An agreement between a company and its members or creditors to restructure the business in some way; the procedure is mainly used when the company is in financial difficulties or to effect a *takeover. It must be approved by a majority in number (holding 75% in value) of those creditors or members at separate meetings and sanctioned by the court. All creditors or members involved in the scheme are bound by it, although the court can make special provision for those who dissent. Agreements with company creditors can often be more conveniently concluded by a *voluntary arrangement. **2.** An agreement between a debtor and his or her creditors to arrange the debtor's affairs to satisfy the creditors. The debtor usually agrees to such an arrangement in order to avoid bankruptcy (see feature BANKRUPTCY LAW on p. 52). If the arrangement is agreed when no bankruptcy order has been made, it may take the form of either an ordinary private contract or a *deed of arrangement. An arrangement agreed after a bankruptcy order has been made is governed by the statutory provisions relating to bankruptcy (*see* VOLUNTARY ARRANGEMENT).

scope economies (economies of scope) The increases in efficiency and sales that can result from producing, distributing, and marketing a range of products, as opposed to a single product or type of product. *Bancassurance is often seen as an example of scope economies.

scorekeeping One of the functions of *management accounting in which the performance of the managers and operators is monitored and reported in accounting statements to the appropriate levels of management.

scrap **1.** What is left of an asset at the end of its useful life, which may have a *salvage value. **2.** The waste arising from a production process, which may have a *salvage value.

scrap value *See* SALVAGE VALUE.

scrip The certificates that demonstrate ownership of *stocks, *shares, and *bonds (capital raised by sub*scrip*tion), especially the certificates relating to a *scrip issue.

scrip issue (bonus issue; capitalization issue; free issue) The issue of new share certificates to existing shareholders to reflect the accumulation of profits in the reserves of a company's balance sheet. It is thus a process for converting money from the company's reserves into issued capital. The shareholders do not pay for the new shares and appear to be no better off. However, in a 1 for 3 scrip issue, say, the shareholders receive one new share for every three existing shares they own. This automatically reduces the price of the shares by 25%, catering to the preference of shareholders to hold lower-priced shares rather than heavy shares; it also encourages them to hope that the price will gradually climb to its former value, which will, of course, make them 25% better off. In the USA this is known as a **stock split**.

SDLT Abbreviation for *stamp duty land tax.

SDRT Abbreviation for *stamp duty reserve tax.

SEAQ Abbreviation for *Stock Exchange Automated Quotations System.

seasonality The seasonal variability of certain economic or financial factors, for example unemployment or commodity prices.

SEATS Abbreviation for *Stock Exchange Alternative Trading Service.

SEC Abbreviation for *Securities and Exchange Commission.

secondary auditor The *auditor of a subsidiary company who is not also the auditor of the parent company. *See also* PRIMARY AUDITOR.

secondary market A market in which existing securities are traded, as opposed to a *primary market, in which securities are sold for the first time. In most cases a *stock exchange largely fulfils the role of a secondary market, with the flotation of new issues representing only a small proportion of its total business. However, it is the existence of a flourishing secondary market, providing *liquidity and the spreading of risks, that creates the conditions for a healthy primary market.

second-hand goods scheme An arrangement in which the *value added tax due on second-hand goods sold is calculated on the trader's margin, rather than the total selling price of the goods. This applies regularly with sales of second-hand cars. In order to qualify, the trader must retain detailed records of car purchases and sales, which must be available for inspection at a VAT control visit.

second-tier market A market for investors to buy and sell shares in new and developing companies. Companies have access to new sources of finance and do not have to follow the complex rules that the main market requires. The *Alternative Investment Market of the *London Stock Exchange is an example of a second-tier market.

secret reserve *See* HIDDEN RESERVE.

secured creditor A *creditor who holds either a fixed or a floating *charge over the assets of a debtor.

secured liability A debt against which the borrower has provided sufficient assets as security to safeguard the lender in case of non-repayment.

Securities and Exchange Commission (SEC) A US government agency established in 1934 to protect investors by regulating behaviour in the securities markets. Each year the SEC brings between 400–500 civil enforcement actions against individuals and companies that break the securities laws. The SEC is also responsible for monitoring and controlling corporate financial reporting and auditing practices. In this aspect of its remit it follows, to a very large extent, the accounting and auditing pronouncements of bodies organized by the public accounting profession, such as the *Financial Accounting Standards Board and the *Auditing Standards Board.

(⊕) SEE WEB LINKS

• Website of the SEC

Securities and Futures Authority Ltd (SFA) The *Self-Regulating Organization formed from the merger of The Securities Association Ltd (TSA) and the Association of Futures Brokers and Dealers Ltd (AFBD) in April 1991. Its responsibilities were taken over by the *Financial Services Authority in December 2001.

Securities and Investment Board (SIB) A regulatory body set up by the *Financial Services Act 1986 to oversee London's financial markets. Each market (e.g. the stock exchange, life assurance, unit trusts) had its own *Self-Regulating Organization (SRO), which reported to the SIB. It was superseded by the *Financial Services Authority in December 2001.

securitization (asset securitization) The process of turning assets into *securities. Generally this involves an arrangement in which one party (the originator) sells a portfolio of assets, such as house mortgages or bank loans, to a *special purpose vehicle (the issuer), who finances the purchase by packaging the cash flows from these assets as tradable financial instruments (securities), which are sold to investors. The arrangement may be a form of *off-balance-sheet finance and now falls under the regulations of *Financial Reporting Standard 5, Reporting the Substance of Transactions, and *International Accounting Standard 39, Financial Instruments: Recognition and Measurement. The prevalence of complex derivative products based on the securitization of subprime mortgages (*see* SUBPRIME LENDING) was widely seen as a key factor in the global financial crisis of 2008–09. *See also* STRUCTURED FINANCE; TOXIC ASSETS.

security 1. An asset or assets to which a lender can have recourse if the borrower defaults on the loan repayments. In the case of loans by banks and other moneylenders the security is sometimes referred to as *collateral.

2. A financial asset, including shares, government stocks, debentures, bonds, unit trusts, and rights to money lent or deposited. It does not, however, include insurance policies. *See also* BEARER SECURITY; FIXED-INTEREST SECURITY; GILT-EDGED SECURITY; LISTED SECURITY.

3. Precautions taken in e-commerce to ensure that the following attributes are safeguarded:

• **Authentication**. Are parties to a transaction who they claim to be? This is ensured by using *digital signatures.

• **Privacy and confidentiality**. Is transaction data protected? The consumer may want an anonymous purchase. Are all non-essential traces of a transaction removed from the public network and have all intermediary records been eliminated?

• **Integrity**. Are the messages sent complete? Checks are needed to ensure that messages have not been corrupted.

• **Non-repudiability**. Could the sender deny sending the message? It is essential that measures are in place to protect against repudiation.

seed capital The small amount of initial capital required to fund the research and development necessary before a new company is set up. The seed capital should enable a persuasive and accurate business plan to be drawn up.

segmental reporting **1.** The disclosure in the *annual accounts and report of certain results of major business and geographic segments of a diversified group of companies. Segmental reporting is required by company law, the *stock exchange, and *Statement of Standard Accounting Practice (SSAP) 25. The argument for segmental reporting is that the disclosure of profitability, risk, and growth prospects for individual segments of a business will be of use to investors. Under SSAP 25 companies should disclose, for both *business segments and *geographic segments, turnover, profit or loss before tax, minority interests, extraordinary items, and net assets. *See also* ORIGIN OF TURNOVER.
2. The approach in *management accounting in which the financial and quantitative performance of each definitive part of an organization is reported to both the management of the business segment and of the organization as a whole.

SEHK Abbreviation for Stock Exchange of Hong Kong. *See* HONG KONG STOCK EXCHANGE.

self-assessment A system that enables taxpayers to assess their own *income tax and *capital gains tax liabilities for the year. Major changes to the UK system occurred in the year 1996–97, since when a self-assessment section has been contained in the *tax return, in addition to the part requiring details of *taxable income, *chargeable gains, and claims for *personal allowances. At present the self-assessment is voluntary; if the taxpayer prefers to let HM Revenue and Customs calculate his or her liability, then the tax return must be submitted by September 30 following the end of the year of assessment, rather than the usual January 31. The introduction of self-assessment was accompanied by the Revenue being granted extensive audit powers to enquire into any tax return.

(⊕) SEE WEB LINKS
• Guide to self-assessment from the HMRC website

self-assessment for companies A scheme for the self-assessment of tax by companies. In the UK, self-assessment of *corporation tax was introduced for all companies with an accounting period ending after 1 July 1999. Tax returns must be completed and filed within 12 months of the end of the accounting period. Smaller companies must pay their tax liability within nine months of the end of the accounting period; large companies must make payments on account in advance of this date.

(⊕) SEE WEB LINKS
• Guide to corporation tax self-assessment from the HMRC website

self-employed taxpayers Persons who are not employees and who trade on their own account. They are taxed on the profits of their trades rather than by *PAYE and their *National Insurance contributions differ from those of employees.

Self-Employment Individuals Retirement Act *See* KEOGH PLAN.

Self-Regulating Organization **(SRO)** One of several organizations set up in the UK under the *Financial Services Act 1986 to regulate the activities of investment businesses and to draw up and enforce specific codes of conduct. By 1995 the SROs recognized by the *Securities and Investment Board, to whom they reported, had been reduced to three: the *Securities and Futures Authority Ltd (SFA), the *Investment Management Regulatory Organization (IMRO), and the *Personal Investment Authority (PIA). All regulatory functions of SROs were taken over by the *Financial Services Authority as of December 2001.

self supply The *value added tax charge on a commercial building, which is used for an exempt purpose, on the grant of an interest in the building. *Output tax is charged on the land and the building costs. *Input tax is allowed on the building costs. The self supply is due to be assessed and paid within three months of the initial occupation.

selling overhead (selling costs) The expenses incurred by an organization in carrying out its selling activities. These would include salaries of sales personnel, advertising costs, sales commissions, etc.

selling price variance *See* SALES MARGIN PRICE VARIANCE.

semi-fixed cost (stepped cost) An item of expenditure that increases in total as activity rises but in a stepped, rather than a linear, function (*see* LINEAR COST FUNCTION). For example, the costs of one supervisor may be required for a particular range of activity, although above this level the cost of an additional supervisor would be incurred.

semi-variable cost An item of expenditure that contains both a *fixed-cost element and a *variable-cost element. Consequently, when activity is zero, the fixed cost will still continue to be incurred. For example, in the UK the cost of gas is made up of a standing charge plus a cost per unit consumed; therefore while the consumption of gas varies with production the fixed standing charge will still be incurred when production is zero.

senior capital Capital in the form of secured loans to a company (*see* SECURED CREDITOR; SECURED LIABILITY). In the event of a liquidation, the senior capital is repaid before the *shareholders' equity.

sensitivity analysis A form of analysis used in approaches to business problems, in which possible changes to the variables are subjected to the decision-making technique to examine the range of possible outcomes and to determine the sensitivity of the projected results to these changes. For example, in a *discounted cash flow calculation possible changes to interest rates, cash flows, and timing may be built into the calculation to determine the sensitivity of the project to each change.

separable assets and liabilities *See* IDENTIFIABLE ASSETS AND LIABILITIES.

separate assessment Before April 1990, an election that could be made by one party to a marriage in the UK enabling each party to pay his or her own tax. Unlike an election for *separate taxation of wife's earnings, this saved no tax. Husband and wife are now subject to *independent taxation.

separate-entity concept *See* ACCOUNTING ENTITY.

separate taxation of wife's earnings An election available before April

1990, in which both parties to a marriage agreed to treat the wife's earnings separately from the husband's, usually as a means of reducing tax. Spouses' earnings are now treated separately (*see* INDEPENDENT TAXATION).

separation point (split-off point) In *process costing, the point at which the *by-products or the *joint products separate and are subsequently processed independently of each other.

serial bonds *Bonds that mature in instalments, rather than on one maturity date.

Serious Fraud Office (SFO) A body established in 1987 to be responsible for investigating and prosecuting serious or complex frauds in England, Wales, and Northern Ireland. It is part of the UK criminal justice system. Serious and complex fraud cases can go straight to the Crown Court without committal for trial. That court can hold preparatory hearings to clarify issues for the jury and settle points of law.

((⊕)) SEE WEB LINKS
• Website of the SFO

SERPS Abbreviation for State Earnings-Related Pension Scheme. *See* STATE SECOND PENSION.

service An economic good consisting of human worth in the form of labour, advice, managerial skill, etc., rather than a *commodity. **Services to trade** include banking, insurance, transport, etc. **Professional services** encompass the advice and skill of accountants, lawyers, architects, business consultants, doctors, etc. **Consumer services** include those given by caterers, cleaners, mechanics, plumbers, etc. Industry may be divided into extractive, manufacturing, and service sectors. The **service industries** make up an ever increasing proportion of the national income.

service contract (service agreement) A contract between an employer and a director or other very senior employee. Service contracts must be kept at the registered office of a company and be open to inspection by members of the company. The Companies Act 2006 prohibits service contracts that give an employee guaranteed employment for more than two years, without the company having an opportunity to break the employment as and when it needs to. This measure prevents directors with long service agreements from suing companies for loss of office in the event of a takeover or reorganization. The 2006 Act also broadened the definition of a service contract to include a *contract for services as well as a *contract of employment. *See also* COMPENSATION FOR LOSS OF OFFICE; GOLDEN PARACHUTE.

service cost centre (indirect cost centre; service department; support cost centre) A *cost centre to which costs are allocated or apportioned in *absorption costing; though the service cost centre is necessary to carry out the production process, it is incidental to it and does not handle the *cost unit. Examples of service cost centres are stores, canteens, and boiler houses.

service department *See* SERVICE COST CENTRE.

set-off An agreement between the parties involved to set off one debt against another or one loss against a gain. A banker is empowered to set off a credit balance on one account against a debit balance on another if the accounts are in the same name and in the same currency. It is usual, in these circumstances, for the bank to issue a **letter of set-off**, which the customer countersigns to indicate agreement. A letter of set-off is also needed if the accounts are not in the same name, e.g. differently named companies in the same group.

SETS Abbreviation for *Stock Exchange Trading System.

settled property Property that is included in an *interest-in-possession trust. A person entitled to benefit from the settled property is known as the life tenant. When the estate of the life tenant is assessed for *inheritance tax, the value of the settled property is included, provided the property does not comprise excluded property. The inheritance tax attributable to the settled property is payable by the trustees of the interest-in-possession trust and this is shown separately in the inheritance-tax computation of the life tenant. Further information regarding this complex topic can be obtained from HM Revenue's Inheritance Tax Manual.

Settlement Code A set of statutory provisions under which income arising from property that has been gifted is taxed as if it were income of the donor and not of the donee. Broadly, the provisions apply whenever there is a gift and the circumstances are such that it is possible for either income or capital to pass back to the donor at a later date. They thus apply to an outright gift, as well as to a gift into *trust. The Settlement Code is designed for three purposes. The first is to attempt to ensure that a trust cannot be used as a piggy bank, in which income can be taxed at a lower rate than that which applies to the settlor, but is then passed back to the settlor. The second is to restrict income-splitting opportunities within the family between parents and minor children. The third is to restrict the possibility of income being assigned to a person subject to a lower rate of tax.

settlement day The day on which trades are cleared by the delivery of the securities or foreign exchange.

set-up time The time taken to prepare a machine, process, or operation to carry out production. It may involve such operations as tool setting, calibration, and the initialization of the production process.

Seventh Company Law Directive (Seventh Accounting Directive) A directive approved by the European Commission in 1983 and implemented in the UK by the Companies Act 1989 concerning *consolidated financial statements prepared by groups. It has been superseded by the *Company Reporting Directive of 2006.

several liability *See* JOINT AND SEVERAL LIABILITY.

severe long-term restrictions Restrictions that hinder the exercise of the rights of a *holding company over the assets or management of a *subsidiary undertaking. Severe long-term restrictions may be used as grounds for excluding a subsidiary from *consolidation; if it is so excluded, a subsidiary should be treated as a fixed-asset investment. *See also* EXCLUSION OF SUBSIDIARIES FROM CONSOLIDATION.

SFA Abbreviation for *Securities and Futures Authority Ltd.

SFAC Abbreviation for *Statement of Financial Accounting Concepts.

SFAS Abbreviation for *Statement of Financial Accounting Standards.

SFLG Abbreviation for *Small Firms Loan Guarantee.

SFO Abbreviation for *Serious Fraud Office.

shadow advance corporation tax A system applying to any unrelieved surplus *advance corporation tax (ACT) on 6 April 1999, when ACT was abolished. It preserved the right to carry forward surplus ACT but did not result in any reduction in the *corporation tax liability for periods after 6 April 1999. Companies were given the choice of opting out of shadow ACT and writing off unrelieved surplus ACT at 6 April 1999.

shadow director A person in accordance with whose instructions the directors of a company are accustomed to act although that person has not been appointed as a director. A shadow director influences the running of the company and some provisions of the Companies Act, including *wrongful trading and the regulation of loans to directors, relating to directors also extend to shadow directors.

shadow price The *opportunity costs that arise in the solution to a *linear programming model.

shallow discount bond A bond issued in a *primary market at a price exceeding 90% of its face value, i.e. a bond in which the discount does not exceed 10%. *Compare* DEEPLY DISCOUNTED SECURITY.

sham transaction A transaction in which the parties intend to create one set of rights and obligations but perform acts or enter into documents that they intend should give other parties (often HM Revenue and Customs) the appearance of creating different rights and obligations. Tax benefits arising from sham transactions may be denied by the courts.

Shanghai Stock Exchange (SSE) The main stock market of the People's Republic of China. Its roots go back to the late 19th century but it was established in its present form in 1990. It is now the fifth largest stock exchange in the world by market capitalization. The main indicator is the SSE Composite Index.

share One of a number of titles of ownership in a company. Most companies are limited by shares, enabling investors to limit their liability if the company fails to the amount paid for (or owing on) the shares. A share confers on its owner a legal right to part of the company's profits (usually by payment of a *dividend) and to any voting rights attaching to that share (*see* VOTING SHARES; A SHARES). Companies are obliged to keep a public record of the rights attaching to each class of share. The common classes of shares are: *ordinary shares, which have no guaranteed amount of dividend but carry voting rights; and *preference shares, which receive dividends (and/or repayment of capital on winding-up) before ordinary shares, but which have no voting rights. Shares in public companies may be bought and sold in an open market, such as a stock exchange. Shares in a private company are generally subject to restrictions on sale, such as that they must be offered to existing shareholders first or that the directors' approval must be sought before they are sold elsewhere. *See also*

CUMULATIVE PREFERENCE SHARE; DEFERRED ORDINARY SHARE; FOUNDERS SHARES; FULLY PAID SHARE; PARTLY PAID SHARE; REDEEMABLE SHARES; SHARES OUTSTANDING.

share capital That part of the finance of a company received from its owners (i.e. its members or *shareholders) in exchange for *shares. *See also* AUTHORIZED SHARE CAPITAL; CALLED-UP SHARE CAPITAL; ISSUED SHARE CAPITAL; PAID-UP SHARE CAPITAL.

share certificate A document that provides evidence of ownership of shares in a company. It states the number and class of shares owned by the shareholder and the serial number of the shares and is usually signed by at least one director and the company secretary. It is not a negotiable instrument. *See* BEARER SECURITY.

shareholder An owner of shares in a limited company or limited partnership. A shareholder is a member of the company.

shareholder debt A risk-bearing equity that is treated as debt for tax purposes (i.e. interest paid is tax deductible). Shareholder debt is a feature of the highly leveraged funding arrangements associated with *private equity firms.

shareholders' equity (shareholders' funds) **1.** The *share capital and *reserves of a company. Formerly, *Financial Reporting Standard (FRS) 4, Capital Instruments, required that share capital be split into *equity and *non-equity shares. The latest regulations are found in FRS 25, Financial Instruments: Disclosure and Presentation, and International Accounting Standards 32 and 39. **2.** The market value of a company's equity shares.

shareholders' perks Benefits offered by a company to its shareholders as a reward for their loyalty. The benefits are given in addition to dividends and are tax-free.

shareholder value An approach to business planning that places the maximization of the value of shares to those who hold them other business objectives. Normally, shareholder value can be increased in three ways: dividend payments, appreciation in the value of the shares, and cash repayments. However, this focus has been widened by companies buying back shares to increase earnings and the demerging of parts of a group in order to unlock the value of individual components by means of a separate flotation. Shareholder value can also be influenced by maximising *economic value, either by undertaking positive *present-value decisions or by running the business in such a way as to create a surplus above the market costs of funding. The shareholder-value objective has sometimes been criticized as being too narrow and contrary to the longer-term interests of other *stakeholder groups.

shareholder value analysis (SVA) A method for valuing the entire *equity in a company. SVA assumes that the value of a business is the *net present value of its future cash flows, discounted at the appropriate *cost of capital. Once the value of a business has been calculated in this way, the next stage is to calculate shareholder value using the equation:

shareholder value = value of business – debt.

This method was first developed by Alfred Rappaport in the 1980s. The key difference between traditional financial accounting and SVA is that the latter recognizes the *time value of money. The traditional *balance sheet and *profit and loss account report on the past performance of a company is not helpful when measuring the change in value of the company. See also *value driver.

Share Incentive Plan (SIP) A plan set up by a British company, and approved by HM Revenue and Customs, under which a trustee acquires and holds shares for the benefit of employees. There are significant tax advantages as long as various conditions are met, the chief being that the SIP must be open to all employees and executive directors. *See also* EMPLOYEE SHARE OWNERSHIP TRUST.

share incentive scheme Any scheme in which employees who achieve personal or group performance targets are rewarded with shares in the company. There are many different types of scheme. *See* EMPLOYEE SHARE OWNERSHIP PLAN; EMPLOYEE SHARE OWNERSHIP TRUST; RESTRICTED STOCK; SAVINGS RELATED SHARE OPTION SCHEME; SHARE INCENTIVE PLAN; SHARE OPTION.

share issued at a discount A share issued at a price (the *issue price) below its *par value. The discount is the difference between the par value and the issue price. It is illegal to issue shares at a discount in the UK.

share issued at a premium A share issued at a price (the *issue price) above its *par value. The premium is the difference between the issue price and the par value. Except in special circumstances, the premium must be credited to a *share premium account. *See also* SHARE PREMIUM.

share option 1. A benefit sometimes offered to employees, especially new employees, in which they are given an option to buy shares in the company for which they work at a favourable fixed price or at a stated discount to the market price. The difference between the value of the share acquired (or its sale proceeds) and the amount paid to exercise the option is subject to income tax. The arrangement under which certain Revenue-approved share option schemes enabled the employee to pay capital gains tax rather than income tax on any gains was ended by the Finance Act 2006. **2.** *See* OPTION.

share premium The amount payable for shares in a company and issued by the company itself in excess of their nominal value (*see* NOMINAL PRICE). Share premiums received by a company must be credited to a *share premium account, which cannot be used for paying dividends to the shareholders, although it may be used to make *scrip issues.

share premium account The account to which any *share premium must be credited. The balance on the share premium account may be used for specified purposes:
• the issue of *bonus shares;
• the writing-off of preliminary expenses;
• the writing-off of underwriting commissions;
• the provision of a premium to be paid on the redemption of *debentures;
• the provision of a premium to be paid on the redemption or purchase of *share capital, subject to certain limits.

The share premium account may not be used to write off *goodwill on consolidation. Relief from the creation of a share premium account is available in specified circumstances (*see* MERGER RELIEF).

share register *See* REGISTER OF MEMBERS.

shares outstanding (outstanding shares) The issued *share capital of a company less any shares that have been repurchased by the company. It includes shares not available to the general public, such as those held by officers of the company or reserved as part of an employee *share incentive scheme.

share splitting The division of the share capital of a company into smaller units. The effect of a share split is the same as a *scrip issue although the technicalities differ. Share splits are usually carried out when the existing shares reach such a high price that trading in them becomes difficult.

share transfer (stock transfer) A change in the ownership of a share or stock. Formerly, a **stock transfer form** had to be executed by the seller of registered securities to legalize such a transaction on the London Stock Exchange. The whole process can now be carried out instantaneously in electronic form, using the *CREST system.

share warrant *See* WARRANT.

shell company **1.** A non-trading company, with or without a stock-exchange listing, used as a vehicle for various company manoeuvres or kept dormant for future use in some other capacity. **2.** A company that has ceased to trade and is sold to new owners for a small fee to minimize the cost and trouble of setting up a new company. Some business brokers register such companies with the sole object of selling them to people setting up new businesses. The name and objects of such a company can be changed for a small charge. **3.** A name-plate company set up in a *tax haven.

shirkah *See* ISLAMIC FINANCE.

short-form audit report In the USA, a standard *auditors' report that conforms to the short-form reporting requirements of the *Securities and Exchange Commission and the *American Institute of Certified Public Accountants. The first paragraph of the report indicates what the auditor has done and the second paragraph gives the findings.

short position A position held by a dealer in securities, commodities, currencies, etc., in which sales exceed holdings because the dealer expects prices to fall, enabling the shorts to be covered at a profit. *Compare* LONG POSITION.

short-termism Any policy that aims to maximize current profits rather than long-term development and wealth. For example, cutting back on *research and development reduces immediate costs but may lead to products becoming obsolescent in the future. A company may well experience problems of this kind if managers' salaries or bonuses are linked to short-term results. Likewise the share price for a company may become volatile if projects vary from year to year. Institutional and individual shareholders often overreact to a company's short-term results and policies, causing the company to lose the longer-term focus that is ultimately in the interests of all *stakeholders.

SIAS Abbreviation for *Statement on Internal Auditing Standards.

SIB Abbreviation for *Securities and Investment Board.

SIC Abbreviation for Standard Interpretations Committee. *See* INTERNATIONAL FINANCIAL REPORTING INTERPRETATIONS COMMITTEE.

sight draft *See* DOCUMENTARY DRAFT.

significant influence An influence by one company on the financial and operating policy decisions of another company (including *dividend policy) in which it has an interest. The influence does not need to amount to control. *See also* ASSOCIATED UNDERTAKING; PARTICIPATING INTEREST.

simple interest *See* INTEREST.

simplex method (simplex algorithm) A method of obtaining a *linear programming solution by producing a series of tableaux. The technique, a step by step iterative process, tests a number of feasible solutions in turn until the final optimal solution is obtained. It lends itself to computer applications.

simplified financial statements Simplified versions of the *annual accounts and report intended for readers who do not possess sophisticated financial knowledge. The financial information may be made easier to understand by using simple financial terminology, showing the information in the forms of graphs and diagrams, providing fuller explanations, and reducing the amount of information. One form of simplified financial statement is the *employee report, which is intended for employees and not covered by legislation; another form is the *summary financial statement intended for shareholders and subject to legislation. *See* INFORMATION OVERLOAD; UNDERSTANDABILITY.

simulation A financial modelling technique that considers the likely outcomes of different hypothetical circumstances. Uncertainty may be modelled by the use of random numbers, as in a *Monte Carlo simulation, or worst cases by the use of *stress testing.

SIN Abbreviation for stores issue note. *See* MATERIALS REQUISITION.

single-capacity system *See* DUAL-CAPACITY SYSTEM.

single-entry book-keeping A *book-keeping system that only records one aspect of each transaction, i.e. either a debit or a credit. *Compare* DOUBLE-ENTRY BOOK-KEEPING.

Single Market The concept of a single integrated market that underlies trading in the European Union, as codified in the **Single European Act** 1986, which was introduced in 1987 with a target date of 31 December 1992 for completion. The Single Market came into force on 1 January 1993 with between 90% and 95% of the necessary legislation enacted by all member countries. In practice, however, some of its terms have taken considerably longer to implement. The measures covered by the legislation include:
- the elimination of frontier controls (the full measures have been repeatedly delayed);
- the acceptance throughout the market of professional qualifications;
- the acceptance of national standards for product harmonization;
- open tendering for public supply contracts;
- the free movement of capital between states;
- a reduction of state aid for certain industries;
- the harmonization of VAT and excise duties throughout the market.

single property ownership trust (SPOT) A single property trust; shares in the trust entitle their holder to a direct share of the property's income and capital. A form of *securitization, a share in a SPOT is similar to a *property income certificate (PINC).

sinking fund A holding by a borrower or the borrower's agent of the borrower's own bonds, purchased in the market or otherwise acquired to meet future redemption commitments. The reason may be a requirement of the loan agreement or it may be due to *defeasance.

SIP Abbreviation for *Share Incentive Plan.

situs The place in which an *asset is held to be located. The location determines the proper law to be applied in identifying the rights and liabilities associated with the asset. For *capital gains tax, the disposal of a foreign situs asset does not give a charge to UK capital gains tax if the person making the disposal is not domiciled within the UK, has been in the UK for less than seven years, or has opted (and paid the fee for) *remittance basis, and the proceeds of the disposal are not remitted to the UK. For *inheritance tax, an asset with a foreign situs is an excepted asset.

sleeping partner A person who has capital in a *partnership but takes no part in its commercial activities. He has all the legal benefits and obligations of ownership and shares in the profits of the partnership in accordance with the provisions laid down in the partnership agreement.

slush fund A fund that is used by an individual, political organization, or company for illegal purposes. For example, a company may have a slush fund for bribing potential customers.

small company Under UK company law, a private company that satisfies at least two of the following criteria for the current and preceding financial year:
• its *net worth does not exceed £2.8 million;
• its *turnover does not exceed £5.6 million;
• the average number of employees does not exceed 50.
A company that is in its first financial year may still qualify as a small company if it falls within these limits. Alternatively, if the company has qualified in the two preceding financial years, it may qualify.

Certain small companies may prepare accounts for their members under the special provisions of the Companies Act. In addition, they may prepare and deliver *abbreviated accounts to the Registrar of Companies.

Some small companies with a turnover of less than £1 million (£250,000 for companies that are charities) and assets of less than £1.4 million can also claim total exemption from *statutory audit. A company with a turnover of between £1 million and £5.6 million (and balance-sheet total of not more than £2.8 million) may also take advantage of the small company audit exemption, but will need an audit exemption report.

If a company is a member of a *group containing a public company, a banking or insurance company, or an authorized person under the Financial Services Act 1986, it is not eligible for the exemptions for small companies.

((⊕)) SEE WEB LINKS
• Further details on filing and audit exemptions from the Companies House website

Small Firms Loan Guarantee (SFLG) A UK government scheme introduced in 1980 that guarantees 75% of a company's overdraft for a 2% premium. The bank must accept the risk for the balance of 25%. The scheme is now available to all *small companies and *medium sized companies.

small group A *group that meets two out of three of the following criteria for the current and preceding year, or the two preceding financial years:
• its *net worth should not exceed £2.8 million net or £3.6 million gross;
• its *turnover should not exceed £5.6 million net or £6.72 million gross;
• the average number of employees should not exceed 50.
If a group is in its first financial year, it may still qualify if it falls within these limits.

Under the Companies Act, a parent company is not required to prepare *consolidated financial statements for a financial year in which the group headed by that parent qualifies as a small group. A small group may file *abbreviated accounts instead of full accounts with the *Registrar of Companies.

A group containing a public company, a banking or insurance company, or an authorized person under the Financial Services Act 1986 is ineligible for the exemptions for small groups. *Compare* MEDIUM-SIZED GROUP.

smart card A plastic card that contains a microprocessor that stores and updates information, typically used in performing financial transactions. Unlike an ordinary *debit card or *cash card a smart card memorizes all transactions in which the card is used. Other uses include storing a person's medical records.

Smith Report A report on the role of *audit committees produced by a panel under Sir Robert Smith; it was published with the *Higgs Report on non-executive directors in 2003. The findings of both reports were included in revisions made to the *Combined Code on Corporate Governance.

smurfing Slang for the practice of dividing a large transaction into numerous much smaller transactions, usually for the purpose of *money laundering. Because the individual payments are below the threshold at which financial institutions are required to report them, the attention of regulatory and law-enforcement agencies can often be avoided in this way. Owing to the threat of international terrorism, however, banks have become increasingly alert to any suspicious pattern of activity. The name alludes to the small identical-looking cartoon characters, the Smurfs. A more formal term is **structuring a deposit**.

SNIF Abbreviation for short-term *note issuance facility.

social accounting issues Issues that concern the impact of an entity on society, both within the organization and externally. Social accounting issues may include charitable donations of equipment and time, education initiatives (such as sponsorships and research funding), product safety, community involvement, employment of disadvantaged groups, and the provision of sports equipment or sponsorship. Environmental issues that are often also included under this heading include energy conservation and control of pollution. *See* SOCIAL RESPONSIBILITY REPORTING.

social audit An *audit of the impact of an organization on society. For

example, an *environmental audit is one kind of social audit. *See also* SOCIAL
RESPONSIBILITY REPORTING.

socially responsible investment *See* ETHICAL INVESTMENT.

social responsibility reporting (corporate social reporting) The reporting
of *social accounting issues by a business. These may be discussed in the
*annual accounts and report or form the basis of a separate report. Social
responsibility costs are the costs to the business of e.g. equipment donated,
sponsorship given, or charitable donations. The monetary quantification of
social benefits is much harder to measure and necessarily subjective. Owing to
the concerns of consumers, investors, and other stakeholders, companies are
increasingly obliged to be environmentally and socially conscious. *See also*
GREEN REPORTING; SOCIAL AUDIT.

soft currency A currency that is not freely convertible and for which there is
only a *thin market. *Compare* HARD CURRENCY.

soft landing The situation in which an economy slows down but does not go
into a recession. The term was first used in astronautics journals of the late 1950s
to describe a safe moon landing.

soft loan A special type of government loan in which the terms and conditions
of repayment are more generous (or softer) than they would be under normal
finance circumstances. For example, the interest rate might be less and the
repayment term might be for a longer period.

software The programs used with a computer, together with their
documentation, as opposed to the physical parts of the computer system
(*hardware). A distinction is made between systems software, or those programs
that control the functioning of the computer itself, and *applications software,
such as accounting or *audit software, which is designed to serve a particular
specialized function. *See* BUSINESS SOFTWARE PACKAGE.

sold day book *See* SALES DAY BOOK.

sold ledger *See* DEBTORS LEDGER.

sole practitioner A *sole proprietor who has a professional practice as an
accountant, solicitor, etc.

sole proprietor An individual who runs an unincorporated business on his or
her own. Generally, a sole proprietor of a business is known as a **sole trader** and
a sole proprietor of a professional practice is known as a *sole practitioner.

solicitors' accounts Accounts prepared under the Solicitors' Account Rules,
a key feature of which is that money held on behalf of clients is accounted for
separately from the money owned by the practice.

Solomons Report **1.** *Prospectus for a Profession* (1974), a report by Professor
David Solomons, which deals with the education and training of accountants.
2. *Guidelines for Financial Reporting Standards* (1989), another report by the
same author, which sets out a *conceptual framework for financial accounting.

solvency **1.** The financial state of a person or company that is able to pay all debts as they fall due. **2.** The amount by which the assets of a bank exceed its liabilities.

SONIA Acronym for Sterling Overnight Index Average, a *reference rate computed as a weighted average of sterling overnight funding rates in the interbank market. *Compare* EONIA; EURONIA. *See* OVERNIGHT RATE.

SORP Abbreviation for *Statement of Recommended Practice.

sort code A sequence of numbers on a cheque or a bank card that serves to identify the branch holding the account.

source and application of funds (source and disposition of funds) A statement describing how a business has raised and used its funds for a specified period. Sources of funds are typically trading profits, issues of shares or loan stock, sales of fixed assets, and borrowings. Applications are typically trading losses, purchases of fixed assets, dividends paid, and repayment of borrowings. Any balancing figure represents an increase or decrease in *working capital. Formerly, a statement of source and application of funds (a **funds flow statement**) was required by *Statement of Standard Accounting Practice 10, Statements of Source and Application of Funds, to be produced by a company if its turnover or gross income was above a specified threshold. SSAP 10 was superseded by *Financial Reporting Standard 1, Cash Flow Statements, which replaced the requirement for a funds flow statement with a cash flow projection.

source document The first document to record a transaction.

sovereign risk *see* POLITICAL CREDIT RISK.

sovereign wealth fund (SWF) An investment fund that is owned by a sovereign nation and managed by a central bank, state pension fund, or official investment company. Most such funds originated in foreign-exchange reserves built up from the sale of commodity exports (notably oil). The growing size and influence of SWFs attracted much comment in the late 2000s, when sovereign funds acquired major stakes in many Western banks and financial institutions. Most of the world's largest SWFs belong to developing nations (e.g. Abu Dhabi, Singapore, Saudi Arabia, Kuwait) but important funds are also held by Norway, Russia, and Australia.

Sox Abbreviation for the *Sarbanes–Oxley Act 2002.

S2P Abbreviation for *State Second Pension.

Special Commissioners A body of civil servants who are specialized tax lawyers appointed to hear appeals against assessments to income tax, corporation tax, capital gains tax, and inheritance tax. Hearings are informal and appellants may present their own case or be represented. *See also* GENERAL COMMISSIONERS.

special dividend (extra dividend) A single irregular *dividend payment. It is usually made after an especially profitable year but is sometimes associated with the restructuring of companies.

special purpose vehicle (SPV) A legal entity established for the sake of a single transaction, for example in the *credit enhancement of a *securitization.

special resolution A *resolution of the members of a company that must be approved by at least 75% of the members to be valid. Members must have been given at least 21 days' notice of the meeting at which the resolution is proposed and the notice of the meeting must give details of the special resolution. *See also* ORDINARY RESOLUTION; EXTRAORDINARY RESOLUTION.

specific bank guarantee An unconditional guarantee from the *Export Credits Guarantee Department to a UK bank enabling that bank to finance an exporter's medium-term credit to an export customer without recourse; the arrangement is known as **supplier credit** in contrast to the buyer credit under which the bank finances the overseas buyer to pay the exporter on cash terms.

specific order costing *See* JOB COSTING.

spend management A systematic attempt to optimize a company's spending by achieving best value for money in every area of its expenditure. This is to be distinguished from simple cost cutting, which often achieves only short-term benefits. Spend management begins with an analysis of current spending behaviour and develops a strategic approach integrating such areas as sourcing, procurement, contract management, supply-chain logistics, and a company's invoicing and payment processes. Specialized software is now available.

split-off point *See* SEPARATION POINT.

spoilage *See* WASTE.

sponsor The financial institution, usually a merchant bank or investment bank, that handles the *flotation of a company. It will supervise the preparation of the *prospectus and make sure that the company is aware of the benefits and obligations of being a public company.

SPOT Abbreviation for *single property ownership trust.

spot market A market that deals in commodities or *foreign exchange for immediate delivery. Immediate delivery in foreign currencies usually means within two business days. For commodities it usually means within seven days. *Compare* FORWARD DEALING; FUTURES CONTRACT.

spread **1.** The difference between the buying and selling price made by a *market maker on the stock exchange. **2.** The diversity of the investments in a *portfolio. The greater the spread of a portfolio the less volatile it will be. **3.** The simultaneous purchase and sale of commodity futures (*see* FUTURES CONTRACT) in the hope that movement in their relative prices will enable a profit to be made. This may include a purchase and sale of the same commodity for the same delivery, but on different commodity exchanges, or a purchase and sale of the same commodity for different deliveries.

spreadsheet A computer application used for tabular calculations. A spreadsheet display consists of a large number of cells arranged in rows and columns. Generally, columns are labelled by a letter, or combination of letters, and rows are labelled by numbers. Each cell in the array has a unique identification: A1, A2, etc., B1, B2, etc. The user can enter text, numbers, or formulas into individual cells. The formulas can be used to perform calculations on values in other cells. For example, A1*100/B1 gives the value in cell A1 and expresses it as a percentage of the value in cell B1. A formula of the type sum (A1:A20) adds all the values in the cells from A1 to A20. Values and formulas can be copied from a single cell to a block of cells. In this way it is possible to set up complex calculations for accounting or financial modelling purposes. Spreadsheet programs generally have a facility for producing graphs and charts automatically from the data. Widely used spreadsheets include Excel, Lotus 1-2-3, and Quattro Pro.

SPV Abbreviation for *special purpose vehicle.

square position In financial trading, an *open position that has been covered or hedged.

SRN Abbreviation for stores returns note. *See* MATERIALS RETURNS NOTE.

SRO Abbreviation for *Self-Regulating Organization.

SSAP Abbreviation for *Statement of Standard Accounting Practice.

SSE Abbreviation for *Shanghai Stock Exchange.

SSP 1. Abbreviation for *statutory sick pay. **2.** Abbreviation for *State Second Pension.

stag A person who applies for shares in new issues in the hope that the price when trading begins will be higher than the *issue price. Often measures will be taken by the issuers to prevent excessive stagging; it is usually illegal for would-be investors to attempt to obtain large numbers of shares by making multiple applications. Issuers will often scale down share applications to prevent such quick-profit taking, e.g. by ballot.

stagflation A combination of slow economic growth with rising prices. The UK and the USA experienced stagflation for the first time in the 1970s.

staggered directorships A measure used in the defence against unwanted takeover bids. If the company concerned resolves that the terms of office served by its directors are to be staggered and that no director can be removed from office without due cause, a bidder cannot gain control of the board for some years, even with a controlling interest in the share capital. *See* POISON PILL.

stakeholder pension scheme In the UK, a type of low-cost pension available from April 2001. Employers with five or more employees have to make a stakeholder pension available to their staff. Stakeholder pensions are bought from authorized financial institutions, such as insurance companies, banks, and building societies. The pension providers can only charge a maximum of 1% of the value of the pension fund each year to manage the fund, plus costs and charges. Any extra services and any extra charges not provided for by law, such as advice on choosing a pension or life assurance cover, must be optional. All stakeholder schemes will accept contributions of as little as £20, payable weekly, monthly, or at less regular intervals. The scheme must be run by trustees or by an authorized stakeholder manager.

stakeholders All those with interests in an organization; for example, as *shareholders, employees, suppliers, customers, or members of the wider community (who could be affected by the social or environmental consequences of an organization's activities). Stakeholders may be users of the *annual accounts and report of the organization and dependent to some degree on its financial position and performance. **Stakeholder theory** is an approach to business that attempts to incorporate the interests of all stakeholders in a business, as opposed to the view that a firm is responsible only to its owners (*see* SHAREHOLDER VALUE). It thus attempts to adopt an inclusive rather than a narrow approach to business responsibility.

stale cheque A cheque that, in the UK, has not been presented for payment within six months of being written. The bank will not honour it, returning it marked 'out of date'.

stamp duty A tax collected by stamping the legal documents giving effect to certain transactions: the rate of duty is ½% of the consideration given, the charge always being rounded up to the nearest multiple of £5. Since 1 December 2003 stamp duty proper has been charged solely on traditional stampable documents relating to shares and securities (including bearer instruments). A transfer of shares or securities that is made without a stampable document (i.e. electronically) is charged to *stamp duty reserve tax. A transfer of land is now charged to *stamp duty land tax.

stamp duty land tax (SDLT) A tax charged on the consideration given for the sale of land in the UK. The rate is 1% of the purchase price of properties between £175,000 and £250,000, and 3% of the price of those between £250,000 and £500,000. Above this figure, it is 4%. Interest is charged on late payment and penalties are imposed that parallel those for income tax and corporation tax.

stamp duty reserve tax (SDRT) A tax levied on the transaction when a shareholding is transferred without a document, or when the document is kept outside the UK. The majority of transactions on UK exchanges are now electronic and 'paperless'. Like *stamp duty, stamp duty reserve tax is charged on the consideration given, not on the market value of the shareholding.

standard cash flow pattern In a *discounted cash flow calculation, the situation in which the projected cash flows are made up of an initial cash outflow followed by subsequent cash inflows over the life of the project, there being no net cash outflows in subsequent years. Such patterns are rare in practice.

standard cost In *standard costing systems, a predetermined unit cost of a product or service. It is important to emphasize that standard cost is a unit cost concept.

standard cost allowance Under a *standard costing system, the level of expenditure allowed to be incurred for variable costs, taking into account the actual levels of activity achieved. For example, the standard cost allowance for *direct materials is obtained from the actual number of units produced multiplied by the *standard direct materials cost per unit.

standard cost card In a *standard costing system, a record showing how the *standard cost of each product is built up. The standard cost card records the standard quantities of material and the standard prices, the standard labour times, and the standard rates of pay, as well as the fixed and variable overhead rates per unit of product. Traditionally, this information was kept on a series of cards but it is now invariably held in computer databases.

standard costing A system of *cost ascertainment and control in which predetermined *standard costs and income for products and operations are set and periodically compared with actual costs incurred and income generated in order to establish any *variances. Standard costing systems are very expensive to develop and maintain; they were also designed for traditional manufacturing systems in which direct labour and direct materials are the most important costs. Recent years have seen a decline in the use of such systems as companies become less labour intensive.

standard direct labour cost In *standard costing, a standard cost derived from the standard time allowed for the performance of an operation and the *standard direct labour rate for the operators specified for that operation.

standard direct labour rate A predetermined rate of pay for *direct labour operators used for establishing *standard direct labour costs in a *standard costing system; it provides a basis for comparison with the actual direct labour rates paid.

standard direct materials cost In *standard costing, a standard cost derived from the standard quantity of materials allowed for the production of a product and the *standard direct materials price for the materials specified for that product.

standard direct materials price In *standard costing, a predetermined price for *direct materials used for establishing *standard direct materials costs in order to provide a basis for comparison with the actual direct material prices paid.

standard fixed overhead cost In *standard costing, a standard cost derived from the standard time allowed for the performance of an operation or the production of a product and the standard fixed overhead absorption rate per unit of time for that operation or product.

standard hour A measure of production (not time) that represents the amount of work, number of units produced, etc., that can be achieved within an hour under normal conditions. It is used to calculate the *efficiency ratio and efficiency variances (*see* DIRECT LABOUR EFFICIENCY VARIANCE; OVERHEAD EFFICIENCY VARIANCE).

Standard Interpretations Committee *See* INTERNATIONAL FINANCIAL REPORTING INTERPRETATIONS COMMITTEE.

standard marginal costing In a *marginal costing system, a system of *cost ascertainment and control in which predetermined standards for marginal costs and income generated for products and operations are set and periodically compared with actual marginal costs incurred and income generated in order to establish any *variances.

standard materials usage A predetermined quantity of materials to be used in the production of a product, which is ultimately compared with the actual quantity of material used to provide a basis for *material control. The difference between standard and actual usage is used in *standard costing to calculate the *direct materials usage variance.

standard minute One sixtieth of a *standard hour.

standard mix 1. The predetermined proportions in which a mixture of different materials are intended to be used in a manufacturing process. It is set as a standard for the purposes of calculating the *direct materials mix variance and *direct materials yield variance. 2. The budgeted total volume of sales of an organization expressed in predetermined proportions of its range of related products. It is set as a standard for the purposes of calculating the *sales margin mix variance and *sales margin yield variance.

standard operating cost The total of all the *standard cost allowances for the actual level of activity achieved by an organization.

standard operating profit The *budgeted revenue from an operation less the *standard operating cost.

standard operator performance *See* STANDARD PERFORMANCE.

standard overhead cost A *standard cost for the fixed and/or variable overhead of an operation derived from the standard time allowed for the performance of the operation or the production of a product and the standard overhead *absorption rate per unit of time for that operation or product.

standard performance (**standard operator performance**) A predetermined level of performance for an operator or a process used as a basis for determining *standard overhead costs. For example, standard performance may be expressed as the number of units of production per *standard hour, *standard minute, or per working day.

standard price *See* STANDARD PURCHASE PRICE; STANDARD SELLING PRICE.

standard production cost The *production costs of products and operations calculated from predetermined levels of performance and cost in order to provide a yardstick against which actual production costs can be compared for the purposes of *cost ascertainment and control.

standard purchase price A predetermined price set for each commodity of *direct material for a specified period. These prices are compared with the actual prices paid during the period in order to establish *direct materials price variances in a system of *standard costing.

standard rate 1. The rate of *value added tax applied to all items sold by *taxable persons that are not specified as either *exempt supplies, *zero-rated goods and services, or taxable at a special rate. The rate for 2008–09 is 17.5%, which has been the rate since 1 April 1991. Previously the standard rate was 15%. 2. The marginal rate of tax for most taxpayers. *See* BASIC RATE OF INCOME TAX.

standard rate of pay A predetermined rate of pay set for each classification of labour for a period. These rates are compared with the actual rates paid during the period in order to establish *direct labour rate of pay variances in a system of *standard costing.

Standards Advisory Council (**SAC**) A body of experts who advise the *International Accounting Standards Board (IASB) on priorities in setting accounting standards. The members also inform the IASB of the implications of proposed standards for users and preparers of financial statements and may give other advice to the IASB or the trustees of the *International Accounting

S

Standards Committee Foundation (IASC Foundation). The IASB is required to consult the SAC in advance of decisions on major projects and the trustees of the IASC Foundation must consult the SAC in advance of making any changes to its constitution. See feature INTERNATIONAL STANDARD SETTERS on p. 248.

(⊕) SEE WEB LINKS
- SAC section of the IASB website

standard selling price A predetermined selling price set for each product sold for a specified period. These prices are compared with the actual prices obtained during the period in order to establish *sales margin price variances in a system of *standard costing.

standard time The time allowed to carry out a production task in a *standard costing system. It may be expressed as the standard time allowed or alternatively, when expressed in *standard hours, as the output achieved.

standard variable overhead cost A *standard cost derived from the standard time allowed for the performance of an operation or the production of a product and the standard variable overhead *absorption rate per unit of time for that operation or product.

standby revolving credit *See* REVOLVING BANK FACILITY.

standing data Information held on file in a computer for long-term use because it does not often change. An example is the names and addresses of clients.

star *See* BOSTON MATRIX.

starting rate of income tax In the UK, a former rate of *income tax below the *basic rate of income tax; it replaced the lower rate in 1999. The starting rate of 10% was abolished from April 2008.

start-up costs The initial expenditure incurred in the setting up of an operation or project. The start-up costs may include the capital investment costs plus the initial revenue expenditure prior to the start of operations.

State Earnings Related Pension *See* STATE SECOND PENSION.

statement of affairs **1.** A document that must be prepared by a debtor after a bankruptcy order has been made against him except when the bankruptcy order was made on his own petition or when the court excuses him. It gives details of his assets, debts and liabilities, the names and addresses of his creditors, and what securities they hold. The debtor must send the statement to the official receiver, and the creditors are entitled to inspect it. **2.** *See* VOLUNTARY LIQUIDATION.

Statement of Auditing Standards (SAS) Any of a series of statements issued by the Auditing Practices Board (APB) on basic principles and essential procedures in auditing. Auditors were required to comply with an SAS, except where otherwise stated in the SAS concerned, in the conduct of any audit of *financial statements for periods commencing before 15 December 2004. For periods commencing on or after that date, *International Standards on Auditing (UK and Ireland) are to be applied.

statement of cash flows The usual *International Financial Reporting Standards term for a *cash-flow statement.

statement of changes in equity (SOCE) The usual *International Financial Reporting Standards term for the *reconciliation of movements in shareholders' funds.

statement of changes in financial position A US term for a *cash-flow statement. *See* ALL-FINANCIAL RESOURCES CONCEPT.

Statement of Financial Accounting Concepts (SFAC) In the USA, any of the reports issued by the *Financial Accounting Standards Board to identify the fundamental concepts of *financial accounting and reporting. They reflect the *objectives of financial statements.

Statement of Financial Accounting Standards (SFAS) In the USA, any of the statements detailing the *financial accounting and reporting requirements of the *Financial Accounting Standards Board. These *accounting standards are *generally accepted accounting principles and should be followed by accountants responsible for the preparation of *financial statements.

statement of financial position The usual *International Financial Reporting Standards term for a *balance sheet.

statement of movements in shareholders' funds *See* RECONCILIATION OF MOVEMENTS IN SHAREHOLDERS FUNDS.

Statement of Principles A document first issued by the *Accounting Standards Board in 1995 in an attempt to provide a *conceptual framework for UK accounting standards. There are seven chapters:
1. The Objectives of Financial Statements
2. Qualitative Characteristics of Financial Information
3. The Elements of Financial Statements
4. The Recognition of Items in Financial Statement
5. Measurement in Financial Statements
6. Presentation of Financial Information
7. The Reporting Entity
Various discussion drafts were subsequently issued before the Board published a final Statement of Principles in December 1999.

statement of recognized income and expense (SORIE) The usual *International Financial Reporting Standard term for a *statement of total recognized gains and losses.

Statement of Recommended Practice (SORP) A non-mandatory statement dealing with accounting topics issued by the *Accounting Standards Committee (ASC). Some **franked SORPs** were prepared by other bodies, mainly on an industry basis, and were approved by the ASC, a process known as franking. The ASC's successor, the *Accounting Standards Board, does not issue or frank SORPs.

Statement of Standard Accounting Practice (SSAP) Any of a series of accounting standards prepared by the *Accounting Standards Board and issued by the six members of the *Consultative Committee of Accountancy Bodies. The first SSAP was issued in 1971 and in total 25 SSAPs were issued. Before a SSAP was issued a discussion document known as an exposure draft was circulated for comment. The SSAPs issued are given in the box below, although some of these were withdrawn by the ASC, amended, or superseded by the later *Financial Reporting Standards.

STATEMENTS OF STANDARD ACCOUNTING PRACTICE

1. Accounting for the Results of Associated Companies
2. Disclosure of Accounting Policies
3. Earnings per Share
4. The Accounting Treatment of Government Grants
5. Accounting for Value Added Tax
6. Extraordinary Items and Prior Year Adjustments
7. Accounting for the Changes in the Purchasing Power of Money (provisional)
8. The Treatment of Taxation under the Imputation System
9. Stocks and Work in Progress
10. Statement of Sources and Application of Funds
11. Accounting for Deferred Taxation
12. Accounting for Depreciation
13. Accounting for Research and Development
14. Group Accounts
15. Accounting for Deferred Taxation
16. Current Cost Accounting
17. Accounting for Post Balance Sheet Events
18. Accounting for Contingencies
19. Accounting for Investment Properties
20. Foreign Currency Translation
21. Accounting for Leases and Hire Purchase Contracts
22. Accounting for Goodwill
23. Accounting for Acquisitions and Mergers
24. Accounting for Pension Costs
25. Segmental Reporting

---

statement of total recognized gains and losses (statement of recognized income and expense) A *financial statement showing the extent to which *shareholders' equity has increased or decreased from all the various gains and losses recognized in the period. It includes profits and losses for the period, together with any changes in the value of items shown in the balance sheet. Unlike the *reconciliation of movements in shareholders' funds, it does not include transactions with shareholders, such as dividend payments. Such a statement has been required of UK companies since 1993. The statement is dealt with under *Financial Reporting Standard 3, Reporting Financial Performance; the relevant *International Accounting Standards are IAS 1 and IAS 3.

Statement on Auditing Standards (SAS) Any of the statements laying down accepted US auditing standards issued by the *Auditing Standards Board of the *American Institute of Certified Public Accountants (AICPA). Members of AICPA have to explain any deviation from SAS principles in their audit reports.

Statement on Internal Auditing Standards (SIAS) Any of the statements issued by the Internal Responsibilities Committee of the *Institute of Internal Auditors, based in the USA.

State Second Pension (SSP; S2P) A scheme run by the UK government to provide a pension in addition to the basic state retirement *pension. It was introduced in April 2002 to replace the existing **State Earnings Related Pension** (**SERPS**). Contributions are made through National Insurance payments. Those wishing to contract out of SSP may currently subscribe to an occupational pension scheme or a personal pension scheme; from 2012, however, it will only be possible to contract out through a defined-benefit scheme operated by an employer.

static budget *See* FIXED BUDGET.

statistical sampling The use of random selection and probability theory to determine the size of a *sample and to evaluate the results using this sample. Statistical sampling provides a measure of the sampling risk to assist an auditor to draw conclusions on the total population. *Compare* JUDGMENTAL SAMPLING.

statutory accounts Accounts required by law, as by the Companies Act. *See also* STATUTORY BOOKS.

statutory audit An *audit of a company as required by the Companies Act, subject to *small company exemptions. The auditors are required to report to the company's members on all accounts of the company, copies of which are laid before the company in general meeting. Companies with a *turnover of not more than £5.6 million and a *balance sheet total of not more than £2.8 million may be exempt from the statutory audit. Companies with a turnover of £1 million or less and a balance sheet total of not more than £1.4 million do not need to have any form of accountant's or auditor's report. Companies with a turnover of between £1 million and £5.6 million need a *reporting accountant's *audit exemption report. The government has increased the audit threshold significantly in recent years to reduce costs for small companies.

Statutory Audit Directive An EU directive (2006) designed to enhance public confidence in the auditing profession within the EU, chiefly by increasing accountability. Together with the *Company Reporting Directive, the Statutory Audit Directive is often seen as providing a European equivalent to the US *Sarbanes–Oxley Act (Sox); as such, the two directives are often referred to jointly as **Eurosox**.

statutory books The *books of account that the Companies Act requires a company to keep. They must show and explain the company's transactions, disclose with reasonable accuracy the company's financial position at any time, and enable the directors to ensure that any accounts prepared therefrom comply with the provisions of the act. They must also include entries from day to day of all money received and paid out together with a record of all assets and liabilities and statements of stockholding (where appropriate). *See also* PROPER ACCOUNTING RECORDS.

statutory demand A standard form used for the enforcement of debts. It typically sets out a demand by a creditor to a debtor to honour payment of an amount owing and specifies a period of three weeks for repayment or other satisfactory solution. Failure to comply with the demand by the debtor will be evidence of an inability by the debtor to pay creditors and can be used to support a *compulsory liquidation petition under the Insolvency Act 1986.

statutory sick pay (SSP) Weekly payments by employers to employees unable to work because of sickness; it is payable, after the first three days of sickness, for a period of up to 28 weeks. Formerly all employers were entitled to an 80% reimbursement for SSP by the government, and smaller companies were entitled to full reimbursement after the first six weeks of each SSP claim. However, this has gradually altered since 1994 and in most cases no recoupment is now possible. The only exception is where an employer pays out, in any income-tax month, SSP exceeding 13% of his liability to pay National Insurance contributions in that month. In such circumstances that excess can be recouped.

statutory total income *See* TOTAL INCOME.

stealth tax (hidden tax) A tax, the incidence of which may be hidden from the person who is suffering it. An example could be a tax levied on goods at the wholesale level, which increases the retail price in such a way that the final customer cannot detect either that it has happened or the amount of the extra cost. The term is also applied to various mechanisms by which the government can increase the tax paid by individuals without raising tax rates, notably the abolition or restriction of tax allowances and the adjustment of thresholds.

step-function cost An item of expenditure that when plotted on a graph against activity levels gives a stepped function; i.e. increments of cost are incurred as activity rises. *See also* SEMI-FIXED COST; LINEAR COST FUNCTION.

stepped cost *See* SEMI-FIXED COST.

Sterling Overnight Index Average *See* SONIA.

stewardship A traditional approach to accounting that places an obligation on stewards or agents, such as directors, to provide relevant and reliable financial information relating to resources over which they have control but which are owned by others, such as shareholders. Not only are stewards responsible for providing information, but they must also submit to an audit. *See* ACCOUNTABILITY; AGENCY RELATIONSHIP.

stickiness A tendency for certain economic variables, notably prices and wages, to 'stick' at or near their existing levels despite changes in supply and demand. For example, companies rarely cut the wages of existing employees, even where market forces might seem to demand this; wages (like prices) are therefore said to be 'sticky downward'. Various factors have been cited to explain such stickiness; these include the role of long-term fixed-price or fixed-wage contracts and the hidden costs of repricing (*see* MENU COSTS). *See also* RATCHET EFFECT.

stock **1.** A *fixed-interest security issued by the government, local authority, or a company in fixed units, often of £100 each in the UK and $1000 in the USA. They usually have a redemption date on which the *par value of the unit price is repaid in full. They are dealt in on stock exchanges at prices that fluctuate, but depend on such factors as their *yield in relation to current interest rates and the time they have to run before redemption. *See also* GILT-EDGED SECURITY; TAP STOCK. **2.** The US name for an *ordinary share. **3.** The stock-in-trade of an organization. *See* INVENTORY. **4.** Any collection of assets, e.g. the stock of plant and machinery owned by a company.

stockbroker An agent who buys and sells securities on a stock exchange on behalf of clients and receives remuneration for this service in the form of a commission. Before October 1986 (*see* BIG BANG), stockbrokers on the *London Stock Exchange were not permitted to act as principals (**stockjobbers**) and worked for a fixed commission laid down by the Stock Exchange. Since October 1986, however, many London stockbrokers have taken advantage of the new rules, which allow them to buy and sell as principals, in which capacity they are now known as *market makers. This change has been accompanied by the formal abolition of fixed commissions, enabling stockbrokers to vary their commission in competition with each other. Stockbrokers have traditionally offered investment advice, especially for their institutional investors.

stock budgets *Budgets set under a system of *budgetary control, which plan the levels of stocks of materials, *work in progress, and *finished goods both in volumes and values at various times throughout a *budget period.

stock control *See* INVENTORY CONTROL.

stock exchange (stock market) A market for the sale and purchase of securities, in which the prices are controlled by the laws of supply and demand. The first stock exchange was in Amsterdam, where in 1602 shares in the United East India Company could be traded. UK exchanges date from 1673, with the first daily official price lists being issued in London in 1698. Stock markets have developed hand-in-hand with capitalism, gradually growing in complexity and importance. Their basic function is to allow public companies, governments, local authorities, and other incorporated bodies to raise capital by selling securities to investors. They perform valuable secondary functions in allowing those investors to buy and sell these securities, providing liquidity, and reducing the risks attached to investment. Stock markets were abolished after World War II in communist-dominated states but with the collapse of communism many restarted. The major international stock exchanges are based in New York, Tokyo, London, Shanghai, and Hong Kong. Outside the UK and English-speaking countries, a stock exchange is usually known as a **bourse**.

Stock Exchange Alternative Trading Service (SEATS) A computerized system used on the *London Stock Exchange for trading on the *Alternative Investment Market and for stocks of restricted liquidity. A screen-based service showing current prices and orders, it runs alongside the *Stock Exchange Automated Quotations System (SEAQ).

Stock Exchange Automated Quotations System (SEAQ) A computerized system used on the *London Stock Exchange to record the prices at which transactions in securities have been struck, thus establishing the market prices for these securities; these prices are made available to brokers through *TOPIC. When a bargain is concluded, the details must be notified to the central system within certain set periods during the day. **SEAQ International** is the system used on the London Stock Exchange for non-UK equities; it operates on similar lines to SEAQ. *See also* STOCK EXCHANGE ALTERNATIVE TRADING SERVICE; STOCK EXCHANGE TRADING SYSTEM.

Stock Exchange Automatic Execution Facility (SAEF) A computerized system used on the *London Stock Exchange to enable a broker to execute a transaction through an SAEF terminal, which automatically completes the bargain at the best price with a *market maker, whose position is automatically adjusted. The price of the transaction is then automatically recorded on a trading report and also passes into the settlement system.

Stock Exchange Trading System (SETS) The London Stock Exchange order-driven electronic trading system that came into operation in 1997. It partly replaced the existing quote-driven system (*see* STOCK EXCHANGE AUTOMATED QUOTATIONS SYSTEM). Buyers and sellers enter their orders, which are matched by computer. It covers the 100 shares of the FT-SE 100 index and other *blue chip securities.

stockholders In the USA, individuals, businesses, and groups owning *stocks in a corporation.

stockholders' equity In the USA, the ownership interest of stockholders in a corporation. It is the difference between the total *assets and the total *liabilities.

stock-in-trade *See* INVENTORY.

stockjobber *See* STOCKBROKER.

stock ledger The accounting book in which the movements of *inventories are recorded. The stock ledger records the receipts and issues of material as well as the balance in hand, in terms of both material quantities and values.

stock market *See* STOCK EXCHANGE.

stock out The circumstance that pertains when the balance of the physical stock of a particular commodity has been used and none remains in store.

stock reconciliation *See* STOCKTAKING.

stock record The record in an *inventory control system of movements in items of stock. The stock record may be made up of entries in the *stock ledger, which records stock movements in both quantities and values, or on the *bin cards, which record quantities only.

stock split *See* SCRIP ISSUE.

stocktaking The process of counting and evaluating stock-in-trade, usually at an organization's year end in order to value the total stock for preparation of the accounts. In more sophisticated organizations, in which permanent stock records are maintained, stock is counted on a random basis throughout the year to compare quantities counted with the quantities that appear in the computerized records.

stock transfer *See* SHARE TRANSFER.

stock turnover *See* INVENTORY TURNOVER.

stock valuation *See* INVENTORY VALUATION.

stock watering Any of various practices in which a company inflates the value of its assets or exaggerates its profits as a pretext for issuing an unjustified amount of shares. Fraudulent practices of this kind were particularly associated with the US railway boom of the late 19th century.

stop loss order An order given by an investor to a broker to sell a financial instrument, commodity, etc., when its price falls to a specified level in order to limit loss.

store card *See* BIN CARD.

stores The part of an organization in which *inventories are stored. Depending on the arrangements within particular organizations, there may be separate stores for stationery stocks, maintenance components, production tools, *raw materials, *work in progress, and *finished goods.

stores issue note (SIN) *See* MATERIALS REQUISITION.

stores oncost *See* ONCOST.

stores requisition *See* MATERIALS REQUISITION.

stores returns note (SRN) *See* MATERIALS RETURNS NOTE.

straight bond A *bond issued in the *primary market that carries no equity or other incentive to attract the investor; its only reward is an annual or biannual interest coupon together with a promise to repay the capital at par on the redemption date.

straight-line method A method of calculating the amount by which a *fixed asset is to be depreciated in an accounting period, in which the *depreciation to be charged against income is based on the original cost or valuation, less the asset's estimated *net residual value, divided by its estimated life in years. This has the effect of a constant annual depreciation charge against profits year by year. In some circumstances the net residual value is ignored.

strategic financial management An approach to management that applies financial techniques to strategic decision making. *See also* STRATEGIC MANAGEMENT ACCOUNTING.

strategic investment appraisal An appraisal of an investment decision based on wider grounds than that provided by a purely financial appraisal. It is also necessary to evaluate possible long-term strategic benefits and any intangible factors that may be relevant to the decision, particularly if advanced manufacturing technology is concerned.

strategic management accounting A *management accounting system organized so that it is capable of providing the information needed for long-term strategic decision making, as opposed to the more traditional approach of providing short-term costs. Strategic management accounting, for example, provides information that will assist in the pricing strategy for new products and decisions relating to the expansion of capacity.

strategic misrepresentation In planning and budgeting, the tendency for those presenting projects for approval knowingly to understate costs and overstate benefits. This is a matter of deliberate policy and thus distinct from *optimism bias or simple miscalculation. Those who adopt such a policy would probably justify it as an expected part of the negotiation 'game' and argue that many worthwhile projects would never get approval if the true costs were revealed at the start.

stress testing A method of *risk analysis in which *simulations are used to estimate the impact of worst-case situations. It is commonly used by regulators, rating agencies, and financial institutions, which base their simulations on both historical and hypothetical crises.

strike price *See* EXERCISE PRICE.

structural capital *See* INTELLECTUAL CAPITAL.

structured finance The creation of complex debt instruments by *securitization or the addition of *derivatives to existing instruments. Structured finance typically involves the pooling of assets, the tranching of liabilities (*see* TRANCHE), and the creation of *special purpose vehicles to limit risk. The prevalence of structured finance products based on *subprime mortgages is generally seen as a key factor in the financial crisis of 2008–09.

structured investment vehicle (SIV) An *arbitrage fund that raises finance by selling asset-backed *commercial paper (CP) and *medium-term notes and invests predominantly in *asset-backed securities (ABSs). The SIV makes its profit from the difference between the short-term rate paid to the holders of CP and the longer-term rate earned on the ABSs. By late 2008 all known SIVs had failed as a result of the global financial crisis.

structuring a deposit *See* SMURFING.

subjective goodwill The *goodwill of an enterprise calculated by deducting its net tangible assets from the *net present value of its estimated future *cash flows.

subjective probabilities *See* PROBABILITY.

sublease A *lease granted from a *head lease.

subordinated debt A debt that can only be claimed by an unsecured creditor, in the event of a liquidation, after the claims of secured creditors have been met. In **subordinated unsecured loan stocks** loans are issued by such institutions as banks, in which the rights of the holders of the stock are subordinate to the interests of the depositors. Debts involving *junk bonds are always subordinated to debts to banks, irrespective of whether or not they are secured.

subprime lending The provision of loans (especially home loans) to borrowers with a poor credit rating. Because such loans are considered high risk, the costs of borrowing are also higher. Reckless subprime lending by US financial institutions, compounded by the *securitization of these loans in high-risk off-balance-sheet instruments, precipitated the financial and banking crisis of 2008. *See* TOXIC ASSETS.

subrogation The principle that, having paid a claim, an insurer has the right to take over any other methods the policyholder may have for obtaining compensation for the same event. For example, if a neighbour is responsible for breaking a person's window and an insurance claim is paid for the repair, the insurers may, if they wish, take over the policyholder's legal right to claim the cost of repair from the neighbour.

subscribed share capital *See* ISSUED SHARE CAPITAL.

subsidiary undertaking (group undertaking) An undertaking that is controlled by another undertaking (the parent or *holding company). The extent of the control needed to define a subsidiary is given in the Companies Act. The financial statements of a subsidiary undertaking are normally included in the *consolidated financial statements of the group. *See also* QUASI-SUBSIDIARY; WHOLLY OWNED SUBSIDIARY.

substance over form An important concept in accounting, according to which transactions and other events are accounted for by their commercial reality rather than their legal form. *Off-balance-sheet finance and *creative accounting depended on accounting according to the legal form, often established in complex agreements. The purpose of *Financial Reporting Standard 5, Reporting the Substance of Transactions, was to give more strength to the substance aspect as well as guidance in specific transactions. However, its provisions are complex and apply only to a small number of transactions, typically involving very large amounts. The principle of substance over form is explicitly set out in the revised *International Accounting Standard 8.

substantial donor A person who makes a series of gifts to a charity that total £25,000 or more in any 12-month period or £100,000 or more during a six-year period. The charity is penalized by the denial of tax relief (or, sometimes, the imposition of a tax charge) if a property is sold to, or purchased from, or is let to, or is let from that substantial donor. This tax treatment also applies to the provision of services, exchanges of property, the provision of financial assistance and investment by the charity in the business of a substantial donor.

substantive tests Audit tests designed to check the completeness, ownership, existence, valuation, and disclosure of the information contained in the accounting records and financial statements of an organization being audited. These tests may include *vouching, inspection, and *analytical review.

subsubsidiary A *subsidiary undertaking of a company that is itself a subsidiary company.

summary financial statement An abbreviated form of the *annual accounts and report that, providing certain conditions are met, may be sent by *listed companies to their shareholders instead of the full report. *See also* ABBREVIATED ACCOUNTS; SIMPLIFIED FINANCIAL STATEMENTS.

sum-of-the-digits method A method of calculating the amount by which a *fixed asset is depreciated in an accounting period. The estimated life is expressed in years, and the digits for each year of its life are totalled. The proportion of the asset's cost or valuation less residual value to be written off as depreciation in a particular year is determined by the number of years remaining before the asset's removal from commission, expressed as a proportion of the sum of the years; the greatest amount is therefore written off in the early years of the asset's life. For example, for an asset with an estimated life of 5 years, the sum of the digits is $5 + 4 + 3 + 2 + 1 = 15$. Thus 5/15 is written off in the first year, 4/15 in year 2, 3/15 in year 3, and so on. In some circumstances the *net residual value is ignored.

sundry expenses Costs incurred as small items of expenditure, which do not lend themselves to easy classification under any other heading. Sometimes they refer to a specific area, such as sundry office expenses or sundry production costs.

sunk costs 1. (sunk capital) Expenditure, usually on capital items, that once having been incurred can be included in the *books of account as an asset, although this value cannot be recovered. An example of this form of expenditure would be creating a railway embankment or dredging to create a berth in a harbour. **2.** In *management accounting, expenditure that has already been incurred and that cannot be recovered. Such costs are not relevant to any subsequent decisions. An example of a sunk cost is the *original cost of a machine when the decision is whether or not to replace this machine. *Compare* RELEVANT COST.

superannuation *See* OCCUPATIONAL PENSION SCHEME.

supplier credit *See* SPECIFIC BANK GUARANTEE.

supply risk 1. The inherent risk in *project financing that the raw materials necessary for the operation of the plant to be constructed may become unavailable. *Compare* COMPLETION RISK; TECHNOLOGICAL RISK. **2.** The risk of disruption of inputs into a firm.

support cost centre *See* SERVICE COST CENTRE.

surcharge liability notice A notice issued when a trader is late with a *value added tax return or with the payment of the tax. The surcharge period is specified on the notice and it will run to the anniversary of the end of the period in which the default occurred. Any default in the liability notice period will result in a further notice extending the notice period to the anniversary of the end of the VAT period in which the second default occurred.

surplus advance corporation tax Formerly, the *advance corporation tax paid in an accounting period in excess of the maximum available for set-off against *gross corporation tax. Advance corporation tax was abolished with effect from 1 April 1999.

surrender value The sum of money given by an insurance company to the insured on a life policy that is cancelled before it has run its full term. The amount is calculated approximately by deducting from the total value of the premiums paid any costs, administration expenses, and a charge for the *life-assurance cover up to the cancellation date. There is little or no surrender value to a life policy in its early years. Not all life policies acquire a surrender value; for example, term assurance policies have no surrender value.

sushi bond A bond issued by a Japanese-registered company in a currency other than yen but targeted primarily at the Japanese institutional investor market.

suspense account A temporary account in the books of an organization used to record balances to correct mistakes or balances that have not yet been finalized (e.g. because a particular deal has not been concluded).

SVA Abbreviation for *shareholder value analysis.

swap A means by which a borrower can exchange the type of funds most easily raised for the type of funds required, usually through the intermediary of a bank. For example, a UK company may find it easy to raise a sterling loan when they really want to borrow euros; a German company may have exactly the opposite problem. A swap will enable them to exchange the currency they possess for the currency they need. This is called a **currency swap**. The other common type of swap is an **interest-rate swap**, in which borrowers exchange fixed- for floating-interest rates. The essence of a swap is that the parties exchange the net cash flows of different types of borrowing instruments on an *over-the-counter market.

swaption An *option to enter into a *swap contract.

SWF Abbreviation for *sovereign wealth fund.

swingline bank facility (swingline loan) A facility that enables a borrower to avail itself of funds at very short notice, usually on a same-day basis, often to cover shortfalls in other credit arrangements. It may form part of a multi-option facility.

SWOT analysis An analysis of the *s*trengths, *w*eaknesses, *o*pportunities, and *t*hreats of an organization as a form of appraisal of its current position at a particular time and future potential.

SWX Europe An order-driven electronic market for pan-European *blue chip securities. As **virt-x** it was created in 2001 from London's Tradepoint Investment Exchange with the involvement of *SWX Swiss Exchange. A *Recognized Investment Exchange under the UK *Financial Services Authority, it acquired its present name in 2008.

SWX Swiss Exchange The main stock exchange in Switzerland, based in Zurich. It was created in 1995, when the exchanges in Zurich, Geneva, and Basle adopted a single automated system for trading, clearing, and settlement (the Berne exchange remains independent). The price level is given daily by the **Swiss Market Index (SMI)**.

syndicated bank facility (syndicated loan) A very large loan made to one borrower by a group of banks headed by one lead bank, which usually takes only a small percentage of the loan itself, syndicating the rest to other banks and financial institutions. The loans are usually made on a small margin. The borrower can reserve the right to know the names of all the members of the syndicate. If the borrower states which banks are to be included, it is known as a **club deal**. A syndicated bank facility is usually a *revolving bank facility. There is only one loan agreement.

synergy The added value created by joining two separate firms, enabling a greater return to be achieved than by their individual contributions as separate entities; i.e. the overall return is greater than the sum of its parts. The synergy is usually anticipated and analysed during merger or takeover activities; for example, one firm's strength in marketing would be complementary to the other firm's versatility in new product development. Although synergy is often optimistically sought, it can be hard to achieve in practice owing to resistance to change, particularly after a contested takeover. The corporate culture that each participant may have built up over many years of separate existence may prove too inflexible to enable a productive merger to be achieved without friction. The condition that arises when, far from adding value, a merger produces an outcome that is less than the sum of the parts is known as **anergy**.

systems-based audit An approach to auditing based on the concept that by studying and assessing the internal control system of an organization an auditor can form an opinion of the quality of the accounting system, which will determine the level of *substantive tests needed to be carried out on the items in the financial statements. This approach is now less popular than formerly because it does not focus on *audit risk. The *risk-based audit is now generally considered to be more flexible, efficient, and effective.

systems control and review file (SCARF) An *embedded audit facility in a computer that consists of a program code or additional data provided by an auditor and incorporated into a computerized accounting system. The auditor designates files as SCARF or not and also specifies a monetary value threshold. All transactions posted to a SCARF file that are above the threshold are also written to a SCARF file, the contents of which can only be altered or deleted by the external auditors of the company. *See also* INTEGRATED TEST FACILITY.

systems development controls The *internal controls ensuring that the development of a computerized system is properly controlled. For example, segregation of duties should ensure that an employee involved in the development of a system should not usually be involved in testing the system.

S

T account A common accounting form in the enlarged shape of the capital letter T. The left-hand side represents the *debit side of an account and the right-hand side the *credit. Entries to the T account are made following the *debit and credit rules.

Taffler's Z score *See* Z SCORE.

takeover bid (offer to purchase) An offer made to the shareholders of a company by an individual or organization to buy their shares at a specified price in order to gain control of that company. In a welcome takeover bid the directors of the company will advise shareholders to accept the terms of the bid. This is usually known as a *merger. If the bid is unwelcome, or the terms are unacceptable, the board will advise against acceptance. In the ensuing **takeover battle**, the bidder may improve the terms offered and will then usually write to shareholders outlining the advantages that will follow from the successful takeover. In the meantime bids from other sources may be made (*see* GREY KNIGHT; WHITE KNIGHT) or the original bidder may withdraw as a result of measures taken by the board of the *target company (*see* POISON PILL). In an **unconditional bid**, the bidder will pay the offered price irrespective of the number of shares acquired, while the bidder of a **conditional bid** will only pay the price offered if sufficient shares are acquired to provide a controlling interest. Takeovers in the UK are currently subject to the rules and disciplines of the *City Code on Takeovers and Mergers, although a new code is due to be issued under the Companies Act 2006.

Takeover Panel *See* CITY CODE ON TAKEOVERS AND MERGERS.

tangible assets Literally, *assets that can be touched, i.e. physical objects such as land, buildings, or machinery. However, tangible assets may also include leases and company shares. They are therefore best defined as the *fixed assets of an organization excluding such *intangible assets as goodwill, patents, and trademarks, which are even more intangible than leases and shares.

taper relief Formerly, a relief applied in computing the *capital gains tax (CGT) charge on a capital gain. The maximum reduction available was 40% for a non-business asset and 75% for a business asset. Taper relief was introduced in 1998 and abolished from April 2008, largely because of disquiet at the extent to which *private equity firms were using it to avoid paying tax on their profits. It was replaced by an *entrepreneurs' relief on the disposal of business assets

tap stock A *gilt-edged security from an issue that has not been fully subscribed and is released onto the market slowly when its market price reaches predetermined levels. **Short taps** are short-dated stocks and **long taps** are long-dated taps.

TAR Abbreviation for throughput accounting ratio. *See* THROUGHPUT ACCOUNTING.

target company A company that is subject to a *takeover bid.

target costing A method of costing products or services to reflect the price that customers are willing to pay. Target costing has four stages.

(1) Identify the **target price** that customers will pay for the product. This involves market research to identify competitors' products and prices.

(2) Identify the **target cost** by deducting a target profit margin from the target price. The target profit margin will vary from company to company. Sony is an example of a company that would require a high profit margin to cover the investment in new technology.

(3) Forecast the **actual cost** of the product.

(4) If the forecast actual cost is greater than the target cost, the company will have to identify ways of lowering the forecast actual cost. Product designers may have to change the design so that it is cheaper to manufacture. Manufacturing engineers may also look into ways of making the production processes more efficient. If the company cannot bring actual costs down to the target cost, then the product should not be manufactured.

This approach to pricing is very different from *cost-plus pricing.

TARP Abbreviation for Troubled Asset Relief Program: a US government initiative designed to restore market stability and revive bank lending in the wake of the *subprime lending fiasco and the ensuing financial crisis. TARP enables the government to buy up to $700 billion of so-called troubled or *toxic assets held by banks and other institutions, chiefly mortgages and complex instruments based on the *securitization of mortgages. The programme was introduced in October 2008 but later underwent several major modifications. *Compare* ASSET PROTECTION SCHEME.

taxable income Income liable to taxation. It is calculated by deducting *income tax allowances and any other tax-deductible expenses from the taxpayer's gross income. *See* NON-TAXABLE INCOME.

taxable person An individual, partnership, limited company, club, association, or charity as defined by the *value added tax legislation. Value added tax is charged on *taxable supplies made by taxable persons in the course or furtherance of a business.

taxable supply A supply of goods or services made in the UK, other than an *exempt supply. The term is used in *value added tax legislation.

tax accountant A person who assists a taxpayer in preparing a *tax return.

tax advantage A benefit enjoyed as a result of a reduction in a charge to taxation.

tax allocation The allocation of a charge to tax between different sources of income.

tax allowance *See* CAPITAL ALLOWANCES; INCOME TAX ALLOWANCES; PERSONAL ALLOWANCE. *See also* TAX RELIEF.

tax assessment A schedule issued by HM *Revenue and Customs showing a calculation of a taxpayer's liability to income tax. The income sources are identified separately on the tax assessment and an individual could receive several tax assessments for each *fiscal year, depending on the number of different sources of income for the year. These assessments can be based on estimated figures, in which case the schedule is known as an *estimated assessment.

taxation A levy on individual or corporate bodies by central or local government in order to finance the expenditure of that government and also as a means of implementing its fiscal policy. Payments for specific services rendered to or for the payer are not regarded as taxation. In the UK, an individual's income is taxed by means of an *income tax (*see* PAYE), while corporations pay a *corporation tax. Increases in individual wealth are taxed by means of a *capital gains tax and by *inheritance tax.

tax avoidance Minimizing tax liabilities legally and by means of full disclosure to the tax authorities. *Compare* TAX EVASION. *See also* TAX PLANNING; WESTMINSTER DOCTRINE.

tax base The specified domain on which a tax is levied, e.g. an individual's income for *income tax, the estate of a deceased person for *inheritance tax, the profits of a company for *corporation tax.

tax bracket Figures between which income is subjected to a specific rate of tax. *See* BASIC RATE OF INCOME TAX; HIGHER RATE OF INCOME TAX.

tax break A tax advantage for a particular activity.

tax code **1.** *See* INCOME TAX CODE. **2.** The body of tax law applicable in a country, in which the tax law is codified rather than laid down by statute.

tax commissioners *See* GENERAL COMMISSIONERS; SPECIAL COMMISSIONERS.

tax credit **1.** The tax allowance associated with the *dividend paid by a company. The shareholder is given allowance for the tax paid at source by the tax credit, at the same rate, 10/90; i.e. a dividend of £90 received by the shareholder has an associated tax credit of £10. For those whose taxable income does not exceed £37,400 there is no further tax to pay. For those whose income is higher, the excess is chargeable at a rate of 32.5%. **2.** Any other allowance against a tax liability. **3.** In the UK, a social security payment such as the Working Tax Credit or Child Tax Credit that is administered by HM Revenue and Customs. Despite their titles, neither of these payments affects the amount of tax that is payable.

tax-deductible Denoting an amount that can be deducted from income or profits, in accordance with the tax legislation, before establishing the amount of income or profits that is subject to tax.

tax deposit certificate A certificate issued by HM Revenue and Customs to a taxpayer who has made an advance payment in anticipation of future income tax, capital-gains tax, or corporation tax. The initial payment must not be less than £500 and should be made to HMRC; payments of £100,000 or over can be made directly to the Bank of England. The certificates bear interest, which is liable to tax. The interest rate depends on whether the certificate is withdrawn for cash or surrendered to meet a tax demand. A higher rate is paid on the latter. Interest normally runs to the date of encashment but if the certificate is used to pay tax, it runs only to the due date of payment of the liability, not the actual date of payment.

tax-effective Denoting a procedure that is in accordance with the tax legislation and results in a reduction in the tax charge.

Taxes Management Act 1970 The UK legislation consolidating the law relating to the administration and collection of *income tax, *corporation tax, and *capital gains tax.

tax evasion Minimizing tax liabilities illegally, usually by not disclosing that one is liable to tax or by giving false information to the authorities. If a person marries in order to reduce his tax burden he is practising *tax avoidance; if he tells the Revenue that he is married when he is not, he is guilty of tax evasion. As Denis Healey once remarked 'The difference between tax avoidance and tax evasion is the thickness of a prison wall.'

Tax Exempt Special Savings Account (Tessa) A UK savings account with a bank or building society, introduced in 1991, in which savers were allowed to invest up to £9000 over a five-year period with no tax to pay on their interest, provided that certain conditions were met. Tessas were replaced by *Individual Savings Accounts (ISAs) in April 1999; however, existing Tessas were allowed to continue under the same arrangements until their term expired.

tax exile A person with a high income or considerable wealth who chooses to live in a *tax haven to avoid high taxation in his or her own country.

tax-free Denoting any payment, allowance, benefit, etc., that is not subject to taxation.

tax harmonization The process of increasing the compatibility of various taxation systems by limiting the variations between them. The main areas of difference in taxation are the *tax base and the rates of tax applicable. There is often strong resistance to tax harmonization between independent states as, by setting limits within which the tax rates can be set, the authority of individual governments is eroded. The level of taxation is often a cornerstone of government policy.

tax haven A country or independent area that has a low rate of tax and therefore offers advantages to wealthy individuals or to companies that can arrange their affairs so that their tax liability falls at least partly in the low-tax haven. In the case of individuals, the cost of the tax saving is usually residence in the tax haven for a major part of the year. For multinational companies, an office in the tax haven, with some real or contrived business passing through it, is required. Monaco, Liechtenstein, the Bahamas, and the Cayman Islands are examples of tax havens. *See also* OFFSHORE FINANCIAL CENTRES.

tax holiday A period during which a company, in certain countries, is excused from paying corporation tax or profits tax (or pays them on only part of its profits) as an export incentive or an incentive to start up a new industry.

tax invoice A detailed *value added tax invoice that must be provided by a *taxable person to another taxable person when the *taxable supply is made for over £100. The tax invoice must show:
- the supplier's name, address, and VAT registration number;
- the tax point and invoice number;
- the name and address of the customer;

- a description of the transaction and the goods supplied;
- the amount of VAT and the amount excluding VAT.

A less detailed invoice is required for a supply of less than £100.

tax loss A loss made by an organization in one period, that can be carried forward to another period to reduce the tax payable by that organization in the subsequent period. *See* LOSS RELIEFS.

taxman An informal name for an *Inspector of Taxes.

tax month Under the UK taxation system, the month running from the 6th day of one month to the 5th day of the following month. This ensures that there are 12 complete tax months in the *fiscal year. Similarly, a **tax week** is any of the series of weeks starting 6 April: the first tax week ends on 13 April, the second ends on 20 April, etc.

tax period The period covered by a *value added tax return, usually three calendar months. The VAT return should be completed and sent to HM Revenue and Customs within one month of the end of the tax period.

tax planning The arrangement of a taxpayer's affairs, in accordance with the requirements of the tax legislation, in order to reduce the overall charge to tax. *See* TAX AVOIDANCE.

tax point Under the *value added tax rules, the date on which goods are removed or made available to a customer or the date on which services to a customer are completed. The tax point determines the tax period for which the *output tax must be accounted for to HM Revenue and Customs.

tax rebate A repayment of tax paid. A *repayment claim must be made and approved by an *Inspector of Taxes and the refund due to the taxpayer will be made by the *Collector of Taxes following the Inspector's instructions.

tax relief A deduction from a taxable amount, usually given by statute. In the UK, income-tax reliefs are given in respect of income from tax-exempt sources (e.g. ISAs), as well as tax-deductible expenses, personal allowances, tax credits, and *gift aid. *See* INCOME TAX ALLOWANCES.

The reliefs against *capital gains tax include an annual exemption, exemption from the proceeds of the sale of an only or a principal private residence, and *entrepreneurs' relief.

For *inheritance tax there is an annual relief as well as relief in respect of gifts between spouses and gifts to political parties and charities; agricultural and business reliefs are also available.

tax return A form upon which a taxpayer makes an annual statement of income and personal circumstances enabling claims to be made for personal allowances. In the UK an income tax return also requires details of *capital gains in the year. The onus is on the taxpayer to provide HM Revenue and Customs with the appropriate information even if the taxpayer receives no tax return. Categories of tax payer who can expect to receive a tax return include the self-employed, company directors, people with a high investment income, and those acting as trustees or personal representatives. Since 1996–97 income tax returns have included a section for *self-assessment, in which the tax payer calculates his or her own liability for income tax. Separate returns are required for *inheritance tax purposes and in respect of VAT and excise duties. It is now possible to complete and send back a tax return over the Internet.

((()) SEE WEB LINKS
• Information on making an online tax return from the Gov.co.uk website

tax shelter (tax shield) Any financial arrangement made to lower a person's or a company's tax liabilities. *See* ABUSIVE TAX SHELTER.

tax system The means by which taxes are raised and collected in accordance with the tax legislation.

tax tables Tables issued by HM Revenue and Customs to employers to assist them in calculating the tax due from their employees under the pay-as-you-earn system (*see* PAYE). The tables are provided either for weekly or monthly payments. In practice, employers now calculate salaries, wages, and tax deductions by computer, using a program into which the tax tables are incorporated.

tax treaty An agreement between two countries, identifying the treatment of income, profits, or gains that are subject to tax in both countries. The amount of double taxation relief will be specified in the treaty (*see* DOUBLE TAXATION AGREEMENT).

tax voucher *See* DIVIDEND.

tax year *See* FISCAL YEAR.

technological risk **1.** The inherent risk in *project financing schemes that the newly designed plant etc. will not operate to specification. *Compare* COMPLETION RISK; SUPPLY RISK. **2.** The risk to a business from changing technology.

teeming and lading *See* LAPPING.

telegraphic transfer (TT) A method of transmitting money overseas by means of an electronic transfer between banks. The transfer is usually made in the currency of the payee and may be credited to his account at a specified bank or paid in cash to the payee on application and identification.

telephone banking A *home-banking facility enabling customers to use banking services by means of a telephone link.

temporal method A method of converting a foreign currency involved in a transaction in which the local currency is translated at the exchange rate in operation on the date on which the transaction occurred. If rates do not fluctuate significantly, an average for the period may be used as an approximation. Any exchange gain or loss on translation is taken to the *profit and loss account. This contrasts with the *closing-rate method of translation, which uses the exchange rate ruling at the balance-sheet date for translation and takes exchange differences to *reserves. *Statement of Standard Accounting Practice (SSAP) 20, Foreign Currency Translation, allows either method to be adopted. This area is now governed by the detailed regulations in *Financial Reporting Standard 23, The Effects of Change in Foreign Exchange Rates, which replaced SSAP 20 in 2004. The relevant *International Accounting Standard is IAS 21.

temporary diminution in value A fall in the value of an *asset that is only expected to be for the short term. Under *historical-cost accounting, no adjustments are made for temporary diminutions (unless they become permanent). *See also* PERMANENT DIMINUTION IN VALUE.

tender bond A guarantee given by a company that it will not withdraw from a contract, if it is awarded, after having submitted a tender.

tender panel A group of banks forming a panel to tender competitively to lend money to a company.

tenor The time that must elapse before a *bill of exchange or *promissory note becomes due for payment, as stated on the bill or note.

ten-year charge An *inheritance tax charge made every ten years on most forms of *discretionary trust (now defined as *relevant property trusts). As a discretionary trust does not attach to the life of an individual there is no inheritance-tax charge on passing through the generations. To compensate for this a ten-year charge, calculated at 30% of the lifetime rate, is assessed, so that a full charge is made every 33.33 years. Assets are valued at *market value at the tenth anniversary of the trust after 31 March 1984, and every ten years thereafter. The current rate is 6%, being 30% of the current lifetime rate of 20%.

terminal bonus An additional amount of money added to payments made on the maturity of an insurance policy or on the death of an insured person, because the investments of the insurer have produced a profit or surplus. Bonuses of this kind are paid at the discretion of the life office and usually take the form of a percentage of the sum assured.

terminal-loss relief Relief for a loss made by a company, partnership, or sole trader during the last 12 months of trading. The business or profession must be permanently discontinued. The trading loss arising in the accounting period in which the trade ceases may be carried back and offset against the profits of the three years ending immediately before the commencement of the final period of trading. *See* LOSS RELIEFS.

terminal value (TV) The value of an investment at the end of an investment period taking into account a specified rate of interest over the period. The formula is the same as that for compound *interest, i.e.

$$TV = P(1 + r)^t,$$

where *TV* is the final amount at the end of period, *P* is the principal amount invested, *r* is the interest rate, and *t* is the time in years for which the investment takes place.

term loan A loan from a bank to a company. The term of the loan is fixed and it is drawn down (*see* DRAWDOWN) immediately or within a short period of signing the loan agreement as set out in the *amortization schedule.

terotechnology The branch of technology that involves the use of management, financial, and engineering skills in installing, operating, and maintaining plant and machinery. *See* LIFE-CYCLE COSTING.

Tessa Abbreviation for *Tax Exempt Special Savings Account.

test data Data used by an auditor in computer processing to check the operation of an organization's computer programs. The main use of test data is in conducting *compliance tests on *application controls; for example, to check that batch totals are being correctly produced. *See also* COMPUTER-ASSISTED AUDIT TECHNIQUES; EMBEDDED AUDIT FACILITY; INTEGRATED TEST FACILITY; SYSTEMS DEVELOPMENT CONTROLS.

theory of constraints (TOC) A systematic approach that aims to identify and eliminate all bottlenecks in a production system. TOC aims to increase profits while simultaneously reducing stock levels and operating expenses.

Examples of TOC solutions include:
- providing additional training for employees to improve working speeds;
- replacing an existing bottleneck machine with a faster one;
- changing the design of a product to reduce manufacturing time.

thin capitalization An arrangement in which a company is incorporated (typically in another jurisdiction) with a small share capital and financed by a large loan from its parent company. The arrangement is often designed to give tax relief on the interest payment on the loan, whereas no relief would be available on dividends paid on shares. In the UK a special tax regime is applied in certain instances of thin capitalization, so that excessive interest paid on the loan is treated as if it were a non-tax-deductible dividend.

thin market A market for a security, commodity, currency, etc. in which there are currently few transactions. In such a market any sizable transactions will have a direct effect on prices. Large investors tend to avoid a thin market because of its low liquidity. *Compare* DEEP MARKET.

third-party debt order An order made by a judge on behalf of a creditor restraining a third party (often a bank) from paying money to a *judgment debtor until sanctioned to do so by the court. The order may also specify that the third party must pay a stated sum to the judgment creditor, or to the court, from the funds belonging to the judgment debtor. It was formerly called a **garnishee order**.

three-column cash book A *cash book in which details of *discounts allowed and *discounts received are included in addition to receipts and payments made. Periodically these totals will be posted to the discounts allowed and received accounts, respectively. *Compare* TWO-COLUMN CASH BOOK.

throughput accounting An approach to short-term decision making in manufacturing in which all *conversion costs are treated as though they were fixed and products are ranked if a particular *constraint or scarce resource exists. Decisions are made using the **throughput accounting ratio (TAR)** as follows:

return per factory hour / cost per factory hour,

where return per factory hour =

(sales price – material cost) / hours on scarce resource;

and cost per factory hour =

total factory cost / total available hours of constraint.

More recently, throughput accounting has been applied in more general areas of *management accounting.

tied adviser *See* INDEPENDENT FINANCIAL ADVISER.

time card (clock card) A card on which is recorded the time spent by an employee at the place of work or the time spent on a particular job. The card is usually marked by mechanical or electronic means by recording the starting and ending times, enabling the elapsed time to be calculated.

time draft *See* DOCUMENTARY DRAFT.

time of supply The date on which goods are removed or made available to a customer or when services for a customer are completed, i.e. the *tax point. Goods on sale or return are treated as supplied on the date of adoption by the customer or 12 months after despatch, whichever is the earlier. Continuous services paid for periodically are charged to tax on receipt of payment or issue of each tax invoice, whichever is the earlier.

time sheet A form on which is recorded the employee time or machine time spent on each activity during a period. It is used for costing jobs, operations, or activities.

time value of money The concept, used as the basis for *discounted cash flow calculations, that cash received earlier is worth more than a similar sum received later, because the sum received earlier can be invested to earn interest in the intervening period. For the same reasons, cash paid out later is worth less than a similar sum paid at an earlier date.

TLF Abbreviation for *transferable loan facility.

Tobin's Q *See* Q RATIO.

TOC Abbreviation for *theory of constraints.

Tokyo Stock Exchange (TSE) The principal stock exchange of Japan, which is also the second-largest in the world by market capitalization. Electronic trading for all transactions was introduced in 2000. The main market indicator is the Nikkei Stock Average of 225 Japanese industrial companies.

tombstone An advertisement in the financial press giving brief deals of the amount and maturity of a recently completed bank facility. The names of the *lead managers are prominently displayed, as well as the *co-managers and the managers. It is customary for the borrower to pay although he or she receives little benefit from the advertisement.

tonnage tax A means of calculating the charge to *corporation tax of a ship-owning company. Since 2000 a company may elect to pay corporation tax on the basis of the net registered tonnage of its shipping, rather than on the basis of the profit or loss made.

TOPIC *Acronym for* Teletext Output Price Information Computer. This computerized communication system provides brokers and market makers on the *London Stock Exchange with information about share price movements and bargains as they are transacted. Input is from the *Stock Exchange Automated Quotations System (SEAQ). It is now run by a private company independently of the stock exchange.

top rate of income tax *See* HIGHER RATE OF INCOME TAX.

Toronto Stock Exchange (TSX) The main exchange for Canadian shares.

Trading has been entirely electronic since April 1997, when the physical trading floor was closed. The main market indicators are the TSX 60 index and the wider TSX Composite index.

total absorption costing *See* ABSORPTION COSTING.

total cost of production *See* PRODUCTION COST.

total costs The sum of all the expenditure incurred during an accounting period, either within an organization, on a product, or on a process. It is often convenient to analyse the total costs into *fixed costs and *variable costs.

total income The income of a taxpayer from all sources. This is often referred to as **statutory total income** and comprises income from some sources calculated on the basis of the income of the current *fiscal year and income from other sources calculated on the basis of the accounting period ending in the current fiscal year. This artificial concept is used to calculate a person's income tax for a given year. *See* BASIS OF ASSESSMENT.

total profits Profits chargeable to *corporation tax (PCTCT), including profits from trading, property, investment income, overseas income, and chargeable gains, less charges.

Total Quality Management (TQM) An approach to managing people and business processes that emphasizes the importance of customer satisfaction and sees *continuous improvement as the means to achieve this. For example, manufacturing companies can save money by continuously improving the quality of their products as there will be less scrap and fewer returns from customers. TQM programs usually entail improved workplace training, a degree of *employee empowerment, and a redesign of work processes. *See also* KAIZEN COSTING.

total standard cost The *total standard production cost plus the *standard cost allowance for the non-production overhead.

total standard production cost The total of *standard direct materials cost, *standard direct labour cost, the *standard fixed overhead cost, and the *standard variable overhead cost.

total standard profit The difference between the sales at *standard selling prices and the *standard overhead cost of these sales.

town clearing Formerly, a special same-day clearing service for high-value cheques drawn on accounts within the City of London and paid into another City account. From 1995 the town clearing service was replaced by electronic transfer of funds via CHAPS (*see* ASSOCIATION FOR PAYMENT CLEARING SERVICES).

toxic assets (troubled assets) Financial instruments for which there is no longer a functioning market. This occurs when the value of assets in a particular class has become highly uncertain and those holding them are unable to sell at the very low prices that buyers would demand. The term was popularized in the financial crash that followed the *subprime lending crisis of 2008, when banks were unable to accept current market prices for the complex derivative products in which they had invested. *See also* TARP.

TQM Abbreviation for *Total Quality Management.

trade The *income tax charge on trading income (previously Schedule D Case I; *see* SCHEDULE) only applies when there is 'a trade' (Income Tax Trading and Other Income Act 2005). If there is no trade, a transaction is likely to be subject to capital gains tax and not income tax. (This gives a lower tax charge.) When deciding whether there is a trade, courts have usually adopted the formulation of the Royal Commission on Trade (1955), which stated that the existence of a trade might be determined by considering the six **badges of trade**, namely:
(1) the subject matter of the transaction;
(2) the length of period of ownership of the property realized in the transaction;
(3) the frequency or number of similar transactions by the same person;
(4) supplementary work on or in connection with the property realized;
(5) the circumstances that were responsible for the realization;
(6) motive.

trade creditors *See* ACCOUNTS PAYABLE.

trade debtors *See* ACCOUNTS RECEIVABLE.

trade discount A reduction in the list price of goods; for example, a discount given to a customer who makes bulk purchases.

trademark A distinctive symbol that identifies particular products of a trader to the general public. The symbol may consist of a device, words, or a combination of these. A trader may register a trademark at the Register of Trade Marks, which is held at the Intellectual Property Office. The trader then enjoys the exclusive right to use the trademark in connection with the goods for which it was registered. Any manufacturer, dealer, importer, or retailer may register a trademark. Registration is initially for 10 years and is then renewable. The right to remain on the register may be lost if the trademark is not used or is misused. The owner of a trademark may assign it or, subject to the Registrar's approval, allow others to use it. If anyone uses a registered trademark without the owner's permission, or uses a mark that is likely to be confused with a registered trademark, the owner can sue for an injunction and *damages or an account of profits. A trademark is a form of *intellectual property and as such is an *intangible asset. Since April 1996 it has been possible to obtain Community Trade Marks for the whole of the EU.

trade reference A reference concerning the creditworthiness of a trader given by another member of the same trade, usually to a supplier. If a firm wishes to purchase goods on credit from a supplier, the supplier will usually ask for a trade reference from another member of the same trade, in addition to a *banker's reference.

trading account The part of a *profit and loss account in which the *cost of sales is compared with the money raised by their sale in order to arrive at the *gross profit.

trading profit The *profit of an organization before deductions for such items as interest, directors' fees, auditors' remuneration, etc.

traditional costing system Any of the systematic costing methods that prevailed before the rise of *activity-based costing in the 1990s. Because they rely on an essentially *arbitrary allocation of *indirect costs, such systems do not give managers accurate product cost information, which means that accurate calculation of product profitability is not possible. The overhead rate in a traditional costing system would typically be calculated using direct labour hours, machine hours, or units. This could lead to accurate product costs when direct costs were high and indirect costs were low, as was the case 50 years ago; however, modern organizations typically have low direct costs and higher indirect costs.

The strengths of traditional costing systems are:

- simplicity – the calculation of overhead rates is relatively straightforward;
- they are widely understood in the business;
- they are not expensive to operate;
- until the late 1980s they were seen as fairly accurate;
- they are still being used after many decades.

The weaknesses of traditional costing systems are:

- their reliance on arbitrary rather than *cause-and-effect allocation of overheads;
- their inability to give accurate product costs in multiproduct companies;
- their failure to analyse non-manufacturing costs.

tranche (French: slice) **1.** A part or instalment of a large sum of money. In the *International Monetary Fund the first 25% of a loan is known as the **reserve** (formerly **gold**) **tranche**. In **tranche funding**, successive sums of money become available on a prearranged basis to a new company, often linked to the progress of the company and its ability to reach the targets set in its *business plan. **2.** In a *securitization, any of several classes of debt instrument created from the same pool of assets but having different risk–return profiles to attract different classes of investor. The junior tranches bear a higher level of *credit risk than the senior tranches and consequently pay a higher coupon. *See* STRUCTURED FINANCE.

transaction An external event (e.g. purchase or sale) or internal event (e.g. depreciation of an asset) that gives rise to a change affecting the operations or finances of an organization.

transaction costs The costs incurred in making a transaction, over and above the benefit exchanged. They typically include research costs, bargaining costs, and enforcement costs; there will also be agency costs if an agent is used (*see* AGENCY RELATIONSHIP). A simple example of a transaction cost is the commission paid to a broker when buying or selling securities.

transaction date The date on which a transaction in the money market took place.

transaction exposure The risk that the cost of a transaction will change because of exchange-rate movements between the date of the transaction and the date of settlement.

transaction file A computer file used to record an external or internal *transaction. *Compare* STANDING DATA.

transferable loan facility (TLF) A bank loan facility that can be traded between lenders, in order to reduce the credit risk of the bank that provided

the loan. It is a form of *securitization but can have an adverse effect on
*relationship banking.

transfer credit risk The *credit risk that arises, especially on long-term
contracts, as a result of a foreign debtor's inability to obtain foreign currency
from the central bank at the appropriate time. This may occur even when the
debtor is able and willing to pay. *Compare* POLITICAL CREDIT RISK. *See also*
COUNTRY RISK.

transfer of a going concern Under *value added tax (VAT) regulations, the
disposal of a business by a *registered trader to another VAT-registered trader, on
which VAT is not charged. In the 2004 Budget new measures were introduced to
crack down on VAT-avoidance schemes using the rules on transfer of a going
concern. HM Revenue and Customs is responsible for applying the rules.

transfer prices The prices at which goods and services are bought and sold
between divisions or subsidiaries within a group of companies.
   The transfer price is a cost to the receiving division and revenue to the
supplying division: therefore the transfer price will affect the profitability of
each division. In a complex organization there may be several buying and
selling divisions in a group. Transfer prices can also apply between *cost
centres.
   Managers need to consider a complex range of issues when setting a transfer
price. This is because transfer pricing can be used for several quite different
purposes:
• to provide information that motivates managers to make good economic
  decisions;
• to provide information for evaluating the managerial and economic
  performance of divisions;
• to maintain divisional autonomy;
• to move profits between divisions, which may involve moving profits from one
  country to another to minimize tax on profits. (In the UK the scope for doing
  this has been greatly reduced by legislation passed in 2003.)
As a result, those setting transfer prices may find that they face a conflict of
objectives. For example, senior managers of a group may want to maximize
profitability even though this will means reducing the autonomy of divisional
managers. This may result in short-term increases in profitability but at the
expense of the motivation of divisional managers in the long run.
   There are six main transfer-pricing methods: *see* COST-PLUS TRANSFER PRICES;
DUAL-RATE TRANSFER PRICES; FULL-COST TRANSFER PRICES; MARGINAL-COST
TRANSFER PRICES; MARKET-BASED TRANSFER PRICES; NEGOTIATED TRANSFER
PRICES.

translation exposure (**accounting exposure**) A risk that arises from the
translation of the assets and liabilities in a *balance sheet into a foreign currency.

treasurer **1.** A person who is responsible for looking after the money and other
assets of an organization. This may include overseeing the provision of the
organization's finances as well as some stewardship over the way in which the
money is spent. **2.** In more recent usage, the manager responsible for an
organization's relationship with financial markets.

Treasury, HM The UK government department responsible for the country's financial policies and management of the economy. It is run by the Chancellor of the Exchequer.

- HM Treasury area of Gov.co.uk: includes latest economic indicators and forecasts for the UK economy

treasury stock A US term for shares that have been repurchased by the issuing company, thereby reducing the number of its shares on the open market.

trend analysis The analysis of the performance of a company or industry over a period, by the use of *accounting ratios.

trial balance A listing of the balances on all the accounts of an organization, with debit balances in one column and credit balances in the other. If the rules of *double-entry book-keeping have been accurately applied, the totals of each column should be the same. If they are not the same, checks must be carried out to find the discrepancy. The figures in the trial balance after some adjustments, e.g. for closing stocks, prepayments and accruals, depreciation, etc., are used to prepare the final accounts (profit and loss account and balance sheet). *See also* EXTENDED TRIAL BALANCE.

Troubled Asset Relief Program *See* TARP.

true and fair view Auditors of the published accounts of companies are required to form an opinion as to whether the accounts they audit show a 'true and fair view' of the organization's affairs. This is an important concept in the UK and may be used as an override to depart from legal requirements. Despite its importance there is no legal definition of the expression. The meaning of 'true and fair view' develops over time as standards are issued and new accounting issues are debated. The US and *International Accounting Standards equivalent of the concept is *fair presentation.

Trueblood Report A report, *Objectives of Financial Statements*, prepared by a committee chaired by Robert M. Trueblood and published by the *American Institute of Certified Public Accountants in 1971. The report identified the basic *objective of financial statements as the provision of information useful for making economic decisions. It was influential in the preparation by the US *Financial Accounting Standards Board of Statement of Financial Accounting Concepts No. 1.

trust An arrangement enabling property to be held by a person or persons (the *trustees) for the benefit of some other person or persons (the beneficiaries). The trustee is the legal owner of the property but the beneficiary has an equitable interest in it. A trust may be intentionally created or it may be imposed by law (e.g. if a trustee gives away trust property, the recipient will hold that property as constructive trustee for the beneficiary). Trusts are commonly used to provide for families and in commercial situations (e.g. pensions trusts). *See also* DISCRETIONARY TRUST; 18–25 TRUST; INTEREST-IN-POSSESSION TRUST; RELEVANT PROPERTY TRUST.

trust deed The document creating and setting out the terms of a *trust. It will usually contain the names of the trustees, the identity of the beneficiaries, and the nature of the trust property, as well as the powers and duties of the trustees.

Trusts of land must be declared in writing; trusts of other property need not be although there is often a trust deed to avoid uncertainty.

trustee A person who holds the legal title to property but who is not its beneficial owner. Usually there are two or more trustees of a *trust and for some trusts of land this is necessary. The trustee may not profit from the position but must act for the benefit of the beneficiary, who may be regarded as the real owner of the property. Either an individual or a company may act as trustee. It is usual to provide for the remuneration of trustees in the trust deed, otherwise there is no right to payment. Trustees may be personally liable to beneficiaries for loss of trust property.

trustee in bankruptcy A person in whom the property of a bankrupt is vested for the benefit of the bankrupt's creditors. The trustee in bankruptcy must collect the bankrupt's assets, sell them, and distribute the proceeds among those with valid claims against the bankrupt. Some claims take preference over others (*see* PREFERENTIAL DEBT).

trustee investments *See* AUTHORIZED INVESTMENTS.

TT Abbreviation for *telegraphic transfer.

Turnbull Report A report (1999) providing directors of UK listed companies with guidance on *risk management and *internal controls and their obligations with regard to both under the *Combined Code on Corporate Governance. It was prepared by a working party of the Institute of Chartered Accountants in England and Wales and endorsed by the London Stock Exchange. Revised guidelines were issued in 2005.

((⊕)) SEE WEB LINKS
• Free downloadable pdf of the 2005 Turnbull Guidance from the FRC website

turnover **1.** The total sales figure of an organization for a stated period. Turnover is defined in the Companies Acts as the total revenue of an organization derived from the provision of goods and services, less trade discounts, VAT, and any other taxes based on this revenue. **2.** More generally, the rate at which some asset is sold and replaced by one of the same class. *See* INVENTORY TURNOVER; RATE OF TURNOVER. **3.** The total value of the transactions on a market or stock exchange in a specified period.

turnover ratio *See* RATE OF TURNOVER.

Turquoise An electronic pan-European trading platform for equities, established by a consortium of nine leading investment banks in 2008.

TV Abbreviation for *terminal value.

two-column cash book A *cash book that records receipts and payments made but does not record discounts allowed and discounts received. *Compare* THREE-COLUMN CASH BOOK.

two-tier board A method of running a large organization in which, in addition to a board of management, there is a supervisory board. It is claimed that this provides an effective method of *corporate governance, as seen in some European countries. In the UK, the normal practice is for a single board to consist of both executive and *non-executive directors.

UBR Abbreviation for Uniform Business Rate. *See* BUSINESS RATES.

UCITS Abbreviation for Undertakings for Collective Investment in Transferable Securities: *unit trusts or *investment trusts that are permitted to operate throughout the EU on the basis of their admission by the domestic regulator in one member state. A set of rules making this possible was drawn up in 1989.

UITF Abbreviation for *Urgent Issues Task Force.

UK Financial Investments (UKFI) A limited company established by the UK government to manage its shareholding in those banks that accepted state investment totalling some £50 billion as part of its bank rescue package during the financial crisis of 2008. The chief recipients were Lloyds and the Royal Bank of Scotland Group.

UK National Accounts An annual publication of the *Office for National Statistics. It is often known as the **Blue Book** and is now available online as well as in printed form. It provides figures for the *gross domestic product and separate accounts of production, income, and expenditure.

ULS Abbreviation for *unsecured loan stock.

ultimate holding company (ultimate parent company) A company that is the *holding company of a group in which some of the subsidiary companies are themselves *immediate holding companies of their own groups. *See also* SUBSUBSIDIARY.

ultra vires (Latin: beyond the powers) Denoting an act of an official or corporation for which there is no authority. The powers of officials exercising administrative duties are limited by the instrument from which their powers are derived. If they act outside these powers, their action may be challenged in the courts. Until recently, a company's powers were limited by the *objects clause in its *memorandum of association; if it entered into an agreement outside these objects, the agreement could be challenged. The Companies Act 2006 removes the requirement for a company to restrict its objects in this way: an act by a company that falls outside the scope of its constitutional documents is now only voidable in law if the company is a charity.

unamortized cost 1. The *historical cost of a *fixed asset less the total *depreciation shown against that asset up to a specified date. **2.** The value given to a fixed asset in the accounts of an organization after *revaluation less the total depreciation shown against that asset since it was revalued.

unappropriated profit The part of an organization's *profit that is neither allocated to a specific purpose nor paid out in *dividends. *See* APPROPRIATION.

unbundling 1. The separation of a business into its constituent parts, generally by selling off certain subsidiaries or business lines. **2.** The selling off of separate parts of a security, for example its *coupon.

uncommitted facility An agreement between a bank and a company in which the bank agrees in principle to make funding available to the company but is under no obligation to provide a specified amount of funding; if a loan is made it will be for only a short period. Examples of an uncommitted facility include a *money market line or an *overdraft. *Compare* COMMITTED FACILITY.

unconsolidated subsidiary An *undertaking that, although it is a *subsidiary undertaking of a group, is not included in the *consolidated financial statements of the group. *See* EXCLUSION OF SUBSIDIARIES FROM CONSOLIDATION.

uncontrollable costs (non-controllable costs) Items of expenditure appearing on a manager's *management accounting statement that are not able to be controlled or influenced by that level of management. Costs regarded as uncontrollable by one level of management may, however, be controllable at a higher level of management. There is always potential for disagreement over what is or is not an uncontrollable cost. Correctly identifying such costs is important for *performance measurement. *Compare* CONTROLLABLE COSTS. *See also* CONTROLLABILITY CONCEPT.

undated security A *fixed-interest security that has no *redemption date.

underabsorbed overhead (underapplied overhead) In *absorption costing, the circumstance in which the *absorbed overhead is less than the overhead costs incurred for a period. This *adverse variance represents a reduction of the budgeted profits of the organization. *Compare* OVERABSORBED OVERHEAD. *See also* OVERHEAD TOTAL VARIANCE.

undercapitalization The state of a company that does not have sufficient *capital or *reserves for the size of its operations. For example, this may be due to the company growing too quickly. Although such a company may be making profits it may be unable to convert these profits sufficiently quickly into cash to pay its debts. *Compare* OVERCAPITALIZATION; THIN CAPITALIZATION.

underlying The asset, measure, or obligation on which a *derivative, such as an option or futures contract, is based.

understandability The principle that the financial information provided by a company should be such that its significance is capable of being perceived by a person with a reasonable knowledge of business and accounting and a willingness to study it with reasonable diligence. The information should not leave out anything material, but should not be so comprehensive that the main points of significance are obscured. The concept is defined in the Accounting Standards Board's *Statement of Principles and in *Financial Reporting Standard 18, Accounting Policies. It is also recognized in the International Accounting Standards Board's *Framework for the Preparation and Presentation of Financial Statements. *See* ACCOUNTING CONCEPTS.

undertaking A *body corporate, *partnership, or an *unincorporated association carrying on a trade or business with a view to making a *profit.

underwriter **1.** A person who examines a risk, decides whether or not it can be insured, and, if it can, works out the premium to be charged, usually on the basis of the frequency of past claims for similar risks. Underwriters are either employed by insurance companies or are members of Lloyd's. The name arises from the early days of marine insurance, when a merchant would, as a sideline, *write* his name *under* the amount and details of the risk he had agreed to cover on a slip of paper. **2.** A financial institution, usually a *merchant bank, that guarantees to buy a proportion of any unsold shares when a new issue is offered to the public. Underwriters usually work for a commission, and a number may combine together to buy all the unsold shares, provided that the minimum subscription stated in the prospectus has been sold to the public. **3.** A person who provides a guarantee for a financial transaction.

underwriting group A group of financial institutions that receive a fee for underwriting a new securities issue.

undischarged bankrupt A person whose *bankruptcy has not been discharged. Such persons may not obtain credit (above £500) without first informing the creditor that they are undischarged bankrupts, and may not carry on a business without disclosing the name under which they become bankrupt. Undischarged bankrupts may not hold office as a JP, MP, mayor, or councillor.

undistributable reserves (capital reserves) *Reserves that may not be distributed according to the Companies Act. They include *share capital, *share premium account, *capital redemption reserve, certain *unrealized profits, or any other reserve that the company may not distribute according to some other Act or its own constitutional documents. In the USA such reserves are known as **restricted surplus**. *Compare* DISTRIBUTABLE PROFITS.

undistributed profit Profit earned by an organization but not distributed to its shareholders by way of *dividends. Such sums are available for later distribution but are frequently used by companies to finance their activities. *See* RETAINED EARNINGS.

unearned income Income not derived from trades, professions, or vocations, or from the emoluments of office. In the UK, it was formerly taxed more heavily than *earned income, on the grounds that investment income was more permanent than earned income and did not depend on the labours of the taxpayer. This was achieved by an investment-income surcharge, which was an extra 15% over the normal rate of income tax. In the UK earned and unearned income are now taxed at essentially the same rates (with minor differences in the treatment of income from savings and company dividends).

unexpired cost The balance of an item of expenditure, recorded in the books of account of an organization, that has not been written off to the profit and loss account. For example, the *net book value of an asset represents the unexpired cost of that asset.

unfavourable variance *See* ADVERSE VARIANCE.

unfranked investment income Formerly, any investment income received by a company that did not qualify as *franked investment income.

unfunded pension system *See* PAY-AS-YOU-GO PENSION SYSTEM.

Uniform Business Rate (UBR) *See* BUSINESS RATES.

uniform commercial code In the USA, a legal code that standardizes business law. It consists of regulations on *commercial paper, uncertified cheques, security agreements, written agency agreements, and *bankruptcy, among other matters.

uniform costing The use of the same basic costing system by a number of different organizations who adopt common costing principles and practices.

unilateral relief Relief against double taxation given by the UK authorities for tax paid in another country with which the UK has no *double-taxation agreement.

unincorporated association An association of people that is not a *corporation and has no legal personality distinct from its members.

unissued share capital The excess of the *authorized share capital over the *issued share capital, i.e. that part of the authorized share capital that has not yet been issued.

unit cost Expenditure incurred by an organization expressed as a rate per unit of production or sales. It may be difficult to make valid comparisons of unit costs between organizations. The main problem is the *arbitrary allocation of *fixed overhead costs.

unit-level activities *See* ACTIVITY.

unit of account **1.** A function of *money enabling its users to calculate the value of their transactions and to keep accounts. **2.** The standard unit of currency of a country. **3.** An artificial currency used only for accounting purposes.

unit price The price paid per unit of item purchased or charged per unit of product sold.

units of production method of depreciation *See* PRODUCTION-UNIT METHOD.

unit standard operating profit The *standard operating profit, expressed as a rate per unit of production or sales.

unit standard production cost The *standard production cost, expressed as a rate per unit of production or sales.

unit standard selling price The *standard selling price, expressed as a rate per unit sold.

unit trust **1.** In the UK, an investment fund shared by a large number of different investors. A unit trust is an 'open-ended fund', which means that the fund gets bigger as more people invest and smaller as people withdraw their money. A fund manager is responsible for the fund and makes the investment decisions. The fund is divided into segments called 'units'. Investors take a stake in the fund by buying these units, the price of which will vary as the value of the investments the trust has invested in increase or decrease. The *Financial Services Authority (FSA) authorizes firms that sell unit trusts, most of which belong to the Investment Management Association (IMA). Investors should always look carefully at the charges associated with unit trusts. Basic-rate tax is deducted from the dividends paid by unit trusts and capital gains on the sale of a holding are subject to capital gains tax. In the USA unit trusts are called **mutual funds**. **2.** A trust scheme (also called a **unit investment trust**) in the USA in which investors purchase **redeemable trust certificates**. The money so raised is used by the trustees to buy such securities as bonds, which are usually held until they mature. Usually both the number of certificates issued and the investments held remain unchanged during the life of the scheme, but the certificates can be sold back to the trustees at any time.

unlimited company A type of *company whose members have an *unlimited liability. Thus on winding-up, the company can make demands upon its members until it has sufficient funds to meet the creditors' claims. The risk that members of unlimited companies assume is balanced by certain advantages: an unlimited company (unless it is a parent or subsidiary of a limited company) does not have to deliver its accounts to the Registrar of Companies and it has more freedom to deal with its capital than a limited company. Unlimited companies may be formed with an *authorized share capital, thus enabling them to issue shares and raise working capital, but members' liability is not limited to the nominal value of these shares.

unlimited liability A liability to pay all the debts incurred by a business. For a *sole proprietor or *general partner, liability is not limited to the amount he or she has agreed to invest. All debts of the business must not only be paid out of the assets of the business but also, if necessary, out of personal assets. *See also* UNLIMITED COMPANY.

unlisted securities (unquoted securities) Securities (usually *equities) in companies that are not on an official stock-exchange list. They are therefore not required to satisfy the standards set for listing (*see* LISTED SECURITY). Unlisted securities are usually issued in relatively small companies and their shares usually carry a high degree of risk. In London, unlisted securities were traded on the Unlisted Securities Market (USM) until 1995, when it was replaced by the *Alternative Investment Market. Other exchanges have similar markets.

unpaid cheque A cheque that has been sent to the payee's bank and then through the clearing process only to be returned to the payee because value cannot be transferred. If the reason is lack of funds the bank will mark the cheque 'refer to drawer'.

unrealized profit/loss A profit or loss that results from holding *assets rather than using them; it is therefore a profit or loss that has not been realized in cash. *Compare* REALIZED PROFIT/LOSS.

unsecured creditor A person who is owed money by an organization but who has not arranged that in the event of non-payment specific assets would be available as a fund out of which that person could be paid in priority to other creditors.

unsecured debenture *See* UNSECURED LOAN STOCK.

unsecured loan stock (ULS; unsecured debenture) A loan stock or *debenture in which no specific assets have been set aside as a fund out of which the holders could be paid in priority to other creditors in the event of non-payment.

Urgent Issues Task Force (UITF) A body established in 1991 as part of the *Accounting Standards Board. It is responsible for tackling urgent matters not covered by existing standards in which the timescale of the normal standard-setting process would not be practicable.

usage rate The speed at which a commodity, raw material, or other resource is used up.

usage variance *See* DIRECT MATERIALS USAGE VARIANCE.

usance **1.** The time allowed for the payment of short-term foreign *bills of exchange. It varies from country to country but is often 60 days. **2.** Formerly, the rate of interest on a loan.

useful economic life The period for which the present owner of an *asset will derive economic benefits from its use.

u

valuation risk The risk that arises from problems of valuation. For example, it can be difficult to value a business during the acquisition process or to put an accurate value on an option on the *over-the-counter market.

value-added statement (added-value statement) A *financial statement showing how much wealth (value added) has been created by the collective effort of capital, employees, and others and how it has been allocated for an *accounting period. Value added is normally calculated by deducting materials and bought-in services from *turnover. The value added is then allocated to employees in the form of wages, to shareholders and lenders in the form of dividends and interest, and to the government in the form of taxes, with a proportion being retained in the company for reinvestment.

value added tax (VAT) A charge on *taxable supplies of goods and services made in the UK by a *taxable person in the course or furtherance of a business. Where appropriate, each trader adds VAT to sales and must account to HM *Revenue and Customs for the *output tax. The *input tax paid on purchases can be deducted from the output tax due. VAT, indirect taxation that falls on the final customer, was introduced in 1973 when the UK joined the European Economic Community. Unless they are *zero-rated goods and services, *exempt supplies, or taxed at a special rate, all goods and services in the UK are currently taxed at a temporary rate of 15% (the full rate of 17.5% is due to be restored from 1 January 2010).

((🌐)) SEE WEB LINKS
• VAT area of the HMRC website

value-at-risk (VAR) A measure of risk developed at the former US bank J. P. Morgan Chase in the 1990s, now most frequently applied to measuring *market risk and *credit risk. It is the level of losses over a particular period that will only be exceeded in a small percentage of cases. A cut-off value for gains and losses is established that excludes a certain proportion of worst-case results (e.g. the bottom 1% of outcomes); the value-at-risk is then measured relative to that cut-off value. VAR was initially designed to measure the overnight risk in certain highly diversified *portfolios. It has since developed into a finance industry standard and has been incorporated into the regulatory requirements applying to financial institutions. In the wake of the financial crisis of 2008–09 there have been claims that VAR methodology helped to create false confidence and encourage excessive risk taking.

value chain The chain of activities by which a good or service is produced, distributed, and marketed. Each step of the chain (which may consist of the activities of one company or of several) creates different amounts of value for the consumer. There are five value-creating activities:
• inbound distribution
• operations

- outbound distribution
- marketing
- after-sales service;

and four supporting activities:

- buying
- research and development
- human resource management
- infrastructure of the firm.

For management, the main application of the value-chain concept is that a company should examine its costs and performance at each stage, and decide, among other things, whether it is best to carry out a particular stage in house or externally. The value chain can provide the basis for a strategic analysis in terms of the search for competitive advantage.

value date The time at which a remittance sent through the bank *clearing cycle becomes available to the payee for use.

value driver Any variable that significantly affects the value of an organization. In his development of *shareholder value analysis, Alfred Rappaport identified seven key drivers of value:

- sales growth rate
- operating profit margin
- tax rate
- fixed capital investment
- working capital investment
- planning period
- cost of capital

Of these, the first five can be used to forecast the future cash flows of a business, whereas the remaining two can be used to calculate the *present value of these cash flows.

In practice, different companies will have different value drivers. For example, Sony is a company that produces high-quality products for which customers are prepared to pay a relatively high price. Maintaining a high operating profit margin is therefore more important for Sony than sales growth. For another company, however, sales growth may well be the more important factor.

value for money audit An *audit of a government department, charity, or other non-profitmaking organization to assess whether or not it is functioning efficiently and giving value for the money it spends.

value in use The value of an *asset calculated by discounting the future cash flows obtainable from its continued use (*see* DISCOUNTED CASH FLOW). This would include any costs associated with its disposal.

value investment An investment strategy guided by a view of the real underlying value of a company and its long-term potential for growth, as opposed to one that tries to make short-term gains from market fluctuations.

value to the business The value of an *asset taken as the lower of the *replacement cost and the *recoverable amount. The latter is the greater of the *net realizable value and *net present value. It is claimed that generally an asset should never be worth more to a business than its replacement cost, because if the business were deprived of the asset it would replace it. If an asset is not worth replacing it would be sold (net realizable value), unless the net present value were higher. The concept is also known as the **deprival value** and was a feature of *current-cost accounting as set out in *Statement of Standard Accounting Practice 16.

vanilla finance *See* PLAIN VANILLA.

VAR Abbreviation for *value-at-risk

variable cost An item of expenditure that, in total, varies directly with the level of activity achieved. For example, *direct materials cost will tend to double if output doubles, a characteristic being that it is incurred as a constant rate per unit. In practice, there are few examples of true variable costs or true *fixed costs, most costs being *semi-variable costs.

variable costing *See* MARGINAL COSTING.

variable cost ratio The ratio of *variable cost to *sales revenue, expressed as a percentage.

variable overhead cost The elements of an organization's indirect costs for a product that vary in total in proportion to changes in the levels of production or sales. Examples can include power, commission earned by sales personnel, and consumable materials.

variable overhead efficiency variance In a system of *standard costing, the difference arising between the actual labour hours worked and the *standard time allowed for the quantity actually produced, valued at the standard variable overhead absorption rate per hour. *See* OVERHEAD EFFICIENCY VARIANCE.

variable overhead expenditure variance In a system of *standard costing, the difference arising between the variable overhead budgeted and the variable overhead incurred. *See* OVERHEAD EXPENDITURE VARIANCE.

variable overhead total variance In a system of *standard costing, the total difference arising between the standard variable overhead absorbed for the actual units produced and the actual variable overhead expenditure incurred. *See* OVERHEAD TOTAL VARIANCE.

variable production overhead The elements of an organization's indirect manufacturing costs that vary in total in proportion to changes in the level of production or sales. Examples can include factory power and depreciation of machinery using the *production-unit method.

variable-rate note (VRN) A *bond, usually with a fixed maturity, in which the interest coupon is adjusted at regular intervals to reflect the prevailing market rate (usually a margin over the *London Inter Bank Offered Rate). A VRN differs from a *floating-rate note in that the margin is not fixed and will be adjusted to take into account market conditions at each coupon setting date.

variable-rate security A *security in which the interest rate varies with market rates. *Floating-rate notes, *eurobonds, and 90-day *certificates of deposit are examples of variable-rate securities.

variance In *standard costing and *budgetary control, the difference between the standard or budgeted levels of cost or income for an activity and the actual costs incurred or income achieved. If the actual performance is better than standard then a **favourable variance** results, while if actual performance is worse than standard there is an **adverse variance**. Adverse variances may be subjected to detailed analysis in order to pinpoint their precise causes. *See* ANALYSIS OF VARIANCE.

variance analysis *See* ANALYSIS OF VARIANCE.

VAT Abbreviation for *value added tax.

VATman An informal name for an employee of HM *Revenue and Customs dealing with *value added tax. It is often used to refer to a VAT Inspector responsible for routine VAT inspections.

VCT *See* VENTURE CAPITAL TRUST.

vendor placing A type of *placing used as a means of acquiring another company or business. For example, if company X wishes to buy a business from company Y, it issues company X shares to company Y as payment with the prearranged agreement that these shares are then placed with investors in exchange for cash. Vendor placings have been popular with some companies as a cheaper alternative to a *rights issue. *See also* BOUGHT DEAL.

venture capital *See* RISK CAPITAL.

venture capital trust (VCT) An *investment trust that provides *risk capital for businesses of the same kind that qualify under the *Enterprise Investment Scheme (broadly, small unlisted trading companies). The trust managers accept sums of money from investors who wish to share in the profits of the trust. This form of investment has certain tax advantages in the UK, in that any profits are free of *capital gains tax and income is untaxed. They have the additional advantages that up to £200,000 can be invested in any year; 30% of any investment in a VCT can be claimed back from previously paid tax, provided the VCT is held for three years. By investing a taxable gain in a VCT that is held for three years, the payment of the capital gains tax is deferred until the VCT investment is sold (and the annual exemptions from capital gains tax can be carried forward).

verification A *substantive test in an audit that checks on the existence, ownership, and valuation of *assets and *liabilities. It is used to perform a *balance-sheet audit or to gather general *audit evidence.

vertical form The presentation of a *financial statement in which the debits and credits are shown one above the other. *Compare* HORIZONTAL FORM. *See* BALANCE-SHEET FORMATS; PROFIT AND LOSS ACCOUNT FORMATS.

vertical integration The combination of two or more companies at different stages in the *value chain. For example, a manufacturer might purchase one of its suppliers or an organization involved in distributing its products. **Vertical disintegration** is said to occur when a business withdraws from a stage in the value chain, usually because it decides that it would be cheaper to pay another company to carry out these activities. *Compare* HORIZONTAL INTEGRATION.

vested interest **1.** In law, an interest in property that is certain to come about rather than one dependent upon some event that may not happen. For example, a gift to 'A for life and then to B' means that A's interest is **vested in possession**, because A has the property now. B's gift is also vested (but not in possession) because A will certainly die sometime and then B (or B's estate if B is dead) will inherit the property. A gift to C 'if C reaches the age of 30' is not vested, because C may die before reaching that age. An interest that is not vested is known as a **contingent interest**. **2.** An involvement in the outcome of some business, scheme, transaction, etc., usually in anticipation of a personal gain.

view to resale The grounds on which a *subsidiary undertaking is excluded from the *consolidated financial statements of a group, because the group's interest in the subsidiary is held exclusively with a view to subsequent resale. *Financial Reporting Standard 2, Accounting for Subsidiary Undertakings, defines the circumstances appropriate for this exclusion as if a purchaser has been identified or is being sought for a subsidiary and it is reasonably expected that the interest will be disposed of within approximately one year of its date of acquisition. The subsidiary undertaking should not previously have been consolidated in group accounts prepared by the *holding company. Where a subsidiary undertaking is excluded on these grounds, it should be recorded in the consolidated financial statements as a *current asset at the lower of cost and *net realizable value. The relevant *International Financial Reporting Standard is IFRS 5, Non-current Assets Held for Sale and Discontinued Operations. *See also* EXCLUSION OF SUBSIDIARIES FROM CONSOLIDATION; HELD-FOR-SALE.

virement In some systems of *budgetary control, an agreed practice in which funds may be transferred from one part of the budget to another during a financial year. So, for example, a projected surplus under one budget head may be used to make up for a deficit under another.

virt-x *See* SWX EUROPE.

VocaLink *See* ASSOCIATION FOR PAYMENT CLEARING SERVICES.

volume variances *See* FIXED OVERHEAD VOLUME VARIANCE; SALES MARGIN VOLUME VARIANCE.

voluntary arrangement **1.** (**company voluntary arrangement; CVA**) A procedure provided for by the Insolvency Act 1986, in which a company may come to an arrangement with its creditors to pay off its debts and to manage its affairs so that it resolves its financial difficulties. This arrangement may be proposed by the directors, an *administrator, or a *liquidator and must be approved by meetings of both the company and its creditors. Once approved, the arrangement becomes binding on all the parties and a qualified insolvency practitioner is appointed to supervise it. The aim is to assist the company to solve its financial problems without the need for a winding-up (*see* LIQUIDATION). **2.** (**individual voluntary arrangement; IVA**) A similar agreement between a debtor and his or her creditors under the Insolvency Act 1986. It takes the form of either a *scheme of arrangement or a *composition and can be made either before or after a bankruptcy order is made. The terms of the arrangement must be agreed at a meeting between the debtor and his or her creditors and an insolvency practitioner appointed. If no agreement is reached, or the debtor subsequently fails to comply with the terms of an IVA, bankruptcy proceedings may be initiated or resumed. See feature BANKRUPTCY LAW on p. 52.

voluntary liquidation (voluntary winding-up) *See* CREDITORS VOLUNTARY LIQUIDATION; MEMBERS VOLUNTARY LIQUIDATION.

voluntary registration Registration for *value added tax by a *taxable person whose taxable turnover does not exceed the registration threshold.

voting shares Shares in a company that entitle their owner to vote at the annual general meeting and any extraordinary meetings of the company. Shares that carry **voting rights** are usually *ordinary shares, rather than *debentures. The company's articles of association will state which shares carry voting rights.

voucher A receipt for money or any document that supports an entry in a book of account.

vouching A *substantive test in an audit to check that the underlying records correctly show the nature of transactions entered into by the business being audited.

VRN Abbreviation for *variable-rate note.

WACC Abbreviation for *weighted average cost of capital.

wages The remuneration paid to hourly paid employees for the work done, usually based on the number of hours spent at the place of work.

wages costs *See* LABOUR COSTS.

wages oncost *See* ONCOST.

waiting time The period during which the operators of a machine or the machinery itself are idle or waiting for work, material, or repairs. *See also* IDLE TIME.

walk-through test An audit test that takes a few transactions from the records of a business and follows them through every stage of the accounting system. For example, a walk-through test of a purchases system would follow through from the material requisition to settlement of the supplier's invoice.

Wall Street 1. The *New York Stock Exchange, which stands on Wall Street in New York. 2. The financial institutions, collectively, of New York, including the stock exchange, banks, money markets, commodity markets, etc.

warehousing 1. The storage of goods in a warehouse. 2. Building up a holding of shares in a company prior to making a *takeover bid, by buying small lots of the shares and 'warehousing' them in the name of nominees. The purpose is for the bidder to remain anonymous and to avoid having to make the statutory declaration of interest. This practice is contrary to the *City Code on Takeovers and Mergers.

war loan A government stock issued during wartime; it has no redemption date and pays only 3½% interest.

warrant 1. (share warrant) A security that offers the owner the right to subscribe for the *ordinary shares of a company at a fixed date, usually at a fixed price. Warrants are themselves bought and sold on *stock exchanges and are equivalent to stock options. Subscription prices usually exceed the market price, as the purchase of a warrant is a gamble that a company will prosper. They have proved increasingly popular in recent years as a company can issue them without including them in the balance sheet. 2. A document that serves as proof that goods have been deposited in a public warehouse. The document identifies specific goods and can be transferred by endorsement. Warrants are frequently used as security against a bank loan. Warehouse warrants for warehouses attached to a wharf are known as **dock warrants** or **wharfinger's warrants**.

waste 1. (spoilage) The amount of material lost as part of a production process. Acceptable levels of waste, known as a *normal loss, are part of the cost of production and as such are allowed for in the product costs. *See also* ABNORMAL LOSS; PROCESS COSTING. 2. Any process or activity that does not add value.

wasting asset An *asset that has a finite life; for example, a lease may lose value throughout its life and become valueless when it terminates. It is also applied to such assets as plant and machinery, which wear out during their life and therefore lose value.

watered stock *See* STOCK WATERING.

WDA Abbreviation for *writing-down allowance.

WDV Abbreviation for *written-down value.

wealth tax A tax used in some European countries, not including the UK, consisting of an annual levy on assets. In practice, the implementation of a wealth tax requires a clear identification of the assets to be charged and an unassailable valuation of these assets.

wear and tear A diminution in the value to an organization of a *fixed asset due to the use and damage that it inevitably sustains throughout its working life. It is one of the causes of *depreciation.

weighted average (weighted mean) An arithmetic average that takes into account the importance of the items making up the average. In calculating the value of a share index, the share prices are usually weighted in some way, most often by the market capitalization of the company.

> **EXAMPLE**
>
> A trader buys a commodity on three occasions – 100 tonnes at £70 per tonne, 300 tonnes at £80 per tonne, and 50 tonnes at £95 per tonne. The purchases total 450 tonnes. The simple average price would be $(70 + 80 + 95)/3 = £81.7$. However, the weighted average, taking into account the amount purchased on each occasion, is:
>
> $$[(100 \times 70) + (300 \times 80) + (50 \times 95)]/450 = £79.4 \text{ per tonne.}$$

weighted average cost *See* AVERAGE COST.

weighted average cost of capital (WACC) A method for calculating the average cost of a company's different sources of finance. The WACC is calculated on the assumption that the company will maintain the same *debt–equity ratio. Managers should only use the WACC as an appropriate *discount rate for a project when the project has about the same level of risk as the company. The most difficult part of the calculation is the estimate for the cost of equity.

   In theory, a company can lower its weighted average cost of capital by increasing the proportion of debt. However, this could become a problem for shareholders, who may feel that higher levels of debt will increase the risk of their investment.

   See also COST OF CAPITAL.

> **EXAMPLE**
>
> A company has a capital structure of 50% debt and 50% equity. If it is assumed that the after-tax cost of *loan capital is 8% and the cost of *equity share capital is 16%, then the weighted average cost of capital can be calculated as follows:
>
> (proportion of loan capital × cost of loan capital) + (proportion of equity capital × cost of equity capital) = $(0.5 \times 8\%) + (0.5 \times 16\%) = 12\%$

weightless **1.** Denoting a business that has very few *tangible assets, especially one involved in *Internet trading. **2.** Denoting that part of the economy that is based on ideas and information rather than trade in physical goods.

Westminster doctrine In UK tax law, the principle that a person is entitled to make any lawful arrangement that he or she sees fit in order to reduce liability to tax. It is named after the ruling in the case *Commissioners of Inland Revenue v the Duke of Westminster* (1936), in which the House of Lords upheld the Duke's right to pay his gardener through a covenant scheme, thus reducing his liability to surtax. *Compare* RAMSEY PRINCIPLE.

white knight A person or firm that makes a welcome *takeover bid for a company on improved terms to replace an unacceptable and unwelcome bid from a *black knight. If a company is the target for a takeover bid from a source of which it does not approve or on terms that it does not find attractive, it will often seek a white knight, whom it sees as a more suitable owner for the company, in the hope that a more attractive bid will be made. *Compare* GREY KNIGHT.

Wholesale Market Brokers' Association (WMBA) The trade association for UK brokers in the *money market. The WMBA provides the *SONIA and *EURONIA indexes for overnight lending in the sterling and euro markets respectively.

wholly owned subsidiary A *subsidiary undertaking that is owned 100% by a holding company (i.e. there is no *minority interest).

will A document giving directions as to the disposal of a person's property after death. It has no effect until death and may be altered as many times as the person (the testator) wishes. To be binding, it must be executed in accordance with statutory formalities. It must be in writing, signed by the testator or at the testator's direction and in the testator's presence. It must appear that the signature was intended to give effect to the will (usually it is signed at the end, close to the last words dealing with the property). The will must be witnessed by two persons, who must also sign the will. The witnesses must not be beneficiaries.

windfall gains and losses Gains and losses arising from actual or prospective receipts that differ from those originally predicted or from changes in the *net present value of the receipts as a result of differences in discount rates.

winding-up *See* LIQUIDATION.

winding-up petition A document presented to a UK court seeking an order for a company to be put into *compulsory liquidation.

window dressing Any practice that attempts to make a situation look better than it really is. It has been used extensively by accountants to improve the look of balance sheets. For example, banks used to call in their short-term loans and delay making payments at the end of their financial years, in order to show spuriously high cash balances. Another example is when a company borrows cash from an *associated undertaking to disguise a short-term liquidity problem. These practices now fall within the remit of the *Accounting Standards Board. *See* CREATIVE ACCOUNTING; OFF-BALANCE-SHEET.

WIP Abbreviation for *work in progress (or process).

withholding tax Tax deducted at source from *dividends or other income paid to non-residents of a country. If there is a *double taxation agreement between the country in which the income is paid and the country in which the recipient is resident, the tax can be reclaimed.

without prejudice Words used as a heading to a document or letter to indicate that what follows cannot be used in any way to harm an existing right or claim, cannot be taken as the signatory's last word, cannot bind the signatory in any way, and cannot be used as evidence in a court of law. For example, a solicitor may use these words when making an offer in a letter to settle a claim, implying that the client may decide to withdraw the offer. It may also be used to indicate that, although agreement may be reached on the terms set out in the document on this occasion, the signatory is not bound to settle similar disputes on the same terms.

without recourse (*sans recours*) Words that appear on a *bill of exchange to indicate that the holder has no recourse to the person from whom it was bought, if it is not paid. It may be written on the face of the bill or as an endorsement. If these words do not appear on the bill, the holder does have recourse to the drawer or endorser if the bill is dishonoured at maturity.

with the exception of *See* EXCEPT FOR.

working capital (working assets) The capital that is used to finance the day-to-day operations of a company. Working capital is part of the *balance sheet and is calculated as the difference between *current assets and *current liabilities.

The size and composition of working capital will vary between different types of business. For example, at any given moment a manufacturing company needs to hold raw materials, *work in progress, and *finished goods. Typically, manufacturing companies sell goods on credit, thereby generating *accounts receivable. A supermarket has very different working capital requirements as it only needs to hold finished goods and will sell goods for cash. For a typical supermarket, the accounts receivable in the balance sheet will be much higher than stocks held. This is good for the supermarket, as it can get the cash from its customers before it has to pay suppliers. By contrast, a manufacturing business may have to pay suppliers many months before it is able to get cash from its customers.

Working capital is an investment in short-term assets and as such its management is very important to a business. Holding sufficient levels of finished goods to meet customer requirements is important, but managers should also be aware of the cost of holding these goods.

working-capital adjustment (monetary working-capital adjustment) A *current-cost accounting adjustment made to the *working capital of a business. Bank balances and overdrafts may fluctuate with the volume of stock held, the *debtors, and the *creditors. If the bank balances and overdrafts arise from such fluctuations, they too should be included in the monetary working capital, together with any cash required to support the daily operations of the business.

working-capital ratio *See* CURRENT RATIO.

work in progress (WIP) The balance of partly finished work remaining in a manufacturing operation or a long-term contract at a particular time. It is normally valued at the lower of cost or *net realizable value, using either the *first-in-first-out cost, the *last-in-first-out cost, or the *average cost method of valuation. In the USA, **work in process** is the more common term.

work measurement An estimate of the time required to carry out a series of manufacturing procedures, by studying the operations involved by means of time, methods, and work studies.

World Bank The name by which the *International Bank for Reconstruction and Development combined with its affiliates, the International Development Association and the International Finance Corporation, is known.

World Congress of Accountants An international conference of accounting professionals first held in St Louis, USA, in 1904. It is now held at four-yearly intervals under the auspices of the *International Federation of Accountants. The 18th Congress will be held in Kuala Lumpur, Malaysia, in 2010.

World Economic Forum A not-for-profit organization that holds an annual meeting of business leaders, politicians, academics, and opinion formers, usually in Davos, Switzerland. It also holds several regional meetings each year. The Forum, which first met in 1971, has its headquarters in Geneva; there are also offices in New York and Beijing.

World Trade Organization (WTO) An international trade organization formed under the *General Agreement on Tariffs and Trade (GATT) to replace GATT and implement measures agreed at the Uruguay Round (1994). It began operating on 1 January 1995. The WTO's aims are to continue the work of GATT in agreeing international trading rules and furthering the liberalization of international trade. The WTO extends its jurisdiction into such aspects of trading as intellectual property rights. WTO rules are very important in international trade contracts. The highest authority of the WTO is the Ministerial Conference, held at least every two years. By 2009 the WTO had 153 member states.

(⊕) SEE WEB LINKS
• Website of the WTO: includes a comprehensive statistics database

World Wide Web *See* INTERNET.

write off 1. To reduce the value of an asset to zero in a balance sheet. An expired lease, obsolete machinery, or an unfortunate investment would be written off. 2. To reduce to zero a debt that cannot be collected (*see* BAD DEBT). Such a loss will be shown in the *profit and loss account of an organization.

writing-down allowance (WDA) A *capital allowance available to a UK trader. Any additions to *plant and machinery are added to the *written-down value of assets acquired in previous years and the writing-down allowance is calculated as 25% of the total. For cars the allowance is restricted to £3000, for vehicles whose initial cost is in excess of £12,000. For industrial buildings the allowance is calculated at 3% of the initial cost, on the *straight-line method. For certain long-life assets it is calculated at 10% in the same way. *See also* ANNUAL INVESTMENT ALLOWANCE.

writ of execution An order issued by a court to enforce a judgment; it is addressed to a court officer instructing that officer to carry out an act, such as collecting money or seizing property. A **writ of delivery** is a writ of execution directing the High Court Enforcement Officer (formerly the sheriff) to seize goods and deliver them to the plaintiff or to obtain their value in money, according to an agreed assessment. If the writ does not offer the defendant the option to retain the goods by paying the assessed value, the writ is a **writ of specific delivery**.

written-down value (WDV) The value of an *asset for tax purposes after taking account of its reduction in value below the initial cost, as a result of its use in the trade. An asset acquired for a trade is eligible for *capital allowances. A *writing-down allowance of 25% is available in the year of purchase, which is deducted from the initial cost to establish the written-down value. In the following year the written-down value is subject to the 25% writing-down allowance, which is deducted to arrive at the written-down value at the end of the second year.

written resolution Under the Companies Act 2006, a *resolution signed by a majority of company members and treated as effective even though it is not passed at a properly convened company meeting. A *special resolution requires the support of 75% of members to become effective. Private companies can, in most circumstances, pass resolutions in this way; other companies may have power to do so under their *articles of association. Under previous legislation, a written resolution required the signature of all members.

wrongful trading Trading during a period in which a company had no reasonable prospect of avoiding insolvent *liquidation. The liquidator of a company may petition the court for an order instructing a director of a company that has gone into insolvent liquidation to make a contribution to the company's assets. The court may order any contribution to be made that it thinks proper if the director knew, or ought to have known, of the company's situation. A director would be judged liable if a reasonably diligent person carrying out the same function in the company would have realized the situation: no intention to defraud need be shown. *Compare* FRAUDULENT TRADING.

WTO *See* WORLD TRADE ORGANIZATION.

W

Yankee bond A bond issued in the USA by a borrower that is not a US-resident company.

year of assessment *See* FISCAL YEAR.

Yellow Book The colloquial name for *Admission of Securities to Listing*, a book issued by the Council of the *London Stock Exchange that sets out the regulations for admission to the *Official List and the obligations of companies with *listed securities. *See* LISTING REQUIREMENTS.

yield 1. The income from an investment expressed in various ways. The **nominal yield** of a fixed-interest security is the interest it pays, expressed as a percentage of its *par value. For example, a £100 stock quoted as paying 8% interest will yield £8 per annum for every £100 of stock held. However, the **current yield** (also called the **interest yield**, **running yield**, **earnings yield**, or **flat yield**) will depend on the market price of the stock. If the 8% £100 stock mentioned above was standing at a market price of £90, the current yield would be 100/90 × 8 = 8.9%. As interest rates rise, so the market value of fixed-interest stocks (not close to redemption) fall in order that they should give a competitive current yield. The capital gain (or loss) on redemption of a stock, which is normally redeemable at £100, can also be taken into account. This is called the **yield to redemption** (**gross redemption yield** or **maturity yield**). The redemption yield consists approximately of the current yield plus the capital gain (or loss) divided by the number of years to redemption. Thus, if the above stock had nine years to run to redemption, its redemption yield would be about 8.9 + 10/9 = 10%. The yields of the various stocks on offer are usually listed in commercial papers as both current yields and redemption yields, based on the current market price. However, for an investor who actually owns stock, the yield will be calculated not on the market price but the price the investor paid for it. The annual yield on a fixed-interest stock can be stated exactly once it has been purchased. This is not the case with *equities, however, where neither the dividend yield (*see* DIVIDEND) nor the capital gain (or loss) can be forecast, reflecting the greater degree of risk attaching to investments in equities. Yields on fixed-interest securities and equities are normally quoted gross, i.e. before deduction of tax. 2. The income obtained from a tax.

yield curve A curve on a graph in which the *yield on deposits or fixed-interest securities is plotted against the length of time they have to run to maturity. The yield curve usually slopes upwards, indicating that investors expect to receive a premium for holding securities that have a long time to run. However, a downward-sloping or **negative yield curve** may occur when the market anticipates falling interest rates or deflation. A flat or 'humped' yield curve is usually taken as a sign of market uncertainty.

yield management *See* REVENUE MANAGEMENT.

yield to maturity *See* GROSS REDEMPTION YIELD.

ZBB Abbreviation for *zero-base budget.

zero-base budget (ZBB) A *cash-flow budget in which the manager responsible for its preparation is required to prepare and justify the budgeted expenditure from a zero base, i.e. assuming that initially there is no commitment to spend on any activity. *Compare* INCREMENTAL BUDGET.

zero coupon bond A *bond issued at a discount to mature at its face value; the discount is set so that no interest is paid during the life of the bond. It is the ultimate deep discount bond (*see* DEEPLY DISCOUNTED SECURITY). *See also* COUPON STRIPPING.

zero-rated goods and services Goods and services that are taxable for *value added tax purposes but are currently subject to a tax rate of zero. These differ from *exempt supplies in that the VAT attributable is allowable for *input tax credit. Zero-rated supplies include:
•most food items,
•sewerage and water services for non-industrial users,
•periodicals and books,
•certain charitable supplies,
•new domestic buildings,
•transport fares for vehicles designed to carry not less than 10 passengers,
•banknotes,
•drugs and medicines,
•clothing and footwear for children,
•all exports.

Z score A multivariate formula, devised by Edward I. Altman in 1968, that attempts to measure the susceptibility of a business to failure. It is computed by applying *beta coefficients to a number of selected ratios taken from an organization's final accounts using the technique of multiple discriminant analysis. A UK-based version was introduced by Richard J. Taffler in 1983. *See* CORPORATE FAILURE PREDICTION.